D0208825

Religions of the World

Second Edition

REFERENCE BOOK
Not to be taken from the Library

Religions of the World

Second Edition

A COMPREHENSIVE ENCYCLOPEDIA OF BELIEFS AND PRACTICES

Volume Five: N–R

J. GORDON MELTON
MARTIN BAUMANN
Editors

TODD M. JOHNSON
World Religious Statistics

DONALD WIEBE
Introduction

ABC-CLIO

Santa Barbara, California • Denver, Colorado • Oxford, England

REFERENCE BOOK
asph/
WISSER MEMORIAL LIBRARY
Ref.
BL80.3
.R45
2010
v.5
c.1

Copyright 2010 by ABC-CLIO, LLC

All rights reserved. No part of this publication may be reproduced, stored in a retrieval system, or transmitted, in any form or by any means, electronic, mechanical, photocopying, recording, or otherwise, except for the inclusion of brief quotations in a review, without prior permission in writing from the publisher.

Library of Congress Cataloging-in-Publication Data

Religions of the world : a comprehensive encyclopedia of beliefs and practices / J. Gordon Melton, Martin Baumann, editors ; Todd M. Johnson, World Religious Statistics ; Donald Wiebe, Introduction. — 2nd ed.

p. cm.

Includes bibliographical references and index.

ISBN 978-1-59884-203-6 — ISBN 978-1-59884-204-3

1. Religions—Encyclopedias. I. Melton, J. Gordon. II. Baumann, Martin.

BL80.3.R45 2010

200.3—dc22 2010029403

ISBN: 978-1-59884-203-6
EISBN: 978-1-59884-204-3

14 13 12 11 10 1 2 3 4 5

This book is also available on the World Wide Web as an eBook.
Visit www.abc-clio.com for details.

ABC-CLIO, LLC
130 Cremona Drive, P.O. Box 1911
Santa Barbara, California 93116-1911

This book is printed on acid-free paper ♾
Manufactured in the United States of America

Contents

A–Z List of Entries

Note: Core essays are indicated with the symbol ◆; country essays are indicated with the symbol ■.

Volume One

Volume Two

Volume Three

Volume Four

Volume Five

Volume Six

Religions of the World

Second Edition

A COMPREHENSIVE ENCYCLOPEDIA
OF BELIEFS AND PRACTICES

Volume Five: N–R

N

Nagarjuna

3rd century CE

As a writer and the founder of one of the most important early schools of Buddhism, Nagarjuna is considered a seminal figure in the emergence of Buddhism on the world stage. At the same time, he is one of the more elusive figures in Buddhist history, with little actual known data about his life, including his birth and death dates. He became an honored figure in the Buddhist community, and when biographies were finally attempted after the passing of many centuries, they were filled with unreliable legendary and mythical material.

He is believed to have lived in southern India in the third century CE, though he is identified with Nalanda University, which was located in Bihar state. There is some reason to consider him to have been born in a Brahmin family. He is known primarily through his writings, which together form a body of commentary on the wisdom (*prajnaparamita*) texts, consisting of some 40 separate works such as the Heart Sutra and the Perfection of Wisdom Sutra. He developed a widely utilized methodology that reduced many arguments to absurdity and arrived at a middle position that eliminated dichotomies and extremes. His major work is the *Mula Madhyamaka-karika* (*Memorial Verses on the Middle Teaching*).

His teachings became the basis of the Madhyamika, or Middle Way, School. Central to his thought is an understanding of the non-essentiality of phenomenal reality and the related concept of *shunyata,* or emptiness. Nagarjuna concluded that the self is essentially "empty," that is, lacking in ego. This emptiness is also equivalent to the absolute. Thus he reasoned that union with the absolute is a form of liberation or release. The idea of emptiness was so central to Nagarjuna's thought that the Madhyamika School was popularly referred to as the Shunyatavada, or emptiness, School.

Edward A. Irons

See also: Mahayana Buddhism; Nalanda.

References

Burton, David. *Emptiness Appraised: A Critical Study of Nagarjuna's Philosophy.* Richmond, Surrey, UK: Curzon 1999.

Kalupahana, David J. *Nagarjuna: The Philosophy of the Middle Way, the Mulamadhyamakakarika of Nagarjuna.* Albany: State University of New York Press, 1986.

Nagarjuna. *The Fundamental Wisdom of the Middle Way: Nagarjuna's Mulamadhyamakakarika.* New York: Oxford University Press, 1995.

Nagarjuna. *Madhyamaka'sastram of Nagarjuna.* 2 vols. Delhi: Motilal Banarsidass, 1988.

Walser, Joseph. *Nagarjuna in Context: Mahayana Buddhism and Early Indian Culture.* Irvington, NY: Columbia University Press, 2005.

Nagorno Karabakh Republic

The Nagorno Karabakh Republic, also known as Artsakh, is a territory on the eastern end of the Armenian Plateau, now completely surrounded by the nation of Azerbaijan. In the fourth century CE Armenia was on the battle line between the Persian and Byzantine empires, and was partitioned between the two powers in

387 CE. Artsakh became part of what was called Caucasian Albania (nothing to do with the present state of Albania in the southern Balkans). The region subsequently came under strong Armenian influence. The region became part of the larger world of Armenian culture and religion (including the Armenian Apostolic Orthodox Church), but existed through the centuries sometimes as an independent nation and sometimes as a part of neighboring states. Because of the mountainous nature of the region, rule from outside was always difficult.

In 1747, Muslim rule from Persian was established through the Karabakh Khanate, a semi-autonomous feudal state. In 1805 Russia won control of the region, but was not able to make its hegemony effective until 1813, when Persia formally ceded all claims to it. Russia abolished it and replaced it with a military occupation. The Russians encouraged Muslims to leave the land and welcomed Christians who formerly resided in Persia, a policy that made the land even more culturally homogeneous.

Russian rule continued through World War I and then the region passed to the Soviet Union. After the war, local forces and the great powers debated Karabakh's future. Locally, an Armenian Assembly of Nagorno-Karabakh declared independence and went about setting up a national government. Later, Ottoman troops entered Karabakh, meeting armed resistance by Armenians. New plans for self-governance in the region ended with the Soviet Union occupying Karabakh in 1920 and all of Armenia and Azerbaijan the following year. In 1923, the Soviet Union designated the Nagorno-Karabakh Autonomous Oblast as a territory within Azerbaijan SSR. As the Soviet Union began to disintegrate in the early 1990s, the majority Christian Armenian population of Karabakh repudiated its ties to the dominantly Muslim Azerbaijan and moved to unite with Armenia.

Karabakh declared independence in 1991. At the latest estimates, the territory claimed by the newly independent nation included 4,457 square miles of territory inhabited by 145,000 (2002) people. This number represents a drop from an estimated 190,000.

The attempt to set up a new country ignited a war between Azerbaijan and the former Autonomous Oblast, which ended with the Azerbaijanis having lost control of the territory that separated Karabakh from Armenia. Russia negotiated a ceasefire in 1994. The area has remained disputed territory, with the United Nations still attempting to broker a cease fire as late as 2008.

Religiously, the people of Nagorno Karabakh largely express their religion in alignment with their ethnicity. According to the government, the country is 95 percent Armenian, meaning that the people are overwhelmingly members of the Armenian Apostolic Church, whose ruling bishop is located in Echmiadzin, Armenia. This figure represents a sharp rise from a decade earlier when Armenians represented only about 75 percent of the people. The change is largely a result of the migration out of the region by the 40,000 Azerbaijanis.

The remaining 5 percent of the population include communities of Kurds, Russians, Greeks, and Assyrians. Of these groups, three follow a form of Orthodoxy. The Assyrians (Iraqis) follow the Apostolic Catholic Assyrian Church of the East, the Greek the Greek Orthodox Church, and the Russians the Russian Orthodox Church (Moscow Patriarchate). Most Kurds are Muslims. While known to follow different forms of Islam, most are Shia Muslims (as are most Azerbaijanis). There are also a very small number of Protestant and evangelical Christians in Karabakh.

J. Gordon Melton

See also: Apostolic Catholic Assyrian Church of the East; Armenian Apostolic Church (Holy See of Echmiadzin); Russian Orthodox Church (Moscow Patriarchate).

References

Boyajian, Artashes. *Failed Transition? The Nagorno-Karabakh Conflict and Armenia's Transition to Democracy*. Saarbrücken, Germany: VDM Verlag Dr. Müller, 2009.

Chorbajian, Levon. *The Making of Nagorno-Karabakh: From Secession to Republic*. London: Palgrave Macmillan, 2001.

Cornel, Svante E. "The Nagorno-Karabakh Conflict." Report no. 46, Department of East European Studies, Uppsala University, 1999. http://www.silkroadstudies.org/new/inside/publications/1999_NK_Book.pdf. Accessed May 15, 2009.

Nalanda

Known as "the Buddhist University," Nalanda ("the place that confers the Lotus") was a vast Buddhist monastic complex. Located in northeastern India near present-day Bihar, Nalanda was visited by such Chinese travelers to India as Xuan Zong and Yi Jing. They left colorful descriptions of the place. At its height Nalanda housed more than 10,000 monks studying the full range of Buddhist topics, including mathematics, medicine, and logic. However, as it grew in influence its curriculum was increasingly influenced by Hinduism.

Traditional accounts say that Nalanda was first founded by the Magadha dynasty in the fifth century CE. However no archaeological evidence has been uncovered to back this up. It was almost certainly founded by rulers of the Gupta dynasty (320–ca. 620). It was also strongly supported by the Pala rulers (eighth–12th centuries). The complex was ultimately destroyed in the Muslim invasions of the 12th and 13th centuries, beginning with the attack of Mohammad Bakhtyar in 1193. The site of Nalanda was first excavated in 1872 by Alexander Cunningham.

Nalanda was most significant as a site of contact with Tibet. A second Nalanda University was founded in Tibet, near Lhasa, by the monk/scholar Rongston Sengge (1347–1449). More recently, a Nalanda Monastery was founded in Toulouse, France, in 1981, by Lama Zopa Rinpoche and Lama Thubten Yeshe.

Today, tourists may visit the vast ruins of Nalanda. In recent years a Nalanda Institute of Pali Studies, established adjacent to the ruins, has attempted to capture the past glory of the site.

Edward A. Irons

See also: Buddhism; Foundation for the Preservation of the Mahayana Tradition; Tibetan Buddhism.

Ruins of Nalanda in present-day Bihar, India. Nalanda was a university and Buddhist center that dates back to at least the fifth century BCE. (AP Photo/Prashant Ravi)

References

Chauley, G. C. *Art and Architecture of Nalanda.* New Delhi: Sundeep, 2002.

Mani, C. *The Heritage of Nalanda.* New Delhi: Aryan Books International, 2008.

Mishra, B. N. *Nalanda.* 3 vols. New Delhi: B. R. Publishing Corporation, 1998.

Uphendra, Thakur. *Buddhist Cities in Early India: Buddha-Gaya: Rajagrha: Nalanda.* Columbia, MO: South Asia Books, 1996.

■ Namibia

Namibia is a sparsely populated and largely desert land on the southwest coast of Africa, between Angola and South Africa. Its 318,700 square miles of territory is bounded on the east by Botswana. The Europeans who finally focused attention on Namibia in the 19th century found it inhabited by some 11 different African peoples. Today, among the 2,089,000 people of the country, the more populous groups are the Hereros, the Ovambos (making approximately half of Namibia's population), and the Demaras.

Germany, which came late to the European quest for colonial glory, annexed Namibia in 1884. In the meantime, explorers found it to be wealthy in a variety of minerals, from diamonds to uranium. Following World War I, Germany was stripped of Namibia, which became a trust territory assigned to South Africa by the League of Nations. Then, after World War II, South Africa announced its intentions to completely annex the land, thus beginning a struggle with the United Nations, which had supported Namibia's independence. In 1968 the UN declared South Africa's presence in Namibia to be illegal, but was unable to act as the major Western powers supported South Africa. In the mid-1960s, Namibians organized the South West African

Rhenish mission church in Namibia, built in 1895. (Bildagentur/Stockphotopro)

Namibia

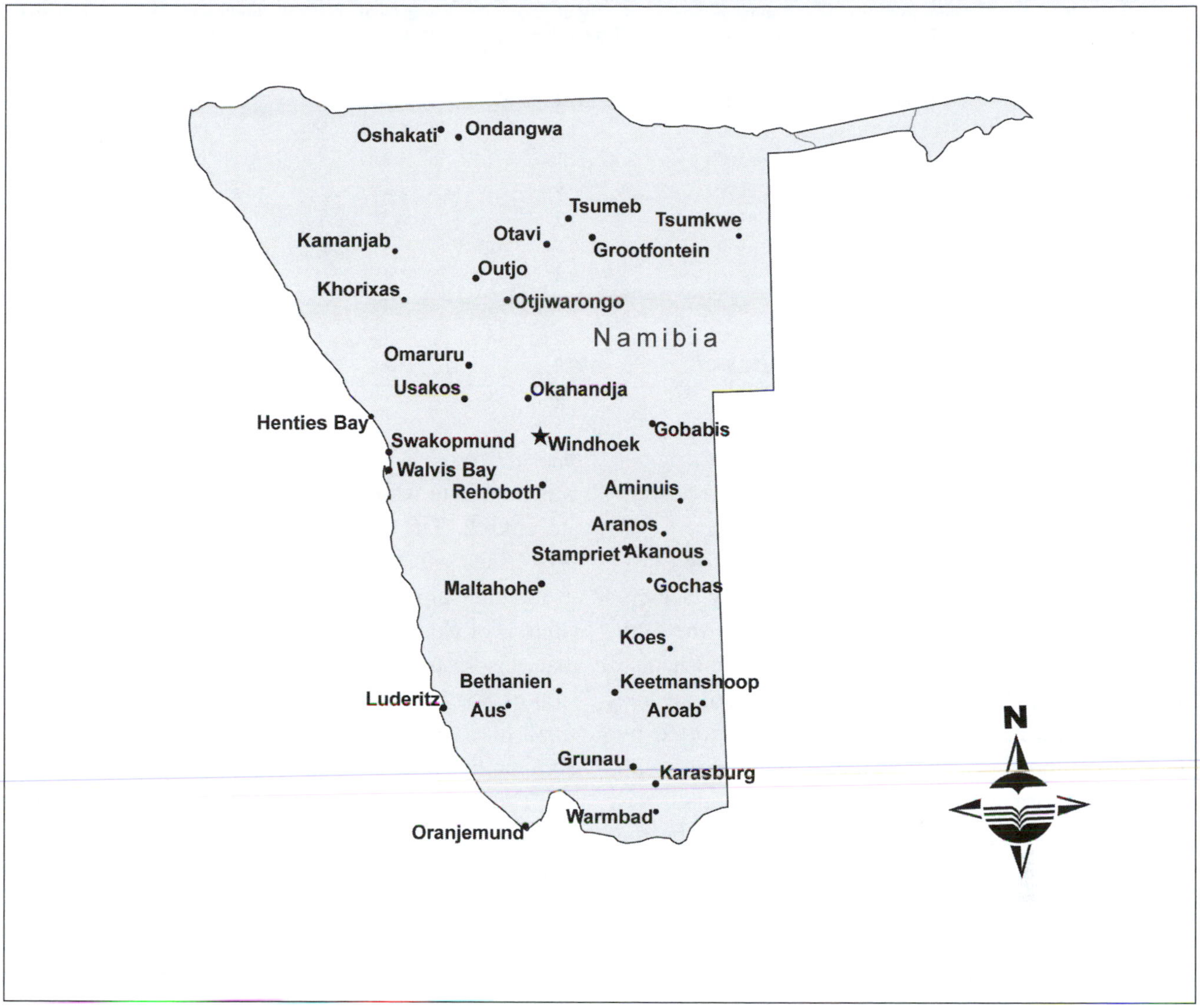

People's Organization (SWAPO) to work for their liberation. A 25-year struggle ensued that often erupted into warfare.

Finally, as changes in the region were undoing the apartheid regime, South Africa finally released its hold on Namibia. In November 1989 the first free elections were held, and SWAPO delegates were swept into power. Independence was formally proclaimed in 1990. The new leadership moved to deal with the effects of apartheid with government actions, including the improvement of living conditions for the Native Africans and the strengthening of literacy programs.

Religion in Namibia today is in many ways shaped by the country's colonial past. Traditional religions do survive among several of the Namibian peoples, especially the Ambo, the Herero, the Heikum, and the Kung (or San) bushpeople. Although each group has its own particular religious community, they all share some common beliefs, such as that in a supreme God who is very distant. Because this deity is removed from everyday life, attention in the traditional religions in Namibia tends to be directed to more immediate realities, ancestor spirits, and magical operations. Traditional religion continues to decline in the face of Christian

Namibia

Religion	Followers in 1970	Followers in 2010	% of Population	Annual % growth 2000–2010	Followers in 2025	Followers in 2050
Christians	715,000	1,967,000	91.2	1.37	2,356,000	2,798,000
Protestants	402,000	1,282,000	59.4	3.90	1,489,000	1,687,000
Roman Catholics	116,000	455,000	21.1	5.02	625,000	740,000
Independents	63,200	260,000	12.1	1.94	310,000	400,000
Ethnoreligionists	56,100	128,000	5.9	1.45	110,000	90,000
Agnostics	0	40,000	1.9	6.33	60,000	100,000
Baha'is	300	10,400	0.5	1.45	18,000	30,000
Muslims	0	8,500	0.4	1.45	12,000	16,000
Jews	600	2,600	0.1	1.45	3,000	4,800
Atheists	0	500	0.0	1.48	1,000	2,000
Total population	**772,000**	**2,157,000**	**100.0**	**1.45**	**2,560,000**	**3,041,000**

evangelism and is now followed by less than 5 percent of the population.

Christianity was introduced to Namibia by European missionaries. The London Missionary Society made an initial survey of Namibia early in the 19th century and was a catalyst in establishing the Rhenish Mission, which began missionary work among the Herero people in 1842. The Mission, supported by members of the Evangelical Church in Germany with a combined Lutheran and Reformed background, was soon joined by a second mission established by the Finnish Lutheran Mission. These two missions grew side by side, working with different African peoples. A third Lutheran group, serving only white members, arose in the 20th century.

At the end of the 19th century the Roman Catholic Church began to build a presence in Namibia, in the area immediately south of the Angolan border, among the Ovambo people. Originally assigned to the Diocese of Cimbebasia (Angola), the mission was designated a prefecture in 1892. The Vicariate of Windhoek was established in 1926, becoming a diocese in 1994. A second missionary thrust in the southern part of Namibia was organized as the Vicariate of Keetmanshoop in 1909. Keetmanshoop was also elevated to diocese status in 1994.

Following the takeover of Namibia by South Africa, South Africans moved into the land and brought with them a number of churches, the largest of which was the Dutch Reformed Church, whose membership was limited to whites though it had an all-black affiliate church. The Methodist Church of South Africa established a black mission, and approximately half its membership was black. The United Congregational Church of Southern Africa developed a membership that was 95 percent black. The Apostolic Faith Mission of South Africa, a Pentecostal church, has had a small black membership in what has remained a predominantly white church.

The Anglicans, though the first Christian group in Namibia, did not develop a mission until the 1920s. That work among the Ambo people was originally assigned to the Diocese of Damaraland (South Africa), but more recently a Diocese of Namibia within the Church in the Province of South Africa has been erected, with its bishop stationed at Windhoek.

African Initiated Churches began to appear in Namibia with the successive waves of unrest among members of the Rhenish Mission, the majority of whom were Herero. In 1946 a group left the Rhenish Mission and affiliated with the African Methodist Episcopal Church, a church based in the United States with affiliated work in South Africa since 1892. Then in 1955 a large group of Herero left to found the Oruuano (Community). Then in the 1960s that church split into three factions.

Since World War II, a spectrum of Protestant churches has appeared, many if not most having grown from South African churches establishing congregations in Namibia. There are also a few independent churches from Botswana, on Namibia's western border, such as the Spiritual Healing Church and the Apostolic Spiritual Healing Church, as well as the Moshoeshoe Berean Bible Readers' Church from Lesotho. Both the Church of Jesus Christ of Latter-day Saints and the Jehovah's Witnesses are also active in Namibia.

A Council of Churches in Namibia was organized in 1978. It is now an affiliate council to the World Council of Churches. The Jewish community in Namibia emerged in the early 1920s, and a synagogue was established in Windhoek in 1924. The several hundred members continue their relationship to the community in South Africa. Namibia has not been considered a major target of Hindu and Buddhist groups, which are very active in South Africa, and support for Islam is minuscule. There are several assemblies of the Baha'i Faith.

J. Gordon Melton

See also: African Initiated (Independent) Churches; African Methodist Episcopal Church; Apostolic Faith Mission of South Africa; Baha'i Faith; Church in the Province of South Africa; Church of Jesus Christ of Latter-day Saints; Dutch Reformed Church; Evangelical Church in Germany; Jehovah's Witnesses; London Missionary Society; Methodist Church of Southern Africa; Rhenish Mission; Roman Catholic Church; United Congregational Church of Southern Africa; World Council of Churches.

References

Beris, A. P. J. *From Mission to Local Church: One Hundred Years of Mission by the Catholic Church in Namibia, with Special Reference to the Development of the Archdiocese of Windhoek and the Apostolic Vicariate of Rundu.* Windhoek: John Meinert, 1996.

Buys, G. L., and S. V. V. Nambala. *History of the Church in Namibia 1805–1990, an Introduction.* Windhoek: Gamsberg Macmillan, 2003.

Hellberg, Carl J. *Mission, Colonialism, and Liberation: The Lutheran Church in Namibia, 1840–1966*. Windhoek: New Namibia Books, 1997.

Hunke, N. *Church and State: 100 Years of Catholic Mission in Namibia.* Windhoek: RCC/John Meinert Printers, 1996.

Katjavivi, P. H., P. Frostin, and K. Mbuende, eds. *Church and Liberation in Namibia*. London: Pluto Press, 1990.

Nammbala, S. V. V. *Church and State in Namibia, 1806–1989.* St. Paul, MN: Luther Northwestern Theological Seminary, 1990.

Nammbala, S. V. V. *History of the Church in Namibia*. Lutheran Quarterly, 1994.

Voipio, R. *History of the Evangelical Lutheran Ovambo Kavango Church.* Oniipa: ELOK, 1972.

Nanak, Guru

1469–1539

Guru Nanak, the founder of the Sikh religion, was a mystic and visionary caught within the conflicts between Hindus and Muslims for the support of the Indian people.

Nanak was born on April 15, 1469, in Talwandi-Rai-Bhoe in the District of Shekhupur (Pakistan), west of Lahore. He was the son of a land-surveyor and small farmer of the Khatri tribe, a warrior people, of the Bedi tribe.

The devotion to God that marked his mature life began to manifest even in his youth; he seemed often in a meditative state even as he watched over the family's cattle. Stories of his childhood tell of him beginning to utter mysterious sayings at the age of five. When he was seven, he was taken to a teacher from whom he was to learn to read, and he lapsed into silence. Stories also later arose of miracles that occurred during his childhood.

His tendency to withdraw led acquaintances of his parents to suggest that they should move for an early marriage. He eventually married Sulakhani, a Khatri from the Chona sub-caste, and they had two sons, Lakhmi Das and Siri Chand. As he grew to manhood, Nanak learned three languages. He took his basic education in the local Indian dialect, but also studied Sanskrit (the language of the Indian holy books) and Persian, whose poetry he mastered.

Of the many mystical experiences that dotted his life, an early one was particularly important. One day he went to the river to bathe. While there he was approached by "messengers of God" who whisked him

Portrait of Nanak, early-sixteenth-century Indian religious leader, founder of Sikhism, and the first guru of Sikhs. (Michael Freeman/Corbis)

away to a divine court where they fed him sweet nectar. No one saw him for three days, and then upon his return he declared his basic insight that there were neither Hindu nor Muslim. He had arrived at a state of internal harmony and equanimity. He now began to teach with the ideals of love, equality, justice, selfless service, and devotion to God as his central themes. He also denounced religious hypocrisy.

Guru Nanak emerged as a leader of the devotional (*bhakti*) movement, while simultaneously calling for reform of unjust Indian social and religious customs. He dedicated himself to awakening the consciousness of the people even as he attacked the oppression of the caste system, discrimination, and injustice.

In founding the Sikh tradition, Nanak sought to integrate Buddhist, Hindu, and Islamic insights that contributed to the virtuous life and enlightenment. As he began to travel through India and beyond, he attacked the caste system and freely mingled with people of all castes. By precept and example, he called for an end to idol worship and what he considered pseudo-religious beliefs (those lacking a spiritual content). He used money he received to set up common kitchens, where all could relax and eat together with any who chose to hear his teachings apart from any consideration of their caste or status.

Three basic teachings formed the essence of his message. First, he called upon his followers to practice Naam Japna, the meditation on the One God through repeating and studying God's Name and virtues (also termed *japna* yoga). The inner life thus developed would support a life of righteousness. Second, his followers were to live as householders to earn their living through honest physical and/or mental labor. The life of righteousness is marked by truthfulness and the highest spiritual, moral, and social values. Third, Sikhs were to share their possession with others of the community. The community lives from the common good.

Nanak's teachings set the goal of human existence as achieving self-perfection while living and then assisting others to do the same (in logical not necessarily temporal order). He also emphasized the importance of the guru's grace and will in transforming one's life.

Throughout his life, Nanak's teachings were transcribed and the manuscripts passed to his successor Guru Angad Dev (1504–1553), the second guru of the Sikhs. These manuscripts were put together with the writings of his several successors by Guru Arjan Dev (1563–1606), to create the Adi Granth, the sacred book of the Sikhs.

J. Gordon Melton

See also: Devotion/Devotional Traditions; Nanak's Birthday, Guru; Sikhism/Sant Mat; Yoga.

References

Banerjee, Anil Chandra. *Guru Nanak and His Times.* Patalia, India: Punjabi University, 1971.

Dhillon, Harish. *The First Sikh Spiritual Master: Timeless Wisdom from the Life and Techniques of Guru Nanak.* Woodstock, VT: Skylight Paths Publishing, 2006.

Kapur, Prithipal Singh, ed. *The Divine Master: Life and Teachings of Guru Nanak.* Jalandhar, India: ABS Publications, 1988.

McLeod, W. H. *Guru Nanak and the Sikh Religion.* London: Oxford University Press, 1968.

Talib, Gurbachan Singh. *Guru Nanak: His Personality and Vision.* Delhi: Gur Das Kapur & Sons, 1969.

Nanak's Birthday, Guru

1469–1539

Guru Nanak was the founder of Sikhism, which he created by merging what he felt was the best of Islam and Hinduism. The religion and its community steadily evolved over the next several hundred years under the leadership of nine gurus who in turn succeeded Nanak. The last of the gurus decreed that the Guru Granth Sahib, the book of writings of Nanak and the several gurus, would from that time forward be the community's new guru. Through the book, Guru Nanak's teachings have remained uppermost in the development of Sikhism.

Nanak was was born in Talwandi, now known as Nankana Sahib, a village near Lahore, in what is now Pakistan. His birth occurred, according to the Hindu lunar calendar then in effect, on the third day of the light half of the month of Baisakh of the year 1469 CE. This date has now been calculated to be on or about Saturday, April 15, 1469, on the Common Era calendar.

The Sikh community is in a transition concerning its celebration of Nanak's birthday. Until the 1990s, it was celebrated in November. However, in the 1990s, a new Sikh calendar was adopted. The calendar is a solar calendar named the Nanakshahi calendar after Guru Nanak and based somewhat on the Common Era calendar. March 14 on the Common Era calendar is the first day of the New Year on the Nanakshahi calendar. The new calendar places Guru Nanak's birthday on Vaisakh 1 (or April 14). Most Sikhs now acknowledge that day.

Guru Nanak's birthday is one of 12 Gurpurbs, holidays that commemorate the birth or death of one of the 10 Sikh gurus. Sikhs will celebrate the Gurpurb for Guru Nanak by performing an Akhand Path, a public reading of the Sikh holy scriptures, at both the Golden Temple in Amritsar, the main Sikh temple, and in *gurdwaras* around the world. To read the entire Guru Granth Sahib from beginning to end requires two days. The reading will begin two days before the holiday to be commemorated and will end early in the morning of the holy day. Each person chosen to participate will read aloud for two to three hours.

Where possible, on the day prior to the actual birthday celebration, a procession may be held. It will include singers and musicians, and five men who dress to represent the Panj Piare (or Five Beloved Ones), the first five members to be formally initiated into the Sikh community.

On the day of the celebration, Sikhs will gather at the gurdwara, which will be decorated for a time of prayer, talks on various aspects of Sikhism, and the singing of *kirtans*, holy songs (in this case from the Guru Granth Sahib), followed by a communal meal. Activities for all ages may continue all day.

J. Gordon Melton

See also: Calendars, Religious; Common Era Calendar; Devotion/Devotional Traditions; Nanak, Guru; Sikhism.

References

Dhillon, Haresh. *The First Sikh Spiritual Master: Timeless Wisdom from the Life and Techniques of Guru Nanak*. Woodstock, VT: Skylight Paths Publishing, 2006.

Duggal, K. S. *Sikh Gurus: Their Lives and Teachings*. New Delhi: UBSPD, 2005.

Kapoor, Sukhbor Sing. *Sikh Festivals*. Vero Beach, FL: Rourke Publishing Group, 1989.

Khalsa, Parmatma S. *Guru for the Aquarian Age: The Life and Teachings of Guru Nanak*. Santa Cruz, NM: Yogiji Press, 1997.

Naqshbandiya Sufi Order

The development of the Sufi *tariqa* Naqshbandiya can be traced back to Khwaja Abu Ya'qub Yusuf-i Hamadani (d. 1140), who was the key figure for the genesis of Sufi associations in Transoxiania. After Hamadani's death, his tariqa split into two *silsilas* from which the two major tariqas in Transoxiania emerged: the Yassawiya, members of which were mainly Turkic-speaking nomads, and the Khwajagan, which found its followers predominantly among the Persian-speaking urban population. The seventh in the line of the Khwajagan Shaykhs was Shah Baha' ad-din-i Naqshband (d. 1389), the founder and name patron of the Naqshbandiya tariqa. His shrine is situated at Čar Bakr near Bokhara in today's Republic of Uzbekistan.

Because of the urban social background of the Naqshbandiya, the interpretations of the normative Islamic texts made by the traditional Islamic scholars, the *ulama,* had a substantially greater influence on the population than, for instance, on the Yassawiya. This perhaps explains why the doctrines of the Naqshbandiya are often described as "pietistic," compared to those of other tariqas from a rural or even nomadic milieu. For example, an absolute prerequisite for the knowledge of the esoteric dimension of Islam is, as it is in the teachings of the most Sufi tariqas, the conscientious execution of the daily religious duties (including fasting in the month of Ramadan and performing the *hajj*). Above that, the silent dhikr (*dhikr-i khufiya*), the remembrance of God by contemplative seclusion (*khalwa*), plays the central role. The aim is not, as in many other tariqas, to cut off the driving soul (*nafs*) by ascetic practices, but to purify the heart (*qalb*) by the way of love (*'ishq*) in daily active life (*hayat al-'amal*).

By stressing a much wider interpretation of the Koranic term *'amal* than was usual, the Naqshbandiya emphasized a much stronger inner-worldliness than most Sufi tariqas in the Middle Ages. This provided it with an immense potential for the reformation of society (*tajdid*). Therefore it seems quite understandable that, from the late Timurid period (late 15th century) on, the Naqshbandiya became ever more concerned with social, economic, and political issues. In fact, it appears that the Naqshbandi saw himself as mediator between the ruler and the ruled, whose task it was to make sure their actions corresponded with the normative requirements of the Koran and the prophetic Sunna. This political intervention of the Naqshbandiya in Transoxiania is connected to individuals such as 'Abd ar-rah man-i Jami from Herat (d. 1492), his disciple 'Ali Shir Nawa'i (d. 1501), and, above all, Khwaja 'Ubayd-allah Ahrar of Samarkand (d. 1490).

The third of the major doctrines concerning Naqshbandi practice is the projection of love (*rabitat al-'ishq*) by the adept on his spiritual master in order to obtain the experience of spiritual unity as a substitute to the ultimate entering into God (*fana'*). In the context of the third doctrine one must refer to the role played by the monistic philosophy of Muhyi d-din b. 'Arabi (d. 1240). His famous philosopheme of the "Oneness of Existence" (*wahdat al-wujud*) allows equal knowledge of the creation with knowledge of the creator. The Naqshbandiya doctrine of the rabitat al-'ishq seems to be based on this theory of Ibn 'Arabi. Therefore his texts became quite popular among Naqshbandis by the 15th century, as we can see from statements made by such important figures as the above mentioned Jami, Nawa'i, and Khwaja Ahrar.

In the 15th century, with Khwaja Ahrar, the center of the Naqshbandiya shifted from Bokhara to Samarkand. He became a close confidant of the Timurid ruler and thus carried out mediation in armed conflicts. The Naqshbandis spread into the territory ruled by the last

Čaghatayid princes and were finally among the followers of Babur (d. 1530) to India, where Babur established the dynasty of the Mughals. The "Baburnama" gives the names of some of those Naqshbandis, among them two spiritual successors (*khalifa*) of Khwaja Ahrar.

Not much is known about the Naqshbandiya in India from that time until the appearance of Muhammad Baqi'-billah "Bi-rang" Simaqi (d. 1603) in imperial Delhi, where he established a convent (*khanaqah*) and gathered a huge number of disciples around him. As an indirect khalifa, or successor, of Khwaja Ahrar, he openly advocated the idea of the *wahdat al-wujud* against the already known idea of the "Oneness of the Testimony" (*wahdat ash-shuhud*) in India, which was developed by the Kubrawiya Shaykh 'Ala' ad-din Simnani (d. 1336).

Baqi'-billah's most famous and effective disciple was without doubt Shaykh Ahmad Faruqi Sirhindi (d. 1668), who was later given the epithet "Renewer of the Second Millennium" (*mujaddid-i alf-thani*). By rigorously advocating the idea of the *wahdat ash-shuhud*, found primarily in his epistles ("Maktubat-i imam-i rabbani"), Sirhindi introduced a new doctrine into the Naqshbandiya and was thus responsible for the divide of the tariqa. The debate over the wahdat al-wujud issue became essential in doctrinal terms, and its advocates constituted the Ahrariya silsila whereas the followers of Sirhindi formed the Mujaddidiya silsila.

With the decline of the Mughal Empire in the 18th century, representatives of both silsilas tried to focus on more pragmatic issues and thus to reunite the Naqshbandiya. A central figure in this context was Shah Wali-allah Dihlawi (d. 1762), whose influence on the various political and intellectual trends in India is still undiminished. Dihlawi tried to resolve the debate over wahdat al-wujud and wahdat ash-shuhud by describing them as referring to two different objects: wahdat ash-shuhud designates an epistemological viewpoint while wahdat al-wujud is an ontological category. More important for Shah Wali-allah Dihlawi was the unity of the Muslim umma to become able to act.

Nevertheless, the two silsilas are still separate today. Although the Mujaddidiya began in the 18th century to establish itself in Transoxiania, where it is connected with names such as Sufi Allahyar Bukhari (d. ca. 1723), and in the Middle East and in Anatolia by mediation of the Indian Murtasa az-Zabidi (d. 1791), the Ahrariya can be found in many south Asian socio-religious movements and institutions that developed in the 19th century: for example, the Dar al-'ulum at Deoband, the Nadwat al-'ulama' in Lucknow, or the movement of the Ahl-i hadith.

Jan-Peter Hartung

See also: Islam; Sufism.

References

Fusfeld, Warren E. "The Shaping of Sufi Leadership in Delhi: The Naqshbandiyya Mujaddidiyya 1750–1920." PhD. diss., University of Pennsylvania, 1981.

Garborieau, Marc, A. Popovic, and Th. Zarcone, eds. *Naqshbandis. Cheminements et situation actuelle d'un ordre mystique musulman.* Istanbul: Institut Français d'Études Anatoliennes, 1990.

Hermansen, Marcia K. *The Conclusive Argument from God: Shah Wali Allah of Delhi's Hujjat Allah Baligha*. Leiden: Brill, 1995.

Paul, Jurgen. *Doctrine and Organization. The Khwâjagân/Naqshbandîya in the First Generations after Bahâ'uddîn*. Berlin: Das Arabische Buch, 1998.

Rahman, Fazlur. *Selected Letters of Shaykh Ahmad Sirhindi*. Karachi: Royal Books, 1968.

Nara

Nara, Japan's capital city in the eighth century BCE, would be founded just as Buddhism was making its first significant push into the country and would continue to serve as the major center from which Buddhism permeated the country for several centuries. The relatively small city became the home of six Buddhist groups whose temple-schools specialized in the study and teachings of particular Buddhist texts, and from whom young monks received their training. The Ritsu School especially concerned itself with the *Vinaya* (*Precepts*), the document from the early Pali canon of Buddhist scripture outlining the rules by which monks lived. It is difficult to determine the exact order and dates when most of the schools arrived in Japan from Korea and China through the seventh century, though

The Buddhist Todai-ji Temple in the Japanese city of Nara is the largest wooden building in the world and houses some of the world's largest statues of the Buddha. (Holger Mette/Dreamstime.com)

the Kegon (aka Huayen or Flower Garland) School was the last to organize (751).

Nara was located on Japan's main island, Honshu, a short distance south of present-day Kyoto. It was a planned city modeled on the Chinese capital, Chang'an (now Xian City in Shaanxi Province). The site remained Japan's capital from 710 to 784.

In the 730s a smallpox epidemic spread across Japan, and the Emperor Shomu (r. 724–749) called upon Buddhists to assist the government in meeting the crisis. He ordered each province of the country to build a Buddhist temple and make copies of Buddhist scriptures. Then in 743 as the disease receded, he oversaw the creation of a giant statue of the bodhisattva Vairocana Buddha, the primary character in the Flower Garland Sutra. It was formally dedicated in 752, its creation being directly connected to the arrival and establishment of the Kegon School. In the meantime, Todai-ji, which would become both the head temple of the Kegon School and the lead temple of all the Buddhist temples across the country, had been completed. The statue of Vairocana was erected in a building adjacent to Todai-ji. In 754, Ganjin, an Itsu priest from China, oversaw the creation of a formal place (a *kaidan,* or platform) for the ordination of Buddhist monks at Todai-ji. As the monks at the several Nara schools finished their course of study, they were all officially ordained at Todai-ji following the format common in China.

By building the Buddhist center in the nation's capital, the government showed both its support of the new faith and its intention to control it. It has also been suggested that with the growth of Buddhism, its role and influence on the court grew beyond what had been expected of it, and hence the emperor finally decided to move to Heian (Kyoto). After the government relocated in 794, all of the Buddhist groups opened branch temples in close proximity to the imperial court through which they continued to exert their power for the next centuries. Nara's power only began to wane with the establishment of the shogun's capital at Kamakura in 1185. The new capital became the new center of Buddhism and the home of a whole new set of groups that would replace the Nara sects as the dominant force in the Buddhist community.

The temple-schools at Nara would face a variety of challenges in the centuries after the capital moved to Kyoto. In 805, Saicho, the founder of the rival Tendai School of Buddhism on Mount Hiei, obtained permission to train monks apart from the Nara schools. At first, the monks had to go to Nara for ordination, but in 827 the Tendai center completed its ordination platform and began ordaining its own monks in the mode Saicho had seen at T'ian-tai Mountain in China. Meanwhile, Kukai (aka Kobo Daishi), the former head of Todai-ji, left Nara and moved to Mount Koya to begin the dissemination of Shingon Buddhism.

In a more mundane sphere, the temples at Nara were largely constructed of wood and at various times fell victim to both war and weather. Most at one point had been destroyed and had to be rebuilt. In the 11th century, Todai-ji was destroyed and the Vairocana Buddha statue damaged. The statue was restored and rededicated in 1195. The process of restoring the statue became the occasion for the building of the second giant Buddha statue, this time of Amida (Amitabha) Buddha, at the new capital of Kamakura. The main hall of Todai-ji that houses the statue was last destroyed in the late 16th century. It was rebuilt and, though slightly smaller than the building it replaced, survives today as the largest wooden building in the world.

Today, Nara is known primarily as a place to see the old temples originally erected in the eighth century and the still impressive statue of Vairocana. Three of the original groups have survived and maintain their national headquarters at Nara—the Kegon, Ritsu, and Hosso Buddhist schools. Beginning with the establishment of the Tendai School on Mount Hiei, however, the Nara schools, which had never developed a popular following, began to be left behind. With the establishment of Kamakura, the new schools—Zen, Pure Land, and Nichiren—became the dominant element in Buddhism, and the Nara schools never again assumed an important role in Japanese life.

Edward A. Irons

See also: Amitabha's Birthday; Hiei, Mount; Kamakura; Nara, Six Buddhist Schools of; Nichiren; Pure Land Buddhism; Saicho; Zen Buddhism.

References

Hakudo, Inoue. *Nar/ the Yamato Road: Villages of Spirit and Body.* Kyoto, Japan: Kyoto Shoin, 1988.

Kasahara, Kazou, ed. *A History of Japanese Religion.* Tokyo: Kosei Publishing, 2001.

Martin, John H., and Phyllis C. Martin. *Nara: A Cultural Guide to Japan's Ancient Capital.* Rutland, VT: Tuttle Publishing, 1994.

Matsuoka, Asako. *Sacred Treasures of Nara.* Tokyo: The Hokuseido Press, 1935.

Nara. Tokyo: The Japan Times, 1972.

Ooka, Minoru. *Temples of Nara and Their Art.* Trans. by Dennis Lishka. New York: Weatherhill, 1973.

Yanagishima, Hikosaku. *Kyoto and Nara: Where the Japanese Heart Goes Alive Everywhere.* Kyoto, Japan: Ranshobo Co., 1960.

Nara, Six Buddhist Schools of

The Six Schools of Nara Buddhism were six temple-schools of Buddhism established in the seventh century at the new capital of Japan. Together, the schools constituted a massive academic center for the study of Buddhism, the training of monk-scholars, and offering leadership to the slowly developing national Buddhist movement. The imperial government assigned Buddhist leadership with conducting rites and ceremonies for the protection of the nation and the imperial family and the promotion of a comprehensive study of Buddhist culture, not just their narrow specialty. That being said, each temple-school represented a single scholastic tradition and approach to Buddhism, known in Japan as the Kusha, Jujitsu, Sanron, Hosso, Kegon, and Ritsu schools. All of these schools were introduced from China (or Korea). Given their primary task relative to the emperor and the nation, the Nara schools had limited direct impact on the religious life of the general population. However, they did lay the foundation upon which Buddhism would later expand. Their efforts provided the basis for the subsequent development of Japanese Buddhism. Buddhist monk-priests became increasingly influential in the Nara court, forcing Emperor Kammu (r. 781–806) to relocate his government to Heian (Kyoto), a move that encouraged Saicho (767–822), founder of the Tendai School, and Kukai (774–835), founder of the Shingon School, to experiment with more broadly based Buddhist movements.

Adherents of all six Nara schools shared Gautama Buddha's original concern for human suffering and his analysis of its cause, remedy, and extinction. Through the succeeding centuries, first in India and then in China, different teachers attempted to clarify the meaning of the Buddha's insight on such issues as interdependency of phenomena, ultimate enlightenment (*nirvana*), the non-self (*anatman*), and the Middle Way. Their divergent understandings created more than a dozen Buddhist intellectual traditions by the time that Buddhism began to move out of its homeland.

Buddha's insight on the interdependence of all phenomena (usually termed co-dependence arising) led directly to his attaining the enlightenment for which he is named. He opined on the fact that all sentient beings possess the essence of enlightenment, but because of the false notions and attachments of the mind, remain in an unenlightened state. The insight that all existences are mutually dependent in time and space reaffirmed the prevailing belief in transiency (*anitya*) and the moral efficacy of reincarnation and karma. Buddha also asserted his understanding of

Kiyomizu-dera (pure water temple) was founded in 780 CE and is associated with the Hosso sect of Japanese Buddhism. (Mihai-bogdan Lazar/Dreamstime.com)

no-self (anatman). The self lacks any substantial reality, and the notion of eternal and self-sustaining entities (that is, the eternal soul or spirit) is fiction.

Buddha offered the Four Noble Truths as a new perspective on the basic human problem. The third of the Four Truths claims the ultimate enlightened state (nirvana) to be the antidote for entrapment in the transitory world of *samsara*. The fourth Noble Truth points to the Eightfold Path as the means by which a person can purge the mind of incorrect views. From this beginning, Buddhists thinkers concentrated their rumination on the nature of the mind. They asked questions such as: What does it know? How does it know? How can it be known? What does it do?

A selection of the many schools of Buddhism developed in India was transmitted to China, from China to Korea, and from both China and Korea to Japan. These traditions were living schools, so as they existed through time and moved into new countries and were expressed in new languages, they changed, even as their proponents continually returned to the texts from which each took their inspiration.

The Kusha School The Japanese scholar-monks Dasho (638–700), Joe (644–714), Chitatsu (dates unknown), and others who studied in China introduced the Kusha (or Dharma Analysis Treasury) School to Japan. It is based on the *Abhidharmakosha* (Japanese: *Abidatsumakusha; Treatise on the Higher Dharma*), written by the Indian Buddhist monk Vasubandhu (ca. 320–400). It was originally translated into Chinese by the Indian monk Paramatha (499–569) and later re-translated by Xuanzhang (600–664). Dasho, Joe, and Chitatsu studied with Xuanzhang's direct disciples.

The Kusha School continued the Indian Sarvastivada School that sought to rationally demonstrate the truth of Buddha's insight of no-self (anatman) and to establish a method to realize enlightenment (nirvana). To accomplish their goal, they attempted to clarify the relationship between transiency (anitya), no-self (anatman), and interdependence (*pratityasamutpada*) by analyzing the elemental building blocks of phenomenal reality (the *dharmas*). They suggested that phenomena were of two types—conditioned (*samskrta*) and unconditioned (*asamskrta*). Conditioned and unconditioned dharmas mix and match through a multiplicity of causes and conditions to momentarily establish and maintain the human personality and the material world. The conditioned elements of reality that constitute the ever-changing phenomenal experience of human existence consist of 72 dharmas that are grouped into four sub-categories: (1) the five sense organs and their objects, (2) mind, (3) psycho-physical (sense and thought) data, and (4) non-mental and physical elements. Dharmic events do not occur simply through a single cause, but are the result of a multiplicity of causes and conditions. The school identified six direct and four indirect causes and five varieties of results that explain the causal efficacy of conditioned dharmas and their effects. In the act of perceiving, conceiving, willing, thinking, and doing, an individual continually generates karmic energy that collectively constitutes an ever-evolving personal existence. In addition to such basic sentient psychophysical functions of sensation, volition, conceptualization, and remembering, the Kusha school identified attendant good (or efficacious) mental faculties, defiled (or inefficacious) mental faculties that relate to the realization of nirvana, and indeterminate mental faculties.

Enlightenment (nirvana), one of the three unconditioned dharmas, identifies a spiritual condition wherein a person has extinguished the karmic energy generated by thought, speech, and body through wisdom that recognizes the fiction of an enduring and substantial self. In order to transcend samsara, the world of suffering and change, a person must cultivate wisdom that extinguishes ignorance of the truth of interdependence (pratityasamutpada) and clinging to the belief in a substantial self (atman).

The other unconditioned dharmas are space and the quiescence that is the result of the absence of causes. The Kusha exploration concerning the mind and its functions anticipates the insights posed by the Hosso School.

The Jujitsu School The Jujitsu School takes its lead from the *Satyasiddhi śastra* (*Establishment of Truth*), a text written by the Indian monk Harivarman (ca. 250–350). Kumarajiva (344–413) later produced a Chinese translation of the text that provoked considerable interest due to the presence within it of both Theravada and Mahayana ideas. It appears that the Korean monk Hyegwan (or Ekwan) transmitted Jujitsu teachings to Japan along with those of the Sanron School into Japan in the 620s as part of the original phase of Buddhism's reception of the new religion a century before Nara existed.

Harivarman criticized the Kusha (in India the Sarvastivada) approach to Buddhism as overly intellectual in its attempt to prove the validity of anatman. Harivarman hoped to re-instill the spirit of the Four Noble Truths as the path to enlightenment by emphasizing nirvana and its attainment. He also introduced 27 stages for spiritual advancement from the 4 stages of the arhat, the ideal enlightened personality of early Buddhism.

Harivarman suggested that individual existence was composed of five psychophysical factors (form, feeling, conceptualization, volition, and consciousness) as well as 84 dharmas that affirm the rationality of anatman. Unlike the Kusha, Harivarman saw the dharmas as non-substantial. Rather than assert or deny the substantiality of dharmas and the self, he suggested that dharmas are provisionally true (*samvrti satya*) in their transitory aspects, but are ultimately true (*paramatha satya*) in their essential non-substantial aspect. Interestingly, however, in the 27 stages of spiritual awareness he proposed, Harivarman speaks of the elimination of clinging to the self, but is silent on the issue of clinging to dharmas.

The Sanron School The Sanron (Three Treatise) School represents a number of strands of Indian

Buddhist thought that emerged from the writings of Indian monk Nagarjuna (ca. 100–200), including the *Dvadasadvara śastra* (*Treatise of Twelve Categories*) and the *Mulamadhyamaka karika* (*Middle Stanzas*); Pigala's commentary on the latter work; and the *Sata śastra* (*Treatise of One Hundred Verses*) by Aryadeva (third century). These texts advocated the refutation of all views that impede the attainment of enlightenment and the establishment of correct views through the Middle Path of the two levels of truth.

To dissuade persons from holding on to false ideas concerning reality, Nagarjuna and his disciples developed a dialectic that reduced all assertions to absurdity. By claiming that all assertions concerning existence or non-existence are false, the Sanron Buddhist refutes (1) the Brahmanic idea of atman, (2) the Kusha belief in the eternal existence of dharmas, (3) the Jujitsu assertion of the emptiness of the self and dharmas, and (4) any Mahayanists who assert the truth of *sunyata,* or emptiness.

The Sanron perspective was introduced to Japan along with the Jujitsu School by Hyekwan, a Korean monk, in 625, during the reign of the Empress Suiko (d. 629), a century before Nara was constructed. Thus it had already been an integral part of the Japanese scene when the new capital was conceived. The Sanron tradition would never develop an independent following, but the study of its central texts continues to the present.

The Sanron position resonates with the Buddha's reluctance to speculate on the nature of the transcendental—to do so contributes nothing to the relief of human suffering. The realization of nirvana, the unconditioned, stands in contradistinction to samsara, and thus transcends both existence and non-existence. Since nirvana/enlightenment is an intuitive experience that could not be expressed, the early Buddhists described it by explaining what it was not and in the process cast an unduly negative perception of the phenomenal world. The Sanron position rejected both the claim of the eternal reality of dharmas and the assertion of the nominal reality of dharmas and the self by affirming the Middle Way by utilizing the idea of sunyata (emptiness). In his effort to explain nirvana, Nagarjuna describes emptiness to be an experience devoid of all false thoughts. A person dwelling in sunyata is empty of thoughts and exists in selflessness.

In the *Middle Stanzas* Nagarjuna identifies the real and the ideal with the Middle Way. In the second verse he writes: "'*Pratityasamutpada*' (interdependence) is 'sunyata' (emptiness), it alone is the Middle Path." In the fourth verse he identifies samsara (this world of transitions) with nirvana (enlightenment). "Samsara has nothing that distinguishes it from nirvana. The limit of nirvana is the limit of samsara." Pratityasamutpada, sunyata, nirvana, and samsara refer to the same reality. Their distinction lay in how they are perceived. *Paramatha satya* (absolute truth) refers to an intuitive experience; with the cessation of conceptual thought, reality is perceived to be of a single uniform and undifferentiated experience. Sunyata, nirvana, and anatman point to this indescribable experience. In contrast, *samvrti satya* (conventional truth) refers to commonsense truth; it is the realm of samsara and pratityasamutpada. These two levels of truth are central to Sanron perceptions and to subsequent Mahayana thought. The Middle Path is simply to live in the world of samsara; to reside in nirvana is to be aware of the world's pitfalls.

The Hosso School The Hosso (also known as the Vijñanavada, the Yogacara, or the Consciousness-only) School derives its name from its special interest in the characteristics of dharmas associated with the various phases of cognition; "hosso" (*dharma laksana*) means "characteristics of dharma." The school is based on the writings of three Indian teachers, Maitreya (ca. 270–350, not to be confused with Maitreya, the future Buddha); Asanga (ca. 410–500); and Vasubandhu, the author of the *Abhidharmakosha*, who posited a Buddhist version of idealism, the notion of mind or consciousness-only, and that the phenomenal realities that we know are manifestations of mental functions. These thinkers do not deny the reality of the physical world; rather they maintain that we know the world through the sensory and cognitive data that are manipulated by the mind.

The most important text of this school is Dharmapala's (439–507) *Vijnaptimatratasiddhi* (*Joyuishikiron*; *Perfection of Consciousness-only*), with its 10 annotated commentaries on Vasubandhu's *Vijnaptimatrat*

Trimśika (*Yuishiki sanjuron*; *Consciousness-only in Thirty Verses*). Vasubandhu reflects on the characteristics of dharmas and explores the process of transformation from ignorance to enlightenment that had been neglected by the other schools.

Unable to locate key documents in his homeland, the monk-traveler Xuanzhang fled China and made his way to Nalanda University in India to study with the Yogacara master Silabhadra (592–645). On his return in 645 he translated the *Vijnaptimatratasiddhi* and established the Faxiang (Hosso) School. The Japanese priest Dosho (628–700) who studied with Xuanzhang returned home with its teachings.

In contrast with the earlier Kusha's limited interest in the functions of mind, the Yogacara system distinguishes eight varieties of mind-consciousness. The first five associated with the sensory organs are the consciousnesses of sight, sound, smell, taste, and touch. The sixth is mind-consciousness that coordinates the sensory information that is received from five organs of sense and cognitive data from the seventh. The seventh is *manas*-consciousness, which receives data from the exterior world processed through mind-consciousness and compares them with information stored in the eighth or *alaya*-consciousness and reroutes the synthesized information to the sixth-consciousness, enabling it to respond. These multiple levels of mind account for the cognitive understanding of the physical world, imagination, dreams, and memory. The functioning of each of the eight consciousnesses is dependent on activities of other levels of mind.

The alaya-consciousness or storehouse-consciousness is the repository of discrete bits of *bijas,* or seeds, which evolved from the mind's apprehension of sensory and mental impressions. Dharmic data are not simply impressed on a passive mind, but are processed, distorted, and retained in the alaya-consciousness until retrieved. Bijas serve as a template with which the mind-consciousness compares with sensory dharmic data to make sense of the world. When eye-consciousness spots a long-lost face, the bija or bijas that are associated with that face are retrieved to confirm the fact. In addition to the task of recognition, cognitive experience is often tinted by emotional and other associative factors. If the long-lost face is that of friend, recognition also arouses joy. If the face is that of a tormentor, it may arouse anger. These earlier impressions were deposited in the alaya-consciousness and color the respective manner in which individuals may view subsequent events. The same event gives rise to differing emotions. While most Americans associate the events of 9/11 with horror and grief, those who perpetuated the attack on the World Trade Towers view the events with triumph and joy. Each person's comprehension of the "objective" world is created from past associations and present conditions; this does not mean that the object does not exist, only that the unenlightened do not perceive its true nature.

The soteriological task for the Hosso devotee is to transform the alaya-consciousness into *adanajnana,* or mirror-wisdom, which will no longer falsely apprehend and fabricate sensory data and mental images. The purification of the alaya-consciousness forms the basis for the transformation of the other seven consciousnesses.

By positing the alaya-consciousness the Yogacarins were able to deflect criticism on the tenability of anatman. Dharmapala, however, asserts that the alaya-consciousness is a separate reality, a position that is found nowhere else in Buddhism.

The Hosso School went on to explain that the mind, depending on the spiritual maturity, perceives "three natures" to any "reality" that appears before it. They are: *parikalpita-laksana* (illusionary and discriminative nature), *paratantra laksana* (dependent nature), and *parisnispanna-laksana* (perfected or true nature). The unenlightened person perceiving the parikalpita-laksana character of the phenomenal world believes phenomena to be independent and eternal, when in fact they are simply manifestations of mind. The person who sees the paratantra-laksana nature of phenomena understands that phenomenal reality is dependent and in constant flux. The enlightened person who grasps the parisnispanna-laksana aspect of phenomenal reality understands that reality is illusionary and temporary manifestations of mind. This understanding transcends both illusionary and temporary reality in the Middle Way. Ultimate reality exists, but not phenomenally; again ultimate reality does not exist, but it is not phenomenal non-existence. It is synonymous with sunyata and nirvana. Imbued with perfect understanding, the enlightened being resides and works in the world of suffering and illusion, an important feature of the Mahayana enlightenment.

The Kegon School The Kegon (or Hauyen) School is based on the Avatamsaka (or Flower Garland) Sutra that first appeared in northeast India between the first and second centuries CE. It emerged as an independent tradition in China through the efforts of Dushun (558–640); Jiyan (602–667); and especially Fazang (643–712), who developed a taxonomy of the several Buddhist schools (and their scriptures). Two of Fazang's disciples, Daoxuan and Shenxiang, visited Japan where they were able to present Fazang's approach to Buddhism to Emperor Shomu (724–748). The emperor responded quite positively to the teachings, and as a result ordered the building of Todai-ji and the casting of a large image of Vairocana Buddha, the major character in the *Avatamsaka Sutra*.

Kegon masters explored the vision that transformed Gautama into the Buddha, the Enlightened One, who on the morning of the enlightenment saw that all dharmas (phenomena) appearing before his mind's eye were mutually related and interdependent. From this vision, they reasoned that the realm of dharmas, or the *dharmadhatu,* is embraced within a single thought and proceeded to describe a psycho-cosmic "metaphysics" that they crystallized in the doctrine of *hokkai engi.* Hokkai engi includes four visions of reality that correspond to the four levels of spiritual maturity. First, *jihokkai,* or the world of phenomenal reality, is the commonsense understanding that all existents are independent and distinct. Second, *rihokkai,* or the realm of universal truth, is the realm that sustains the phenomenal world; it is the realm of sunnyata that can be only intuitively apprehended. Third, *rijimuge hokkai*, the realm of the non-obstruction of phenomena and truth, is a vision that can be seen only by enlightened beings. Enlightened beings apprehend the truth present in every individual existence. Fourth, *jijimuge hokkai*, the realm of the interfusion of things, articulates the Kegon vision that all existents, while maintaining their individual identity, mutually interrelate and interfuse with each other to create a harmonious whole. The final chapter of the *Avatamsaka Sutra* also describes the various mental disciplines that need to be mastered to realize the dharmadhatu.

In its early years, the Kegon School enjoyed a certain privilege among the several Nara schools, given the emperor's favor and its hegemony over the megastatue of vairocana and the ordination platform for monks that were erected in Todai-ji. However, through the succeeding centuries it failed to attract a large following. On two occasions, monk-teachers attempted to revive the tradition—Myoe (1185–1333) during the Kamakura period and Hotan (1657–1738) in the Tokugawa period—but both failed. Kegon exerted considerable influence on later Buddhist developments, particularly Zen, but survives as one of the smaller Japanese groups.

Ritsu School While five of the Nara schools focused on the philosophical issues raised in Buddhist thought, the Ritsu, or Precepts, School was most concerned with the practical matters of faith and the maintenance of the institution, especially the sangha. "Ritsu" focuses on the Buddhist Precepts or Vinaya, the original Buddhist codes of moral and monastic guidelines. The Vinaya was an essential text of the Pali canon of scripture so valued by the Theravada Buddhists.

The original purpose of the Vinaya was a confession of faith and affirmation of community. However during the Buddha's life time the community instituted 250 articles for monks and 348 for nuns that set forth the rules that govern ordination, retreats, study, the celibate life, judicial codes, voting, and decision making. A second aspect of the code deals with safeguards against crimes and prohibitions against killing, stealing, lying, sexual misconduct, and imbibing intoxicants. Serious violations of the code meant expulsion from the community; lesser violations involved confession and ablution. The Ritsu School maintained that the commitment to and faithful observance of the *Vinaya* are essential steps to the purification of the mind and to enlightenment. The study of the *Vinaya* as canonical text has always been part of the Buddhist curricula for all traditions, though Mahayana interpretations vary somewhat from the Theravada.

In Japan, Emperor Shomu (r. 724–749), who took a considerable amount of his time to interact with the Nara schools, was highly concerned that an ordination procedure be put in place to ensure that future monks had a proper understanding of the responsibilities of their position. He commissioned two priests, Eiei and Fusho, to travel to China and determine how best to introduce the vivaya to Japan. As they began their studies, they quickly discovered that to be considered a monk, a candidate must pledge to observe the 250 *Vinaya* rules at the time of ordination. Both startled and concerned, they begged their Chinese colleague Dao Xuan (702–760) to leave for Japan immediately and begin informing the authorities in Nara of the demands of the Vinaya. He arrived in 736.

It would be almost 20 years later before Jianzhen (known in Japan as Ganjin, 687–763) arrived in Nara (754) with the invitation to formally establish the Ritsu School. Two months after his arrival, the ordination platform was constructed at Todai-ji, and 80 monks of the several schools received their priestly ordination, while other laypersons received the lay precepts. In China and subsequently in Japan a person was not considered to be a cleric until he or she had stepped on the *kaidan,* or ordination platform, and pledged to observe the Vinaya codes. The Chinese kaidan evolved from the early Buddhist *sima*, a sacred site in which the ordination took place. The candidate alighted the ordination platform by ascending three steps, representing the emptiness of self, dharmas, and both self and dharmas. The formal ceremony required the presence of at least 10 clerics who would determine the suitability of the candidate.

While Buddhism had been in Japan for more than a century, the transmission of the *Vinaya* from China to Japan formalized the actual establishment of a Buddhist community in the country. For the next generation, the Ritsu School acted as the exclusive interdenominational guardian of the ordination of the clergy. Its exclusive hold on the rites of ordination would be breached by Saicho (767–822), the founder of Japanese Tendai, who obtained the permission of the emperor to begin to train a few monks at Mount Hiei. The year after his death, permission was given to the Tendai Buddhists to establish an ordination platform on Mount Hiei. But for several centuries, Todai-ji remained the primary place for Buddhist monks to be ordained.

While Ganjin was able to establish the kaidan, it was also the case that Ganjin had to deal with several politically influential clerics who had persuaded the government to set guidelines for clerical conduct that fell short of those demanded in the *Vinaya*. Ganjin found himself lending legitimacy to this watered-down ordination process and in 758 Ganjin resigned his post at Todai-ji. The next year, he received permission to establish a center for Buddhist studies at Toshodaiji along with a rival kaidan. Because of the problems at Todai-ji and the rise of the Mahayana *Vinaya* on Mount Hiei, however, formal *Vinaya* discipline never took hold in Japan.

J. Gordon Melton

See also: Buddhism; Hiei, Mount; Mahayana Buddhism; Saicho; Zen Buddhism.

References

Buddhist Denominations and Schools in Japan. Tokyo: Bukkyo Dendo Kyokai, 1984.

Dutt, Sukumar. *Buddhist Monks and Monasteries of India.* London: George Allan and Unwin, 1962.

Frauwallner, Erich. *Studies in Abhidharma Literature and the Origins of Buddhist Philosophical Systems.* Trans. by Sophie Francis Kidd. Albany: State University of New York Press, 1965.

Kasahara, Kazou, ed. *A History of Japanese Religion.* Tokyo: Kosei Publishing, 2001.

Matsunaga, Daigan, and Alicia Matsunaga. *Foundation of Japanese Buddhism.* Vol. 1, *The Aristocratic Age.* Los Angeles: Buddhist Books International, 1974.

Murthy, K. Krishna. *Buddhism in Japan*. Delhi: Sundeep Prakashan, 1989.

Ryukoku, Daigaku. *Bukkyō yoron*. Kyoto: Hakkaen, 1972.

Saunders, E. Dale. *Buddhism in Japan, with an Outline of Its Origins in India*. Philadelphia: University of Pennsylvania Press, 1964.

Takakusu, Junjiro. *The Essentials of Buddhist Philosophy.* Honolulu: University of Hawaii Press, 1947.

Naropa

956–1040

Naropa, a key figure in the development of Indian Tantric Buddhism, is honored as one of the primary links in the lineage of the Kagyu School of Tibetan Buddhism, where the Six Yogas of Naropa form an essential element in the advanced teachings. He played an essential role in the transmission of Vajrayana Buddhism to both Tibet and Nepal.

Naropa was the subject of several reverential biographies (hagiographies); however, their contradictions call into question significant facts about his life. Some sources place his birth in Kashmir, while others suggest eastern India. A Tibetan source presents him as a prince who became a monk during his young adult years, while other sources claim that he had a more humble social origin as the son of a liquor dealer. Most sources agree that he was an excellent debater, and he most certainly spent years at Nalanda, the famed Buddhist university complex in Bihar. He seems to have served as the warden at Nalanda's northern gate, where he was assigned the task of discussing Buddhism with visiting scholars.

It is said that he eventually tired of life at Nalanda. Drawn toward the esoteric practices of Tantra, he sought out the Vajrayana teacher Tilopa. Among the more heralded events in his life, Naropa was required to pass through a set of 12 ordeals. Only after his successful completion of the ordeals did Tilopa accept him as a student. The highly motivated Naropa then became Tilopa's most accomplished student, his studies culminating in his full realization of Mahamudra, a direct understanding of the nature and essence of the mind. Soon afterward he settled at Pulahari, a retreat center not far from Nalanda. Through the years he attracted numerous students, the most notable being Marpa Lho-brag-pa (1012–1097), who played a key role in the passing of what became the Kagyu lineage of Tantric Buddhism to Tibet.

Several important works on Vajrayana Buddhism are attributed to Naropa, including commentaries on the *Sekoddesha,* the latter an important work associated with the secretive Kalachakra Tantra. He is also credited with originating a widely hailed advanced set of techniques known among Tibetans as the "Six Yogas of Naropa."

J. Gordon Melton

See also: Kagyupa Tibetan Buddhism; Nalanda; Tantrism.

References

Guenter, Herbert V., trans. *The Life and Teaching of Naropa.* Oxford: Clarendon Press, 1963.

Mullin, Glenn H., trans. *Tsongkhapa's Six Yogas of Naropa.* Ithaca, NY: Snow Lion, 1996.

Yeshe, Lama. *Becoming Vajrasattva: The Tantric Path of Purification*. Somerville, MA: Wisdom Publications, 2004.

Nation of Islam

The Nation of Islam, popularly known as the Black Muslim movement, emerged in 1930s Detroit. Its militant doctrine combined Islam and Black Nationalism; over the course of the 20th century, it became an influential religious community and an important African American political voice. Its leaders and spokesmen, including such individuals as Elijah Muhammad, Malcolm X, and Louis Farrakhan, influenced not only the Nation's membership, but also played a significant role in the development of African American political identity and served as a counterpoint to the Civil Rights movement.

In 1930 a charismatic salesman named Wallace Fard traveled the streets of Detroit, visiting homes and preaching a new religious doctrine that combined Islam and Black Nationalism. Within three years, he built a substantial following with a cohesive organizational structure that included a school and a security force. From this foundation, the Nation of Islam developed.

Fard disappeared in the early 1930s. His appointed successor, Elijah Muhammad (1897–1975), taught that Fard was Allah incarnate, and that he was his Messenger. White Americans were identified as white devils, and black Americans as Allah's chosen people. The Muslims anticipated an imminent "Fall of America," which would see white America destroyed and black Americans rising to their rightful place as world leaders.

In *Message to the Blackman in America*, Muhammad directed the Muslims to adhere to a strict moral code and attain a "knowledge of self." They were encouraged to follow strict dietary regulations, which included prohibitions on pork and a "slave diet" (foods

Nation of Islam security guards flank the stage as their leader, Louis Farrakhan, speaks behind bullet-proof glass during the Million Man March in Washington, D.C., October 16, 1995. (AP/Wide World Photos)

such as corn bread and black-eyed peas), and they were forbidden to smoke, drink alcohol, take drugs, and gamble. Muhammad also encouraged racial pride. Many members took the surname "X" to symbolize both the mysterious origins and the power of the black American community.

In the late 1940s, the Nation converted Malcolm Little. He adopted the name Malcolm X (1925–1965), and rapidly advanced through the movement's ranks. He was a minister and recruiter; among those he converted were Cassius Clay and Louis Farrakhan. A rift developed between Elijah and Malcolm in the early 1960s, which eventually led to Malcolm's expulsion from the Nation. He converted to orthodox Islam, and founded a new movement, but was assassinated on February 21, 1965.

Elijah Muhammad led the Nation until his death in 1975. His son Wallace succeeded him, and, following trends that emerged late in Elijah's leadership, rapidly moved the Nation toward orthodox Islam. Although most Muslims accepted these changes, some did not. Among those who did not was Louis Farrakhan. He left in 1978, returned to Elijah Muhammad's original doctrine, and re-established the Nation of Islam.

Farrakhan's charisma, coupled with his attention to proselytism, saw the movement grow rapidly. Several events soon made him notorious with the American public. In 1984, when Jesse Jackson ran for the leadership of the American Democratic Party, Farrakhan declared that he would, for the first time, register to vote, and encouraged his followers to do the same. His vocal support for Jackson, however, brought media attention to anti-Zionist themes in his rhetoric. As well, during this period the Nation received several large financial gifts from Libya (including one loan for

$5 million). By the close of the 1980s, however, Farrakhan had moved the Nation closer to a more traditional form of Islam, observing Friday prayers and Ramadan, and encouraging members to engage in Koranic study. During the 1990s, Farrakhan and the Nation worked toward reconciliation with Wallace Muhammad (Warith Deen Muhammad) and the more orthodox Muslim American Society, a notable milestone in Farrakhan's move toward orthodox Islam. Scholars suggest that this trend will eventually culminate with Farrakhan moving the Nation's followers to traditional Islam. In this decade, too, he continued to engage the larger American political community. In October 1995, he orchestrated the Million Man March on Washington, a controversial "day of atonement" for black American men. The March drew hundreds of thousands of participants, a success that emphasized the importance of Farrakhan's political voice.

The 2008 election of Barack Obama as president of the United States posed a significant challenge to the Nation of Islam; the organization's doctrine in part reflects the view that African Americans have no effective access to political power. In an interview following the election Farrakhan stated that he never thought he would live to see the day that a black man became president, and that America was "changing." Indeed, should America allow the black community to demonstrate its excellence, Farrakhan commented, it might well be that America has evolved into a "post-racial" nation. His comments on these developments further suggest that in the future, both Farrakhan and the Nation will move closer to the religious and political mainstream.

The headquarters of the Nation of Islam are in Chicago, and its mosques can be found across the United States, as well as in Canada, France, and the United Kingdom. It continues to publish *The Final Call*, a newspaper that publicizes its doctrine (available online at http://www.finalcall.com) and comments on current religious and political events.

Nation of Islam
7351 South Stoney Island Ave.
Chicago, IL 60649
http://www.noi.org

J. Gordon Melton

See also: Islam; Warith Deen Mohammad, Ministry of.

References

Curtis, Edward E. *Black Muslim Religion in the Nation of Islam, 1960–1975*. Chapel Hill: University of North Carolina Press, 2006.

Farrakhan, Louis. *A Torchlight for America*. Chicago: FCN Publishing, 1993.

Gardell, Mattias. *In the Name of Elijah Muhammad, Louis Farrakhan and the Nation of Islam*. Durham, NC: Duke University Press, 1996.

Muhammad, Elijah. *History of the Nation of Islam*. Cleveland, OH: Sectarius Publications, 1994.

Nation of Yahweh

The Nation of Yahweh is a relatively small group that continues the tradition of black nationalism within the African American community. It was founded by Hulon Mitchell, Jr., better known by his religious name, Yahweh ben Yahweh (1935–2007). Raised as a Pentecostal, as a young man he joined the Nation of Islam and rose to become the leader of a mosque. However, he left the mosque and began to call African Americans together as Black Israelites, the followers of Yahweh.

Drawing themes from the teachings of Black Jews that had appeared throughout the 20th century in the United States, Yahweh ben Yahweh taught that there was only one God, that his name was Yahweh, that he had black woolly hair, and that he had sent his son, Yahweh ben Yahweh, to the African American people as their savior and deliverer. He identified African Americans as the true lost tribes of Israel, and upon accepting Yahweh, members take the last name "Israel" as a means of rejecting their slave past. Those who oppose God, of whatever color, are the devil. Though Yahweh had a special love for black people and a special animus for white people as the oppressor, ultimately individual white people could be saved by faith in Yahweh ben Yahweh.

Through the 1980s, the Yahwehites spread across the United States, their white clothing becoming a familiar sight in the African American community. By the end of the decade, centers had been established in

Nation of Yahweh service. The Nation of Yahweh moved to Miami in 1979 and set up the Nation of Yahweh under the leadership of Yahweh Ben Yahweh. (Ed Kashi/Corbis)

37 cities and members owned a number of businesses associated with the movement. Movement leaders saw themselves as establishing a united moral power within the African American community that would support voter registration, black-owned businesses, health education, scholarships for college, better housing, and strong family ties. They opposed the spread of drugs in the community.

However, during the late 1980s, stories began to circulate that leaders in the group had engaged in multiple acts of violence and murder, especially in the early 1980s. These rumors surfaced in 1986 after some people were shot during an eviction procedure in an apartment house owned by the Yahwehites. Then in 1988, a former member confessed to 4 murders and implicated Yahweh ben Yahweh and 12 other leaders. Yahweh ben Yahweh and several other members were arrested and in the early 1990s convicted in federal court of conspiracy to murder. They received lengthy sentences, though Yahweh ben Yahweh was released in 2001, on the condition that he not associate with the group he had founded.

The group has survived, but it no longer is the growing enterprise that it had become at the time of the trial that brought down their founder. Headquarters were relocated from Miami to Quebec, Canada, where it reorganized legally as the Abraham Foundation. Its publishing branch, the P.E.E.S.S. ("Politically, Economically, Educationally, Socially, Spiritually") Foundation, with offices in suburban Montreal and in Seguin, Texas, publishes and circulates the group's materials.

Nation of Yahweh
P.E.E.S.S. Foundation
PO Box 520
Kirkland, PQ
Canada H9H
www.yahwehbenyahweh.com/.

J. Gordon Melton

See also: Nation of Islam.

References

Freedburg, Sydney P. *Brother Love: Murder, Money, and a Messiah*. New York: Pantheon Books, 1994.
Hamill, Pete. "Mr. God Raises Hell." *Esquire* 115 (1991): 34.
"Nation of Yahweh." New Religions Web Site. http://religiousmovements.lib.virginia.edu/nrms/nyah.html. Accessed September 15, 2001.

National Association of Congregational Christian Churches

During the Puritan era in the 17th century, believers who agreed upon particulars of Reformed theology disagreed upon church polity, some opting for congregationalism and others the presbyterian system. While Presbyterians dominated in England, Congregationalists settled in the American colonies and became the favored elite in New England through the 18th century and into the 19th.

In the 20th century, the Congregational churches took a leading role in the ecumenical movement and demonstrated their leadership with two important mergers. The first was in 1931 with congregations from the Christian Church, a church with a congregational polity from the Free church tradition. Then in the 1950s the Congregational Christian churches moved toward union with the Evangelical and Reformed Church, a church with which they shared many theological affinities but one that had a presbyterian organizational background. At stake was congregational ownership of parish property versus some centralized ownership based in presbyteries and synods.

In 1957 the union was consummated and the United Church of Christ came into being with mixed elements of congregational and presbyterian polity. Among the Congregationalists were individuals who feared and rejected any compromise on the congregational polity they had come to enjoy. Anticipating the 1957 union, they met in 1955 in Detroit and formed the National Association of Congregational Christian Churches. That meeting had been sponsored by two anti-union organizations, the League to Uphold Congregational Principles and the Committee for the Continuation of Congregational Christian Churches.

The National Association was formed as a fellowship of autonomous congregations that cannot and does not make pronouncements binding upon the local churches. However, it does undertake cooperative programs that extend the ministry of the local churches. Such programs have been initiated in ministerial career development, Christian education at all levels, church extension, and communications. One important area of cooperation has been in home and foreign missions. The association has supported the development of new congregational churches in the United States and missions in 12 countries in different parts of the world.

In 2001, the association reported 65,000 members in 432 congregations. It is a member of the International Congregational Fellowship.

National Association of Congregational Christian Churches
8473 S. Howell Ave.
PO Box 1620
Oak Creek, WI 53154-0620
http://www.naccc.org/

J. Gordon Melton

See also: International Congregational Fellowship; United Church of Christ.

References

Burton, Malcolm K. *Destiny for Congregationalism*. Oklahoma City, OK: Modern Publishers, 1953.
Cowen, Gerald P. *Who Rules the Church? Examining Congregational Leadership and Church Government*. Nashville: B&H Publishing Group, 2003.
Kohl, Manfred Waldemar. *Congregationalism in America*. Oak Creek, WI: Congregational Press, 1977.

National Association of Free Will Baptists

The National Association of Free Will Baptists continues the tradition of Arminian theology that has divided the Baptist community over the centuries. Baptists emerged as one element in the larger Puritan community, the English phase of the spread of Reformed theology. Reformed theology, as originally stated by John Calvin (1509–1564), had emphasized the sovereignty of God and hence the predestination of those who would be saved by Christ's saving act. As the Reformation became established in Holland, Dutch theologian Jacob Arminius (1560–1609) developed a Reformed theology that left a place for the human response in faith to God's grace. Arminian theology left the door open for the role of human free will in Protestant theology.

In the United States, the institutionalization of Free Will Baptist theology came in 1727 with the organization of a church at Perquimans, Chowan County, North Carolina, by Paul Palmer (d. ca. 1770). Other churches were subsequently formed, and in 1752 some 16 churches associated together in a yearly meeting. As this growth continued, they formed a general conference in 1827. A statement of belief was issued in 1834. A similar development of Free Will Baptists occurred in the northern states, and a 1896 Triennial Convention included congregations from across the South and as far north as Ohio. In 1911 the Free Will Baptists in New England merged into the North Baptist Convention (now the American Baptist Churches in the U.S.A.). Meanwhile, a number of disconnected Free Will congregations in the West (Texas, Nebraska, Kansas, Oklahoma, and Missouri) joined together as the General Co-operative Association of Free Will Baptists. They established headquarters in Tecumseh, Oklahoma, where they opened a school.

In 1935 the general conference in the South united with the General Co-operative Association to form the National Association of Free Will Baptists. Like most Baptists elsewhere, the new association championed the autonomy of the local congregations while providing an effective instrument for cooperative action, especially in church growth, education, and missions.

Free Will Baptists had existed in Canada since the early 19th century. They came together in 1832 as the Christian Conference Church, later renamed the Free Christian Baptists. In the 1870s, George W. Orser, one of the ministers, began to call for a new biblical church order. He opposed formal education of ministers and the paying of ministerial salaries. He eventually withdrew from the Free Christian Baptists and formed the Primitive Baptist Conference of New Brunswick, Maine, and Nova Scotia. The church eventually centered on Hartland, New Brunswick, where it had formed its own educational institution, the Saint John Valley Bible College. In 1981 the church joined with the National Association of Free Will Baptists as its Canadian conference.

The Association has its headquarters at Antioch, Tennessee. It supports four colleges. In 2005 it reported 187,193 members in some 2,399 congregations in the United States with an additional 10 congregations in the associated Atlantic Canada Conference. Although foreign missions had begun in the 19th century, the formation of the association allows a more effective mission program to develop. Currently, work is supported in Spain, Panama, Cuba, Brazil, Uruguay, France, the Ivory Coast, India, and Japan. The national associations from around the world are now united in the International Association of Free Will Baptist Churches (http://www.ifofwbc.org/).

Free Will Baptists are unique among Baptist bodies as one of the groups that supports three ordinances: baptism, the Lord's Supper, and foot washing (a practice derived from their reading of the Bible, John 13:4–17). The national Association remains theologically conservative. It joined the National Association of Evangelicals for a period but eventually withdrew. It has not associated with the Baptist World Alliance.

National Association of Free Will Baptists
PO Box 5002
Antioch, TN 37011-5002
http://www.nafwb.org/

J. Gordon Melton

See also: American Baptist Churches in the U.S.A.; Arminius, Jacob; Baptist World Alliance; Calvin, John.

NEW YORK INSTITUTE
OF TECHNOLOGY

References

Cox, Violet. *Missions on the Move*. Nashville: The Woman's National Auxiliary Convention, [1966].

Davidson, William F. *The Free Will Baptists in America*. Nashville: Randall House Press, 1985.

Picirilli, Robert E. *History of the Free Will Baptist Associations*. Nashville: Randall House Publications, 1976.

National Baptist Convention of America

The National Baptist Convention of America emerged out of a controversy regarding the newly formed National Baptist Convention, U.S.A. When the latter Convention formed in 1895, it followed the organizational pattern of the American Baptists, allowing a considerable amount of autonomy to its boards and agencies. Among these was the National Baptist Publishing Board, a structure incorporated prior to the formation of the convention. While serving as the convention's publishing arm, R. H. Boyd (1843–1922), the head of the board, increasingly operated independently and even contrary to the wishes of the Convention.

The issues between the board and the Convention culminated in 1915 with a court case that established the independence of the board. Following the ruling, Boyd and his supporters withdrew from the Convention and formed the National Baptist Convention of America. There were no doctrinal issues at stake, and the two conventions developed parallel programs. Through the rest of the century, the National Baptist Convention of America would grow, but it never rivaled its parent body.

The new Convention aligned itself with the Lott Carey Baptist Foreign Mission Convention, through which the Convention would focus its foreign missionary activity. That cooperation ended in the 1940s, and the Convention organized its own foreign missions board.

The strength of the Convention has been the publishing concern, both the literature it prints and the leadership it provides. However, the issue of its independence arose again in the 1980s and led to a split and the formation of the National Baptist Missionary Convention in 1989. Again, no doctrinal issues were at stake in the controversy.

The National Baptist Convention of America is organized congregationally, and the Convention facilitates fellowship and cooperation between affiliated congregations. The Convention supports missionary work in Jamaica, Panama, and several African nations. It co-sponsors two seminaries with the National Baptist Convention, U.S.A. The Convention is a member of the Baptist World Alliance and the World Council of Churches. In 2000, the Convention reported 3,500,000 members.

National Baptist Convention of America
777 S R Thornton Frwy., Ste. 210
Dallas TX 75203
http://www.nbca-inc.com/

J. Gordon Melton

See also: Baptist World Alliance; National Baptist Convention, U.S.A.; World Council of Churches.

References

Fitts, Leroy. *A History of Black Baptists*. Nashville: Broadman Press, 1985.

Pelt, Owen D., and Ralph Lee Smith. *The Story of the National Baptists*. New York: Vantage Press, 1960.

National Baptist Convention of Mexico

The National Baptist Convention of Mexico traces its roots to the organization of the first Baptist congregation in Mexico on January 30, 1864, in Monterrey. The congregation was formed by James Hickey, then in Mexico as an agent of the American Bible Society. This church would reproduce itself six times over the remainder of the decade. One member of the original church, Thomas Westrup, served as a missionary of the American Baptist Home Missionary Society (now a constituent part of the American Baptist Churches in the U.S.A.). John Westrup, Thomas's brother, organized three churches in northern Mexico during the late 1870s. In 1880 he was hired as a missionary by the Southern Baptist Convention's Foreign Mission Board, but he was assassinated before the year was out. However, through the rest of the century, both Baptist organizations sent more than 50 missionaries into Mexico. The first regional conventions were organized in 1884 and 1885.

In 1903 representatives from congregations of both American groups and some independent congregations affiliated with the National Sunday School Convention met in Mexico City and formed what became the National Baptist Convention of Mexico. Among its first tasks was the election of delegates to the 1905 gathering of the Baptist World Association.

The Baptist work in Mexico spread until 1910 but was decimated during the Revolution (1910–1917), when both property and lives were lost. Meetings of the Convention were suspended in 1912. The secular government established in 1917 nationalized church property, restricted church worship, and allowed only Native Mexicans to lead congregations. Only 54 churches were represented at the 1919 meeting of the Convention. Although the Convention revived its evangelism in Mexico City and along the Rio Grande Valley, the Southern Baptists extended its missionary activity independently, especially in the creation of several institutions. In 1977 two of these, a seminary in Mexico City and a hospital in Guadalajara, were turned over to the Convention. The Southern Baptists also agreed to work in a coordinated fashion with the Convention. By 1993 the Southern Baptist work was fully integrated into the Convention, which that same year was registered with the government as a separate religious organization.

In 2007 the Convention reported 150,000 members in 1,550 churches. It publishes a periodical, *La Luz Bautista*, and supports two seminaries. It has extended its work to include 10 of the different language groups of the Native inhabitants of Mexico, which is a predominantly Spanish-speaking country. It also began missionary work in Honduras. The two American bodies continue to support the work of the Convention, and other groups such as the North American Baptist Convention and the Baptist General Conference have added their support of personnel and money. At the same time, through the decades following World War II, a variety of other Baptist groups launched independent missionary efforts, that of the fundamentalist Baptist Bible Fellowship International being the most successful. The Convention is a member of the Baptist World Alliance.

National Baptist Convention of Mexico
Vizcainas Oriente No. 16 Ote.
060080 Mexico, D.F.
Mexico
http://www.bautistas.org.mx/ (in Spanish)

J. Gordon Melton

See also: American Baptist Churches in the U.S.A.; Baptist Bible Fellowship International; Baptist World Alliance; Southern Baptist Convention.

References

Carnett, Daniel B. *Contending for the Faith: Southern Baptists in New Mexico, 1938–1995*. Albuquerque: University of New Mexico Press, 2002.

Patterson, Frank W. *A Century of Baptist History in Mexico*. El Paso, TX: Baptist Spanish Publishing House, 1979.

National Baptist Convention, U.S.A.

The National Baptist Convention, U.S.A., the largest African American religious body in the world, is rooted in the efforts of American Baptists to evangelize African Americans throughout the 19th century. The first African American Baptists had appeared during the colonial era, and in 1758 the first congregation was formed in Virginia. Many blacks in the northern states were attracted to the church, and independent congregations began to form in communities with a significant African American presence. However, it was not until the 1830s that large numbers of black people were attracted to the church. The first African American Baptist association was formed in Ohio in 1934.

Prior to the American Civil War, most African American Baptists were members of the several predominantly white Baptist bodies, and after the war the American Baptists (now the American Baptist Churches in the U.S.A.) made special efforts to cultivate black Baptist membership. However, although many blacks were happy to remain a part of the larger American Baptist Fellowship, others rejected their exclusion from the highest levels of the denomination

Nannie Helen Burroughs holds the banner of the Women's Convention of the National Baptist Convention, 1900. (Library of Congress)

and began to create institutions controlled by African Americans.

A variety of organizational attempts led in 1880 to the formation of the Baptist Foreign Mission Convention of the U.S.A. (generally accepted as the founding date of the National Baptists). A structure for congregational fellowship, the American National Baptist Convention, was formed in 1886. The Baptist National Educational Convention emerged in 1893. These three bodies merged in 1895 to form the National Baptist Convention, U.S.A. (Many African Americans continued to affiliate with the American Baptists and today constitute approximately one-third of that body's membership.)

The new denomination followed the organizational pattern of the American Baptists, with the semi-autonomous boards that served the cause of Christian education and foreign missions relating directly to the affiliated congregations. Controversy arose immediately, and those who wished to continue a relationship with the American Baptists in the area of missions withdrew to form the independent Lott Carey Baptist Foreign Mission Convention.

The next major controversy to hit the Convention occurred because of its failure to create a publishing house. Publishing for the Convention was primarily handled by the National Baptist Publishing Board, which had been incorporated separately under the leadership of R. H. Boyd (1843–1922). He began to operate independently of the directions offered by the Convention, and in 1915 the board's independence was upheld in court. The trial became the occasion for

Boyd and his supporters to found the rival National Baptist Convention of America.

Under the leadership of Reverend Elias Camp Morris (1855–1922), however, the National Baptist Convention, U.S.A., recovered from its losses and moved forward with a newly founded, Convention-controlled publishing house and went on to eclipse the older Methodist denominations in membership. The Morris era was followed by lengthy presidential terms for Lacey K. Williams (1871–1940), D. V. Jemison (1875–1954), and Joseph H. Jackson (1900–1990).

During Jackson's lengthy tenure (1953–1982), opposition to his philosophy of civil rights developed with the rise of Martin Luther King, Jr. (1929-1968), a young Baptist pastor in Alabama who had become the center of a movement centered on nonviolent confrontation with the authorities and the demand for the immediate end to racial segregation in the American South. King's approach ran counter to Jackson's belief in the gradual elimination of discriminating structures. Those most supportive of King and most opposed to Jackson's continued domination of the Convention left in 1961 to form the Progressive National Baptist Convention.

Jackson's lengthy tenure finally ended in 1982, and he was succeeded by Theodore J. Jemison. The election of Jemison, an activist in the Civil Rights movement in Louisiana, represented a change of direction for the formerly conservative Convention. Jemison also led the National Baptists into finally building a national headquarters building in Nashville, Tennessee, though the official headquarters of the Convention continues to be centered in the church pastored by the president.

In the 1990s, the Convention was traumatized when its president, Henry Lyons, was arrested and convicted of embezzling church funds. In 1999, the current president, Dr. William J. Shaw, pastor of White Rock Baptist Church in Philadelphia, assumed office and immediately moved to reorganize the Convention's financial affairs to pay off the debt incurred by Lyons and to create a system that would prevent such occurrences in the future.

The National Baptist Convention, U.S.A., is led by its president but is organized congregationally. There are various estimates of the membership of the convention's churches, but in 2004, it reported five million members. It supports one college, two universities, and four theological seminaries. The Convention is a member of the Baptist World Alliance and the World Council of Churches.

The National Baptist Convention, U.S.A.
1700 Baptist World Center Dr.
Nashville, TN 37207
http://www.nationalbaptist.com/

J. Gordon Melton

See also: American Baptist Churches in the U.S.A.; Baptist World Alliance; National Baptist Convention of America; Progressive National Baptist Convention; World Council of Churches.

References

Fitts, Leroy. *A History of Black Baptists*. Nashville: Broadman Press, 1985.

Jackson, Joseph H. *A Story of Christian Activism*. Nashville: Townsend Press, 1980.

Pelt, Owen D., and Ralph Lee Smith. *The Story of the National Baptists*. New York: Vantage Press, 1960.

National Evangelical Synod of Syria and Lebanon

Protestantism entered the territory of the former Ottoman Empire early in the 19th century, when Reformed missionaries from the United States and the British Isles established a mission. Missionaries working in what is today Lebanon and Syria were recognized by the Ottoman authorities in 1848. That year, an initial congregation was established in Beirut. Throughout the rest of the century additional missions were initiated by various Protestant bodies from France, Switzerland, Denmark, and Holland.

Following the fall of the Ottoman Empire, the present state of Lebanon was carved out of the empire's former territory. At that time, the National Evangelical Synod of Syria and Lebanon was formed by the association of several small presbyteries that had been established in Lebanon. In 1959 the Synod assumed responsibility of a number of the missions that had been established in Lebanon and Syria. Worship in these churches is primarily in Arabic.

In 2005 the Synod reported approximately 20,000 members in 38 congregations. It has a presbyterian polity and directs a ministry through its many schools and medical facilities. The Synod is a member of the World Alliance of Reformed Churches, the Middle East Council of Churches, and the World Council of Churches.

National Evangelical Synod of Syria
PO Box 70890
Rabieh, St. 34
Antelias
Lebanon

The Synod is closely related to the National Evangelical Union of Lebanon, which also carries the heritage of evangelical church life prior to the establishment of the state of Lebanon. The original congregation in Beirut became a center around which a small number of congregations gravitated, drawing on it for pastoral care and administrative guidance. These congregations made their relationship official in the early 1960s with the formation of the National Evangelical Union of Lebanon. In contrast to the Synod, the Union is organized with a congregational polity. In the 1990s it reported 9 congregations and 2,000 members. The Union is a member of the World Alliance of Reformed Churches and the Middle East Council of Churches.

National Evangelical Union of Lebanon
PO Box 11 5224
Al Kanissa Al Injiliah
Beirut
Lebanon

The Union and the Synod are related to each other through the Supreme Council of the Evangelical Community in Syria and Lebanon, which also includes the Armenian Evangelical Churches in the Near East. The members of the Council support the Near East School of Theology in Beirut. All three churches suffered during the Civil War (1975–1991), which led to the destruction of much church property and the migration of many members to the United States and Australia.

J. Gordon Melton

See also: Middle East Council of Churches; World Alliance of Reformed Churches; World Council of Churches.

Reference

Chopourian, G. H. *The Armenian Evangelical Reformation: Causes and Effects*. New York: Armenian Missionary Association of America, 1972.

National Presbyterian Church in Mexico

The National Presbyterian Church in Mexico dates to the beginning of Presbyterian work in Mexico by the United Presbyterian Church of North America (now an integral part of the Presbyterian Church [U.S.A.]) in Mexico City following the granting of religious freedom in the country in 1857. Other churches soon followed, including the Presbyterian Church in the U.S. (now also a part of the Presbyterian Church [U.S.A.]), the Congregationalists (now part of the United Church of Christ), and the Associate Presbyterian Church. The work of the United Presbyterians spread south and east from Mexico City toward Yucatan.

The first presbytery was established in Zacatecas in 1883, and others soon followed. The previous year a theological seminary was opened in Mexico City. What became the National Presbyterian Church began in 1901 when the United Presbyterian Church and the Presbyterian Church in the U.S. decided to unite their work in Mexico. The process of developing indigenous leadership that had begun with the founding of the seminary was greatly accelerated by the adoption of the new Constitution by Mexico in 1917, which allowed only Native Mexicans to lead congregations. In 1920, with the assistance of the Reformed Church in America, the National Presbyterian Church expanded into Chiapas.

In the years immediately after World War II, the church experienced two schisms. A local controversy led to the formation of the Independent Presbyterian Church in 1947. Then in the 1950s, Reverend Carl McIntire (b. 1906–2002), a Fundamentalist Presbyterian from the United States, brought to Mexico his fight against the modernist tendencies he saw invading mainstream Presbyterianism and found some support among Mexican Presbyterians. In the early 1950s his supporters formed the National Conservative Presbyterian Church.

The National Presbyterian Church in Mexico became a part of the world ecumenical community, joining both the World Alliance of Reformed Churches and the World Council of Churches though it has subsequently withdrawn from the latter. Closer to home, in 1995 it joined with the Presbyterian Reformed Church and the Associate Presbyterian Reformed Church to create the Alliance of Presbyterian and Reformed Churches in the Republic of Mexico.

The church has a presbyterial polity, and its general assembly is the highest legislative body. It recognizes the Heidelberg Catechism, the Canons of the Synod of Dort, the Westminster Confession, and the Belgic Confession in a statement it authored on its doctrinal perspective. In the 1990s it reported 1.2 million members in 4,800 congregations. The work is organized into 40 presbyteries and 7 synods. Six of the presbyteries are located in southern Mexico working among the indigenous peoples of the states of Chiapas, Oaxaca, and Huasteca Potosina. The seminary in Mexico City has now been joined by five additional ministerial training schools.

National Presbyterian Church in Mexico
Arenal 36
Col. Agri. Chimalistac
01050 Mexico, D.F
Mexico

J. Gordon Melton

See also: Presbyterian Church (U.S.A.); Reformed Church in America; United Church of Christ; World Alliance of Reformed Churches; World Council of Churches.

Reference

Bauswein, Jean-Jacques, and Lukas Vischner, eds. *The Reformed Family Worldwide: A Survey of Reformed Churches, Theological Schools, and International Organizations*. Grand Rapids, MI: William B. Eerdmans Publishing Company, 1999.

National Spiritualist Association of Churches

The National Spiritualist Association of Churches (NSAC) is the oldest and largest organization of churches to emerge out of the 19th-century Spiritualist movement in the United States. As Spiritualism developed, it was given structure by a number of state Spiritualist associations. The movement was seen by many of its earliest exponents as having a "scientific" purpose—to demonstrate life after death—rather than as a new religion. However, in the decades after the Civil War, Spiritualist churches were founded and many began to advocate a Spiritualist approach to theology. Thus, in 1893, a number of leading Spiritualists, including Chicago medium Cora L. Richmond (1840–1923) and two former Unitarian clergymen, James M. Peebles (1822–1922) and Harrison D. Barrett (1863–1911), founded the National Spiritualist Association (later adding the words "of Churches" to the title). They initially drew support from some of the state associations and a few of the prominent camp meeting establishments. Among the reasons for forming such a national movement was the need to attack fraudulent mediumship, which many had seen as harming the movement.

In 1899, the Association adopted a six-article Declaration of Principles, later expanded to nine articles. These articles expressed the authors' faith in life after death as being a proven fact, demonstrated by the phenomena of Spiritualism. The NSAC has tended to focus upon mental phenomena, that is, mediumship, rather than the physical phenomena that were so much at issue in charges of fraud directed at the larger Spiritualist movement. The Association also called for a moral life based upon the biblical Golden Rule, "Do unto others as you would have them do unto you." Drawing upon contemporary science, the Declaration of Principles looked upon nature as an expression of God or infinite intelligence, and it noted that happiness is a result of following nature's laws. It affirmed the existence of both physical and spiritual laws.

The NSAC has generally taken a negative stance toward two issues of importance to Spiritualists. First, it has not upheld the belief in reincarnation that was so staunchly advocated by the Theosophical Society and some Spiritualists early in the 20th century who accepted the idea from competing organizations. Second, Spiritualists have carried on a lengthy debate over the relation of Spiritualism to Christianity. Many individual Spiritualists see the experiences that are common in the movement as similar to experiences described in the Bible. However, the Association as a whole sees Spiritualism as distinct from Christianity, though they draw a distinction between primitive Christianity (with which they feel an affinity) and contemporary Christianity, which they see as a very different reality.

The Association has a fraternal connection to the National Spiritualist Church of Canada in Ontario and Quebec but has only cursory relationships with the Spiritualist movement in Great Britain and has been at odds with Spiritualists in France and Brazil where reincarnation is widely accepted. In 2009, the NSAC reported 89 member congregations. Seven state associations and 13 camps are affiliated with the NSAC.

National Spiritualist Association of Churches (U.S.)
Morris Pratt Institute
11811 Watertown Plank Road
Milwaukee, WI 53226
http://www.nsac.org/

Marika Speckmann

See also: Spiritualism; Theosophical Society (America).

References

Holms, A. Campbell. *The Fundamental Facts of Spiritualism*. Indianapolis, IN: Stow Memorial Foundation, n.d.

Judah, J. Stillson. *The History and Philosophy of the Metaphysical Movements in America*. Philadelphia: Westminster Press, 1967.

Leonard, Todd Jay. *Talking to the Other Side: A History of Modern Spiritualism and Mediumship: A Study of the Religion, Science, Philosophy and Mediums That Encompass This American-Made Religion*. New York: iUniverse, Inc., 2005.

One Hundredth Anniversary of Modern American Spiritualism. Chicago: National Spiritualist Association of Churches, 1948.

Native American Church

In the early 1890s many of the traditional Indian ways of worship were being banished. However, at that time, the longstanding ritual use of the cactus plant peyote (*Lophophora williamsii*) was formalized into new ceremonies. Under the inspiration of the medicine men Quanah Parker (ca. 1845–1911; parents: Comanche, white) and John Wilson (ca. 1840–1901; parents: Delaware, Caddo-French), two different traditions of the new peyote religion, which today is called the Native American Church (NAC), diverged into distinct practices known as the Comanche Half Moon (also Little Moon and Way of the Sioux) and the Wilson Big Moon (also Cross Fire and Old Way). Both ritual forms fuse ancient Mexican, Plains Indian, and Christian themes. The Wilson Big Moon variant typically omits the water ceremonies that Quanah Parker had established, including the ritual water call and the blessing of people with water, celebrating an old Indian belief that water is a life-giving substance.

Peyote grows naturally only in north-central Mexico and in a limited area on the dry, rocky hills north of the Rio Grande River near Laredo, Texas. It contains at least 57 alkaloids, including the psychoactive alkaloid mescaline. Since the 1880s peyote from this region was cut and dried for shipment to communicants in the United States. Probably the Carrizo culture, which once occupied the area that extends from Laredo to the Gulf of Mexico, was instrumental in the early development of peyote meetings. Carrizo peyote rituals that were observed in 1649 included all-night dancing around a fire, but without the tepee or lodge used today. The western neighbors of the Carrizo, the Lipan Apache, seem to have transformed the Carrizo ceremony before teaching it to the Kiowa, Kiowa-Apache, and Comanche.

The Half Moon ritual appears to have been formalized by the Comanche in the 1880s. The Big Moon rite was also formalized about 1880. It spread between 1890 and 1908 among the Shawnee, Caddo, Seneca, Delaware, Quapaw, Potawatomi, and above all the Osage, and it was carried and transformed by different local "prophets," such as Jonathan Koshiway (b. 1886; father: Sauk and Fox, mother: Otoe) and John Rave (ca. 1855–1917; Nebraska Winnebago). From the Kiowa,

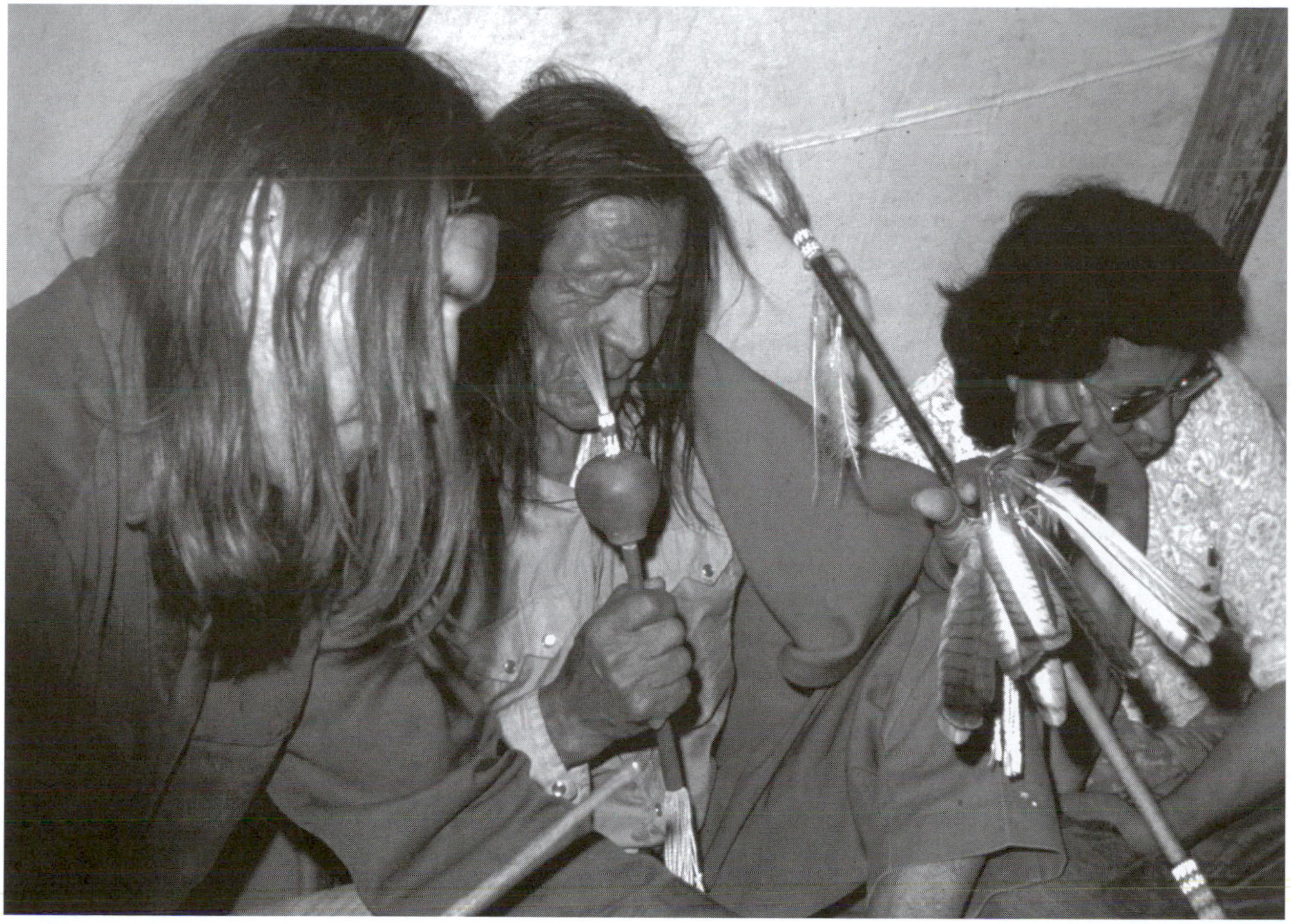

Navajo Indians at a peyote ceremony near Pinon, Arizona. The hallucinogen peyote is considered sacred by Native Americans and is used in religious practices to combat spiritual, physical, and other social ills. (Richard Erdoes/MPI/Getty Images)

the Comanche, and the Caddo, the new religion spread to the eastern Great Basin, in Colorado, by 1896. It appeared throughout the Great Basin and into southern Canada beginning in the 1910s.

In 1918 the state of Oklahoma repealed an earlier territorial ban against the peyote sacrament and granted a charter authorizing the NAC. Peyotists in other states received similar authorization, and a national church was formed in 1934–1944. In 1945–1955 the NAC was organized into the NAC of Oklahoma and the NAC of North America. The main purpose of those incorporations was to legalize peyote as a sacrament.

The NAC ethical code constitutes a way of life, which is called Peyote Road. This ethic has four main parts: brotherly love, care of family, self-reliance, and avoidance of alcohol, in addition to truthfulness, economic self-sufficiency, praying for the sick, and praying for peace. There is no formal teaching or learning of the rituals through books, schools, or lectures. In the Christian element, which is mostly confined to Siouan-speaking groups, members are free to interpret Bible passages according to their own understanding.

From its earliest days the ceremony has consisted of an all-night prayer meeting in a tepee, lodge, or hogan around a crescent-shaped mound of earth, a sacred fire, and a special peyote button, today called Grandfather Peyote or Chief. Roadman, Cedar chief, and Drummer chief sit together opposite the door. The Fireman sits on the opposite side of the circle next to the door. Around the sacred elements in the center of the lodge, the water drum, gourd rattle, and staff are passed while peyote songs are sung, prayers are offered, sacred tobacco is smoked, cedar is burned, and peyote is ingested. At midnight the ritual is interrupted by special songs and a bucket of water is brought in to be blessed, mostly by the Fireman. At dawn there is another water ceremony, as the Water Woman carries holy water into the meeting along with her prayers. The morning water is followed by a ritual breakfast of corn, water, fruit, and meat, prepared by women. The singing, drumming, and praying last all night (10 to 14 hours). Finally the morning sun is greeted with hands raised to heaven and thanks given to the Creator.

In the first part of NAC history, women were usually not admitted to take part in ritual. Yet the importance of male and female complementarity is reflected in NAC myth and ritual. It is widely believed that being inside the tepee represents being inside the womb of the Mother, and the drum is the sound of the fetal heartbeat. According to many peyote origin myths, this religion was brought to the Indians by a woman, called Peyote Woman, and it is kept by men. In Navajo Peyotism the cactus itself is referred to as Female Medicine (*'azee' ba'áád*) or Mother (*shimá 'azee'*).

For some, the NAC serves as a bridge between the ancient and modern systems of belief. Praying in peyote meetings appears to have much of the psychological flavor of the old vision quest. The NAC has often been bracketed with the Ghost Dance religion, which also taught the value of peaceful intertribal relations. (Although many other authors have repeated this idea, first set forth by Shonle [1925], historical documents establish that Peyotism had become an active ritual before Wovoka had directed the first Ghost Dance about 1889.) However, claims for the therapeutic effect of peyote are controversial, although several published reports have attempted to determine whether peyote used in the ritual of the NAC is effective in the treatment of alcoholism.

After 1965, the ceremonial use of peyote by Indians was protected by federal regulation. Although 28 states had by then enacted laws in conformance with the federal regulation, 22 states had not done so. In 1990 the Supreme Court prohibited the use and possession of peyote for all Americans. A 1995 law provided an exemption, declaring that although possession of peyote and its derivatives is illegal in the United States, Native Americans may use it for religious purposes.

The NAC has no professional paid clergy. Beyond the Roadmen, who lead the meetings, there are official leading positions for chairmen and the president of the NAC. The church is organized into regional, state, and national groups throughout North America. The members belong to some 70 Native American nations. In the continental United States, every state west of the Mississippi has at least one chapter; in all there are 80 chapters.

The NAC is the most widespread religion currently practiced by American Indians. By 1930, it was estimated that half the Indian population belonged to the church. The NAC membership in Navajoland ranged from 12 to 14 percent in 1951 to 40 to 50 percent in the 1980s. At the end of the 1960s there were an estimated 250,000 Peyotists, one-quarter of all Indians in the United States and Canada. In the 1980s the membership from more than 50 North American Indian tribes included some 100,000 adherents. In 1995 there was again a total membership of around 250,000, belonging to more than 70 Native American nations. A directory of Native American Churches has been developed by the Utah branch (http://web.archive.org/web/20050308162749/www.utah-nac.org/nacindex.html).

The spread of Peyotism beyond North America is not known. An example of non-Indian membership can be found in 1968, when a group with young whites took peyote in a ritual way, which was incorporated in New Mexico as the American Church of God and had a steady membership of some 200 people. Four-fifths of the group were whites. The rest were Indians, mostly 50 to 70 years old, from tribes all over the Southwest.

The peyote ritual in the United States was first reported by J. Lee Hall in 1886, an Indian agent for the U.S. government. Then in 1890 it was described by James Mooney, who researched peyote meetings among the Kiowa in Oklahoma. The earliest general historical and comparative study was written by Weston La Barre, who traveled to and studied peyote meetings among 15 tribes in the United States in 1935 and 1936. During the years after 1936 Omer Stewart visited peyote meetings; since 1960 he appeared in court to help defend the right of Peyotists (see, for example, Stewart

1987). Slotkin published a famous fieldwork report in 1956. Fieldwork accounts written by David Aberle (for example, 1966) specialized in Navajo Peyotism.

Among more recent work, a study about the NAC written by Silvester Brito (1989) is remarkable as he is the first Indian Peyotist to write an academic work about his religion. Peter Gerber (1975) explains the NAC as a crisis movement. In 1996 Huston Smith and the NAC Roadman Reuben Snake compiled testimonies of NAC members showing the church's struggle to survive in the face of constitutional debates. Marika Speckmann (1999) describes the NAC morning water ceremony, comparing it with other Indian rituals and myths.

Marika Speckmann

See also: Native American Religion.

References

Aberle, David F. *The Peyote Religion among the Navaho.* Chicago: Aldine Publishing Company, 1966.

Brito, Silvester. *The Way of a Roadman.* American University Studies, Series 21, Regional Studies Vol. 1. New York, Bern, Frankfurt am Main, and Paris: Peter Lang Publishing, Inc., 1989.

Gerber, Peter. *Die Peyote-Religion. Nordamerikanische Indianer auf der Suche nach einer Identität.* Zurich: Lang Druck, 1980.

La Barre, Weston. *The Peyote Cult.* Hamden, CT: Archon Books, 1975.

Shonle, Ruth. "Peyote—Giver of Visions." *American Anthropologist* 27 (1925): 53–75.

Slotkin, J. S. *The Peyote Religion: A Study in Indian-White Relations.* Glencoe, IL: University of Chicago and The Free Press, 1956.

Smith, Huston, and Reuben Snake, eds. *One Nation under God: The Triumph of the Native American Church.* Santa Fe, NM: Clear Light Publishers, 1996.

Speckmann, Marika. *Panindianische Mythologie am Beispiel der Peyote-Religion.* Stuttgart: Marika Speekmann, 1999.

Stewart, Omer C. *Peyote Religion: A History.* The Civilization of the American Indian Series, 181. Norman: University of Oklahoma Press, 1987.

Native American Religion: Roman Catholicism

Roman Catholicism as practiced by indigenous people in the United States and Canada has undergone major changes over the 20th century, going from a mission-type institution to an almost full-fledged Native Church. It has spearheaded the enculturation of Christianity in those countries and granted Natives equal participation in the workings of the Universal Church. Though in the last decades it has been faced with declining membership like the other major Christian denominations in Native communities, on and off reservations, it now displays a rich variety of tribal expressions and keeps gathering momentum in the campaign to obtain the canonization of Kateri Tekakwitha. The social, spiritual, liturgical, and pastoral impact of eenculturation will be addressed here along with the symbolic function of Kateri.

In Canada, it is estimated that 55 percent of the 1.3 million self-identified Native people are Catholics. In the United States, the figure is estimated at around 17 percent, or less than 500,000 people out of the 2.5 million who identify as Native. Regarding religious activity, one can divide Natives into three major groups: those who have retained some form of Christianity and may have also retained their traditional ways, but are not very active; those who have rejected Christianity altogether, and will tend to have reverted forcefully to traditional spiritualities; those who prove strongly committed Christians, and may also have kept some of their traditional practices. This last group divides along several lines: many have left the old churches to join newcomers, notably Pentecostalism and, in the western and central states and provinces, Mormonism (the Church of Jesus Christ of Latter-day Saints); some shift affiliation within the major groups; some remain fervent adepts of their churches such as the Native Catholics who are taking their religious life into their hands as they are also gaining more social and political clout nationally. To accompany them, the Roman Catholic Church has devised a new mode of evangelization called enculturation.

Enculturation The idea of enculturation implies that the church should no longer impose a Western

Roman Catholic bishops and Native Americans pass a ceremonial pipe at the 60th Annual Tekakwitha Conference on the Gonzaga University campus in Spokane, Washington. (AP Photo/Jeff T. Green)

European model on its non-Western membership, and relative to Native Americans must bring to the fore those elements of Christianity that have always existed in Native cultures. Enculturation originated in discussions initiated before, but carried forward mostly after, the Second Vatican Council. The term was coined by a Belgian Jesuit, Pierre Charles, who gave it the same anthropological meaning as "enculturation," the process whereby one acquires one's own culture; the term was first publicly used during the 32nd General Congregation of the Society of Jesus (1974–1975), and was introduced to the Roman Synod on Catechesis (1977) by Pedro Arrupe (1907–1991), then general of the Society. Pope John Paul II (1920–2005) elaborated on the concept, yet he warned that the Christian message was transmitted through a specific apostolical dialogue that cannot be completed severed from its territorial origins. The message must be rooted in the culture of the evangelized communities even more than in the past. Cultural diversity is sought in a dialogue with the mother church that must respect ethnic expressions and seek to include them in its liturgy in order to ease the access of non-Western communities to the hidden mystery of the Christian message and to help them produce original celebrations of life and of the divine out of their own traditions (*Catechesi tradendae* 53).

Enculturation moves the institution to adjust its focus toward the vernacular, the local, and the laity, in order to meet the challenges brought about by modernity and decolonization; it has seen its major theological developments in Africa. In North America, the Jesuits, the Benedictines, and the Oblates of Mary Immaculate have been most innovative in the field. In Canada in 1984 John Paul II said that faith is expressed in many manners, and not only is Christianity pertinent for Native peoples but through the limbs of his Body, Christ himself is an Indian.

Theology and Ritual Enculturation has given rise to a new theology combining the Christian message and indigenous spirituality that has been formulated by a number of Native nuns and priests, including Sisters Priscilla and Eva Solomon, C.S.J. (Chippewa from northern Ontario), Sister Marie Therese Archambault, O.S.F. (Lakota Hunkpapa), Sister Kateri Mitchell, S.S.A. (Mohawk from Akwesasne), and Father John Hascall, O.F.M. Cap. (Sault Ste Marie Chippewa), to name but a few. All are very active in pastoral care and teaching and have articulated vibrant texts that illuminate the Christian message for Native communities. They emphasize its loving and healing power to mend the scars caused by colonization and its accomplice, imperial and authoritarian evangelization. By condemning Native cultures as Pagan and savage, previous missionaries robbed a whole people of its pride and self-esteem, wreaking havoc in its psychical, physical, and social makeup.

Emboldened by the new openness from Rome, these leaders have retrieved their Indian heritage from oblivion to re-empower Natives, claiming it is as important to Christianity as that of the Hebrews. They have developed the concept of the Two Old Testaments completing each other. The Native one contains the spiritual knowledge that tribes passed down often in clandestine ways to the younger generations, thus preparing them to receive the New Testament. As Sister Priscilla Solomon noted, "Our Aboriginal spirituality is our way back to God, to find eternal life. The teaching of my own tradition points to Jesus Christ, to the grace that he brings to us." For them, the message of Christ is above culture, and above the wrongdoings a human institution such as the church may have inflicted on helpless converts.

Native theology is acted out in the introduction of tribal mores in ceremonies. To celebrate Mass, just as John Paul II wore fringed leather vestments in Aboriginal Canada (1987), priests wear theirs decorated with the symbolical patterns of the local tribe, found as well on altar covers. The drum and the flute will prevail over organ music. The offerings will be presented to the four directions. Prayers will be recited in tribal languages. Instead of incense, the thurifer will use local plants to perform smudging, using a feather fan to blow the smoke over the altar and the attendees. A baptism ceremony will blend the Catholic and the indigenous name-giving rituals, the participants moving in a pattern corresponding to the cosmic order of the tribe.

The retribalization of religious culture is also expressed in the architecture and the decoration of churches and spiritual centers. Whereas the typical religious buildings in Indian lands and in the rest of the two countries have remained European in style, many communities have chosen designs pertaining to their own vision of sacred geography in order to affirm their regained cultural pride. Where Indians lived in teepees, one finds round churches pointing to the sky; on the northwest coast they are made of large cedar beams and masts. Inside, the four directions are marked with the colors attributed by the respective tribes, and Native paintings, quilts, and sculptures adorn the aisles, often alongside classical representations of Saint Anne, Saint Joseph, or the Virgin of Guadalupe. One figure has gained more and more recognition in the past decades, Kateri Tekakwitha (1656–1680), from whom Native Catholicism today is inseparable.

Kateri Tekakwitha Tekakwitha was born in 1656 at Gandaougué, near present-day Auriesville in New York State. Her father was Mohawk, her mother a Catholic Algonquin; both were killed by smallpox, which marked Kateri's face forever and damaged her eyesight. At four, she was adopted by her uncle. Jesuits visited the village and confirmed what she had learned from her mother. When she came of age to be married she refused all proposals, much to the surprise of her people for whom celibacy and virginity had no value. Later, Father Lamberville taught her more and baptized her on Easter day in 1676 as Catherine.

In spite of her uncle's refusal, she settled in Sault Saint-Louis mission near Montreal. On the day of the Annunciation she pronounced her vows. Since she constantly mortified her body, she became sick and died at the age of 24. Her face underwent a transfiguration, the smallpox scars disappearing altogether.

Her cause was introduced in 1884 by the U.S. bishops in plenary council in Baltimore, and in 1885 by several Indian tribes from Canada and the United States. The *Positio super virtutibus* was published in 1938, and she was pronounced Venerable in 1943. With one miracle recognized, she was beatified in 1980. In

2009 the file on a new miracle (needed for canonization) was sent to Rome.

As the only blessed Native, she serves as a role model. The group most focused on promoting her cause is the Tekakwitha Conference. A 1939 meeting in Fargo, North Dakota, of Northern Plains Catholic missionaries to discuss the problems they faced with evangelization became yearly. The fathers then placed it under the patronage of Kateri. Nuns asked to take part since they were in the front line as teachers on the reservations. Lay Natives were not included until the 1970s. It is now a large network of Native Catholics whose headquarters is in Great Falls, Montana, with Sister Kateri Mitchell as the executive director (since 1998). It runs various seminars and activities, the most prestigious being the annual conference. It is organized in different cities by the local Catholic Natives, often united in Kateri Circles, and is attended by about 1,000 Native people, many nuns and clergy. The unfolding is meticulously planned to incorporate local tribal particularities into the canonical ritual that culminates in the daily high Mass celebrated by several bishops, showing the appreciation the church authorities pay to the Conference.

The workshops address the major social, family, and individual problems faced by Natives as well as spiritual healing (blending charismatic and traditional Native handling of sickness); testimonies and addresses by leaders strengthen the bonds between the members and their communities and impart them with the courage to face the future, in the footsteps of Kateri.

In Ontario, Eva Solomon organized the Kateri Conference in 1987 but it ceased to exist in 1995. Several pastoral and spiritual activities are still set up there around the figure of Kateri.

The success of "Katerian Catholicism" must not hide the fact that in both countries vocations to shepherd the flock are scarce, as in Europe. Whereas there are many Native nuns, there are very few priests, celibacy and the need to study far from home never appealing to Native men. As in the church at large, the diaconate is one of the solutions currently explored but it has not yet met with enough success to guarantee regular pastoral care in all Catholic parishes.

Still, the new forms of enculturated theology and rituals have proved to be a major ferment among Native communities. The new assessments of the universality of Christ's message, best expressed in particular ethnic cultures, have allowed a reduction of tension for Native Catholics feeling torn between their two identities as Native people and Christian. They have found ways to affirm both their deep-rooted Indianness and an intense commitment to Christ. Enculturation has allowed a new ability to face criticisms leveled by traditionalists who lash out at them for what they consider their betrayal of authentic Native values. In the 21st century, Native Catholicism has emerged as a significant force within the Catholic Church in North America. Current signs of vitality appear to be the product of improved theological and pastoral leadership, both Native and non-Native.

Bernadette Rigal-Cellard

See also: Benedictines; Church of Jesus Christ of Latter-day Saints; Easter; Iroquois Confederacy; Jesuits; Modernity; Pentecostalism; Roman Catholic Church; Saints.

References

Archamnault, Marie Therese, Christopher Vecsey, and Mark G. Thiel, eds. *The Crossing of Two Roads: Being Catholic and Native in the United States*. Maryknoll, NY: Orbis Books, 2003.

Holmes, Paula Elizabeth. "Symbol Tales: Paths Towards the Creation of a Saint." Ph.D. diss., McMaster University, 2000.

Peelman, Achiel, OMI. *Christ Is a Native American*. Maryknoll, NY: Orbis Books, 1995.

Rigal-Cellard, Bernadette. *Missions extrêmes en Amérique du Nord: des Jésuites à Raël*. Bordeaux : Pleine Page, 2005.

Treat, James. *Native and Christian: Indigenous Voices on Religious Identity in the United States and Canada*. New York: Routledge, 1996.

Vecsey, Christopher. *The Paths of Kateri's Kin*. Notre Dame, IN: University of Notre Dame Press, 1997.

Vecsey, Christopher. *Where The Two Roads Meet*. Notre Dame, IN: University of Notre Dame Press, 1999.

Native Baptist Church

The English Baptist Alfred Saker (1814–1880) began work in the Cameroon in 1845 and continued for the next three decades. Then in 1884, the Baptist churches that had been founded were handed over to the German-based Basel Mission when the Germans began their colonial rule, and these churches soon found their local autonomy threatened by the Basel Mission structures. In response, members formed their own independent church, the Native Baptist Church (NBC), in 1888, the same year that a similar church began in Lagos. The German colonial authority moved to restrict its activities.

The first leader of the NBC was Joshua Diboundou, who resigned his leadership in 1910 when he became a polygamist, to be followed by Albert Tobo Diedo. For a brief period (1917–1932), the NBC was in federation with Baptists of the Berlin Mission and the Basel church. Adolph Lotin Sami (1882–1946), a pastor in the Berlin Baptist Mission, was excluded from the pastorate by the missionaries in 1922 because of a "desire to earn money" and his practice of baptizing polygamists. Refusing to comply, Lotin began to reorganize the NBC, which was revived in 1932 with Lotin as its president. He composed many hymns sung to traditional Douala tunes. When he died in 1946, his place was taken by Moise Mathi Mathi, who changed the name of the NBC to Cameroon Baptist Church in 1949. The CBC was almost exclusively Douala and had more than 5,000 members by 1945, but it was in a state of decline in the 1990s.

Estimates of membership in 2009 are about 55,000. In 1995 the Native Baptist Church (Eglise baptiste camerounaise) was admitted to the World Council of Churches and began a process of internal reform, including renewing links with the Baptist Missionary Society in Britain.

Native Baptist Church
BP 4237
Douala Akwa
Cameroon

Allan H. Anderson

See also: African Initiated (Independent) Churches; Basel Mission; World Council of Churches.

References

Brutsch, L. R. "Origine et Développement d'une Eglise Independante Africaine." *Le Monde Non-Chrétien* 12 (October–December 1949): 408–424.

Gifford, Paul. *African Christianity: Its Public Role*. London: Hurst, 1998.

Joseph Church, Richard A. "State and Society in Colonial Cameroon." *International Journal of African Historical Studies* 13 (1980): 5–32.

■ Nauru

Nauru is an island republic in the South Pacific, northwest of Australia and south of the Marshall Islands. With only 8 square miles of land, it joined the United Nations in 1999 as the world's smallest independent republic. The island was originally settled by Polynesians and Micronesians. It was called to the attention of the West after its initial visit by American whalers, who called it Pleasant Island. In 1888 it was annexed by Germany. At the beginning of World War I, Australia took control of Nauru, a suddenly wealthy land due to the discovery of rich deposits of phosphate. It would remain under Australian control until 1968, except for a period under Japanese rule during World War II. Australia brought in a number of immigrant workers, including many Chinese, to work the mines. Today (2008), some 13,700 people reside on Nauru.

Nauru, which became independent in 1968, is a most unusual land. It has retained its rural character, and no cities have been built. The mining has made the nation wealthy, paying for all education, medical care, and housing. The influx of immigrants from many places to work in the mines has given the Nauru a very ethnically pluralistic culture. Only about 50 percent of the residents are Native Nauruans.

The indigenous religion of the Nauruans survived into the 20th century but appears to have disappeared in the decades since World War II. Although Germany controlled the island early on, the first missionaries were Congregationalists from the London Missionary Society. They assumed the work of translating the Bible into the Native language. Their work grew into the Nauru Congregational Church. As expatriates of other Protestant traditions moved to Nauru, they were

Nauru

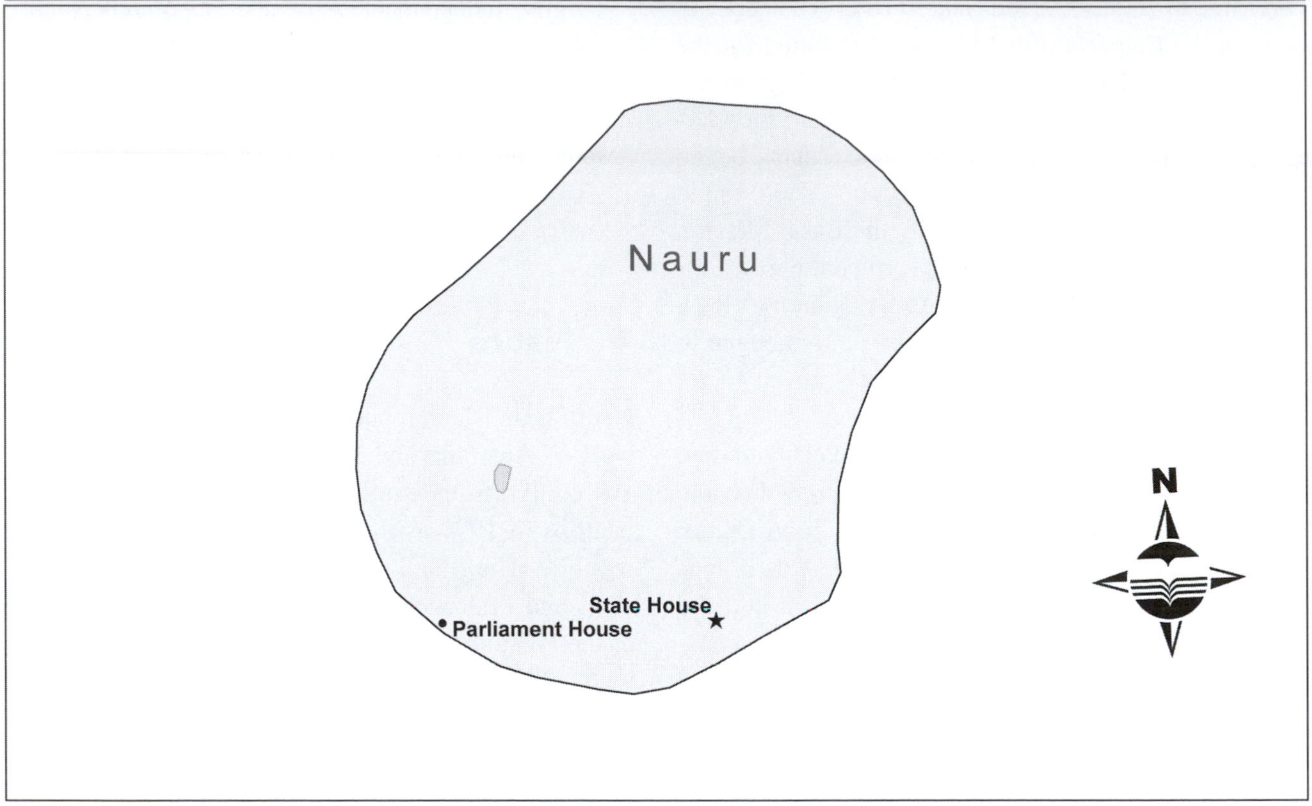

Nauru

Religion	Followers in 1970	Followers in 2010	% of Population	Annual % growth 2000–2010	Followers in 2025	Followers in 2050
Christians	5,400	7,700	74.9	–0.01	7,800	7,200
Protestants	2,700	5,400	52.4	0.21	5,300	5,000
Roman Catholics	1,200	3,400	33.0	2.23	3,800	3,900
Independents	0	700	6.8	1.30	900	1,200
Chinese folk	600	1,100	10.3	0.13	1,100	1,100
Baha'is	100	1,000	9.7	0.14	1,300	1,500
Agnostics	300	390	3.8	3.83	500	700
Buddhists	150	140	1.4	0.14	300	400
Total population	**6,500**	**10,300**	**100.0**	**0.15**	**11,000**	**10,900**

welcomed into the Congregational Church, which is still the only Protestant body on the island.

The Roman Catholic Church began work on Nauru in 1902. At present the parishes are part of the Diocese of Tarawa (Gilbert and Ellice Islands). Members of the Anglican Church moved to Nauru following the takeover of the island by Australia. Its work is now a part of the Anglican Church in Aotearoa, New Zealand, and Polynesia.

Besides the three Christian church bodies, there is also a small group practicing the Baha'i Faith and some Chinese who follow the ubiquitous Chinese folk religion (a mixture of Buddhism, Daoism, and Confucianism).

J. Gordon Melton

See also: Baha'i Faith; Nauru Congregational Church; Roman Catholic Church.

References

McDaniel, Carl N., and John M. Gowdy. *Paradise for Sale: A Parable of Nature*. Berkeley: University of California Press, 2000.

Petit-Skinner, S. *The Nauruians*. San Francisco: MacDuff Press, 1981.

Nauru Congregational Church

The Nauru Congregational Church dates to around 1889 and the arrival on Nauru Island of Timoteo Tabwia, a Gilbert Islander who had been converted by missionaries of the American Board of Commissioners for Foreign Missions (ABCFM), an association of American Congregationalists. He was later joined by two Americans, Philip A. and Salome Delaporte, who arrived in 1899, mastered the Nauruan language, and translated the Bible. The ABCFM continued their work through the early decades of the 20th century, during which time the island was invaded by a variety of European companies that wanted to mine the calcium phosphates discovered in 1900.

In 1917, the ABCFM turned over its responsibilities in Nauru to the London Missionary Society, a British Congregationalist group. Through midcentury and following Japanese occupation of the island, Nauruan Congregationalists became closely affiliated with the Congregational Union of Australia.

Although the church had grown significant indigenous leadership during this time, the first Nauruan minister to receive seminary training, Itubwa Amram, was not ordained until 1956. Subsequently, the church became autonomous of the LMS but kept close ties with Australia. It is a member of the International Congregational Council, the Council for World Mission (the successor body to the LMS), and the Pacific Conference of Churches. It was a member of the World Council of Churches but has recently withdrawn.

Some 65 percent of the island's 10,000 residents are members of the church's 7 congregations. The church faces the challenge of diminishing mineral resources, the likely negative economic impact of the ending of mining operations, and the destruction of the majority of the island by the mining operations.

Nauru Congregational Church
PO Box 232
Nauru
Central Pacific

J. Gordon Melton

See also: American Board of Commissioners for Foreign Missions; London Missionary Society; World Council of Churches.

Reference

Bauswein, Jean-Jacques, and Lukas Vischner, eds. *The Reformed Family Worldwide: A Survey of Reformed Churches, Theological Schools, and International Organizations*. Grand Rapids, MI: William B. Eerdmans Publishing Company, 1999.

Navajo, The

The Navajo refer to themselves as the Dine (the People). Originally a seminomadic tribal group of Athapascan stock from western Canada and Alaska, they began settling in the Four Corners region of the American Southwest in the 11th century CE.

The Navajo world was created when the Diyin-Dine (Holy People) emerged from four underworlds into this, the fifth world. The most important of these Holy People are First Man and First Woman, whose inner natures are, respectively, "Thought" and "Speech." Together they created a world where the most important value is *hozho*. Most commonly translated as "beauty," hozho encompasses much more—harmony, peace, health, happiness, balance, and the general good.

For the Navajo, life itself is movement, and it is through good intentions and prayer that men and women participate in keeping the world in harmony. Although the original harmonic patterns were created when the Holy People emerged into this world, the Navajo continue to participate in this ongoing creative act by ritually associating themselves with these supernatural beings through thought and speech. Beauty is not something to be discovered in nature but it is to

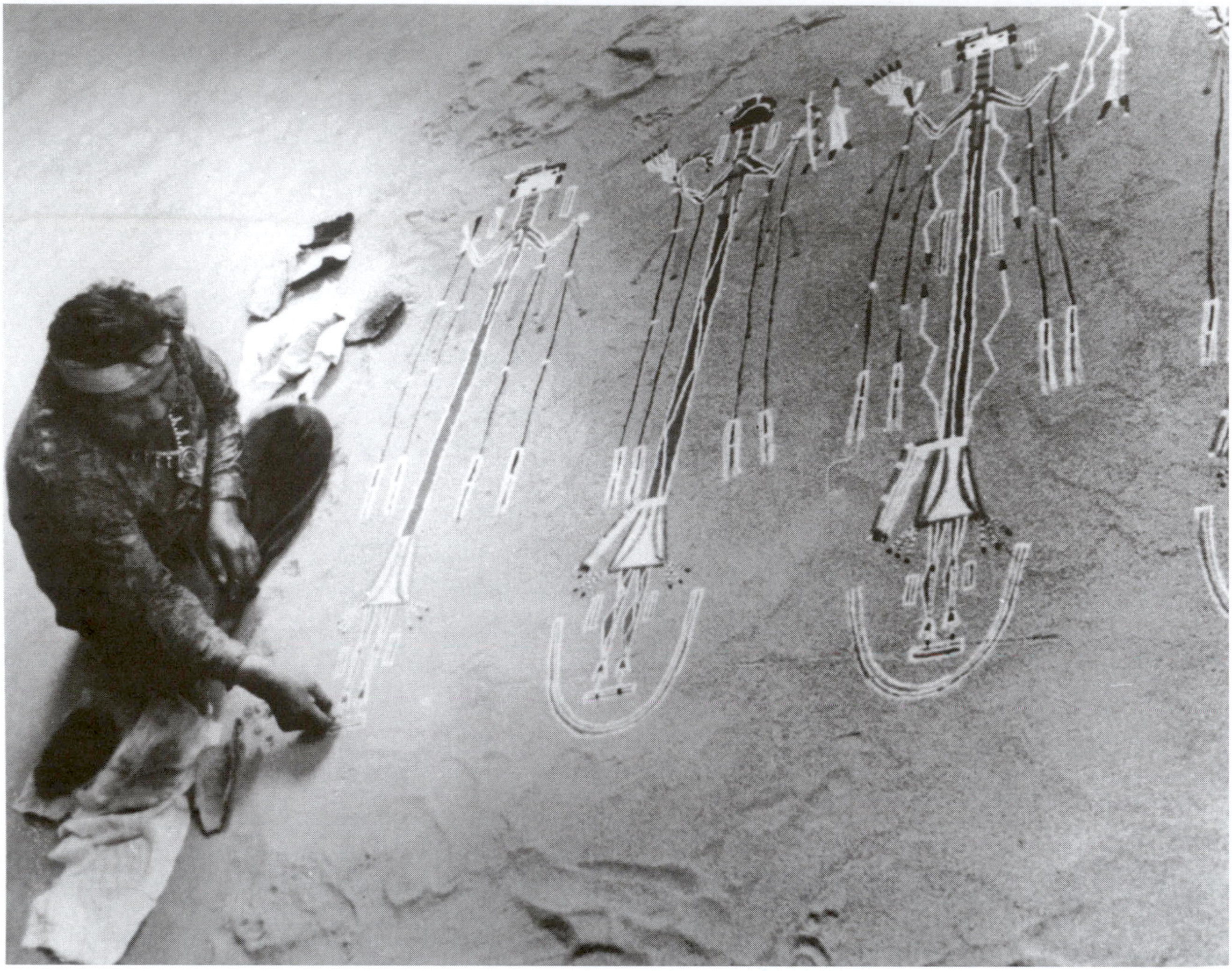

Navajo medicine man Deschinni Nez-Begav of Rough Rock, Arizona, draws a Red Ant Chant sandpainting using loose sand on the floor of the Museum of Navajo Ceremonial Art in Santa Fe, New Mexico, 1963. (AP Photo)

be created, first in the mind as thought and then projected out into the world as speech. Speech is, in fact, the outer form of thought.

The Navajo walk in harmony and beauty through everyday activities that are rich with symbolism. Symbols seem to be the very grounding and basis for thought. Every morning, for example, men and women emerge from their *hogons* (circular homes), each of which is the symbolic center of the cosmos, to chant the world into existence by identifying themselves with First Man and First Woman. Through such ritual actions as scattering cornmeal in four directions and chanting beauty into the world at sunrise, the Navajo become active participants in creation itself.

All Navajos should work to create hozho, because then they will live long and prosperous lives, and their communities will continue in harmony. In this context, illness signifies a disruption in the harmonious fabric of living. A sick person, with the assistance of friends and family, will try to determine why his or her world is out of balance. Perhaps the ill person failed to fulfill some social or religious obligation. Or perhaps, even more seriously, a man returning from war has been polluted by violence and death. In the first instance only a portion of a Blessingway ritual might need to be performed some evening. In the second case a full-blown Enemyway ceremony of three or four days' duration will be needed to restore hozho.

There are at least 60 major ceremonies among the Navajo that preserve and restore hozho. It usually takes several years of apprenticeship for the ritual specialist, called a singer, to master one of these rites. Although both men and women may become singers, only men will prepare the sandpaintings that are usually integral to the ceremonies. Few singers learn more than one major rite, and only very rarely will any individual know more than a couple. Religious knowledge is therefore widely dispersed across the Navajo nation. A singer will diagnose the cause of illness and determine whether the patient should be referred to another singer or undergo this specialist's ceremony. This is critical, because the person *will* be healed if the diagnosis is correct, if the singer does the ritual properly, and if the wills of the singer and the people taking part in the healing are strong enough to forge a connection between the patient and the Holy People.

The singer creates the conditions for the complete merger of this world and the supernatural world by purifying the patient, most commonly through chanting prayers in a sweat lodge, and by overseeing the drawing of a sandpainting in the center of a hogon that creates the activities of the first Holy People in an action corresponding to the cause and cure of the patient's illness. The nearly naked patient then sits or lies on his or her corresponding deity in the sandpainting. Chanting, shaking rattles, touching, and other symbolic activities effect the cure by restoring hozho to the patient's life.

The Navajo do not fear dying when their cycle of life is completed. But a premature death signals the malevolent activity of sorcerers. The most common way for a sorcerer to harm an individual is to sing the parts of a religious ceremony in reverse order, thereby creating chaos in the place of harmony. Sorcerers must operate in secret because they cannot resist the direct onslaught of a singer's benevolent energy and will be destroyed by their own evil energy when it is returned to them.

Despite the many ways that hozho can be disrupted, the Navajo are remarkably optimistic. As long as they continue to participate with the Holy People in maintaining and creating hozho in the world, they can be assured that their world will be beautiful and harmonious and that they will live healthy and prosperous lives.

According to the 1990 census, there were more than 225,000 Navajo, of whom nearly 145,000 live on reservation and trust lands in Arizona, New Mexico, and Utah. Since religious and cultural practices are indistinguishable for the Navajo, most attend rituals at least occasionally, even though some also practice forms of Christianity. Not infrequently, Navajo sense the need to return to a ritual healing when they feel polluted by death. Numerous healing chants, for example, were held for veterans who returned from Vietnam, even those who lived in cities away from the reservation.

Thomas V. Peterson

See also: Native American Church.

References

Gill, Sam. *Sacred Words: A Study of Navajo Religion and Prayer*. Westport, CT: Greenwood Press, 1981.

Reichard, Gladys A. *Navaho Religion: A Study of Symbolism.* Princeton, NJ: Princeton University Press, 1974.

Witherspoon, Gary. *Language and Art in the Navajo Universe.* Ann Arbor: University of Michigan Press, 1977.

Navaratri/Dashain

The Navaratri (Navaratra), or "Nine Nights," Festival is celebrated in September–October (Hindu lunar month of Ashvin) for 9 nights (and 10 days). This is a pan-Indian festival, which, as Holi welcomes the spring, welcomes the autumn season. Also, like Holi, it takes very different forms in different regions. In neighboring Nepal, as the national holiday, Dashain, it is the largest festival of the year, involving both Hindu and non-Hindu Nepalis alike in celebration.

In most Hindi-speaking areas of North India Navaratri is centered on Rama, like Krishna an incarnation of the deity Vishnu. It is celebrated with a drama, the Rama Lila (the mysterious divine magic of Lord Rama), drawn from the Ramayana epic story. Here there are recitations every day from the medieval Hindi Tulsidas Ramayana, and in most places plays that depict scenes from the Ramayana story are presented in smaller or grander scale.

The largest of the Rama Lila play is staged across the river from Benares, where the king (maharajah) of Benares established an immense ground that represents the Ramayana story. Actors go from station to station on different days as the story develops. On Vijayadashami—variously described as the culminating day of Navaratri or the day after Navaratri—the effigies of Rama's enemy, the demon king Ravana, along with his son Meghanada and his brother Kumbhakarna, are burned to celebrate the victory of Rama over the forces of the demons or Rakshasas.

In Bihar, Bengal, and Assam the Navaratri Festival, and in Nepal, Dashain is celebrated as a Durga festival. Durga *pujas,* or worship services, are done for her on the last three days of the festival. The festival begins by awakening Durga, who is asleep, and continues by manufacturing a temporary image of her which is enlivened for the purpose of the festival.

On Vijayadashmi, the image of Durga will be taken in a great procession to be immersed in the local body of water, be it a river or the ocean or a large tank. Lively festivities follow. In south India the goddess Sarasvati, the goddess of learning and the arts, is worshipped on the seventh day of the festival and Durga only on the eighth day. On the ninth day there is a worship of instruments and implements of livelihood, which are taken out to be honored with mantras and small offerings.

An additional tradition surrounding Durga and Navaratri concerns the Pandava brothers, important characters in the great Indian epic, the Mahabharata. Great warriors, all five brothers were married to one woman named Draupadi. At one point, they lived through a 14-year exile followed by a one-year period of incognito during which time they had to put away their distinctive weaponry. They hid it in a Shami tree near their residence. When their incognito year was finished, they went to the tree and retrieved their weaponry. For its safe preservation, they offered worship and thanksgiving both to the Shami tree and the goddess Durga, the deity of strength and victory. Meanwhile, their rivals, the Kauravas, had invaded the region looking for them. After completing their devotions, the Pandavas went directly to engage in the Battle of Kurukshetra, at which they won a decisive victory. That day subsequently became known as Vijayadashami ("Vijaya" is Sanskrit for "Victory"). Today, on Vijatadashami, people give Shami leaves with a wish that the recipient might have victory in his or her efforts.

Constance A. Jones

See also: Calendars, Religious; Holi.

References

Eck, Diana L. *Banaras, City of Light*. New York: Columbia University Press, 1999.

Harshananda, Swami. *Hindu Festivals and Sacred Days.* Bangalore: Ramakrishna Math, 1994.

Mukuncharandas, Sadhu. *Hindu Festivals (Origin Sentiments & Rituals).* Amdavad, India: Swaminarayan Aksharpith, 2005.

Sharma, Nath. *Festivals of India.* New Delhi: Abhinav Publications, 1978.

Shekar, H. V. *Festivals of India: Significance of the Celebrations.* Louisville, KY: Insight Books, 2000.

Welbon, Guy, and Glenn Yocum, eds. *Religious Festivals in South India and Sri Lanka.* Delhi: Manohar, 1982.

Nazareth

Nazareth, a small town situated inside a bowl atop the Nazareth ridge north of the Jezreel valley in Galilee in what today is Israel, was the hometown of Jesus, who was referred to as the Nazarene. Nazareth is west of the Sea of Galilee and some 65 miles north of Jerusalem. In Jesus' day, Nazareth was a relatively isolated village of only some 200 residents. Its lack of status as a community was reflected in the statement ascribed to one of Jesus' future apostles, "Can anything good come out of Nazareth?" (John 1:46).

Nazareth emerges out of obscurity in the New Testament account of Jesus' mother Mary, who, after being engaged to marry Joseph, was visited by the angel Gabriel who announced to her the birth of Jesus (Luke 1:26–33). Though not the father of Jesus, Joseph married the pregnant Mary and the two then left Nazareth for Bethlehem to be counted in the census ordered by Caesar Augustus. Jesus subsequently spent his boyhood years in Nazareth, where he reput-

Israeli city of Nazareth, the center of Jesus' ministry and one of Christianity's most sacred areas. Archaeological excavations reveal the ancient village of Nazareth was actually located on the hillside above the modern city. (Corel)

edly learned carpentry from Joseph. After beginning his ministry when he was about 30, he moved his home to Capernaum, but returned to teach in the synagogue of Nazareth twice more. He was rejected both times (Mark 6:1–6). On one occasion the townspeople were so outraged at Jesus that they tried to throw him off a cliff to his death (Luke 4:16–30).

Very little is known about Nazareth from the ancient sources. It is not mentioned in pre-Christian records and then again falls into obscurity after the New Testament period. It is rediscovered only after the Roman Empire decriminalizes Christianity in the fourth century and the Holy Land emerges as a primary pilgrimage site. More recent archaeological excavations have confirmed that the city was only a small agricultural village during the Hellenistic and early Roman periods.

During the period of the Crusader kingdom, Nazareth became the center of a bishopric. A Byzantine-style church was built over a cave that had been designated as the spot where the angel Gabriel announced the birth of Jesus. In 1966 the Roman Catholic Church began constructing a new basilica over the remains of that church, and today this new Church of the Annunciation is the largest church building in the Middle East. Nearby is a Greek Orthodox church that was built over a well that also has been claimed as the site of the Annunciation, a claim that derives from one of the apocryphal gospels, the "Proto-evangelium of James," that pictured the scene of the Annunciation occurring as the Virgin Mary was drawing water.

In contemporary Israel, Nazareth's population has grown to more than 60,000, mostly Arab Christians.

J. Gordon Melton

See also: Jerusalem; Mary, Blessed Virgin; Pilgrimage.

References

Braun, Herbert. *Jesus of Nazareth. The Man and His Time*. Philadelphia: Fortress Press, 1979.

Brown, Raymond E. *The Birth of the Messiah: A Commentary on the Infancy Narratives in Matthew and Luke*. Rev. ed. Mahwah, NJ: Paulist Press, 1994.

Emmett, Chad. *Beyond the Basilica: Christians and Muslims in Nazareth*. Chicago: University of Chicago Press, 1995.

Kenyon, K. *Archaeology in the Holy Land*. 4th ed. New York: W. W. Norton & Company, 1979.

Pixner, Bargil. *With Jesus through Galilee According to the Fifth Gospel*. Rosh Pina: Corazin.

Nazareth (Nazarite) Baptist Church

The largest of the African Initiated Churches (AIC) among the Zulu, the Nazareth Baptist Church, better known as the amaNazaretha, or Isonto LamaNazaretha, or Shembe Church, was founded by Mdliwamafa Mloyisa (Isaiah) Shembe (ca. 1869–1935), who experienced several visions and audible inner voices from an early age. These revelations later told him to leave his four wives and children and to use no medicine, and they showed him people in white gowns who would follow him. He began his Christian life as a Methodist but was baptized in William Leshega's African Native Baptist Church (an early African secession from the white Baptists) in about 1900, by which time he was already a renowned healer. He was ordained an evangelist and began to baptize in the sea near Durban, a practice of many coastal African churches today.

In about 1911, Shembe seceded from the African Native Baptist Church, which did not insist as he did on taking off shoes in worship, leaving the hair uncut, not eating pork, night Communion services with foot washing, and the seventh day Sabbath. He founded the amaNazaretha and applied biblical references to Nazarites to his followers, who were to obey these laws. In 1916 he established a "high place," called Ekuphakameni, outside Durban, and a holy mountain, Nhlangakazi—sites for annual festivals in July and January, respectively. Shembe wielded great influence in Zulu society. When he died in 1935, a sacred mausoleum was built over his grave at Ekuphakameni, now the headquarters of the church, and his son Johannes Galilee Shembe inherited the leadership.

On Galilee's death in 1976, a fierce and acrimonious schism resulted, with court cases, violent clashes, and even killings between the two factions. A small part of the church followed Galilee's son Londa Shembe, who was murdered in 1989 in the midst of the KwaZulu Natal violence, leaving no clear successor. The majority of members followed Isaiah's other son, Amos Khula Shembe. As an indication of the prestige attained by the Shembe family, Nelson Mandela attended Amos's funeral in 1995. His son Mbusi Vimbeni Shembe, who seems to have retained the loyalty of the vast majority of the church, succeeded him.

The amaNazaretha's great veneration for their founder has been interpreted to mean that he is seen as an African Christ, a mediator between his people and God, standing at the gate of heaven to admit only his followers. amaNazaretha greet their leader with the shout "He is holy!" Shembe is believed to have "risen from the dead"; he appears to people in revelations and is believed to reveal God to the Zulus, and in his name prayer is directed. The criticisms of this movement have centered on the person of Isaiah Shembe and reflect prevalent assumptions made by earlier Western theologians about the AICs.

Evidence from the amaNazaretha themselves, however, is ambiguous. In the opinion of at least some of his followers, Shembe has very extraordinary, perhaps even divine powers, and divine and messianic titles are ascribed to him. But most frequently, amaNazaretha describe Shembe in lesser, more mortal terms. Instead of being a divine Messiah or Black Christ, Isaiah Shembe is a human "servant of the Lord," "the man sent by God," who is obedient to the bidding of God.

amaNazaretha wear white robes and remove their shoes in worship, men are circumcised (a custom not practiced elsewhere in Zulu society), polygyny is allowed, and members may not shake hands with outsiders, eat pork, drink alcohol, or take medicines. Isaiah Shembe composed more than 200 hymns that are sung by church members, some of which are accompanied by sacred dancing in African dress, and some of which are believed to have been written after his resurrection. Baptism by immersion, communion at night, and foot washing are practiced as sacraments, and the Sabbath is observed as well as the *hlonipha* (respectful avoidance) rules of the Zulu. The amaNazaretha have greatly influenced the rituals of other Zulu AICs (especially Zionists), and they represent a unique blend of Christianity with the best of Zulu culture. There are approximately a million amaNazaretha in South Africa today.

Allan H. Anderson

See also: African Initiated (Independent) Churches; Native Baptist Church.

References

Anderson, Allan H. *African Reformation: African Initiated Christianity in the Twentieth Century*. Trenton, NJ: Africa World Press, 2001.

Hexham, Irving, and G. C. Oosthuizen, eds. *The Story of Isaiah Shembe: History and Traditions Centered on Ekuphakameni and Mount Nhlangakazi*. Lewiston: Edwin Mellon Press, 1996.

Sundkler, Bengt G. M. *Bantu Prophets in South Africa*. Oxford: Oxford University Press, 1961.

Bhairabnath Hindu temple and evening market, Bhaktapur, Nepal. (Szefei/Dreamstime.com)

■ Nepal

The modern state of Nepal is strung out along the Himalayas northwest to southeast between Tibet to the north and India to the south. It is home to 28,560,000 people who represent a variety of ethnicities. It consists of 56,800 square miles of territory.

Nepal was created by King Prithvi Narayan Shah of Gurkha (1723–1775). He conquered the Kathmandu Valley in 1768–1769 and went on to conquer great swaths of the Himalayan foothills, west as far as Kangra and east to Sikkim. After a war with the British East India Company in 1814–1816, the boundaries of the state of Nepal were fixed largely as they are today, Nepal's autonomy was recognized, and the British right to recruit soldiers within Nepal was also granted.

In the period preceding 1769 and the unification of the country as seen by nationalist historians, there were numerous small kingdoms in the hills, ruled by families claiming prestigious Hindu descent from Indian Rajputs, who had supposedly fled to the Himalayas to escape Muslim depredations in Rajasthan. The high mountain region was inhabited by small pockets of Tibetan people, most of whom practiced a form of Myingma Tibetan Buddhism. The Sherpas, for instance, were migrants from Tibet who came over the high passes in the 16th and 17th centuries. In the middle hills to the south there were a number of tribal peoples: from west to east, the Magars, Gurungs, Tamangs, Rai, and Limbu, as well as other smaller groups. (These are the names that are used for these groups today; in some cases the names were not current before the 19th, or even early 20th, century and the groups did not see themselves as distinct groups until so classified by the Hinduizing state.) Of these tribal groups, the Magars were the most Hinduized, the Tamangs the most Tibetanized. All of them possessed lively shamanic traditions, which loomed largest among the Rai and Limbu, collectively known as Kirantis.

NEPAL

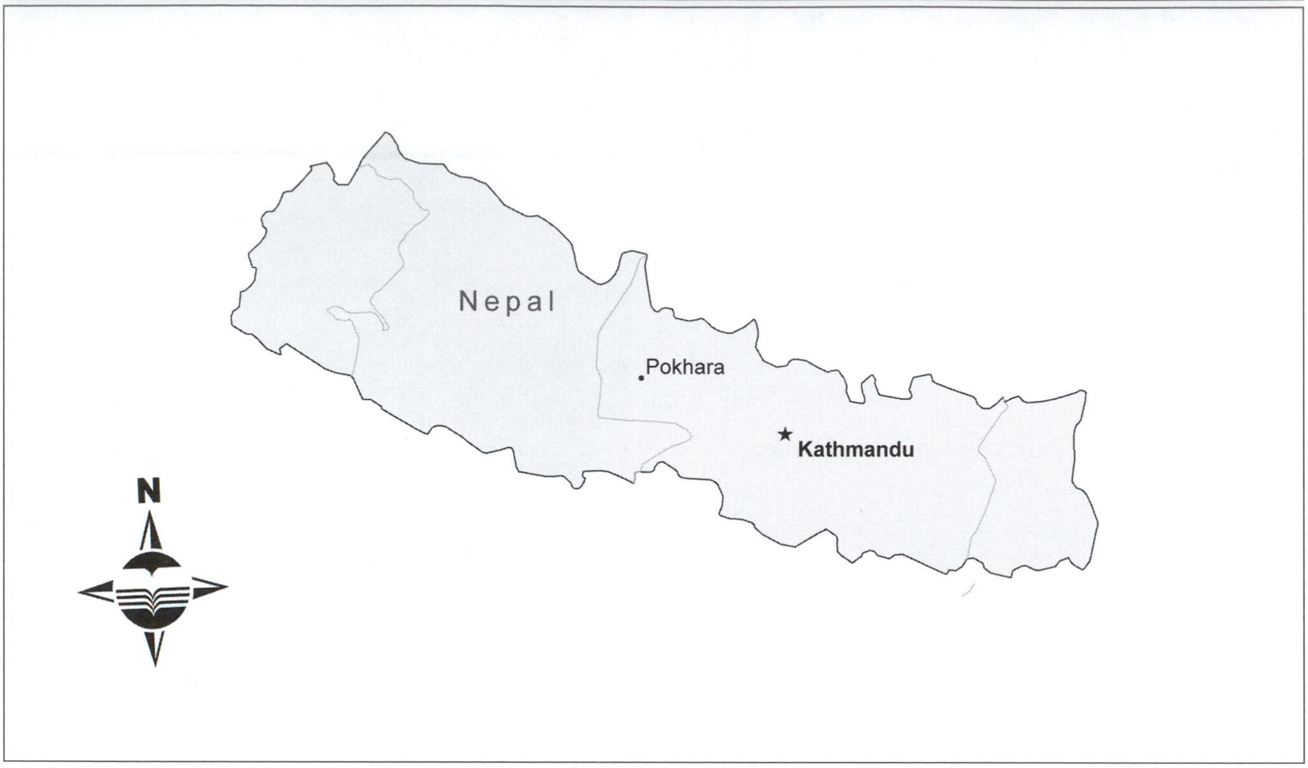

In this early period the largely forested plains (Tarai) region was inhabited mainly by tribal groups practicing shifting agriculture, most of whom now think of themselves as Tharus. There were, however, some areas of longer settlement, notably around Janakpur, where the populations were Hindu and culturally similar to those over the border in India. Finally, in the Kathmandu Valley, housing the three cities of Kathmandu, Lalitpur (Patan), and Bhaktapur, the Newar people practiced both Hinduism and Buddhism, both strongly influenced by Tantric ritualism.

Both of these forms of religion were highly conservative, harking back to forms of religious practice once much more widespread in the subcontinent. The Newar Buddhism is of particular significance, as the last direct descendant of Indian Mahayana Buddhism, which was exported and translated to the rest of Asia before dying out in the land of its birth. As the great French Sanskritist Sylvain Lévi (1863–1935) pointed out, studying Newar Buddhism is a window onto early Indian Mahayana Buddhism and the Hindu-Buddhist context in which it grew up and eventually went into decline. Also present in the Kathmandu Valley since at least the 17th century, and perhaps from the 16th, was a minority of Muslim traders.

From 1845 to 1951 Nepal was ruled by a hereditary system of Rana prime ministers. State-sponsored Hinduism played a key role in legitimating the rule of the Ranas and in welding their culturally and linguistically diverse kingdom into some form of unity. This sponsorship took the form of encouraging the countrywide observance of major festivals, in particular, that of Dasain focusing on the goddess Durga, which legitimated royal power as well as the position of leading men within patrilineages. It also took the form of introducing a national legal code that gave formal judicial backing to hierarchical Hindu notions of status.

The Rana regime fell in 1951, and after an abortive experiment with parliamentary democracy, King Mahendra (1920–1972) introduced Partyless Panchayat Democracy in 1960. The new constitution declared Nepal a Hindu state. The legal code was modernized and caste was no longer recognized. But there was no positive discrimination on behalf of Untouchables

Nepal

Religion	Followers in 1970	Followers in 2010	% of Population	Annual % growth 2000–2010	Followers in 2025	Followers in 2050
Hindus	9,018,000	20,630,000	69.0	2.00	26,576,000	35,754,000
Ethnoreligionists	1,353,000	3,665,000	12.3	2.04	4,200,000	4,700,000
Buddhists	1,400,000	3,220,000	10.8	2.11	4,200,000	5,650,000
Muslims	332,000	1,305,000	4.4	2.10	1,695,000	2,260,000
Christians	7,400	935,000	3.1	5.11	1,908,000	3,062,000
Independents	5,500	720,000	2.4	4.72	1,500,000	2,250,000
Protestants	600	200,000	0.7	6.77	400,000	800,000
Roman Catholics	300	7,500	0.0	1.35	15,000	30,000
Agnostics	30,000	80,200	0.3	2.10	170,000	300,000
Chinese folk	0	20,900	0.1	2.10	40,000	70,000
Atheists	10,000	18,800	0.1	2.10	30,000	40,000
Sikhs	0	10,500	0.0	2.10	15,000	25,000
Jains	2,500	7,500	0.0	2.10	10,500	15,000
Baha'is	3,000	4,500	0.0	2.10	10,000	15,000
Total population	**12,155,000**	**29,898,000**	**100.0**	**2.10**	**38,855,000**	**51,891,000**

or other disadvantaged groups, as in India, and the entire population was governed by the same civil code. The Panchayat period was one of conscious nation-building. A Hindu cultural identity was a part of this; Buddhism, along with Jainism and Sikhism (barely present in Nepal), was declared to be a branch of Hinduism—a point that modernist Buddhist activists were not at all happy to concede.

In the 1930s Theravada Buddhism was first introduced, initially by Newars, but from the 1980s on there were increasing numbers of recruits from non-Newar backgrounds. A major expansion of Tibetan Mahayana Buddhism also occurred in Kathmandu and other major towns, sponsored both by Tibetan refugees and by urbanized and upwardly mobile Nepalis from Buddhist backgrounds (Gurungs, Tamangs, and others). Rais and Limbus began to organize in the 1990s around their shamanic indigenous religion, which they named Kirantism. After 1990 and the fall of the Panchayat regime, it became increasingly possible to assert a non-Hindu or even anti-Hindu identity, and many started to do so.

The 1991 census, out of a total population of 18.4 million, revealed 86.5 percent Hindus, 7.8 percent Buddhists, 3.5 percent Muslims, 1.7 percent Kirantis, and 0.2 percent Christians. (Buddhist activists have long claimed that the censuses, even that of 1991, underestimate the numbers of Buddhists.) Inducing people to convert remained illegal, but the penalties for conversion were no longer applied. Large numbers began to convert to Christianity, and a number of individuals from non-Muslim backgrounds also converted to Islam. The influx of the modern world and global culture meant that various new religions, such as Reiyukai and Tenrikyo from Japan, Sai Baba, Rajneesh (now Osho Commune International), S. N. Goenka's *vipassana* movement, and many others, established a presence in the capital and elsewhere. The new Constitution of 1990 continued to define Nepal as a Hindu state, but this was more controversial than ever before.

David N. Gellner

See also: Buddhism; Jainism; Mahayana Buddhism; Newar Buddhism; Nyingma Tibetan Buddhism; Osho and the International Osho Movement; Reiyukai; Sikhism; Tenrikyo; Theravada Buddhism; Vipassana International Academy.

References

Bennett, L. *Dangerous Wives and Sacred Sisters: Social and Symbolic Roles of High-Caste Women in Nepal*. New York: Columbia University Press, 1983.

Gellner, D. N. *Monk, Householder, and Tantric Priest: Newar Religion and Its Hierarchy of*

Ritual. Cambridge: Cambridge University Press, 1992.

Gellner, D. N., J. Pfaff-Czarnecka, and J. Whelpton, eds. *Nationalism and Ethnicity in a Hindu Kingdom: The Politics of Culture in Contemporary Nepal*. Amsterdam: Harwood, 1997.

Hitchcock, J., and R. L. Jones, eds. *Spirit Possession in the Nepal Himalayas*. Warminster: Aris and Phillips, 1976.

Höfer, A. *The Caste Hierarchy and the State in Nepal: A Study of the Muluki Ain of 1854*. Innsbruck: Universitätsverlag Wagner, 1979.

Ortner, S. *High Religion: A Cultural and Political History of Sherpa Buddhism*. Princeton, NJ: Princeton University Press, 1989.

Nepal, Indigenous Religions in

Nepal was until 2006 the only kingdom in the world to be officially Hindu. Following the movement for democracy, however, in which the king's power was severely curtailed, the Nepali Parliament altered the Constitution in January 2007 to make Nepal a "secular state." Indigenous religions in Nepal, in their richness and diversity, deny any such categorizations or attempts at secularization. The numerous tribal groups in the Nepalese hills present complex religious systems, which interrelate the various key influences of Hinduism, Tibetan Buddhism, spirit possession, shamanism, and "folk" traditions. Each religious system of hill Nepal, whether that of the Rai and Limbu (the Kirantis), or of the Tamang, Magar, Sherpa, Gurung, Newar, Sunuwar, or of the Indo-Nepalese Damai, Sarki, Bahun, or Chetri, combines these strands in their own unique way depending, for example, on their location, history, myths, and social structure. Studies of religion in hill Nepal have so far tended to focus on the separate strands of Hinduism, Tibetan Buddhism, and spirit possession. They have shown that for many groups there is a particular tribal identity and culture represented in their myths and rituals and through tribal ritual specialists. The Rai and Limbu (Kirantis), for example, developed in the 1990s their own pan-Kiranti identity around their indigenous religion, which they called Kirantism.

One of the key features of Nepal religions, as with South Asian religions in general, is the use of multiple specialists to communicate with the spiritual world, to carry their tribal knowledge, to propitiate divinities, and to act as psychopomp. These specialists are of central significance since for those living in Nepal the world is teeming with spirits of all kinds—including evil spirits, malevolent divinities, protective ancestors, moody ancestors, ghosts of the dead (some shared with other groups and some tribal-specific), as well as Buddhas and Hindu gods and goddesses. The tribal practitioners tend toward inclusivity in their rituals since omission of any god or spirit is likely to incite the wrath of the neglected. Common ailments such as diarrhea, backache, fever, or indigestion as well as severe illnesses are understood in terms of disturbance in the relationship between humans and one or more of these superhuman beings. To counter illness and misfortune people in the hills may seek support from Buddhist lamas and the authority of sacred texts, from Hindu practices, or from the power of shamans and ritual sacrifice. Shamans are the spiritual specialists, who are able to enter a trance state at will to communicate with spirits and gods on behalf of the community. They specialize in dreamlike revelatory states; from their journeys into the cosmos they can divine the future or sources of misfortune and illness, and return lost souls. Soul flight and spirit possession are prevalent and shamans from any ethnic group may be sought out. The Nepali term for the magico-religious specialist who is prevalent throughout the Nepalese hills is *jhankri*. These specialists are usually initially possessed involuntarily by spirits or gods and often undergo prolonged periods of illness before they learn to control the unintegrated dead or malevolent divinities.

Charlotte Hardman

See also: Ancestors; Possession; Sacred Texts; Secularization; Spirit Possession.

References

Desjarlais, Robert. *Body and Emotion: The Aesthetics of Illness and Healing in the Nepal Himalaya*. Philadelphia: University of Pennsylvania Press, 1992.

Hardman, Charlotte E. *Other Worlds: Notions of Self and Emotion among the Lohorung Rai*. Oxford: Berg, 2000.

Hitchcock, J. T., and Rex Jones. *Spirit Possession in the Nepal Himalayas*. New Delhi: Vikas Publishing House, 1976.
Holmberg, David H. *Order in Paradox: Myth, Ritual and Exchange among Nepal's Tamang*. Ithaca and London: Cornell University Press, 1989.

■ Netherlands, The

The Netherlands is a Western European nation with a long coastline on the North Sea. To its south lies Belgium, with Germany to its east. Its 16,000 square miles is mostly flat coastal land, with a significant proportion having been reclaimed from the sea, the highest point in the country rising little more than 100 feet above sea level.

The Netherlands is a typical trade country, and therefore it is an open society; since around 1970, it has been a multicultural society as well. The capital is Amsterdam; the place of government, The Hague. The population amounts to 17.5 million (2008). Dutch is the official language; in Friesland, also Frisian. The main religions are the Reformed branch of Christianity, divided into many churches (greater and smaller) and small communities, and, especially in the southern part of the country, the Roman Catholic Church. The important minority group (about one million) is the Muslim community from Turkey and North Africa, divided into national and religious-determined mosque-associations. The Netherlands is an open trade country and has therefore a wide spectrum of religious groups representative of the variety of the world's religions. Most Dutch citizens accepted the presence of the different religions, and a spirit of tolerance existed side by side with a special attachment to the Reformed branch of Christianity. In recent times the traditional spirit of tolerance has decreased.

The Netherlands has many political parties. The main political parties are the CDA (Christian Democratic Party, rather conservative), the PvdA (Partij van de Arbeid, a moderate Socialist party), the VVD (Volkspartij voor Vrigheid en Democratie, a Conservative party), the SP (Socialistischie Partij, a radical Socialist party), and recently the PVV (Partij voor de Vrijheid, an anti-Muslim party). Smaller political parties are D'66 (a Liberal party), Groen Links (a Progressive party), the CU (Christian Union, the representative of some progressive Reformed Christians), and the SGP (Staatskundig Gereformeede Partij, a party of very conservative Christians).

Basilica of St. Servas, a Catholic church in the southern city of Maastricht, the Netherlands. (iStockPhoto.com)

As early as the Middle Ages, the Low Countries (a former name for The Netherlands) took a special place on the field of religion. At that time the Roman Catholic Church was the only religion legally allowed. But many heretical movements of all kinds emerged, especially in the many towns. In the 14th century the Brethren of the Common Life, with Geert de Groot (1340–1384) as its "founding father," gained many adherents, primarily in the towns and villages. That movement became very popular in many parts of Europe, from Sweden to Spain and Portugal. The Brethren promoted education in elementary schools, a modest way of life for the priests, and a personal belief. Of special importance to the Brethren was the now-classic devotional text *The Imitation of Christ*, written by Thomas à Kempis (1379/1380–1471), now available in numerous languages.

The Lutheran Reformation drew significant response for a short time, again especially in towns like Amsterdam. But the Reformers John Calvin (1509–1564), Ulrich Zwingli (1484–1531), Heinrich Bullinger (1504–1575), and others drew the attention away from the Lutherans. Their views on personal obedience to God and personal responsibility provided a rationale for denying allegiance to the lord of the Low Countries—that is, the king of Spain. The Eighty Years' War (1568–1648) found support from those who believed in a right of resistance when the king or other authorities did not obey the will of God. At the same time, the Bible-oriented Humanism of Desiderius Erasmus (1469–1536) and Dirck Coornhert (1522–1590) rose in importance, influencing especially the upper classes, who generally reigned in the cities.

During the post-Reformation era, The Netherlands was relatively tolerant of other beliefs: while churches other than the Reformed Church were officially forbidden, they were in practice tolerated. At that time the Low Countries knew Lutherans; revolutionary Anabaptists, ultimately reorganized as the Mennonite Church under the guidance of Menno Simons (1496–1559); Roman Catholics; and (Sephardic) Jews.

After the fall of Antwerp in 1585 (Spain occupied that important trade city and harbor), many strict Calvinists took refuge in the Low Countries and became important to the wealth of those regions. In 1685 many Huguenots (French Calvinists) came to this region because of the abolition of the Edict of Nantes. They organized themselves into the Eglises Wallones, now one of the classes of the former Netherlands Reformed Church, which recently merged into the new Protestant Church of the Netherlands. At that time another important part of what was to become part of the Dutch population fled from Spain: the Portuguese (Sephardic) Jews built their famous synagogue in Amsterdam. Amsterdam and other towns therefore in later centuries had two important Jewish groups: the Ashkenazi and Sephardic Jews. The Low Countries became very important through their publishers (Elsevier and others); books forbidden in other countries could be published there. All the foreigners and refugees made the Golden Age of 1600 to 1650 possible.

Through the 17th century, the leaders of the country were moderate Calvinists and somewhat tolerant, although most of the common people and the ministers were strict Calvinists. The leaders had been strongly influenced by the mainly English writers of the Nearer, or "Nadere," Reformation Puritans, who were important because of their personal belief and emphasis upon the necessity of experiencing conversion.

During the 17th century the northern Netherlands became for the Roman Catholic Church *partes infidelium*. Some Catholics disagreed and decided on a schism, the result being the founding of the Old Catholic Church of the Netherlands in 1723. Of particular influence in that action was the theological perspective of the Dutchman Cornelius Jansen or Jansonius (1585–1638), a Roman Catholic bishop in Ypres (Belgium) whose study of the works of Saint Augustine convinced him that the Roman Catholic Church had deviated from orthodox traditions.

The 19th century became for the Reformed Church an age of schisms, marked by the Separation movement of 1834 and the movement of Nonconformism in 1886. Both movements nurtured the beginnings of Reformed denominations with their distinct names. Since the Reformation, the Roman Catholic Church had been only tolerated, but in 1853 it was allowed the legal right of its own organization. Since that time of emancipation, the church has constructed a number of new buildings (to replace the churches that had been confiscated in the 16th century), and Catholics founded many denominational schools (from primary schools to universities such as Tilburg and Nijmegen), newspapers, and a political party. For the next century, The Netherlands was divided into four socio-political and socio-religious groups: the Roman Catholics; the Reformed believers; the Socialists; and the so-called common group. Each group had its own broadcasting company, newspapers, and organizations in every possible field. The Roman Catholics and Reformed groups had their own schools.

At the end of the 19th century some new religions (primarily Christian sectarian expressions) from North America and other Anglo-Saxon countries attained

The Netherlands

some popularity, but only in small groups. These were the Jehovah's Witnesses, the Seventh-day Adventist Church, several Pentecostal movements (which have led to the formation of many independent communities), and, to some extent, the Church of Jesus Christ of Latter-day Saints.

World War II caused dramatic changes in Dutch religious life, and in the subsequent half-century, several dominant trends were documented: (1) an increase of the process of secularization, so that about 50 percent of the Dutch consider themselves unbelievers, and Humanist organizations have begun to appear; (2) Indian religions have gained a noticeable popularity among young adults, and Hindu-based movements (such as the Ananda Marga Yoga Society, the International Society for Krishna Consciousness, and the movement around Bhagwan Rajneesh) have emerged; (3) so-called youth religious groups, such as the Children of God (now the Family International) and the Church of Scientology, have grown in popularity; (4) Christian ministers and evangelists from the United States (Billy Graham and others) have achieved great popularity among many independent communities, utilizing a common broadcasting organization (Evangelische Omroep, the Evangelical Broadcasting Company); and (5) there are many new religions originating from the Far East (such as Zen Buddhism and the Unification movement), some arriving by way of the

The Netherlands

Religion	Followers in 1970	Followers in 2010	% of Population	Annual % growth 2000–2010	Followers in 2025	Followers in 2050
Christians	11,651,000	10,653,000	64.6	–0.36	9,591,000	8,840,000
Roman Catholics	5,367,000	4,800,000	29.1	–1.81	4,600,000	4,200,000
Protestants	4,709,000	3,050,000	18.5	–1.32	2,850,000	2,620,000
Independents	166,000	400,000	2.4	1.25	550,000	800,000
Agnostics	1,166,000	4,071,000	24.7	2.13	5,017,000	5,410,000
Muslims	60,000	1,072,000	6.5	2.22	1,316,000	1,572,000
Atheists	100,000	300,000	1.8	5.56	480,000	650,000
Buddhists	4,000	200,000	1.2	2.84	300,000	450,000
Hindus	1,000	115,000	0.7	3.19	150,000	180,000
Jews	30,000	25,100	0.2	0.50	25,000	25,000
Spiritists	3,000	25,500	0.2	0.50	29,000	35,000
Sikhs	0	13,500	0.1	0.50	15,000	18,000
New religionists	7,000	12,000	0.1	0.41	14,000	18,000
Chinese folk	15,000	7,200	0.0	0.50	12,000	20,000
Baha'is	2,700	6,800	0.0	1.12	10,000	15,000
Ethnoreligionists	0	700	0.0	0.50	1,000	1,500
Zoroastrians	0	300	0.0	2.89	300	300
Total population	**13,039,000**	**16,502,000**	**100.0**	**0.50**	**16,960,000**	**17,235,000**

United States and already assimilated into the Western world.

In addition, around 1948 the process of decolonization began for The Netherlands. First from the East Indies, many so-called South Moluccans came to The Netherlands with their own Christian denominations and forms of worship. Only a very small group of the Moluccans was Muslim. In the 1960s began the decolonization of Surinam, with its many different religions, and many Surinamese moved to The Netherlands. At that time, many "guest workers" from countries around the Mediterranean migrated to The Netherlands. They became the major source of the current Dutch Islamic community. In the 1980s many refugees found The Netherlands a safe haven. They came (and continue to arrive) from several countries in Africa and Asia. Although some of these refugees are Christians, others are Hindu, Buddhist, and Muslim. Many Chinese refugees—very visible because of the Chinese restaurants now found throughout the country—are adepts of Confucianism and the unique Chinese mixture of Daoism and Buddhism. African and Asian Christians have formed tight communities that provide essential social contacts and a range of services. They have also developed an active program to re-Christianize the Dutch people, whom they see as having lost their original belief.

The Dutch government allows all religions and spiritual perspectives to build their own places of worship, and the Buddhists, Hindus, and Muslims have their own (small) broadcasting organizations modeled on the larger ones sponsored by Catholic and Reformed believers. For many centuries the Dutch people have provided an ongoing example of toleration in the midst of the world's growing religious pluralism.

E. G. Hoekstra

See also: Ananda Marga Yoga Society; Calvin, John; Calvinism; Church of Jesus Christ of Latter-day Saints; Church of Scientology; Confucianism; International Society for Krishna Consciousness; Jehovah's Witnesses; Mennonite Church; Netherlands Reformed Church; Old Catholic Church of the Netherlands; Roman Catholic Church; Seventh-day Adventist Church; Unification Movement; Zen Buddhism.

References

Blei, Karel. *The Netherlands Reformed Church, 1571–2005*. Grand Rapids, MI: William B. Eerdmans Publishing Company, 2006.

Blom, J. C. H., R. G. Fuks-Mansfeld, and I. Schoffer, eds. *The History of the Jews in the Netherlands*. Oxford: Littman Library of Jewish Civilization, 2007.

Brienen, T., et al. *De Nadere Reformatie en het Gereformeerd Piëtisme*. 's Gravenhage: Boekencentrum, 1989.

Buijs, Frank J., Froukje Dernant, and Alef Hamdy. *Strijders van eigen bodem. Radicale en democratische moslims in Nederland*. Amsterdam: University Press, 2006.

Eijnatten, Joris, and Fred van Lieburg. *Nederlandse religiegeschiedenis*. 2nd ed. Hilversum: Verloren, 2006.

Hoekstra, E. G., and M. H. Ipenburg. *Handboek christelijk Nederland. Kerken, gemeenten, samenkomsten en vergaderingen*. Kampen: Kok, 2008.

Hoekstra, E. G., and M. H. Ipenburg. *Wegwijs in religieus en levensbeschouwelijk Nederland: Handboek religies, kerken en stromingen*. 3rd ed. Kampen: Kok, 2000.

Jongeneel, J. A. B., R. Budiman, and J. J. Visser, eds. *Gemeenschapsvorming van Aziatische, Afrikaanse en Midden- en Zuidamerikaanse christenen in Nederland: Een geschiedenis in wording*. Zoetermeer: Boekencentrum, 1996.

Knippenberg, Hans. *De religieuze kaart van Nederland: Omvang en geografische spreiding van de godsdienstige gezindten vanaf de Reformatie tot heden*. Assen and Maastricht: Van Gorcum, 1992.

Meijering, Eginhard. *Het Nederlandse christendom in de twintigste eeuw*. Amsterdam: Balans, 2007.

Selderhuis, Herman, ed. *Handboek Nederlandse kerkgeschiedenis*. Kampen: Kok, 2006.

Shadid, W. A. R., and P. S. Van Koningsveld. *Moslims in Nederland. Minderheden en religie in een multiculturele samenleving*. 2nd ed. Houten: Bohn Stafleu and Van Loghum, 1997.

Stoutenbeek, Jan, and Paul Vigeveno. *Joods Nederland: Een cultuurhistorische gids*. Amsterdam: Em. Querido, 1989.

■ Netherlands Antilles

The Netherlands Antilles consists of two sets of islands on opposite sides of the Caribbean Sea tied together by their relationship to the Netherlands. One group, located off the coast of Venezuela, consists of Curaçao and Bonaire. The other group, located between Anguilla and Antigua, consists of Saba, St. Martin, and St. Eustatius islands. The total land area is 370 square miles with a population of some 225,000 residents (2008). The original inhabitants of Curaçao and Bonaire, the Caiqueti people, were enslaved by the early Spanish explorers and deported to Hispaniola. The original inhabitants of St. Martin and St. Eustatius met a similar fate.

The Dutch took Curaçao from the Spanish in 1634. After receiving Bonaire in the Treaty of Westphalia in 1648, the Dutch began to repopulate the islands with enslaved Africans. Slavery was not abolished until 1863. Economically depressed over several generations, the islands came alive when refineries were built to handle the oil being produced in Venezuela.

In 1954, the islands were granted local autonomy. As a move was afoot to grant complete independence, in 1986 Aruba, which had been part of the Antilles, pulled out and became a separate country. That left Willemstad, on Curaçao, as the only city in the Antilles.

A variety of religions have been represented on the islands over the years. The Roman Catholic Church began a mission in the 16th century but was expelled when the Dutch took control of Curaçao in 1634. Several Jesuits re-established the Catholic presence in 1705. A vicariate was created on Curaçao in 1842, and the Diocese of Willemstad in 1958. Among Curaçaoans, 85 percent profess Catholicism, with lesser percentages on the other islands.

Protestantism came to Curaçao following the Dutch takeover, when the Dutch began settlement in 1650. Eventually, Reformed churches were established on Curaçao and Bonaire. Dutch Lutherans also migrated to the islands, and in 1825 Dutch authorities forced a union of the Reformed and Lutheran churches that produced the Protestant Church. In 1931, members of the Protestant Church in Curaçao created the Reformed Church in Curaçao and assumed as a major

Netherlands Antilles

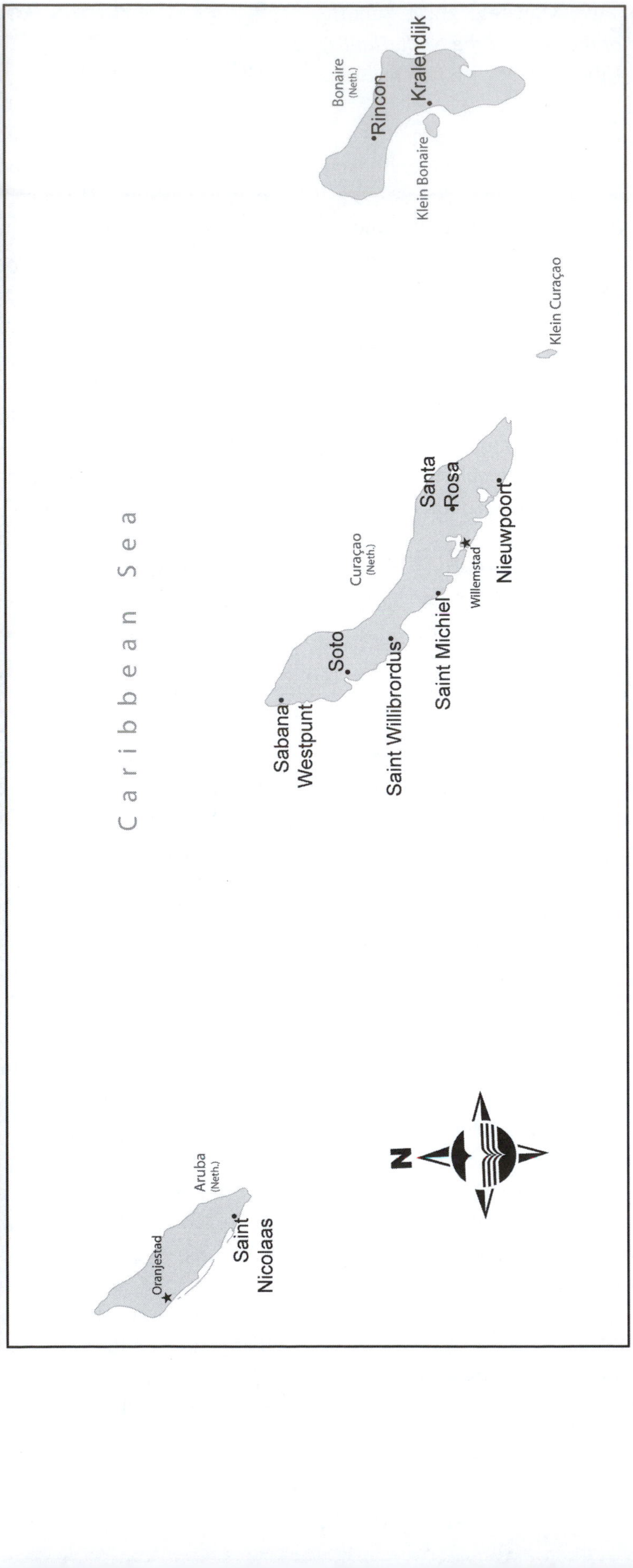

Netherlands Antilles

Religion	Followers in 1970	Followers in 2010	% of Population	Annual % growth 2000–2010	Followers in 2025	Followers in 2050
Christians	154,000	187,000	93.8	0.58	189,000	162,000
Roman Catholics	134,000	152,000	76.4	–0.70	151,000	125,000
Protestants	17,100	32,000	16.1	1.22	36,000	35,000
Marginals	1,000	4,000	2.0	2.74	7,000	9,000
Agnostics	2,900	6,400	3.2	2.14	10,000	14,000
Spiritists	0	2,200	1.1	0.62	2,800	3,000
Buddhists	400	1,000	0.5	0.62	1,400	1,600
Jews	600	620	0.3	–0.55	850	850
Baha'is	250	500	0.3	0.65	800	1,100
Hindus	100	410	0.2	0.63	600	800
Muslims	250	400	0.2	0.61	800	1,000
Atheists	0	310	0.2	0.63	500	700
Chinese folk	500	300	0.2	0.66	400	400
New religionists	50	150	0.1	0.58	300	400
Total population	**159,000**	**199,000**	**100.0**	**0.63**	**207,000**	**186,000**

task the ministry to members of the Reformed Churches in the Netherlands (one of the several Reformed denominations operating in Holland) who had migrated to the Antilles. This group merged with the Protestant Church to create the United Protestant Church of Netherlands Antilles in 1984. It is the largest Protestant church in the Antilles.

Methodists began work in the Antilles among Africans in St. Eustatius. In the mid-1780s, an African slave known only as Black Harry (and not to be confused with Black Harry Hosier, the contemporary Methodist preacher in the United States) had gathered a small group that the Methodists termed a "class." When Methodist Superintendent Thomas Coke (1747–1814) arrived in 1787, he found 20 people in this group and during his visit organized additional similar classes. He returned a year later to find Harry had been banished by slave owners, fearful of religious organization among the slaves.

Although Methodism grew in the Antilles during this time, it was not until the early 1800s that nonhostile relations with the Dutch authorities developed. Methodism spread to St. Martin in the 1840s and to Curaçao in the 1930s. Methodist work there is now included in the Methodist Church in the Caribbean and the Americas.

Through the 20th century, a spectrum of churches began work in the Netherlands Antilles, the Salvation Army, the Assemblies of God, and the Seventh-day Adventist Church being among the more successful.

The Jewish community in the Antilles originated in the short-lived Dutch settlement of Brazil. Jews who had been living quietly under Portuguese rule in Recife openly organized after the Dutch arrived. When the Dutch were forced out of Brazil, many Jews left and came to Curaçao, where in 1651 João d'Ylan led in the construction of what is now the oldest synagogue in the Western Hemisphere.

Islam in the Antilles developed in the 20th century with the movement of laborers from Lebanon and Syria to Curaçao. They formed the Muslim Community of Curaçao, which sponsors a mosque in Willemstad.

There are a few adherents of the Baha'i Faith, and some members of the Liberal Catholic Church, the theosophical body that has one of its strongest followings in the Netherlands, and the Ancient and Mystical Order Rosae Crucis.

J. Gordon Melton

See also: Ancient and Mystical Order Rosae Crucis; Assemblies of God; Baha'i Faith; Liberal Catholic Church; Methodist Church in the Caribbean and the

Americas; Reformed Churches in the Netherlands; Roman Catholic Church; Salvation Army; Seventh-day Adventist Church; United Protestant Church of Netherlands Antilles.

References

Bauswein, Jean-Jacques, and Lukas Vischner, eds. *The Reformed Family Worldwide: A Survey of Reformed Churches, Theological Schools, and International Organizations*. Grand Rapids, MI: William B. Eerdmans, 1999.

Emmanuel, Isaac S., and Suzanne A. Emmanuel. *History of the Jews of the Netherland Antilles*. Cincinnati, OH: American Jewish Archives, 1970.

Lutz, William. *Netherlands Antilles*. New York: Chelsea House Publications, 1987.

Netherlands Reformed Churches

The Netherlands Reformed Churches (Nederlands Gereformeerde Kerken) were founded in 1979 through a conflict in the Reformed Churches in the Netherlands (Liberated). Some members wanted to enter into conversation with the General Synod of the Reformed Church in the Netherlands (GKN) (now an integral part of the Protestant Church in the Netherlands). They were suspended from membership and some 20 percent of the members and 30 percent of the ministers left the church. The Dutch Reformed Churches represent, on the whole, the perspective of the Reformed Churches in the Netherlands around the 1970s. Like most Reformed groups in the Netherlands, it accepts the authority of the Catechism of Heidelberg, the Canons of the Synod of Dort, and the Dutch Confession.

In 2007, the church included 32,250 members, 76 ministers, and 95 local parishes. Ministers are educated at the Theological University of the Christian Reformed Churches in the Netherlandses at Apeldoorn. The church now has (partly) its own academy. The parishes are different in their practice: some are very traditional Reformed, others rather progressive; some refuse to allow women to be elders, others have no problems with women holding office.

The church is not a member of any of the several international ecumenical organizations, but it maintains ecumenical contact with the Christian Reformed Church in North America, the Reformed Churches in Australia and New Zealand, the Orthodox Presbyterian Church in America, the Églises Reformées Evangéliques Indépendantes in France, and the Geredja Bebas in Eastern Soemba, Indonesia.

Netherlands Reformed Churches
Medeblikhof 39
6843 BC Arnhem
The Netherlands
http://www.ngk.nl/ngken.html

E. G. Hoekstra

See also: Christian Reformed Church in North America; Orthodox Presbyterian Church; Protestant Church in the Netherlands; Reformed Churches in the Netherlands (Liberated).

References

Hoekstra, E. G., and M. H. Ipenburg. *Handboek christelijk Nederland. Kerken, gemeenten, samenkomsten en vergaderingen*. Kampen: Kok, 2008.

Informatieboekje voor de Nederlands Gereformeerde Kerken. Amsterdam: Buyten & Schipperheyn, 1974–.

Moggré, A. J. *Kinderen van één Vader*. Kampen, 1994.

Neturei Karta

Neturei Karta (Aramaic: Guardians of the City) is the name adopted by a group of Orthodox Jews who have resided in Palestine for many generations but who refuse to recognize the existence or authority of the state of Israel. They have become well known for their history of demonstrating in support of their position, including staged burnings of the Israeli flag. Neturei Karta was founded in Jerusalem in 1938 by Rabbis Amram Blau and Aharon Katzenelbogen as a splinter group of Agudath Israel (or Agudas Yisroel), an Orthodox Jewish organization that was originally opposed to Zionism, the movement for the return of the Jewish people to Palestine and Jewish sovereignty over the territory of ancient Israel. In the early 20th century, Agudath Israel dropped its opposition to Zionism.

Ultra-Orthodox men from the Neturei Karta take part in a protest outside the United Nations headquarters in Jerusalem, July 22, 2007. The protesters called on the UN to recognize them as an oppressed people by Israeli authorities. (AP Photo/Kevin Frayer)

The Neturei Karta originally were known as Hevret ha-Hayyim, only assuming their present name over the years. Their leader Rabbi Amram Blau (1895–1976) spent much of his life planning and leading demonstrations against the Israeli authorities. Following the establishment of the modern state of Israel, Neturei Karta members found themselves in a high state of tension with authorities. They tended to describe the founders and leaders of the state as Zionists rather than as fellow believers.

Neturei Karta has opposed the state of Israel on the grounds that the idea of a sovereign Jewish state is contrary to Jewish law, and it stands against the practice of uprooting centuries-old Jewish communities around the world in order to build the Jewish population in Israel. Members continue the position assumed by many 19th-century Jewish rabbis who believed Zionism was contrary to the Talmud—the oral tradition believed by Orthodox Jews to have been given to Moses while he was on Mount Sinai receiving the Torah (the Law). They believe that the true state of Israel will only be established without the use of human force, and they claim that Jews should not revolt against established nations but rather seek to live as loyal citizens.

Over the years, many Neturei Karta members have left Israel for more hospitable environments. Neturei Karta centers have now been established in several countries, including the United Kingdom and the United States. There are three synagogues in Brooklyn, New York. Closely associated with Neturei Karta is the Friends of Jerusalem, an organization that has taken the lead in furthering the various causes of the Neturei Karta by organizing demonstrations against Israel and participating in a spectrum of activities (including meetings with heads of state) to advocate strong opposition to Zionist programs.

In recent years, Neturei Karta has divided into two factions. The more activist faction has come together under the names Neturei Karta International and Jews United Against Zionism. They are led in Israel by Rabbi Moshe Hirsch (the son-in-law of Aharon Katzenelbogen) and his son Rabbi Yisrael Meir Hirsch, and in New York by Rabbi Yisroel Dovid Weiss and Rabbi Moshe Ber Beck. This group has been most demonstrative and is regularly the focus of news reports. Rabbi Hirsch had served in the cabinet of the late Palestinian leader Yasser Arafat (1929–2004) as the minister for Jewish affairs. More recently leaders of the group in New York met with Nation of Islam leader Louis Farrakhan while leaders of the Israeli branch traveled to Iran (2006) to meet with Mahmoud Ahmadinejad. This faction's main synagogue, Ohel Sarah, is located in one of the oldest neighborhoods of Jerusalem.

The more moderate, less activist faction of the Neturei Karta is led by Rabbi Zelig Reuven Katzenelbogen (the grandson of the group's two founders). It claims the allegiance of the majority of Neturei Karta members. Its main synagogue, Toireh veYiroh, is also located in the old section of Jerusalem not far from Ohel Sarah.

The Neturei Karta claims several thousand committed members and a sympathetic constituency in the hundreds of thousands, which would include some of the anti-Zionist Hasidic movements such as Satmar. As Satmar Hasidism grew, the Neturei Karta placed itself under its care and guidance. The relationship had unforeseen consequences in 1965, when Rabbi Blau married a former Roman Catholic who had converted to Judaism. Satmar Rabbi Yoel Teitelbaum (1887–1979) forced the ouster of Blau from his leadership role. Most recently, following the visit of the several rabbis to Iran, some of whom described themselves as Satmar rabbis, the Satmar leadership denounced the rabbis and separated themselves from their actions and statements.

Neturei Karta International
PO Box 1316
Monsey, NY 10952
http://www.nkusa.org/

J. Gordon Melton

See also: Hasidism; Nation of Islam; Orthodox Judaism; Satmar Hasidism; Zionism.

References

Domb, I. *The Transformation: The Case of the Neturei Karta*. London, 1958.

Lawrence, Bruce. *Defenders of God: The Fundamentalist Revolt against the Modern Age*. Columbia: University of South Carolina Press, 1995.

Odenheimer, Micha. "We Do Not Believe, We Will Not Follow." *Guilt and Pleasure* 2 (Spring 2006). http://www.guiltandpleasure.com/index.php?site=rebootgp&page=gp_article&id=17. Accessed March 24, 2009.

Zimmer, Uriel. "The Guardians of the City." http://www.nkusa.org/Books/Publications/guardians.cfm. Accessed March 24, 2009.

New Acropolis Cultural Association

Founded in 1957 in Buenos Aires, Argentina, by Jorge Angel Livraga Rizzi and his wife, Ada Albrecht, the New Acropolis Cultural Association claims to have more than 10,000 members in more than 40 countries. Professor Livraga Rizzi was born in Buenos Aires in 1930 of Italian ancestry, and he died in 1991 in Madrid, Spain. He allegedly studied medicine, philosophy, and the history of art at a university in Buenos Aires and was the author of numerous books and articles: the study of ancient cultures and civilizations, novels, philosophical essays, and reflections on the contemporary world, among others. His house in Buenos Aires is now a museum, maintained by the New Acropolis Cultural Association, where his achievements are honored and preserved. Some of Livraga's books and articles, as well as those of some of his disciples, are available in an electronic format on the Internet at: www.acropolis.org.

New Acropolis Cultural Association is a post-Theosophical movement that combines elements from many sources: Theosophy, Esoteric thought, alchemy, astrology, and Eastern and Greek philosophy. Although it claims to be a Humanist organization, independent of political and religious ties, some of its former members in France have accused the organization of being right-wing and promoting Fascist and neo-Nazi ideas. The alleged use of paramilitary language, symbols, and forms of organization, along with more recent charges of brainwashing, have led to many criticisms of the New Acropolis in Europe, especially in France, since the mid-1970s.

The New Acropolis movement promotes the idea of a universal "philosophy" or "tradition" upon which the world's different religions and Esoteric traditions are based. However, it emphasizes Western rather than Eastern Esotericism and particularly focuses on Greek philosophy in the tradition of Pythagoras and Plato, according to Italian lawyer/sociologist Massimo Introvigne.

The stated aim of New Acropolis is to help each member reach his or her Higher Self and to reclaim a higher consciousness that, while normally dormant, is preserved in the esoteric schools and accessible through symbols, the active use of imagination, the study of one's own dreams, and other techniques. The Higher Self, in turn, is a gateway to the Cosmic or Universal Self, described as a collective archetypal reality. When an adequate number of human beings achieve that Higher Self, the Universal Self may emerge as collective consciousness and may have important social and political implications. Although the society inspired by the collective consciousness of the archetypal Universal Self has been described in different ways throughout the history of the movement, it is certainly different from modern democracy. Indeed, the founder's criticism of contemporary democracy (quoting Plato and other authors) is often offered by critics of New Acropolis as evidence of the movement's "reactionary" or "fascist" attitude, although other texts by Livraga and his successors unequivocally condemn Nazism, Fascism, and more recently the National Front in France.

The New Acropolis website lists member organizations in the following countries: Argentina, Costa Rica, Japan, Paraguay, Slovenia, Sweden, Turkey, the United States, and Venezuela. Also, other organizations that use a similar name are known to exist in Mexico, Colombia, Belgium, and France.

New Acropolis Cultural Association
Amenabar 863
Buenos Aires 1426
Argentina
www.acropolis.org

Clifton L. Holland

See also: Alchemy, Daoist; Astrology; Theosophical Society (America); Western Esoteric Tradition.

References

Introvigne, Massimo. "Defectors, Ordinary Leave-takers and Apostates: A Quantitative Study of Former Members of New Acropolis in France." www.cesnur.org. Accessed June 15, 2009.

New Acropolis Cultural Association. www.acropolis.org.

New Age Movement

The New Age movement, which rose to public prominence in the West in the 1970s and 1980s, was a millennial revivalist movement that swept through the groups of the Western Esoteric tradition, leading to the expansion of many older groups, the emergence of a new set of Esoteric organizations, and a general reappraisal of the tradition by the general public. The movement's name derived from its orientation around a vision of a coming New Age of peace and wisdom, which was believed to be dawning upon humanity as the 21st century approached. The initial exponents of the movement were followers of offshoots of older Esoteric groups (the Theosophical Society, the Arcane School, and others) and the churches of the New Thought tradition. The movement waned in the 1990s as the idea of an imminent New Age lost support and the movement as a whole was attacked for some of its more questionable assertions.

The Western Esoteric tradition, at least in its popular phase as the purveyor of occult teachings over against the dominant Christian worldview, experienced a new rebirth in the 19th century following a century of decline under the combined challenge of Protestant Christianity and the Enlightenment. Its reemergence paralleled that of science, and the new occultists attempted to align magical teachings with the emerging scientific world. Leading the way was Austrian physician Franz Anton Mesmer (1734–1815), who proposed the existence of a universal magnetic force that he

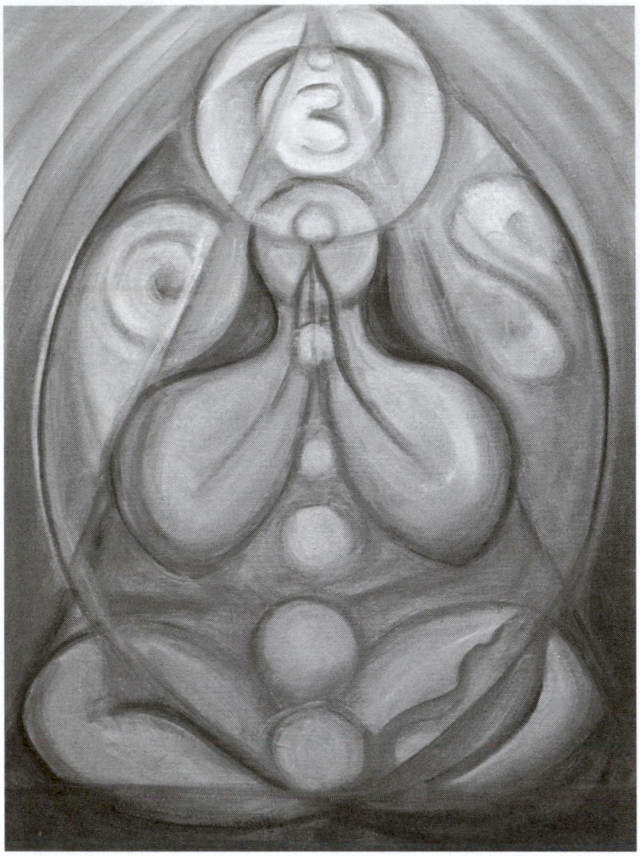

New Age painting depicts meditation in pursuit of the higher self. (Loveliestdreams/Dreamstime.com)

believed underlay spiritual healing. Though denounced by the French Royal Academy of Science, "mesmerism" became a popular movement throughout the West in the early 19th century.

Building upon Mesmer's thought, Eliphas Levi (1810–1875) identified the universal energy with the cosmic agent evoked while working magic. Levi's several books launched a revival of magic in Europe. A century later, the elitist initiatory magic promoted by Levi and later exponents such as Aleister Crowley (1875–1947) would find its popular expression in neo-Pagan Wicca or Witchcraft. The renewed practice of magic supported the simultaneous rebirth of interest in various divinatory practices such as palmistry, astrology, and tarot reading. Astrology has been the most popular occult belief, and the very visible rise of the new 20th-century "science of astrology" provides a framework for understanding the appeal of occultism as a whole.

In North America, the very successful mesmerist movement was superseded in the middle of the 19th century by a movement centered upon contact and communication with the spirits of the recently deceased. Spiritualism began in Hydesville, New York, in 1848, and through the 1850s it spread across America and then to England and France, where it enjoyed an even greater response. Over the last decades of the 19th century, Spiritualist activity could be found in the major cities of Europe and such unlikely places as Cairo and Rio de Janeiro.

The alternative healing emphasis of the magnetist movement that popularized Mesmer's ideas supported the development of a host of alternative healing practices in 19th-century America, setting the context for the discovery by Mary Baker Eddy (1821–1910) of a new kind of healing. After decades of fighting illnesses, in 1866 she came to a realization of the Allness of God, from which she concluded that all illness was a monstrous illusion of limited minds, an erroneous perception of the nature of reality. To embody her new insight, Eddy founded the Church of Christ, Scientist. In the 1880s, one of her leading students, Emma Curtis Hopkins (1849–1925), began an independent ministry, now seen as the beginning of a new movement, New Thought, today embodied in several metaphysical church/movements: the Unity School of Christianity, Divine Science Federation International, Religious Science, and Seicho-No-Ie.

To Esotericists and occultists of the 19th and 20th centuries, history was of secondary interest at best, a practical means of relating to a mundane world from which they were trying to escape. Attention was focused on a set of occult (hidden) realities believed to lie behind the visible universe. However, toward the end of the 20th century, an attempt to ascribe some importance to the mundane world as a place of spiritual unfolding began with Madame Helena Petrova Blavatsky (1831–1891), a cofounder of the Theosophical Society. She suggested that the real goals of the Theosophical Society were to cooperate with the evolution of the race and to prepare for the coming of Lord Maitreya, one of the Masters of the Great White Brotherhood, the adepts who from a lofty estate actually guide humanity on its way. Maitreya's coming would initiate a new cycle for humanity.

Blavatsky's initial idea about Maitreya was developed more fully by Annie Besant (1847–1933), who became the president of the Society early in the 20th century, and by a former Anglican priest, Charles Webster Leadbeater (1854–1934). Leadbeater identified the vehicle of the coming Maitreya as one Jiddu Krishnamurti (1895–1986), a young boy whom Leadbeater spotted on a beach near the Theosophical Society's international headquarters at Adyar, India. Besant took control of the situation and provided for Krishnamurti's education. The society prepared him for his role as the Coming World Savior, and through the 1920s, Krishnamurti appeared at numerous Society-sponsored events.

Initially, Krishnamurti appeared to be following the Theosophical program, and the Society mobilized international support for the designated Savior figure. Then in 1929, he suddenly abandoned his predestined role and left the Society to deal with both the problems of his resignation and the Great Depression. The Society never recovered. Meanwhile, a new teacher, Alice A. Bailey (1880–1949), was just emerging as a prominent figure in the movement. Bailey had left the Theosophical Society to begin an independent effort built around her direct communications with one of the Masters, Djwhal Khul, whom she usually referred to as the Tibetan. Annie Besant disapproved both of the material received from the Tibetan and the process by which it was received—channeling, or mediumship. Bailey withdrew from the society in 1923 and with the assistance of her husband, Foster, founded the Arcane School.

Toward the end of her life, Bailey began to call her students' attention to the reappearance of the Christ, which she believed would occur during the last years of the 20th century. In the 1950s, many left the Arcane School, and students of her works founded a spectrum of independent Baileyite organizations—the "Light" groups—which engaged in channeling spiritual light (cosmic energy) into the world for its uplift and healing. The members of these groups also prepared for the expected World Savior.

As early as the 1960s, leaders of several British Baileyite groups would be the first to propose the New Age vision of a transformed world. They suggested that a transformation could result if an international network of Light groups would channel spiritual energy to the planet. A rudimentary vision began with the networking of several groups: the Wrekin Trust (England), the Universal Foundation (London), and the Findhorn Foundation (near Inverness, Scotland). By the end of the decade, Anthony Brooke (b. 1912), the former ruler of Sarawak and the head of the Universal Foundation, was touring and promoting the formation of additional Light groups. Groups emerged in several countries around the world.

In the mid-1970s, David Spangler (b. 1945), co-director of the Findhorn Foundation, authored several books that elucidated a broad vision of an emerging New Age. His 1976 volume, *Revelation: The Birth of a New Age*, and several subsequent titles offered a more fully developed statement of New Age possibilities, which became immediate fuel for an emerging revival. Spangler suggested that in the generation maturing in the last quarter of the 20th century, human beings could seize a unique opportunity to create a new social order that would replace the current world, characterized so much by war, poverty, starvation, and other social ills.

The New Age would begin with the transformation of individuals, who would be healed, changed, uplifted, and enlightened. Their transformation would be accomplished by the use of many old occult tools (astrology, palmistry, and meditation and concentration practices), new information received through channeling from evolved spiritual beings, and an array of alternative healing disciplines. Transformation could on occasion be quick and dramatic, but any change was but the beginning of a long-term process of development that would lead to new levels of spiritual experience and realization.

As ever-greater numbers of individuals were transformed, the larger goal, the transformation of society, would follow. The emergence of this new social and cultural situation was the real New Age. Spangler argued that if individuals would share the wisdom and energy they received as they were transformed, through the uniting of light and love the entire planet would be transformed into a New Age for humanity.

Spangler cited two sources for the New Age. First, the present moment (the late 20th century) was a propitious moment, when the heavens were being aligned for release of new levels of cosmic spiritual energy, which would power the New Age. Thus the idea of the New Age aligned with the notion of the Aquarian Age, which astrologers had predicted as occurring at some imprecise time in the 20th or 21st century. Significant points in the progression of the Earth through the zodiac and the initiation of a new astrological age are seen as occurring about every 2,000 years.

However, the cosmic energy of the stars could not do it alone. The second source for the New Age would be people—working, cooperating, and uniting. The New Age would require the effort of large numbers of transformed people channeling the cosmic energies. If people failed to act, the opportunity would be lost.

The New Age movement reached its zenith in the 1980s. During the decade people who had previously adhered to the Western Esoteric tradition caught the vision of the New Age, while hundreds of thousands of others around the world who had no background in the tradition also discovered the movement. New Age publishers and bookstores appeared in urban centers throughout the Western world, and New Age networks linked the largely decentralized movement. New Agers gathered annually in large New Age expositions that were organized so the various, often divergent elements of the movement could share experiences.

Under its new label, the Western Esoteric tradition continued to promote the older occult arts but remolded them for the New Age world. Ancient divinatory practices, including astrology and the tarot, were now offered to the public as scientific transformative tools. They were taken from their former deterministic worldview, in which they offered predictions of the future, and were now utilized primarily as instruments of personal insight and self-revelation.

Crystals emerged in the 1980s as a prominent New Age tool. Crystals had been mentioned in the channeled readings of seer Edgar Cayce (1877–1945), whose insights were published in a small booklet by the Association for Research and Enlightenment. Cayce's linkage of crystals and ancient Atlantis inspired Frank Alper, of the Arizona Metaphysical Center, who claimed that crystals had great potential for their ability to store and release transformative spiritual energies. Enthusiastic New Agers added crystals to their attire, meditated in their presence, and placed them in their ritual spaces in the belief that their energizing powers would thus effect spiritual evolution.

Mediumship, now termed "channeling," emerged as the most definitive practice of the New Age movement. Channelers brought messages from a spectrum of authoritative spiritual entities (God, the Ascended Masters, spirits, extraterrestrial beings, the channeler's higher self) who provided guidance and direction for the movement. Some channels provided individuals with personal messages for their own particular and immediate concerns. The most well-known channels (JZ Knight, Jach Pursel, Kevin Ryerson, Ken Carey, Pat Rodegast, and others) brought more philosophical teachings that were applicable to the larger New Age public.

Among the more interesting New Age organizations was Share International, which structured the teaching activity of Benjamin Crème (b. 1922), a student of the Bailey writings, who in the 1970s began channeling messages from Maitreya and announcing his imminent appearance. When Crème's prediction of Maitreya's appearance in 1982 failed, he was largely dismissed by the rest of the movement.

The New Age culminated in 1989 with the airing of the television version of actress Shirley MacLaine's autobiographical book, *Out on a Limb.* MacLaine (b. 1934) had followed a New Age pilgrimage for a decade; however, her own transformation coincided with a very different change undergone by the movement itself. During the 1980s leaders were feeling the critiques of reporters and scholars, especially those directed at the underlying claims of paranormal realities related to crystals and channeling. Scientists denounced pseudoscientific claims about the power of crystals to store and release energy and raised doubts about the existence of the spiritual entities who spoke through channels. As the 1980s came to a close, several prominent New Age spokespersons (including writer David Spangler and publisher Jeremy Tarcher) revealed their conviction that they had erred in believing in the possibility of social transformation. That so many people had experienced a personal transformation justified the existence of the New Age movement, but it was time to give up any hope in a more pervasive social transformation.

In the 1990s the great majority of New Agers came to agree with Spangler and Tarcher, and they abandoned hope in a coming New Age. By this time millions of people across the Western world had been attracted to the Western Esoteric tradition, still called the New Age in the larger society. (Adherents remained a small minority in the West, still dominated by Christianity.)

The great majority of New Agers were content with the personal spirituality they had found. Many were associated with the organizations most identified with the movement—the Association for Research and Enlightenment, the Church Universal and Triumphant, and Ramtha's School of Enlightenment, to name just a few. Through the 1990s, new groups emerged that attempted to continue belief in the New Age, now defined as an ever-increasing global interest in spirituality that over the next centuries will lead to new levels of spiritual awareness and produce a flourishing new culture. This transformed New Age vision was given voice in a book by James Redfield in *The Celestine Prophecy* (1994), which became a bestseller and spawned a set of related texts and a new movement, the New Civilization Network. This new phase of the movement has been referred to as the Next Age, especially in Europe.

The New Age suffered greatly in the aftermath of the September 11, 2001, bombings of the World Trade Center in New York and Pentagon in Washington, D.C. Over the next few years, the large convention/expositions were either cancelled or held in a reduced low-key manner. Many New Age businesses collapsed and only slowly has the movement recovered. The many New Age religious groups fared the best but suffered from a loss of a venue to contact prospective new members and distribute their literature.

As the movement recovered from the 9/11 disaster, it also became attuned to new millennial expectations built around the date, December 12, 2012. This date was originally posed as significant by students of the ancient Mayan calendar, who noted that it ran out in 2012. Others have added to the expectations around the year, though opinions as to what might occur in 2012 vary widely.

The New Age is best seen as a burst of growth in the Western Esoteric tradition. The movement greatly enlarged the number of people adhering to an esoteric worldview, created new currents of esoteric expression, and bequeathed to the tradition a fresh, more positive image in the Western world. As the New Age movement emerged, older adherents of the Western Esoteric tradition expressed a range of opinions about it. Some openly supported it, others watched and observed from a distance, and not a few voiced their strident hostility to the movement's shallowness. In any event, the movement created a new situation out of which future Western Esoteric activity will operate.

J. Gordon Melton

See also: Arcane School; Association for Research and Enlightenment; Bailey, Alice Ann; Church of Christ, Scientist; Church Universal and Triumphant; Crowley, Aleister; Divine Science Federation International/United Divine Science Ministries International; Ramtha's School of Enlightenment; Religious Science; Seicho-No-Ie; Spiritualism; Theosophical Society (America); Unity School of Christianity; Western Esoteric Tradition; Wiccan Religion.

References

Benedict, Gerald. *The Mayan Prophecies for 2012*. London: Watkins, 2008.

Drury, Nevill. *The New Age: The History of a Movement*. London: Thames & Hudson, 2004.

Introvigne, Massimo. *New Age and Next Age*. Casale Monferrato, Italy: Piemme, 2000.

Hanegraaff, Wouter J. *New Age Religion and Western Culture*. Leiden: E. J. Brill, 1996.

Heelas, Paul. *The New Age Movement*. Oxford: Blackwell Publishers. 1996.

Klimo, Hjon. *Channeling: Investigations on Receiving Information from Paranormal Sources*. Berkeley, CA: North Atlantic Press, 1998.

Lewis, James, and J. Gordon Melton, eds. *Perspectives on the New Age*. Albany: State University of New York Press, 1992.

Melton, J. Gordon. *Finding Enlightenment: Ramtha's School of Ancient Wisdom*. Hillsboro, OR: Beyond Words, 1998.

Melton, J. Gordon, Jerome Clark, and Aidan Kelly, eds. *New Age Encyclopedia*. Detroit: Gale Research Company, 1990.

Redfield, James. *The Celestine Prophecy*. New York: Warner Books, 1994.

Spangler, David. *Revelation: The Birth of a New Age*. San Francisco: Rainbow Bridge, 1976.

Sutcliffe, Steven. *Children of the New Age: A History of Spiritual Practices*. London: Routledge, 2003.

New Apostolic Church

The New Apostolic Church, is one of the largest new religious movements founded in Europe, with an international following of some 11 million.

The Catholic Apostolic Church, established in England in the wake of the revival led by Edward Irving (1792–1834), though he was not its founder, was particularly successful in Germany. It taught, however, that no new Apostles should be appointed after the death of its 12 original founders. This created serious problems, since only the Apostles were empowered to consecrate Bishops, and only Bishops can ordain priests. This was not a major problem for the Catholic Apostolic Church, however, because the end of the world was expected to occur quite soon. This did not happen, of course, and one after the other the original Apostles died. Following short-lived attempts to solve the problem within the German branch, between 1897 and 1898 Fritz Krebs (1832–1905) proclaimed himself an Apostle, and proceeded to appoint other Apostles who, in turn, elected him as *Stammapostel* ("Root-Apostle" and chief of the church). In order to distinguish this splinter group from the Catholic Apostolic Church, it was legally established as the New Apostolic Church.

The New Apostolic Church's success was outstanding, thanks to the efforts of Krebs and his successors Hermann Niehaus (1848–1932) and Johann Gottfried Bischoff (1871–1960). Although the Catholic Apostolic Church almost died out (and is currently reduced to a small remnant), the New Apostolic Church gathered millions of members throughout the world. Around the end of Bischoff's life, a millenarian movement erupted within his church, in the expectation of an imminent end of the world. Schisms followed, although Bischoff's successor, Walter Schmidt (1891–1978), was eventually able to explain why the prophecy had failed (God had changed his plans), and to keep most of the members within the fold. Today the New Apostolic Church, the current Stammapostel being German-born Wilhelm Leber, includes, according to most outside observers, some 11 million members, with 72,000 local communities throughout Europe, with the strongest concentrations in Germany and Switzerland, and the world (with the largest communities in Australia, the Philippines, the United States, and Canada).

The New Apostolic Church has come to the conclusion that Apostles in today's world should number more than 12. There are at present 28 main "District Apostles" and some 300 other Apostles. Under the Apostles' leadership are Bishops, elders, pastors, evangelists, priests, and deacons. Although the structure of the New Apostolic Church is reminiscent of the Catholic Apostolic Church (except, of course, that in the latter the number of Apostles never exceeded 12), the doctrine is more similar to evangelical Protestantism and includes a pre-millennial, pre-tribulationist belief in the rapture. The liturgy, on the other hand, maintains elements of the Catholic Apostolic Church (in turn derived from the Church of England), and includes the celebration of three sacraments: baptism, a kind of confirmation celebrated 18 months after baptism, and Communion. It is because of these liturgical elements, and its belief in the crucial role of the apostolic hierarchy, that evangelical Protestants do not normally regard themselves as being in communion with New Apostolics.

New Apostolic Church
Gutleutstraße 298
60327 Frankfurt am Main
Germany
http://www.nak.org

Massimo Introvigne and PierLuigi Zoccatelli

See also: Catholic Apostolic Church; Church of England.

References

Guide for the Administration: Brothers of the New Apostolic Church. Frankfurt am Main, Germany: Apostles College of the New Apostolic Church, 1967.

Question and Answers Concerning the New Apostolic Church. Frankfurt am Main, Germany: J. G. Bischoff, 1978.

Rockenfelder, Gottfried. *Geschichte der Neuapostolischen Kirche*. Frankfurt am Main: Neuapostolische Kirche, 1953.

New Caledonia

See Kanaky.

New Kadampa Tradition–International Kadampa Buddhist Union

The New Kadampa Tradition–International Kadampa Buddhist Union (NKT-IKBU) is a network of Buddhist centers and temples operating under the guidance of the Tibetan-born Gelugpa monk, Geshe Kelsang Gyatso (b. 1931). The organization aims to have a presence in all the major cities of the world. It is currently (2008) represented in 40 countries across 5 continents but with the majority of centers in Europe and America. The NKT headquarters are located in the United Kingdom, where there are around 50 centers each of which acts as a satellite for Buddhist teaching activities in other towns in the area. The NKT is one of the largest schools of Buddhism in the United Kingdom. There are now also nearly 40 centers in the United States.

The NKT-IKBU was founded by the Tibetan national, Gelugpa monk, and teacher Geshe Kelsang Gyatso. Geshe Kelsang was invited to the United Kingdom in 1977 by the Foundation for the Preservation of the Mahayana Tradition (FPMT) to head one of their centers. He and his students declared independence from the FPMT in 1991. Since that time the organization has grown rapidly and spread across the globe.

The NKT-IKBU practices include meditation, the taking of refuge in Buddha, acknowledgment of the Dharma (or truth of impermanence), participation in the Sangha (or community of truth-seekers), and the recitation of ritual texts (*sadhanas*). Practitioners may receive empowerments for such rituals, which carry concomitant commitments to regular practice, from Geshe Kelsang or his senior followers. The texts, which are spoken in the vernacular, are represented as translations of traditional Gelugpa practices.

Central to the movement are three graded study programs: the open and introductory General Programme, the Foundation Programme for more committed practitioners, and the demanding Teacher Training Programme that is adapted from the Tibetan Geshe degree. Successful completion of the study programs is the primary goal for practitioners since only those who know the teachings can pass them on to others. The programs are based on commentaries by Geshe Kelsang on traditional Gelugpa texts such as the Lamrim. NKT teachers may be lay or monastic followers. Monks and nuns have equal status. They wear traditional Tibetan robes and take identical ordination precepts that have been developed by Geshe Kelsang for the Western context. The organization has developed internal rules partly as a result of scandals involving sexual misconduct among high profile monastics.

The NKT-IKBU promotes an exclusive path, stressing the need to study and practice only within Geshe Kelsang's teaching lineage and to avoid "mixing" NKT-IKBU practices with those of other schools. This contrasts with the approach of the Dalai Lama, who favors an inclusive, nonsectarian presentation of Tibetan Buddhism. This difference in emphasis, which is rooted within long-standing Tibetan debates, has become focused on the nature and status of the protector deity, Dorje Shugdan. Although some Gelugpa practitioners, including the Dalai Lama, regard Dorje Shugdan as a troublesome and sectarian worldly deity of dubious origin, for Geshe Kelsang and his teachers before him, Dorje Shugdan is a manifestation of the Buddha and also the most powerful and appropriate protector of Western practitioners. Practices focused on Dorje Shugdan remain central to NKT-IKBU ritual. The NKT-IKBU's uncompromising stance, which runs counter to some popular Western images of Buddhism and has been perceived to threaten the unity of the exiled Tibetan community, has attracted criticism from other Western Buddhist groups and from the Gelugpa school. The NKT-IKBU is nonetheless a member of the UK Network of Buddhist Organisations and it is by no means alone among Western Buddhist movements in attracting criticism from ex-members and from other Buddhist organizations.

Manjushri Centre
Ulveston, Cumbria LA12 9QQ
United Kingdom
http://www.kadampa.net

Helen Waterhouse

See also: Foundation for the Preservation of the Mahayana Tradition; Gelugpa; Meditation; Tibetan Buddhism.

References

Cozort, D. "The Making of the Western Lama." In *Buddhism in the Modern World*. Oxford: Oxford University Press, 2003.

Kay, David. "The New Kadampa Tradition and the Continuity of Tibetan Buddhism in Transition." *Journal of Contemporary Religion* 12, no. 3 (1997): 277–293.

Kay, David. *Tibetan and Zen Buddhism in Britain: Transplantation, Development and Adaptation.* Abingdon: RoutledgeCurzon 2003.

New Year's Day

Most contemporary religions operate on a calendar based on the annual circulation of the Earth around the Sun (Islam being a prominent exception), have designated a beginning point from which to measure that circulation, and acknowledge a New Year's Day (Christianity being a prominent exception). For most religious communities, the new year begins on January 1 of the Common Era calendar or the Vernal or Spring Equinox. In the ancient world, the Winter and Summer solstices and the Spring and Fall equinoxes were among the most well known astronomical events.

Some ancient calendars, such as the Babylonian, used the Vernal Equinox as the new year. The Babylonians invented the Zodiac and calculated the movement of the Sun through its 12 signs. They passed this system to the Chaldeans and Assyrians and on to Egypt. The Hebrews were influenced by the Babylonian calendar during the years of captivity when they picked up the Babylonian days of the months and moved their New Year celebration (Rosh Hashanah) to the fall. Rosh Hashanah actually falls on Tishri 1, the first day of the seventh month in the Hebrew calendar, The first month (Nissan) comes in the spring. Rosh Hashanah is a prescribed day of rest, like the Sabbath. Its exact date relative to the Common Era calendar varies from year to year, and also must not fall on a Sunday, Wednesday, or Friday.

Julius Caesar revised the Roman calendar as a strictly solar calendar, established January 1 as the beginning of the New Year, and ensured the beginning of spring (the Spring Equinox) always occur in March. These strictures were carried forward in the Gregorian reforms and are maintained in our Common Era calendar today.

The Christian church adopted the Julian calendar as its official calendar at the Council of Nicaea in 325 CE. January 1 was not a particularly significant date on the annual liturgical calendar, though once the date of Jesus' birth was set as December 25, the New Year was acknowledged as the date of the Feast of the Circumcision. It was assumed that in Hebrew society circumcision of males would be held on the eighth day after birth. The feast of the circumcision is somewhat lost, falling as it does between Christmas and Epiphany (January 6). That fact, along with the downplaying of the liturgical calendar in general in Protestant circles, has contributed greatly to the almost complete secularization of New Year's Day in the Christian West.

Chinese New Year's Day While as in the West, the Chinese New Year's celebration has largely become a secular affair, it still retains elements of its religious past in Chinese traditional religion. It is celebrated on the first day of the first month of the Chinese lunar year and has always been a joyful event marking the end of winter and the beginning of spring. That date appears to have been largely set during the Han dynasty (221–206 BCE), which adopted the Taichu calendar that set the first day of the year across the land. Some elements of the festival—staying up all night on New Year's Eve, the lighting of lanterns, fireworks, the drinking of wine—also began to spread at this time. During the Tang dynasty (618–907), the focus of the festival gradually shifted from one of protecting one's self from ghosts and demons to enjoying life and expecting good in the year ahead. The celebration took on a lighter, more joyful tone. In later dynasties, more ritualized aspects of the celebration were added and the variety of entertainments—including lion dancing, dragon dancing, and boat races—was significantly increased. In many places, visits to the temple of the local deity became part of the day's activity.

Front door in Beijing, China, decorated with banners to ensure good luck for the New Year. (Lightbrush/ Dreamstime.com)

The New Year's Day festivities have become the most important and celebrated holiday in both China and the Chinese diaspora. Preparation will begin as much as a week ahead of time. Those who have moved to the city in the last few decades will return to their rural home and extended family. The celebration, which begins on New Year's Eve, may last for a few days or stretch for as much as two weeks. In fact, preparation will have begun during the 12th month of the lunar year with the Laba (Lantern) and New Year Preliminary Festivals (Small New Year), built around the kitchen god. It was also a time for spring cleaning.

On New Year's Eve, the family will gather and seal the door of their home with red paper, to prevent their good fortune from escaping. They will offer food to the deities on their home altar and pay respects to their ancestors. They will rise early on New Year's Day and remove the paper around the door as it is time to welcome the good fortune of the new year into their homes. The welcoming is accompanied by firecrackers.

At this time, one would encounter a variety of decorations carrying various forms of well wishes for the coming year. Written on strips of papers they would be displayed in front of shops and on the doors of homes. The front gates of homes might also have pictures of two guardians and a tiger. This practice is derived from an old Daoist story in which two brothers fought demons and fed them to the tigers, believed to be the enemy of evil spirits and any who would harm the deceased.

New Year's Day is also a time to indulge in food. Enough for everyone for several days will have been prepared ahead of time. One popular practice is to place coins in dumplings (amid the meat dumplings) with being served such a dumpling being considered a sign of coming good luck. Presents may be exchanged.

In both China and Taiwan, the secularization of the holiday and the following of practices of the traditional culture without taking note of the spiritual reasons that lie behind them have become the norm. A most important sign of the transformation is the opening of retail businesses so that holiday goers may spend New Year's Day shopping.

Islamic New Year's Day Islam follows a lunar calendar of 354 days, which means that relative to the Common Era calendar, the new year will begin 11 days earlier each year. The Islamic New Year (Maal Hijra) is celebrated on the first day of Muharram (the first month of the Islamic calendar).

New Year is approached as a time for quiet and sober reflection. There are special prayers for the occasion that will be repeated by those who gather at a mosque. For Sunni Muslims, possibly the most important activity is to repeat the story of the Prophet Muhammad's *hijra* (the flight from Mecca to Medina in 622), and to reflect upon one's life and moral state.

For Shi'a Muslims, New Year's Day has a completely different meaning. It marks the beginning of the 10-day Remembrance of Muharram, when Shi'a

Muslims recall the Battle of Karbala and mourn the death of Imam Husayn ibn Ali, Muhammad's grandson, at the hands of the army of the Sunni Muslim caliph Yazid I. The time of mourning culminates on the 10th day, the holy day called Ashura, the anniversary of the actual day of the battle. During this period, people will gather in mosques for the re-enactment of scenes of the Battle of Karbala. Women will wear black. Groups will begin to construct a replica of Husayn's tomb that will later be carried through the streets in a procession led by a horse, recalling Husayn's horse, Dul Dul.

Baha'i New Year's Day The Baha'i Faith has published its own calendar that operates within its community for scheduling religious events. It is built around 19 months of 19 days each, plus additional days to keep it aligned to the Common Era calendar. The first day of the year on the Baha'i calendar is always March 21, thus tying it to the Spring Equinox, even if in any given year the exact equinox occurs on March 20 or 22. Traditionally, the Persian calendar begins the year on March 21.

The Baha'i New Year's Day is termed Naw-Ruz (a name meaning "new day," taken from the same day in the Persian calendar). It marks the end of the annual 19-day month of Alá, which is a time for fasting, and is celebrated with a banquet feast. It is also one of the nine holy days of the year when work and school are suspended.

Indian New Year's Day In 1957, the Indian government introduced the new Saka calendar, a solar calendar that corresponds in many ways with the Common Era calendar, but begins on the day after the Vernal Equinox, on the first day of the month of Chaitra. That day is usually March 22, but will be March 21 during a leap year. Many Hindus focus upon Brahma, the Creator, as they believe that he began creating the world on this day.

India is a relatively new country, having been created by the British as it brought the many states of the Indian subcontinent into a single colonial regime. The various states retain ancient languages and customs, and in places their own calendars. In most states of modern India, there are local celebrations of New Year's Day and most of these local celebrations fall on the first day of the month of Chaitra. Among the different New Year's days is Puthandu, celebrated as New Year's Day in Tamil Nadu. Puthandu is observed on the first day of the month of Chithirai in the Tamil calendar (April 13 or 14). Celebrating New Year's on April 13 or 14 is also the traditional way in Nepal and the Indian states of Kerala, Orissa, and West Bengal.

Sikh New Year's Day Among the Sikhs, New Year's Day continues an old harvest festival in the Punjab called Baisakhi or Vasakhi, which happens to fall on April 13 or 14 in the Common Era calendar. This day attained a heightened meaning for Sikhs as one of their gurus, Gobind Singh, created the Khalsa, the collective body of all Sikhs, on this day by performing the Amrit (baptism) ceremony in the year 1699. Traditionally, for 48 hours prior to the beginning of the day, a continuous reading of the Guru Granth Sahib is held and the morning of Baisakhi begins with a completion ceremony. The gathered congregation then sings divine hymns and listens to discourses on the importance of Baisakhi. It is a day for those who wish to identify with the Sikh community to take Amrit. Following the activities at the *gurdwara,* all will engage in a wide variety of *sewa* (religious work).

Other Religions Most newer religions have adopted the dominant calendar in the place of their origin, and only a few have engaged in any attempt to create a new calendar for the special use of their group. For most new religions, January 1 on the Common Era calendar is their New Year's Day, though they might attempt to give the day new significance or involve members in special activities. Various religious groups will take advantage of the general holiday spirit during the period (including released time from work and suspension of school activities) from Christmas to New Year's Day in many Western countries to hold retreats, seminars, and other events for their members. Every year, a few days before New Year's Day, the Church of Scientology organizes a gathering of church members in a large auditorium in the Los Angeles Area at which the year, especially the accomplishments of the organization, is reviewed and celebrated and goals for the future are projected. This event is recorded and then sent to all the churches worldwide so that it might be shown at gatherings to be held on New Year's Eve.

Among the groups proposing a different New Year's Day are the Wiccans and neo-Pagans. They build their year around eight evenly placed high holidays, the Summer and Winter solstices, the Spring and Fall equinoxes, and four holidays halfway between the equinoxes and solstices. Samhaim (Summer's End) occurs on October 31, halfway between the Fall Equinox and Winter Solstice. It traditionally marks the end of the harvest season, though few modern Wiccans/Pagans engage in agriculture or even reside in rural areas, and hence they have come to emphasize the day as a festival for the deceased. In Samhaim gatherings, those who have died in the previous year are acknowledged and contact with the spirit world attempted. It is believed that the veil between this world and the next is thinnest on the evening of Samhaim.

Many scholars believe that Samhaim was the beginning of the Celtic year, and modern Wiccan/Pagans have picked up that idea, along with the convergence of Samhaim with the Christian celebration of All Saints' Day (November 1) and All Saints' Eve or Halloween (October 31).

J. Gordon Melton

See also: Baha'i Faith; Calendars, Religious; Church of Scientology; Fall Equinox; Rosh Hashanah; Sikhism; Spring Equinox; Summer Solstice; Winter Solstice.

References

Algül, Hüseytinj. *The Blessed Days and Nights of the Islamic Year*. Somerset, NJ: Light, 2005.

Gregory, Ruth W. *Anniversaries and Holidays*. Chicago: American Library Association, 1983.

Latsch, Marie-Luise. *Traditional Chinese Festivals*. Singapore: Greaham Brash, 1984.

Liming, Wei. *Chinese Festivals: Traditions, Customs, and Rituals*. Hong Kong: China International Press, 2005.

Mukundcharandas, Sadhu. *Hindu Festivals (Origin, Sentiments & Rituals)*. Amdavad, India: Swaminarayan Aksharpith, 2005.

Mukundcharandas, Sadhu. *Hindu Rites & Rituals (Sentiments, Sacraments & Symbols)*. Amdavad, India: Swaminarayan Aksharpith, 2007.

Parise, Frank, ed. T*he Book of Calendars*. New York: Facts on File, 1982.

Plunket, Emmeline. *Calendars and Constellations of the Ancient World*. New York: Cosimo Classics, 2005.

Richards, E. G. *Mapping Time: The Calendar and Its History*. New York: Oxford University Press, 2000.

Talley, Thomas J. *The Origins of the Liturgical Year.* Collegeville, MN: Liturgical Press, 1991.

■ New Zealand

Religion in New Zealand begins with the story of the history of Maori and Pakeha (non-Maori, especially White) immigrants. New Zealand was first settled by Polynesian people called Maori in the period between 500 and 1000 CE. Traditional Maori religion is based upon two realms: the world of physical existence and the world of supernatural beings. The latter is populated by beings including *atua* (gods), *wairua* (spirits), *tipuna* (ancestors), and *kehu* (ghosts). There are no clear-cut divisions between the two realms; gods or spirits frequently visit the physical world. The majority of Maori rituals aim to influence the gods and spirits so that their actions in the physical world are beneficial. All things are considered sacred, including nature and the land.

Dutch sea captain Abel Tasman (ca. 1603–1659) was the first European to discover New Zealand, in 1642, but it was not until the visit of Captain James Cook (1728–1779) in 1769 that moves were made toward settlement by the British. New Zealand's missionary period began in July 1814, when two tradesmen-missionaries, Thomas Kendall (1778–1832) and William Hall, distributed religious literature to Maori people and held shipboard services. It is claimed that the first Christian service was held in New Zealand on Christmas Day, 1814, by Samuel Marsden (1764–1838). Marsden was an Anglican chaplain from Australia and a representative of the Church Missionary Society. His sermon, delivered in English, was translated into Maori.

Representatives from other Christian churches began to arrive in the small European settlement that

Interior of St. Mary of the Angels, a Roman Catholic church in Wellington, New Zealand. (Tupungato/Dreamstime.com)

was mainly established in the north of the country. The year 1819 saw the arrival of the first ordained Anglican priest, John Butler, and the first Wesleyan missionary, Samuel Leighton. By 1838 2,000 settlers had come, including the first Catholic, Bishop Jean Baptiste Pompallier, in 1838. The first Presbyterian, John McFarlane, preached at Petone in 1840.

In 1840 Governor William Hobson (1793–1842) signed the Treaty of Waitangi with Maori chiefs, annexing New Zealand as a British colony. The treaty ceded Maori sovereignty to the British queen in return for guaranteed possession of their property and the rights of British subjects. These events are still controversial, particularly the interpretations of the treaty and the circumstances under which it was signed.

With the advent of organized settlement, a new period of religious colonization began. By 1840 a number of Maori had already professed to be Christian, their conversion being assisted by exposure to Christianity through schools, hospitals, and chapels. The major Christian denominations continued to grow. The first Anglican bishop, George Augustus Selwyn (1809–1878), was consecrated in 1841, and in 1848 the Presbyterians founded their own settlement at Otago. In 1850 Anglicans established themselves at Canterbury, and the first Baptist church formed in Nelson in 1851. At its first meeting, in 1854, the newly formed House of Representatives asserted the principle of religious equality for all denominations, endorsing the pluralism that was already a feature of the new colony.

Maori responded to the Christian influence by developing indigenous Christian sects that helped maintain their Maori identity. The basic theology of the Maori-Christian syncretism identifies the Hebrew Jehovah with Io, a figure in Polynesian myth. It is debatable whether Io's traditional role is that of a supreme being and thus comparable to the Christian God, but that is clearly the case in syncretistic Maori religious movements. This correlation then allows the genealogies of both traditions to be aligned, providing Maori with an ethnic identity that can be placed within Jewish, Christian, Mormon, and even Rastafarian belief systems. Although Maori have undoubtedly participated in this construction, the origin of these concepts can also be attributed to Samuel Marsden. An emphasis on charismatic prophets and imminent millenarianism is also a common feature of these movements.

From 1830 to 1850 10 religious movements arose based on this theology, and in the 1850s another 9 arose, mainly based on healing. Disputes between Maori and the new colonials regarding sovereignty, land ownership, and land confiscation led to the onset of the Land Wars from 1860 to 1865, a further catalyst for Maori to develop religious movements that suited their circumstances. At least 16 major prophetic movements arose, including the Pai-Marire, more commonly known as Hauhau. A prophetic movement, Hauhau transposed Old Testament prophecies about the Promised Land into the contemporary Maori situation. One of the most important movements arising in this period was Ringatu, a movement that has continued to thrive. Ringatu was founded in 1867 by Te Kooti, who identified himself with Moses and the Maori as Hurai (Jews), the lost tribes of Israel.

While indigenous Christian sects had been growing, so too had the major Christian denominations. By the 1860s Anglican, Presbyterian, Methodist, Catholic, and Baptist congregations were present in most major cities and towns. The 1877 Education Act established a free, secular, and compulsory national system of education, further evidence of the separation of church and state in New Zealand. By 1900 a number of religious groups, including Congregationalists, Churches of Christ, Quakers, Plymouth Brethren, Seventh Day Adventists, Latter-day Saints, and Lutherans, were also represented, in smaller numbers. A second major indigenous Christian sect was founded by Tahupotiki Wiremu Ratana in 1925. The Ratana Church understands itself as the mouthpiece of Jehovah and also stresses faith healing. Ratana is notable for its role as a major force in Maori politics and continuing growth. It holds a monopoly of the Maori parliamentary seats and is strongly linked with the New Zealand Labour Party.

In the 1960s there was a decline in the number of adherents to mainstream Christianity in New Zealand, with groups also splitting from the major denominations and forming evangelistic sects. The 1970s saw a growth in Pentecostalism and neo-Charismatic groups.

The 1996 census revealed that 60.5 percent (2,189,580) of the country identify as Christian. The three largest Christian denominations are Anglican (17.5 percent), Catholic (13.1 percent), and Presbyterian (12.7 percent). These figures have tended to decline over recent years, with the exception of Catholicism, which has remained fairly static. The next largest religious groups are Christian nondenominational (5.2 percent), Methodist (3.4 percent), Pentecostal and Assemblies of God (1.9 percent), Baptist (1.5 percent), Latter-day Saints (1.1 percent), Ratana (1 percent), Brethren (0.6 percent), and Jehovah's Witnesses (0.5 percent). An increase in the Christian nondenominational groups from 1.3 percent in 1986 to 5.2 percent in 1996 may account for some of the decreases among the major denominations. However, some denominations are growing; the number of Pentecostals has more than quadrupled since 1981, when they accounted for 0.2 percent of the population. The percentage of people not specifying their religion has increased sharply, from 1.8 percent in 1991 to 5.2 percent in 1996, and a similar rise in the number of people professing to no religion has also appeared, from 17 percent in 1986 to 24 percent in 1996.

Maori currently account for 9 percent of the New Zealand population, of which 60 percent are Christian, belonging to a variety of denominations: Anglicans (15.6 percent), Catholics (13.3 percent), Presbyterians (4.5 percent), Mormons (4.4 percent), Methodists (3.4 percent), Pentecostal and Assemblies of God (2.3 percent), and Christian nondenominational (5.3 percent). Of the indigenous churches, Ratana claims 6.7 percent and other indigenous Christian sects another 1.7 percent. Anglican and Catholic churches are becoming more Maori and Polynesian and less English or Irish. Buddhists have grown from 0.2 percent of the population in 1986 to 0.8 percent in 1996; Hindus, from 0.2 percent to 0.7 percent; and Islam, from 0.2 percent to 0.4 percent. The Jewish community, which dates to the arrival in 1831 of Sir Moses Montefiore (1784–1885), remains small, though a number of Jews have held high and responsible positions in the government and academia. The 3,300 Jews now account for 0.1 percent

NEW ZEALAND

Three Kings Islands
Hikurangi
Dargaville
Auckland
Waiuku
Whangamata
North Island
Hamilton
Te Awamutu
Rotorua
Te Kuiti
Taupo
Gisborne
New Plymouth
Napier
Taihape
Hawera
Hastings
Wanganui
Castlecliff
Waipawa
Palmerston North
Masterton
Porirua
Upper Hutt
Nelson
Blenheim
Wellington
Westport
New Zealand
Greymouth
South Island
Christchurch
Chatham Islands
Timaru
Oamaru
Dunedin
Gore
Invercargill
Stewart Island
Bounty Islands
The Snares
Antipodes Islands
N
Auckland Islands
Campbell Island

New Zealand

Religion	Followers in 1970	Followers in 2010	% of Population	Annual % growth 2000–2010	Followers in 2025	Followers in 2050
Christians	2,690,000	2,998,000	70.0	0.43	3,018,000	3,149,000
Protestants	852,000	792,000	18.5	0.18	739,000	750,000
Anglicans	877,000	640,000	14.9	−0.30	600,000	600,000
Roman Catholics	426,000	430,000	10.0	−1.00	420,000	450,000
Agnostics	84,400	924,000	21.6	3.14	1,230,000	1,428,000
Hindus	3,800	90,800	2.1	2.15	150,000	195,000
Buddhists	1,400	98,600	2.3	8.21	135,000	155,000
Atheists	15,000	54,000	1.3	6.00	75,000	90,000
Ethnoreligionists	9,000	40,000	0.9	2.90	32,000	30,000
Muslims	1,000	37,000	0.9	2.72	60,000	80,000
Chinese folk	7,000	15,000	0.4	2.64	22,000	26,000
Sikhs	300	10,000	0.2	1.23	15,700	20,500
Baha'is	2,600	7,600	0.2	1.95	10,000	15,000
Jews	3,800	4,800	0.1	1.23	7,000	7,500
New religionists	1,000	4,200	0.1	2.58	7,000	10,000
Spiritists	1,000	1,200	0.0	1.04	2,000	2,500
Total population	**2,820,000**	**4,285,000**	**100.0**	**1.23**	**4,764,000**	**5,209,000**

of the population. Adherents to Spiritualism and New Age religious movements add another 0.3 percent.

To a large degree the census figures reflect the effect of regional migrations. For example, the lack of immigrants from continental Europe has resulted in comparatively low numbers of Lutherans, while the recent increase in the number of Buddhists is largely due to Asian immigration, not conversion. Religious practice in New Zealand can be characterized as the adoption of nominal religious identity; census statistics are much higher than actual church membership and attendance, which can be attributed to only 12 to 15 percent of self-identified Catholics and Presbyterians, for example. It can almost be argued that civil religious practices such as ANZAC day or rugby are more important to contemporary New Zealanders than commitment to institutional religion.

Michelle Baker

See also: Anglican Church in Aotearoa, New Zealand, and Polynesia; Assemblies of God; Associated Churches of Christ in New Zealand; Baptist Union of New Zealand; Church Missionary Society; Church of Jesus Christ of Latter-day Saints; Jehovah's Witnesses; Maori Religion; Methodist Church of New Zealand; New Age Movement; Pentecostalism; Presbyterian Church of Aotearoa New Zealand; Selwyn, George Augustus; Spiritualism.

References

Colless, Brian, and Peter Donovan, eds. *Religion in New Zealand Society*. 2nd ed. Palmerston North, NZ: Dunmore, 1985.

Davidson, Allan K. *Christianity in Aotearoa: A History of Church and Society in New Zealand*. 2nd ed. Wellington, NZ: Education for Ministry, 1997.

Donovan, Peter, ed. *Religions of New Zealanders*. Palmerston North, NZ: Dunmore Press, 1990.

Ellwood, Robert S. *Islands of the Dawn: The Story of Alternative Spirituality in New Zealand*. Honolulu: University of Hawaii Press, 1993.

Hill, Michael, and Wiebe Zwaga. "Religion in New Zealand: Change and Comparison." In *The Changing Face of Religion,* edited by James A. Beckford and Thomas Luckmann, 64–87. London: Sage Publications, 1989.

Stenhouse, John, and Jane Thomson. *Building God's Own Country: Historical Essays on Religion in New Zealand.* Dunedin, NZ: University of Otago Press, 2005.

Newar Buddhism

The Newar society of the Kathmandu Valley in Nepal has a good claim to being the oldest continuous local tradition of Buddhism. Although the Buddhism of modern Newars is a diverse and evolving tradition, the term "Newar Buddhism" is used to refer to a distinct form of Vajrayana Buddhism. Its only professional religious are married priests of the Vajracarya/Sakya caste, who live in monastic courtyards carefully organized into public Mahayana and secret Vajrayana spaces. They draw their clients from mercantile, artisanal, and agricultural castes. They are unique among modern Buddhists in that their canonical language is Sanskrit, a trait that marks them as the last surviving descendants of the Indian Buddhist tradition. Together with Hindu Newars they draw on a common Indic inventory of gods and rituals. For example, all Newars worship Ganesha before any significant undertaking, worship the Eight Mother Goddesses, and take part in fasting vows (Sanskrit: *vratas*) according to the lunisolar calendar.

Scholars believe that Buddhism took root in Nepal at the time of Ashoka (d. 232 or 238 BCE). The great *caitya* (stupa or religious shrine) of Svayambhu, one of two foci of Newar Buddhist practice, may date from this time. The other great Newar site, the Lokesvara at Bungamati, was well established as part of the pan-Asian Amoghapasa cult by the eighth century, and in this period Newar Vajrayana attained its early coherence. Nepalese Vajrayana retained its distinct local identity even as it helped to form high Pala Vajrayana of India, which returned to Nepal as refugees were driven from the great Indian Buddhist universities with their destruction around 1200.

From the 13th century on, Newar Vajrayana settled into its later form, emphasizing Chakrasamvara and the Mother Tantras but still preserving the Bodhisattva Amoghapasa Lokesvara and the Buddha Vairocana as key figures. Nepal had long been a training ground for Tibetan Buddhists, but the Newar *sangha* (order) now turned inward, preserving Indic texts and forms while retaining strong commercial contacts with Tibet. By 1450 the extinction of Indian Buddhism led to a crisis in Newar Buddhism, which reinvented itself as an independent tradition and produced the last great Sanskrit Buddhist sutras (texts). These show a complex mix of Mahayana and Vajrayana ritual, thought, and iconography.

After 1768, with the advent of the modern Nepalese state, Newar Buddhism entered a long phase of decline. There was a period of intense creativity in the early 1800s, but the anti-Buddhist ideology of the Gorkha state pushed middle-class Buddhists to adopt Hindu names and affiliations.

In the 20th century, the opening of Nepal fostered a more complex and indeterminate practice among Newar Buddhists. As a result of the emergence of Newar Theravada in the 1930s, the influx of Tibetan refugees after 1950, and the development of Kathmandu as a site on the "Hippy Trail," Newar Buddhists found their homeland converted into a center of modern eclectic Buddhism. Even though traditional high Newar Vajrayana is still taught and practiced by Vajracarya priests, its transmission is closed and secret. However, middle-class Newar Buddhists may go to Theravada monasteries for lifecycle rituals, some Vajracaryas and Sakyas have links with charismatic Tibetan lamas, and Japanese Buddhist pilgrims now visit the great Newar monasteries.

Will Tuladhar-Douglas

See also: Ashoka; Theravada Buddhism; Tibetan Buddhism.

References

Gellner, David N. *Monk, Householder, and Tantric Priest: Newar Buddhism and Its Hierarchy of Ritual.* London: Cambridge University Press, 1992.

Lewis, Todd T. *Popular Buddhist Texts from Nepal: Narratives and Rituals of Newar Buddhism.* Albany: State University of New York Press, 2000.

Locke, John K., S.J. *Karunamaya.* Kathmandu Tribhuvan University, 1980.

von Rospatt, Alexander. "On the Conception of Stupa in Vajrayana Buddhism: The Example of the Svayambhucaitya of Kathmandu." *Journal of the Nepal Research Centre* 11 (1999): 121–147.

Ngunzist Churches (Congo)

At the same time that the Kimbanguist Church was developing in the 1920s, an alternative Kimbanguist movement known as Ngunzism (from the Kikongo word *ngunza,* or prophet) began to appear. This movement, like some of the Harrist movements in West Africa, went much further than the prophet Simon Kimbangu (ca. 1887–1951) had intended: seeing Kimbangu as a political figure, a black messiah who would dramatically return from prison and destroy the colonialists with a holy war. Some said he would restore the ancient Kongo Empire. Many legends about miracles surrounding Kimbangu after his arrest were propagated. Borrowing elements from the Salvation Army, which had arrived in the Congo in 1934, several Ngunzist groups were formed, including the independent Congolese Salvation Army.

André Matswa founded the Amical Balali movement for the liberation of the French Congo (Brazzaville). His movement was at first a movement for political liberation. Matswa was imprisoned in 1930, where he remained until his death in 1942. He, like Kimbangu before him, was transformed by his followers into a religious figure—a savior and messiah who would come back to free his people from oppression and restore the old Kongo Empire.

In 1939 Simon-Pierre Mpadi, who trained as a Salvation Army officer, founded the Mission of the Blacks, the best-known of the Ngunzi movements. The colonial authorities saw all these groups as belonging to one Kimbanguist movement and they sought to destroy them, even though the Kimbanguists and Kimbangu himself had repudiated the views of Ngunzism. Mpadi's even more powerful movement was known as Mpadism, or the Khaki movement, after the khaki uniforms worn by his followers. Mpadi became the second and "greater" prophet of this Congolese church, and he built on the traditions surrounding Kimbangu and Matswa. He tried to unite various Ngunzist groups and succeeded in bringing Amicalism into his movement after Matswa's death. Mpadi himself was arrested in 1949 and imprisoned in the same prison as Kimbangu, and during that time his followers formed one of the most influential churches in the Congo.

A decree on Christmas Eve 1959 by the colonial administration gave recognition to the existence of religious "sects." On his release from prison in 1960, when a general amnesty was given to African prophets in preparation for independence, Mpadi refused to join the Kimbanguists when invited to do so. He reorganized his Mission of the Blacks as the Church of the Blacks and Africa. He declared that Kimbangu had appointed him head of the Kimbanguist Church. In contrast to the Kimbanguists, Mpadi's church made polygyny compulsory and encouraged dancing, drumming, and displays of ecstasy. Mpadi was a messiah-like figure who wore a red gown with a crown and a scepter and claimed to have been resurrected 14 times.

Relationships between the prophetic churches and the government in the Congo (Kinshasa) were strained. In 1971 President Mobutu Sese Seko (1930–1997) forced the consolidation of most of the churches in the country by declaring an approved list of only six churches, one of which was the Kimbanguist Church. Even harsher laws were imposed in 1979, severely curtailing the activities of any unregistered religious groups. Several significant African Initiated Churches had to seek and obtain registration by affiliating with the Iglise du Christ au Congo (Church of Christ in the Congo), the recognized Protestant ecumenical council.

The Ngunzist movement differs from the Kimbanguist Church in several ways. Unlike the latter, Ngunzism is a heterogeneous movement located largely in the western Congo Basin, consisting mostly of small, unorganized groups loyal to a local prophet. Christian hymns, prayers, and the Bible are of secondary importance, and the main emphasis is on "organized quaking" and the beating of drums, accompanied by collective ecstasy, shrieking, and trance, which are believed to manifest possession by the Holy Spirit. Although many of these ecstatic manifestations were found in the ministry of Kimbangu, the Kimbanguists later discouraged any excessive emotionalism. Traditional African rituals and customs, including polygyny, are usually promoted in the Ngunzist movement.

Different religious groups in the region begin as movements of cultural and religious renaissance, others as political and anti-white protest movements, but most have made use of the mystique associated with the name of one of Africa's greatest prophets, Simon Kimbangu.

Allan H. Anderson

See also: African Initiated (Independent) Churches; Church of Christ in the Congo; Kimbanguist Church; Native Baptist Church.

References

Anderson, Allan H. *African Reformation: African Initiated Christianity in the Twentieth Century*. Trenton, NJ: Africa World Press, 2001.

Andersson, Efraim. *Messianic Popular Movements in the Lower Congo*. Uppsala: Studia Ethnographica Upsaliensia, No. 16, 1958.

MacGaffey, Wyatt. *Modern Kongo Prophets: Religion in a Plural Society*. Bloomington: Indiana University Press, 1983.

Wamba-dia-Wamba, Ernest. "Bundu dia Kongo: A Congolese Fundamentalist Religious Movement." In *East African Expressions of Christianity*, edited by Thomas Spear and Isaria N. Kimambo, 213–228. Oxford: James Currey, 1999.

Nicaea

Nicaea, now known as Yznik, was an important Christian center from the fourth to the 11th centuries. It was located on the Sea of Marmara some 50 miles east of Constantinople. It became the site of two of the seven Ecumenical Councils at which the early church established orthodox doctrine. The most ubiquitous statement of Christian faith is named the Nicene Creed for the city and the council that promulgated it.

Originally founded in 310 BCE, Nicaea became an important Roman port city and an early Christian center in the region. With the emergence of the emperor Constantine (ca. 272–337) and his favoring of Christianity, the city's bishop and his headquarters at St. Sophia Cathedral quickly rose in status, all the more so after the church was chosen as the seat of the first Ecumenical Council in 325. This council, which gathered just two years after persecution against the church was formally ended, was called to consider the views of the priest Arius (d. 336). Attempting to understand in what sense Christ could be considered God and hence the object of worship, Arius proposed that since Christians believed that God the Father begat the Son, the Son of God must have had a beginning, that there was a time when he was not, but that his substance was like nothing in the rest of creation. The Council of Nicaea condemned the beliefs of Arius and wrote the first version of the now famous Nicene Creed proclaiming that the Son was of one substance with the Father.

A second all-church council was called in 736 and held its substantive sessions in 737. It dealt with the iconoclastic controversy, specifically with the issue of the use of iconic representations of Jesus and other holy personages. It ruled in favor of the icons, suggesting that representational art was quite in harmony with the history of the spread of the gospel. Such art provided confirmation that the God becoming man was real and not just imaginary.

Nicaea remained a Christian city until it fell to the Turkish Muslim Seljuk dynasty in 1078. The Ottomans took control in 1331. In subsequent years the Christian presence dwindled and today St. Sophia lies in ruins. As the Muslim city of Yznik, the city became noted for the quality ceramics it produced. Presently, Nicaea is a modest town of some 34,000 residents.

J. Gordon Melton

See also: Arius; Athanasius; Constantine the Great; Istanbul.

References

Bellitto, Christopher M. *The General Councils: A History of the Twenty-one General Councils from Nicaea to Vatican II.* New York: Paulist Press, 2002.

Davis, Leo Donald. *The First Seven Ecumenical Councils (325–787): Their History and Theology.* Wilmington, DE: M. Glazier, 1987.

Faroqhi, Suraiya N. *The Cambridge History of Turkey.* Cambridge: Cambridge University Press, 2006.

Hughes, Philip. *The Church in Crisis: A History of the General Councils 325–1870.* Garden City, NY: Hanover House, 1961.

Rubenstein, Richard E. *When Jesus Became God: The Struggle to Define Christianity during the Last Days of Rome*. Orlando, FL: Harvest Books, 2000.

Taylor, Jane. *Imperial Istanbul: A Traveller's Guide: Includes Iznik, Bursa and Edirne.* London: Tauris Parke Paperbacks, 2007.

■ Nicaragua

The Republic of Nicaragua, the largest country in Central America, is located between Honduras and Costa Rica and bordered by the Caribbean Sea and the Pacific Ocean. The nation has an area of 49,998 square miles, slightly smaller than New York State, and had a population of 5.6 million in 2006. Its major languages (according to the 1995 census) are Spanish, 97.5 percent; Miskito, 1.7 percent; and other, 0.8 percent. English Creole (Afro-Caribbean) and Amerindian languages are mainly spoken on the Caribbean coast, also known as the Miskito Coast.

The Miskito Coast (La Mosquitia) of Nicaragua is a wide coastal lowland along the Caribbean Sea that stretches from Honduras to Costa Rica, which contains mangrove swamps, lagoons, rivers, savannas, and tropical rain forests. It has a population of about 118,000 inhabitants, consisting of 57 percent Miskito (Afro-Amerindian); 22 percent Creoles (Afro-Caribbean); 15 percent *mestizo* (European and Amerindian); 4 percent Sumo (Amerindian); 1 percent Garifuna (or Black Carib, Afro-Amerindian); 0.5 percent Chinese; and 0.5 percent Rama (Amerindian). The Miskito Coast's principal cities are Bluefields in the south and Puerto Cabezas in the north.

The Nicaraguan Constitution of 1987 provides for freedom of religion and the government generally respects this right in practice. Although there is no official state religion, because of its historical presence in the country since colonial times, the Roman Catholic Church has often enjoyed a close relationship with the government and has wielded significant political influence, especially under Conservative administrations.

The national census of 2005 reported religious affiliation in Nicaragua as follows: Roman Catholic, 58.6 percent (down from 72.9 percent in 1995); Protestant, 23.2 percent (up from 12.2 percent in 1995); other religions (including marginal Christian groups), 2.5 percent (up from 2.0 percent in 1995); and none/no response, 15.7 percent (up from 8.5 percent in 1995).

In 1950, Roman Catholic adherents were 95.8 percent and Protestant adherents were 4.1 percent of the national population, which shows a significant shift in religious affiliation that is characteristic of the Central American region: the Catholic population has declined at the expense of rapid and widespread Protestant church growth. Also, secularization has taken its toll on the Nicaraguan population, with about 16 percent now claiming no religious affiliation.

Nicaraguans have endured humid climate, perpetual poverty and underdevelopment, natural disasters (hurricanes, floods, earthquakes, and volcanic eruptions), civil wars and foreign military intervention, repressive dictatorships, and corrupt democratic governments. These conditions motivated many people to abandon their homeland during the 1970s and 1980s and seek refuge elsewhere. Although this mass exodus of Nicaraguan refugees caused families to be separated, it has also generated millions of dollars of support from those living abroad who send remittances to help their relatives in Nicaragua.

Turmoil continues to plague the nation today as political factions wage unending verbal warfare against their opponents, while seeking to gain advantage in the next elections. Historically, since 1821, the nation's various Conservative and Liberal political parties have vied for power and control of the executive, legislative, judicial, and military branches of government. However, today, the nation's two major political parties are (1) the leftist Sandinista National Liberation Front (FSLN), led by President Daniel Ortega Saavedra (r. 1985–1990, 2000–present)—also a member of the ruling junta (1979–1984); and (2) the Constitutionalist Liberal Party (PLC), led by former President Arnoldo Alemán Lacayo (r. 1997–2002) who inherited the legacy of the Liberal Somoza dynasty.

During the period 1821 to 1909, Nicaragua experienced continued civil strife, which encouraged the development of a variety of private armies controlled by the political and commercial interests of Conservatives and Liberals. In 1893, Liberal President José Santos Zelaya (r. 1893–1909) came to power and enacted a series of progressive reforms, which included improving public education, building railroads, establishing steamship lines, and enacting constitutional reforms that provided for equal rights, property guarantees,

The Catholic Church of Guadalupe in Granada, Nicaragua, was built in 1626 by Fray Benito Baltodano. (Holger Mette/ Dreamstime.com)

habeas corpus, compulsory vote, compulsory education, the protection of arts and industry, minority representation, and the separation of state powers. However, in late 1909, due to ongoing conflicts with domestic and foreign powers (both political and commercial), President Zelaya resigned as president, turned over the government to José Madriz Rodríguez (who governed from December 1909 to August 1910), and fled into exile.

The chaotic political situation in Nicaragua prompted U.S. President William Howard Taft (r. 1909–1913), a Republican, to send the U.S. Marines to occupy the country (1912–1933) in order to provide political stability and safeguard U.S. economic and political interests. Between 1910 and 1926, the Conservative Party ruled the country under a series of 10 presidents, amid continued rivalry and civil conflict between Conservative and Liberal factions.

Liberal President Juan Bautista Sacasa (r. 1933–1936) took office in January 1933, and named General Anastasio Somoza García (1896-1956), nicknamed "Tacho," as commander of the National Guard, at the insistence of the U.S. ambassador. In February 1934, Somoza assassinated Augusto César Sandino, who had led a guerrilla rebellion between 1926 and 1933, and several of his aides. Two years later, Somoza seized power in a coup d'état and established a family dynasty that ruled Nicaragua for more than 40 years (1936–1979).

General Somoza García was the de facto dictator of Nicaragua from 1936 until his assassination in 1956. His eldest son, Luis Somoza Debaye (1922–1967), succeeded his father as president (r. 1956–1967). In May 1967, Luis's brother Anastacio Somoza Debayle (1925–1980, nicknamed "Tachito") was elected president (r. 1967–1972, 1974–1979). While Luis Somoza had ruled more gently than his father, Tachito was intolerant of opposition of any sort; civil liberties were restricted and corruption was widespread. Because he was prohibited legally from immediate presidential re-election, Tachito worked out a deal that allowed him to run for re-election in 1974: he was replaced as president in 1972 by a three-man junta consisting of two Liberals and one Conservative, while he retained control of the National Guard and was the de facto ruler of the country.

On December 23, 1972, a magnitude 6.2 earthquake and several large aftershocks hit the nation's capital, virtually destroying the city: about 80 percent of Managua's commercial buildings were destroyed, an estimated 5,000 to 6,000 of the city's 400,000 residents were killed, and 20,000 were injured. Two-thirds of Managua's residents were displaced and faced starvation and disease due to infrastructural damages and crippled emergency services. General Somoza immediately declared martial law and appointed himself as head of the National Emergency Committee. Then he and his inner circle proceeded to embezzle foreign aid monies and resell supplies sent for earthquake relief and rebuilding efforts. Somoza's greed and corruption began to alienate a large portion of the country's influentials, including a significant sector of the Catholic clergy who began to speak out against the dictatorship. One of his fiercest critics was leftist Jesuit priest Ernesto Cardenal, who was an advocate of Marxist-inspired Liberation Theology.

As criticism mounted, support for the leftist Sandinista National Liberation Front (FSLN) was growing inside and outside the country. During the early 1970s, a coalition of leftist guerrilla groups under the FSLN launched armed revolutionary activities in the northeastern mountain region of Nicaragua, with limited financial and logistical support from Cuba and the Soviet Union. The Sandinista insurgency attracted the support of groups throughout the country, including progressive religious leaders and their parishioners, among both Catholics and Protestants. In 1975, President Somoza sent National Guard units to conduct a fierce military campaign against the FSLN and its supporters throughout the country. Opposition to the despotic Somoza government now included prominent national leaders, such as newspaper publisher and editor Pedro Joaquín Chamorro Cardenal (1924–1978) of Nicaragua's leading daily, *La Prensa,* who was assassinated, allegedly under orders from Somoza, in 1978.

After the Somoza dictatorship was finally overthrown by the Sandinistas in 1979, FSLN commander Daniel Ortega became a member of the five-person Junta of National Reconciliation. The National Guard, without its top commanders, virtually disintegrated following the Sandinista victory, and a new professional army had to be built from scratch from the various guerrilla combat units. The new Sandinista government, led by Daniel Ortega, inherited an underdeveloped nation that was riddled with corruption and bureaucratic mismanagement and handicapped by poverty, infrastructural destruction, and economic ruin. The nation had more than $1.5 billion in debts and only about $3.5 million in international reserves. Human and material losses due to the civil war were staggering. An estimated 30,000 to 50,000 Nicaraguans had been killed; about 100,000 were injured; an estimated 150,000 were homeless; at least 150,000 had fled to neighboring Costa Rica or Honduras; and tens of thousands more had become internal refugees. Large-scale international efforts provided emergency relief, prevented starvation, and averted immediate economic collapse, but the task of national economic recovery and reconstruction was overwhelming. Also, the eyes of the world were on Nicaragua to see what would develop under revolutionary leadership, which included both Marxist and non-Marxist political components.

In 1981, U.S. President Ronald Reagan condemned the FSLN and authorized the CIA to begin financing, arming, and training rebels, some of whom were

NICARAGUA

former National Guard officers, as anti-Sandinista guerrillas, who became known collectively as the Contras (a nickname for contra-revolutionaries, which President Reagan called "freedom fighters"). Between 1980 and 1989, more than 30,000 Nicaraguans died in the Contra conflict with the Sandinista government.

In November 1984, in the midst of the Contra war, Ortega allowed national elections; he won the presidency with 63 percent of the vote and took office in January 1985. According to the vast majority of independent observers, the 1984 elections were perhaps the freest and fairest in Nicaraguan history. The seven political parties that participated in the elections represented a broad spectrum of political ideologies.

However, in the 1990 presidential elections, Ortega lost to Violeta Barrios de Chamorro, his former colleague in the Junta of National Reconciliation, which finally brought an end to the illegal U.S.-backed Contra war. Chamorro was supported by a 14-party anti-Sandinista alliance known as the National Opposition Union (UNO), whose members ranged from Conservatives and Liberals to Marxists.

In Ortega's concession speech the day after the election, he vowed to keep "ruling from below," a reference to the power that the FSLN still wielded among various social sectors. Ortega ran for election again in October 1996 and November 2001 but lost on both occasions to Arnoldo Alemán Lacayo of the Constitutionalist Liberal Party (PLC) and to Alemán's former vice president Enrique Bolaños, respectively, both of whom had received substantial financial support from the U.S. government. In these elections, a key issue was the allegation of corruption by the ruling party.

In addition to its political divisions, Nicaragua has long been a nation divided by its geography and ethnicity. A central mountain range divides the country from north to south, and there are few roads on the broad Caribbean coastal plain—an area making up more than half of the national territory that is dissected by hundreds of rivers and streams. Historically, the Caribbean coast and the central mountain region have been thinly populated, whereas the Pacific coastal region has been more heavily populated, originally by Amerindian peoples and later by Spanish settlers and their descendants.

Prior to Spanish colonization, the Caribbean coast was populated by the Miskito, Sumo, and Rama peoples of Macro-Chibchan origin (the predominant group in Colombia) who lived in scattered fishing villages on the coast and along the inland waterways, whereas the Pacific coast was largely home to ethnolinguistic groups that migrated south along the Pacific coast from present-day Mexico as early as 1000 BCE: Chontales, Chorotegas (Dirianes and Nagrandanos), and Nicaraos (Nahua-Náhuatl-Pipil speakers of Uto-Aztecan origins).

Today, descendants of the latter ethnic groups live in the departments of Matagalpa (Misumalpan), León (Subtiaba), and Masaya (Monimbó), although they no longer speak their mother tongues. However, the Amerindian groups on the Caribbean coast still speak their original languages and many are bilingual in English and/or Spanish. Overall, about 194,000 Amerindian peoples were reported to exist in 1990, the majority of whom were Roman Catholics on the Pacific coast, whereas the majority of the Miskitos, Sumos, and Ramas on the Caribbean coast are Protestant (mainly adherents of the Moravian Church).

Spanish Colonial Period and Development of the Roman Catholic Church Christopher Columbus (1451–1506) discovered the territory of Nicaragua during his fourth voyage to the New World in 1502, when he sailed along the Caribbean coast and explored the area of Cabo Gracias a Dios at the mouth of the Coco River. It was not until 1522, however, that a formal military expedition, under Gil González Dávila, led to the first Spanish conquest of Nicaraguan territory.

In 1523, the governor of Panama, Pedro Arias Dávila (known as Pedrarias), appointed Francisco Hernández de Córdoba (d. 1517) to resume the conquest of Nicaragua, and he and his small army succeeded in establishing the first permanent Spanish settlements in Nicaragua in 1524: Santiago de los Caballeros de León and Granada, which later became the centers of colonial Nicaragua.

Although the Spanish conquerors were successful on the Pacific coast, their efforts were unfruitful on the Caribbean coast, which was dominated by the Miskito people and smaller Amerindian groups. Later, the British Empire established an alliance with the Miskitos that lasted for several hundred years. In 1894, Nicaraguan President José Santos Zelaya took control of the Miskito coast by military force, and the British, not wishing to go to war for a territory of little value to the British Empire, recognized Nicaraguan sovereignty over the region.

The first Roman Catholic Church was established in Granada in 1524 by Franciscans, but most missionary work during the colonial period was done by the Jesuits. The Diocese of León was erected in 1531, which included all the territory of Nicaragua and present-day Costa Rica, with diocesan priest Diego Alvarez de Osorio (1485–1536) as its first bishop. His successor as bishop was Padre Francisco de Mendavia (1537–1540), Order of Saint Jerome, who previously served as prior of a monastery in Victoria de Salamanca, Spain. Mendavia's successor was Dominican Friar Antonio de Valdivieso (1544–1549). During the 16th century, 10 bishops served the Diocese of León. In 1850, the Diocese of Costa Rica was separated from the Diocese of León. A Concordat between the Vatican and the Republic of Nicaragua was established in 1861.

In 1894 and following, the government of President José Santos Zelaya (r. 1893–1909) passed anti-Catholic legislation and other progressive reforms that provoked a protest from Bishop Francisco Ulloa y Larrios (1819–1902), which resulted in the bishop being banished to Panama. Upon his death in 1902, he was succeeded by Bishop Simeone Pereira (1863–1921). Although the Catholic Church had been the official state religion since the first Constitution of 1826, under Zelaya's administration church and state were separated and freedom of religion was constitutionally guaranteed to all forms of religious worship.

Traditionally, the hierarchy of the Roman Catholic Church in Nicaragua generally supported the Somoza family, which ruled from 1936 to 1979 under the umbrella of the Nationalist Liberal Party, and other members of the ruling oligarchy, although the bishops were partial to the various Conservative factions. However, beginning in the 1960s, many Catholic priests begin to actively oppose the despotic Somoza regime, especially priests from the United States and Spain who became more dedicated to the Sandinista cause than were many Nicaraguan priests.

Diverse tensions arose within the Nicaraguan Catholic Church during the 1960s and following years, which resulted from challenges posed by the Second Vatican Council (1962–1965), the Conference of Latin American Bishops held in Medellín (Colombia) in 1968, Latin American Liberation Theology, and the Catholic Charismatic Renewal movement. These powerful new currents polarized Catholic bishops, priests (diocesan and religious), lay brothers and sisters (members of religious orders), and the laity in general into various factions. *Traditionalists* wanted the church to remain as it was prior to the reforms approved by the Second Vatican Council (mid-1960s), with an emphasis on apostolic authority, orthodox theology, the sacraments, and personal piety. *Reformers* generally supported the church's post–Second Vatican Council stance of modernization and toleration of diversity based on its official social doctrine. *Progressives*, inspired by reforms approved at the Second Vatican and Medellín conferences, sought to implement the new vision for "a preferential option for the poor" through social and political action aimed at transforming Nicaraguan society and establishing greater social justice through peaceful democratic means. *Radicals* adopted the Marxist-inspired Liberation Theology and advocated violent revolution by the people as a means of overthrowing the Somoza dictatorship and creating a Socialist state that would serve the poor marginalized masses. *Charismatic agents* sought to transform the spiritual and communal life of Catholics by means of the power and gifts of the Holy Spirit (including the "baptism of the Holy Spirit and speaking in tongues"), rather than by political and social activism.

Several radical Catholic priests (advocates of Liberation Theology) who supported the Sandinista uprising against the Somoza dictatorship were named to key posts in the new Sandinista government, following its July 1979 victory. Progressive and radical social and political advocacy among Catholics in Nicaragua was first apparent among priests, often Jesuits, who taught in private Catholic high schools and universities. By the mid-1970s, many of their former students, often children of wealthy families, had joined the Sandinista rebellion. And, as the fight against the Somoza regime intensified, several priests joined Sandinista guerrilla units in the field, while others helped organize people in poor neighborhoods via "church base communities" (called CEBs, *comunidades eclesiales de base*) in preparation for the "popular" insurrection. Many Catholic parishes played an indirect role in the Sandinista uprising by stockpiling food and medicine, giving first aid courses, or providing direct assistance to Sandinista guerrillas (including hiding combatants in their homes and churches).

The Sandinistas overthrew the Somoza regime with the help of a large segment of the Catholic Church, including the tacit approval of five out of seven bishops. However, following the Sandinista victory in July 1979, strains developed between the Catholic hierarchy and the Sandinista government. Archbishop Miguel Obando y Bravo of Managua, who opposed the Somoza regime but refrained from endorsing the Sandinista rebellion, became increasingly critical of the new leftist government while many Catholics in the "popular church" still supported it.

One of the particularly bothersome issues for the Catholic bishops of Nicaragua was the fact that five Catholic priests held high-level administrative positions in the Sandinista government. On May 13, 1980, the bishops asked for the resignation of the priests who worked in government positions. Pope John Paul II tried to persuade the rebellious priests to step down from their government posts as a condition of his visit to Nicaragua in March 1983. But he received only a compromise whereby the priests agreed to steer clear of the pontiff during his activities. Among the pope's reported aims was to strengthen Catholic unity in the country in the wake of the Sandinista victory, due to concerns about the existing polarization between Somoza loyalists and Sandinista supporters.

In December 1984, the Sandinistas suffered some embarrassment due to pressure from the Vatican over the issue of priests serving in government posts. After five years of warnings, the Society of Jesus expelled priest Fernando Cardenal Martínez when he refused to resign as minister of education. Finally, in May 1985, the Vatican issued the suspension order to the three rebellious priests: Foreign Minister Miguel d'Escoto, Culture Minister Ernesto Cardenal, and Minister of Social Welfare/OAS Ambassador Edgard Parrales.

In 2000, the Nicaraguan Catholic Church administered 8 dioceses (including the Vicariate of Bluefields) with 243 parishes, served by 247 diocesan priests and 127 religious priests (total of 374), of which 75 percent were native-born and 25 percent were foreign-born. Also, there were 196 religious brothers and 977 religious sisters (nuns) in the country. The current archbishop of Managua, Monsignor Leopoldo José Brenes Solórzano, was appointed in 2005 as the successor to Cardinal Miguel Obando y Bravo (b. 1926, archbishop from 1970 to 2005) who retired in 2005. In many of the rural areas of the Nicaraguan interior, the presence of the Catholic Church has been weak or nonexistent due to a lack of clergy, especially in the North-Central Region and South Atlantic Autonomous Region.

The Catholic Cathedral of Managua, built in 1920, survived a 1931 earthquake but was severely damaged by the massive 1972 earthquake and was condemned. This eventually led to the construction of a new cathedral, called Catedral Metropolitana de la Purísima Concepción (Metropolitan Cathedral of the Immaculate Conception), inaugurated in 1993. Each town and city has annual celebrations (*fiestas patronales*) for its patron saints, and special religious celebrations are held all over the country during Holy Week that ends on Easter Sunday.

The Protestant Movement Protestant missionary activity in eastern Nicaragua can be traced to Anglican efforts in the 1760s, although an Anglican influence was present as early as the 1620s among the scattered British trading settlements and logging camps on the Caribbean coast, known as the Miskito Shore. The Wesleyan (British) Methodists made a weak and unsuccessful attempt to establish themselves in the port of Bluefields in the 1830s, mainly among the Creoles (English-speaking Afro-Americans from the British West Indies). However, serious efforts to evangelize the Creoles and Amerindians in eastern Nicaragua did not begin until the arrival of the German United Brethren (Moravian Church) in the port of Bluefields in 1847. From this base of operations, the Moravians began evangelizing the various ethnolinguistic groups on the Miskito Shore: Amerindians (Miskitos, Sumos and Ramas), Garifunas (or Black Caribs, an Afro-Caribbean people deported by the British from the Island of St. Vincent in the Caribbean to the Bay Islands of Honduras in 1789; the Garifuna community in Nicaragua is located at Sandy Bay, north of Bluefields), and Creoles (English-speaking West Indians) who were concentrated in the port settlements. The Jamaican Baptists were active in the Corn Islands of Nicaragua during the 1850s, and the Anglicans (now a diocese in the Episcopal Church) renewed their efforts on the Miskito Shore during the 1880s.

Prior to 1900, few Protestant attempts had been made among the Spanish-speaking population of western Nicaragua, either in the Pacific coastal region or in the central highlands. However, several successful missionary efforts had begun to produce fruit among the Hispanicized population (descendants of the original

Amerindian peoples: Matagalpa, Subtiaba, and Monimbó tribes) by 1940. The independent Central American Mission began its labors in 1900, independent Pentecostals in 1911, the American Baptists (now the American Baptist Churches in the U.S.A.) in 1917, and the Assemblies of God in 1936. The Seventh-day Adventist Church, which initiated mission work on the Caribbean coast among the Creoles in 1904, did not begin to expand their efforts to western Nicaragua until the 1940s.

Protestant church growth was slow in Nicaragua prior to the mid-1960s. In 1937, only 7 Protestant mission agencies had begun work on either coast; however, by 1965, 26 Protestant denominations were active in Nicaragua and, by 1978, 46 new denominations had arrived. In 1980, there were at least 72 Protestant denominations in Nicaragua with about 1,500 organized congregations that were served by more than 300 ordained national pastors, 760 lay workers, and 83 foreign missionaries (up from 41 missionaries in 1973).

In 1936, 75 percent of Protestant church members were Amerindians and Creoles on the Caribbean coast, and only 25 percent were Hispanics on the Pacific coast. In 1980, the situation was reversed: 70 percent of the Protestant membership lived on the Pacific coast (including the central mountain region) and only 30 percent lived on the Caribbean coast, which represented a drastic shift in the strength of Protestantism in Nicaragua during the previous 45 years.

Under the Somoza dynasty (1936–1979), Protestant denominations benefited from the principle of separation of church and state, with the Constitution guaranteeing religious freedom to all Nicaraguan citizens and to foreign residents. Consequently, most Protestant groups grew unhindered, engaging in evangelistic activities and planting churches at will, supported by constitutional law and the power of the civil authorities. Protestants, in general, felt that the civil authorities were "ordained of God" for the common good and could be counted on for protection in times of crises.

As a rule, Protestants abstained from assuming a critical stance toward the Somoza family dynasty, even though the National Guard increasingly used repression to stop political dissent, often with brutal and bloody consequences for political opponents or even those suspected of supporting the Sandinista insurgency during the 1960s and 1970s. For many Protestants, the revolutionary movement, led by the FSLN against the corrupt Somoza dictatorship, created a climate of fear, confusion, and uncertainty, for both the present and the future. Nevertheless, some Protestants, especially young people, openly embraced the Sandinista cause; others adopted a more cautious "wait-and-see" attitude in an attempt to remain politically neutral; and some even openly supported the Somoza government in submissive resignation to the belief that "the powers that be are ordained of God."

Prior to the 1960s, most cooperative efforts among Protestants were fostered by foreign mission agencies, rather than by national church organizations, which were just beginning to develop as autonomous bodies. However, during the 1960s, national evangelical leaders and their respective ecclesiastical organizations played a more significant role in cooperative efforts than did the foreign missionaries.

In 1966, preoccupations over church-state issues and basic religious liberties compelled nine of the larger Protestant denominations to form the National Evangelical Council of Churches in an effort to counteract intensified Roman Catholic activities against evangelicals. In the early 1960s, the Catholic Church sponsored the "Santa Misión" program, which was probably a reaction to growing evangelical visibility and credibility among nominal Catholics during the 1950s and 1960s, especially in Managua. There, evangelicals had conducted several mass evangelistic crusades in public places, had marched down city streets by the thousands carrying banners with Bible verses and evangelical slogans, had begun dozens of radio programs and even founded an evangelical radio station, along with massive campaigns for Bible distribution, house-to-house visitation, prayer cells and Bible studies, and literacy efforts. The Catholic program to counteract activities by evangelicals was a logical reaction, especially when Nicaragua entered the modern period of mass communications. However, the National Evangelical Council was largely ineffective due to internal strife and the nonparticipation of influential evangelical leaders and their churches, such as those of the Baptist Convention.

Nevertheless, following the disastrous Managua earthquake in 1972, some 40 Protestant denominations and service agencies joined forces to organize the Evangelical Committee for Relief and Development (CEPAD). Later, the General Assembly of CEPAD formed a committee of pastors to promote interdenominational activities through a socio-pastoral action department. This committee, called RIPEN (Interdenominational Representatives of Evangelical Pastors in Nicaragua), organized regional pastoral committees in many parts of the country. CEPAD held training seminars, workshops and inspirational retreats and conferences, at both the national and regional levels, during the 1970s.

In the new environment following the overthrow of the Somoza dictatorship in 1979, there were lingering doubts among many evangelicals about the direction the Sandinista government was headed and about the enthusiastic support given by CEPAD and RIPEN to the Junta of National Reconciliation. Consequently, a group of about 50 evangelical pastors from a dozen or so small independent churches, but also from a few of the larger denominations, decided to form a new association of pastors in Managua during February 1980. This organization was called the National Council of Evangelical Pastors of Nicaragua (CNPEN), composed of individual pastors and not associations of churches (denominations) like CEPAD.

A national study of the Protestant movement in 1979, conducted by INDEF-CEPAD as part of the Central American Socio-Religious Studies Project (PROCADES), reported a total of 1,531 Protestant congregations (churches and missions) with 78,387 baptized members among 72 church associations (denominations and independent church bodies). It also revealed that the Pacific Region of the country, with 63.5 percent of the population, contained 52.3 percent of the Protestant congregations; the North-Central Region, with 29.4 percent of the population, contained 23.3 percent of the Protestant congregations; and the Atlantic Region, with 7.1 percent of the population, contained 24.5 percent of the Protestant congregations.

The main Protestant denominations in Nicaragua in 1979, according to the National Protestant Church Directory produced by INDEF-CEPAD in 1980, were the Moravian Church in Nicaragua (123 congregations with 12,950 members), Assemblies of God (186 congregations with 8,500 members), the Seventh-day Adventist Church (83 congregations with 6,073 members), Church of God (Cleveland, Tennessee) (116 congregations with 5,250 members), Baptist Convention of Nicaragua (174 congregations with 4,659 members), Baptist International Mission (21 congregations with 3,040 members), Apostolic Church of Faith in Jesus Christ (60 congregations with 3,600 members), the independent United Pentecostal Evangelical Mission—a split from the Assemblies of God in the mid-1950s (49 congregations with 3,004 members), and the Free Apostolic Church (43 congregations with about 3,000 members). Pentecostals represented 45 percent of all Protestants; the Adventists, 7.8 percent; liturgical groups (Lutheran, Episcopalian and Reformed-Presbyterian), 2.4 percent; other non-Pentecostal denominations (Moravian, Baptist, Brethren, Church of Christ, Nazarene, Central American Mission–related churches, Mennonite, etc.) 44.2 percent; and unclassified groups, 0.6 percent.

The National Protestant Church Directory, produced by INDEF-Nicaragua in 1998, reported 220 Protestant church associations and at least 113 independent churches in Nicaragua in 1997, for a total of 4,402 churches with a Protestant population of 534,284, or 12.2 percent of the national population (1995 census). Geographically, it also revealed that the Pacific Region of the country, with 56.6 percent of the population, contained 46.5 percent of the Protestant congregations; the North-Central Region, with 31.1 percent of the population, contained 31.8 percent of the Protestant congregations; and the Atlantic Region, with 13 percent of the population, contained 21.7 percent of the Protestant congregations.

The largest Protestant denominations in 1997 were the Assemblies of God (603 congregations with 65,315 members), the Moravian Church (144 congregations with 52,274 members), Full Gospel Church of God (Cleveland, Tennessee) (363 congregations with 21,308 members), United Pentecostal Evangelical Mission

Nicaragua

Religion	Followers in 1970	Followers in 2010	% of Population	Annual % growth 2000–2010	Followers in 2025	Followers in 2050
Christians	2,380,000	5,597,000	96.0	1.32	6,711,000	7,624,000
Roman Catholics	2,168,000	5,000,000	85.7	1.00	5,800,000	6,350,000
Protestants	118,000	1,050,000	18.0	3.57	1,350,000	1,600,000
Independents	19,700	420,000	7.2	3.17	650,000	880,000
Spiritists	4,000	85,000	1.5	1.35	104,000	130,000
Agnostics	3,800	94,000	1.6	3.19	180,000	310,000
Ethnoreligionists	2,000	27,500	0.5	1.35	32,000	30,000
Baha'is	2,800	12,000	0.2	1.35	20,000	30,000
Buddhists	1,000	7,800	0.1	1.35	12,000	20,000
Atheists	500	3,000	0.1	1.35	6,000	10,000
Chinese folk	1,000	3,000	0.1	1.35	4,500	8,000
New religionists	200	1,100	0.0	1.34	2,000	3,000
Muslims	0	1,000	0.0	1.37	3,000	4,000
Jews	200	200	0.0	1.36	200	200
Total population	**2,395,000**	**5,832,000**	**100.0**	**1.35**	**7,075,000**	**8,169,000**

(273 congregations with 19,200 members), Pentecostal Church of God of Puerto Rico (211 congregations with 12,529 members), Apostolic Church of Faith in Jesus Christ (187 congregations with 12,122 members), Church of God of Prophecy (170 congregations with 11,870 members), Baptist Convention of Nicaragua (112 congregations with 10,158 members), Assembly of Christian Churches from New York City (98 congregations with 8,321 members), Pentecostal Mission of Christian Churches—a split from the United Pentecostal Evangelical Mission in 1975 (117 congregations with 6,024 members), Free Apostolic Churches (90 congregations with 5,727 members), and Church of the Nazarene (98 congregations with 5,066 members). All other Protestant denominations reported fewer than 5,000 members each in 1997.

Also, the 1998 National Protestant Church Directory listed 1,182 congregations in the city of Managua, which had a population of 1,093,760 in 1995. By comparison, in 1979, there were only 253 Protestant congregations in the city of Managua with a population of 511,767, according to the PROCADES study.

Moravian and Anglican-Episcopal communities are concentrated on the Atlantic coast, while other evangelical churches dominate the Pacific and North-Central regions. There is a strong correlation between ethnicity and religion within the various regions. Creoles (Afro-Caribbean) predominate in the coastal towns where English-speaking congregations were established by Baptist and Methodist immigrants from the British West Indies during the 19th and 20th centuries, whereas Seventh-day Adventist missionaries from the United States first arrived in 1904. Most of the other Protestant denominations that now exist in Zelaya Department (now divided into the North and South Atlantic Autonomous regions) did not begin work there until after 1950, and most of their congregations are Spanish-speaking. Amerindians (Miskito, Rama, and Sumo) who live along the Caribbean coast are more likely to belong to Moravian, Anglican-Episcopal, or Seventh-day Adventist churches.

Some evangelical denominations (mainly Pentecostal) have a strong presence in the remote towns of the North-Central Region and South Atlantic Autonomous Region, where Spanish-speaking migrants arrived to clear the forest and create new communities and farms since the 1940s. However, the North-Central Region of the country experienced the most significant Protestant church growth in Nicaragua between 1979 and 1997 (18 years). In 1979, the North-Central Region, with 29.4 percent of the population, had 23.3 percent of the Protestant congregations, whereas in 1997, the North-Central Region, with 31.1 percent of the population, had 31.8 percent of the Protestant congregations.

According to research conducted by the Latin American Socio-Religious Studies Program (PROLADES, the geographically expanded version of PROCADES), the highest rate of Protestant church growth in Nicaragua took place during the 1970s (12.2 percent annually), which corresponds to the period of greatest civil conflict between the Sandinistas and the Somoza dictatorship. The proportion of Pentecostal adherents in Nicaragua increased from 44.8 percent of all Protestants in 1979, to 51.5 percent in 1991, and to 55.7 percent in 1997; whereas the evangelical non-Pentecostal proportion decreased from 44.5 percent in 1979, to 34.7 percent in 1991, and to 32.4 percent in 1997. Therefore, the evidence shows that Pentecostal membership was growing more rapidly than non-Pentecostal membership between 1979 and 1997.

In 2007, the largest Protestant denomination in Nicaragua was the Assemblies of God with more than 860 congregations and an estimated 200,000 baptized members (mainly Spanish-speaking). Also, the Assemblies of God has a megachurch with more than 10,000 members in Managua. The second largest denomination was the Moravian Church with 188 congregations and 82,944 members (predominantly among Miskitos).

Today, there are four private Protestant universities that operate with official government authorization: the Nicaraguan Polytechnic University (founded by Baptists), Martin Luther King Evangelical University (nondenominational), the Adventist University (founded by Seventh-day Adventists), and Bluefields Indian and Caribbean University (founded by Moravians). Also present are dozens of evangelical Bible institutes and several theological seminaries that train pastors and lay workers.

Many of the more conservative Protestant denominations are associated with the Consejo Nacional Evangélico de Nicaragua (National Evangelical Council), which is affiliated with the Latin American Confraternity of Evangelicals (CONELA) and the World Evangelical Alliance (WEA). The Baptist Convention and the Moravian Church are the only members of the Latin American Council of Churches (CLAI) in Nicaragua, which is affiliated with the World Council of Churches (WCC).

Other Christian Groups Also present in Nicaragua are the following non-Protestant Christian groups: Jehovah's Witnesses (322 congregations and 19,003 adherents in 2005); the Church of Jesus Christ of Latter-day Saints (founded in 1953; reported 92 congregations and 59,886 adherents in 2007); the Light of the World Church (from Guadalajara, Mexico); Philadelphia Church of God; the Universal Church of the Kingdom of God and the God Is Love Pentecostal Church (from Brazil); and the Voice of the Cornerstone, Mita Congregation and the People of Amos (from Puerto Rico). The Growing in Grace International Ministry (with headquarters in Miami, Florida) claims to have at least 1,000 members in Nicaragua and has been active since 1997.

Immigrant groups include Palestinian Christians (Eastern Orthodox) whose ancestors came to Central America in the early 1900s, as well as Chinese and Korean Christians who arrived after the 1960s. Several other Christian groups (Eastern- and Western-rite) are reported to exist in Nicaragua as well: the Orthodox Apostolic Catholic Church–Virgin of Perpetual Help Mission (Padre Basilios Victorino Castro Mejías) and the Orthodox Church of the East/Church of Utrecht in America. The latter group was founded in the United States by Richard A. Marchenna (1932–1982), who was also associated with the Old Roman Catholic Church; he was succeeded by Derek Lang of the episcopal diocese of Nicaragua. The Nicaraguan Mission operates St. Martin's Seminary in La Esperanza, Zelaya. In addition, the Eastern Orthodox Catholic Church has one "religious community" of monks and nuns, the Monastic Community of Saint Basil, located at St. John's Monastery in Nicaragua. Its headquarters are at Our Lady of Sitka Monastery in Cleveland, Ohio.

Additional Religious Groups World religions in Nicaragua include the Baha'i Faith; Buddhism: Bodhichitta Buddhist Center, Compassion Buddhist Center, Paget Sayers Buddhist Center; Hinduism: Devanand Yoga Center, International Society for Krishna Consciousness, International Sri Sathya Sai Baba Organization, the transcendental Meditation Movement (now led by the Global Country for World Peace; Islam, and Judaism (see below); Western Esoteric Tradition: Ancient and Mystical Order Rosae Crucis (AMORC),

Grand Universal Fraternity–Order of Aquarius (from Venezuela), and the Universal Gnostic Movement (Samael Aun Weor); Spiritualist-Psychic-New Age movements: Ishaya Techniques, Kardec School of Spiritualism, and Unification movement (Reverend Sun Myung Moon). In addition, there are numerous psychics, mediums, clairvoyants, and astrologers who announce their services in local newspapers.

Although there are few adherents of pre-Columbian religions in the country, there has been a "freedom movement" within the Moravian Church to allow some Amerindian spiritual expression, often through music. Animistic groups include traditional Amerindian religions among the Miskito, Sumo, and Rama; Myalism-Obeah among Creoles; Garifuna religion (Afro-Amerindian) among the inhabitants of Sandy Bay, located north of Bluefields; and "popular Catholicism" among the Hispanic population (syncretistic), which includes the use of magic, witchcraft (*brujería*), folk healing (*curanderismo*), and spiritual guides (*chamanismo*).

The Jewish community has only about 50 adherents (including expatriates); they gather for religious holidays and Sabbath dinners but do not have an ordained rabbi or a synagogue. According to community members, the last synagogue in the country was firebombed by a Sandinista street mob in 1978.

There are approximately 1,200 to 1,500 Muslims in Nicaragua, mostly Sunnis who are resident aliens or naturalized citizens from Palestine, Libya and Iran.

Clifton L. Holland

See also: American Baptist Churches in the U.S.A; Ancient and Mystical Order Rosae Crucis; Apostolic Church of Faith in Jesus Christ of Mexico; Assemblies of God; Baptist Convention of Nicaragua; Church of God (Cleveland, Tennessee); Church of God of Prophecy; Church of Jesus Christ of Latter-day Saints; Church of the Nazarene; Episcopal Church; Franciscans; Garifuna Religion; Global Country of World Peace; International Society for Krishna Consciousness; Jehovah's Witnesses; Jesuits; Mita Congregation; Moravian Church in Nicaragua; Roman Catholic Church; Seventh-day Adventist Church; Spiritism; Spiritualism; Unification Movement; Universal Church of the Kingdom of God; World Council of Churches; World Evangelical Alliance.

References

Dussell, Enrique, et al. *Historia General de la Iglesia en América Latina.* Vol. 6, *América Central.* Salamanca, Spain: Ediciones Sígueme, 1985.

Gooren, Henri. "Latter-day Saints under Siege: The Unique Experience of Nicaraguan Mormons." *Dialogue: A Journal of Mormon Thought* 40, no. 3 (Fall 2007): 134–155.

Grimes, Barbara F., ed. *Ethnologue: Languages of the World.* 12th ed. Dallas, TX: Summer Institute of Linguistics, 1992.

Holland, Clifton L., ed. *World Christianity: Central America and the Caribbean.* Monrovia, CA: MARC-World Vision, 1981.

INDEF-CEPAD. *Directorio de Iglesias, Organizaciones y Ministerios del Movimiento Protestante: Nicaragua.* San José, Costa Rica: INDEF, 1980.

INDEF. *Directorio de las Iglesias Protestantes en Nicaragua, 1996–1997.* Managua, Nicaragua: Departamento de Investigaciones Socio-Religiosos, Instituto Nicaragüense de Evangelismo a Fondo, 1998.

Matamoros Ruiz, Bartolomé. *Historia de las Asambleas de Dios en Nicaragua.* Managua, Nicaragua: Distribudora Vida, 1984.

Millett, Richard. *Guardians of the Dynasty: A History of the U.S. Created Guardia Nacional de Nicaragua and the Somoza Family.* Maryknoll, NY: Orbis Books, 1977.

PROLADES–Religion in the Americas Database. "Religion in Nicaragua," http://www.prolades.com/cra/regions/cam/nic/ingles/nica-rd.htm.

Revista de Historia del Protestantismo Nicaragüense. Managua, Nicaragua: CIEETS, September 1993.

Rudolph, James D. *Nicaragua: A Country Guide.* Washington, DC: U.S. Government Printing Office, 1982.

U. S. Department of State. *International Religious Freedom Report 2007: Nicaragua.* http://www.state.gov/g/drl/rls/irf/2007/90261.htm.

Nichiren

1222–1282

Nichiren was a 13th-century Buddhist reformer whose advocacy of the exclusive superiority of the Lotus Sutra, one of the more important Mahayan Buddhist scriptures, led to the formation of a new school of Japanese Buddhist life. Nichiren Buddhism is best known for its central practice, the calling upon the Buddha through the Lotus Sutra by reciting the mantra, "nam myoho renge kyo." Nichiren taught that as "myoho-renge-kyo" was the title of the Lotus Sutra, it represented the essence of the sutra's teaching.

Nichiren was born Zennichi-maro in Tojo Village, Awa Province, Japan. As a boy of but 11 years, he began his study of Buddhism at a nearby temple of Tendai Buddhism. He was ordained in 1237, and subsequently moved to Kamakura, which became his base for travels across Japan to study at different centers.

Tendai Buddhists had developed an approach to the many Buddhist scriptures that ranked them hierarchically, with the Lotus Sutra ranked at the top. Nichiren accepted the central Tendai observation that the Lotus Sutra contained the highest Buddhist teachings, and hence was superior to the other Buddhist sutras, but took the teaching one step further and concluded that the Lotus Sutra had supplanted the other sutras. It was all that a Buddhist needed. Simultaneously, he concluded that he had been entrusted with the mission of Bodhisattva Superior Practices, an important character in the Lotus Sutra to whom the task of propagating the Dharma in the Latter Days had been entrusted. Nichiren assumed that his work included emphasizing the superiority of the Lotus Sutra while at the same time pointing out the errors of the other Buddhists, including the very popular Pure Land Buddhist groups and his former Tendai colleagues.

Launching his mission in 1253 at Seicho-ji, a temple on Mount Kiyosumi near his birthplace, he

Nichiren Calming the Storm by Utagawa Kuniyoshi, ca. 1835, portrays the Japanese Mahayana master as one capable of influencing natural events. (Historical Picture Archive/Corbis)

assumed the new name by which he would henceforth be known—Nichiren (Sun Lotus). He also preached an initial sermon on the Lotus Sutra that included an attack on the Pure Land Buddhists and their central practice of reciting the *Nembutsu* (the mantra by which they called upon Amida Buddha in hopes that they would be delivered to the western paradise [or Pure Land] over which he was believed to have hegemony). The untactful attack led to an immediate reaction by the local Pure Land believers. Nichiren immediately retreated and went back to Kamakura. He spent the rest of his decades recruiting an initial following that included the first members of what would become the inner core of monk-disciples.

In 1260, while residing in Kamakura, now the capital of Japan, Nichiren renewed his public debate with the Pure Land Buddhists. In 1260 he took the occasion of a crisis that Japan had experienced due to a series of natural disasters to present his treatise *On Establishing the Correct Teaching for the Peace of the Land* to government authorities. He suggested that Japan's problems derived from the widespread slander that he and his followers of the true Buddhism had experienced at the hands of the Pure Land Buddhists and others. He warned of further possible disasters. As people learned of the content of his writing, an angry mob sought Nichiren and he chose to leave the city. When feelings seemed to calm, he tried to return, but the shogunate sent him into exile on the Izu Peninsula, where he remained for the next three years. Finally the exile order was lifted and he was allowed to return to his hometown.

Back in Kamakura in 1268, Nichiren penned a letter reminding the shogun and the public that eight years earlier he had predicted the current threat, namely, an imminent invasion by Mongol forces. When a drought hit in 1271, he used the occasion to ridicule Ryokan, a leading Shingon Buddhist in Kamakura, questioning his ability to have any effect in ending the drought. Nichiren was arrested and threatened with execution, though in the end the shogun again exiled him for three years. Nichiren made use of the time to write some of his more important and substantive writings.

When he returned to Kamakura in 1274, the shogun offered him the opportunity to establish and have Nichiren Buddhism recognized on an equal footing with the other Buddhist schools. He rejected the offer and asserted that his teachings were superior and could not be reduced to just another Buddhist variant. He abandoned Kamakura for Mount Minobu, in Yamanashi Prefecture, where he founded the Kuon-ji Temple. He would remain there until just before his death.

Nichiren spent his last years writing and training the small group of disciples who would lead the movement after his death. It was also during this time (1279) that he inscribed the giant mandala-like Object of Worship, the Gohozon, which he dedicated to the attainment of Buddhahood by all humanity. Early in the new decade, his health began to fail. After making arrangements to transfer leadership to six senior disciples, in 1282, for the first time since his arrival, he left the mountain to visit a hot springs in hope of recovering his health. He died along the route.

After Nichiren's death, his disciples had a falling out over the care of his tomb on Mount Minobu. One of the six, Nikko (1246–1333), accused the others of neglecting the tomb and then went on to suggest that they were becoming tolerant of wrong practices. Nikko broke relations with his brethren and established himself separately at a temple near Mount Fuji. The effort of the five disciples would be continued by the Nichiren-shu, the largest group of Nichiren's followers. Nikko's following organized as what became known as the Nichiren Shoshu, or the Fuji School. In the 20th century, the Nichiren Shoshu would see the formation of a lay organization now known as the Soka Gakkai International. In the years after World War II, Soka Gakkai International became a large Japanese phenomenon and spread Nichiren's teachings worldwide. It became the largest Buddhist group in many Western countries. Then in the 1980s, the Soka Gakkai split with the Nichiren Shoshu and has now become a separate third large independent Nichiren group.

Edward A. Irons

See also: Mahayana Buddhism; Nichiren Shoshu; Nichirenshu; Pure Land Buddhism; Soka Gakkai International; Tian Tai/Tendai Buddhism.

References

Masaharu, Anesaki. *Nichiren, the Buddhist Prophet.* Cambridge: Harvard University Press, 1916.

Montgomery, Daniel B. *Fire in the Lotus: The Dynamic Buddhism of Nichiren*. London: HarperCollins, 1991.

Nichiren. *The Writing of Nichiren Daishonin*. Tokyo: Soka Gakkai, 2003.

Petzold, Bruno. *Buddhist Prophet Nichiren: A Lotus in the Sun.* Tokyo: Hokke Janaru, 1978.

Rodd, Laurel Rasplica, ed. *Nichiren: Selected Writings*. Honolulu: University of Hawaii Press, 1980.

SGI-USA Study Department. *The Untold History of the Fuji School: The True Story of Nichiren Shoshu*. Santa Monica: World Tribune Press, 2000.

Yamblosky, Philip B. *Selected Writings of Nichiren*. New York: Columbia University Press, 1990.

Nichiren Shoshu

Nichiren Shoshu is a Japanese Buddhist religious sect founded by Nikko (1246–1333), one of the disciples of Nichiren (1222–1282). After the death of Nichiren, his disciples agreed that the guardianship of his tomb should rotate among his six senior disciples. Two years later when the rotation finished, Nikko broke away from the Nichirenshu and in 1290 founded Taiseikiji Temple, the present head temple of Nichiren Shoshu, at the foot of Mount Fuji. Over the centuries other Nichiren sects also developed. After the Maiji Restoration in 1868, followers in Nikko's lineage were forced into association with the other Nichiren sects. However, in 1900 it became independent and took the name Nichiren Shoshu in 1912.

In the 1920s, Tsunesaburo Makiguchi (1871–1944), the founder of Soka Gakkai, a Nichiren Shoshu lay association, was converted to Nichiren Shoshu. Although remaining small through the 1930s, after World War II Soka Gakkai International emerged as an aggressive proselytizing organization through which Nichiren Shoshu experienced dramatic growth and spread worldwide. Although Soka Gakkai had provided funds and buildings to Nichiren Shoshu, friction between the two organizations occurred almost from the beginning of the foundation of Soka Gakkai.

The conflict grew through the 1980s, and in 1991 Nichiren Shoshu pronounced excommunication on Soka Gakkai, on the grounds that Soka Gakkai had gone against Nichiren Shoshu teachings. The process of separating the two organizations took several years, and in 1997 the leadership of Nichiren Shoshu ordered all of its members to completely disaffiliate with Soka Gakkai by November 30, 1997, or lose their membership status. In the break, the majority of members (especially those residing outside Japan) adhered to Soka Gakkai, but a large minority of the non-Japanese believers remained loyal, and Nichiren Shoshu has retained its presence throughout the Japanese diaspora.

Members of Nichiren Shoshu believe that in *mappo* (the last period of history: a degenerate age in which the Buddhist law is no longer observed), only Nichiren and the Lotus Sutra can save this world, and that the government should endorse Nichiren Buddhism and establish it as the state religion—a principle known as *obutsu myogo* (a polity fundamentally united with Buddhism). This policy has led Nichiren Shoshu into the political arena, and in the last half of the 20th century it had close relations with a new political party. That party, the Komei Kai, adhered to Soka Gakkai after 1991. It has officially dropped any organizational ties to any religious organizations in the wake of the changes in Japan following the Aum Shinrikyo disaster in 1995.

Nichiren Shoshu reveres Nichiren as the religious founder (*shuso*) and Nikko as the sectarian founder (*haso*). As with other Nichirenist sects and movements, chanting "daimoku: namu myoho rengekyo" (adoration to the Lotus Sutra) is of central importance because it is believed that the invocation has a miraculous power to fulfill one's wish and lead to enlightenment.

Nichiren Shoshu is currently led by Abe Nikken. Its reported membership in 2000 was 338,000. It is a member of the Japan Buddhist Federation. In the United States, there are six temples, including one in Hawaii.

Nichiren Shoshu Headquarters
Taisekiji, 2057 Kamijo
Fujinomiya-shi, Shizuoka Prefecture 418-0116
Japan

http://www.cebunet.com/nst/ (in English)
http://www.nichirenshoshu.or.jp/ (in Japanese)

Keishin Inaba

See also: Aum Shinrikyô/Aleph; Japan Buddhist Federation; Nichiren; Nichirenshu; Soka Gakkai International.

References

The Doctrines and Practice of Nichiren Shoshu. Fujinomiya, Shizuoka. Japan: Nichiren Shoshu Overseas Bureau, 2002.

Hori, Ichiro, et al., eds. *Japanese Religion: A Survey by the Agency for Cultural Affairs*. Tokyo: Kodansha International, 1972.

Wilson, Bryan, and Karel Dobbelaere. *A Time to Chant: The Soka Gakkai Buddhists in Britain.* Oxford: Oxford University Press, 1994.

Nichirenshu

The term "Nichirenshu" refers to a collection of Japanese Buddhist sects that have grown out of the life and work of Nichiren (1222–1282). Nichiren studied Tendai Buddhism at Mount Hiei and came to believe that the Lotus Sutra, the most famous Buddhist Sanskrit text, was also the most important Buddhist scripture and that it taught the ways of transformation, bliss, and law. Followers were taught to call upon the Lotus Sutra through the Daimoku, a chanting of "namu myoho renge kyo" (adoration to the Lotus Sutra). The repetition of this phrase is the most distinctive practice of the Nichirenshu and groups derived from it, and it is believed that its frequent use has a miraculous power to lead to enlightenment. Worship and repetition of the Daimoku is performed in front of the Gohonzon, a mandala upon which the chant is inscribed along with the names of various Buddhas, bodhisattvas, and other Buddhist deities.

In 1260, Nichiren presented the teaching of *Rissho ankoku ron* (the establishment of righteousness and the security of the nation), stating that Japan would suffer from natural calamities and social ills if the government did not adopt the teaching. He also presented a view of world history divided into three millennia. The first, *shobo*, began with the Buddha's death and constituted the period of true law. The second, *zobo*, or image law, followed. The third period, which began in 1052 CE, is called *mappo*, the end of the law. It will last, not just 1,000 years, but 10,000. During mappo, the Lotus Sutra is the way of salvation.

During his lifetime, Nichiren harshly attacked other religious groups, and in turn Nichiren's sect itself later split into a number of subsects, including Kenpon Hokkeshu, Nipponzan Myohoji, Nichiren Shoshu, and Hokkeshu. There are also numerous Nichiren-related new religions such as Reiyukai, Rissho Kosei Kai, and Soka Gakkai International.

The head temple of Nichirenshu is Minobesan Kuonji, located in Yamanashi Prefecture. It is currently led by Fujii Nikko. With a membership in 2000 of 3,845,986, it is currently one of the largest Buddhist groups in Japan. It is also a member of the Japan Buddhist Federation. It sponsors Rissho University in Tokyo and Minobusan Junior College in Minobu, Yamanashi-ken.

Nichirenshu has a significant following overseas, especially in Korea, the United States, and Brazil. In 2008, there were 15 Nichirenshu temples in the United States and one in Canada.

Nichirenshu Headquarters
Ikegami Honganji
1-32-15 Ikegami
Ota-ku, Tokyo 146-8544
Japan
http://www.nichiren-shu.org/ (in English)
http://www.nichiren.or.jp/ (headquarters in Tokyo, in Japanese)

Keishin Inaba

See also: Japan Buddhist Federation; Nichiren; Nichiren Shoshu; Nipponzan Myohoji; Reiyukai; Rissho Kosei-kai; Soka Gakkai International.

References

Agency for Cultural Affairs. *Shukyo Nenkan*. Tokyo: Gyosei, 2001.

Anesaki, Masaharu. *History of Japanese Religion.* London: Kegan Paul Trench Trubner & Co., 1930.

Anesaki, Masaharu. *Nichiren, the Buddhist Prophet.* Cambridge: Harvard University Press, 1949.

Buddhist Denominations and Schools in Japan. Tokyo: Bukkyo Dendo Kyokai, 1984.

Christensen, J. A. *Nichiren: Leader of Buddhist Reformation in Japan*. Fremont, CA: Jain Publishing Company, 2001.

Nichiren-Buddhist Service Companion. Chicago: Headquarters of the Nichiren Buddhist Temple of North America, 1968.

■ Niger

Niger is a large landlocked country in central West Africa. It is surrounded by Algeria, Libya, Chad, Nigeria, Benin, Burkina Faso, and Mali. Four-fifths of its 489,000 square miles of territory is in the Sahara Desert, and thus most of its 12,273,000 people reside in the southern part of the country immediately north of the border with Nigeria. This area has been inhabited for several thousand years. A kingdom, the Nok Empire, arose in southern Niger and had hegemony for many centuries prior to its decline in the sixth century. Its cities were important stops on the trade routes across the Sahara to the north and eastward to the Nile River valley. Successive regimes appeared through the centuries of the modern era.

The French entered the area in the 19th century, in 1922 annexing Niger as a French colony. They attempted to introduce cash crops for export, leading to periodic food shortages. At the time it became an independent nation in 1960, Niger was among the poorest of the African nations. On the heels of a major drought in the early 1970s, the army took control of the government and introduced a number of reforms. An economic boom followed, which ended in 1980 with a fall in prices of uranium, one of the country's few mineral assets. (Based on forged documents, in 2003 Niger was accused of attempting to sell uranium to Saddam Hussein, then the ruler of Iraq, for the purpose of creating nuclear weapons.)

Children sing at the small Evangelical church in the town of Maradi, Niger. (AP Photo/Schalk van Zuydam)

NIGER

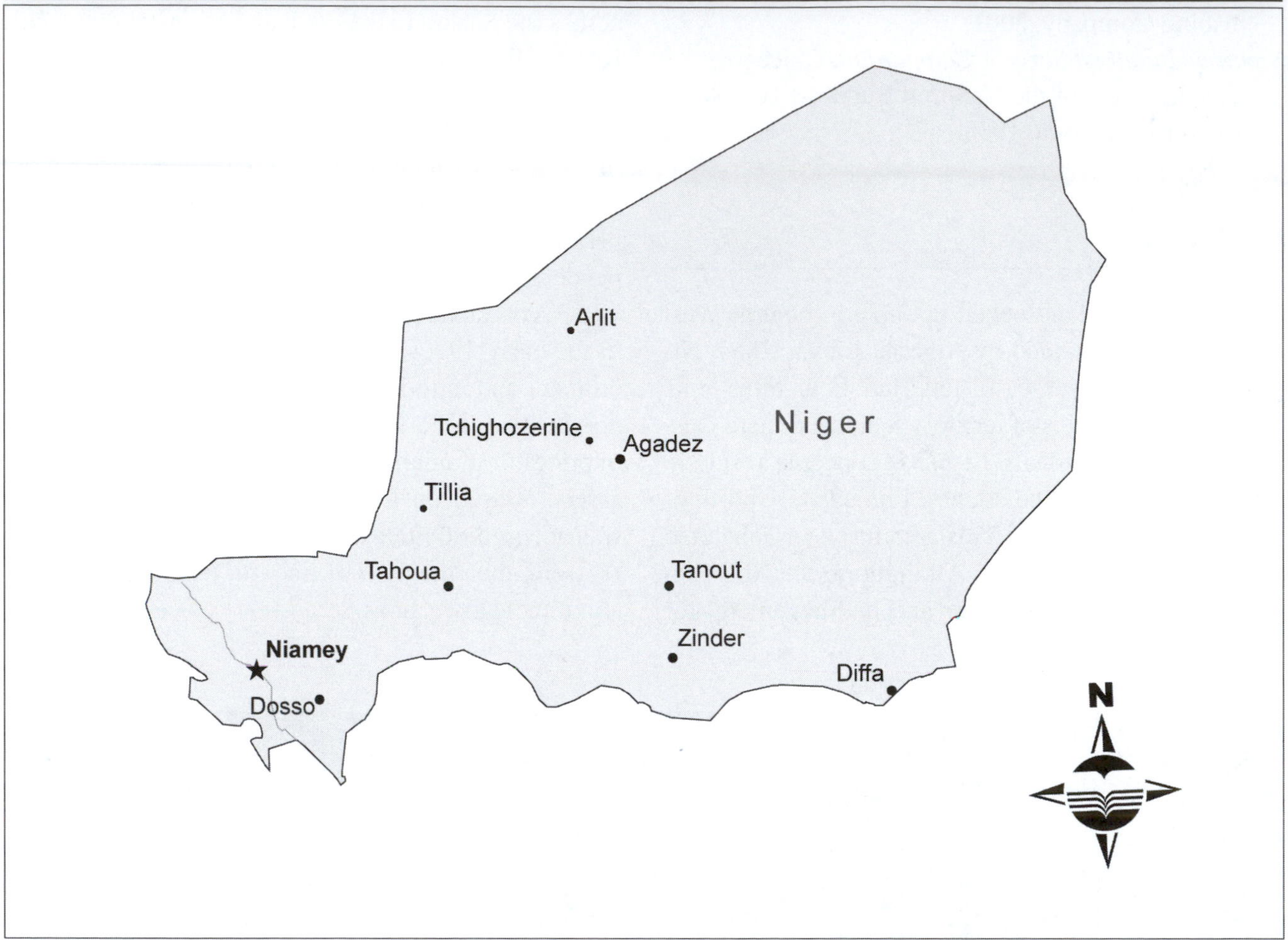

Islam entered Niger in the 11th century along the trade routes from the Mediterranean Coast. Most Muslims are of the Sunni Malikite School, but the Tijaniyya Sufi Order is especially strong among the Tuareg, Kanuri, Fulani, and Hausa peoples. A school for the training of religious leaders is found in Say, a Muslim holy city. Although Islam largely replaced the traditional beliefs of the various Native people of Niger, traditional beliefs remain strong among the Kurfei and Mauri peoples. And resistance to Islam is notable among the Serma-Songhai and Beriberi.

It was not until the 20th century that Christianity arrived in Niger. The Sudan Interior Mission, an independent evangelical sending agency, sent its representatives into the area in 1923. They opened the initial mission station at Zinder the next year. Their work resulted in the present-day Evangelical Church of Niger, which supports a hospital at Galmi, one of the important medical facilities in the country, and a Bible school in Niamey. In 1991 the church faced a major schism that led to the founding of two additional denominations, the Union of Evangelical Protestant Churches of Niger and the Evangelical Church Salama of Niger.

Evangelical Baptist Missions, a sending agency dedicated to the spread of Christianity in French-speaking countries, began work in 1929 that led to the present-day Union des Églises Evangéliques Baptistes. A rather limited spectrum of Protestant churches entered through the remainder of the century: the Cherubim and Seraphim, one of several African Initiated Churches from Nigeria, and the New Apostolic Church from Germany showing some limited response. No

Niger

Religion	Followers in 1970	Followers in 2010	% of Population	Annual % growth 2000–2010	Followers in 2025	Followers in 2050
Muslims	3,634,000	14,616,000	92.6	3.66	24,858,000	51,346,000
Ethnoreligionists	565,000	1,100,000	7.0	2.70	1,258,000	1,567,000
Christians	16,900	57,100	0.4	2.12	94,500	179,000
Roman Catholics	13,400	15,000	0.1	–3.79	17,000	25,000
Independents	1,000	27,000	0.2	5.40	45,000	90,000
Protestants	2,400	14,000	0.1	6.69	30,000	60,000
Agnostics	0	9,200	0.1	4.09	20,000	40,000
Baha'is	800	5,700	0.0	3.58	14,000	25,000
Sikhs	0	3,300	0.0	3.58	4,000	5,000
Atheists	0	200	0.0	3.60	700	1,000
Total population	**4,217,000**	**15,791,000**	**100.0**	**3.58**	**26,250,000**	**53,163,000**

churches or church associations based in Niger are members of the World Council of Churches or the World Evangelical Alliance.

The Roman Catholic Church came to Niger from an earlier base in Dahomey (now Benin) in 1931. It had very little success among the local population, and the great majority of its members are expatriates residing in Niger, many from neighboring African states. Nevertheless, a diocese was created in 1961. In 1972 the ordination of the first Niger priest became a cause for national celebration. Among those in attendance was the grand imam of Niamey, a leading figure in the Muslim community.

There is a small community of the Baha'i Faith in Niger, but other major religious traditions beyond those already mentioned are as yet unrepresented.

J. Gordon Melton

See also: African Initiated (Independent) Churches; Baha'i Faith; Cherubim and Seraphim/Eternal Sacred Order of the Cherubim and Seraphim; Malikite School of Islam; New Apostolic Church; Roman Catholic Church; Tijaniyya Sufi Order; World Council of Churches; World Evangelical Alliance.

References

Aidou, Ousseina. *Engaging Modernity: Muslim Women and the Politics of Agency in Postcolonial Niger*. Madison: University of Wisconsin Press, 2005.

Bauswein, Jean-Jacques, and Lukas Vischner, eds. *The Reformed Family Worldwide: A Survey of Reformed Churches, Theological Schools, and International Organizations*. Grand Rapids, MI: William B. Eerdmans Publishing Company, 1999.

Fugelstad, Finn. *A History of Niger 1850–1960.* Cambridge: Cambridge University Press, 1983.

Masquelier, Adeline. *Prayer Has Spoiled Everything: Possession, Power, and Identity in an Islamic Town of Niger*. Durham, NC: Duke University Press, 2001.

Norris, H. T. *Sufi Mystics of the Niger Desert: Sidi Mahmud and the Hermits of Air*. Oxford: Clarendon Press, 1990.

Stoller, Paul. *Fusion of the Worlds: An Ethnography of Possession among the Songhay of Niger.* Chicago: University of Chicago Press, 1997.

■ Nigeria

Nigeria, with a population of more than 150 million, is the most populous country in sub-Saharan Africa. The country is located in western Africa and has a total area of 356,669 square miles. It shares land borders with the Republic of Benin in the west, Chad and Cameroon in the east, and Niger in the north. Its coast lies on the Gulf of Guinea, a part of the Atlantic Ocean, in the south. Nigeria contains a vast diversity of ethnic and cultural backgrounds, comprising more than 400 languages. There are more than 250 ethnic groups, creating a country of rich ethnic diversity. The largest ethnic groups are the Fulani/Hausa, Yoruba, and Igbo, while the minority groups include Edo, Ijaw, Kanuri, Ibibio, Nupe, and Tiv, to mention a few.

The country gained political independence from the British imperial regime in October 1960. Nigeria is presently comprised of 36 states and the Federal Capital Territory in Abuja. It is a federal constitutional republic with a three-tier system of government comprising the executive, the judiciary, and the legislature. Nigeria reintroduced democracy in 1999, ending a protracted military rule that lasted from 1966 until 1999, and excluding the short-lived second republic between 1979 and 1983, aborted by military dictators who seized power in coups d'état and counter-coups during the Nigerian military juntas of 1966–1979 and 1983–1998.

The religious landscape of this geopolitical entity is highly complex and dynamic. Essentially, it is characterized by a multiplicity of religious traditions, including the traditional local religions and worldviews, the various strands of Christianity and Islam, as well as newer Spiritual Science movements. Many of the most recent manifestations of these various religions have come to be subsumed under the category of new religious movements. Another recent phenomenon that is easily noticeable within Nigeria's multifaith scenario is what has been described elsewhere as civil religion.

Accurate statistics for each tradition are difficult to come by and are largely a matter of conjecture. However, it is evident that the major religions in Nigeria are Christianity and Islam, both influenced in part by indigenous religious traditions. The politicization of religious statistics has become even more controversial with the enduring debate about whether Nigeria is a secular or a religious state. Whatever the case, religious ideas and worldviews continue to shape the ways that Nigerians explain, predict, and control the events and life circumstances that surround them. Religion has served and is still serving as a significant source through which many Nigerians seek understanding of their complex reality and existence, and it serves as a panacea for their various existential problems of day-to-day living.

The indigenous religions (also called ethnoreligions) of the various ethnic and cultural groups in Nigeria are apparently the oldest religious forms in the region. Examples of indigenous religion have come to be referred to, especially in academic circles, by the name of the respective language groups: Yoruban religion, Igbo religion, Edo religion, Kalabari religion, Hausa religion, Tiv religion, and so on. This categorization does not in any way presuppose a kind of uniformity of beliefs and rituals among these peoples. Indigenous religions are more or less localized; some beliefs may be more widespread while others may vary from one ethnic group or subgroup to another. What the categorization suggests instead is an aggregation of shared, similar, and related but sometimes quite different belief and ritual systems, often shaped by particular ethnic and social groups, power structures, and even the characteristics of natural phenomena in each respective locality. The indigenous religions do not lay claim to any specific historical origins but are believed to have been transmitted from one generation to another. One essential characteristic shared by the Nigerian indigenous religions is the belief in a Supreme Being, as well as various divinities, spirits, ancestors, and mysterious powers such as witchcraft, sorcery, and magic. However, it must be noted that the names, attributes, and significance of these supramundane entities may vary from one locality to another. The concept of God is called Olodumare or Olorun among the Yoruba, Osanobua among the Edo, and Chukwu or Chineke among the Igbo.

The description of these groups as "indigenous" or "traditional" does not in any way suggest that they are static and moribund. Their dynamism is partly exemplified by their tendency toward growth and innovation, a development that has given birth to what is now described as neo-traditional movements. A case in point is Ijo Orunmila, a movement founded in the 1930s by Yoruba Christians seeking to re-establish links with their traditional religious heritage. In 1963 the Arousa Cult (Edo National Church), which developed from Bini indigenous religion, fused with another neo-traditional movement, the National Church of Nigeria, to form what is now referred to as Godianism. The Bori Cult, a neo-traditional movement prominent among

A mosque in Abuja, Nigeria. Islam is one of Nigeria's major religions. (iStockPhoto.com)

Hausa women, draws partly on Islamic beliefs and practices. Also significant here are the various transformations of the Nigerian indigenous religions in diaspora, including Santeria, Candomblé, and the numerous Orisa cults. These are only a few examples of the creativity and innovation inherent in these indigenous religions.

The prevailing wave of modernization and social change has resulted in the decline of some features of the indigenous religions even as it has brought about a revitalization and modification of other aspects of the indigenous practices and modes of thought. The claim that Christianity and Islam totally outweighed the indigenous religions in their religious encounter is somewhat problematic. It becomes especially questionable when one considers how and to what extent these "external" religious traditions have engaged the indigenous religions in their attempt to contextualize and to make their messages more intelligible and acceptable to the Nigerian people. The indigenous religious worldview or aspects of it still largely pervade, consciously or unconsciously, the religious outlook and vision of many Nigerians, irrespective of their new religious convictions and background. The pertinence and reality of the indigenous religions for many individuals and communities in contemporary Nigeria are evident in the growing popularity of cults of divinities such as Ogun, Osun, and Oya. Religious festivals such as the Osun Oshogbo festival are gaining prominence among adherents and non-adherents alike, and the annual event is assuming international popularity. Kingship rituals such as the Igue Festival in Benin City, secret societies such as the Ogboni Society in western Nigeria, masquerades such as Egungun and Eyo among the Yoruba, divination, healing, and oracle systems such as Arockukwu among the Igbo and Ifa among the Yoruba are instances of the various ways and avenues through which the indigenous religions manifest their resilience in the face of a complex, multireligious, and rapidly changing society.

Islam touched on the Nigerian soil long before Christianity. It made its debut as early as the 11th century, entering from the interior of the continent across the West African savannahs and the Sahara Desert to the north. Through the activities of Arab and Berber merchants from the western Sudan and North Africa, Islam made inroads in many cities in the north, especially in the Kingdom of Kanem-Bornu. In the late 14th and early 15th centuries, Islam was also introduced through the influence of Wangarawa-Dyula traders in the city-kingdoms of Hausaland. Before the 16th century, Islam in northern Nigeria was very much mixed with Hausa traditional religion. The earliest attempts at propagating Islam produced what remained essentially a religion of the merchants, of the towns, the *ulama* (learned men), and the ruling class. It was only in the 17th century that it started to expand among other segments of the population. By 1700, Islam of the Sunni Malekite School began to generate immense support among all levels of Hausa society. The influence of the religion started to be felt in southwestern Nigeria only in the 18th century through the incursion of Hausa traders.

During the 19th century, a number of reform movements aimed at purifying Islam and more or less characterized by militancy were launched throughout West Africa. Another motivation of these reform movements was to create theocratic states based on *shariah*, the Islamic law. The successful *jihad* (holy war) under the leadership of Uthman Dan Fodio (d. 1817) in 1804 turned Islam into a religion of the masses and further resulted in a theocratic state, the Sokoto Caliphate. In this state there was extensive autonomy for emirates, who recognized the spiritual authority of the caliph (sultan). More than 30 emirates were created during the course of the 19th century. The successful execution of the jihad also enhanced the spread of Islam within and beyond the north. Through military conquest, the Caliphate expanded south into the Middle Belt region, thus leading to the forceful incorporation of other ethnic groups and non-Muslims into the emirates of the Islamic polity.

During the 17th century, the Oyo Kingdom had already been in contact with Hausa Muslims through trade. In 1817 the revolt by the pastoral Fulani, Hausa slaves, and Muslim Yoruba converts in Ilorin dealt a death blow to the Oyo Kingdom, followed by a series of internecine civil wars around Yorubaland. By the 20th century, Islam had spread to northern Yorubaland with an emirate in Ilorin, from where it moved on to other Yoruba towns such as Osogbo, Ibadan, Oyo, and Iwo. Islam experienced hostility in southeastern Nigeria because of the annexation of Ilorin and northern Yorubaland by the Sokoto Caliphate. However, Muslim traders gradually reestablished themselves in Yoruba commercial towns, thus leading to the integration of Yoruba Islam into traditional society. The evangelization of the southwest by Hausa traders and preachers was largely carried out through peaceful means and involved several Islamic organizations. Some of these towns had a predominantly Islamic population, even in the face of competition with Christianity, which was already well established in Yorubaland at the time Islam came. The integration of Islam into Yoruba indigenous culture gave it a distinct character that makes it different from Islam in northern Nigeria.

The diversity and complexity of Islamic movements in Nigeria is partly exemplified by the Sufi orders or brotherhoods. Two major movements that were involved in the Islamization process in Nigeria were the Qadiriyya and the Tijaniyya. The former is much older and has spread widely in northern Nigeria since the 19th century. The Qadiriyya emphasizes intellectual pursuits more than the Tijaniyya and was also introduced in the 19th century. The two brotherhoods have witnessed tension and rivalry for several decades of their existence. Other Islamic organizations oppose these two brotherhoods on the basis of doctrine. Yoruba Muslims have formed various societies whose task is to provide Muslims with a modern education that does not conflict with Islamic values. The Ahmadiyya Muslim movement has made significant impact in the southwest, where it is very popular. In 1923 a group broke away and formed the Ansar-ud-Deen Society. Both movements have enhanced the development of secular education, particularly in southwest Nigeria. The Ansar-ud-Deen was probably the most popular of these Muslim educational organizations. By 1960 it already ran numerous primary and secondary schools and training colleges.

The Izala (Jamaatu Izalat al-Bida) emerged in 1978, enjoining its members to reject innovation and instead work for the preservation of the Sunna. The leading representative of Izala until his death in 1992 was Abubakar Gumi, whose most important concern was to try to unite Muslims politically. However, between 1978 and 1985, many northern Nigerian towns and cities were shaken by the armed insurrections led by Mohammed Marwa Maitatsine (d. 1980) and his Yan Tatsine movement. Maitatsine had a long history of fomenting Islamic unrest in northern Nigeria. The source of his inspiration was the belief, especially in Sufi Islam, that a *mujaddid* (reformer) will arise each century to purify and revitalize Islam. Maitatsine's brand of Islam seemed to largely combine traditional Muslim conceptions with local indigenous elements.

One of the very visible effects of Islam in Nigeria has been the demand for and subsequent declaration of sharia in some states of the federation, a development that has produced protests and huge criticisms from the Christian population. The incessant religious riots in northern Nigeria have been given an added impetus with this recent development. Religion has become a matter of political significance and a source of tension in Nigeria. This religious tension has a clear connection with the growth of uncompromising Muslim and Christian activism. The relationship between Islam and

Christianity has led to a growing culture of religious violence, particularly in northern Nigeria. Since the 1980s, there have been many violent clashes between Muslims and Christians, especially in the northern cities of Kano, Kaduna, Kafanchan, and Zaria. Nigeria provides a fertile ground for exploring the role of religious organizations in civil society and politics. Although there are three major religions, religious and political issues and conflicts have revolved largely around the activities of and the interrelationships between Islam and Christianity. Their involvement in regional and national politics is aptly illustrated by their activities in post-independence politics in Nigeria.

Christianity spread along the West African coast, via the Atlantic Ocean, to the south. The first attempt at planting Christianity in Nigeria was in the late 15th and 16th centuries, a period that witnessed the activities of Portuguese Catholics in the Warri and Benin kingdoms and the Niger Delta area. The Portuguese missionaries placed political and economic considerations over and above religious interests, leading to a dismal failure of this first attempt at evangelization. A more profound attempt at Christianization was made in the 19th century, especially following the abolition of the obnoxious trade in human slaves.

Many of the liberated slaves who had already converted to Christianity worked with foreign missions and later became the "native agents" in the eventual spread of Christianity among their own people. An example is the case of Samuel Adjai Crowther (ca. 1809–1891) and his missionary role within the Church Missionary Society (Anglican) in Yorubaland. Christianity was accompanied by Western education, a feature that was immensely attractive to potential converts. The success of this mission attempt was witnessed along the coastal towns of Lagos, Badagry, and Abeokuta, where a large number of people were attracted to Christianity and the accompanying Western education. This impact, which was first witnessed in Yorubaland, later spread to the Niger Delta and eastern Nigeria. The early missionaries who spearheaded this second evangelization process were Anglicans of the Church Missionary Society, Methodists, Baptists, and later Roman Catholics. These different bodies competed among themselves in a bid to carve out spheres of influence. With the intensification of mission work into the hinterland in the early 20th century, Christianity expanded rapidly throughout the southwest and the central areas of Nigeria.

The British administration, under the system of indirect rule, and the emirates deliberately prohibited Christian evangelization in Muslim areas. As a result, Western education developed very slowly in northern Nigeria as compared to the southwestern part of the country. It was only at the latter part of the 20th century that Christianity started to make inroads in the north, already the stronghold of Islam. The missionary enterprise to northern Nigeria was carried out partly by the Sudan Interior Mission (SIM). The SIM, an independent sending agency, devoted its energies to spreading the Christian gospel in northern Nigeria via church planting, literature development and dissemination, general education, and medical work. The SIM gave birth to a number of churches that together adopted the name Evangelical Church of West Africa (ECWA).

Just as the West African coast was the first home and indigenous breeding ground for the mission churches in the 19th century, so it fulfilled the same function for the indigenous African churches in the 20th century. African instituted churches can be understood basically by examining three phases of development. The first and earliest phase refers to the group of churches that broke away from the existing mission churches owing to a number of irreconcilable issues. These flourished mainly in South Africa (Ethiopian Churches) and West Africa (African Churches) in the 19th century. They all emerged out of similar circumstances, such as rigid white (European) missionary control and domination, discrimination against local African leadership, disputes over resources, a general feeling of marginalization among educated Africans, and apartheid (mainly in the South African context). Some of the churches that seceded from the historic churches in Nigeria are the United Native African Church (1891) and the African Church (Bethel) (1901) from the Anglican Church, and the United African Methodist Church (1917) from the Methodist Church. One notable feature of these churches was that in spite of the change in church leadership, they were still tied to the apron

NIGERIA

strings of the mission churches in their liturgical and hierarchical structures. Some of them still depended largely on the parent churches for financial resources.

The 1920s and 1930s witnessed the second wave of new beginnings within African Christianity, which include the Aladura churches in Nigeria. These are also variously referred to as "prophetic" and "healing" churches. The most dramatic aspect of 20th-century Christianity in Nigeria was the growth of the prophetic churches. These churches share certain basic characteristics in their worldview that helped to create a rather Nigerian brand of Christianity. These basic features include the centrality of the Bible, prayers, healing, prophecy, visions and dreams, elaborate rituals, flexible modes of worship, unstereotyped liturgy, and a charismatic leader (that is, a prophet or prophetess). The prophetic churches embrace a functional theology, and their pragmatic approach to life and existential problems endeared them to many Nigerians. Though they utterly condemn and reject the traditional religion as "fetish" and "demonic," their belief systems and ritual structure appear to have affinities with traditional cosmologies. That is why they derive much of their membership not only from within the mainline churches, but also from other Christian and non-Christian groups (Islam and traditional religion).

In spite of the affinities that abound among the prophetic churches, it is important to note that each has its own religious dynamic. There are differences in specific doctrines and in the details of ritual acts and performance, just as in their histories of emergence. Their pattern of emergence is twofold. The first were those that emerged from or had their nucleus as "prayer bands" or "fellowship groups" within a mainline church, but that later broke away to form an independent group. In Nigeria, the Garrick Braide movement was the earliest movement in this category, breaking away from the Niger Delta Pastorate Church as early as 1916.

Other churches that fall under this category include the Cherubim and Seraphim (1925), the Church of the Lord, Aladura (1930), and the Christ Apostolic Church (1930). The second category refers to those groups that did not emerge out of conscious schism from an existing mainline church. They were founded through the visionary experience of a charismatic figure and independently of any existing mission church. A typical example is the Celestial Church of Christ, founded by Samuel Bilewu Oschoffa (1909–1985) in 1947. Most of the indigenous churches of both categories belong to a continental ecumenical movement, the Organization of African Instituted Churches (OAIC).

The most recent development within Nigerian Christianity is the emergence and increasing proliferation of Pentecostal and Charismatic churches, especially from the 1950s on. A huge proliferation of new Pentecostal churches was witnessed in the last two decades of the 20th century in Nigeria. In an attempt to forge ecumenical links and cooperation, both among themselves and between themselves and other churches, a majority of the churches have now come under an umbrella called the Pentecostal Fellowship Association of Nigeria (PFN).

There are two waves of Pentecostal movements. First there are the indigenous Pentecostal groups such as the Redeemed Christian Church of God, the Deeper Life Bible Church, and the Mountain of Fire and Miracles Church. Then there are Pentecostal groups and organizations that have established branches in Nigeria but have their headquarters situated in the West or elsewhere outside Nigeria. These include the International Church of the Foursquare Gospel, the Full Gospel Businessmen Fellowship International, Youth with a Mission, and Christ for all Nations. The former are largely independent and hardly rely on any external assistance, some even embarking on mission activities by planting branches in the United States, Canada, Europe, and other parts of the world. Many groups in the latter category rely heavily on their mission headquarters for funds, literature, and sometimes personnel.

One underlying feature of the Pentecostal churches is the emphasis on a specific conversion experience, spiritual rebirth ("born againism"), and the manifestation of charismatic gifts such as speaking in tongues (glossolalia), healing, and prophecy. Some are more or less holiness movements, more interested in religious experience than in rituals. Some are noted for the prosperity gospel they preach, which has become very popular among Nigerians. The gospel of prosperity teaches that God is a rich God and intends his followers to prosper in all their endeavors in life. It promises a miraculous escape from poverty, unemployment, ill health, lack of promotion, poor examinations, and the like, offering a "short-cut" to riches by tithing and giving to the poor and less privileged. Some of these groups have assimilated some ideas and features originating in American Pentecostalism. On the other hand, their commitment to the gospel of prosperity fits in well with values of the Nigerian indigenous culture, where elaborate religious rituals are engaged to ensure prosperity, health, and protection from malevolent forces. That is why Christian groups such as the Pentecostal churches, the Aladura, and prophetic churches that seek to address day-to-day, existential problems have continued to expand in contemporary Nigeria.

One difference between the prophetic and Pentecostal groups is that many founders of the prophetic churches were semiliterate; their counterparts in the Pentecostal churches were in most cases university graduates and had worked in nonreligious professions. For instance, William Kumuyi, who founded the Deeper Life Bible Church in 1973, was a lecturer in mathematics at the University of Lagos. Chris Okotie, who founded the Household of God Fellowship in 1987, was a lawyer. Dr. David Oyedepo, the founder and bishop of the Winners Chapel (1983), was originally an architect by profession. The Christ Chapel Church (aka Voice of Faith Ministries) was founded in 1980 by a medical doctor, Tunde Joda. Following their callings, these founders have abandoned their erstwhile professions to undertake full-time church ministry. These churches are very appealing to youths, graduates, and professionals. The Pentecostal churches also emphasize in-depth study of the Bible through theological training, Bible courses, camp meetings, seminars, revivals, and retreats.

The Spiritual Science movements are an extremely heterogeneous collection of groups and organizations. One distinguishing feature of these movements is their quest for spiritual knowledge and power, higher states of consciousness and direct religious experience, as

Nigeria

Religion	Followers in 1970	Followers in 2010	% of Population	Annual % growth 2000–2010	Followers in 2025	Followers in 2050
Christians	22,694,000	72,302,000	45.7	2.58	99,194,000	139,000,000
Independents	3,076,000	26,500,000	16.7	2.87	37,000,000	52,000,000
Protestants	3,959,000	23,800,000	15.0	3.81	32,000,000	45,000,000
Anglicans	2,941,000	21,500,000	13.6	2.31	30,000,000	42,000,000
Muslims	23,057,000	72,306,000	45.7	2.58	99,200,000	139,000,000
Ethnoreligionists	7,870,000	13,160,000	8.3	1.99	10,800,000	9,143,000
Agnostics	100,000	420,000	0.3	2.43	700,000	1,100,000
Atheists	20,000	50,000	0.0	2.52	100,000	200,000
Baha'is	11,400	36,500	0.0	3.57	80,000	160,000
New religionists	11,100	24,000	0.0	2.53	32,000	48,000
Buddhists	500	8,500	0.0	2.53	15,000	30,000
Chinese folk	0	4,600	0.0	2.53	7,000	14,000
Jews	0	1,100	0.0	2.54	1,200	1,300
Total population	**53,764,000**	**158,313,000**	**100.0**	**2.53**	**210,129,000**	**288,696,000**

well as the use of procedures, techniques, and practices that draw upon hidden or concealed forces in order to manipulate the course of events. Some of them are very eclectic in nature, drawing upon Western Esotericism, Eastern spirituality, and indigenous traditions. Groups primarily drawing on Western esoteric traditions are the Ancient Mystical Order Rosae Crucis (AMORC), the Aetherius Society, the General Church of the New Jerusalem, the Institute of Religious Science, and the Superet Light Mission. The largest Rosicrucian body internationally, AMORC has become quite popular in Nigeria, with headquarters in Lagos and branches in several parts of the country. AMORC does not claim to be a religion but describes itself as a "mystical philosophy," a "worldwide cultural fraternity," and an age-old brotherhood of learning. One of its main aims is to help people to discover their secret powers of inner vision and cosmic consciousness and to develop their psychic power of attraction.

The Eastern-related Spiritual Science movements include the ECKANKAR or Secret Science of Soul Travel, the International Society for Krishna Consciousness, the Unification movement, the Subud Brotherhood, the Grail movement, the Baha'i Faith, and Soka Gakkai International, a Japanese religion that has branches in Lagos and Zaria. The ECKANKAR Society of Nigeria, with headquarters in Lagos, began in 1973 in Benin City. In 1981 it began an extensive campaign to launch the movement in the country. It has more than 70 branches scattered all over Nigeria. The Unification Church was registered in Lagos in 1980, and although it has existed in Nigeria for some years, it has not had much success.

A typical example of an indigenous Spiritual Science movement in Nigeria is the Sat Guru Maharaj (the "Perfect Master"), which combines Sat Mat and Hinduism with elements of Christianity and Islam. The headquarters of the group is situated at the Ibadan end of the Lagos-Ibadan Expressway. Members of this group are easily identified by their red, flowing gowns and a distinct haircut. Although the presence and activities of the various Spiritual Science movements do not rival Christian and Islamic movements, the religious map of Nigeria would be incomplete without taking notice of their presence.

Afe Adogame

See also: African Instituted (Independent) Churches; Ahmadiyya Movement in Islam; Aladura Churches; Ancient and Mystical Order Rosae Crucis; Baha'i Faith; Candomblé; Celestial Church of Christ; Cherubim and Seraphim/Eternal Sacred Order of the Cherubim and Seraphim; Christ Apostolic Church; Church Missionary Society; Church of the Lord;

Deeper Life Bible Church; ECKANKAR; Ethnoreligions; Evangelical Church of West Africa; General Church of the New Jerusalem; Grail Movement, The; International Church of the Foursquare Gospel; International Society for Krishna Consciousness; Malikite School of Islam; Organization of African Instituted Churches; Pentecostalism; Qadiriyya Sufi Order; Religious Science; Roman Catholic Church; Santeria; Soka Gakkai International; Subud; Sufism; Tijaniyya Sufi Order; Unification Movement; Western Esoteric Tradition; Yoruban Religion.

References

Falola, T. *Culture and Customs of Nigeria.* Westport, CT: Greenwood Press, 2001.

Hackett, R. I. J., ed. *New Religious Movements in Nigeria.* Lewiston, NY: Edwin Mellen, 1987.

Isichei, E. *A History of Nigeria.* London: Longman, 1983.

Kalu, O. U. *Christianity in West Africa: The Nigerian Story.* Ibadan, Nigeria: Daystar, 1978.

Olupona J. K., and T. Falola, eds. *Religion and Society in Nigeria—Historical and Sociological Perspectives.* Ibadan: Spectrum Books, 1991.

Nigerian Baptist Convention

Nigeria was one of the early mission fields selected by the newly formed (1845) Southern Baptist Convention. Thomas Jefferson Bowen arrived in 1850 as the Convention representative and settled at Badagry in the southwestern part of the country. The work progressed slowly, due in part to the American Civil War, during which funds were cut off. However, after 1874 the work began to make some progress. In 1888 the mission experienced a schism when some 200 members left to form the Native Baptist Church (not to be confused with the church of the same name in Cameroon), one of the first of what are now referred to as African Initiated Churches.

Because of the schism, the mission increased its efforts, and the Native Baptist Church also adopted a vigorous evangelistic stand. Both groups had grown by the time they reunited in 1914 as the Yoruba Baptist Association. Five years later the Yoruba Association became the Nigerian Baptist Convention. Over the next 20 years, the membership grew from approximately 3,000 to more than 21,000, more members coming from the Yoruba people. However, the work also began to expand into the rest of Nigeria, including the northern part of the country controlled by Muslims. In the 1930s a new rule against polygamy led to a schism among members in Oya state, who established the United African Baptist Church.

During the last half of the 20th century, the Convention experienced significant growth and by the mid-1990s reported 600,000 members in 4,656 churches. During the last quarter of the century, the number of missionary personnel also dropped significantly, indicative of the Convention's continued progress at recruiting indigenous leadership.

The Convention has developed a major center of activity at Ogbomosho that includes a theological seminary, a medical center, a nursing school, a children's home, and a media center. Other similar institutions are found across the country. Literature is now published in English, Hausa, and Yoruban, with worship services being carried out in more than a dozen additional languages. The Convention, after the pattern of the Southern Baptists, has encouraged the development of a Women's Missionary Union, which has emerged in spite of the secondary role generally assigned women in traditional Nigerian society. The Union carries out a variety of evangelistic and social programs, from teaching literacy to assisting mothers in homemaking and child care.

The Convention has developed its own foreign mission program in Sierra Leone and Cote d'Ivoire. It is a member of the Christian Council of Nigeria, the Baptist World Alliance, and the World Council of Churches. In 2005, the convention reported 3 million members worshipping in its 8,500 congregations.

Nigerian Baptist Convention
The Baptist Building
P.M.B. 5113
Ibadan, Oyo State
Nigeria

J. Gordon Melton

See also: African Initiated (Independent) Churches; Baptist World Alliance; Southern Baptist Convention; World Council of Churches.

References

Ademola, Ajayi S. "The American Civil War of 1861–1865: A Major Challenge to the Survival of Early Baptists' Ventures in Nigeria." *Baptist History and Heritage* (2008). http://www.thefreelibrary.com/The+American+Civil+War+of+1861-1865:+a+major+challenge+to+the...-a0184132777. Accessed December 15, 2008.

Cillins, Travis. *The Baptist Mission of Nigeria, 1850–1993*. Ibadan, Nigeria: Associated Book-Makers Nigeria Limited, 1993.

Duval, Louis M. *Baptist Missions in Nigeria*. Richmond: FMB, Southern Baptist Convention, 1928.

High, T. O. *Outline Notes on the Expansion of Baptist Work in Nigeria, 1850–1939*. Ibadan: Caxton Press, Ltd., 1970.

Okedara, J. T., and S. Ademola Ajayi. *Thomas Jefferson Bowen: Pioneer Baptist Missionary to Nigeria, 1850–1856*. Ibadan: John Archers, 2004.

Whirley, Carlton F. *The Baptists of Nigeria: A Story to Tell*. Nashville: Convention Press, 1988.

Nipponzan Myohoji

Nipponzan Myohoji is a Japanese Buddhist organization in the tradition of Nichiren (1222–1282) that maintains a conspicuous presence in the contemporary peace movement despite its small membership of approximately 150 celibate monks and nuns (predominantly Japanese) and 1,500 lay followers. Its beliefs and practices have been determined by the life and career of its founder, Fujii Nichidatsu (1885–1985).

Fujii was ordained a Nichiren priest at the age of 19 and graduated from Nichiren University at 23. In 1916, while fasting, praying, and performing austerities in a waterfall, he had a vision that would prove decisive: Jyogyo Bodhisattva appeared to him carrying the child Buddha on his back and beating a hand drum. Thereupon Fujii vowed to unify all people according to the teachings of the Lotus Sutra by instituting the practice of *gyakku-senryo*, beating a fan-shaped hand drum while chanting "namu myo ho ren ge kyo," the sutra's title. This and periodic fasting continue to be prominent aspects of Nipponzan Myohoji practice.

Fujii went to Manchuria and established Nipponzan Myohoji temples in each of its districts, the first in 1918. These temples served as bases for proselytization and catered to the spiritual needs of the expatriate Japanese community. The first Nipponzan Myohoji temple in Japan was established in 1924 at the foot of Mount Fuji in Tagonoura. In 1930 Fujii vowed to realize Nichiren's prophecy that Japanese Buddhism would return to India (*saiten kaikyo*). He arrived in India in 1931 and established temples in Bombay (1932) and Calcutta (1935). While in Ceylon he received Buddha relics that would be an integral part of his teaching thereafter. In 1933 he met Mahatma Gandhi and was impressed by his teachings of equality and nonviolence.

Despite Fujii's claims that he was opposed to World War II, the evidence suggests that Nipponzan Myohoji activities were conducted in full accord with national policy. Fujii supported Japanese expansion as the bringing of (Buddhist) "civilization" to the Asian continent. The role of Nipponzan Myohoji clergy before and during the war was closely connected to the military—clergy members conducted prayer services for victory, remembered war victims, and spiritually purified military and political leaders.

With the Japanese defeat in 1945, Fujii began to advocate absolute pacifism, and Nipponzan Myohoji became the first Japanese Buddhist group to campaign actively for peace. Fujii's teachings strongly denounced modern materialistic culture, and he identified the United States as the foremost embodiment and proponent of the values of materialism. The group first gained international notoriety when its yellow-robed, head-shaven monks and nuns protested nuclear and hydrogen bomb testing after Japanese fishermen were exposed to radiation off Bikini atoll in 1952, and it continues to campaign for a total ban on such weapons. Group members have also consistently opposed the presence of U.S. military bases in Japan, the most famous incident being in 1954 at the U.S. air base in Sunagawa, where protesting monks were attacked and seriously wounded by police. Nipponzan Myohoji was also prominent in demonstrations of opposition to the Vietnam War.

Nipponzan Myohoji peace pagoda in Milton Keynes, England. Built in 1980, it was the first peace pagoda established in the Western Hemisphere. (iStockPhoto.com)

Walking is considered a spiritual discipline by Nipponzan Myohoji, and its members engage regularly in peace walks, some for up to a year, throughout Japan and the world. Their other main form of practice is the building of "peace pagodas"—stupas containing Buddha relics—as symbols of peace. Fujii initiated the building of the first pagoda in Japan immediately after the war in 1945. There are now many more worldwide, some of which maintain small communities. They do not proselytize. In the United States, the group has forged special ties with Native American communities. They also have ties with the Sarvodaya Shramadana movement based in Sri Lanka.

Nipponzan Myohoji has no head temple and there is no spiritual successor to Fujii. Administrative leaders are chosen from among senior members and are appointed for three-year terms.

Nipponzan Myohoji, Tokyo Office
8-7 Shinsen-cho
Shibuya-ku, Tokyo-to 150-0045
Japan

Nipponzan Myohoji, Osaka Office
1-3-11 Minami-Senba
Chuo-ku
Osaka-shi, Osaka-fu 542-0081
Japan
http://www.peacepogoda.org (Nipponan Myohoji Sangha at Leverett, Massachusetts)

John S. LoBreglio

See also: Nichiren; Relics.

References

Fujii. *Buddhism for World Peace: Words of Nichidatsu Fujii.* Trans. by Miyasuku Yumiko. Tokyo: Japan-Bharat Sarvodaya Mitrata Sangha, 1980.

Fujii. *My Non Violence: An Autobiography of a Buddhist.* Trans. by Yamaori Tetsuo. Tokyo: Japan Buddha Sangha Press, 1975.

Green, Paula. "Walking for Peace: Nipponzan Myohoji." In *Engaged Buddhism in the West,* edited by Christopher S. Queen, 128–156. Somerville, MA: Wisdom Publications, 2000.
Kisala, Robert. *Prophets of Peace: Pacifism and Cultural Identity in Japan's New Religions.* Honolulu: University of Hawaii Press, 1999.

■ Niue

Niue is an autonomous island state in the South Pacific, between Tonga and the Cook Islands, which has strong ties to New Zealand. Its original inhabitants had a unique Polynesian dialect that led to its separation from its closest neighbors in the eyes of Europeans in the 19th century. Only 100 square miles in size, it has steadily lost population over the last generation (from 5,200 in the mid 1960s to some 1,500 in 2008). Many left for New Zealand.

Niue was originally settled in the prehistoric past by Samoans and Tongans. It was first visited by Europeans in 1774 when James Cook (1728–1779) arrived. The British established their hegemony in the 19th century and incorporated Niue into a protectorate jointly with the Cook Islands in 1900. Four years later Niue was separated from the Cook Island administration. It attained autonomy in 1974 as the Aotearoan Association Territory. It has an independent local government, with New Zealand continuing to handle its defense and foreign affairs.

The first effort to establish Christian missionary work on the island was in 1830. Unfortunately, the work of John Williams (1796–1839) of the London Missionary Society (LMS) was unsuccessful, as were periodic attempts over the next 15 years. Finally, in 1846 a Niuean who had attended a school sponsored by the LMS on Samoa returned home. Three years later, a Samoan classmate came to the island, and together they were able to launch a missionary effort. It would not be until 1861 that a European missionary, William George Lawes (1839–1907), settled on the island. Lawes stayed for seven years and was succeeded by his brother, Frank E. Lawes (d. 1910).

Under the Laweses and their successors, the mission developed strong ties to the Congregational Union of New Zealand, as some 15,000 Niueans reside in New Zealand. The church attained independence in 1966 as the Ekalesia Niue. It is by far the largest religious body on the island and a member of both the Council for World Mission and the World Alliance of Reformed Churches.

The dominance of the Ekalesia Niue has been challenged by the Seventh-day Adventist Church, whose Tonga-Niue Mission was started in 1895; the Church of Jesus Christ of Latter-day Saints, which began work in 1952; and the Jehovah's Witnesses, who arrived in 1960. There is also a small Anglican presence, part of the Diocese of Polynesia of the Anglican Church in Aotearoa, New Zealand, and Polynesia, serving mostly British and New Zealand expatriates.

J. Gordon Melton

See also: Anglican Church in Aotearoa, New Zealand, and Polynesia; Church of Jesus Christ of Latter-day Saints; Ekalesia Niue; Jehovah's Wit-

Niue

Religion	Followers in 1970	Followers in 2010	% of Population	Annual % growth 2000–2010	Followers in 2025	Followers in 2050
Christians	5,000	1,500	97.0	–2.86	1,200	1,300
Protestants	3,700	900	60.0	–2.91	750	750
Marginals	500	380	25.3	0.57	400	500
Roman Catholics	220	150	10.0	0.00	150	150
Agnostics	0	30	2.0	4.36	40	60
Baha'is	10	10	0.7	–1.89	10	10
Chinese folk	0	10	0.3	–5.59	10	20
Total population	**5,000**	**1,500**	**100.0**	**–2.76**	**1,300**	**1,400**

NIUE

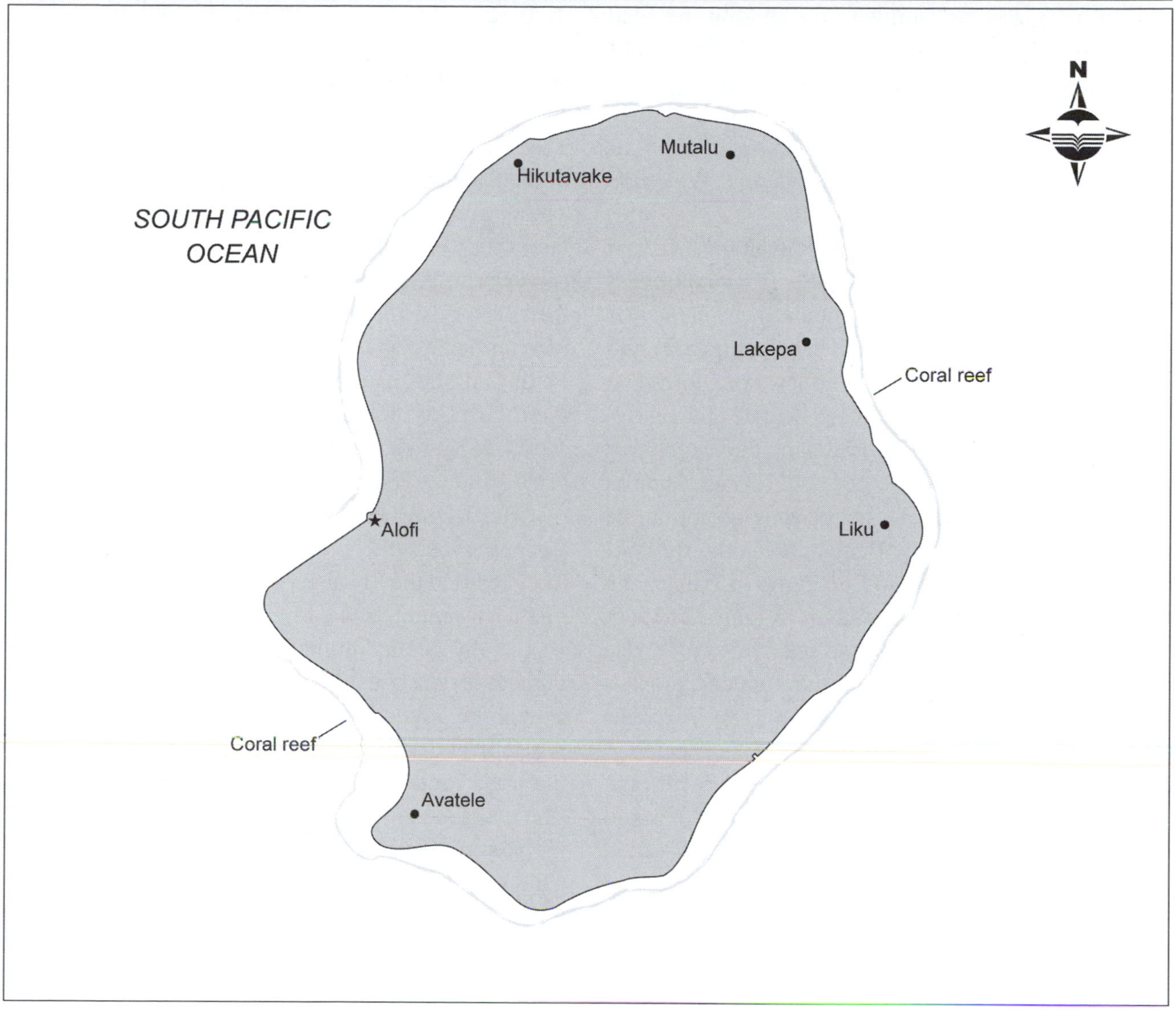

nesses; London Missionary Society; Seventh-day Adventist Church; World Alliance of Reformed Churches.

References

Britsch, R. Lanier. *Unto the Islands of the Sea: A History of the Latter-day Saints in the Pacific.* Salt Lake City: Deseret Books, 1986.

Chapman, T. M., et al. *Niue: A History of the Island.* Suva, Fiji: Institute of Pacific Studies of the University of the South Pacific and the Government of Niue, 1982.

Forman, Charles H. *The Island Churches of the South Pacific: Emergence in the Twentieth Century.* Maryknoll, NY: Orbis, 1982.

Loeb, E. M. *History and Traditions of Niue*. 1926; rpt.: New York: Kraus Reprint, 1978.

Nomiya Luo Church

The first African Initiated Churches (AICs) to emerge in Kenya were churches that began among Luo Anglicans around Lake Victoria in the Province of Nyanza, an area administered at the time by the Church Missionary Society in the Diocese of Uganda. One of the earliest AICs was the Nomiya Luo Mission, founded by a former Catholic, Johana Owalo (d. 1920), in 1914 and emerging as a deliberate and consciously syncretistic movement combining elements of Unitarian Christianity, Islam, Judaism, and Luo traditional religion in reaction against both Catholic and Protestant forms of Christianity.

The angel Gabriel appeared to Owalo in 1907 and told him to preach that people should worship God only, not Jesus or Mary. In a vision of heaven, he was told to circumcise his male followers (contrary to Luo custom), teach people to obey the laws of Moses and keep the seventh-day Sabbath, and baptize them in rivers. Owalo died suddenly in 1920, and the church was plagued with division over who should succeed him as leader. Eventually Petro Ouma became bishop, to be followed after his death by Benjamin Oundo. By 1944 the movement had spread to Luo living in Tanganyika and had more than 50,000 members in Kenya by 1966.

In 1960 the Holy Spirit descended on several Nomiya people who began speaking in tongues, prophesying, revealing sins, and jumping in ecstasy. A former Catholic, Jaote Pesa, began preaching and healing, claiming to be the successor to Owalo, and in 1967 the supporters of this Holy Spirit movement were expelled from the church. They formed a new church called the Nomiya Luo Roho (Spirit) Church under Bishop Zablon Ndiege, who has been archbishop since 1978. This church has suffered several schisms: Jaote Pesa started the Holy Ghost Coptic Church, and Cornell Bunde began the Nomiya Luo Roho Gospellers Church. The Nomiya Roho Sabbath Church started in 1974 out of a desire to return to the Sabbath observance that had been abandoned by the Nomiya Luo Roho Church.

Allan H. Anderson

See also: African Initiated (Independent) Churches; Church Missionary Society; Islam; Judaism.

References

Clark, Debbie. "History of Nomiya Luo Roho Church." Unpublished paper, 1984. Harold Turner Collection. University of Birmingham, UK.

Hoehler-Fatton, Cynthia. *Women of Fire and Spirit: History, Faith and Gender in Roho Religion in Western Kenya*. Oxford: Oxford University Press, 1996.

■ Northern Marianas

The Northern Marianas are a chain of islands in an area of the Pacific Ocean generally designated Micronesia. The several islands together have 177 square miles of land which is home to some 87,000 people (2008).

Prior to World War II, the islands shared much of their history with Guam and the Federated States of Micronesia. They were claimed for Spain in 1521 by Ferdinand Magellan (ca. 1480–1521). They were given their name in 1668 by Father Luis Diego Sanvitores (1627–1672) to honor the Austrian princess Maria Ana (1634–1696), then the regent of Spain.

The islands had originally been settled by the Chamorros people, possibly as early as 1500 BCE. They resisted the Spanish occupation that began in the mid-17th century and carried on a 20-year revolt that was finally quelled in the late 1680s. The indigenous population was greatly affected by the influx of Spanish culture, especially as it was reinforced by a growing number of Filipinos who came to the islands along the trade route that Spanish traders had established. The development of a new breed of Chamorros from the intermarriage of the Native people with the Spanish and Filipinos was accelerated by the relocation of many of the Marianas people to Guam in the 18th century. They were not allowed to return until after 1885.

Germany claimed the islands in 1885 but did not receive official control until Spain sold them in 1899, following the loss of its other Pacific territories to the United States in the Spanish-American War. Germany moved government administrators in early in the new century. The islands were lost to Japan as World War II began, and as the United States moved to end the war it fought fierce battles to take the islands, especially Saipan and Tinian. Tinian became the base from which the atomic bombs were dropped on Japan in 1945.

The Marianas were given to the United States as a trust following World War II. In a 1975 referendum they were separated from Guam (the southernmost island) and from the rest of Micronesia as a free associated state with a special continuing relationship to the

Northern Marianas

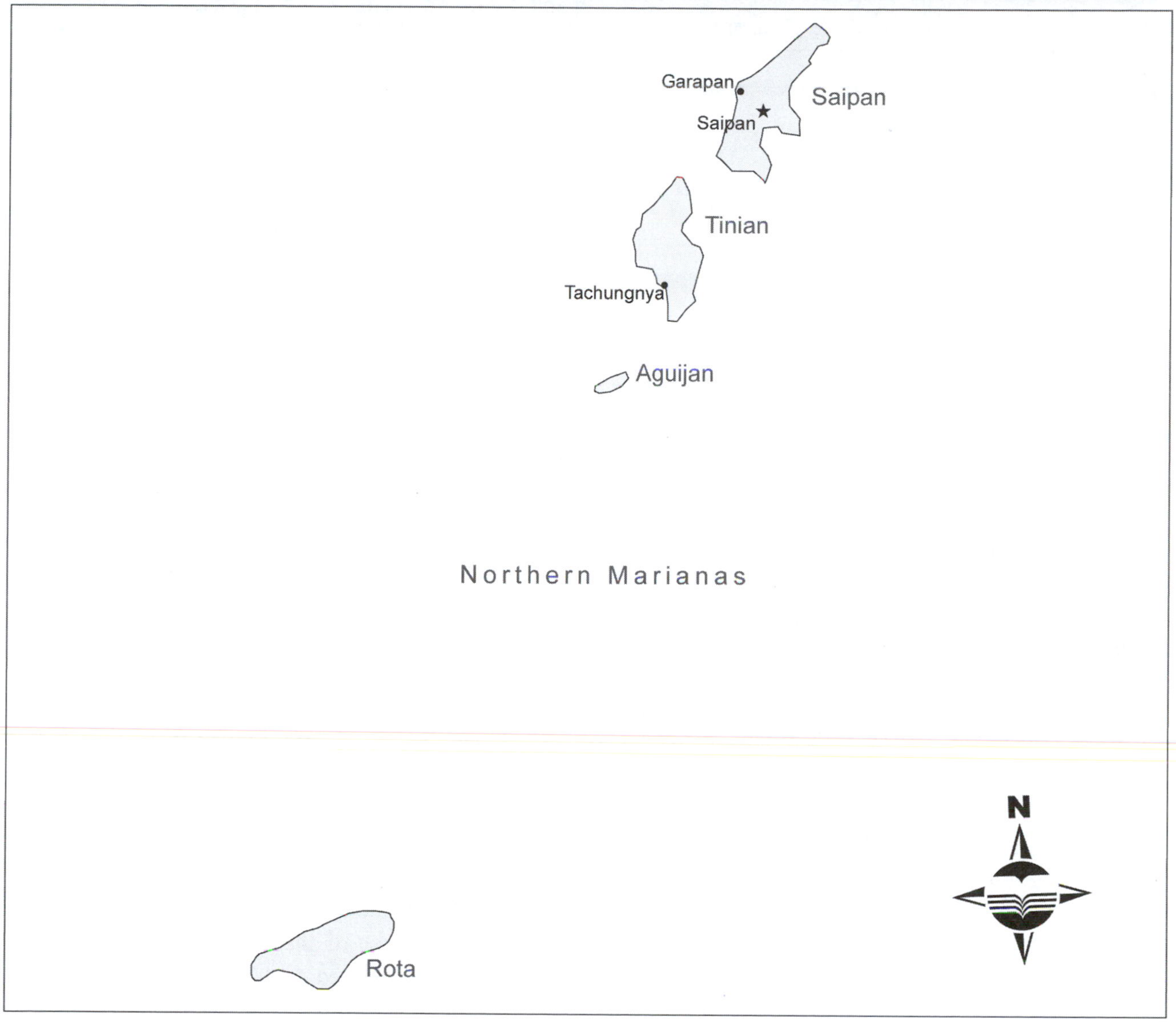

United States. In 1986 the islands gained commonwealth status with the United States, and the citizens of the Marianas are now considered U.S. citizens (though without the right of voting in federal elections). The president of the United States is the official head of state, but there is a locally elected government that resembles a U.S. state government.

The Marianas have radically changed since 1970. The population has grown from approximately 10,000 to more than 85,000. Many of the newer residents are expatriates from Korea, China, and the Philippines.

The Roman Catholic Church initiated work in the Marianas in 1668, when six Jesuit priests, including Father Sanvitores, launched a mission. They had little success until after the local revolt was quelled in the 1680s. With the influx of Filipinos in the 18th century and intermarriage of the Spanish colonists with the local population, a very different indigenous culture developed and a unique form of Spanish Catholicism emerged, which is now practiced by the majority of the population. The church's parishes are included in the Diocese of Agaia (Guam).

Northern Marianas

Religion	Followers in 1970	Followers in 2010	% of Population	Annual % growth 2000–2010	Followers in 2025	Followers in 2050
Christians	12,700	71,900	81.2	3.04	88,700	120,000
Roman Catholics	11,400	71,300	80.6	2.31	84,500	108,000
Protestants	1,100	7,500	8.5	1.36	10,200	15,000
Independents	0	9,100	10.3	6.22	12,500	17,800
Buddhists	0	9,400	10.6	3.07	11,800	16,100
Chinese folk	20	4,300	4.9	3.07	5,400	7,400
Agnostics	0	900	1.0	5.65	2,000	3,500
Muslims	0	610	0.7	3.09	800	1,100
New religionists	0	600	0.7	3.07	900	1,400
Baha'is	40	430	0.5	3.06	800	1,200
Ethnoreligionists	200	310	0.4	3.04	400	450
Confucianists	0	110	0.1	3.06	200	300
Atheists	0	20	0.0	3.13	50	100
Total population	**13,000**	**88,500**	**100.0**	**3.07**	**111,000**	**152,000**

Protestants appear to have begun work in the Marianas only after World War II. In 1947 the General Baptist Foreign Missionary Agency sent a couple to Saipan to launch a mission that has grown into the Saipan Baptist Mission and now the Marianas Association of General Baptists. More recently the Seventh-day Adventist Church and the Assemblies of God have initiated work on the islands.

Work by the Church of Jesus Christ of Latter-day Saints began in the 1970s on Saipan but was then withdrawn. Restarted in 1975, it subsequently spread to Rota (1982) and Tinian (1986). It is attached to the Micronesia Guam Mission. There is also a small Baha'i Faith community in the Marianas.

J. Gordon Melton

See also: Assemblies of God; Church of Jesus Christ of Latter-day Saints; Roman Catholic Church; Seventh-day Adventist Church.

References

Driver, Marjorie J. *Fray Juan Pobre de Zamora and His Account of the Mariana Islands*. Mangilao, Guam: Micronesian Area Research Center, University of Guam, 1984.

Farrell, D. A. *History of the Northern Mariana Islands*. Saipan: Public School System/ Commonwealth of the Northern Mariana Islands, 1991.

Flood, Bo. *Marianas Island Legends, Myth and Magic*. Honolulu: Bess Press, 2001.

Forman, Charles H. *The Island Churches of the South Pacific: Emergence in the Twentieth Century*. Maryknoll, NY: Orbis, 1982.

■ Norway

Norway, the country along the westernmost edge of the Scandinavian Peninsula, shares a large peninsula with Sweden. It includes some 125,000 square miles of land area. Much of the country is surrounded by water and an estimated 50,000 islands huddle along the irregular edge of the mainland. The coastline, one of the longest in the world, reaches from the North Sea to the Norwegian Sea to the Arctic Ocean. Though a number of Norwegian towns are located within the Arctic Circle, the great majority of its 4,650,000 people reside in the most southern part of the country.

Norway appears to have been inhabited for some 10,000 years by the Germanic tribes that moved into the area following the retreat of the last Ice Age. Sense of nationality arose around 800 CE with the emergence of the Vikings, the seagoing people whose home base was Norway. Harald Harfagre (ca. 865–933) is considered the father of the nation. He consolidated power in the 890s following a battle at Hafrsfjorf, near

Stavanger, and brought much of modern Norway into a single political entity. As the Viking kingdom expanded, explorers crossed the Atlantic to Greenland and even North America.

At the height of the Norwegian expansion, during the reign of Haakon IV (1204–1263), the kingdom included Iceland, Greenland, the Scottish Islands, and the Faeroe Islands. The Black Death killed close to half of all Norwegians, hitting the upper classes especially hard. The Norwegian kingdom subsequently fell apart. In 1397 Norway was brought into a united Scandinavia and remained a province of Denmark for the next four centuries. At the close of the Napoleonic era in 1814, Denmark surrendered Norway to Sweden. Norway spent much of the 19th century in a struggle to free itself. In 1884 a constitutional monarchy was adopted, and in 1905 Norway gained its independence and crowned Prince Carl of Denmark as King Haakon VII (1872–1957). Norway has remained a sovereign power ever since. It was overrun by Germany during World War II, and Haakon ran a government in exile from England. Christianity was introduced into Norway in the 10th century by a Roman Catholic representative of the archbishop of Bremen/Hamburg in Germany. The spread of Christianity was greatly aided by several Christian kings, especially Haakon the Good (d. ca. 961), who had been educated in England. A certain resentment toward the church developed as the bishops assigned to administer the church, who were residing in Denmark, proved a significant force blocking Norway's attempt to free itself from Danish control. In 1523 the Norwegian administrative council acted to obtain independence. The Catholic bishops blocked the council's attempt to obtain Swedish support. Eventually, in 1536, the council was abolished. The Protestant Reformation gained control in Denmark the following year, and Norway quickly accepted the reorganization of the church along Lutheran lines and the dismissal of the Catholic bishops.

In 1937 the Church of Norway was established, with the king of Denmark and Norway at the head. The church, which was established on the basis of the Lutheran (Augsburg) Confession, was a rather staid institution, largely isolated from the various renewal and Pietist movements that so affected the life of Lutheranism in Germany. The first renewal of significance appeared in the early 19th century under the leadership of Hans Nielsen Hauge (1771–1824). He organized Pietist religious societies across the country that protested an emphasis upon liturgical worship and a rational orthodox theology. Other movements appeared periodically through the 19th century, some emphasizing enthusiasm for foreign missions.

St. Mary's Church (Mariakirken), a Lutheran church in Bergen, Norway. (iStockPhoto.com)

The Church of Norway remains the dominant force in Norwegian life. The relatively high church membership, however, is contrasted with a very low church attendance. The Lutheran Church was established as the state religion, and the king and the majority of his cabinet were required to be professed members. The strong ties between church and state continue, but reforms through the 20th century gave the church more autonomy.

In the mid-19th century, free churches began to challenge the exclusive hegemony of the Church of Norway over the religious life of the citizenry. Possibly the first to appear were the Baptists. Danish sailor

Norway

Batsfjord
Hammerfest
Vardo
Vadso
Alta
Lakselv
Kirkenes
Tromso
Harstad
Narvik
Bodo
Mo
Sandnessjoen
Mosjoen
Namsos
Steinkjer
Trondheim
Molde
Alesund
Andalsnes
Floro
Norway
Hermansverk
Lillehammar
Gudvagen
Bergen
Hamar
Drammen
Oslo
Moss
Haugesund
Stavanger
Skien
Tonsberg
Egersund
Arendal
Kristiansand
N

Frederick Ludvig Rymker began to preach in Norway in 1857 and founded several Baptist churches. By 1877, when the Norwegian Baptist Union was formed, churches had been founded in all parts of the country, though their actual membership was relatively small.

Methodism in Norway began in 1849 when Ole Peter Petersen (1822–1901), a sailor converted by Methodists in New York, returned to his hometown and began to share his new faith. A revival spread and Petersen began to preach. In 1850 he returned to the United States, pursued studies for the ministry, and was ordained. He returned to Norway in 1853. In 1856, Christian Willerup was sent from New York to superintend the work in Norway, and he eventually extended his work across Scandinavia. The first congregation was formally organized soon after Willerup arrived, and the annual conference met first in 1876. The church in Norway was founded as an extension of the Methodist Episcopal Church and has, through several mergers, become an integral part of the United Methodist Church.

Two revival movements in the Lutheran Church led to new Free church bodies that more closely adhered to the core of Lutheran doctrine, the Evangelical Lutheran Free Church of Norway (1877) and the Mission Covenant Church of Sweden (1984). The latter church is related to the Covenant Church movement in Sweden that had roots in Methodist Pietism.

The Salvation Army entered Norway in 1888. Although most know it as a social service agency, the army is also a Holiness church, and in Norway it had spectacular success in attracting members. By the middle of the 20th century, it was by far the largest of the several bodies in the country, with almost 100,000 members.

Pentecostalism came to Norway in 1906, when Thomas Ball Barratt (1862–1940), a Methodist minister who had received the baptism of the Holy Spirit and converted to the Pentecostal position while visiting New York, returned home to Oslo and began to preach about his experience. As a result of his preaching, he was forced to withdraw from the Methodist Church. The growth of Pentecostalism in Norway led to the founding of the Norwegian Pentecostal Assemblies, which is now second only to the Salvation Army in size. Pentecostalism has also been strengthened by the addition of British missionaries with the Apostolic Church and American missionaries with the Apostolic Faith Mission.

There is an active Christian ecumenical movement in Norway. More liberal Protestant churches that are members of the World Council of Churches are associated together in the Christian Council of Norway. More conservative churches are members of the Evangelical Alliance in Norway and affiliated with the World Evangelical Alliance. A number of evangelical churches are indigenous to Norway, most founded by former members of the Church of Norway, including the Maranatha Revival Church, the Congregation of God at Vegardshei, and the Free Pentecostal Friends.

The Roman Catholic Church was allowed to reestablish itself in the early 19th century, and the first new parish was opened in 1842. The church experienced slow growth, there still being a great deal of anti-Catholic prejudice in the 19th century. A vicariate was erected in Oslo in 1931 and a diocese in 1953. The national episcopal conference includes the diocese and the two territorial prelatures of Trondheim and Tromsö.

As in most other Western European countries, 20th-century Norway saw the development of a pluralistic religious culture that now includes the broad spectrum of the world's religions—from the Church of Scientology to Tibetan Buddhism. The variety of organizations serving primarily expatriate communities include the Greek Orthodox Church and the Sikh community. The Jewish community, dating to the mid-19th century, consists of approximately 2,000 people, most residing in Oslo and Trondheim.

There is a relatively new Muslim community, originally centered on the Muslim Union of Oslo. It grew steadily through the last decade of the 20th century into the first decade of the new century, with a second site of concentration in Akershus. By 2005, the total community had grown to more than 100,000, most with origins in Pakistan. Most Muslims are of the Hanafite School of Sunni Islam, and many of their mosques have associated together in the Islamsk Råd Norge (Islamic Council Norway).

A variety of new Buddhist and Hindu groups, most seeking membership from young adults, including the International Society for Krishna Consciousness, have come to Norway since World War II, though most have only one or two centers. Esotericism is

Norway

Religion	Followers in 1970	Followers in 2010	% of Population	Annual % growth 2000–2010	Followers in 2025	Followers in 2050
Christians	3,829,000	4,370,000	91.4	0.22	4,583,000	4,911,000
Protestants	3,924,000	4,164,000	87.1	0.10	4,302,000	4,527,000
Roman Catholics	10,100	61,000	1.3	1.91	95,000	130,000
Independents	20,500	50,000	1.0	1.35	80,000	130,000
Agnostics	30,400	180,000	3.8	6.66	280,000	350,000
Muslims	4,000	150,000	3.1	9.40	250,000	300,000
Atheists	10,000	28,500	0.6	1.45	35,000	42,000
Buddhists	100	36,000	0.8	5.91	50,000	85,000
New religionists	500	7,000	0.1	–0.04	12,000	20,000
Baha'is	1,200	2,800	0.1	1.38	4,500	6,500
Sikhs	0	2,300	0.0	2.43	3,000	3,500
Ethnoreligionists	0	1,300	0.0	0.65	1,600	1,800
Chinese folk	0	1,800	0.0	6.89	2,500	4,000
Jews	900	900	0.0	0.67	900	900
Spiritists	0	540	0.0	0.66	700	900
Total population	**3,876,000**	**4,781,000**	**100.0**	**0.66**	**5,223,000**	**5,726,000**

represented in the Theosophical Society and the Ancient and Mystical Order Rosae Crucis.

The Church of Jesus Christ of Latter-day Saints (LDS) has been active in Norway since 1850, although many of its 19th-century converts migrated to the United States and the church is not as strong as it could have been. Norway was the home of one of the more interesting LDS splinter groups, the Independent Church of Jesus Christ of Latter-day Saints, which opened headquarters in Oslo and subsequently established congregations in Denmark and the United States.

J. Gordon Melton

See also: Ancient and Mystical Order Rosae Crucis: Apostolic Church; Apostolic Faith Mission; Church of Jesus Christ of Latter-day Saints; Church of Scientology; Evangelical Lutheran Free Church of Norway; Free Churches; Hanafite School of Islam; International Society for Krishna Consciousness; Mission Covenant Church of Sweden; Norwegian Baptist Union; Salvation Army; Theosophical Society (America); United Methodist Church; World Council of Churches; World Evangelical Alliance.

References

The Church of Norway. Hegdehaugen, Norway: Church of Norway Information Service, 1990.

Furseth, Inger. *A Comparative Study of Social and Religious Movements in Norway, 1780s–1905*. Lewiston, NY: Edwin Mellen Press, 2002.

Hale, Frederick. *Norwegian Religious Pluralism: A Trans-Atlantic Comparison*. Lewiston, NY: Edwin Mellen Press, 1992.

Hunter, L. S. *Scandinavian Churches: A Picture of the Development and Life of the Churches of Denmark, Finland, Iceland, Norway, and Sweden*. London: Faber & Faber, 1965.

Wilson, T. B. *History of Church and State in Norway from the Tenth to the Sixteenth Century*. Westminster (London): A. Constable & Co., 1903.

Norwegian Baptist Union

Unlike many Baptist fellowships in Europe, those in Norway had American rather than German roots. However, prior to the arrival of any Baptists, Lutheran pastor G. A. Lammers (1802–1878) had built a Baptist-like movement in Norway. Lammers became convinced of the truth of believer's baptism (as opposed to infant baptism, then the standard practice in the state-sponsored Church of Norway), and in 1856 he left the state church. Lammers and his fellow believers formed an Apostolic Free Church, congregations of which began to appear in various locations through the mid-19th century. As it grew, the movement split over the necessity of rebaptizing people who had been baptized as infants.

In 1857 Frederick Ludwig Rymler, a Norwegian who had been converted to the Baptist faith in the United States, returned to Norway and settled in Porsgrunn. Finding some initial support from those previously affiliated with Lammers's movement, Rymler organized the first Baptist church in Norway in 1860. The first association of churches was organized in 1872, and a Norwegian Baptist conference, including 14 congregations, was established in 1877. The Norwegian church was greatly assisted by Swedish Baptists.

The Norwegian Baptists had a steady membership gain through the early 20th century, in spite of losses to the Pentecostal movement. In 1910 they were able to open a theological school (superseded after World War II by a new seminary in Oslo). In 1963, in order finally to obtain government recognition, they adopted a confession of faith, thereby fulfilling one of the government's requirements. The church, a conservative body, has also issued a separate statement on the Bible as "God's inspired word." Membership peaked in the 1940 at around 7,500 and has since declined.

In the 19th century, the Norwegian Baptist Union supported missionaries through the American Missionary Baptist Union. It formed its own missionary organization in 1915 and commissioned its first missionary, Bernard Aalbu, in 1918. Aalbu began work in the Congo (Zaire) in 1920. More recently, the Union has tried to open work in Nepal. For many years it has worked with other Scandinavian Baptist churches in support of a Seaman's Mission in San Francisco, California.

In 2008 the Norwegian Baptist Union reported some 5,430 members in 78 churches. It is a member of the Baptist World Alliance. In the changed atmosphere of Norwegian religious life in the last generation, the church has moved from a position of hostility in relation to the Church of Norway to one of dialogue and cooperation.

Norwegian Baptist Union
Michelets vet 62
N-1320 Stabekk
Norway
http://www.baptist.no/ (in Norwegian)

J. Gordon Melton

See also: Baptist World Alliance; Baptists.

References

McBeth, H. Leon. *The Baptist Heritage: Four Centuries of the Baptist Witness*. Nashville: Broadman Press, 1987.

Rushbrooke, J. H. *The Baptist Movement in the Continent of Europe*. London: Kingsgate Press, 1923.

Stiansen, P. *History of the Baptists in Norway.* Chicago: Blessing Press, 1933.

Westin, Gunnar. *The Free Church through the Ages*. Nashville: Broadman Press, 1958.

Nyingma Tibetan Buddhism

Nyingma (Tibetan: *rNying ma*), which literally means "old," is the earliest tradition of Tibetan Buddhism. It is not a tightly structured institution, but a variety of traditions encompassing monastic practice, householder yogi lineages, and other diverse forms of Buddhist practice. Historically, the Nyingma tradition declined in significance in Tibet as its political importance was eclipsed by other schools, particularly the Gelugpa (Tibetan: *dGe lugs pa*). However, it has retained a number of significant monastic centers including Mindroling and Samye in central Tibet, others in eastern Tibet, and has a strong presence at village level. The advent of the Tibetan diaspora since the late 1950s has also witnessed the development of Nyingma monasteries in India and Nepal and Nyingma-affiliated Dharma centers in most countries in the West. Changes to Tibetan political and religious life that accompanied the development of the diaspora and the formation of the Tibetan government-in-exile made it desirable for the Nyingma to appoint a single "head," a nontraditional position that has now been filled by a number of notable lamas.

The teachings and practices of Nyingma are said to represent those brought from India during the period of the early spread of Buddhism in Tibet. Although

Established in 1676, Mindroling Monastery in central Tibet is one of the centers of Nyingma Buddhism. (Ethel Davies/StockphotoPro)

this tradition may have commenced as early as the seventh century, it is thought to have gained real momentum during the reign of King Trisong Detsen (Tibetan: *Khri srong lDe brtsan*) (ca. 740–798 CE). Tradition has it that this king invited the noted monk and abbot of Nalanda monastery, Santaraksita, to travel to Tibet and found the country's first Buddhist monastery, Samye (Tibetan: *bSam yas*). According to legend, the new religion was vigorously opposed by various autochthonous spirits and deities, who by night would pull down the walls of Samye that had been built during the day. In turn, Santaraksita called upon the renowned Indian tantric master Padmasambhava (Lotus Born) (eighth century) to subjugate the opposition.

Padmasambhava, also known as Guru Rinpoche, the "Precious Guru," is venerated in Tibet as highly as the historical Buddha himself. Guru Rinpoche inspired the translation of many Buddhist texts into Tibetan and hid many texts and blessed objects (Tibetan: *gter-ma,* pronounced "terma," meaning treasure), with the intention that they would be thus protected and then rediscovered at an appropriate time. Terma are of great importance within the Nyingma tradition. Although texts and sacred objects had been concealed in pre-Buddhist Tibet, this practice was strongly emphasized by Padmasambhava and his disciples. Those who discover these hidden terma are called "treasure finders" (Tibetan: *gter ston,* pronounced "terton") and are held in high esteem and often identified as reincarnations of Padmasambhava's disciples and other famous teachers.

The terma are a vital and dynamic part of the Nyingma textual collections. Although the term "Nyingma" indicates an emphasis on old traditions, the promotion of terma texts creates the opportunity for innovation. These texts of mysterious authorship enable new practices to be introduced that are responsive to changing needs. One of the most important terma texts of recent times was the Longchen Nyinthig (Tibetan: *rDzogs-pa Chen-po Klong-chen Thig-le*, or *Klong-chen sNying-thig*), the Innermost Spirituality of Longchenpa, which was promulgated by Jigme Lingpa (Tibetan: *Jigs med gling pa*) (1730–1798). This text, coupled with the teaching legacy of Jigme Lingpa, established the main Dzogchen (Tibetan: *rDzogs chen*, or Great Completion) teachings in the contemporary period and laid the foundation for the Ris Med, or nonsectarian, movement. Dzogchen teachings emphasize recognizing intrinsic awareness.

The Longchen Nyinthig gave the Ris Med movement an emphasis on yogic self-discipline rather than imposed monastic discipline and emphasized a conception of the enlightened state as pure and open, beyond all logic and conventional description. Jigme Lingpa's teaching lineage flourished in eastern Tibet around Dege (Tibetan: *sDe dge*), and after his death three incarnations were recognized as being his emanations. The most famous of these was Jamyang Khyentse Wangpo (Tibetan: *'Jam dbyangs mKhyen brtse'i dbang po*) (1820–1892). Khyentse Wangpo joined with Jamgon Kongtrul (Tibetan: *'Jam mgon Kong sprul*) (1813–1899) in an extensive search across Tibet for rare treasure teachings. This search resulted in the creation of the most valued collection of these materials, the Rin chen gTer mdzod, the *Precious Collection of Treasures*. This collection is still growing, and was updated by important lamas in the 20th century.

The Nyingma tradition, like that of its pre-Buddhist predecessors, the Bonpos, includes both non-celibate householder (Tibetan: *sngags-pa*) lamas and monastic communities. The most eminent 20th-century Nyingma lamas, such as Dilgo Khyentse Rinpoche and other Khyentse incarnations, all carried this important heritage, which emphasizes treasure teachings, the Longchen Nyinthig, and Dzogchen. The most recent head of the Nyingmapa, appointed in 2001, was Minling Trichen Rinpoche (Tibetan: *sMin gling Khri chen*) (1930–2008). Like so many other greats in this tradition, Minling Trichen was a yogi-householder. His successor is yet to be announced.

The largest Nyingma monastery outside of Tibet is the Palyul Namdroling Monastery (PO Bylakuppe, Distt. Mysore, Karnataka, India 571-104), which was until recently under the direction of the previous head of the Nyingma, Penor Rinpoche (1932–2009). The emphasis in the Nyingma tradition on mystical experience and a deep appreciation of householder life has helped ensure its popularity in the West. Early residents in the West include Dudjom Rinpoche (1904–1987), a former head of the Nyingmapa, Tarthang Tulku (head of the Nyingma Institute, Berkeley, California), Sogyel Rinpoche (head of the Rigpa Fellowship), and Chagdud Tulku (head of the Chagdud Gonpa Foundation), all of whom have founded impressive institutions. There are also less well-known resident lamas and also regular visitors of no fixed address with retreat centers in Western countries, India, and Tibet.

There is also a new generation of Tibetan lamas who were born in the Tibetan diaspora since the 1960s. Among these are Dzongsar Khyentse Rinpoche (b. 1961) (head of the Khyentse Foundation) and Jigme Khyentse Rinpoche (b. 1960). One of the most recent important incarnations is Khyentse Yangsi Rinpoche (b. 1993), recognized as the reincarnation of Dilgo Khyentse Rinpoche, who is being educated in Bhutan. Some of the Westerners who came into contact with Nyingma lamas since the 1960s have also established a significant presence in the Nyingma tradition. Most notable is Matthieu Ricard (b. 1946), who studied with Dilgo Khyentse Rinpoche from 1967 to 1991. He is notable for his photography, translation work, teaching, and the surprising achievement of being dubbed "the happiest man in the world" as a result of his participation in scientific analysis of brain function.

Despite setbacks in the 1960s and 1970s in Tibet, the movement of important lamas and institutions to regions outside of Tibet has created a new and vital diaspora. The Nyingma School has had considerable success both in asserting its presence within this diasporic community and in transmitting its teachings into the broader non-Tibetan environment, thus successfully managing its transition from being an almost exclusively Tibetan religion to one with adherents around the globe. In the process significant inroads have been made into the task of translating its massive scriptural canon.

Diana Cousens and Keith Richmond

See also: Gelugpa; Khyentse Foundation, The; Nyingma Tibetan Buddhism; Padmasambhava; Rigpa Fellowship; Tibetan Buddhism.

References

Rinpoche, Dudjom, and Jikdrel Yeshe Dorje. *The Nyingma School of Tibetan Buddhism, Its Fundamentals and History*. 2 vols. Boston: Wisdom Publications, 1991. Vol.1, The Translations. Trans. and ed. by Gyurme Dorje with the collaboration of Matthew Kapstein. Vol. 2. Reference Material. Gyurme Dorje and Matthew Kapstein.

Snellgrove, David L. *Indo-Tibetan Buddhism, Indian Buddhists and Their Tibetan Successors*. Boston: Shambhala, 1987.

Snellgrove, David L., and H. E. Richardson. *A Cultural History of Tibet*. London: George Weidenfeld and Nicolson, 1968. Rev. ed., Boston: Shambhala, 1986.

O

Occupied Territories

The Israeli-occupied territories (official name: the Palestinian Authority, but also referred to as "Palestine") constitute land captured from surrounding nations during the Six-Day War in 1967, including the West Bank, East Jerusalem, the Gaza Strip, and the Golan Heights. The Sinai Peninsula was also captured at this time, but was returned to Egypt as per the Camp David Accords of 1977. The combined population for the occupied territories exceeds 3.7 million.

These western Asian areas are rich with religious history and represent a modest number of world religions. However, because the occupied territories are not a unified body and lack reliable census data, it is difficult to give precise estimates of religious adherents in these areas. Although calculations of exact percentages vary, the three largest religious groups in the occupied territories are Muslims, followed by Jews, then Christians. There also exist many religiously unaffiliated individuals in the region (agnostics and atheists).

Muslims Palestine came under Islamic rule in the seventh century CE and remained so until the British Mandate of Palestine in 1920. The vast majority of the residents of the occupied territories are Sunni Muslim (more than 80 percent of the population). Palestinian Arabs are the largest Muslim people group in the territories, but there are also smaller populations of Egyptian, Bedouin, and Syrian Arabs. Muslims in these areas represent at least two of the four schools of *fiqh* (expansion of *sharia* law based on the Koran and Sunnah in the Sunni tradition), the Shafii School and Hanafi School. Shafii is the largest school practiced in the occupied territories and is considered one of the more theologically conservative. The Palestinian Basic Law serves as a temporary Constitution for the Palestinian Authority in lieu of independence from Israel. It claims Islam as the official religion of the territory with sharia law as its source of legislation and Arabic as its official language. In addition, the Basic Law states that respect be given to adherents of all other religions in the region.

The Gaza Strip is currently governed by Hamas, a term meaning "zeal" in Arabic, but that also serves as an abbreviation for Islamic Resistance Movement. Due to its militaristic efforts, including suicide bombing and use of short-range missiles, Hamas is considered a terrorist group by the European Union and the United States. Ninety-nine percent of residents in the Gaza Strip are Sunni Muslims, many of whom support Hamas because of their humanitarian work in the region (funding schools, orphanages, mosques, and other institutions that are not typically provided by the Palestinian Authority). The region is decisively marked by its more strict observance of Islam as compared to other Palestinian areas in the occupied territories, most conspicuously the appearance of women—nearly all appear in proper Islamic dress, including *hijab* (scarf) and *jlibab* (coat).

The Noble Sanctuary (also known as the Temple Mount) in East Jerusalem is considered one of the most holy sites of Islam. Islamic tradition states that the angel Gabriel visited the Prophet Muhammad while he was in the Kaaba in Mecca and brought him on a wild steed to Jerusalem (Isra) to visit the Masjid Al Aqsa (the Farthest Mosque). Muhammad then ascended to the circles of heaven (Mi'raj) and was given the command by Allah of five daily prayers (*salat*). The Noble Sanctuary also includes the Dome of the Rock, where,

The Dome of the Rock in Jerusalem, an important Muslim shrine that stands adjacent to the Western Wall, an important Jewish holy site. (iStockPhoto.com)

according to Islamic tradition, Muhammad ascended into heaven from the rock contained within. Jerusalem was the first *qibla* (direction of prayer) for Muslims before being replaced by Mecca, and the Masjid Al Aqsa is visited by thousands of Muslims for weekly Friday prayers. Historically, the area has been under many jurisdictions, though the Noble Sanctuary is currently under Muslim control. However, Jews still lay claim to the area, many of whom believe that a final temple will be built on the Temple Mount, destroying the Islamic presence there at the coming of the promised Messiah.

Jews According to the account found in the Tanakh (Hebrew Bible) and other rabbinical sources, Jews claim to be settlers of the land of Palestine since antiquity. The expulsion of the Jews by the Roman Empire in 70 CE, however, contributed to the Jewish diaspora that continues to this day. This expulsion was only the last in a series of invasions and deportations that contributed to the disinheritance of the Jews from the land. The conviction of the necessity for the Jews to return to their biblical homeland was heightened by the rise of modern political Zionism beginning in the late 19th century. Israeli settlements in the occupied territories—which many countries and human rights groups have claimed are in violation of international law—are highly controversial and the cause of much strife in the region for Muslims, Jews, and Christians. There are more than 444,000 Jews in the occupied territories—arriving both before and after the Six-Day War—with numbers nearly evenly split between the West Bank and East Jerusalem, with smaller populations in the Gaza Strip and the Golan Heights.

Nearly 95 percent of Jews in the West Bank are ultra-Orthodox, significantly contributing to population growth in the region due to high birth rates. Many ultra-Orthodox Jews move to the region not for political reasons, but for economic (cheaper housing compared to Jerusalem) or personal (opportunity to live in a closed Orthodox community) ones. Notably, these ultra-Orthodox Jews typically do not adhere to the political Zionist ideology. There is also a considerable population of Russian Jews in the West Bank who arrived in the late 1980s and early 1990s from the former Soviet Union. Many of these individuals—like Jewish populations all over the world, including Israel and the occupied territories—are only moderately observant to Judaism, or are entirely secular (Jewish by ethnicity, not religious practice).

East Jerusalem contains some of the holiest sites of Judaism, Christianity, and Islam. For Jews, Jerusalem's Old City, the Temple Mount, and the Western Wall are of the utmost importance for religious expression in the Holy Land. The Western Wall is visited by millions of individuals a year, both Jewish and non-Jewish alike. As of 2005, residents of East Jerusalem were 53 percent Muslim and 42 percent Jewish. Tensions between the two communities continue, and are often violent. Though attempts to achieve a peace agreement between Israel and the Palestinian Authority persist, the city is still highly contested.

In addition to the larger Jewish population in the occupied territories, the West Bank is home to a small community of Samaritans, a Jewish sect dating back to the eighth century. The Samaritans reject both the Mishnah and the Talmud (classic Jewish rabbinical texts), have their own version of the Torah, and consider Mount Gerizim the place that God has chosen for worship, not Jerusalem. Though estimates vary, it is likely that there are fewer than 1,000 Samaritans worldwide, half of whom live in Nablus, a Palestinian city located between Mount Ebal and Mount Gerizim in the northern West Bank.

Christians Since the establishment of the modern state of Israel in 1948, the Israeli-Palestinian conflict has caused hundreds of thousands of Palestinian Christians to leave their historic homelands (the territories were 17 percent Christian in 1900 but only 2 percent today), in which they have been present since the first century CE. Reasons for this exodus include better economic opportunities and political stability abroad, in conjunction with the desire for greater religious freedom. Many Palestinian and western Christian scholars claim that the Palestinian Christian population is on the verge of extinction if current statistical trends continue.

Despite dwindling numbers, the Christian community in the occupied territories is diverse in affiliation. Although most Christians in these areas are Greek Orthodox, there is also a significant Roman Catholic community. Other groups include Anglicans, Protestants (including evangelicals), and Independents (including Pentecostals). The largest Christian denomination is the Greek Orthodox Patriarchate of Jerusalem, considered of great importance for Orthodox Christians because of its claimed historical ties to the Jerusalem church established on the Day of Pentecost (as recorded in Acts 2). In Palestine, 99 percent of the members of the Greek Orthodox Church are Arab and are Arabic- or Arabic/Greek-speaking Christians. With 10 congregations in 2005, this church makes up 41 percent of affiliated Christians and 0.88 percent of the population in the occupied territories. The second largest Christian denomination in the occupied territories is the Roman Catholic Church, with 43 congregations in 2005, but it has a slowly diminishing population growth rate. In 2000, the Holy See and the Palestinian Liberation Organization (PLO) signed the Basic Agreement Treaty, which addresses, among other topics, freedom of religion and conscience, equality of citizenship despite religious affiliation, and respect for the legal code (the *Status Quo*) of the holy sites of Christianity. In May 2009 Pope Benedict XVI visited the Holy Land, making one stop in the occupied territories—Bethlehem—where he met with Palestinian Authority President Mahmoud Abbas and visited various sites, including the Palestinian Aida refugee camp.

Religious Freedom Though religion is only moderately regulated by law through the government (both Israeli and Palestinian), the occurrences of social regulation of religion and religious persecution run high in the occupied territories. The 2008 Report on International Religious Freedom raised several issues in regard to the region, especially particular cases of religious persecution of Muslims, Jews, and Christians against each other during the reporting period. The Palestinian Authority Basic Law does provide for religious freedom; however, many religious minorities (such as select churches) are not recognized by the Authority.

There have been several accounts of discrimination and persecution from Orthodox Jews against non-Orthodox Jews, especially when an individual did not meet Orthodox requirements for being considered truly Jewish. There are also often violent clashes between Jewish and Muslim groups, especially in areas such as East Jerusalem, where tensions are high and adherents of each religion live in close proximity. In addition, proselytizing groups such as evangelical Christians often cite instances of discrimination and violence because of their forward attempts to spread their religious convictions. The issue of religious freedom in the occupied territories is a fragile blend of ethnic, religious, and political threads that often results in social strain and pressure on all religious groups in the region.

Gina Ann Bellofatto

See also: Agnosticism; Atheism; Greek Orthodox Patriarchate of Jerusalem; Gush Emumin; Islam; Islamism; Jerusalem; Mecca; Mosques; Orthodox Judaism; Roman Catholic Church; Women, Status and Role of.

References

Choshen, Maya, ed. *Statistical Yearbook of Jerusalem: No. 22—2006*. Jerusalem: The Jerusalem Institute for Israel Studies, 2007.

Goldscheider, Calvin. *Cultures in Conflict: The Arab-Israeli Conflict*. Westport, CT: Greenwood Press, 2002.

Grim, Brian J., and Roger Finke. "International Religion Indexes: Government Regulation, Government Favoritism, and Social Regulation of Religion." *Interdisciplinary Journal of Research on Religion* 2 (2006), Article 1, referenced in The Association of Religious Data Archives: Israeli Occupied Territories (Palestine).

Johnson, Todd M., ed. *World Christian Database*. Leiden: Brill, 2007.

Lybarger, Loren D. *Identity and Religion in Palestine*. Princeton, NJ: Princeton University Press, 2007.

U.S. Department of State. "International Religious Freedom Report 2008: Israel and the Occupied Territories." International Religious Freedom. http://www.state.gov/g/drl/rls/irf/2008/108484.htm. Accessed July 7, 2009.

Old Believers (Russia)

The Old Believers (or Old Ritualists) originated out of an intense controversy within the Russian Orthodox Church in the middle of the 17th century. Over the centuries, various practices had been introduced into the Russian Church at variance from those of the Orthodox in the Mediterranean Basin, especially in those churches in the jurisdiction of the Ecumenical Patriarchate of Constantinople. Shortly after assuming office in 1652, the new Patriarch Nikon (1605–1681) moved to revise ritual books used in the church that had become corrupted over the years and bring them in line with the Greeks. For example, a seemingly minor practice, the Russians had been making the sign of the cross with two fingers rather than three as was common to most of Orthodoxy. Nikon introduced the first reforms almost immediately and continued them through the work of several synods in 1654 and 1655. In 1655 he began to publish the revised liturgy books. A synod in 1666 ordered the excommunication of any who continued to adhere to the old rites and use the old books. Each change led to the opposition party growing stronger, with most radical groups believing that Nikon's innovations signified the beginning of the reign of the Antichrist.

The execution of Archpriest Avvakum Petrov in 1682 became a rallying point for those who opposed Nikon and who gradually became known as Old Believers, that is, those who followed the rituals and practices as they were prior to his term of office. Those in sympathy with the Old Believers may have constituted as much as 10 percent of the population. As the Czar Alexey Michailovich (1645–1676) backed Nikon's reforms, they found themselves under the government's thumb. Many were imprisoned, some executed, and others exiled. Many more fled from the czar's land.

Over time, the Old Believers split into as many as a dozen recognizable groups, though the majority

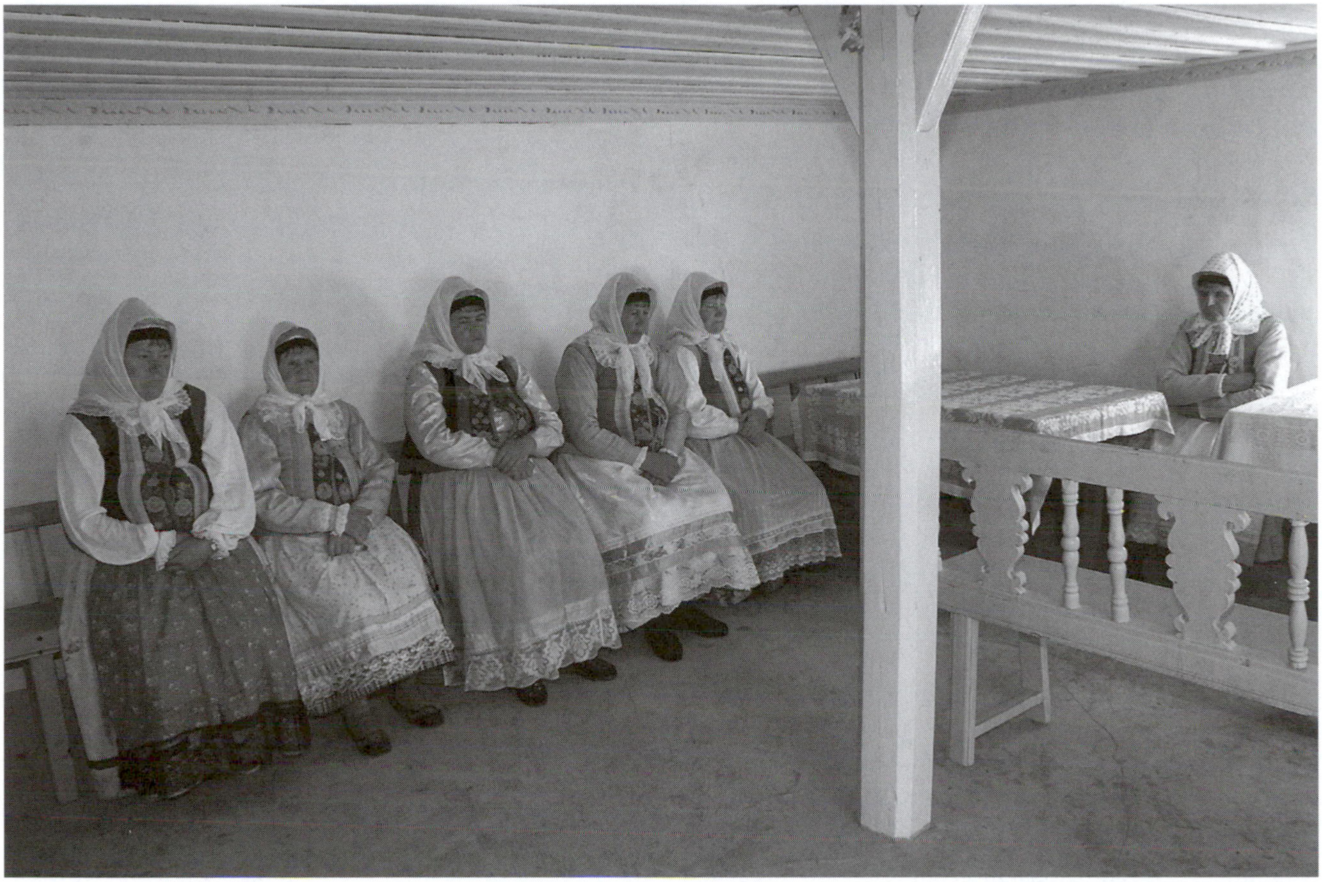

Old Believers, Russian Christians, pray at the village of Gorelovka south of the Georgian capital of Tbilisi. (AP Photo/Shakh Aivazov)

adhered to one of two main groupings: the Popovtsy ("with priests") and the Bespopovtsy ("without priests"). While loyal to the tradition, the Old Believers were presented with a major problem as no Orthodox bishop had aligned with their cause. Without a bishop they lost their apostolic succession and the episcopal authority to ordain priests. The Popovtsy absorbed priests as they left the Russian Orthodox Church; the Bespopovtsy adapted to life without priests and sacraments. The Popovtsy found a friend in 1847 in the person of the former Orthodox Metropolitan Ambrosios of Sarajevo (Bosnia), who consecrated two bishops, thus providing for the establishment of an episcopal hierarchy.

In the 18th and 19th centuries, the civil rights of the Old Believers remained severely restricted, with occasional periods of liberalization, such as under Catherine the Great (1762–1796) when they were allowed to return from abroad and given incentives to set up businesses in developing industrial areas of Russia. This gave rise to the phenomenon of the Old Believers' entrepreneurship that made enormous contributions to the transformation of the Russian economy in the 19th century, with their families such as the Morozovs, the Ryabushinskys, the Konovalovs constituting the country's economic elite.

Finally, in 1905, Czar Nicholas II issued the Edict of Toleration that considerably expanded the Old Believers' freedom to worship but retained the ban on their joining the civil service. During the Soviet years, those who remained in Soviet Russia were initially treated favorably by the Bolshevik government as those who had been oppressed by the czarist regime; however, from the late 1920s on they began to suffer the same persecution from the atheist government as all other believers. In 1971 the Russian Orthodox Church and some groups within the Old Believers lifted the mutual anathemas they had previously pronounced, which reflected both the sense of common fate under the Soviet regime and the government's intent to unify Russian Orthodox groups to make them more controllable.

As recently as 2000, Patriarch Alexy II, the then head of the Russian Orthodox Church, took visible steps to bring the Old Believers back into the church and had admitted the error of past persecution and restrictions. There are an estimated 2 to 2.5 million Old Believers in Russia. The headquarters of the largest priestly group of Old Believers, the Bielaia Krinitsia Church, is in the Ukraine, established at a time when the headquarters town was in Austrian territory. After the end of the Communist period, the Russian church was led by Metropolitan Alimpyj of Moscow and All Russia (1929–2003) who was elected in 1988. During his term a seminary was opened in Moscow (1996) and Metropolitan Ambrosios was canonized as a saint (1997). Since 2005 the head of the church has been Metropolitan Korniliy (Titov). The Bielaia Krinitsia Church is aligned with the Old Ritualist Orthodox of Romania who are led by Metropolitan Leonty of Braila, Romania. A second Russian group of Popovtsy is led Archbishop Aristarch of Novozybkov, Moscow, and All Russia. He resides in Novozybkov, and has associated bishops in several Russian communities as well as Georgia and Belarus.

A number of Bezpopovtsy moved to Lithuania in the late 17th century. An initial community was established in the Anyksciai region in 1709, and a monastery was opened in the Ignalina region in 1728. In the 1930s some 53 communities of the Old Believers with about 34,000 people could be found. Today, they make up approximately 1.43 percent of the population. Leadership is found in the Supreme Council of the Old Believers (Volunges N9–68, 2055 Vilnius, Lithuania). Similar groups in neighboring countries are organized into the Union of Latvian Old Believer Congregations (Maskavas 116, Riga LV-1003 Latvia) and the Union of Old Believer Parishes of Estonia. The revival of the Old Believers in post-Soviet Estonia is being assisted by the Society of Old Believer Culture and Development (Soola 5, Tartu 50013, Estonia).

Old Believers have also moved to the West. Bishop Sofrony (elected 1996) heads Old Believers in the United States, Canada, and Australia from his residence in Gervais, Oregon. Some 10,000 members reside in Oregon and there is a small community in Alaska. There are approximately 500 in Canada and membership in the 3 countries exceeds 10,000 believers.

Old Believers Moscow
c/o Metropolitan Alimpyj of Moscow and All Russia
Rogozhovsky pos. 29
Moscow, Russia

Old Christ Rite Church (Romania)
c/o H. H. Leonti, Metropolitan
No. 5 Zidari St.
601 Braila
Romania

Old Believers Australia
c/o Old Orthodox Church of Holy Nativity
20 Norval St.
Auburn NSW 2144
Australia

Marat S. Sterin

See also: Russian Orthodox Church (Moscow Patriarchate).

References

Bolshakoff, Serge. *Russian Nonconformity*. Philadelphia: Westminster Press, 1950.

Conybeare, Frederick C. *Russian Dissenters*. Cambridge: Harvard University Press, 1921.

Pokrovsky, N. N., and Richard A. Morris, eds. *Traditional, Spiritual, and Material Culture of Russian Old Believer Settlements in Europe, Asia and America*. Novosibirsk: Nauka Press, 1992.

Robson, Roy R. *Old Believers in Modern Russia*. Rockford, IL: Northern Illinois University Press, 1996.

Wigowsky, Paul J., comp. *Collection of Old Believer History and Tradition*. http://www.geocities.com/Athens/Agora/2827/collection.html. Accessed March 10, 2009.

Old Catholic Church in Switzerland

Confronted with the growing prerogatives entrusted to the papal institution and with the determined opposition of the leadership of the Roman Catholic Church to modern ideas in the 19th century, Catholic liberals—

especially in Germany and Switzerland—had become increasingly suspicious of Rome. After the proclamation of the dogma of the infallibility of the pope at the First Vatican Council in 1870, some did not accept the new doctrine and broke with the Roman Catholic Church. They founded national Old Catholic Churches, which would join forces within the Union of Utrecht together with a group of Dutch Catholics who had separated from Rome in the 18th century and preserved the episcopate within their ranks.

In Switzerland, the leaders of the movement were primarily laymen, although a few priests joined the resistance too. The movement enjoyed a strong political support in those cantons where liberals were at the helm. It built upon a long desire of liberal political circles to create a national church, not submitted to any foreign leadership: several proposals to erect a national diocese had already been advanced over the previous decades. Large meetings of liberal Catholics took place during the spring of 1871. In a few cantons (Berne, Geneva), the governments decided that parishes had to elect their own ministers and, since the Roman Catholic Church forbade its faithful to take part in such elections, the parishes were then entrusted to priests ready to comply with the wishes of the local government. In such cases of government-enforced schism, only a minority of the faithful were ready to follow, and most of those parishes finally returned to the Catholic Church, once Rome allowed the faithful to vote in the elections for parish priests. In other cases, however, the movement had real popular support, and a few parishes freely decided to break with Rome.

Some participants in the movement wanted to go as far as to abolish the episcopate. But the episcopal function was finally preserved, although its power would be limited. The first National Synod took place in Olten in 1875 and marked the official beginning of the Old Catholic Church in Switzerland as a constituted body. Actually—this remains specific to the Swiss branch of Old Catholicism—it adopted the name of Christian Catholic Church of Switzerland (Christkatholische Kirche der Schweiz). The priest Eduard Herzog (1841–1924) was elected as the first bishop of the Christian Catholic Church and consecrated the same year by the Old Catholic bishop of Germany.

The newly formed church very soon introduced reforms, which had already been introduced on their own by some priests in their parishes, including use of the vernacular in the Mass and abolition of clerical celibacy. As early as 1874, the government of the Canton of Berne had decided to sponsor the creation of a liberal Catholic theological faculty at the local university, which allowed the church to develop a well-trained clergy. In 1948, the Old Catholic Church of Switzerland became one of the founding members of the World Council of Churches. It made the headlines in the Swiss media when it ordained its first woman priest in 2000.

The Christian Catholic Church still enjoys today a public law status in nine Swiss cantons, which means among other things the right to raise church taxes. The church forms an acknowledged part of the Swiss religious landscape, but the number of its adherents has constantly decreased over the years: while there may have been some 70,000 members in the mid-1870s and there were still more than 35,000 in 1930, there are today less than 14,000 Old Catholics in Switzerland.

The Christian Catholic Church has its headquarters at Willadingweg 39, 3006 Bern, Switzerland. It has an Internet site at http://www.christkath.ch/.

Jean-François Mayer

References

Flückiger, Wilhelm, and Carlo Jenzer. *Christ-katholisch: Die Christkatholische Kirche der Schweiz in Geschichte und Gegenwart*. Zurich: Benziger Verlag, 1978.

Gschwind, Paulin. *Geschichte der Entstehung der Christkatholischen Kirche der Schweiz*. Solothurn: Verlag Gassmann, 1910.

Küry, Urs. *Die Altkatholische Kirche: Ihre Geschichte, ihre Lehre, ihr Anliegen*. 2nd ed. Stuttgart: Evangelisches Verlagswerk, 1978.

Moss, Claude Beaufort. *The Old Catholic Movement, Its Origins and History*. London: SPCK, 1948.

Old Catholic Church of Austria

The beginning of the Old Catholic Church of Austria dates to October 1871, when the Catholic minister Alois Anton celebrated the first Old Catholic liturgy at Vienna. In that same year religious services started also in Warnsdorf (now in the Czech Republic) and in Ried

(Upper Austria). As early as 1877, the government of the Austrian monarchy accepted the Old Catholic Church as one of the official religions in Austria. The first official synod, in May 1879, introduced the first changes from the contemporary practice of the Roman Catholic Church, namely, the right of laypeople to vote for and be elected to positions within the church, the use of the native tongue (in this case German) instead of Latin for the liturgy, and the abrogation of both priestly celibacy and confession. Though the church had gained followers, the Austrian government prohibited the election of a bishop for the diocese, refused to recognize the validity of marriages by Old Catholic priests, and did not allow members to direct tax money to the support of their priests.

During the next decades the church established several new parishes, but after World War I some of their territories were lost to Hungary and the Czech Republic. Thus in 1921 a new Austrian diocese had to be formed, and three years later Adalbert Schindelar was elected the first bishop of the Austrian Old Catholic Church. During World War II the church was incorporated within the Catholic Diocese of the Old Catholics in Germany, but since the end of that war the independent Austrian diocese is functioning again.

At present there are 19,000 members of the church living in Austria, organized within 12 parishes. Each parish is headed by a minister, who is supported in his or her pastoral works by a committee. The whole church is headed by a bishop who is elected by the synod and a committee (Synodalrat) consisting of three ordained individuals and six laypersons. The bishop, the ministers, and the deacons serve as liturgical authorities. In 1991 and 1995 the synod decided to allow women to be ordained to these church offices, and in 1998 Karin Leiter and Elfriede Kreuzeder were ordained as the first female ministers. In February 2008, Johannes (John) Ekemezie Okoro was ordained as bishop and head of the Church in Austria. For the theological training of future ministers there are no special university facilities as there are in the Evangelical Church of the Augsburg and Helvetic Confession and the Roman Catholic Church, which have their own faculties of confessional theology at the state universities. A university degree in Old Catholic theology can be acquired, however, at the University of Berne (Switzerland).

The Austrian Old Catholic Church has long been involved in cooperation with other churches. Soon after the founding of the Union of Utrecht in September 1889, the representatives of the Austrian Old Catholic Church joined the Union, rejoining it again after the reorganization of the diocese in 1921. (The Union of Utrecht was formed as a cooperative association of the Old Catholic bishops of the Netherlands, Germany, and Switzerland.) Since its beginning in 1958, the Ecumenical Council of Churches of Austria has recognized the Old Catholic Church as one of its members, and there are active ecumenical meetings throughout Austria, mainly with the Evangelical Church and the Anglican Church but also with the Roman Catholic Church. In 1986 the Evangelical and the Old Catholic Church agreed to intercommunion; the Roman Catholic Church did not join this agreement. The church is also a member of the World Council of Churches.

Old Catholic Church of Austria
Schottenring 17
A-1010 Wien
Austria
http://www.altkatholiken.at (in German)

Manfred Hutter and J. Gordon Melton

See also: Catholic Diocese of the Old Catholics in Germany; Roman Catholic Church; World Council of Churches.

References

Halama, Christian. *Altkatholiken in Österreich. Geschichte und Bestandsaufnahme.* Vienna: Böhlau, 2004.

Zankl, Wilhelmine. "Die altkatholische Kirche." In *Religionen. Ein Friedensbuch,* edited by Brigitte Hantschk-Vavra and Christian Hantschk, 96–101. Vienna: Horn, 1986.

Old Catholic Church of Mariavites/ Catholic Church of Mariavites

Mariavitism started as a Catholic movement aiming at the moral reform of Polish Catholicism at the end of the 19th century. The movement assumed a more formal existence on December 15, 1903, when Felicja or

Church of the Old Catholic Church of Mariavites in Plock, Poland. (Fotosearch/StockphotoPro)

Feliksa (later Maria Franciszka) Kozlowska (1862–1921) established the Association of Mariavites of Continuous Adoration in Supplication. The new organization was denounced by the Vatican in 1904, and two years later Kozlowska was excommunicated. Following the excommunication, the movement became a legally independent "sect."

The highly controversial marriage of the Mariavite archbishop Johann Kowalski (1871–1942) and his three bishops to nuns in 1922 was followed by trials of the archbishop (1928) and other priests. In 1931 the archbishop was sentenced to three years of imprisonment, later reduced to two years. The first consecrations of women priests, including a bishop, took place in 1929. The split of the movement in 1935 resulted in formation of the Old Catholic Church of Mariavites (OCCM), critical of the activities of M. Kowalski, and the Catholic Church of Mariavites (CCM), the smaller of the two bodies, which adhered to all of the innovations introduced in the 1920s. OCCM discontinued the priesthood for women in 1938.

OCCM is based on principles of the Old and New Testaments as well as the tradition of the undivided church determined by the first seven general, or ecumenical, councils. The message received by Kozlowska on God's mercy is also fundamental; it says the sinful world can be saved through the veneration of the Holy Sacrament and by the help of the Virgin Mary. No new dogmas are accepted in the OCCM, as it is thought that the power to do so should rest only with a council that is ecumenical, that is, representative of the whole of Christianity. The church does not accept the primacy of any bishop in the truly Catholic Church or the infallibility of humanity in matters of faith and morality. Neither excommunication nor interdicts are administered in OCCM.

The aim of the church is to spread the worship of Jesus Christ hidden in the Holy Sacrament and to remind people of their need for constant help from the Most Holy Mother in the face of the worldly hostilities against God. The veneration of the Holy Sacrament consists of frequent holy Communion. Every member has to devote one hour per week to individual adoration of the Holy Sacrament and one hour per month to communal and ceremonial adoration. Participation in the Sunday Mass is obligatory as well. Priests and nuns have to practice the adoration daily. The entire liturgy is conducted in Polish.

In 1924 the church dropped strictures requiring the celibacy of the clergy, despite the views of Kozlowska on this issue. Instead, the stress has been put on leading the Franciscan life. The variety of services offered by the church (baptism, marriage, burial, and so on) are free, and acceptance of any payment for the conduct of the Holy Mass (as has been common in the Roman Catholic Church) is forbidden.

There are seven sacraments. Confession received by a priest is obligatory for children and youth and optional for people older than 18. However, adults are obliged to make the general confession to Christ himself, which is followed by absolution of sins by a priest. The holy Eucharist is distributed in two forms (bread and wine) to all believers. Though the church honors religious pictures and memorabilia of saints, it does not accept the claims made for so-called wondrous relics and paintings. In the beginning, most controversies around the Mariavites concerned its erosive influence on the Roman Catholic Church. During the partition of Poland, many believed any movement directed against the church was antinational.

OCCM is divided into 3 dioceses that cover 42 parishes and have 45 churches and chapels. There are 32 priests. OCCM counts approximately 26,000 members (1997) who live in Poland, mainly in the area of Plock and Siedlce as well as Lodz, Lublin, and Warsaw. The highest supervising body of the church is the synod. In periods between synod meetings, the General Chapter (the organization to which all priests belong) provides supervision. The main administrative body is the Council of the Church. The church is led by its head bishop. OCCM publishes the monthly periodical *Mariawita* and is a member of the World Council of Churches.

CCM is divided into 2 "custodies," or dioceses, with 23 parishes. Among 18 priests, 12 are women. The head of the church is the Highest Council of Superiors. The 3,000 members of CCM reside in Poland.

Starokatolicki Kosciol Mariawitow
(Old Catholic Church of Mariavites)
ul. Kazimierza Wielkiego
09-400 Plock
Poland

Kosciol Katolicki Mariawitow w RP
(Catholic Church of the Mariavites)
Felicjanow k. Plocka
09-470 Bodzanow
Poland

Leslaw Borowski

See also: Mary, Blessed Virgin; Roman Catholic Church; Women, Status and Role of; World Council of Churches.

References

Anson, Peter. *Bishops at Large*. London: Faber and Faber, 1964.

Ginter, Wladyslaw. *Informator o Kosciele Starokatolickim Mariawitow*. Plock, 1989.

Mazur, Krzysztof. *Mariawityzm w Polsce*. Krakow: Nomos, 1991.

Rybak, Stanislaw. *Mariawityzm. Studium historyczne.* Warsaw: Lege, 1992.

Old Catholic Church of the Netherlands

Old Catholic Church of the Netherlands (usually called Oud-Katholieke Kerk and officially titled Roomsch Katholieke Kerk van de Oud-Bisschoppelijke Clerezie) was founded on April, 23, 1723, but considers itself as the continuation of the Old Catholic Church that existed in the north Netherlands before the Reformation. The church traces its beginnings to 695, with the nomination of the Irish missionary Willibrord (ca. 658–739) to be the first archbishop of Utrecht. A problem arose in 1651, when the pope nominated Frederik Schenck van Toutenburg to the archbishop's chair, whereas since 1559, the year of the new grouping of the dioceses, the chapters of all the dioceses had been given the right to elect their own archbishops.

Another problem arose as result of the introduction of the Reformation into the Republic of the Seven United Netherlands. Rome failed to nominate new bishops as vacancies appeared, and it also refused to accept the nominations of the king of Spain, who at that time still formally held authority over the Netherlands. Eventually episcopal leadership fell to Sasbout Vosmeer (1548–1614), who in 1602 was appointed as the archbishop of Philippi *in partibus infidelium* (or in the regions of the infidels, a title usually given to bishops in non-Christian countries). Rome had intended to nominate him as archbishop of Utrecht, but the Peace of Münster in 1648 (ending the Thirty Years' War between Spain and the new Dutch Republic) blocked Vosmeer's elevation. Nevertheless, the Old Catholic Church claims that Vosmeer and his successors continued the Catholic worship and organization.

At the end of the 17th century the Roman Catholic Church tried to centralize its power over all Roman Catholics. Rome considered the Dutch Republic as a missionary country, to be governed by a nuncio directly out of Rome. The republic and the old Clerezie (priesthood) refused to accept the nuncio and instead acknowledged each other.

In the 17th century the Old Catholic Church adopted the perspective of Bishop Jansenius (1585–1638), popularly known as Jansenism. He emphasized a return to the authentic sources of Christian beliefs: the Bible and the writings of the fathers of the church, especially Augustine. Very important were his ideas about original sin: the fall of humanity has so depraved human nature that human beings, even after christening, cannot voluntarily do anything else but sin. Only the mercy of Christ makes it possible for humans to voluntarily do things that please God. Jansenius also championed spirituality and placed great emphasis on the inner life and on the dignified preparation for the receipt of the Holy Sacraments. In the field of the canon law, he stressed the governing power of the bishops and the council of prelates over and against that of the pope. This latter point became especially important later, as part of the schism between the Roman Catholic Church and the Old Catholic Church.

The definitive break with Rome occurred in 1723, when the Chapter of Utrecht elected Cornelis Steenoven (d. 1742) to be archbishop. He was consecrated by Dominicus Maria Varlet, a French archbishop. Most Catholic believers in the Netherlands continued to follow Rome, even though there were no bishops until 1853, when the hierarchy of the Roman Church was re-established in the Netherlands.

The early history of the Old Catholic Church as a separate entity was dominated by a series of internal and external problems. In 1742 the bishop of the Diocese of Haarlem and in 1758 the bishop of Deventer (without a diocese) were consecrated to secure the episcopal succession. Then began a period of struggle for the defense of the old beliefs and practices. The church refused to accept the dogma of the Immaculate Conception of the Blessed Virgin Mary proclaimed by Pope Pius IX on December 8, 1854.

Other Old Catholic churches arose from religious and ethical concerns over the decrees on the dogma of the infallibility of the pope, proclaimed by Rome at the First Vatican Council of 1870. For example, under the leadership of theologian Johann Joseph Ignaz von Döllinger (1799–1890), Catholics in Germany separated from the Roman Catholic Church in 1871. They sought connection with the Dutch Old Catholic Church, and subsequently J. H. Reinders was appointed as the first bishop in Germany, and in 1873 he was consecrated by Hermannus Heykamp, the bishop of Deventer (Netherlands). In Switzerland a fear of the loss of political freedom led to the formation in 1889 of the Union of Utrecht, a cooperative association of the Old Catholic bishops of the Netherlands, Germany, and Switzerland.

The Council of the Old Catholic Church of the Netherlands is the supreme ecclesiastical organ and can decide on binding points of doctrine. All Old Catholic churches are therefore members of the Council. Old Catholics accept the Bible as the scriptural reproduction of the original revelation and therefore the primary source for the religious doctrine of the church and for personal life. The Bible is understood through the tradition of the church. The ideal ecclesiastical situation and the canon of faith for the Old Catholic Church is the old and undivided church of the first 10 centuries; the conclusions of the councils of this early period provide the basics for Old Church believers. In this there is no difference with the tradition of the Roman Catholic Church.

Old Catholics also emphasize the doctrine of the redemption of humanity: no one can find the solution to life's problems and fulfillment in life without God. Only God can restore the broken relationship between God and humanity, and only through such restoration is some cooperation between God and humans possible. Redemption through faith is only possible in the community of the church.

The Old Catholic Church accepts seven sacraments, the intermediaries of salvation. They facilitate the construction of the community of saints. The sacraments support believers in their faith and equip them for holy conduct in life. In the sacrament of holy Communion, Christ is seen as really present in the elements of bread and wine, though the Roman Catholic doctrine of transubstantiation is not accepted. The Apostolic succession is essential for preaching and doctrine as well as for the succession of the priestly offices. The Apostolic succession—very essential in the Old Catholic Church—is linked with the consecration of bishops.

Old Catholic buildings closely resemble Roman Catholic churches. The altar, as token of Mount Golgotha (where Jesus was crucified), has a central place. In the middle of the altar there is an open space where during the consecration of the altar some relics of martyrs are enclosed. The church is decorated with various liturgical colors reflective of the different periods of the ecclesiastical year. The celebration of the Eucharist is the essential act of Sunday worship services.

The Old Catholic Church has an episcopal structure. There are two dioceses: the Archdiocese of Utrecht and the Diocese of Haarlem. Until 1982 the church also had a titular bishop of Deventer. The archdiocese encloses the whole country except the province of North Holland and has 18 parishes, with 8 priests, 5 deacons, and 4 priests for special services. The Diocese of Haarlem has 12 parishes, 12 priests, and 1 deacon. In addition, the church also supports stations with believers in regions without a priest or parish.

The bishops are elected by the priests and by some believers entitled to vote. The Chapter of Utrecht is very important in the organization of the church. Decisions are made by the provincial synod of the clergy and by the general synod, but they need the approbation of the episcopate. Clergy education is provided for by the church's seminary at Amersfoort, connected with the State University of Utrecht or the Catholic University of Utrecht. There are some 10,000 Old Catholic Church members in the Netherlands.

Internationally, the several Old Catholic Churches around the world are associated in the Union of Utrecht promulgated on September 24, 1889. Now, as a new century begins, Union member churches include Old Catholics in the Netherlands, Germany, Switzerland, Austria, countries of the former Yugoslavia, Poland, France, Sweden, Italy, the United States, and Canada. The International Old Catholic Bishops' Conference handles all questions with regard to other churches and makes decisions on matters of belief and ethics. Worldwide, the Old Catholic Church counts some 600,000 believers (with 400,000 in Germany and 25,000 in the United States).

The Old Catholic Church has a special place in the ecumenical world as a result of its genesis. As early as 1873 and 1874 the so-called Bonner Unionskonferenzen (Conferences) between the Roman Catholic Church, the Anglican Church, and the Eastern Orthodox churches had occurred. A special place in this process was assumed by the Anglican Church, though it was not until 1931 that full communion was restored between the Church of England and the Old Catholics. The several Old Catholic churches have been active in the World Council of Churches. Meanwhile, the relationship with the Roman Catholic Church remains laborious. The Old Catholic Church has made several attempts at reconciliation, without results until 1966. Relations have been hampered by the special proclamation of Pope Pius XII (1950) of the dogma of the physical assumption to heaven of the Blessed Virgin Mary. However, in 1966 Pope Paul VI removed the restrictions on dialogue between the two churches, and in 1972 the International Conference of Bishops of the Old Catholic Church and the Roman Catholic Secretary for the Unity of All Christians decided to cooperate in matters in the pastoral and sacramental sphere.

Old Catholic Church of the Netherlands
Kon. Wilhelminalaan 3
3818 HN Amersfoort
The Netherlands
http://www.okkn.nl/ (in Dutch)

E. G. Hoekstra

See also: Church of England; Eastern Orthodoxy; International Old Catholic Bishops' Conference; Roman Catholic Church; World Council of Churches.

References

Hoekstra, E. G., and M. H. Hoekstra. *Handboek christelijk Nederland. Kerken, gemeenten, samenkomsten en vergaderingen.* Kampen: Kok, 2008.

Kleef, B. A. *Geschiedenis van de Oud-Katholieke Kerk van Nederland.* Rev. ed. Assen, the Netherlands: Van Gorcum, 1953.

Küry, U. *Die alt-katholische Kirche. Ihre Geschichte, ihre Lehre, ihr Anliegen.* Frankfurt am Main: Ev., 1966.

Maan, P. J., K. Ouwens, F. Smit, and J. Visser. *De Oud-katholieke Kerk van Nederland. Leer en leven.* Hilversum, the Netherlands: Gooi & Sticht, 1979.

Moss, C. B. *The Old Catholic Movement.* Eureka Springs, AK: Episcopal Book Club, 1948.
Tans, J. A. G., and M. Kok. *Rome-Utrecht.* Hilversum, the Netherlands: Paul Brand, 1966.
Visser, J., F. Smit, and P. J. Maan. *Onafhankelijk van Rome, toch katholiek. 250 jaar oud-katholieke geschiedenis.* Hilversum, the Netherlands: Gooi & Sticht, 1973.

Old Catholicism

The Old Catholic movement traces its beginning to differences that developed in the Roman Catholic Church in France and the Low Countries around the teachings of Cornelius Jansen (1585–1638), who in the 17th century found himself in opposition to the Jesuits. However, the more immediate catalyst for the movement was the declaration of papal infallibility at the First Vatican Council in 1870–1871.

Portrait of seventeenth-century Flemish theologian Cornelius Jansen. He challenged the Catholic Church's doctrine of grace, giving rise to a movement known as Old Catholicism. (Library of Congress)

Jansen, a Dutch theologian residing at Port Royal, France, was accused by the Jesuits of Protestant tendencies because of his denial of free will. From that point the controversy surrounding his work expanded. Moving from France to Holland, Jansen found support in the person of Peter Codde (1656–1710), the bishop of Utrecht. Pope Clement XI (r. 1700–1721), however, favored the Jesuit position; he deposed Codde and did not replace him. Some years later, Dominique Marie Varlet, who had recently been consecrated the bishop of Babylon and was on his way to his new post, stopped in Holland, where he confirmed a number of children. A bishop is needed for confirmation, and there had been no confirmation in Codde's diocese since his being deposed. Varlet was consequently deposed, and he settled in Amsterdam. In 1724 he agreed to consecrate a new archbishop for Utrecht, and he subsequently consecrated bishops for Deventer and Haarlem as well. Thus, an administrative schism existed in Holland while Dutch Catholics appealed their situation to a church council.

In 1870 the first church council since the Council of Trent in the 16th century was called, in part in reaction to the problems the church encountered with the rise of secular governments in Europe and the resultant loss of its power. In Italy, the church was dealing with the loss of the papal state, as modern Italy was being created. The actions of the First Vatican Council strengthened the authority of the papal office, especially in the affirmation of papal infallibility, long sought in some parts of the church. This widely misunderstood doctrine stated that the pope was infallible on those rare occasions when he spoke "ex cathedra," or as the head of the church, in the act of defining doctrine. The doctrine elevated the pope's role as the prime teacher of the church and gave renewed importance to all of the documents, the encyclicals, issued by the pope, though these were not included among the documents declared infallible.

Some within the church opposed the new definition as a departure from tradition in ecclesiastical doctrine. In 1871, in anticipation of the Council's pronouncement, a conference was called by those who saw themselves as the defenders of the status quo. The conference was attended by delegates from both the Church of England and the schismatic diocese in Holland. The conference voted to organize the Old Catholic Church in hopes that large numbers of Catholics, including bishops and priests, would drop their alignment to Rome. That did not occur, but enough people did support the Old Catholics to allow national churches to be formed in Germany, Switzerland, Australia, and several other countries. Receiving no acknowledgment of their protest from the Roman Catholic Church, the three dioceses in Holland reorganized as the Old Catholic Church of the Netherlands and supplied episcopal orders to the other Old Catholic churches. (The Old Catholic Church's episcopal orders are considered valid by the Roman Catholic Church, but it considers the exercise of the powers of their office by the various bishops illegal.)

Over the next decades, the Old Catholics began to make a number of changes in religious practice, such as dropping compulsory fasting and private confession of sins to a priest. In 1874 they dropped requirements for priestly celibacy, and in 1880 moved toward a Mass in local languages in place of the Latin Mass.

In 1874–1875, the Old Catholics organized two Union Conferences in Bonn, Germany, to which Eastern Orthodox, Anglicans, and even Protestants were invited. These conferences located a wide range of theological agreement among the participants, though no administrative moves toward closer alignment were made. Then in 1889, the Old Catholic bishops created the Union of Utrecht. They established an annual bishops' conference and formulated principles to guide their common life. The Union was extended to include other Old Catholic bodies such as the Polish National Catholic Church and its European affiliate, the Polish Catholic Church. Then in 1931, representatives of the Church of England signed the Bonn Agreement, which created full sacramental intercommunion between the Church of England and the Old Catholic churches. That intercommunion had been made possible by the Old Catholic recognition of Anglican orders in 1925.

The intercommunion has since been extended to the various churches of the worldwide Anglican Communion. The relationship between the two communions has been disturbed over the years by the Anglican moves to ordain and even consecrate women, though those issues were largely resolved in the mid-1990s, when the Old Catholics began to admit women to the priesthood and the bishopric. The first Old Catholic woman was ordained by the Catholic Diocese of the Old Catholics in Germany in 1996. However, to monitor the ongoing relationship, in the late 1990s Anglican and Old Catholic authorities established the Anglican/Old Catholic International Coordinating Council. The Old Catholics have yet to come into communion with Protestants; however, in 1985 the Old Church in Germany reached an agreement with the Evangelical Church in Germany that allows members of both churches to share in the Eucharist at congregations of either church.

In the last century, the Old Catholic movement has developed along two different paths. The churches of the Union of Utrecht exist as substantial church bodies, with thousands of members. The Dutch, Austrian, German, and Swiss churches are members of the World Council of Churches. Representatives of the International Old Catholic Bishops' Conference meet annually with the representatives of the other world Christian communions. A second group began in 1908, when the bishop in Holland consecrated Arnold Harris Mathew (1852–1919), a former Anglican priest, under the assumption that he was leading a substantial body of people who wished to be Old Catholics. No such following existed, and contrary to his agreement, without the sanction of Utrecht, he consecrated others to the episcopacy. These orders were then transferred to North America, where a series of new independent Old Catholic jurisdictions were established by bishops who founded dioceses in the hope that a church would emerge around them. Over the years more than 100 such bodies have been founded, and through the 20th century, the phenomenon of bishops without churches spread across Europe. The independent Old Catholic churches have been joined by independent Anglican and Orthodox churches that have followed a similar pattern.

J. Gordon Melton

See also: Anglican Communion/Anglican Consultative Council; Catholic Diocese of the Old Catholics in Germany; Church of England; Evangelical Church in Germany; International Old Catholic Bishops' Conference; Jesuits; Old Catholic Church of the Netherlands; Polish National Catholic Church and Polish Catholic Church; Roman Catholic Church; World Council of Churches.

References

Anson, Peter F. *Bishops at Large*. London: Faber and Faber, 1964.

Bess, Douglas. *Divided We Stand: A History of the Continuing Anglican Movement*. Nashville: Apocryphile Press, 2006.

Huelin, George. *Old Catholics and Anglicans, 1931–1981*. New York: Oxford University Press, 1983.

Moss, C. B. *The Old Catholic Movement*. Eureka Springs, AK: Episcopal Book Club, 1977.

Plummer, John P. *The Many Paths of the Independent Sacramental Movement*. Nashville: Apocryphile Press, 2006.

Pruter, Karl, and J. Gordon Melton. *The Old Catholic Sourcebook*. New York: Garland Publishing, 1983.

Queen, Andre J. *Old Catholic: History, Ministry, Faith & Mission*. Lincoln, NB: iUniverse, 2003.

Ward, Gary L. *Independent Bishops: An International Directory*. Detroit, MI: Apogee Books, 1990.

Old Rite Romanian Orthodox Church

The Old Rite Romanian Orthodox Church traces its beginnings to October 1924, when the Romanian Orthodox Church introduced the Gregorian calendar to its members. Prior to that time, the church had followed the Julian calendar (instituted by Julius Caesar in 46 BCE). The Gregorian calendar, followed by most of the world by that time, differed from the Julian calendar by some 13 days.

A number of the Orthodox faithful rejected the new calendar, and some monks left the monasteries that had instituted the new calendar and built new churches and monasteries. These Old Rite Romanian Orthodox Christians continued the Orthodox belief and practice, with the exception of the dates when the various church festivals and holy days were observed. Their leaders argued that the festivals of the church had been established by the councils of Nicaea (325) and Antioch (345) and could not be changed. Consequently, any alteration of the calendar was regarded as a violation of the decisions made by the fathers of the church. In this matter, they made common cause with the Monastic Community on Mount Athos in Greece.

In 1930 the Romanian authorities began a period of harassment and persecution of the Old Rite believers. A number of their priests were arrested. However, the church persisted, and in 1936 the Romanian Council on Ministries decided that the Old Rite believers were to be integrated back into the Romanian Orthodox Church. More than 30 of the Old Rite church buildings were demolished. Following World War II, the priests were released from prison. They gathered the remaining body of believers (some 12,000) and demanded that their confiscated goods be returned. In 1945 the new Ministry of Cults granted the freedom to practice their faith to the Old Rite Church. A new center for the church was established at Suceava.

In 1948 a new General Status of Religious Denominations Law was passed, failing to recognize the Old Rite as a legal entity. A new wave of persecution hit the church in 1953. Again, most of the churches were closed and priests were arrested. Three church buildings were demolished, as were two monasteries. It was not until 1990 that Romanian authorities again officially recognized the church. The church quickly revived and by 1992 reported 18 churches, 8 monasteries, and 23,634 members, most of whom resided in the Suceava and Neamt districts.

At the same time as the Old Rite Church was forming in one part of Romania, others who similarly rejected the calendar change gathered in northern Moldavia, where they formed several large communities and monasteries. Although generally following Orthodox belief and practice, these believers have a special regard for the authority of the Synod of Constantinople and pay special attention to the Pilalion, a collection of religious canons approved by that synod, which they regard as the "guide of the church until the end of the world." In 1945, during the reprieve in the persecution, they had been reduced to approximately 2,000 believers and 6 associated monasteries. In 1990 the Moldavian believers were recognized as the Traditional Christian Church with an administrative center in Minceşti.

The Old Rite Romanian Orthodox Church is currently led by Metropolitan Vlasie, president of the Synod of the True Orthodox Church of Romania. He is assisted by seven additional bishops. The church is in communion with the True (Old Calendar) Orthodox Church of Greece under the jurisdiction of Metropolitan Cyprian and the Old Calendar Church in Bulgaria. In 2008, it reported 130 parishes, 13 monasteries, and 21 *sketes* (communities of hermits).

Old Rite Romanian Orthodox Church
c/o Monastery of the Transfiguration
Slatioara, Moldavia
Romania
http://www.mitropoliaslatioara.ro/ (in Romanian)

J. Gordon Melton

See also: Romanian Orthodox Church; True (Old Calendar) Orthodox Church of Greece.

References

Branzea, Nicolae I., and Stefan Lonita. *Religious Life in Romania.* Bucharest: Editura Paideia, 1999.

Bujor, Constantin. *Resisting unto Blood: Sixty-five Years of Persecution of the True Old Calendar Orthodox Church of Romania, October 1924–December 1989.* Etna, CA: Center for Traditionalist Orthodox Studies, 2002.

Cuciuc, Constantin. *Atlasul Religiilor şi al Monumentelor Istorice Religioase din Romania.* Bucharest: Editura Gnosis, 1996.

Olympus, Mount

Rising 9,577 feet, Mount Olympus, located about 70 miles from Thessaloniki, Macedonia, is the highest mountain in Greece, and one of the highest mountains in Europe. In ancient Greek Pagan religion, Olympus was believed to be the home of the gods and especially the Twelve Olympians, the 12 principal Greek deities, whose stories would be told in the writings of Homer and Hesiod.

The Olympians came to power when Zeus and his siblings overthrew their father Cronos and the other old deities (the Titans), who were hurled down to the abyss of Tartarus. Once in power, Zeus, fearing that he would in turn be the victim of one of his sons, consumed his first wife Metis. But she was already pregnant and the two within his stomach gave Zeus a hearty case of nausea. Eventually his daughter Athena would emerge fully grown and dressed as a warrior from Zeus's head. Others of the 12 were either Zeus's siblings—Hera (also Zeus's wife), Hades/Pluto, Poseidon, Aphrodite, Demeter, and Hestia—or his offspring—Ares, Apollo, Artemis, Hermes, and Hephaestus. The number and makeup remained somewhat fluid and different lists include additional deities in the Olympian household. The extended family would also be enlarged by the likes of the Muses, also known as the Olympiades, daughters of Zeus who were seen as residing in the deep ravines of the mountain.

In ancient Greek religion, each of the different deities had responsibility and primary concern for different regions of Earth and/or areas of human life. Olympus was their common space. They would also be joined in their work by additional deities with whom both the Olympian deities and humans interacted. The other deities would come to the mountain home when summoned by Zeus.

The Zeus family of deities were seen, not as residing on the mountain proper, but in a palace, higher up above the clouds. Here they lived a life of relative leisure, feasting on ambrosia and nectar and being entertained by Apollo playing his lyre and by the Graces and the Muses.

The Olympian deities would be worshipped in temples found throughout Greece. One appropriate form of worship was the offering of animals for sacrifice. It was believed, for example, that the Olympians loved the smell of beef and mutton being cooked, but did not care for their taste. Thus mortals would sacrifice sheep and cattle to them, and afterward the temple officials would either consume the meat themselves or sell it to support the temple. Festivals were a regular and frequent part of Greek life, with each deity enjoying special days and her or his own primary following.

Zeus wielded his authority from his seat on a large polished black marble throne, heavily trimmed with gold. Each of the seven steps of the pedestal upon which it rested was decorated in one of the seven colors of the rainbow. At his right arm was a ruby-eyed golden

View of Mount Olympus, Greece. In Greek mythology, Mount Olympus was home to the 12 Olympians, the highest gods in the Greek pantheon. (iStockPhoto.com)

eagle. He sat on a purple ram's fleece, which could when needed be used for rainmaking. Zeus and Hera had lodgings at the south end of the palace. The view out their window overlooked the prominent Greek cities—Athens, Thebes, Sparta, Corinth, Argos, and Mycenae. The other deities lived around the open square in the center of the palace. Athena provided the gods' and goddesses' clothing, while things of a more solid nature were made of metal by Vulcan (or Hephaestus) who was architect, armourer, and chariot builder on Olympus.

In the time that the Olympian gods and goddesses dominated the religious life of Greece (until the fourth century CE, when Christianity emerged in power), the main sanctuary of the Macedonians, who had come to power through Alexander the Great and his successors, was located at Dion, a site located between Mount Olympus and the nearby Thermalhos Sea. Here the Macedonian kings would come to make sacrifices before engaging in war. The site had a number of temples to the Olympian deities (Zeus, Demeter, Artemis) to which were added temples to Egyptian deities such as Isis and Sarapis, the Egyptian religion spreading through the Macedonian Empire in the decades after Alexander's death. Near the base of Olympus, a number of towns and cities maintained temples where worship of the Olympian deities and the related pantheon was conducted. Included would be the cities of Petra, Pimbleia, Leivithra (believed to be the home of Orpheus), Pieris, Atira, and Pythio (where the god Apollo was especially worshipped).

In 2003, Greece asked the United Nations Educational, Scientific and Cultural Organization (UNESCO) to consider Olympus for a place on the list of World Heritage Sites. It remains under consideration.

J. Gordon Melton

See also: Athens; Wiccan Religion.

References

Burkert, Walter. *Structure and History in Greek Mythology and Ritual*. Berkeley: University of California Press, 1982.

Graf, Fritz. *Greek Mythology: An Introduction*. Baltimore: Johns Hopkins University Press, 1996.

Woodard, Roger D. Th*e Cambridge Companion to Greek Mythology*. Cambridge: Cambridge University Press, 2007.

■ Oman

One of several countries on the Arabian Peninsula, Oman occupies 82,310 square miles of its easternmost corner. It is bounded on the south and east by the Arabian Sea and on the north by the Gulf of Oman. To the west are the United Arab Emirates, Saudi Arabia, and Yemen. The oil-rich country is home to 3,300,000 people, most of whom live along its lengthy coastline.

Even though much of Oman is desert, the inhabitable portions were already a prosperous trading site as early as the third century BCE. Traders developed oceangoing routes across the Indian Ocean to Indonesia and Vietnam. Most residents of the area converted to Islam in the seventh century, and as a result, some dissidents left the country and founded the city of Zanzibar on the East African coast.

Since the eighth century, the secular and religious leadership in the country has been united in the person of the sultan. The area has been the scene of numerous wars, as different neighboring powers attempted to seize the country's wealth. Finally, in 1507 the Portuguese arrived and assumed control of the area for more than 150 years. A 20-year revolt finally succeeded in driving the Portuguese out in 1650, and Omanis eventually recaptured related territory along the African coast, including Zanzibar (1698).

Through the 18th century, Oman expanded its territory, eventually stretching from the Gulf of Oman to Madagascar. In 1832 the capital was moved to Zanzibar. This occurred just as the British presence was growing in the lands surrounding the Indian Ocean,

Sultan Qaboos Grand Mosque in Muscat, capital of Oman. (AP/Wide World Photos)

and in 1856, the two heirs to the throne divided the African and Arabian portion of their land, forming two separate countries. In 1891 the British made present-day Oman a protectorate. An internal fight for power led to the division of Oman in 1920, but it was reunited in 1955, primarily in response to British pressure.

The present sultan, Qaboos ben Said, came to power in 1970 after overthrowing his father. He has brought his country into a strong alliance with the United States, which has been interested in its oil reserves and its strategic location relative to Iran, the Persian Gulf, and Middle Eastern oil fields.

Oman appears to have accepted Islam in a relatively peaceful fashion in the year 630, when the two rulers agreed to submit to the faith. Islamic states in the region were dividing into Sunni and Shia (Shiite)

Oman

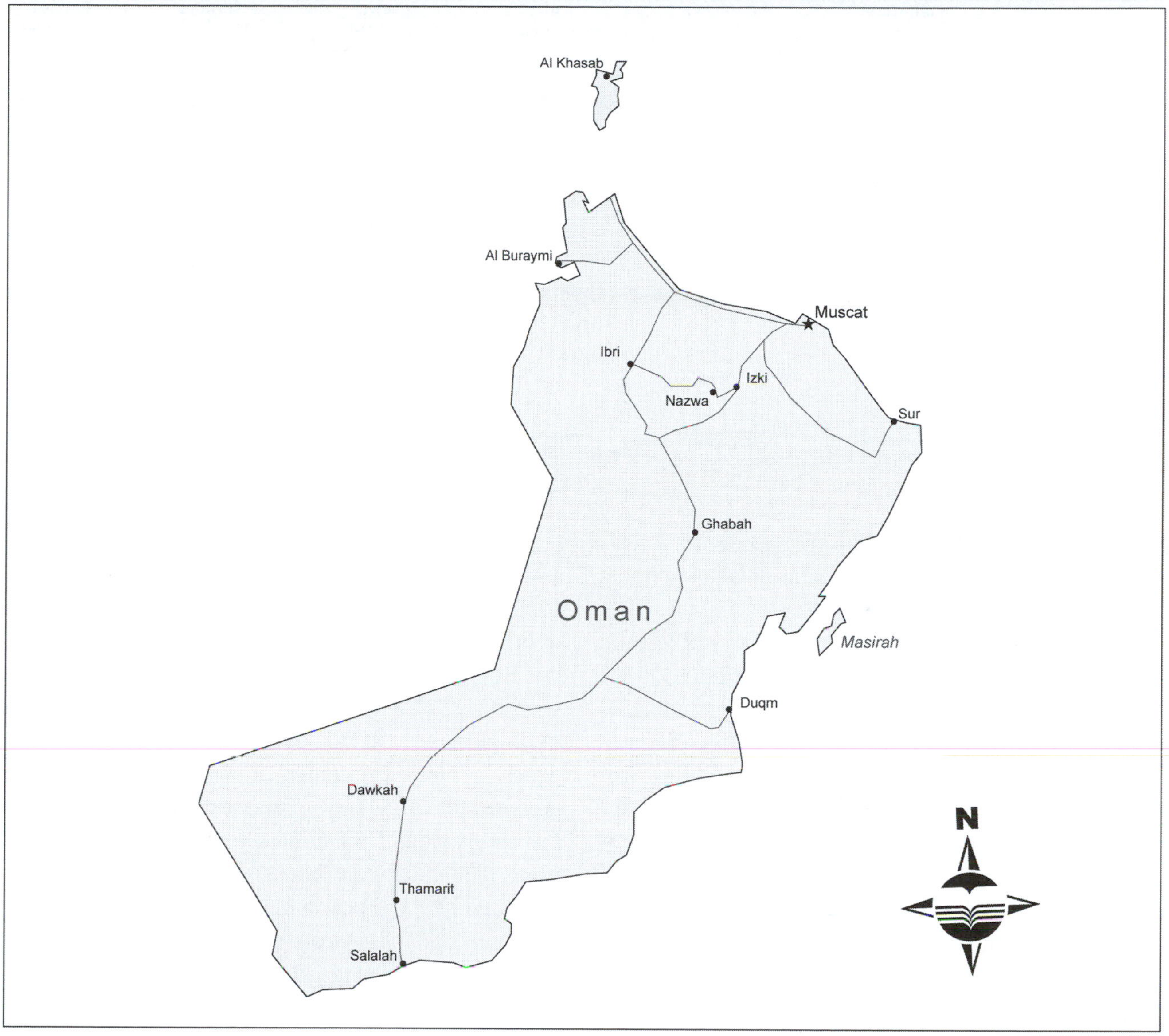

camps. The primary issue dividing the community concerned succession, the Sunnis placing leadership in the hands of the descendants of the tribe of the Prophet Muhammad, and the Shias placing it in the hands of members of the Prophet's family. Oman took a third option that has come to be known as the Ibadi School of Islam. The Ibadis believe that leadership should go to the best candidate in the Muslim community. That belief allowed Omani leadership to rise, but it also meant that continual strife and even wars would be experienced during the process of choosing a new leader.

Dissent on the issue of succession placed the Ibadi leaders at odds with both the Shia and the Sunni peoples who surrounded them, on the one hand, and on the other hand, it led them to develop a level of tolerance toward people of other religions that developed into a doctrine of quietism. Unlike those with extremely evangelical approaches to Islam, the Ibadi have tended to allow non-Ibadi people in realms under their control to retain their faith. This approach also served the needs of Ibadi traders as they moved about non-Muslin areas of Africa. Today the majority of Omani Muslims are

Oman

Religion	Followers in 1970	Followers in 2010	% of Population	Annual % growth 2000–2010	Followers in 2025	Followers in 2050
Muslims	739,000	2,429,000	87.8	0.86	3,110,000	3,919,000
Hindus	2,000	150,000	5.4	–0.19	220,000	300,000
Christians	3,800	131,000	4.7	2.22	190,000	273,000
Roman Catholics	470	75,000	2.7	2.23	110,000	150,000
Orthodox	1,200	20,400	0.7	2.07	30,000	42,000
Independents	620	24,000	0.9	2.47	35,000	58,000
Buddhists	0	21,500	0.8	0.86	35,000	50,000
Sikhs	0	18,500	0.7	0.86	28,000	40,000
Baha'is	300	10,000	0.4	0.86	20,000	35,000
Agnostics	1,600	6,500	0.2	0.86	10,000	20,000
Ethnoreligionists	0	550	0.0	0.86	300	500
New religionists	0	300	0.0	0.90	500	800
Atheists	0	200	0.0	0.82	500	1,000
Total population	**747,000**	**2,767,000**	**100.0**	**0.86**	**3,614,000**	**4,639,000**

Ibadi, but as many as one-third of the country's residents are followers of various Sunni (Wahhabi, Shaffite, Hanbalite) and Shia beliefs.

Oman is officially a Muslim country, and Islamic law dominates the judicial system. Sultan Qaboos ben Said has voiced his opinion that various religious groups have a right to establish their faith communities in the country as long as they are law abiding. Religious life is guided from the government's Ministry of Awqaf and Religious Affairs (*awqaf* refers to religious endowments, such as mosques and schools and the state-administered revenues for their upkeep). Authorities monitor mosques for departures from orthodoxy. The sultan has granted land to a variety of different non-Muslim religious groups for the erection of religious facilities, but these must be placed behind high walls. Non-Muslims may not proselytize within the Muslim community—a regulation that also limits the circulation of any religious literature outside of the group's membership. Islam is a requirement for citizenship, but approximately 40 percent of the population are expatriates who have moved to Oman for various reasons, primarily to work in the oil fields.

There is no evidence that Christianity had penetrated to Oman by the time that the country adopted Islam in the seventh century. Thus, Christianity is believed to have first entered the land with the coming of the Portuguese in 1507–1508 and also to have departed with them. A new era began in 1889–1890 with the arrival of James Cantine and Samuel Zwemer (1867–1952) in Muscat, Oman's capital. Their visit was part of their work with the American Arab Mission. In 1894 the Reformed Church in America (RCA) assumed sponsorship of their work, which extended throughout the region. The RCA opened a hospital in Muscat, which became the center of the nation's Christian presence for many years. This work, now known as the Protestant Church of Oman, includes Protestants of many denominational backgrounds and continues to be served by RCA personnel. Its work is concentrated in Muscat and in the nearby communities of Ruwi and Ghala. The sultan also granted to the church parcels of land in Salalah and Sohar.

The Roman Catholic Church re-established itself in the area in 1841 with the assignment of personnel to Aden (Yemen). That work grew successively into a prefecture (1854) and a vicariate (1888), and in 1889 it gave birth to the Vicariate of Arabia, now administered from Abu Dhabi (United Arab Emirates) and responsible for Catholics in Oman. The first Catholic church in Oman was erected in 1977 in Muscat, and subsequently, as the community has grown, other churches have appeared.

In recent decades, a number of religious communities have emerged among the expatriate population. The Anglican Church has been one of the strongest.

Anglican congregations are under the jurisdiction of the Episcopal Church in Jerusalem and the Middle East. In 1960, in response to the sultan's request for a physician, Dr. Bruwell Kennedy moved to the Buaimi Oasis in the northeast corner of Oman. Sponsored by The Evangelical Alliance Mission (TEAM), an American-based evangelical sending agency, Kennedy was given unusual liberty to carry out both medical and religious work among the Bedouins of the area. The TEAM staff soon numbered more than 20 members.

A large percentage of the expatriate community has come from India. Among the first group to request and accept the sultan's recognition were Christians from Kerala state in India, who organized the initial congregation of the Syrian Orthodox Church of Malabar and of the Mar Thomas Syrian Church. There are also various Indian-based Pentecostal and evangelical groups. Many of the Indian residents in Oman are Hindus, and the sultan has been as generous to them as to the Christians. The Hindu community is centered on the Shiva and Bajrangbali Temple in Muscat and additional temples in other towns dedicated to Govindrayji, Shree Ganesh, and Devi Kalaka.

J. Gordon Melton

See also: Episcopal Church in Jerusalem and the Middle East; Hanbalite School of Islam; Ibadhi Islam; Islam; Mar Thoma Syrian Church; Muhammad; Reformed Church in America; Roman Catholic Church; Shia Islam; Syrian Orthodox Church of Malabar; Wahhabi Islam; Zwemer, Samuel Marinus.

References

Alhinai, Abdulrahman Bin Ali. *Ceremonies and Celebrations of Oman*. Reading, Berkshire, UK: Garnet Publishing, 2000.

Bierschenk, T. *Religion and Political Structure: Remarks on Ibadism in Oman and the Mzab (Algeria)*. Bielefeld, Germany: University of Bielefeld, 1983.

Ghubash, Hussein. *Oman Islamic Democratic Tradition*. London: Routledge, 2006.

Horner, N. A. "Present-day Christianity in the Gulf States of the Arabian Peninsula." *Occasional Bulletin of Missionary Research* 2 (April 1978): 53–63.

Maamiry, A. H. *Oman and Ibadhism*. 2nd ed. New Delhi: Lancers Books, 1989.

Owtran, Francis. *A Modern History of Oman: Formation of the State since 1920*. London: I. B. Tauris, 2004.

Omoto

Like Tenrikyo and Tensho Kotai Jingukyo, Omoto (Great Origin) was founded in Japan by a peasant woman, Deguchi Nao (1836–1918). Before she founded Omoto in 1892, Deguchi Nao had been involved in a new religion called Konkokyo. In 1897 she met the mystic and spiritualist Ueda Kisaburo (1871–1948), who became her son-in-law by marrying her daughter Sumi. He later changed his name to Deguchi Onisaburo and from 1904 became known as the *kyosu,* or doctrinal founder, of the movement while Deguchi Nao held the title of *kaiso,* or spiritual founder.

Although fiercely loyal to Japan and supportive of its expansionist policy in the Far East, both of these figures expressed literally and symbolically a deep hatred of the modernizing reforms introduced by the Meiji government (1868–1912) and its taxation policies in the rural areas. They challenged not only the government's modernization program but also the core myth on which the imperial system was based: that Amaterasu was the divine ancestor of the imperial line. Deguchi Onisaburo went so far as to claim that he himself was the authentic leader of Japan. This opposition led the movement to develop a powerful utopian vision of the ideal society and to construct a model of such a society in Kyoto Prefecture, at Ayabe City, at the center of which is the Miroku-den (Hall of the Future Buddha, Maitreya) and the Choseiden sanctuary.

Government persecution followed the establishment of this center; the movement's buildings were destroyed in 1921 and in 1935, and Deguchi Onisaburo was imprisoned on the charge of lèse-majesté. In 1935 the movement was dissolved. At this stage the estimated size of the membership was 2 million. Omoto would never again attract so many people.

In January 1946 Deguchi Onisaburo reorganized the movement and registered it as a religious juridical entity with the name Omoto Aizenen (Grand Source of the Community of Love and Virtue). In 1952 it adopted its present name of Omoto.

Omoto's teachings are contained in the Ofudesaki (The Tip of the Divine Writing Brush), written by Deguchi Nao, who is said to have been illiterate, under the inspiration of the deity Ushitora-no-Konjin (Great Father God). In this sacred text Deguchi Nao predicts the destruction of humanity and calls for a return to traditional ways of living and for the construction of the Kingdom of Miroku.

Among Deguchi Onisaburo's contributions to the movement's spiritual development and teaching is his insistence on art as meditation and prayer, as a spiritual discipline in its own right. Omoto also practices a form of meditation known as *chinkon kishin*, which leads to union with God. Once a month Omoto holds a communal service with roots in classical Shinto beliefs that see the divine everywhere in nature. A number of annual festivals convey the same sense of Omoto's Shinto roots, the most important being the Spring Festival, or Setsubun, which commemorates the day on which God revealed himself to Deguchi Nao; the Miroku Festival in April; and the Harvest Festival during which a pilgrimage is made to the Hill of Ten'nodaira (Imperial Flat Hill) where Nao, Onisaburo, and Sumi are buried.

Since Deguchi Nao's death, the movement has been headed by her female descendants. Its current head is Kiyoko, her great-great-granddaughter. Omoto's administrative headquarters are at Kameoka City, Kyoto Prefecture, where it has built the Ten-onkyo (Holy Grounds) and the Bansho-den (Hall of a Million Beatitudes). Although its membership in Japan has declined to around 150,000, Omoto has exercised great influence on the development of the teachings and practices of other Japanese new religions, particularly Seicho-No-Ie (House of Growth) and Sekai Kyusei Kyo (The Church of World Messianity).

Omoto has very few members outside Japan. It is nonetheless very active abroad in pursuit of its objectives. Among its main activities are programs for the protection of the environment, organic farming, the teaching of Esperanto, interreligious dialogue, and ecumenism. It participates in numerous joint projects with Christian, Muslim, and Buddhist movements, among others, and supports the construction of a world government. It sees the nation-state and the teaching of specific languages as dangerously divisive.

Omoto Tokyo Headquarters
2-1-44 Ikenohata
Taito-ku, Tokyo 110-0008
Japan
http://www.oomoto.or.jp/

Peter B. Clarke

See also: Konkokyo; Seicho-No-Ie; Sekai Kyusei Kyo; Tenrikyo; Tensho Kotai Jingukyo.

References

Berthon, Jean-Pierre. *Omoto, esperance millenariste d'une nouvelle religion Japonaise*. Paris (Atelier Alpha Bleue): Cahiers d'Etudes et de Documents sur les Religions du Japan, 1985.

Hardacre, Helen. "Gender and the Millennium in Omotokyo." In *Japanese Civilization in the Modern World,* edited by T. Humasao, H. Hardacre, and H. Nakamaki, 47–62. Osaka: National Museum of Ethnography, 1990.

Hino, I. P. *The Ofudesaki: The Holy Scriptures of Omoto*. Kameoka, Japan: Omoto Foundation, 1974.

Ooms, Emily Groszos. *Women and Millenarian Protest in Meiji Japan: Deguchi Nao and Omotokyo*. New York: Cornell University East Asia Program, 1993.

Ontakekyo

Ontakekyo (Great Mountain Sect) is a Shinto-based Japanese religion. In the early 19th century, Shimoyama Osuke, a devotee of nature worship, founded Ontakekyo. Also known as Mitakekyo, Ontakekyo is one of the religious groups included among the "Sect Shinto" (*kyoha shinto*), those autonomous religious organizations that the Japanese government recognized between 1868 and 1945. The government recognized Ontakekyo as an independent sect within Shinto in 1882. By the late 20th century, an extensive study of Japanese religions carried out by Hori and other Japanese scholars (1981) had identified about 15 groups that were derived from Ontakekyo.

Ontakekyo is a mountain worship sect. Like many other religious movements in Japan, it was initially a voluntary association of people who were interested in climbing mountains as a religious discipline. As a devotional association, Ontakekyo encouraged the ritual climbing of Mount Ontake. The group's founder, Shimoyama, gathered like-minded devotees and established a permanent structure for the pilgrimage to Mount Ontake. Even today the popularity of Mount Ontake among the Japanese as a place of pilgrimage and religious practice is quite apparent in various areas, where small hills, such as the one in Nisshin-shi, Aichi Prefecture, are identified as Ontakesan. By climbing Ontakesan, pilgrims intend to produce newly empowered spiritual strength.

Mount Ontake, 10, 049 feet high, is located on the border between Nagano and Gifu prefectures of central Japan. Among the Japanese, it is popularly called Ontakesan (Great Mountain) and has for centuries been regarded as a sacred mountain. From the latter part of the Sengoku (Civil War) period (1467–1568), the Shinto shrine on the summit of Ontakesan has functioned as an object of worship.

Characteristic features of the Ontakekyo include its stress on ascetic training and the worship of mountain deities. For the members of Ontakekyo, Ontake Okami (the Great Kami of Mount Ontake) is the primary object of worship. As a divine being, Ontake Okami combines three divine bodies: Kunitokotachi no Mikoto, Onamuchi no Mikoto, and Sukunahikona no Mikoto.

Japanese farmers believe mountains such as Ontakesan are holy places where divinities dwell. In early spring, they select a day to worship Ontakesan. This religious practice is connected with the folk belief that the god of the mountain (*yama no kami*) descends from the mountain to the rice fields in spring.

Even today, in summer, pious devotees dressed in white robes climb the mountain to reach Ontake Shrine as an act of religious piety. A bus takes the pilgrims partway up the mountain, but the remainder of the pilgrimage to the summit is an arduous one, particularly in the winter months. In winter, Mount Ontake is covered with snow and only very rarely do pilgrims climb the mountain, as it takes some 12 hours for the journey. Until the early 19th century, women were not allowed to climb Mount Ontake beyond the Mitake Shrine.

As a religious group, Ontakekyo aims to generate purity of heart, to realize divine virtues, and to contribute toward a stable nation, rich with spirituality. Members interpret the vicissitudes of life, such as fortune and misfortune, happiness and unhappiness, as indications of divine will. Although they engage in possession and healing, they also practice ascetic and purification rituals, such as *chinka-shiki* (rite of pacifying fire) and *kugatachi-shiki* (rite of sprinkling hot water), and a variety of divination and breathing exercises.

Ontakekyo
3775 Aza Obuchi
Futana-machi
Nara-shi, Nara-ken 631
Japan

Mahinda Deegalle

See also: Pilgrimage.

References

Bocking, Brian. *A Popular Dictionary of Shinto*. Surrey, UK: Curzon Press, 1996.

Hori, Ichiro, et al., eds. *Japanese Religion: A Survey by the Agency for Cultural Affairs*. Tokyo: Kodansha International, 1981.

Ordo Templi Orientis

The Ordo Templi Orientis is the largest branch of an Esoteric tradition dating back to the occult milieu as it existed in Europe during the first decades of the 20th century. During his long occult career, British magus Aleister Crowley (1875–1947) ultimately took control of the Ordo Templi Orientis (OTO). The organization had been established in Germany by Theodor Reuss (1855–1923), based on certain ideas developed by Austrian businessman Carl Kellner (1850–1905). Not all members of the OTO accepted Crowley's flamboyant authority, however, and several "pre-Crowleyan" OTOs are still in existence to this day. Crowley's death in

1947 was followed by a complicated struggle for succession. At present, there are more than 100 rival "Crowleyan" OTOs (in addition to several "pre-Crowleyan") throughout the world. The largest organization is known as the "Caliphate" OTO, based both on the title of "Caliph" granted to its leaders, and on a joke by Crowley himself on the phonetic similarity between "Caliph" and "California." The Caliphate has successfully claimed rights to the trademark OTO, at least in the United States, and to the copyright on Crowley's writings in certain countries.

Forerunners of the Caliphate OTO include the organization created in the United States by Charles Stansfeld Jones (1886–1950), Crowley's one-time "magickal son", and the Agapé Lodge, founded in Pasadena by Wilfred Talbot Smith (1885–1957), and which claimed rocket scientist Jack Parsons (1914–1952) as its most famous (or notorious) member. The present-day Caliphate OTO traces its direct origins back to German-born Karl Germer (1885–1962), a prominent disciple of Crowley who moved to California and claimed to be his successor (although he was not particularly active in running the OTO as an organization). Germer's own succession is also a somewhat disputed matter. Both in American courts of justice and among a significant section of Crowley's followers in the United States (and several other countries), Grady Louis McMurtry (1918–1985) gained official recognition as Germer's legitimate successor, taking the name Hymenaeus Alpha. In 1982, the Caliphate OTO (with McMurtry as its leader) was legally incorporated in the United States. McMurtry died in 1985, and French-born William Breeze, a member of its New York chapter, became his successor under the name of Hymenaeus Beta.

What is Crowleyan "orthodoxy" and who is, or is not, loyal to Crowley's teaching is a matter of endless debate among the many contentious OTO branches throughout the world. But, be that as it may be, the Caliphate OTO is certainly one of the organizations most loyal to Crowley, whose main writings, published in *The Holy Book of Thelema,* are regarded by the membership as holy scripture, with particular emphasis on the *Book of the Law*, received by Crowley through magical revelation in Cairo in 1904. The Caliphate's initiatory system, in 13 degrees, is also quite similar to Crowley's, and includes the various teachings on sexual magic for which Crowley is both famous and infamous.

At present (2008), the Caliphate OTO counts 3,218 members throughout the world, in 151 official groups in 45 different countries.

Ordo Templi Orientist
Postfach 33 20 12
D-14180 Berlin
Germany
http://oto-usa.org/.

Massimo Introvigne and PierLuigi Zoccatelli

See also: Crowley, Aleister; Thelema.

References

Crowley, Aleister. *Magick.* York Beach, ME: Samuel Weiser, 1973.

Heidrick, Bill. *Magick and Qabalah.* Berkeley, CA: Ordo Templi Orientis, 1980.

The Holy Book of Thelema. York Beach, ME: Samuel Weiser, 1988.

Hymenaeus Beta, ed. *The Equinox* 3, no. 10. New York: Thelema Publications, 1986.

Reuss, Theodor, and Aleister Crowley. *OTO Rituals and Sex Magick.* Ed. by A. R. Naylor. Thames: I-H-O Books, 1999.

Symonds, John. *The Beast 666: The Life of Aleister Crowley.* London: The Pindar Press, 1997.

Organization of African Instituted Churches

The Organization of African Independent Churches (OAIC) was founded in 1978 in Cairo, Egypt. The link with Egypt was significant, for African Initiated Churches (AICs) saw Egypt and Ethiopia as the birthplaces of the oldest independent churches in Africa, the Coptic Orthodox Church and the Ethiopian Orthodox Tawahedo Church, both established alternatives to Western Christianity. Many previous attempts to bring together AICs in ecumenical associations had ended in failure. By 1985 the All Africa Conference of Churches

(AACC) had accepted only 15 AICs into membership and the World Council of Churches (WCC) had admitted only 7, out of literally hundreds of applications to both organizations from across Africa.

Then AIC leaders Reuben Spartas of Uganda and Arthur Gathuna of Kenya pioneered the links with the Coptic Church, first visiting Cairo in 1943. AICs in several African countries began to form national councils, and by 1986 some 95 such councils had been formed, a remarkable achievement although 41 of these councils were in South Africa and Nigeria. The Kenya African United Churches was the first to be established in Kenya, in 1961, through the efforts of James Ochwatta of the African Orthodox Church. This success was short-lived, however, and in 1963 Ochwatta helped form the East African United Churches, which included all the large AICs in Kenya and was supported by politicians like Jomo Kenyatta (ca. 1891–1978), first president of Kenya, and Oginga Odinga (ca. 1911–1994). Zakayo Kivuli of the Africa Israel Church, Nineveh, was grand metropolitan of the organization, Lucas Nuhu of the Holy Spirit Church of East Africa was chairman, and Ochwatta was general secretary. This council unsuccessfully tried to register with the Kenyan government and to join the AACC and the WCC. In 1984 it was renamed the International Holy Spirit and United Indigenous Churches, with Nuhu as chair.

In 1976 Pope Shenouda III (b. 1923), Coptic patriarch of Alexandria, consecrated M. S. Mikhail as bishop of African affairs, and Mikhail took the name Bishop Antonious Markos. From his office in Nairobi, Bishop Markos began an extensive tour of AICs all over Africa, met political and mainline church leaders, and gained financial support for development projects for AICs. Two years later, Pope Shenouda invited 20 significant AIC leaders to the inauguration of the OAIC in Cairo, with the basic aim of facilitating teaching, training, and theological education. The executive elected at this time included (among others) Joseph Diangienda of the Kimbanguist Church in the Congo as a member, Nigeria's Primate E. O. A. Adejobi of the Church of the Lord (Aladura) as chairman, and Bishop Markos as organizing secretary. The second conference was held in 1982 in Nairobi, with representatives from 17 African nations and 31 AICs. A constitution was approved and Bishop Mathew Ajuoga of the Church of Christ in Africa (Kenya) was elected chairman, a post he held for 15 years.

In 1985 the name of the OAIC was changed to the Organization of African Instituted Churches at the request of the Kenyan government, and registration was effected. Bishop Markos resigned as OAIC executive secretary in 1990 after increasing tension with AIC leaders, and in 1995 the OAIC reorganized itself into eight regional groupings. The first issue of an official OAIC magazine, *Baragumu: The African Independent Churches Voice*, was launched in 1996. The third conference of the OAIC was held in 1997, when Nigerian Baba Aladura Dr. G. I. M. Otubu of the Eternal Sacred Order of the Cherubim and Seraphim was elected chairman. The new general secretary was Kenyan Archbishop Njeru Wambugu of the National Independent Church of Africa.

Then a significant shift in policy was made—member churches could become members of the OAIC only through their regional councils and could no longer join by applying directly to the international office. The OAIC office in Nairobi continues to be actively involved in projects for theological education by extension and development. One of the questions facing the OAIC and its member churches at the beginning of a new millennium was how to progress with assistance from the North without losing precious independence and identity to the new form of dependency euphemistically called "partnership." The question becomes all the more relevant as many African countries spiral into greater economic crisis and debt.

Organization of African Instituted Churches
PO Box 21736
Nairobi
Kenya

Allan H. Anderson

See also: Africa Israel Church, Nineveh; African Initiated (Independent) Churches; African Orthodox Church; All Africa Conference of Churches; Cherubim and Seraphim/Eternal Sacred Order of the Cherubim and Seraphim; Church of the Lord; Coptic Orthodox Church; Ethiopian Orthodox Tewahedo Church; Kimbanguist Church; World Council of Churches.

References

Anderson, Allan H. *African Reformation: African Initiated Christianity in the Twentieth Century*. Trenton, NJ: Africa World Press, 2001.

Barrett, David B., and T. John Padwick. *Rise Up and Walk! Conciliarism and the African Indigenous Churches, 1815–1987*. Nairobi: Oxford University Press, 1989.

Consultation with African Instituted Churches, Ogere, Nigeria, 9–14 January 1996. Geneva: World Council of Churches, 1996.

"Organization of African Instituted Churches." *Baragumu: The African Independent Churches Voice* 1 (1996).

Orthodox Church in America

The Orthodox Church in America dates to the arrival of the first Orthodox priests in Alaska from Russia following the Russian discovery of Alaska in 1741. The first convert, an Aleut, was baptized in 1843. The mission expanded slowly through the rest of the century, and in 1794 seven monks came to Paul's Harbor and formally consecrated the first church. In 1824 Father John Veniaminoiv (1797–1879), later consecrated as the first American bishop, arrived. He oversaw the construction of the cathedral in Sitka and of a seminary that was opened in 1841. He later returned to Russia to become head of the Russian Orthodox Church (Moscow Patriarchate) and in 1977 was canonized as Saint Innocent.

A significant change came to the mission diocese in 1867, when Alaska was purchased by the United States from Russia. The church was cut off from its parent, and in 1872 the bishop moved to San Francisco, California; the church was reorganized as the Russian Orthodox Church, Diocese of the Aleutian Islands and North America. The establishment of the church in San Francisco gave Russian Orthodoxy hegemony over the Orthodox community in North America, though that hegemony would later be challenged by the Ecumenical Patriarchate, which has oversight over the Greek Orthodox outside of Greece proper.

Under Bishop Nicholas (r. 1891–1898), beginning in 1891, the church experienced a period of growth. As the mission work in Alaska expanded, thousands of Russians were pouring into the United States and Canada and new parishes were springing up rapidly in the eastern half of the nation. In addition, Orthodox Christians from other lands were also coming to the United States, and initially, most of these believers found their church home in the Russian churches. As the number of non-Russian Orthodox believers grew, ethnic parishes would be organized and eventually new ethnic dioceses formed as autonomous jurisdictions. During the first half of the 20th century the whole spectrum of Eastern Orthodox church life appeared in America. In the process, the head of the American Russian Orthodox was elevated to the office of archbishop and additional dioceses appeared—Alaska, Cleveland (Ohio), Brooklyn (New York), and Pittsburgh (Pennsylvania).

The steady progress of the church was disrupted during World War I by events in Russia. The Russian Revolution swept the czar, with whom the Russian church had always had a special relationship, from power and left the Moscow Patriarchate under the thumb of an aggressively atheist regime. The American church found its funds cut off even as it had to accommodate a new wave of refugees from the revolution. In the 1920s the patriarch of Moscow was arrested, and in 1923 the American leadership was faced with the arrival of representatives of the Russian church loyal to the new government and demanding control of the church and its property. In 1924, the American Archdiocese rejected the Russian representatives, declared its autonomy from Moscow, and reorganized as the Russian Orthodox Greek Catholic Church of America.

Those priests and members who remained loyal to the patriarch in spite of the changes in Russia also reorganized and took the new schismatic (as they saw it) church to court. They scored a major victory, winning the headquarters property, St. Nicolas Cathedral in New York City. This small faction continued under the leadership of Bishop John Kedrovsky (1879–1934). Their position was somewhat undermined by the arrival in 1933 of yet another bishop from Moscow—Benjamin Fedchenkov (1880–1961). He represented a position of accommodation to the presence of the Communist government in Russia, but he was seen as less accepting of its domination of the Patriarchate. He

Russian Orthodox church and cemetery in Ninilchik, Kenai Peninsula, Alaska. (Oksanaphoto/Dreamstime.com)

was thus able to build a following of Russians who wished to remain under the jurisdiction of Moscow. Eventually the Kedrovsky faction merged into what became known as the American Exarchate of the Russian Orthodox Church.

In 1970 the Russian Orthodox Greek Catholic Church and the American Exarchate reached an agreement, the result of many years of negotiation and consideration of the position of the Russian Church as the initial Orthodox body in the United States. The Russian Orthodox Greek Catholic Church changed its name to the Orthodox Church in America and recognized the spiritual leadership of the Russian Patriarchate. The Patriarchate, in return, acknowledged the autonomy of the American church. The Exarchate dissolved and its members and parishes merged into the new Orthodox Church in America. A small number of parishes wished to remain under the direct authority of the patriarch of Moscow and reorganized as the Patriarchal Parishes of the Russian Orthodox Church in the U.S.A. This group remained in possession of St. Nicolas Cathedral in New York City.

In the meantime, as the main body of Russian Orthodox believers had found their way to accommodate the changes in Russia, one group refused to acknowledge the changes in Russia. Under the leadership of several bishops who had been placed in charge of the Russian church in diaspora prior to the revolution, they reorganized as a continuing Russian Orthodox church in vocal opposition to the Moscow Patriarchy and its accommodation with the Communist government. Over the years, this faction, now known as the Russian Orthodox Church Outside of Russia, came to embody the most conservative element of Russian Orthodoxy and has rejected the post-Communist emergence of the Russian Orthodox Church for its movement into the ecumenical world and its attachment to the World Council of Churches.

The Orthodox Church in America is headed by its archbishop, and the U.S. parishes are grouped into 13 dioceses. There are also one Canadian diocese and an Exarchate in Mexico. The Diocese of South America includes one parish in Brazil and three in Venezuela. The church is a leading member of the Standing Conference of Canonical Orthodox Bishops, which includes most of the larger Orthodox bodies in the United States. Also operating under the canonical jurisdiction of the Orthodox Church in America are the Albanian Orthodox Archdiocese and the Romanian Orthodox Episcopate of America—the result of splits in the Romanian and Albanian churches after their home countries fell under Communist control.

The Orthodox Church in America reports some 1 million members while recognizing that its active membership, served by its 700 priests, is far less. It supports St. Tikkon's Orthodox Theological Seminary in South Canaan, Pennsylvania, and St. Vladimir's Orthodox Theological Seminary in Tuckahoe, New York. It is a member of the World Council of Churches. The leader of the church, His Beatitude, Metropolitan Jonah (born James Paffhausen), is a former Episcopalian who converted to Orthodoxy. He was consecrated to the episcopacy and elected as the metropolitan in 2008.

Orthodox Church in America
PO Box 675
Syosset, NY 11791-0675
http://www.oca.org/

J. Gordon Melton

See also: Ecumenical Patriarchate/Patriarchate of Constantinople; Russian Orthodox Church (Moscow Patriarchate); Russian Orthodox Church Outside of Russia; World Council of Churches.

References

Koulomzim, Sophie. *The Orthodox Christian Church through the Ages*. New York: Russian Orthodox Greek Catholic Church of America, 1956.

Tarasar, Constance. *Orthodox America, 1794–1976: Development of the Orthodox Church in America*. Syosset, NY: Orthodox Church in America, Department of Archives and History, 1975.

Orthodox Church in China

Orthodox Christianity came to China in the 17th century, brought in 1686 by Cossacks serving in the Chinese imperial guard. A permanent mission in Beijing was established in 1715, which over the course of several centuries welcomed some 5,000 converts. The church swelled enormously in the 1920s, when some 300,000 believers fled into China from the effects of the Communist revolution in Russia. By the time of the Chinese revolution, there were some 106 Orthodox churches in China. Most participants were Russian expatriates, though some 10,000 members were also among the faithful.

Following the Chinese revolution, all foreign missionaries were required to leave, and many of the members also returned to Russia. In 1957 the church was granted autonomous status, and bishops established in Beijing and Shanghai. The Cultural Revolution (launched in 1966) almost destroyed the church—the churches were closed and all property was confiscated.

It was not until the 1980s that a revival of Orthodoxy in China was possible. Father Grigori Zhu Shi Fu (d. 2000) began regular services again in October 1981, at the Church of the Holy Protection in Harbin-Nangang. A second church was opened later some 16 miles from Harbin, where many Orthodox believers are buried in the cemetery. It is used on special occasions. The church in Beijing has been restored but turned into a museum.

In Xinjiang Province there are some 3,500 orthodox and reconstruction of a church at Urumqi was completed in 1990, though there is no priest to conduct services. Believers in Shanghai and Beijing have as yet not been allowed to organize for services.

On February 17, 1997, the 40th anniversary of the Orthodox Church in China was celebrated. The Russian Orthodox Church (Moscow Patriarchate) accepted a new level of responsibility for the Orthodox believers in China, especially until a new leader of the church can be elected.

The Orthodox Church can be contacted at 270 Bolshoi Prospect, Harbin, China. It is not among the officially recognized religious bodies in the People's Republic of China. As of 2004, there were an estimated 13,000 Orthodox believers in China (not including

Hong Kong) with parishes in Xinjiang, Inner Mongolia, and Harbin. There were as yet no priests serving the parishes.

J. Gordon Melton

See also: Russian Orthodox Church (Moscow Patriarchate).

References

Meyer, Jean François. "Toward a Rebirth of the Orthodox Church in China. Interview with Mitrophan Chin." http://www.orthodoxytoday.org/articles5/MayerChina.shtml. Accessed December 15, 2008.

Orthodoxy in China. http://orthodox.cn/.

Orthodox Church in Czech Lands and Slovakia

Eastern Orthodoxy was introduced into what is now the Czech Republic and Slovakia in the ninth century CE as part of the general spread of Christianity among the Slavic peoples. The area was overrun by the Hungarians in 906, and the Roman Catholic Church became the dominant religious community, though some churches retained the Eastern rite. Only in the 20th century, with the establishment of the independent state of Czechoslovakia in 1918, was Orthodoxy able to reassert its independent existence.

In 1925 the re-established Orthodox Church of Czechoslovakia came under the protection and guidance of the Serbian Orthodox Church and the patriarch residing in Belgrade. The small church experienced a sudden growth when, in 1930, some 25,000 Eastern-rite Catholics converted to Orthodoxy. The church's growth was halted during World War II when the Nazi government disbanded it and executed its leader, Bishop Gorazd (1879–1942), who had been the major force in founding the church.

The church was reorganized after World War II, and since the new government did not recognize Eastern-rite Catholicism, the remaining Eastern-rite Catholics were placed under the Orthodox bishop. Then in 1951, the Serbian Patriarchate recognized the autonomy of the Orthodox Church of Czechoslovakia. In 1968, as new freedoms were introduced into the country, many of the members returned to Roman Catholicism. The rebuilding of Eastern Catholicism created some harsh feelings, as buildings and property were turned over to the new Catholic body. Disputes over property between the two bodies continue to the present.

Following the separation of the former Czechoslovakia into the Czech Republic and Slovakia, the church adopted its present name. There is an archbishop in Prague and one in Presov, Slovakia. In 2005 the church reported some 75,000 members with 167 of its 242 parishes in Slovakia. It supports the Orthodox theological faculty at Presov University, and is a member of the World Council of Churches.

Orthodox Church in Czech Lands and Slovakia
V. Jamé 6
PO Box 655
CZ-111 21, Prague 1
Czech Republic

Orthodox Church in Czech Lands and Slovakia
Budovatelska ul. 1
SK-080 01 Presov
Slovakia

J. Gordon Melton

See also: Eastern Orthodoxy; Roman Catholic Church; Serbian Orthodox Church; World Council of Churches.

References

Giannaras, Chrestos. *The Church in Post-Communist Europe*. Crestwood, NY: Interorthodox Press, 2003.

Novak, G. "The Orthodox Church in Czechoslovakia." *Orthodoxy* (1964): 240–252.

Orthodoxia. Regensburg, Germany: Ostkirchliches Institut, issued annually.

Orthodox Church of Cyprus

Christianity on the island of Cyprus began with the arrival of the biblical Apostles Paul and Barnabas, who had been commissioned as missionaries at Antioch (Acts 13:2) and proceeded to Cyprus as one of the first stops on their initial tour. The church in Cyprus developed under the authority of Antioch until its autonomy was proclaimed by the church's Council of Ephesus in 431 CE. The ruling had the effect of granting the synod of Cypriot bishops the right to select their own archbishop. The church developed in the Eastern Orthodox orb and shares the same faith and practice with other Orthodox bodies.

With the spread of Islam in the seventh century, Cyprus became a target of Muslim raiders. At one point, many of the Christians, including the archbishop, relocated to Nea Justiniana, a city on the Dardanelles, where the Byzantine emperor could more easily provide protection. When the crisis passed and the archbishop returned to Cyprus, he added the title of archbishop of Nea Justiniana to his own; the Cypriot bishop is known by that designation to the present.

As part of a Crusade to recover Jerusalem, the British King Richard the Lionhearted (1157–1199) conquered Cyprus in 1191. The next year it was turned over to Guy de Lusignan (1129–1194), the former king of Jerusalem, whose Christian nation had been wiped out by the Muslim sultan Saladin (ca. 1137–1193) in 1187–1188. De Lusignan and his successors, who were Catholic, attempted to impose Latin Christianity on Cyprus, and for the next three centuries, the Orthodox Church found itself in retreat and fighting to survive.

The dominance of the Roman Catholic Church on Cyprus continued until 1571, when the emergent Turks, having captured Constantinople, overran the island. The new Muslim rulers removed the Roman bishops, recognized the Orthodox Church, and even granted it some degree of autonomy. As was common elsewhere in the expanding Turkish (Ottoman) Empire, Orthodox bishops were assigned a position in the civil government, with authority over the Greek-speaking Cypriots. This situation worked well until 1821, when the Greek citizens staged an unsuccessful revolt. In response, the Turks killed all the Orthodox bishops. New leadership that possessed the required apostolic authority (granted only by ordination and consecration by recognized bishops) had to be reintroduced from Antioch.

Real change came only in 1878, when the British leased the island from Turkey and subsequently annexed it (1914). The British granted independence to Cyprus in 1960. Archbishop Makarios III (1913–1977) became the first president of the new country, a move that continued the traditional political role played by Orthodox bishops but was nonetheless extremely controversial.

In 1973 the three other bishops of the Church of Cyprus created a national crisis by declaring that Makarios was no longer archbishop. The patriarchs of the other Orthodox churches in the region (Antioch, Jerusalem, Alexandria, and the Church of Greece) assumed authority to act and deposed the rebellious bishops. They also assisted in the appointment of three new bishops. However, this crisis was no sooner resolved than the continuing tension between the Greek and Turkish communities on the island became the excuse for Turkey to invade Cyprus and carve out a (still disputed) Turkish nation in the northern third of the island. The Orthodox Church lost many churches that were looted and/or destroyed in the takeover. For the next two decades no Orthodox priests were allowed into the area, though in 1994 two priests were allowed in to lead worship at St. Andrew Monastery, on the Karpas Peninsula.

The church is led by His Beatitude Chrysostomos, archbishop of Nea Justiniana and All Cyprus (b. 1927). Besides the Archdiocese of Nicosia, there are five additional dioceses on Cyprus. In 2005, the church reported 654,000 members. The church is a member of the World Council of Churches.

Orthodox Church of Cyprus, Office of the Archbishop
PO Box 21 130
1502 Nicosia
Cyprus
http://www.church.cy.net

J. Gordon Melton

See also: Roman Catholic Church; World Council of Churches.

References

Englezakis, Benedict. *Studies on the History of the Church of Cyprus, 4th–20th Centuries*. London: Variorum, 1995.

Hackett, John. *A History of the Orthodox Church of Cyprus*. New York: Burt Franklin, 1972.

Ioannou, M. *Studies in the History of the Church of Cyprus, 4th–20th Centuries*. Aldershot, England: Variorum, 1995.

Orthodox Church of Greece

The Orthodox Church of Greece is the 11th-ranking autocephalous church in the Eastern Orthodox communion. It includes the great majority of Orthodox Christians in Greece, where it is officially recognized as the predominant religion in the country. The entrance of Christianity to Greece is recorded in the Bible (Acts 16:9ff.), which tells us that the Apostle Paul responded to a dream calling him to Macedonia. The developing church eventually fell under the direct supervision of the Patriarchate at Constantinople, under whose authority it remained until the 19th century. In the meantime, Greece was conquered (1460) and incorporated into the Turkish Ottoman Empire.

The 1821 Greek revolution against Turkish rule culminated in the sultan's acceptance of Greek independence in the Treaty of Adrianople in 1829. The Orthodox Church had played a prominent role in the revolution and paid a heavy price for it: when the uprising began in 1821, the Ottoman government hanged Ecumenical Patriarch Gregorios V and a number of metropolitans at the gate of the patriarchal compound in Constantinople.

In 1833 the fledgling government of the new Greek kingdom declared the country's Orthodox Church autocephalous and established at its head a five-member permanent synod of bishops presided over by the king. This unilateral break with Constantinople and the establishment of a state-controlled church disrupted relations with the other Orthodox churches. After lengthy negotiations, the situation was regularized on June 29,

Interior of Saint Dimitrios of Thessaloniki, a Greek Orthodox church. (Panagiotis Karapanagiotis/Dreamstime.com)

1850, when Constantinople granted a Tomos, or official declaration, of autocephaly to the Orthodox Church of Greece. This declaration specified that the archbishop of Athens would preside over the Holy Synod and restored relations with the other Orthodox churches.

As Greece annexed more territory at the expense of the Ottomans, more Orthodox dioceses were received into the Orthodox Church of Greece. The large area of northern Greece acquired in 1912 remained under the Ecumenical Patriarchate until 1928, when those dioceses were provisionally placed under the administration of the Greek church. The dioceses in Crete and the Dodecanese Islands, as well as the monastic republic of Mount Athos, have remained under the Ecumenical Patriarchate to this day. Official statistics indicate that 96 percent of the Greek population today self-identifies as Orthodox, 2 percent as Muslim, and 1 percent as Catholic.

Over time, secular influence in church affairs has gradually decreased. However, the present Greek Constitution (1975) continues to recognize Orthodoxy as the "prevailing" religion in Greece and forbids proselytism. It also specifies that the Orthodox Church of Greece is "governed by the Holy Synod of all functioning bishops," and by the permanent Holy Synod made up of members of the "first," a structure that respects the provisions of the 1850 Tomos. The Greek Parliament enacted the current Charter of the Church of Greece in 1977. The Holy Synod is currently made up of 12 bishops and the archbishop of Athens, who presides over it.

The once-flourishing monastic tradition in Greece suffered greatly at the time of independence, when the new government closed most of the monasteries and convents. Subsequent wars and the Communist insurgency in the 1940s weakened it still further, and by the 1960s its future appeared bleak. But a modest revival has taken place since that time, with a significant influx of young men and women into the monasteries, especially on Mount Athos, where the number of monks has doubled since 1980.

There are theology faculties at the universities of Athens and Thessalonica, along with several seminaries for the training of parish priests. Most of the distinguished theologians of the Greek church are laymen. The church has been heavily involved in philanthropic activity, maintaining many orphanages, homes for the aged, and similar institutions. Total church membership is estimated at about 9 million. The Orthodox Church of Greece is a member of the World Council of Churches.

Orthodox Church of Greece
His Beatitude Archbishop Hieronymos II
14 Ioannou Glennadiou St.
GR-115 21 Athens
Greece
http://www.ecclesia.gr/ (Greek and English versions)

Ronald Roberson

See also: Ecumenical Patriarchate/Patriarchate of Constantinople; World Council of Churches.

References

Frazee, C. *The Orthodox Church and Independent Greece, 1821–1852*. London: Cambridge University Press, 1969.

Hammond, P. *The Waters of Marah: The Present State of the Greek Church*. London: Rockliff, 1956.

Roudometof, V. "Orthodoxy as Public Religion in Post-1989 Greece." In *Eastern Orthodoxy in a Global Age: Tradition Faces the Twenty-First Century*, edited by V. Roudometof et al. Walnut Creek, CA: Alta Mira, 2005.

Stavrou, T. "The Orthodox Church of Greece." In *Eastern Christianity and Politics in the Twentieth Century,* edited by Pedro Ramet, 183–207. Durham, NC: Duke University Press, 1988.

Orthodox Church of Poland

The Orthodox Church in Poland (Polski Autokefaliczny Kosciol Prawoslawny) started with the conquests in the East by King Kazimierz the Great (1310–1370) in the 14th century. His efforts for an independent Orthodox Church in Poland resulted in the appointment of a separate Polish metropolitan soon after his death. Some tension arose between the Orthodox Church and the Roman Catholic Church with the introduction of the Gregorian calendar by royal decree in 1582, though the major conflict emerged following the Union of Brzesc in 1596. A newly formed Uniate Church, combining its relationship with the pope with the Orthodox liturgy, started to attract Orthodox bishops. However, an independent Orthodox hierarchy was restored in 1620. In 1667 the metropolitan of Kiev accepted the authority of the patriarch of Moscow, which would later undergird interventions into Polish internal affairs by the Russian czar. The Orthodox Church was strongly supported by the czarist authorities during the partition of Poland. The Union of Brzesc was formally dissolved in the 19th century. Autocephalic status was given to the Polish Orthodox Church by the ecumenical patriarch in 1924, though the Synod of the Russian Church, the mother-church for Poland, accepted the fact only in 1948.

The head of the Polish Orthodox Church, for almost a quarter of a century, was His Eminence, Highly Blessed Bazyli (Wlodzimierz Dorosz Kiewicz, 1914–1998), the late metropolitan of Warsaw and the Whole of Poland. He was succeeded by the present Metropolitan Sawa (Michal Hrycuniak, b. 1938). There are dioceses at Białystok, Gdansk, Lodz, Poznan, Wrocław, Szczecin, Przemyśl, and Nowy Sącz, as well as at Lublin and Chelm. The church's main administrative organization, the General Synod, consists of bishops and representatives of both clergy and laity. The Council of Bishops deals with matters exceeding the competence of particular bishops. The Council is the executive body of the Synod of Bishops chaired by the metropolitan of Warsaw.

The Orthodox Church of Poland took under its jurisdiction the Diocese of Aquilei (Italy) in 1988, the Metropolia of Lisbon along with four Portuguese dioceses in 1991 and a missionary diocese in Brazil. The church counts around 555,000 members residing in 250 parishes. They use 325 churches and chapels supervised by 273 priests (1997). The main press organ is the monthly *Przeglad Prawoslawny/Orthodoxia* (5,000 copies). Additional periodicals include *Biuletyn Informacyjny Kola Teologow Prawoslawnych* (1,000 copies) and *Wiadomosci Bractwa* (1,500 copies).

In 1957, the Section of Orthodox Theology was formed in the Christian Academy of Theology (ChAT) in Warsaw, and there is also an Orthodox seminary in Warsaw. The biggest Polish Orthodox sanctuary and the best-known pilgrimage center is the Holy Mountain Grabarka (south of Białystok), with its monastery of Saints Martha and Mary. Up to 60,000 pilgrims gather here annually on August 19, the Day of the Lord's Transfiguration. Additional important pilgrimage centers include the Monastery of Saint Onufry in Jableczna, and Zabludow, the birthplace of the martyr Gabriel Zabludowski, the only Orthodox saint born within the boundaries of contemporary Poland. Other Orthodox sanctuaries are found at Rogacze, Suprasl, Odrynki, Krynoczka, Puchly, Nowa Wola, Stary, Kornin, Piatienka, Swieta Woda, Saki, and Tokary. The biggest center of Orthodox Christians in Poland is the Cathedral of Saint Nicolas at Białystok (ca. 100,000 people).

Polski Autokefaliczny Kosciol Prawoslawny
(Orthodox Church of Poland)
al. Solidarnosci 52
03-402 Warszawa
Poland

Leslaw Borowski

See also: Calendars, Religious; Eastern Orthodoxy; Roman Catholic Church; Russian Orthodox Church (Moscow Patriarchate).

References

Adamczuk, L., and A. Mirowicz. *Kosciol Prawoslawny w Polsce. Dawniej i dzis*. Warsaw: GUS and Warszawska Metropolia Prawoslawna, 1993.

The Orthodox Eastern Church in Poland. Past and Present. London: Polish Research Centre, n.d.

Orthodox Judaism

Through the 19th century, the European and American Jewish communities experienced the challenges of post-emancipation modern life and an emerging, majority, secular culture that persistently sought to integrate and absorb the Jewish community into itself. In partial response to this new situation, a new form of Judaism that consciously tried to adapt to modern culture developed. Reform Judaism made a number of changes to traditional Jewish life, replacing traditional practices that were deemed nonessential to Jewish identity and inappropriate for the contemporary context. Included in the reforms were the cessation of kosher food standards, the introduction of the vernacular to

An Orthodox Jew prays at the Wailing Wall in Jerusalem. The Wailing Wall is the only wall that remained after the Roman destruction of the Second Temple and it is viewed as one of the holiest places on Earth by many Jews. (Corel)

and abbreviation of the worship services, and the ending of separate seating between men and women at synagogue services.

As Reform Judaism emerged, especially in Germany and also among German Jewish immigrants and their children in the United States, traditional rabbis sought to reinvigorate commitment to traditional standards, even as some allowed for accommodations to the wider culture. Orthodox Judaism is the name now given to all elements of the religious Jewish community that demand strict observance of Jewish law and praxis.

Orthodox Judaism is distinguished by its attachment to the written Torah (the Jewish Bible or Tanakh) and the Oral Torah, a tradition explaining what the written Scriptures mean. Orthodox Jews believe that God gave the scriptures to Moses and then taught him the oral tradition, which has been passed down from generation to generation. Around the second century CE, the oral tradition was committed for the first time to writing in the Mishnah. In the centuries after the Mishnah was produced, additional commentaries elaborating on it, called the Gemara, were written down. The Mishnah and the Gemara together constitute the Talmud. Through succeeding centuries, rabbis continued to apply the Halakic process (a system of legal reasoning and interpretation) to the Torah and to these later sacred texts to determine how best to answer new questions as they arose. The Halakic process has given to the Orthodox community the means of dealing with changing situations, and serves as the basis for Orthodox observance.

Among the earliest champions of Orthodoxy in the face of reform were Samson Raphael Hirsch (1808–1888) in Germany and Isaac Leeser (1806–1868) in the United States. For a quarter of a century, Leeser published *The Occident and American Jewish Advocate*. In the pages of this periodical, he opposed American Reform leader Isaac Mayer Wise (1819–1900) and the spread of Reform Judaism and advocated the unity of the American Jewish community around traditional Jewish practice. Hirsch is known for championing a fully Orthodox belief and practice while living in the modern world; the religious movement he spearheaded in Germany was called neo-Orthodoxy.

The Orthodox in German-speaking communities were the first to feel the full impact of modernity, and they developed an approach that has allowed Orthodox Jewry not only to survive, but, apart from the devastation of the Holocaust, to thrive. Through the 20th century, many flocked to an engaged Orthodoxy as they began to encounter the modern West. As modern Orthodoxy developed, it was distinguished on the one hand from the Reform and Conservative movements, and on the other hand from ultra-Orthodox organizations such as Neturei Karta and Gush Emunim.

Jewish Orthodoxy is split into a number of distinguishable communities. Some of the major divisions are ethnic. The Jews of Central Europe, Eastern Europe, and the Iberian peninsula (Sephardic Judaism) form the major divisions, all of which now appear in strength in North America. Over the centuries, these and other Jewish communities developed a variety of differences that do not affect their status as Orthodox but nevertheless are perpetuated.

Approximately half of the world's 13 million Jews reside in the United States. In the United States the majority of Orthodox Jews are represented by a congregational association and two rabbinical associations. The Union of Orthodox Jewish Congregations of the United States and Canada emerged in the 1880s, soon after the Reform congregations had organized. Rabbis are served by the Union of Orthodox Rabbis in the United States and Canada, uniting originally rabbis of primarily eastern European origin, whose influence has waned in recent decades, and the Rabbinical Council of America, which includes the rabbis who graduate from New York's Yeshiva University. Other Orthodox congregations are associated with the Young Israel movement. Jews of Iberian heritage are associated with the American Sephardi Federation (15 W. 16th St., New York, NY 10010). Hasidism represents a mystical form of Orthodox Jewry.

In most countries of the world, the Orthodox community is organized nationally. The Conference of European Rabbis represents Orthodox Jews in Europe. Some Jewish communities, though by no means all, have selected a chief rabbi. Such an organization is reflected in modern Israel, where there are two chief rabbis for the state, one for Ashkenazic Jews and one for Sephardic Jews. Agudath Israel is an Orthodox Jewish organization that operates a variety of social service programs in the Jewish community worldwide and represents the interests of Orthodox Jewry to local, regional, and federal governments. Founded in 1912, it seeks to place the Torah in a lead position in the Jewish community as it faces the modern world. The organization has spread globally through the Agudath Israel World Organization.

Union of Orthodox Jewish Congregations of America
11 Broadway
New York, NY 10004
http://www.ou.org/

Rabbinical Council of America
305 7th Ave., 12th floor
New York, NY 10001
http://www.rabbis.org/

Conference of European Rabbis
87 Hodford Rd.
London NW11 8NH
United Kingdom
http://www.cer-online.org/

Israel Chief Rabbinate
Heikhal Shelomo
58 King George St.
Jerusalem
Israel

Agudath Israel World Organization
84 William St.
New York, NY 10038

Pamela S. Nadell and J. Gordon Melton

See also: Conservative Judaism; Gush Emunim; Hasidism; Neturei Karta; Reform Judaism; World Sephardic Federation; Young Israel.

References

Davidman, Lynn. *Tradition in a Rootless World: Women Turn to Orthodox Judaism.* Berkeley and Los Angeles: University of California Press, 1991.

Donin, Hayim Halevy. *To Be a Jew*. New York: Basic Books, 1972, 2001.

Gurock, Jeffrey. *Orthodox Jews in America.* Bloomington: Indiana University Press, 2009.

Heilman, Samuel. *Sliding to the Right: The Contest for the Future of American Orthodoxy*. Berkeley: University of California Press, 2006.

Katz, Jacob. *A House Divided: Orthodoxy and Schism in Nineteenth-Century Central European Jewry*. Hanover, NH: Brandeis University Press and University Press of New England, 1998.

Sclossberg, Eli W. *The World of Orthodox Judaism.* Northvale, NJ: Jason Aronson, 1997.

Orthodox Presbyterian Church

The Orthodox Presbyterian Church is the major organizational product of the Fundamentalist-Modernist controversy in the Presbyterian Church in the United States of America (now a constituent part of the Presbyterian Church [U.S.A.]) and currently a leading

American representative of the evangelical movement. As the Fundamentalist controversy continued in the Presbyterian Church into the 1930s, it became evident that the Modernists, who had aligned themselves with the contemporary trends in science, theology, and the critical study of the Bible, had largely taken control of the church. In 1932 a new phase in the battle focused on the 1932 book *Re-thinking Missions* by William E. Hocking (1873–1966). Drawing on his experience of the changing needs of the world missionary enterprise, Hocking suggested that Protestant missionaries should not just work for the conversion of non-Christians but should develop Christian social services, especially medical missions. Challenging Hocking's conclusions was J. Gresham Machen (1881–1937), an eminent conservative professor at Princeton Theological Seminary. Machen had inherited the tradition of conservative theology that had been identified with the school, though more liberal theological spokespersons now dominated its faculty.

Machen charged that the church was sending missionaries to foreign fields who did not believe that Jesus Christ was the only way of salvation. He also began to support the Independent Board of Foreign Missions, an agency that attempted to garner support for the sending of conservative Fundamentalist missionaries apart from the official missionary board of the Presbyterian Church. Machen also expanded his critique to the other agencies of the church. As his criticisms grew, church officials charged him with disturbing the peace of the church. He resigned from Princeton in 1929, and from the Presbyterian Church in 1936, and with his supporters he left to found the Orthodox Presbyterian Church. The new church adopted the Westminster Confession of Faith and the two Westminster catechisms (the Longer and Shorter) as its standards of faith.

Shortly after organizing the church, Machen entered into a second controversy with one of his prominent colleagues, Carl McIntire (1906–2002), pastor of a large congregation in Collingswood, New Jersey. Like many of his Fundamentalist colleagues, McIntire had accepted the method of biblical interpretation that had been developed among the Plymouth Brethren, called dispensationalism. He also had become a premillennialist. Machen rejected both views. McIntire also wanted to continue the work of the Independent Board of Foreign Missions. Machen felt that the work of the Board had been superseded by the new Missionary Board of the Orthodox Presbyterian Church.

Before their differences were resolved, Machen died in 1937. The following year, McIntire left the Orthodox Presbyterian Church and with his followers founded the Bible Presbyterian Church. McIntire would be the leading spokesperson of the continuing Fundamentalist wing of American Presbyterian through the next generation. In the 1940s, he would lead the relatively small community of fundamentalists in the formation of two interdenominational organizations, the American Council of Christian Churches and the International Council of Christian Churches. The Orthodox Presbyterians would, in the meantime, participate in the development of a new neo-evangelical perspective that would retain its emphasis upon biblical authority and traditional Christian affirmation while attempting to engage in dialogue with contemporary intellectual currents and modern culture. That perspective became embedded in the National Association of Evangelicals.

A relatively small body, in 2006 the Orthodox Presbyterian Church reported 28,486 members in 255 congregations; however, it supports missions in Korea, Japan, China, Eritrea, Ethiopia, Kenya, and Surinam. It is a member of the International Conference of Reformed Churches.

Orthodox Presbyterian Church
AT 607 N. Eastern Rd.
Bldg E, Box P
Willow Grove, PA 19090-0920
http://www.opc.org/

J. Gordon Melton

See also: International Conference of Reformed Churches; International Council of Christian Churches; Presbyterian Church (U.S.A.)

References

Galbraith, John. *Why the Orthodox Presbyterian Church?* Philadelphia: Committee on Christian Education, Orthodox Presbyterian Church, 1965.

Hart, D. G., and John Muether. *Fighting the Good Fight: A Brief History of the Orthodox Presbyterian Church*. Willow Grove, PA: Committee for the Historian of the Orthodox Presbyterian Church, 1995.

The Standards of Government, Discipline, and Worship of the Orthodox Presbyterian Church. Philadelphia: Committee on Christian Education, Orthodox Presbyterian Church, 1965.

Osho and the International Osho Movement

Osho, formerly known as Bhagwan Shree Rajneesh (1931–1990), was a controversial spiritual teacher from India whose contemporary devotees include thousands of Americans, Europeans, and Asians.

Since 2000, the Osho spiritual movement has grown increasingly decentralized, and there are local centers in more than 60 countries. With few exceptions, these centers house no more than a few dozen residents, but they attract many more clients and visitors interested in Osho's teachings and meditations. Visiting group leaders, some of whom had direct contact with Osho when he was alive, swell attendance at center classes and events.

The diffuse spiritual movement's official headquarters, Osho Meditation Resort in Pune, Maharashtra, India, has belonged to the Osho (Rajneesh) movement since 1974. It houses a multiversity that offers workshops on personal and spiritual growth and on healing and creative arts. The movement's emphasis, however, is on meditation. There are individual and collective meditations throughout the day and evening.

The Pune meditation resort attracts spiritual tourists, seekers, and longtime Osho devotees alike. Swami Amrito, who was part of an inner circle that Osho appointed to continue his work in the late 1980s, oversees the movement's practical organization.

Around 2000, there was a schism within the Pune inner circle. Amrito successfully supported greater emphasis on Osho's visionary ideas and their diffusion, with less attention to his personal role as an enlightened master. A group led by another member of Osho's last inner circle, Ma Neelam, asserted that Osho's enduring personal legacy could not be separated from his doctrine. She established a competing center in Delhi and later moved to a large headquarters complex open to both devotees and visitors, Nisarga, near the Himalayas in Dharmsala, Himachal Pradesh, India. Despite the tension, many devotees and seekers visit both centers and sustain cordial relations with both, because each group defers to Osho's vision.

Indian spiritual leader and teacher Osho (Bhagwan Shree Rajneesh) at a news conference at the Rajneeshpuram, Oregon on July 20, 1985. (AP Photo/Bill Miller)

From 1958 to 1966, Osho, then known as Rajneesh, taught philosophy, primarily at the University of Jabalpur. He resigned his post in 1966 to travel throughout India as an independent religious teacher. In the early 1970s, he shifted headquarters from his Bombay apartment to the Shree Rajneesh Ashram in Pune.

His synthesis of spirituality with personal growth psychology attracted significant numbers of Westerners. Devotees known as *sannyasins* often received new names signifying their spiritual rebirth. Rajneesh developed unique meditations, a number involving intense, emotionally cleansing activity preceding stillness. Before his death, Osho shifted his emphasis to meditative therapies encouraging individuals' responsibility for their own personal and spiritual growth.

Osho's philosophical approach blends Western and Eastern traditions, with special emphasis on Zen Buddhism. Important themes include dropping the ego and its conditioned beliefs and integrating the material and the spiritual. The ideal human is "Zorba the Buddha," a consummate being, combining Buddha's spiritual focus with the life-embracing traits of novelist Nikos Kazantzakis's character Zorba. Recent interpretations from leadership at Pune underscore the importance of Zorba, on the grounds that it is easier for a life-embracing individual to develop a spiritual focus, than it is for an inner-directed meditator to embrace earthly pleasures.

At the height of his popularity, Osho was controversial throughout India because of his views on sexual freedom and the encounter groups that attracted so many foreigners to the country. The greatest controversy, however, developed in the United States when Osho settled at the Big Muddy Ranch in central Oregon. From the summer of 1981 until the winter of 1986, several thousand sannyasins labored to create the communal city of Rajneeshpuram and a model agricultural collective. Their dream disintegrated because of financial, legal, and political conflicts, and Rajneesh embarked on a world tour before returning to Pune in 1987. Two years later he took the name Osho, which means "dissolving into the totality of existence." He died on January 19, 1990.

In the wake of the exodus from Rajneeshpuram, a number of people left the movement. Several movement leaders were convicted of crimes against outsiders and also other devotees. A few former sannyasins, such as Anand Somendra, Paul Lowe, Margo Anand, and Swami Virato, have become independent spiritual teachers, drawing heavily upon what they learned while associated with the movement.

At Osho International Meditation Resort a core staff hosts thousands of visitors annually. Osho Nisarga, the competing group's much smaller enclave, also offers guest accommodations, workshops, and meditations at the foot of the Himalayas. In the United States, active centers are Osho Academy in Sedona, Arizona; Viha Meditation Center in Northern California; and Osho Padma Meditation Center in New York City.

Osho International
17 Koregaon Park
Pune MS 411001
India
http://www.osho.org

Osho Nisarga
Shilla: Post Office Pantehar
Dharmsala, HP 176057
India
http://www.oshonisarga.com

Marion S. Goldman

See also: Meditation; Zen Buddhism.

References

D'Andrea, Anthony. *Global Nomads: Techo and New Age as Transnational Countercultures in Ibiza and Goa*. New York: Routledge, 2007.

Franklin, Satya Bahrti. *The Promise of Paradise: A Woman's Intimate Story of the Perils of Life with Rajneesh*. Barrytown, NY: Station Hill Press, 1992.

Goldman, Marion. *Passionate Journeys: Why Successful Women Joined a Cult*. Ann Arbor: University of Michigan Press, 1999.

Osho. *India My Love: A Spiritual Journey.* New York: St. Martin's Press, 2002.

Osore, Mount

Mount Osore (aka Osoresan), one of Japan's most sacred sites, is a 2,884-foot-high volcanic mountain in the center of the Shimokita Peninsula on the northernmost reaches of the main island of Honshu. A volcanically active area, the terrain is somewhat desolate and barren, devoid of plant life. Sulfurous gases escaping from the underground color the water and permeate the air. Translated into English, Osoresan means Fear Mountain, and the entire site is often likened to Western (especially ancient Greek) ideas of the hell realm.

Buddhists have been present in the region for more than a millennium, and the Bodaji Temple gives focus to the veneration of Jizo (or Ksitigarbha), the primary bodhisattva worship at Osoresan. Bodaji is located next to Lake Usori. Near the main entrance is a red bridge over a river, Sanzu no Kawa, likened to the River Styx in Greek mythology. Surrounding the lake are eight peaks, familiar from Buddhist descriptions of the afterlife. Just outside the temple are six statues of Jizo, one for each of the six realms of the Buddhist underworld through which Jizo can travel.

Osoresan is seen particularly as an abiding place of the souls of children and unborn babies who are pictured as trying to make their way across the river. To do so, they build piles of pebbles along the river. Jizo's task is to protect them from evil demons who are constantly trying to disperse the piles. The area is now dotted with many piles of small rocks created by parents of deceased children who have visited, and their many offerings in the form of items (often very colorful) associated with children, similar to ex voto offerings often left at Roman Catholic sites. The offerings are seen as items that will assist the children in attaining paradise.

Bodaji is home to a group of trance mediums, the *itako*, who specialize in communication with the souls of deceased children. The itako are especially trained for their work, and in the months prior to the annual Osoresan Festival each year (July 22–24), they perform a variety of austerities as part of a set of purification rituals.

J. Gordon Melton

See also: Bodhisattva; Ksitigarbha's/Jizo's Birthday; Mountains.

References

Blacker, Carmen. *The Catalpa Bow: A Study of Shamanistic Practices in Japan*. London: Allen & Unwin, 1975.

Ivy, Marilyn. *Discourses of the Vanishing: Modernity, Phantasm, Japan*. Chicago: University of Chicago Press, 1995.

Miyazaki, Fumiko, and Duncan Williams. "The Intersection of the Local and the Translocal at a Sacred Site: The Case of Osorezan in Tokugawa Japan." *Japanese Journal of Religious Studies* 28, nos. 3–4 (2001).

Mount Osore. http://www.osorezan.info/Entrance.html. Accessed August 15, 2009.

Schattschneider, Ellen. *Immortal Wishes: Labor and Transcendence on a Japanese Sacred Mountain*. Durham, NC: Duke University Press, 2003.

OTO (Ordo Templi Orientis)

See Ordo Templi Orientis.

Our Lady of All Nations

The devotional life that surrounds Our Lady of All Nations in Amsterdam arose from the apparitions and messages that a Dutch woman, Ida Peerdeman (1905–1996), received between 1945 and 1984. In these visions, Mary revealed herself as Our Lady of All Nations and introduced a peculiar prayer that, coupled with the expected spread of the rosary, was intended to realize the swift promulgation of a new, fifth dogma of Mary as "Coredemptrix, Mediatrix, and Advocate." With this dogma, Mary would achieve a place of her own in God's acts of salvation, an accomplishment that many felt the apparitions at Fatima, Portugal, had pointed toward in 1917. A painting of the apparition, showing The Lady standing on a globe, with her back against the Cross of Christ, functions as an icon for the devotion. The feast days are celebrated on March 25 and May 31.

In view of the parallel themes between Our Lady of All Nations and Our Lady of Fatima, devotees consider the Amsterdam apparitions to be a continuation of Fatima, for the messages of both are concerned with a spectrum of evils in the world: natural disasters, wars, hunger, chaos, apostasy, and Communism endanger the church and the world, and, above all, Satan threatens the world. However, after investigations in 1955 and 1973, the Diocese of Haarlem concluded that there was no ground for accepting a divine origin for the apparitions. Because of active support and promotion in several dioceses and noticeable activity in Third World mission fields, the veneration directed to Our Lady of All Nations became a concern for the Vatican as well, and in 1974 and 1987 it reiterated the conclusions of the Diocese of Haarlem. Nevertheless The Lady continued to enjoy the support and devotion of tens of thousands of Catholics, primarily conservatives. Millions of copies of the devotional card with the contested prayer on the renaming of Mary and the painting of The Lady in dozens of languages have been distributed around the world.

A turning point for the organization promoting Our Lady of All Nations came in 1996, with the death of the visionary, the arrival on the scene of a new administration for the group and of a group of missionary nuns (of the Austrian Family of Mary) who manage its daily activities. A breakthrough for the devotion came from the new bishop Jozef Maria Punt of the diocese. On May 31, 2002, he made public that notwithstanding the earlier investigations he received—"in a moment of mysticism"—the message or insight revealing that the Amsterdam apparitions were indeed of a supernatural character. This acknowledgment of the apparitions and messages led to skeptics within the Dutch church province but gave way to great enthusiasm among the devotees and an international stimulus of the cultus. Pope Benedict XVI, former apparition-skeptic Cardinal Joseph Ratzinger, demanded that the contested words in the prayer—"The Lady who once was Mary"—would no longer be practiced.

The center of worship for Our Lady of all Nations, located in a mansion in Amsterdam, receives about 9,000 Dutch and foreign visitors each year. Beginning in 1997, international prayer days were organized in Amsterdam, with up to 10,000 visitors. In 2001 these days were split into national prayer days for The Netherlands, Germany, England, Austria, Ireland, the Cote d'Ivoire, Japan, the Philippines, Slovakia, and Switzerland, with about 20,000 participants in total. The largest number of adherents are to be found in these countries, but there are increasing numbers in Africa, Asia, and the United States. Following the "apocalyptic" events of September 11, 2001, more than a half million prayer cards of Our Lady of All Nations were distributed in the United States. A missionary "world action" has also been undertaken, in which dozens of copies of the painting of The Lady are traveling the world to expand the devotion.

Within the World Network of Marian Devotion, one encounters devotion to The Lady also among a spectrum of movements, among them the Medjugorje devotees. Devotees of Medjugorje visit the Amsterdam shrine regularly, as they see a link among the three "most important" apparitions of the new Marian era: from its beginning in Fatima (in revelatory messages), through Medjugorje (recruiting "work apostles"), to the consummation in Amsterdam (the realization of the fifth dogma).

Sanctuary of the Lady of All Nations
Diepenbrockstraat 3
1077 VX Amsterdam
The Netherlands
http://www.laudate.org/en/home
http://www.de-vrouwe.nl
http://www.ladyofallnations.org
http://www.fifthmariandogma.com/

Lady of All Nations Action Center
PO Box 31481
St. Louis, MO 63131

Peter Jan Margry

See also: Charismatic Movement; Devotion/Devotional Traditions; Fatima; Marian Devotion, World Network of; Mary, Blessed Virgin; Medjugorje; Roman Catholic Church.

References

Auclair, Raoul. *The Lady of All Nations.* Quebec, Canada: Ed. L'Armée de Marie, 1978.

Klos, Peter. *The Lady of All Nations, Who Once Was Mary.* Santa Barbara, CA: Queenship Publishing Company, 1998.

Künzli, Josef, ed. *The Messages of the Lady of All Nations.* Santa Barbara, CA: Queenship Publishing Company, 1996.

Margry, Peter Jan. "Paradoxes of Marian Apparitional Contestation: Networks, Ideology, Gender, and The Lady of All Nations." In *Moved by Mary: The Power of Pilgrimage in the Modern World,* edited by Anna-Karina Hermkens, Willy Jansen, and Catrien Notermans, 182–199. Aldershot: Ashgate, 2009.

The Messages of the Lady of All Nations. New edition. Amsterdam: The Lady of All Nations Foundation, 1999.

P

Pacific Council of Churches

The Pacific Council of Churches attempts to provide an avenue for fellowship, united ministry, and speaking with a common voice to the many Christian churches scattered throughout the islands of the South Pacific. The South Pacific was among the first targets of the developing world Christian missionary movement in the first half of the 19th century. These churches grew through the 20th century and in the decades since World War II passed through the process of decolonization and the transformation from missions into autonomous denominations.

Talks leading to the formation of the Council began at a church consultation in 1961 and the Council itself was organized in 1966. The Council works through five program areas, but has become known for its work on female equality, economic development at the village level, and opposition to further nuclear testing. Its work has been a challenge given the isolation of many of its members and the vast stretches of ocean between the centers of activity. At the same time, it has found itself dependent on outside sources of income to maintain its existence.

In 2006, it reported 26 member churches, including the Roman Catholic Church, representing 17 nations. It is the regional ecumenical body cooperating with the World Council of Churches.

J. Gordon Melton

See also: Roman Catholic Church; World Council of Churches.

Reference

Van Beek, Huibert. *A Handbook of Churches and Councils: Profiles of Ecumenical Relationships*. Geneva: World Council of Churches, 2006.

Padmasambhava

Eighth century CE

Padmasambhava, popularly known as Guru Rinpoche (Precious Teacher), is credited with introducing Buddhism into Tibet from India in the eighth century CE during the reign of the Tibetan king, Trisong Detsen. Many elements of the story of his life have been questioned and the boundary between fact and legend is often vague. Even his name, which means "Lotus-born," refers to a legend of the miraculous nature of his birth, which occurred at Oddiyana, an area around the border of Afghanistan and Pakistan. According to the story, Padmasambhava initially appeared in the form of an eight-year-old boy sitting in the center of a lotus flower in the middle of a sacred lake. He was then adopted by the local king and raised as a prince in his court. As he matured, he wanted to follow a spiritual life to which the king objected. To free himself from the king's oversight, Padmasambhava arranged the death of a minister's son. For this crime, the king banished him. Padmasambhava would reside for the next years of his life in cremation grounds, understood to be terrifying places of death where those pursuing a spiritual path would go to practice meditation while at the same time overcoming their fears. Reputedly, during this time, he developed the extraordinary spiritual powers for which he would later become renowned. Some derived from his visitation by wisdom *dakinis* (female guides to enlightenment), who initiated him into various esoteric Tantric practices.

Padmasambhava's fame increased year by year, and eventually reached King Trisong Detsen (ca. 740–798 CE) who invited the powerful yogi to Tibet where he hoped that the local demons and other obstructing forces could be defeated and that Buddhism could be established. Padmasambhava is usually associated with the founding of Samyé (775 CE), the first Buddhist monastery in Tibet; and the Nyingma, the oldest School of Buddhism in Tibet, revere him as a "second Buddha." The Nyingma speak of the eight major forms of Padmasambhava, his eight manifestations that range in appearance from a peaceful gentle monk to the wrathful and terrifying Dorje Drolod. The Nyingma dedicate the 10th day of each lunar month in their religious calendar to commemorate a major event in Padmasambhava's life.

Padmasambhava had two primary consorts during his life—the Indian princess Mandarava and the Tibetan noblewoman Yeshe Tsogyal. Pictures of Padmasambhava often include the pair, who will be seen standing to either side of him. Yeshe Tsogyal, who became a Tibetan Tantra teacher in her own right, would pen Padmasambhava's biography and is credited with the process of concealing his more advanced secret teachings as *terma* (treasure). In Tibetan Buddhism, it is believed that many renowned gurus hid their important teachings, which they felt were somewhat ahead of their time. These teachings would then be discovered and released in the future by spiritually advanced ones (*tertons,* or treasure revealers). Padmasambhava is also remembered through the many places around Tibet that he is said to have visited. Across the country there are mountains, lakes, and caves considered to have been blessed as places of spiritual power by his presence.

Toward the end of his life, Padmasambhava left Tibet to continue his work of subduing demons and spreading the Buddha's teaching in wild and untamed lands. Since his passing from this life, he is considered to be a fully enlightened Buddha and as such remains an active presence in this world working from spiritual realms to benefit all sentient beings.

Edward A. Irons

See also: Meditation; Monasticism; Nyingma Tibetan Buddhism; Tibetan Buddhism.

References

Chonam, Lama, and Sangye Khandro, trans. *The Lives and Liberation of Princess Mandarava: The Indian Consort of Padmasambhava*. Boston: Wisdom Publications, 1998.

Evans-Wentz, W. Y., ed. *The Tibetan Book of the Great Liberation: or, the Method of Realizing Nirvana Through Knowing the Mind*. Preceded by an epitome of Padma-Sambhava's Biography. Oxford: Oxford University Press, 1983.

Kunsang, Erik Pema. *Dakini Teachings: Padmasambhava's Oral Instructions to Lady Tsogyal.* Boston: Shambhala, 1990.

Padmasambhava. *Natural Liberation: Padmasambhava's Teachings on the Six Bardos.* Commentary by Gyatrul Rinpoche. Trans. by B. Alan Wallace. Somerville, MA: Wisdom Publications, 1997.

Powers, John. *Introduction to Tibetan Buddhism.* Ithaca, NY: Snow Lion Publications, 1995.

Yeshe Tsogyal. *The Lotus-Born.* Trans. by Erik Hein Schmidt. Boston: Shambhala, 1993.

Pagan Federation

The Pagan Federation was founded in 1971 as the Pagan Front by John and Jean Score, Doreen Valiente, and others to provide information and to counter misconceptions about Wicca. In 1981, the name was changed to the Pagan Federation and around half the membership now practice some form of Wicca or Pagan religious Witchcraft, while the remainder practice various contemporary Pagan spiritualities including Druidry, Heathenry (Odinism, Asatru, Vanatru, and Northern Tradition), Shamanism, and Goddess spirituality.

The aims of the Pagan Federation are to provide contact between Pagan groups and genuine seekers of the Old Ways; to promote contact and dialogue between the various branches of European Paganism and other Pagan organizations worldwide; and to provide practical and effective information on Paganism to members of the public, the media, public bodies, and the administration.

At its core, the Pagan Federation upholds the following three principles:

1. Love and Kinship with Nature, which involves reverence for the life force and its ever-renewing cycles of life and death.
2. The Pagan Ethic: "If it harm none, do what thou wilt." This is a positive morality, expressing the belief in individual responsibility for discovering one's own true nature and developing it fully, in harmony with the outer world and community.
3. Honoring the Totality of Divine Reality, which transcends gender, without suppressing either the female or male aspect of Deity.

Membership is open to people over 16 years of age who consider themselves Pagan.

The Pagan Federation publishes a quarterly journal, *Pagan Dawn* (formerly *The Wiccan*, founded in 1968), and other publications. Conferences and other member events take place frequently throughout the year. In many parts of Europe, the Pagan Federation provides public celebrations of the eight major religious festivals of contemporary Paganism.

From the late 1980s, the activities of the Pagan Federation have been expanding. In 1989, the Pagan Federation took part in a major interfaith festival at Canterbury Cathedral, the seat of the archbishop of Canterbury who is the senior archbishop of the Church of England, and performed the first public Pagan religious ritual in Canterbury for many centuries. Since then, the Pagan Federation has been active in interfaith dialogue and has members in many interfaith organizations in the United Kingdom. It provides prison ministry for the Prison Service. In 2004 the Scottish Pagan Federation secured legal recognition for Pagan religious marriage services in Scotland.

The Pagan Federation is run by an elected committee that reports to a policy-making Council comprised of regional coordinators, honorary members, and other activists. The Pagan Federation has a membership of around 4,500, more than half of whom are women. Most members are United Kingdom–based, but Pagan Federation International has members in most Western European countries and a growing presence in Eastern Europe. There are also members in the United States and Canada.

Current campaigning issues for the Pagan Federation include prevention of discrimination against Pagans, the right to perform legally recognized marriages, recognition as a religious charity (not-for-profit organization), and ensuring that Pagans are accurately included in official statistics.

Pagan Federation
BM Box 7097
London WC1N 3XX, UK
http://www.paganfed.org/

Vivianne Crowley

See also: Church of England; Druidism; Goddess Spirituality; Wiccan Religion; Witchcraft.

References

Hutton, Ronald B. *The Triumph of the Moon*. Oxford: Oxford University Press, 1999.

Pagan Federation. *The Pagan Federation Information Pack*. London: Pagan Federation, 2008.

Weller, P. *Religions in the UK: A Multi-faith Directory*. Derby: University of Derby, 2001.

■ Pakistan

The modern state of Pakistan, a long, narrow country following the Indus River Valley, is sandwiched between Iran and Afghanistan on the west and India on the east. It emerged in the 1930s with the suggestion that a Muslim state be set apart from India, then a British colony. That state was created in 1947, but its eastern half separated in 1971 and is now known as Bangladesh. Present-day Pakistan exists with unstable borders, its northwest border with Afghanistan following the Duran line representing the limit of British hegemony in the area in the 19th century and dividing the Pashtun ethnic community in half. Neither Pakistan nor Afghanistan has ratified the border. At the same time, there are continuing disputes over Pakistan's border with India relative to the Indian state of Kashmir. The remaining state of Pakistan includes 310,000 square miles of territory. Though relatively small geographically, its 172,800,000 citizens (2008) make it the 6th most populous country in the world.

The Indus Valley had been inhabited as early as the third millennia BCE, but its modern history begins with the conquest of the area by Alexander the Great

Badshahi Mosque, Lahore, Pakistan. Built in the sixteenth century, it is one of the most famous landmarks and tourist destinations of Pakistan in addition to being one of the largest mosques in the world. (Naiyyer/Dreamstime.com)

(356–323 BCE). In the middle of the next century, it would be incorporated into the empire of Indian Buddhist ruler Asoka (d. 238 or 232). The history of the rise and fall of the Indian kingdoms was somewhat interrupted at the beginning of the eighth century with the entrance of the Arab Muslims under al-Hajjaj (661–714 CE), whose successors in the next generation came to dominate the whole of the Indus River Valley. From their foothold in Pakistan, Muslim rulers conquered most of India, residents of which were predominantly Hindu.

From the eighth century to the present, the struggle between Hindus and Muslims would be a major theme in the history of the Indian subcontinent. Through most of that history, the Muslim minority would form the ruling elite. Islam did not merge into Hinduism, as the religions of many earlier groups had, although it would give rise to Sikhism out of the effort of Guru Nanak (1469–ca. 1539) to find a synthesis between the two faiths. The decline of Muslim hegemony in India was evident in the 18th century, but its fate was sealed by the advent of the British and the conquest of India in the 19th century. Hindus were much quicker to identify with the British and to accept positions in the colonial administration.

In 1949 the modern state of Pakistan came into existence as an autonomous dominion within the British Commonwealth. The setting apart of Pakistan led to the deaths of hundreds of thousands in riots and the migrations of millions, as Hindus left the region and Muslims moved in. The future of the country was further hindered by the death in 1948 of Muhammad Ali

Jinnah (1876–1948), who had led the fight for an independent Muslim nation. The new country was afflicted with internal disagreement, leading to the October 1958 assumption of power by General Muhammad Ayub Khan (1907–1974) and the imposition of martial law. Ayub Khan ruled the country for a decade but was pushed out of office in 1969. The new government was immediately faced with grievances in eastern Pakistan that would lead in 1971 to its separation and the formation of independent Bangladesh.

The separation of Bangladesh set the stage for the rise of Zufikar Ali Bhutto (1928–1979), head of the Pakistan People's Party. His rule was interrupted by a 1977 coup led by General Zia-ul Haq (1924–1988). When the general was killed in an airplane accident in 1988, former president Bhutto's daughter, Benazir Bhutto (1953–2007), became the first female head of state in a predominantly Muslim country. Though her rule lasted only two years, she re-established constitutional order in the country. Her successors in office attempted to try her for political corruption, but she survived and would briefly return to power in the mid-1990s. In 1999, after a decade of failure by the democratically elected government to deal with the country's economic problems, there was another military coup.

The American invasion of Afghanistan has led to instability in Pakistan, whose leadership has attempted to be friendly with the United States while retaining its status in the larger Muslim world. Its disputed border has become a matter of concern as the Pushtan community has shown widespread support for both al-Qaeda, the group responsible for bombings in the United States, and the Taliban, the former rulers of Afghanistan deposed by the Americans.

For more than 1,000 years, the Indus River Valley has been dominated by Islam. With the immigration of most of its Hindu residents to India after partition in 1947 and the settlement of Indian Muslims in Pakistan at the same time, the country became overwhelmingly Muslim. In 1956 the country declared itself an "Islamic republic," a unique designation in the Muslim world. The 1973 Constitution emphasized Islam as the state religion, and periodically an emphasis on Islamization has been proclaimed by government leaders (and seen by many Shia Muslims as a move to impose Sunni values on the country). Only a Muslim can be president, and the state is mandated to provide Islamic education for all citizens. The government supports the Muslim establishment, oversees mosques and funds collected for charitable purposes, and takes responsibility for the schools at which clergy (imams) are trained. At the same time, the Constitution guarantees the rights of religious minorities and of all citizens to profess, practice, and propagate their religion.

The Pakistani Muslim community is predominantly of the Sunni Hanafite School, though it has manifested an extremely diverse nature. Some 18 percent of Pakistani Muslims are Shias and 6 percent are Sufis, with the Naqshbandiya and Qadiriyya being the largest brotherhoods. The primary struggle in Pakistan has been between traditionalists and modernists, the traditional religious authorities being concerned that movement into the modern world will challenge allegiance to the Koran, the Islamic holy book and authority.

Pakistan is well known as the place of origin of the Ahmadiyya Muslim movement, founded in 1889 by Hazrat Mirza Ghulam Ahmad (1835–1908). In his early years, Ahmad had concluded that Islam was in a state of decline, and it certainly had been pushed aside in British India. He took upon himself a mission to demonstrate the truth of Islam and was termed *mujaddid*, the renewer of the faith in the present age. He launched a proselytization movement to bring his fellow citizens back into the Muslim fold and took his crusade to the West.

Ahmad attempted to challenge Christianity directly. He developed a number of arguments for the superiority of Islam and called a variety of Christian beliefs into question. He asserted, among other things, that Jesus had not died on the cross but had merely swooned and recovered after being placed in the tomb. Eventually, he traveled to Kashmir and died a natural death there.

The Ahmadiyyas existed for many years as an organization within the larger Pakistani Muslim community, but following the death of Ahmad in 1908, the group split into two factions over the status of Ahmad. One group, the Ahmadiyya Muslim movement, wished to consider Ahmad as a prophet, a status equal to that of Muhammad. The other smaller group, while holding Ahmad in esteem, refused to consider him of such a lofty estate. The attempt to proclaim Ahmad a prophet

Pakistan

met with considerable criticism from the larger Muslim community, and in 1974 the Pakistani government formally declared the idea to be heretical and those who believed it as existing outside of the Muslim community. In the wake of that declaration, the small group, the Ahmadiyya Anjuman Ishaat Islam, Lahore (headquartered in Lahore, Pakistan), has had to fight to avoid being included in the general condemnation heaped on the larger faction.

Pakistan is home to several important international Islamic organizations, including the World Muslim Congress, Tanzeem-e-Islami, the World Federation of

Pakistan

Religion	Followers in 1970	Followers in 2010	% of Population	Annual % growth 2000–2010	Followers in 2025	Followers in 2050
Muslims	57,429,000	166,576,000	96.1	1.83	216,065,000	280,542,000
Christians	1,173,000	3,923,000	2.3	1.83	5,083,000	6,604,000
Protestants	592,000	2,150,000	1.2	0.87	2,600,000	3,150,000
Roman Catholics	341,000	1,250,000	0.7	–0.92	1,500,000	1,900,000
Independents	235,000	1,000,000	0.6	1.77	1,500,000	2,250,000
Hindus	890,000	2,260,000	1.3	1.83	2,900,000	3,700,000
Ethnoreligionists	35,000	185,000	0.1	1.83	200,000	200,000
Agnostics	10,000	140,000	0.1	1.83	300,000	500,000
Buddhists	2,000	112,000	0.1	1.83	170,000	240,000
Baha'is	15,100	90,000	0.1	1.83	150,000	300,000
Sikhs	2,000	45,400	0.0	1.83	60,000	80,000
Zoroastrians	5,200	8,000	0.0	1.83	8,000	8,000
Atheists	2,000	8,000	0.0	1.83	14,000	20,000
Chinese folk	1,000	2,600	0.0	1.83	5,000	10,000
Jews	250	900	0.0	1.84	1,000	1,000
Total population	**59,565,000**	**173,351,000**	**100.0**	**1.83**	**224,956,000**	**292,205,000**

Islamic Organizations, and the United Islamic Organization. Nationally, a variety of organizations represent the spectrum of Muslim opinion on political and economic issues, and a number of them are dedicated to establishing Muslim law as the law of the land.

Christianity was introduced into the area now constituting Pakistan at several points, beginning in the eighth century, but no permanent work was begun until the conquest of India by the British in the 19th century was well under way. In 1834 the first permanent work was launched by Presbyterian John C. Lowrie (1808–1900). Over the next few years he was joined by John Newton (1810–1891), Charles Forman (1821–1894), and Andrew Gordon (1828–1887). Their efforts would eventually lead to the formation of the Presbyterian Church of Pakistan (formally established by a merger of two older Presbyterian bodies in 1993). It is now the second largest Protestant church in the country.

The Church Missionary Society brought Anglicanism into Karachi in 1850, and the missionaries, as representatives of the Church of England, enjoyed the approbation of the British colonial authorities. The work spread through the region, and the Diocese of Lahore was formed in 1877. Representatives of the American-based Methodist Episcopal Church (now an integral part of the United Methodist Church) arrived in 1873. They were particularly blessed by rapid growth early in the 20th century. Lutheranism was introduced to Pakistan in 1903 by the Danish Pathan Mission (associated with the Church of Denmark). The work grew slowly but was supplemented by Norwegian and American Lutheran missions, and in 1955 the Pakistani Lutheran Church came into being by a merger of their work. In 1970 the Anglicans, Methodists, Lutherans, and the Presbyterians whose work was initiated in 1856 by the Church of Scotland merged to form the Church of Pakistan, currently the largest Christian body in the country.

The larger Presbyterian body (then the United Presbyterian Church) was heading toward participation in the merger that produced the Church of Pakistan, when in 1968 it was hit with a major controversy over its participation in the ecumenical movement. A group headed by the church's moderator, Kundan Lall Nasir, attacked the liberal views present in the World Council of Churches, and as a result of the disagreements, almost a third of the church members withdrew and established the United Presbyterian Church of Pakistan. The new church then aligned itself with the International Council of Christian Churches, a fundamentalist rival of the WCC.

A variety of different churches began work in Pakistan throughout the 20th century, many before the partition of 1947. Among those receiving the most response were the New Apostolic Church and the Associate Reformed Presbyterian Church. Pentecostalism has had less success in Pakistan in recent decades than in other countries, and there are relatively few new indigenous churches. Among the several uniquely Pakistani churches is the National Virgin Church of Pakistan (1969), formed by former Presbyterians.

The Roman Catholic Church in Pakistan started anew in 1842. Administered under the Vicariate of Hindustan for many years, Lahore became a vicariate in 1886. By the time the new nation was created, the mission work had become centered on Karachi, the capital, and the first archdiocese was established there in 1950. The church rivals that of the slightly larger Church of Pakistan.

Christian ecumenism is manifested in the National Council of Churches in Pakistan, which includes the several larger churches and is affiliated with the World Council of Churches. More conservative groups are members of the Evangelical Fellowship of Pakistan, affiliated with the World Evangelical Alliance. Several of the most conservative churches are members of the International Council of Christian Churches.

Despite the large-scale movement of Hindus out of Pakistan over the years, a large Hindu minority remains in Pakistan. Pakistani Hindus have continued to try to live in peace with their Muslim neighbors. Although only 1 percent of the population, the community numbers more than 1.7 million strong. There are significantly fewer members of the Baha'i Faith and practitioners of Buddhism, Jainism, and Sikhism. At the time of partition, most Sikhs left Pakistan, and most of those who remained were killed in the rioting. The Baha'is, who have been in the area for more than 100 years, are mostly people of Persian (Iranian) heritage.

J. Gordon Melton

See also: Ahmadiyya Anjuman Islaat Islam, Lahore; Ahmadiyya Movement in Islam; Asoka; Baha'i Faith; Church Missionary Society; Church of England; Church of Pakistan; Hanafite School of Islam; International Council of Christian Churches; Naqshbandiya; Presbyterian Church of Pakistan; Qadiriyya Sufi Order; Roman Catholic Church; United Methodist Church; World Council of Churches; World Evangelical Alliance; World Muslim Congress.

References

Banuazizi, Ali, and Myron Weiner. *The State, Religion, and Ethnic Politics: Afghanistan, Iran, and Pakistan*. Syracuse: Syracuse University Press, 2001.

Gabriel, Theodore. *Christian Citizens in an Islamic State: The Pakistan Experience*. Aldershot, Hampshire, UK: Ashgate Publishing, 2007.

Iqbal, A. *Islamization of Pakistan*. Lahore, Pakistan: Vanguard Books, 1986.

Mangus, Marsden. *Living Islam: Muslim Religious Experience in Pakistan's North-West Frontier*. Cambridge: Cambridge University Press, 2006.

Pinault, David. *Notes from the Fortune-Telling Parrot: Islam and the Struggle for Religious Pluralism in Pakistan*. London: Equinox Publishing, 2008.

Rooney, J. *On the Heels of Battles: A History of the Catholic Church in Pakistan, 1780–1986*. Rawalpindi, Pakistan: Christian Study Centre, 1986.

Schimmel, A. *Islam in India and Pakistan*. Leiden: Brill, 1982.

Titus, Murray T. *Islam in India and Pakistan: A Religious History of Islam in India and Pakistan*. New Delhi: Musnhiram Manoharlal, 2005.

Walbridge, Linda. *Christians of Pakistan: The Passion of Bishop John Joseph*. New York: RoutledgeCurzon, 2003.

■ Palau

The nation of Palau includes a chain of 200 islands southeast of the Philippines and north of Papua New Guinea. They include 177 square miles of land inhabited by some 21,000 people. The Palauans are a Micronesian group.

Palau was settled as early as 1000 BCE by Polynesians. The residents' first contact with Europeans occurred in 1543, when Ruy Lopez de Villalobos (d. 1546) of Spain landed. Spain claimed the islands but

Palau

did not occupy them. In 1783 an Englishman, Henry Wilson, was shipwrecked off Ulong Island. The island's chief helped repair Wilson's ship and sent his son to be educated in Europe. The British put Palau in their trading network until the Spanish claimed their property in 1885. Spain turned Palau over to Germany in 1899 following its defeat in the Spanish-American War.

The Germans were overwhelmed by the Japanese as World War II began. The Palauans suffered most in the war, with more than 80 percent of their number being killed in the fighting. After the war the islands became part of the U.S. Trust Territory of Micronesia, but in 1978 it opted to become independent, despite U.S. protest. The people have continually fought the proliferation of any nuclear presence in their country.

The Roman Catholic Church in the Caroline Islands (now part of the Federated States of Micronesia) extended its mission to Palau, but not until 1891. The original Spanish priests were replaced by German Capuchins following the transfer of the islands to German control in 1899. The work, which involved a majority of the island's residents, is a part of the Diocese of the Caroline Islands.

Protestants arrived in 1929, also from the Caroline Islands, through a couple representing the Liebenzell Mission. They were accompanied by a convert from Chuuk Island. Later, the Seventh-day Adventist Church

Palau

Religion	Followers in 1970	Followers in 2010	% of Population	Annual % growth 2000–2010	Followers in 2025	Followers in 2050
Christians	11,100	19,400	94.8	0.74	21,700	23,800
Roman Catholics	4,000	8,500	41.5	–0.23	9,500	10,300
Protestants	2,600	6,300	30.8	2.01	7,200	8,100
Independents	4,400	3,400	16.6	0.03	3,800	4,300
Agnostics	50	560	2.7	6.36	900	1,400
Buddhists	0	180	0.9	0.84	250	300
Baha'is	30	160	0.8	0.84	200	300
Ethnoreligionists	130	120	0.6	0.88	100	100
Chinese folk	20	60	0.3	0.82	70	80
Atheists	0	10	0.0	0.00	10	20
Total population	**11,300**	**20,500**	**100.0**	**0.87**	**23,200**	**26,000**

and the Assemblies of God would begin work in Palau. Missionaries from Baptist Mid-Missions worked there briefly in the 1980s but have subsequently withdrawn.

J. Gordon Melton

See also: Assemblies of God; Roman Catholic Church; Seventh-day Adventist Church.

References

Forman, Charles H. *The Island Churches of the South Pacific: Emergence in the Twentieth Century.* Maryknoll, NY: Orbis, 1982.

Ibanez y Garcia, Luis de. *The History of the Marianas, with Navigational Data, and of the Caroline and Palau Islands: From the Time of Their Discovery by Magellan in 1521 to the Present.* Mangilao, Guam: Micronesian Area Research Center, University of Guam, 1992.

Kubary, John S. *The Religion of the Palauans.* Woodstock, NY: Micronesian Seminar, Woodstock College, 1969.

Shuster, Donald. R. "Islands of Change in Palau Church, School, and Elected Government, 1891–1981." Ed.D. thesis, University of Hawaii, 1982.

Palo Mayombe

Palo Mayombe, now found in Brazil, across the northern shore of South America, in Mexico, and in Cuba, perpetuates religion of the Kongo people of southwest Africa. Its main practitioners are people of West African descent, but it has also found a following among Hispanic people, who call it Palo Monte.

The traditional beliefs of the Kongo people are similar to those of the Yoruban religion in that they recognize a High God, a set of lesser deities (among the Kongo seen as the higher deities personifying the forces of nature), the spirits of nature (that inhabit various natural objects), and the spirits of the dead. It is possible to communicate with these various spirits through particularly gifted people and by possession, when the deity is believed to possess and speak through an individual.

Worship in Palo Mayombe occurs around the *nganga* or *prenda,* a consecrated cauldron that contains various objects including sacred earth, sticks (*palos*), and bones. The cauldron is believed to be inhabited by a spirit, who is thought to be active in any act of worship or magic that the worshippers might perform. Initiates go through a ceremony that links them to this spirit. After initiation, the new member is believed to be protected by the spirit.

Palo Mayombe received some negative publicity following the discovery in 1989 of the bodies of more than a dozen murdered men in Matamoros, Mexico (across the border from Brownsville, Texas). The murders were eventually traced to a gang deeply involved in the border drug trade. In a building on the site where the bodies were found, authorities discovered a nganga, and there was much speculation that the leader, Adolfo Constanzo (1962–1989), had molded the gang into a

Palo Mayombe group and was using human sacrifice to both eliminate rival gang members and build confidence among the gang members that they were magically protected. It was also revealed that members of the group had to watch a movie, *The Believers*, which portrays a group practicing a Hollywood version of Afro-Cuban faith.

As the investigation into the life of Constanzo continued, it was discovered that during the 1980s he had operated in Mexico City as a psychic, and that his services had included foretelling the future and clearing people of what they believed to be curses that had been placed upon them. His work often included animal sacrifices. Eventually his services expanded to include assistance to drug dealers and their staff. For a fee, he offered to make them invisible to police or bulletproof against their enemies. It appears that he made Palo Mayombe part of his practice in 1985, at which time he is believed to have raided a graveyard for human remains to include in his first nganga.

In July 1987, Constanzo became acquainted with the Hernandez brothers, who ran drugs along the Mexico-Texas border. While continuing his activities in Mexico City, he instituted his form of Palo Mayombe at a center near the village of Rancho Santa Elena, 20 miles from Matamoros. Human sacrifices became a regular part of the activities of the group, each sacrifice tied to some benefit the group was to receive. Several months after the police uncovered the activities at Matamoros, Constanzo was killed during a shoot-out with police in Mexico City. Other members of the group received long prison sentences.

Although the events at Matamoros were horrendous, there is no record of parallel violence that would indicate that Palo Mayombe practice is similarly violent and dismissive of human life.

J. Gordon Melton

See also: Possession; Spirit Possession.

References

Canizares, Baba Raul. *The Book on Palo*. Farmingdale, NY: Original Publications, 2002.

Gallerne, Gilbert. *Sacrifices humains à Matamoros*. Paris: Editions Fleuve Noir, 1993.

Humes, Edward. *Buried Secrets*. New York: Dutton, 1991.

Montenegro, Carlos. *Palo Mayombe: Spirits, Rituals, Spells*. Farmingdale, NY: Original Publications, 1998.

Schutze, James. *Cauldron of Blood: The Matamoros Cult Killings*. New York: Morrow/Avon, 1989.

■ Panama

Although the Republic of Panama, which is about the size of South Carolina, is now considered part of the Central American region, until 1903 the territory was a province of Colombia. The Republic of Panama forms the narrowest part of the isthmus and is located between Costa Rica to the west and Colombia to the east. The Caribbean Sea borders the northern coast of Panama, and the Pacific Ocean borders the southern coast. Panama City is the nation's capital, which contains about 40 percent of the nation's population.

The country has an area of 30,193 square miles and a population of 3.3 million (2008). Racially, the majority of the population is considered *mestizo* (70 percent, mixed Amerindian and Hispanic), while the rest are West Indian (14 percent, Afro-Caribbean), Amerindian (8 percent), Caucasian (6 percent), and Asian/other (2 percent). The Amerindian population (285,230 in 2000) includes 6 ethnolinguistic groups: the Guaymí (Ngöbe-Buglé), Kuna, Choco (Emberá-Wounaan), Teribe (Naso), Bokota, and Bribri.

In 2000, about 80 percent of the population were Spanish-speaking, about 9 percent were speakers of Asian or Middle Eastern languages (Chinese, Japanese, Korean, Hindustani, Hebrew, and Arabic), 8.3 percent were Amerindian (speakers of eight languages), and 3.7 percent were English-speaking (mainly West Indian and North American). However, many Panamanians are bilingual, especially in Spanish and English (Standard English and Western Caribbean Creole English). There is also a small population of Negros Congos, who speak an Afro-Hispanic Creole, especially on the Caribbean coast of Colón Province. The national literacy rate was 90.8 percent.

Panama's dollarized economy mainly depends on a well-developed services sector that accounts for 80 percent of GDP. These services include operating the Panama Canal, banking, the Colón Free Trade Zone,

Panama

Religion	Followers in 1970	Followers in 2010	% of Population	Annual % growth 2000–2010	Followers in 2025	Followers in 2050
Christians	1,395,000	3,058,000	87.1	1.81	3,678,000	4,312,000
Roman Catholics	1,316,000	2,360,000	67.3	0.22	2,700,000	3,050,000
Protestants	84,000	500,000	14.2	3.44	660,000	880,000
Independents	13,800	120,000	3.4	3.36	190,000	280,000
Muslims	65,000	155,000	4.4	1.84	190,000	225,000
Agnostics	8,500	108,000	3.1	2.61	160,000	250,000
Baha'is	14,400	46,000	1.3	1.84	60,000	80,000
Ethnoreligionists	8,000	38,000	1.1	1.84	37,500	35,000
Buddhists	2,000	27,300	0.8	1.84	36,000	45,000
New religionists	1,500	21,500	0.6	1.84	28,000	36,000
Atheists	2,000	18,000	0.5	1.84	30,000	50,000
Spiritists	0	17,000	0.5	1.84	21,000	25,000
Hindus	5,000	11,100	0.3	1.84	14,000	20,000
Chinese folk	3,000	5,200	0.1	1.84	7,000	9,000
Jews	2,000	4,400	0.1	1.84	5,000	5,500
Total population	**1,506,000**	**3,509,000**	**100.0**	**1.84**	**4,267,000**	**5,093,000**

insurance, container ports, flagship registry, and tourism. The nation's principal agricultural products are bananas, rice, corn, coffee, sugarcane, vegetables, livestock, and shrimp.

Although Panama's Constitution does not designate the Roman Catholic Church as the country's official religion, it recognizes Roman Catholicism as "the religion of the majority of Panamanians." The archbishop of Panama enjoys privileges usually reserved for government officials, and Catholicism is taught in public schools, although classes in religion are not mandatory. The Constitution guarantees freedom of religion, as long as "Christian morality and order" are respected; allows religious organizations to own property; bars clergy from public office, except in the areas of social welfare, public instruction, and scientific research; and prohibits discrimination in employment based on religion.

According to a January 1996 national public opinion poll conducted by CID-Gallup, the religious affiliation of the Panamanian population was as follows: Roman Catholic, 86.4 percent; Protestant, 7.3 percent; other religions, 2.1 percent; and none/no response, 4.2 percent. In June 2004, the company Latin Dichter & Neira conducted another national poll with the following results: Roman Catholic, 79.1 percent; Protestant, 10.8 percent; other religions, 7.7 percent; and none/no response, 2.4 percent. A comparison of these two polls reveals that Protestant adherents and those affiliated with "other religions" are growing in Panamanian society, while Catholic adherents are declining.

Historically, Panama has played an important role in world commerce, starting in the Spanish colonial period when mineral treasures from the Andean region were brought by ship to Panama and carried overland from the Pacific to the Caribbean coast for transshipment to Spain. During the California Gold Rush (1848–1855) would-be miners arrived by ship in the Caribbean port of Aspinwall, now called Colón, and walked or rode in wagons across the narrow isthmus to Panama City, located on the Pacific Ocean, where they boarded other ships to travel to the gold fields in northern California. In 1850 U.S. businessmen financed the construction of the Panama Railroad between these two major port cities in order to provide transportation for the growing numbers of people who were headed to California. Then, in 1878, a French company acquired the exclusive right to build an inter-oceanic canal on the Isthmus of Panama, which was partially constructed between 1882 and 1889.

With the political and military backing of the U.S. government, the Province of Panama seceded from

Colombia in 1903 and established the independent Republic of Panama. Immediately thereafter, the U.S. and Panamanian governments signed the Hay-Bunau Varilla Treaty, which gave the former the right to build the Panama Canal across the Isthmus and to control a 10-mile strip of land from coast to coast for its operation, maintenance, and protection, which became the U.S.-administered Panama Canal Zone (PCZ). The U.S. Corps of Engineers proceeded to complete the difficult and costly construction of the Panama Canal that was finally opened to shipping in 1914. The U.S.-controlled Panama Canal Company operated the interoceanic waterway until December 1999, when, under the provisions of the Torrijos-Carter Treaty of 1977, the Panama Canal and PCZ were turned over to the government of Panama.

From 1903 until 1968, Panama was a constitutional democracy dominated by a commercially oriented oligarchy. During the 1950s, the Panamanian military began to challenge the oligarchy's political hegemony. Its civilian government was overthrown in 1968 by a military coup, and for 20 years Panama was run by a left-wing military junta led by Generals Omar Torrijos (r. 1968–1981) and Manuel Noriega (r. 1983–1989).

In October 1968, Dr. Arnulfo Arias Madrid (1901–1988), twice elected president (r. 1940–1941, 1949–1951) and twice ousted by the Panamanian military, was ousted for a third time as president by the National Guard after only 10 days in office. A military government was established, and the commander of the National Guard, Brigadier General Omar Torrijos, soon emerged as the principal power in Panamanian political life. Torrijos's regime was harsh and corrupt, but his charisma, populist domestic programs, and nationalist (anti-U.S.) foreign policy appealed to the rural and urban constituencies largely ignored by the oligarchy. In 1979, Torrijos founded the Revolutionary Democratic Party (PRD), with a Social Democratic ideology, described as center-left.

Torrijos's sudden death in 1981 in a mysterious plane crash—rumored to have been caused by CIA operatives—altered the tone but not the direction of Panama's political evolution. Despite the 1983 constitutional amendments, which appeared to proscribe a political role for the military, the Panama Defense Forces (PDF), as they were then known, continued to dominate Panamanian political life behind a façade of civilian government. By this time, General Manuel Noriega was firmly in control of both the PDF and the civilian government.

The U.S. government froze economic and military assistance to Panama in the summer of 1987 in response to the domestic political crisis in Panama and an attack on the U.S. Embassy. In April 1988, President Ronald Reagan invoked the International Emergency Economic Powers Act, freezing Panamanian government assets in all U.S. organizations. In May 1989 Panamanians voted overwhelmingly for the anti-Noriega candidates. The Noriega regime promptly annulled the election, and embarked on a new round of repression. By the fall of 1989 the regime was barely clinging to power, and the regime's paranoia made daily existence unsafe for American citizens.

On December 20, 1989, U.S. President George H. W. Bush ordered his military forces into Panama, allegedly to protect the lives and property of U.S. citizens (about 25,000 resided in the PCZ, both civilians and military personnel), to fulfill U.S. treaty responsibilities regarding the operation and defense of the Panama Canal, to assist the Panamanian people in restoring democracy, and to bring Noriega to justice. The U.S. troops involved in Operation Just Cause achieved their primary objectives quickly, and Noriega eventually surrendered to U.S. authorities on January 3, 1990; and he was immediately taken to Florida on a U.S. military airplane to face criminal charges in a U.S. Federal Court.

On December 22, 1989, the Organization of American States (OAS) passed a resolution deploring the U.S. invasion of Panama and calling for the withdrawal of U.S. troops. On December 29, 1989, the UN General Assembly voted 75–20 with 40 abstentions to condemn the U.S. invasion of the Republic of Panama as a "flagrant violation of international law."

Since the 1989–1990 U.S. invasion and occupation of Panama City and surrounding areas, which ended the 21-year Torrijos-Noriega military dictatorship, Panama has successfully completed three peaceful transfers of power to opposition political parties. Panama's political landscape is now dominated by two major parties and many smaller ones, which are driven more by individual leaders than by ideologies.

Guillermo David Endara Galimany, who won the 1989 presidential election that General Noriega annulled, was later declared the winner after the U.S. invasion and served as president from 1989 to 1994 with the support of a coalition of anti-Noriega parties. Ernesto Pérez Balladares (PRD), who was an ally of General Omar Torrijos, served as president from 1994 to 1999; since leaving office, he has been implicated in charges of corruption. Current President Martin Torrijos (PRD), the son of General Omar Torrijos, succeeded President Mireya Moscoso (1999–2004), the widow of former President Arnulfo Arias Madrid who founded the Panameñista Party (renamed the Arnulfista Party in 1990).

Missionaries of the Roman Catholic Church accompanied the early Spanish explorers and settlers, which led to the establishment of the first Catholic parish in Panama in 1510. This became the seat of the Diocese of Santa María La Antigua del Darién and was the first diocese formed on the mainland of the Western Hemisphere, when Bishop Juan de Quevedo Villegas (d. 1519) arrived with Governor Pedro Arias de Avila (also known as Pedrarias Dávila, ca. 1440–1531) in 1513. The name was changed to the Diocese of Panama in 1520, and this jurisdiction became an archdiocese in 1925.

Many of the colonial churches built by the Spanish were constant reminders of the wealth and power of the Catholic Church in Panama and its temporal powers. One of these colonial treasures, the Cathedral of Old Panama City, was ransacked and burned by Englishman Captain Henry Morgan (1635–1688) and his pirate band in 1671, but its ruins are still the centerpiece of Panamá Viejo and a major tourist attraction.

In 1911, Monsignor F. X. Junguito, S.J., who was appointed bishop in April 1901, resided in Panama City and was assisted by his vicar-general, his secretary, the priest of the parish of the Sagrario, and two other secular priests who labored to supply the spiritual needs of the 30,000 inhabitants, at least two-thirds of whom were Catholics. They were assisted by the resident Jesuit Fathers (seven priests), Lazarists (five priests), and the Discalced Augustinians (three priests and two lay brothers).

The Roman Catholic Church holds a respected, though not very powerful, position in Panamanian society and is a familiar facet of daily life. The Constitution of 1946 provides for freedom of religion, provided that "Christian morality and public order" are respected, and it recognizes that Catholicism is the country's predominant religion, which is taught in the public schools. Such instruction or other religious activity is not compulsory, however.

The basic principles governing the church's activities or its relationship with the government were not affected by the Constitution of 1946. From the early years of independence up until the late 1960s, the Catholic Church continued to emphasize its spiritual role and generally avoided involvement in secular affairs. However, since the Second Vatican Council in 1965 and the Conference of Latin American Bishops in Medellín in 1969, the Catholic Church has become more active in temporal matters, due to its increasing concern for, and commitment to, improving the social conditions of the impoverished masses in Panama and elsewhere.

Traditionally, Panama has had a very low percentage of native-born priests and nuns within religious orders. In 1970, more than 75 percent of the Catholic missionaries in Panama were foreigners, mostly coming from Spain, Italy and the United States, or from other Latin American countries. Present in Panama were religious orders and personnel from Catholic missions in North America that included 28 male religious orders representing the Vincentians (21), Benedictines (1), Holy Cross Fathers (1) and Sulpicians (1), plus 3 diocesan priests and 1 lay brother. In addition, there were 10 female religious groups representing the Maryknolls (6), Mercy of Brooklyn (1), Franciscans of Mary Immaculate (1) and St. Joseph of Medaille (1), as well as 1 lay sister. Also, the Scarborough Foreign Mission Society of Canada had 1 priest in Panama.

However, these religious orders and missionaries from North America represented a small part of the total number of Catholic mission workers in Panama in 1980. Most of the 209 religious priests, 490 sisters, and 58 lay brothers in Panama were from Europe or other Latin American countries. The Jesuits, Carmelites, Paulists, and La Salle Christian Brothers were the major groups represented in Panama, whereas the Visitandinas was the only order of cloistered nuns in the country.

PANAMA

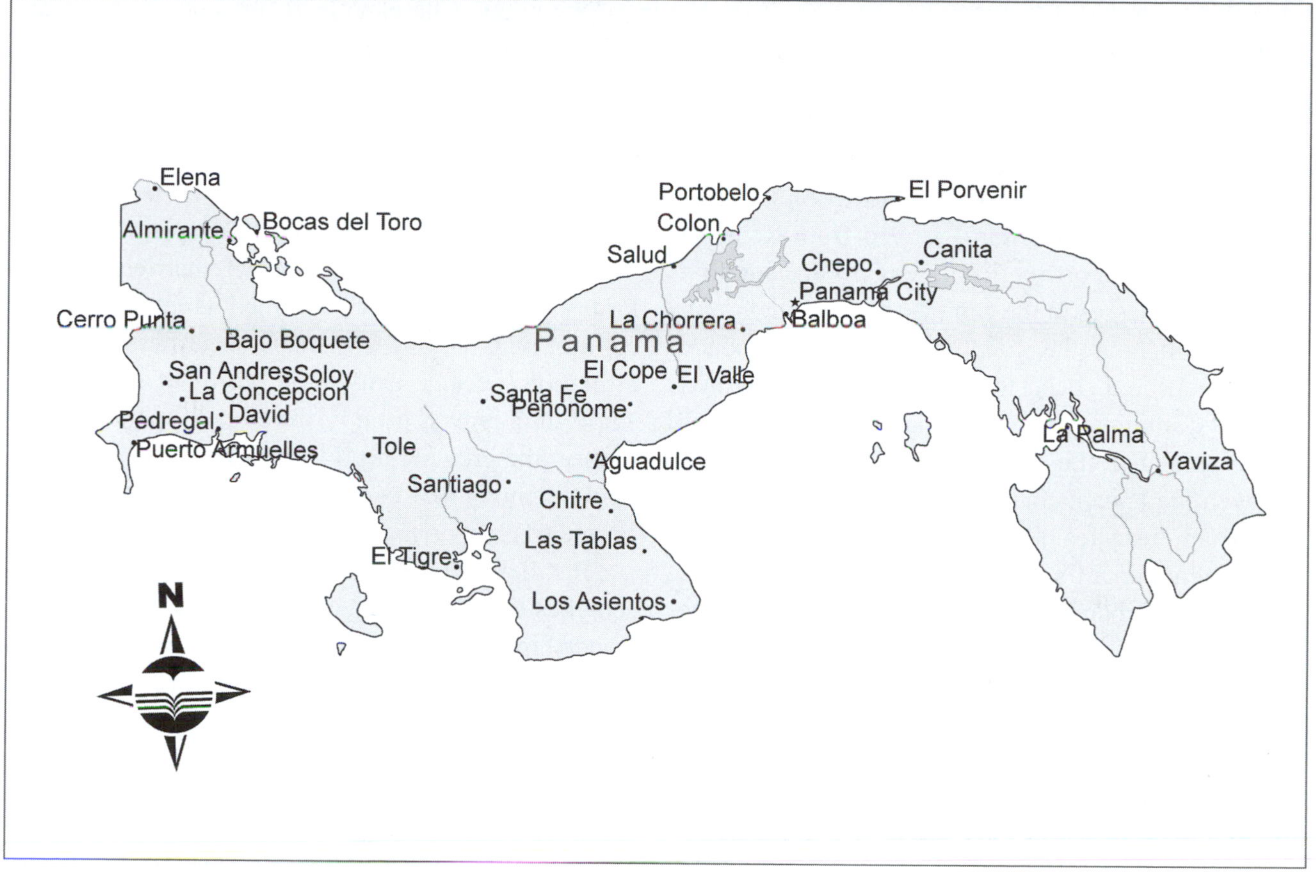

In 1980, approximately 87 percent of the population was considered Roman Catholic and virtually every town had a Catholic church, although many towns did not have a resident priest. Due to the small number of Catholic clergy in Panama, only 1 priest for every 6,299 inhabitants in 1980, many rural Catholics received only an occasional visit from a busy priest who traveled among a number of parishes. While Catholicism permeates the environment of most Panamanians, its impact is not as pronounced as in many other Catholic countries of Latin America.

The Catholic Church in Panama, in 1980, consisted of one archdiocese, three dioceses, a vicariate apostolic in Darien, and a nullius prelate in Bocas del Toro. A papal nuncio also represented the Vatican. At that time, Panama was organized into 133 parishes. Catholic institutions included 70 elementary and secondary schools, a Catholic university, a seminary for training diocesan priests, and numerous charitable programs. Monsignor Marcos Gregorio McGrath (1924–2000) was archbishop of Panama from 1969 to 1994, and he was succeeded by Monsignor José Dimas Cedeño Delgado in 1994.

Until September 2000, when Archbishop Cedeño declared Holy Mary of La Antigua to be the official patroness of Panama, the unofficial patron saint had been the Immaculate Conception of the Virgin Mary, whose feast day is celebrated nationally on December 8 (Mother's Day). Another important religious festival is celebrated annually in Portobelo, Colón province, dedicated to the Miraculous Black Christ, whose statue is paraded through city streets.

In 2004, the Archdiocese of Panama included 88 parishes that were served by 80 diocesan priests and 117 religious priests (a total of 197, or 1 priest for every 3,126 Catholics); in addition there were 161 lay brothers, 218 nuns, and 48 permanent deacons. However, these statistics do not include the dioceses of Chitré,

Darién, David, Penonomé, Santiago de Veraguas, and Colón-Kuna Yala and Territorial Prelature of Bocas del Toro.

Since the 1950s, the Catholic Church has attempted to revive active interest in religious affairs, raise church attendance, and increase the number of church marriages. This has been a continuing effort since 1958, when a lay mission group, La Santa Misión Católica (The Holy Catholic Mission), arrived from Rome to stimulate and support the local clergy. Focusing first on the lower classes in the capital, the campaign soon spread throughout the country. It helped introduce church-sponsored social welfare projects, and served to rouse Catholics from the lethargy that had traditionally plagued the Catholic Church in Panama. However, the Panamanian Catholic Church continues to confront obstacles: a shortage of priests, the indifference of nominal Catholics, and the secular attitudes of a growing urban population, especially among the youth.

During the 1970s, the Catholic Church received moderate public support, which was bolstered at times by militant Catholic action groups, such as federations of Catholic doctors and lawyers, who campaigned for a more dynamic role for the Catholic Church in community life. A growing number of priests and nuns took a more active role in labor movements, in the formation of cooperatives, in concern for the poor, and in activities that sought to produce moderate reform within Panamanian society.

An added dimension during the 1970s was the birth and development of the Catholic Charismatic Renewal (CCR) movement, which began when a Spanish priest and a Panamanian nun were strongly influenced by Catholic Charismatics in the United States. The CCR was officially organized in the Archdiocese of Panama in September 1974, following a retreat led by Friar Alfonso Navarro Castellanos (1925–2003) of the Congregation of the Missionaries of the Holy Spirit in Mexico City, one of the early leaders of the CCR in Latin America. From the beginning, Monsignor Marcos Gregorio McGrath (1924–2000), archbishop of Panama, supported the CCR, which became known in Panama as Renovación Cristiana en el Espíritu Santo. The principal leaders of the CCR in Panama are Monsignor Alejandro Vásquez Pinto, Segundo Cano, David Cosca, Francisco Verar, Teófilo Rodríguez, Reynaldo Karamañites, and Rafael Siú.

Numerous Charismatic Bible study, prayer, and fellowship groups were organized in the early 1970s, along with Charismatic Masses and rallies. Soon, Protestant pastors and laymen were also participating in the Charismatic Renewal movement, which then took on an ecumenical flavor during the 1970s. This new openness and receptivity was most apparent among the middle and upper classes, where barriers between Protestants and Catholics became less important. This spirit of unity among Christians, regardless of church affiliation, became evident as scores of small Bible study and prayer groups developed spontaneously to meet the growing need for fellowship and spiritual nurture among new converts and revitalized older believers who experienced Charismatic renewal.

Parallel to this development, the work of the Assemblies of God in Panama began in 1967 under the leadership of missionaries Richard Jeffery and David and Doris Goodwin, who held extended evangelistic crusades, called "Gran Campaña de Sanidad Divina" (Great Campaign of Divine Healing), throughout much of Panama. The first such crusade was held on Calle Primera, Vista Hermosa, in Panama City. Some of the early converts in these crusades were Hermenia Villarreal and Carmen and Anita González, who began working with the Assemblies of God under the guidance of missionary Richard Larson, who arrived in Panama in 1969 and established a church in the Canal Zone.

Carmen González, a few months after her conversion, traveled to the United States and was strongly influenced by the CCR there. Upon her return to Panama, Carmen worked in an evangelistic ministry in the Province of Chiriquí in western Panama, where she met María Ramos. In 1973, Carmen and María returned to Panama City and became leaders in the early Charismatic Renewal movement there. They met with a large number of Charismatics in the Guadalupe Catholic Church and at Colegio Las Esclavas del Sagrado Corazón de Jesús until they were forced to leave and find another meeting place. In 1975, they began meeting at a house in Barrio San Francisco and became known as the "Interdenominational Charismatic Prayer Group." Later, this group moved to Barrio Bella

Vista and was organized as a church with María Ramos as pastor, under the name Christian House of Prayer (Casa de Oración Cristiana); it became affiliated with the Assemblies of God in 1977, under the pastoral leadership of Mario Vásquez.

By 1980, the Catholic hierarchy attempted to place restrictions on the CCR and to more strongly direct its course in order to avoid losing members to evangelical groups, which were seen as a threat largely due to widespread Pentecostal growth in the capital. The CCR had a considerable impact among members of the upper class, although relatively few became members of evangelical churches. However, a growing spiritual receptivity among the upper class was evidenced by attendance at ecumenical meetings sponsored by the Full Gospel Business Men's Fellowship (FGBMF) and Women's Aglow Fellowship during the 1970s.

The Roman Catholic Church dominated the religious life of Panama until labor opportunities in the PCZ brought many American citizens and other foreign nationals to the country. The rapid influx of thousands of Protestant immigrants to Panama in the early 1900s led to the construction of many Protestant chapels for the largely English-speaking population of the PCZ, which included many African Americans from the British West Indies. The U.S. occupation of the PCZ also provided an open door for many U.S. Protestant mission agencies to begin work in Panama, such as the Salvation Army, the Seventh-day Adventist Church (1904), the Southern Baptist Convention (1905), the Methodist Episcopal Church (now an integral part of the United Methodist Church) (1906), the Church of God (Anderson, Indiana) (1906), and the National Baptist Convention, U.S.A. (1909).

By 1911 about 10,000 residents in the PCZ were being served by 39 Christian churches: Protestant Episcopal (13), nondenominational (8), Roman Catholic (7), Baptist (7), Methodist (3), and Adventist (1). Three additional Protestant groups arrived in the next decade: the Free Methodist Church of North America (1913), the Christian Mission of Barbados (1914), and the Christian Brethren (1918). Also in 1914, the Union Churches of the Canal Zone were organized as nonsectarian, interdenominational community churches. In 1935 the population of the PCZ numbered 14,816 and was served by 54 congregations.

However, the first Protestants to arrive in Panama were a group of 1,200 colonists from Scotland (some of whom were Presbyterian), who attempted to build a commercial colony on the Caribbean coast of the Darien Peninsula in 1698. However, the colony was abandoned in late 1699.

The next Protestants to arrive were Wesleyan (British) Methodists, who were among Afro-Caribbean immigrants to settle in the Bocas del Toro region of the Caribbean coast, beginning in the 1820s. The United Methodist Free Church of England (1870s), the Jamaican Baptists (1880s), and the Jamaican Wesleyan Methodists (1880s) also began work among West Indian immigrants in Panama.

The Church of England (through the Society for the Propagation of the Gospel in Foreign Parts) arrived in the 1850s during the construction of the Panama Railroad. Company officials helped to finance the construction of the first permanent Protestant church building in Panama, Christ's Church-by-the-Sea in Aspinwall, built in 1864–1865. This was the second oldest permanent Protestant church in Central America, with the first being St. John's Anglican Cathedral in Belize City, built in 1825. However, occasional Anglican-Episcopal worship services had been held in Panama since 1849, conducted by clergymen en route to the gold fields in California, which led to the establishment of the first Episcopal congregation in 1851 in the port town of Taboga. An official Isthmian Mission of the Anglican Church was established in Panama in 1853, although missionary work was sparse until 1883.

Prior to the 1950s, Protestant missionary activities were largely centered in the PCZ, where many of the English-speaking people were concentrated. However, over time, some of the Protestant denominations began to evangelize and establish churches among the Spanish-speaking population, mainly in the urban areas adjacent to the PCZ and in the western provinces of the country.

Prior to the 1940s, Southern Baptist work in Panama was largely limited to North Americans and West Indians in the PCZ and in the port cities of Panama City and Colón. In the 1940s increased efforts were made by the Southern Baptist Home Mission Board to launch work in Spanish-speaking communities, and in the 1950s among the Kuna Indians on the Caribbean coast of northeastern Panama. Protestant efforts among the Kunas began in 1913, led by British and American independent missionaries under the sponsorship of the San Blas Mission. During the 1950s, the nondenominational New Tribes Mission and several Mennonite groups began work among Amerindian groups in Panama as well.

Pentecostal work in Panama began with the arrival of the Arthur Edwards family in 1928, sent out from the U.S.-based International Church of the Foursquare Gospel. Early evangelistic efforts by Edwards and his helpers proved quite successful among the Spanish-speaking population during the 1930s and 1940s, especially following revival meetings in the PCZ town of Frijoles, where supernatural "signs and wonders" were reported for several years in the mid-1930s. The mother church of the Panamanian Foursquare movement, the Calle Q Foursquare Church, was founded in 1937 in Panama City and became a training center for missionary efforts throughout the country. The Foursquare Bible School was established at the mother church in 1938. By 1981, the Foursquare Church had grown to include 21,700 baptized members, 206 organized congregations, and 201 preaching points in all nine provinces, with about 97 percent of the membership composed of Spanish-speaking Panamanians. At that time, the Foursquare Church was not only the largest Pentecostal denomination in Panama but also the largest Protestant denomination.

Other Pentecostal denominations in Panama include the Church of God (Cleveland, Tennessee) (1935), the Evangelistic Doctrinal Church of Puerto Pilón (an independent group, founded in 1940), the Church of God of Prophecy (1946), the International Evangelical Church, Soldiers of the Cross (1950), the Pentecostal Church of God–International Mission of Puerto Rico (1956), the Apostolic Assembly of Faith in Jesus Christ (1960), the Church of God in Christ (1964), the New Life Evangelical Church (a 1967 split from the Foursquare Church in the Province of Chiriquí), the Assemblies of God (1967), the Pentecostal Christian Church of the World Wide Missionary Movement (1973) and Missionary Advance (1973), both from Puerto Rico, the Pentecostal Church of Jesus Christ (1974), the United Pentecostal Church (1980), and the International Pentecostal Holiness Church (1988). Also, the Maranatha World Revival Ministry (founded by Apostle Nahum Rosario in Chicago, Illinois) arrived in 2003.

Panama Metropolitan Cathedral in Panama City was built between 1688 and 1796. (iStockPhoto.com)

Small, non-Pentecostal Protestant denominations include the following: the Lutheran Church–Missouri Synod (1942, Iglesia Evangélica Luterana de Panamá), the nondenominational Central American Mission (1944), the independent Churches of Christ (1945), the New Tribes Mission (1952), the Gospel Missionary Union (1952), Conservative Baptist Home Mission Society (1952, renamed Mission to the Americas in 1994), the Church of the Nazarene (1953), the Society of Bible Churches (1958), the Mennonite Brethren Board of Missions and Services (1958), the Church of the Brethren (1958), the United Gospel Church (1961), the Evangelical Mission of Panama (1961), Baptist International Missions (1961), the Association of Lutheran Churches of Panama (1963), the Free Will Baptist Church (1964), American Baptist Churches in the U.S.A. (2001), and the Church of God–Holiness (2003). Also, the Evangelical Lutheran Church in America is engaged in relief and development ministry in Coclé Province, which includes a "Ministry of Reconciliation" between Amerindian peoples (Ngöbe-Buglé) in Penonomé.

In 1980 the largest Protestant denominations in Panama were the Foursquare Church, the Episcopal Church (which assumed responsibility for the Anglican community in 1906 due to growing U.S. influence in the PCZ), the Seventh-day Adventist Church, and the Panamanian Baptist Convention (affiliated with the Southern Baptist Convention).

By 2005, the Assemblies of God had become the largest Protestant denomination as a result of 38 years of strenuous evangelistic and church-planting efforts throughout the country, with 800 congregations (churches and missions) and about 50,000 members. Second largest was the Seventh-day Adventist Church, with 162 congregations and 40,600 members. The International Church of the Foursquare Gospel was third largest, with 415 congregations and 31,200 members. Other large denominations included the Baptist Convention (120 congregations with 12,100 members), the Evangelical Methodist Church and the Wesleyan Methodist Church (combined statistics were 257 congregations and about 12,000 members), the Pentecostal Church of God (103 churches and 154 missions with 8,134 members), the independent Churches of Christ (84 churches with 6,740 members), the New Tribes Mission–related churches (72 churches and 6,090 members), the Anglican-Episcopal Church (23 churches with 5,400 members), the Church of God (Cleveland, Tennessee) with 85 congregations and 5,200 members, the Evangelical Doctrinal Church Association (34 congregations and 4,060 members), and the United Pentecostal Church (77 congregations and 3,850 members). All other Protestant denominations had fewer than 3,000 members each in 2005.

Many of the more conservative Protestant churches are associated with the Panamanian Evangelical Confraternity (Confraternidad Evangélica Panameña [CONEPA]), which is affiliated with the World Evangelical Alliance. Members of the Latin American Council of Churches (CLAI), which is affiliated with the World Council of Churches (WCC), include the Episcopal Diocese of Panama, the Evangelical Methodist Church (affiliated with the United Methodist Church in the U.S.A.), the Wesleyan Methodist Church (affiliated with the Conference of the Methodist Church in the Caribbean and the Americas), and the independent Lutheran Church (Diocese of Panama).

In the area of mass communication, evangelical radio station HOXO (AM transmitter) was founded in 1949 in Panama City, with financial help and technical assistance provided jointly by the Latin America Mission (LAM) in Costa Rica and World Radio Missionary Fellowship, operators of radio station HCJB in Quito, Ecuador. In 1971 an FM radio transmitter was added, called "Radio Vida," and these two radio stations were incorporated in 1974 as the Tropical Broadcasting Association under a Panamanian board of directors. By 2005, at least 13 evangelical radio stations existed in Panama, 5 of which were owned and operated by the Assemblies of God, as well as a TV channel: "Hosanna Visión—Canal 37."

The Ecumenical Committee of Panama (COEPA) is a fraternal association of churches, founded in 1986, which confess Jesus Christ as God and Savior and seek to fulfill their common calling to the glory of God while promoting greater unity, dialogue, and interreligious activities. Its current members include representatives of the Evangelical Methodist Church of Panama, the Roman Catholic Church, the Episcopal-Anglican Church of Panama, Calvary Baptist Church, the Methodist Church in the Caribbean and the Americas, the Greek Orthodox Church, and the Russian Orthodox Church. The president of COEPA is Bishop Pablo Morales of the Evangelical Methodist Church of Panama.

Non-Protestant Christian groups present in the country include the Church of Jesus Christ of Latter-day Saints (1 temple, 93 congregations and 42,606 members in 2007), Jehovah's Witnesses (235 kingdom halls with 11,704 members in 2005), Christadelphians, Voice of the Chief Cornerstone (from Puerto Rico), Mita Congregation (from Puerto Rico), Universal Church of the Kingdom of God (from Brazil, also called Strong Prayer to the Holy Spirit Church), God Is Love Pentecostal Church (from Brazil), Light of the World Church (from Mexico), Unity School of Christianity, Seicho-No-Ie, Philadelphia Church of God, and Evangelical Doctrinal Church of Port Pilón (founded in Panama).

Eastern Orthodox churches in Panama include a small Greek Orthodox community, affiliated with the Greek Orthodox Metropolitanate of Central America under Metropolitan Athenagoras in Panama City; the

Russian Orthodox Greek Catholic Church of Three Saints founded in the United States in 1898, affiliated with the Moscow Patriarchal Parish; and the Russian Orthodox Church, affiliated with the Russian Orthodox Church Outside of Russia—ROCOR.

Also, there are four independent Catholic denominations in Panama. The Apostolic Orthodox Old Catholic Church (under Monsignor Jorge Rodriguez-Villa) represents the Old Catholic Tradition. The Apostolic Community of Our Lady of Beautiful Love of Panama was founded by Friar Orlando Enrique Rojas Bonilla (located in El Común, Tolé Municipality of Chiriquí Province); it is affiliated with Our Lady of Guadalupe Community of Communities, founded in Costa Rica by Monsignor Higinio Alas Gómez in 2007 (previously this group was known as Reformed Apostolic and Catholic Church, 2000–2005). The Reunited Apostolic Catholic Church (Diocese of Central America, Panama and the West Indies) was founded in Costa Rica by Archbishop Monsignor Pablo José de Jesús María (secular name: Francisco Eduardo de la Espriella Torrens); it is affiliated with the Brazilian Apostolic Catholic Church (founded by Monsignor Carlos Duarte Costa, bishop of Maura), the Free Orthodox Church of Ibero-America, and the Byzantine Catholic Church, Inc. (under Patriarch Mar Markus I) of Los Angeles, California. The Ecumenical Catholic Church of Christ is affiliated with the Diocese of Our Mother of God in Costa Rica (under Monsignor Sebastián Herrera Plá) and is part of the Apostolic Administration of Central America, Panama and Cuba (under Monsignor Karl R. Rodig of Miami, Florida).

Today, there are a small number of Rastafarians (founded in Jamaica in the 1930s) and adherents of older African-derived religions, such as the syncretistic religion of the Negros Congos, Myalism, Obeah, "revivalistic sects," and Kumina, almost exclusively among the Afro-Panamanian population. Historically, some of these religions were present in Panama from the beginning of the African slave trade in the Caribbean to the end of the British colonial period. The Negros Congos trace their ancestry to African slaves imported during the Spanish colonial period and speak an Afro-Hispanic Creole, especially on the Caribbean coast of Colón Province, centered in the colonial port city of Portobello. Present among the British West Indian Creole population were the Afro-Caribbean sects of Myalism (a syncretistic religion that appealed to all African ethnic groups in Jamaica and the West Indies) and Obeah (a religion probably of Ashanti origin, characterized by the practice of sorcery and witchcraft, which had been outlawed in the British colonies during the slavery period).

In addition, several "revivalistic" sects originated in Jamaica and the British West Indies during the 1800s: Native Baptists, Spiritual Baptists, and Zion Revivalism (modifications of Myalism, which inserted familiar elements of the Christian faith—the Bible, God, angels, archangels, saints, apostles, and prophets—into worship patterns characteristic of African religiosity); and Kumina (also known as Pukkumina or Pocomania), a post-Emancipation (August 1 is celebrated as Emancipation Day throughout the Caribbean) religious tradition traced to African indentured servants who were brought to Jamaica from Central Africa, in which "spirit possession," ritual healing, and animal sacrifice were central features (similar to Santeria in Cuba and Puerto Rico).

Other religions include traditional Amerindian belief systems (animistic) among the Guaymí (Ngäbe Buglé), Kuna, Choco (Wounaan and Emberá), Bribri, Teribe (Naso), and Buglere (Bokota); "popular religiosity" (syncretistic, practiced by a majority of the Hispanic population); traditional Chinese religions: Daoism, Confucianism, and Buddhism; Hinduism (including the International Society for Krishna Consciousness, International Sri Sathya Sai Baba Organization, and International Society of Transcendental Meditation—TM); Sant Mat (including ECKANKAR, the Path of Light and Sound, Sant Thakar Singh, Surat Shadd Yoga, Sawan Kirpal Ruhani Mission, Science of Spirituality, and Supreme Master Ching Hai Meditation Association); Sikh, Islam, and Subud; Japanese Buddhism (Soka Gakkai International of Panama—Nichiren Shoshu Temple) and Shinto; Judaism; Baha'i Faith; Ancient and Mystical Order Rosae Crucis (AMORC); Wicca; Superet Light Doctrinal Church (a U.S.-based Spiritualist community); New Acropolis Cultural Association; The God, Love and Charity Spiritist Fraternity (founded in 1982); Latin American Federation of Para-Psychological and Similar Sciences; the Saint Germain Foundation, Raelian movement; Ishaya

Techniques; and the Holy Spirit Association for the Unification of World Christianity, popularly known as the Unification Movement, founded in Korea by the Reverend Sun Myung Moon, which publishes the Spanish-language newspaper, *Tiempos del Mundo,* in Panama.

Beginning with the building of the Panama Railroad in the 1850s, many Chinese laborers arrived via Canada and Jamaica, mainly from Guangzhou Province but also from the British crown colony of Hong Kong. Along with the Chinese immigrants came some Buddhist, Daoist, and Confucian traditions that were centered on family altars where devotion was rendered to their ancestors; they include the Fa Yen Religious Society and Yan Wo Religious Society. There were several waves of Chinese immigrants whose descendants today number around 50,000. Since the 1970s, an estimated 80,000 Chinese have settled in Panama from other parts of mainland China: 99 percent are Cantonese-speaking, although Mandarin and Hakka speakers are represented among the newer arrivals. Over time, the older Chinese immigrants and their descendants began assimilating into Panamanian society and, often, that meant converting to Catholicism or Protestantism. The Sacred Heart Chapel in Ancon is now home to a Chinese Roman Catholic congregation, and there are a dozen or more evangelical Chinese churches, mainly located in Panama City and Colón. Some of the evangelical churches are affiliated with the Chinese Christian Mission of Petaluma, California; the Baptist Convention; the Christian and Missionary Alliance; or the Evangelical Free Church.

With independence came the North American canal-building effort, which in turn brought in an international labor force and greater religious diversity. Panama's Hindu and Muslim communities, which initially arrived by way of the British colonies of Guyana and Trinidad-Tobago, first came as canal workers between 1904 and 1913. Most of the Hindus trace their roots back to the states of Gujarat and Sindh, in India and Pakistan, respectively. Many ancestors of today's Muslim community also came from those same places, but this community has since been augmented by Arabs, who arrived via South American countries, and more recently as a result of home-grown converts. The Muslims live primarily in Panama City and Colón, with smaller concentrations in David and other provincial cities. The majority of today's Muslims are of Lebanese, Palestinian, or Asian Indian descent. As of March 1997, there were four Mosques (*masajid*) in the Republic of Panama. There are also a few Sikhs in Panama, almost all of whom trace their roots to the Punjab.

Some of the South Asian subcontinent organizations in Panama are the Sunni Muslim Religious Association, the Panama Muslim Mission (originally named the Sunni Indo-Pakistani Muslim Society, founded in 1929), the Islamic Foundation of Panama (Jama Masajid), the Panamanian Hindu Civic Association, the Krishna Radha Temple Society, the Hindustani Society of Panama (Templo Hindu de Tumba Muerto), the Hindustani Society of Colón, the Islamic Cultural Center of Colón, and the Guru Nanak Sahid Civic Society.

Also, about 10,000 Lebanese (some are Orthodox Christians and others are Muslim) live in Panama, including many investors who have businesses tied to the Colón Free Trade Zone, which re-exports an enormous variety of merchandise throughout the Americas. Begun in 1948, it is now the largest free trade zone in the Americas and second largest in the world.

The small Jewish community (about 9,000) dates from the middle of the 19th century, and includes 5 synagogues: Beth El Synagogue (Orthodox), Shevet Achim Synagogue in Panama City (Orthodox-Sephardic), Ahavat Sion Synagogue (Orthodox-Sephardic), Kol Shearith Israel Synagogue in Panama City (Reform), and Ahvat Ahim Synagogue in Colón. The Baha'i Faith maintains one of the world's seven Baha'i Houses of Worship.

Clifton L. Holland

See also: American Baptist Churches in the U.S.A.; Ancient and Mystical Order Rosae Crucis; Apostolic Assembly of Faith in Jesus Christ, U.S.A.; Assemblies of God; Baha'i Faith; Christadelphians; Church of God (Cleveland, Tennessee); Church of God in Christ; Church of God of Prophecy; Church of Jesus Christ of Latter-day Saints; Church of the Brethren; ECKANKAR; Lutheran Church–Missouri Synod; Roman Catholic Church; Evangelical Lutheran Church in America; International Church of the

Foursquare Gospel; International Evangelical Church, Soldiers of the Cross; International Pentecostal Holiness Church; International Society for Krishna Consciousness; Jehovah's Witnesses; Latin American Council of Churches; Master Ching Hai Meditation Association; Methodist Church in the Caribbean and the Americas; Mita Congregation; New Acropolis Cultural Association; Nichiren Shoshu; Rastafarians; Ruhani Satsang; Russian Orthodox Church (Moscow Patriarchate); Russian Orthodox Church Outside of Russia; Sathya Sai Baba Movement; Seicho-No-Ie; Seventh-day Adventist Church; Sikhism/Sant Mat; Soka Gakkai International; Southern Baptist Convention; Spiritual Baptists; Subud; Unification Movement; United Methodist Church; Unity School of Christianity; Universal Church of the Kingdom of God; World Council of Churches; World Evangelical Alliance.

References

Brierly, Peter, ed. *World Churches Handbook.* London: Christian Research, 1977.

Catholic Encyclopedia (1913). "Republic and Diocese of Panama." http://en.wikisource.org/wiki/Catholic_Encyclopedia_(1913)/Republic_and_Diocese_of_Panama. Accessed March 1, 2009.

Grimes, Barbara F., ed. *Ethnologue: Languages of the World.* 12th ed. Dallas, TX: Summer Institute of Linguistics, 1992.

Holland, Clifton L., ed. *World Christianity: Central America and the Caribbean.* Monrovia, CA: MARC-World Vision, 1981.

Jackson, Eric. "Holy Scriptures Month and Panama's Religious Heritage." *The Panama News* 13, no. 11 (May 20–June 2, 2007).

PROLADES-Religion in the America Database: "Religion in Panama." http://www.prolades.com/cra/regions/cam/pan/pan-rd.htm. Accessed March 1, 2009.

Ravensbergen, Gerriejan Anna. "Protestantism in Panama and Why Middle Classers go Evangelical." Master's thesis in Latin American Studies, CEDLA Inter-university Centre for Latin American Research and Documentation, Amsterdam, 2008.

Statistics for the Archdiocese of Panama. http://www.catholic-hierarchy.org/diocese/dpana.html. Accessed March 1, 2009.

U.S. Department of State, *International Religious Freedom Report 2007: Panama.* http://www.state.gov/g/drl/rls/irf/2007/90262.htm. Accessed March 1, 2009.

Pangestu

Pangestu is one of the new spiritual religions of Indonesia. Its name, which means "blessing" in Javanese, is both an acronym for the organization named Paguyuban Ngesti Tunggal ("association focusing on union") and its common name. The organization was founded in 1949 but its origins lie in the revelation received by Raden Soenarto Mertowardojo (1899–ca. 1965), or Pakde Narto, on February 14, 1932. Pakde Narto was born near Boyolali in Central Java, then lived in Surakarta, where he worked as a clerk in a series of government offices, and died in the mid-1960s. Soon after his initial experience two close followers transcribed the teachings he received through the "True Teacher" (Sang Guru Sejati). These became *Sasangka Jati* (a text translated into English as *True Light*), which contains the core teachings of Pangestu.

Sasangka Jati begins with clarification of the three aspects of God: Suksma Kawekas (the source of life, or God the Father), Suksma Sejati (the True Teacher, messenger of God), and Roh Suci (the Holy Spirit). It proceeds with clarification on the five qualities essential to proper worship of God: non-attachment, acceptance, truthfulness, patience, and noble aspiration; then to five commandments (*Paliwara*); a version of Genesis (*Gumelaring Dumadi*); the One Teaching (*Tunggal Sabda*); the safe path (*Dalan Rahayu*); the "whence and whither" (*Sangkan Paran*); and prayer (*Panembah*).

Pakde Narto lived in a Surakarta world in which virtually all men of his position were involved in a variety of spiritual practices, often simultaneously. He was closely associated with the Mankunegaran, the lesser court of Solo, and through it also with Dutch Protestant missionaries and the Theosophical Society. It is emphasized that Pangestu is neither a new religion nor "mystical." Those terms are disavowed in favor of the "spiritual" to stress that it involves no relations with ancestral spirits or occult powers. Even the term "meditation" is avoided, as in Pangestu this is associated mainly with Hindu and Buddhist philosophies that leaders believe do not focus sufficiently on God. At the same time teachings are presented as a newly received, direct transmission from God, which came without the mediation of an established religious system.

The organization became prominent in the 1950s, when Dr. Sumantri Hardjoprakoso, a Dutch-trained psychiatrist, became its leader. Since then Pangestu has particularly appealed to intellectuals with a modernizing agenda. Within the Javanist world of movements it could be described as the equivalent of Muhammadiyah, Indonesia's leading modernist Muslim movement. It synthesizes many elements of traditional philosophy and literature into a clear system, which appeals strongly to educated Javanists. From the 1950s on, but especially during the Suharto era, it became especially strong within both the army and the civil service. It was estimated in 1970 that membership was around 50,000, but in recent years it has claimed a following of twice that. It has a clearly structured organization throughout Indonesia and lists branches in Europe, but most members everywhere are ethnic Javanese.

J. Gordon Melton

See also: Meditation; Theosophical Society (Adyar).

References

De Jong, Suffridus. *Een Javaanse Levenshouding*. Wageningen: H. Veenman & Zonen B.V., 1973.

Hadiwijono, Harun. *Man in the Present Javanese Mysticism*. Baarn: Bosch & Keuning N.V., 1967.

Hardjoprakoso, Sumantri. *Indonesisch Mensbeeld als Basis ener Psycho-Therapie.* Leiden, 1956.

Mertowardojo, Soenarto. *True Light.* Pangestu, Jakarta, 1972. (English ed.)

Sutrisno, Mudji. "Life Wisdom of 'Sasongko Jati'." http://www.crvp.org/book/Series03/IIID-6/chapter-5.htm. Accessed March 24, 2009.

Pantheism

Pantheism is a widely discussed philosophical position, but one that has rarely led to the formation of religious communities. It is the view that the universe is identical with God, and that God is identical with the universe. A slightly similar position, called panentheism, identifies the universe as divine but also assumes that God is more than the universe and hence remains an object of veneration and worship. Panentheism is often identified with the philosophy of Alfred North Whitehead (1861–1947) and Charles Hartshorne (1897–2000).

Alasdair MacIntyre (1967) suggests that pantheism includes the belief that everything that exists constitutes an all-inclusive "unity" that is in some sense divine. The first prominent pantheist is generally identified as the Dutch philosopher Baruch Spinoza (1632–1677), and British freethinker John Toland (1670–1722) is credited with coining the term "pantheist," which he used synonymously with "Spinozist." However, a number of ancient philosophers, including Plato (ca. 428–348 BCE) and Plotinus (205–270 CE), are identified as pantheists, as are literary lights such as D. H. Lawrence (1885–1930), Walt Whitman (1819–1892), and Ralph Waldo Emerson (1803–1882).

Various movements, such as Daoism, are often identified as inherently pantheistic, as is much mystical and scientific thought. One movement often accused of being pantheistic is the Church of Christ, Scientist, though its founder, Mary Baker Eddy (1821–1910), denied the charge. On the other hand, modern neo-Pagan groups often identify themselves, in their worship of nature, as pantheists.

Among the few groups identifying itself as pantheist is the Universal Pantheist Society, founded in 1975, which describes its beliefs as follows: "The cosmos, taken or conceived of as a whole, is synonymous with the theological principle of God. The Cosmos is divine, and the earth sacred. Pantheists do not propose belief in a deity; rather, they hold nature itself as a creative presence. Pantheism reconciles science and religion through ecology leading to strong environmental awareness" (http://www.pantheist.net). Another pantheist organization is the World Pantheist Union. The Union supports an Earth-honoring, life-affirming, naturalistic form of pantheism, which it hopes to make available as a religious option and a rational alternative to traditional religions.

Universal Pantheist Society
PO Box 3499
Visalia, CA 93278
http://www.pantheist.net/

World Pantheist Union
PO Box 55629
Riverside, CA 92517
http://www.pantheism.net/

J. Gordon Melton

See also: Church of Christ, Scientist.

References

Garrett, Jan. "An Introduction to Pantheism." http://www.wku.edu/~garreje/panthesm.htm. Accessed December 1, 2001.

Harrison, Paul. *Elements of Pantheism.* London: Llumina Press, 1999, 2004.

Levine, Michael P. *Pantheism: A Non-Theistic Concept of Deity*. London and New York: Routledge, 1994.

MacIntyre, Alasdair. "Pantheism." In *Encyclopedia of Philosophy,* edited by Paul Edwards. New York: Macmillan and Free Press, 1967.

Russell, Sharman Apt. *Standing in the Light: My Life as a Pantheist.* New York: Basic Books, 2008.

■ Papua New Guinea

The modern nation of Papua New Guinea brings together the eastern half of the island of New Guinea, the islands of the Bismarck Archipelago, the northern Solomon Islands, and a variety of other islands east of New Guinea. The western half of New Guinea, the second largest island in the world, is part of Indonesia. Papua New Guinea's 175,000 square miles of land is inhabited by its 5,932,000 citizens, which includes a variety of Melanesians, Polynesians, and Micronesians.

The modern state of Papua New Guinea was constructed in steps, beginning with the merger of the former British protectorate of Papua with the German colony of New Guinea after the Germans were displaced during World War I. The land was administered by Australia until independence was proclaimed in 1975.

The islands covered by Papua New Guinea have been inhabited by Melanesian peoples since at least 2000 BCE. They traditionally tended to live in small groups separated by dense jungle, and modern scholars have identified more than 700 Native languages and dialects. When Europeans made their initial contact with the island's inhabitants in the 20th century, many of these groups had only limited use of tools. Some had yet to discover the wheel.

The traditional religions of the Native population continue to be practiced by many of the islanders, but only a few (less than 5 percent) follow it exclusively. Native religion came under heavy attack by the missionaries, the first of whom, Samuel McFarlane (1837–1911), arrived in 1871. McFarlane, representing the London Missionary Society, was joined within a few years by W. G. Lawes (1839–1907), and together they pioneered work on Murray Island and Port Moresby. Their work would grow into the present United Church in Papua New Guinea.

Australian Methodists (now a constituent part of the Uniting Church in Australia) chose New Guinea as their first mission field and sent George Brown (1835–1917) and a team of native church workers from Fiji and Samoa. The mission grew to include the Duke of York, New Britain, and New Ireland Islands. The work was spurred by the 1878 death of four of the Fijians, who were killed by those among whom they were working. Work expanded to Papua in 1890. This work was later incorporated into the United Church of the Solomon Islands.

In 1886 German Lutherans working through the Neuendettelsau Mission Society began what would become one of the more successful missions in Papua New Guinea. Under the leadership of Johann Flierl (1858–1947), the German mission grew with a succession of mass movements early in the 20th century. After World War I, the Australian Lutherans became the dominant force in leadership, and the American Lutheran Church (now a constituent part of the Evangelical Lutheran Church in America) added its resources to assist in recovery from the Japanese occupation.

A Protestant mission church in the mountains of Papua New Guinea. (iStockPhoto.com)

The church became autonomous in 1956 as the Evangelical Lutheran Church of New Guinea. The United Church in Papua New Guinea, the United Church of the Solomon Islands, and the Evangelical Lutheran Church of Papua New Guinea are all members of the World Council of Churches.

The last of the major Christian groups to enter New Guinea, also from Australia, were the Anglicans. Albert Maclaren (1853–1891) launched the Anglican mission at Dogura on the island's northeast coast, and the Diocese of Papua New Guinea was erected in 1898. The diocese existed within the Church of England in Australia until the independent Province of the Church of Papua New Guinea was formed in 1977.

Roman Catholic missionaries actually found their way to the Bismarck archipelago in 1847 but had little effect until 1881, when representatives of the Missionaries of the Sacred Heart came. Thereafter, the work expanded rapidly and a vicariate of British New Guinea was established in 1889. The Roman Catholic Church experienced spectacular growth in Papua New Guinea in the 1960s, but it has had a continuing problem with the recruitment of indigenous priests; the first Native Papuan priest was not ordained until 1937. He later became the first Papuan bishop (1970). As the new century begins, there are 4 archdioceses and 20 dioceses.

Through the 20th century, a spectrum of Christian denominations launched missions in Papua New Guinea. Most of these originated in Australia, with a lesser number coming from the United States (including the Baptist Bible Fellowship International, the Church of the Nazarene, and the Salvation Army). Swedish and Finnish Pentecostals initiated work in the 1960s. The independent Bethel Pentecostal Temple, the first Pentecostal church in the state of Washington, started a small mission in 1948, which has grown to be

Papua New Guinea

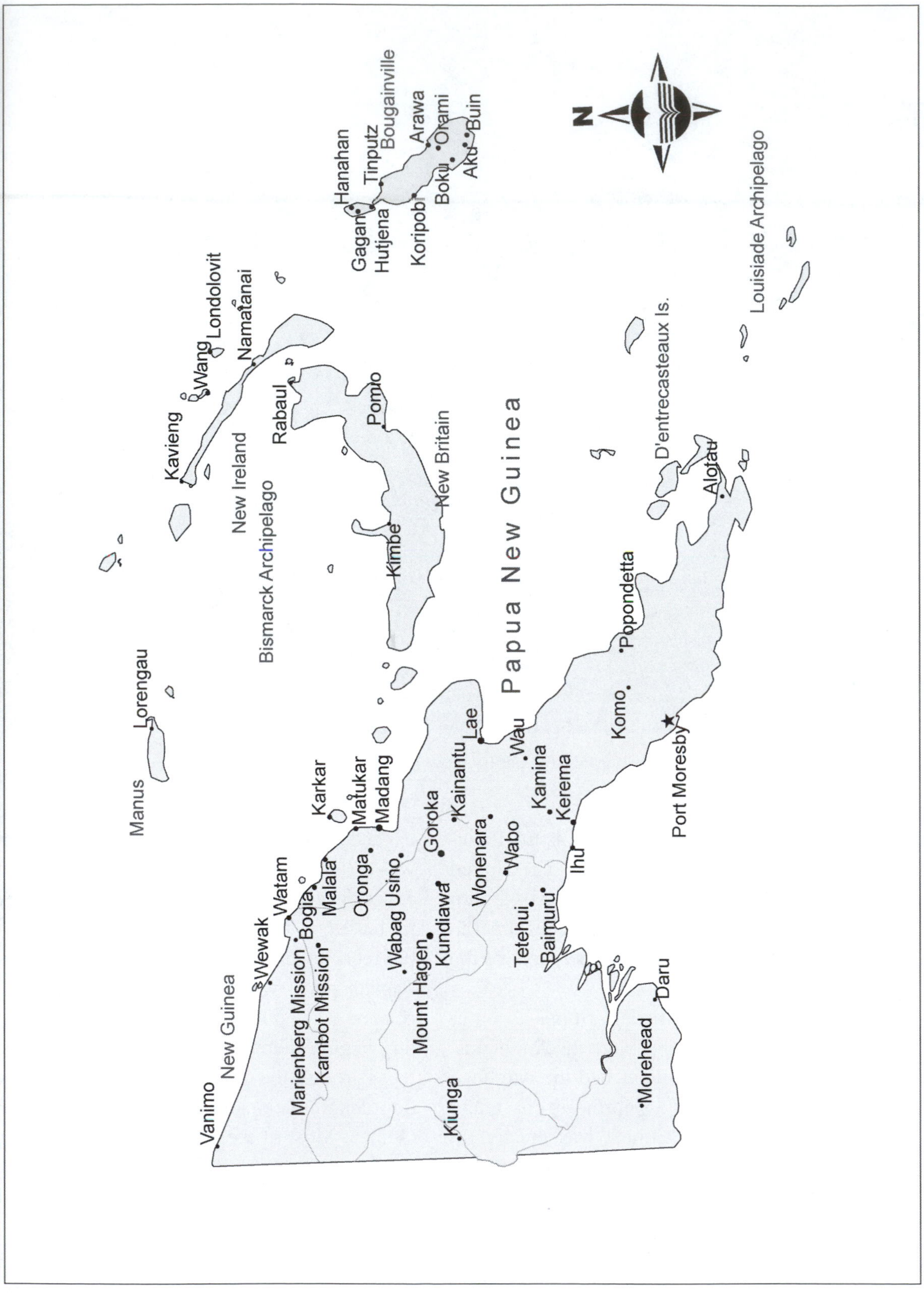

Papua New Guinea

Religion	Followers in 1970	Followers in 2010	% of Population	Annual % growth 2000–2010	Followers in 2025	Followers in 2050
Christians	2,317,000	6,152,000	95.0	2.44	7,855,000	10,182,000
Protestants	913,000	3,840,000	59.3	3.00	4,850,000	6,300,000
Roman Catholics	607,000	1,830,000	28.2	2.47	2,450,000	3,200,000
Independents	23,200	315,000	4.9	2.85	480,000	750,000
Ethnoreligionists	114,000	208,000	3.2	2.27	240,000	290,000
Baha'is	9,300	57,000	0.9	2.64	85,000	120,000
Agnostics	2,000	40,000	0.6	11.08	70,000	110,000
Buddhists	2,000	10,500	0.2	2.49	14,000	19,000
Chinese folk	2,200	4,600	0.1	2.47	5,500	7,000
Atheists	0	1,900	0.0	2.48	3,000	5,000
New religionists	0	1,900	0.0	2.40	3,000	4,000
Muslims	0	1,800	0.0	2.55	3,000	4,500
Jews	300	700	0.0	2.49	700	700
Total population	**2,447,000**	**6,478,000**	**100.0**	**2.47**	**8,279,000**	**10,742,000**

one of the largest evangelical churches in Papua New Guinea, with almost 300 congregations.

The primary indigenous religious movements grew out of World War II and the use of New Guinea as a staging area for the U.S. armed forces. The so-called cargo cults originated from the experience among Native people of seeing cargo planes landing and leaving behind large amounts of supplies. In this context, a variety of local leaders, some with messianic pretensions, arose and began new movements. As the history of contemporary Papua New Guinea has been assembled, the cargo cults have been placed in the larger context of those movements, the first arising as early as the 1890s, through which the indigenous population attempted to respond to the coming of the Europeans. These movements fall in a spectrum, from dominantly Christian to dominantly traditional in belief.

Among the first of these new movements was the movement surrounding the Tokarau Prophet in 1893. Around the beginning of World War I, three new prophets appeared at Saibai on the southwest coast of Papua. However, during and in the years after World War II, more than 100 such groups have appeared, the large number due in part to the many different culture groups inhabiting the various islands. Each group has a rather limited following.

Other groups also operate in the islands. There is a small Buddhist community, primarily made up of Chinese expatriates. The Baha'i Faith has had a steady growth since the 1960s.

J. Gordon Melton

See also: Baha'i Faith; Baptist Bible Fellowship International; Church of England; Church of the Nazarene; Evangelical Lutheran Church in America; Evangelical Lutheran Church of Papua New Guinea; London Missionary Society; Roman Catholic Church; Salvation Army; United Church in Papua New Guinea; United Church of the Solomon Islands; Uniting Church in Australia; World Council of Churches.

References

Note: There are numerous anthropological studies of the indigenous people of Papua New Guinea, most of which concentrate observation on one of the many peoples who inhabit what is a very diverse land.

Alerts, Theo. *Traditional Religion in Melanesia: Introduction*. Port Moresby: University of Papua New Guinea Press, 1996.

Barth, Fredrik. *Cosmologies in the Making: A Generative Approach to Cultural Variation in Inner New Guinea*. Cambridge: Cambridge University Press, 1990.

Forman, Charles H. *The Island Churches of the South Pacific: Emergence in the Twentieth Century.* Maryknoll, NY: Orbis, 1982.

Jebens, Holger. *Pathways to Heaven: Contesting Mainline and Fundamentalist Christianity in Papua New Guinea*. New York: Berghahn Books, 2006.

Kros, Peter. *A Certain Foreign Cult Called Christianity: Do We Need It?* Boroko, Papua New Guinea: Institute of Papua New Guinea Studies, 1975.

Robbins, Joel. *Becoming Sinners: Christianity and Moral Torment in a Papua New Guinea Society*. Berkeley: University of California Press, 2004.

Turner, Ann. *Historical Dictionary of Papua New Guinea*. Methuen, NJ: Scarecrow Press, 2001.

Williams, R. G. *The United Church in Papua New Guinea and the Solomon Islands: The Development of an Indigenous Church*. Rabaul, Papua New Guinea: Trinity Press, 1972.

■ Paraguay

Paraguay is a landlocked South American country, about the size of California, and surrounded by Argentina, Bolivia, and Brazil. Its 406,752 square miles of territory is home to an estimated 6,163,913 people (2008), almost all of mixed Spanish and Amerindian heritage. East of the Paraguay River there are grassy plains, wooded hills, and tropical forests; west of the Paraguay River (the Chaco region) the terrain is low, flat, and marshy plain. The nation is divided administratively into 18 provinces, with the city of Asunción in the Central Province as its capital. The Greater Asunción Metro Area had a population of 1,659,500 in 2002.

Today, Paraguay is a nation of *mestizos* (about 95 percent), a result of the interbreeding of Amerindians with Spanish colonists and later immigrants from Argentina, Brazil, and Europe, mainly Swiss-Italians and Germans. Spanish and Guaraní are the national languages, with the latter being dominant: about 75 percent of Paraguayans speak Spanish (the language of business and government) and 90 percent speak Guaraní. Spanish is dominant in the capital city of Asunción and surrounding areas, while Guaraní is dominant in the interior. Also, German is still spoken among many Lutherans and Mennonites.

Paraguay is a developing country that ranked as the second poorest country in South America in 2007. Paraguay has a market economy marked by a large informal sector that features both re-export of imported consumer goods to neighboring countries, and thousands of small business enterprises. Paraguay's largest economic activity is based on agriculture, agribusiness, and cattle ranching.

Historically, Paraguay's economic potential has been constrained by its geography, but it does have access to the Atlantic Ocean via the Paraná River. Because it is landlocked, Paraguay's economy is very dependent on Brazil and Argentina, its major trade partners. Roughly 38 percent of Paraguay's GDP is derived from trade and exports to Brazil and Argentina. Paraguay, through various treaties, has been granted free ports in Argentina, Uruguay, and Brazil through which its products are exported and imports are channeled.

Paraguay has a serious problem with poverty and inequality. According to government sources, approximately 2.1 million people (about 35 percent of its total population) are considered to be poor. In rural areas, 41 percent of the people lack an adequate monthly income to cover their basic necessities, whereas in urban areas the poverty level is estimated at 27.6 percent. The top 10 percent of the population earns 43.8 percent of the national income, while the lowest ten percent earns less than 1 percent. The current economic recession has worsened income inequality, notably in the rural areas.

Similarly, land concentration in the countryside is one of the highest worldwide: 10 percent of the population controls 66 percent of the land, while 30 percent of the rural people are landless peasants. This inequality has caused a great deal of social and political tension between the landless and the socio-economic elite who control the nation's business, industry, and government.

Religious affiliation in Paraguay today (2002 census) is dominated by the Roman Catholic Church (89.6 percent), with only a small representation of other religious groups: Protestants (6.2 percent), other religions (2.1 percent), none or undesignated (2.1 percent). However, by 2006, a new survey indicated that 84.7

Catholic cemetery with mausoleums in Asunción, Paraguay. (Imagebroker/StockphotoPro)

percent of respondents considered themselves Catholic, a decrease of 5 percentage points from 2002.

The Constitution provides for freedom of religion, and other laws and policies contributed to the generally free practice of religion. The law at all levels protects this right in full against abuse, by either governmental or private actors. The government generally respects religious freedom in practice; however, it occasionally has failed to enforce religious freedom laws when abuses have occurred.

From the 1870s to the present, Paraguay has experienced considerable social progress, mainly due to the arrival of waves of immigrants from neighboring Argentina, the Middle East, North America, and Europe. Some 40,000 new residents from Spain were mainly responsible for developing the livestock, agriculture, and forestry industries. The immigrants included about 5,000 Mennonites from Europe and North America who created agricultural colonies, schools, and small businesses.

Some of these early immigrants were members of Protestant congregations before their arrival in Paraguay: German Lutherans, German and French Calvinists, as well as German-Russian Mennonites during the early 20th century. During the 1930s and after World War II, Japanese Shinto and Buddhist immigrants arrived and settled in agricultural colonies near Asunción and Encarnación; by the 1980s, there were about 8,000 Japanese immigrants in these agricultural colonies. In the early 1970s, thousands of Brazilians began migrating to Paraguay, mainly because of the availability of cheap land; and, by the early 1990s, an estimated 300,000 to 350,000 Brazilians lived in the eastern border region.

Also during the 1970s, an estimated 30,000 to 50,000 immigrants (mainly Buddhists) from Korea, Hong Kong, and Taiwan began arriving in Paraguay. Many of these immigrant groups brought their own religious traditions with them, thereby enriching the religious diversity of Paraguay.

Before the arrival of Europeans, three Aboriginal peoples dominated the Paraguay River valley, which divides the territory into two regions. Upriver, the Guaraní were a settled agricultural people. Downriver, in what is termed the Chaco region, the more nomadic Guaycurús and Payaguás were hunters, gatherers, and fishers. Three other Amerindian groups, united by language, were differentiated into more than 100 subgroups.

The Spanish entered the region by following the tributaries of the large Rió de la Plata, looking for mineral resources. Spanish conquistador Juan de Salazar (1508–1560) and his company of soldiers and colonists founded Fort Asunción in 1537 as part of a campaign to colonize and subdue an estimated 200,000 Amerindians, principally the Tupi-Guaraní. That fort would grow into the present-day capital of Paraguay, Asunción.

The purpose of the pacification of the Amerindians was to provide the Spanish colonists with a source of cheap labor for agricultural and commercial development. Within 20 years of its founding, Asunción boasted a Spanish population of 1,500, a Roman Catholic cathedral, a textile mill, and the beginning of the livestock industry. For more than two centuries, Asunción was a principal center of Spanish power in the Río de la Plata basin, and from Asunción the conquistadors launched expeditions to dominate and colonize the surrounding territories.

The early Spanish colonists failed to recognize the relative agricultural value of the region, and as a result the Amerindians suffered somewhat less than in other countries under Spanish control, at least in the beginning. However, in the late 18th century, many Amerindians were forced to become laborers on the developing cattle ranches and plantations. In 1811, the Spanish governor in Asunción was forced out when the region's planters demanded a free trade policy for their tea and tobacco. Officials of the new republican government established a relatively isolated position in an attempt to escape the chaos they saw in the surrounding Southern Cone countries.

In 1811, Paraguay declared its independence from Spain and from the newly independent government in Buenos Aires. However, the country's first president, Dr. José Gaspar Rodríguez de Francia (1766–1840), established a cruel dictatorship that lasted from 1811 to 1840. Many Spaniards who were the owners of the best lands and businesses were jailed, murdered, or exiled, along with others who criticized his rule. Nevertheless, during this period, the nation prospered due to the hard work of its people and improved methods of agricultural and livestock production.

When Rodríguez de Francia died in 1840, the nation experienced six months of disorder until Carlos Antonio López (1792–1862) came to power and ruled despotically from 1841 to 1862. Carlos Antonio López died in 1862 and was followed in power by his 35-year-old son, Francisco Solano López (1826–1870), who ruled until 1870. The second López was responsible for plunging his weak nation into a savage and bloody war with the combined military forces of Argentina, Uruguay, and Brazil. In the disastrous War of the Triple Alliance (1865–1870), about two-thirds of Paraguay's adult males were killed and much of its territory (99 square miles) was lost to the victors. The country was politically and economically crippled for the next half century.

The country's isolationist policy worked for about two generations (1811–1865) but Paraguay had been involved for years in boundary and tariff disputes with its more powerful neighbors, Argentina and Brazil. The people of Uruguay also had struggled to achieve and maintain their independence from those same powers, especially from Argentina. In 1864, the government of Brazil helped the leader of Uruguay's Colorado Party oust his major opponent, whereupon the military dictator of Paraguay, Francisco Solano López, declared war on Brazil, believing that the regional balance of power was threatened. Paraguay's army numbered about 50,000 men, which was the strongest military force in Latin America at that time. López's action was viewed by many as aggression for self- and national aggrandizement but, as the war wore on, many viewed this as a war of conquest by Argentina. At that time, Paraguay's population was only about 450,000.

In response to López's declaration of war, the governments of Brazil, Argentina, and Uruguay created a political and military alliance, backed by England, against Paraguay that led to the bloodiest conflict in Latin American history to date. The five-year War of the Triple Alliance (1865–1870) led to the deaths of 60 to 80 percent of the Guaraní people, and Paraguay lost almost half of its national territory. All the males who survived were sold into slavery. Those Amerindian groups in the more remote areas suffered fewer ill effects from the war, but to this day women greatly outnumber men in the entire country. As a result, family instability has contributed to the country's lack of stability overall.

The Colorado Party (officially, the National Republican Association [ARN]), nationalistic and ultraconservative, was founded in 1887 by General Bernardino Caballero Melgarejo (1839–1912), a descendant of Spanish nobility who fought in the War of the Triple Alliance and served as president of Paraguay from 1881 to 1886. He was the virtual ruler of the country from 1887 until 1904. After Caballero rigged the 1886 election to ensure the victory of his chosen candidate—Patricio Escobar—some of the general's political opponents founded the Paraguayan Liberal Party (PLP). In response to this challenge, Caballero and his supporters proceeded to found the Colorado Party as a counter measure. Out of office, General Caballero maintained a large degree of political control as commander of the army. Since then, the Colorados and the Liberals have been competing for dominance of the country.

The PLP dominated the government from 1904 until 1936 (and again briefly during 1939 and 1940). In 1936, the PLP lost power largely due to the disastrous results of the Chaco War (1932–1935), which was fought to control the Chaco region's national resources; Paraguay defeated Bolivia at great cost. There were an estimated 100,000 casualties, of which more died from diseases (such as malaria and other infections) than from the actual fighting; about 57,000 of the total casualties were Bolivian. At the same time, the war brought both countries to the brink of economic disaster.

Since then, the Liberal Party has never recovered dominance, and the Colorado Party held power by means of military dictatorships until 1989, most notably the regime of General Alfredo Stroessner Mattiauda (1912–2006). By the end of the Stroessner regime (1954–1989), the Liberal Party no longer existed but its political successor, the Authentic Radical Liberal Party (PLRA), currently is the second largest political party in the country.

From 1947 until 1962, the Colorado Party ruled Paraguay as a one-party state; all other political parties were declared illegal. Finally, after 61 years in power, it was defeated in national elections held in April 2008. The Colorado Party lost the presidential elections to an opposition candidate from the center-left, Fernando Lugo Méndez (a former Roman Catholic bishop). This was a first on two accounts: the free election of an opposition candidate and of a Catholic bishop to the office of president of Paraguay.

The decades of poverty and instability led the way to the emergence in 1954 of General Alfredo Stroessner Matiauda (1912–2006), a Paraguayan military officer who created a corrupt and brutal regime (1954–1989), the second longest dictatorship of the 20th century, surpassed only by that of Fidel Castro, who ruled Cuba from 1959 to 2008. Between 1960 and 1980, an estimated one million Paraguayans migrated to Argentina to find work and to improve their lives. Stroessner himself was overthrown in a coup led by General Andrés Rodríguez Pedotti (1923–1997) in 1989, which resulted in an opening for democracy.

Some observers maintain that opposition from the Catholic bishops is the only reason that General Stroessner did not have absolute control over the country. After the destruction of Asunción University in 1972 by the police, Archbishop of Asunción Ismael Rolón Silvero excommunicated the minister of the interior and the chief of police, and prohibited the celebration of the Mass as a sign of protest against the brutal Stroessner regime. When Pope John Paul II visited Paraguay in 1988, his presence and message bolstered what was already a robust anti-Stroessner movement within the country.

The most serious charges against the Stroessner dictatorship concern Operation Condor, an official, organized, and secret campaign of political repression against alleged leftist dissidents conducted during 1975 and 1976 jointly by the governments of Argentina, Bolivia, Brazil, Chile, Paraguay, and Uruguay, with the collaboration of the American Central Intelligence Agency (CIA). In 1992, archives of the operation were uncovered that contained information about the secret incarceration of an estimated 400,000 alleged subversives, of which about 50,000 were murdered and more than 30,000 were "disappeared" (called *los desaparecidos*), meaning that their whereabouts are unknown and they are presumed dead. These murders, assassinations, and disappearances carried out by national security agencies of the respective countries were categorized as "extra-judicial executions" by international human rights organizations.

General Rodríguez, once closely linked to Stroessner, launched a coup against the dictator in 1989. During his term as president (r. 1989–1993), Rodríguez abolished the death penalty, ended martial law, and tried, convicted, and imprisoned some of the leading members of the Stroessner regime. Also during his presidency, in 1992, the Paraguayan legislature approved a new Constitution that prohibited re-elections for executive positions, which required Rodríguez to relinquish power and hand over the presidency to civilian rule. Wasmosy, who was endorsed by Rodríguez as his successor in the 1993 elections, won with approximately 40 percent of the vote in what is generally acknowledged to be the first honest election in the country's republican history. However, Wasmosy became very unpopular when he failed to continue the limited reforms implemented by Rodríguez. In 2002, after leaving office, Wasmosy was convicted for fraud and embezzlement ($40 million) and was sentenced to four years in prison; however, he appealed his sentence, paid a bond of $830,000, and was placed on parole.

In 1998, Raúl Cubas Grau (b. 1943) won the election; and his main campaign pledge was to free Oviedo. In 1999, Cubas's vice president, Luis María Argaña, who had been named as Cubas's running mate but who opposed him on some key political issues, was brutally murdered. Cubas was immediately implicated in the plot, and his resignation demanded. Cubas's political support virtually evaporated and Congress voted overwhelmingly to impeach him. Faced with certain conviction and removal from office, Cubas resigned immediately and fled to Brazil. Cubas was replaced by the president of the Senate, Luis Ángel Gonzalez Macchi, who completed Cubas's term in office (1999–2003). Cubas returned to Paraguay in 2002 and was immediately arrested and tried for corruption and conspiracy to murder Argaña, but he was later cleared of all charges.

The nation's current president is Fernando Armindo Lugo Méndez, formerly the Roman Catholic bishop of the Diocese of San Pedro, which has the nation's highest poverty rate. Lugo resigned as bishop in 2005 after he had requested laicization (removal of the right to exercise the functions of the priestly office) in order to run for public office. However, the Holy See refused the request on the grounds that bishops could not undergo laicization, and also denied him the requested canonical permission to run for civil elected office. Subsequently, he resigned from the priesthood after announcing his candidacy for the nation's presidency.

Lugo entered the national political arena by backing the peasants' claims for improving land distribution. In October 2007, Lugo registered as a member of the Christian Democratic Party (PDC) in order to become qualified to run for office. In April 2008, he won the presidential election by a margin of 10 percentage points, although far short of a majority. Lugo's swearing-in ceremony marked the first time since Paraguayan independence in 1811 that a ruling party had peacefully surrendered power to an elected member of the opposition.

Roman Catholic Church Iberian Roman Catholicism entered Paraguay with the Spanish conquistadors, and a papal decree created the Bishopric of Our Lady of Asunción in 1547, 11 years after the foundation of Asunción by Juan de Ayolas in 1536. The first bishop was Father Pedro de La Torre (d. 1573), a Franciscan, who arrived at Asunción in 1555 during the second administration of Martinez de Irala. The diocese was directly dependent upon the Holy See in Rome, and its jurisdiction extended over the whole Río de la Plata territory, which was divided into 102 parishes, 6 of which were located in the capital. The present Cathedral of Asunción was formally dedicated on October 27, 1845.

Paraguay

Most important for the development of the Catholic Church, after 1588 Jesuit and Franciscan priests began evangelizing among the Guaraní and other Amerindian groups along various rivers, including areas now part of surrounding nations, with the intent of pacifying and converting them. They developed a system of communal towns that closely paralleled the agricultural society that had previously developed among the Guaraní. They also developed a written form of the Guaraní language.

The Jesuits soon realized they had to protect the Amerindians from enslavement by Spanish and Portuguese colonists if they were going to convert them to the Catholic faith. From 1609 to 1767, the Jesuits established and maintained missions among the Guaraní and other tribes in the upper Rio de la Plata region, where the Natives were settled in a system of communal towns, called Reductions (*reducciones*), under Jesuit administration.

The Treaty of Madrid in 1750 transferred the territory occupied by the Jesuit-Guaraní missions from the jurisdiction of Spain to Portugal. Although Spain, at least officially, no longer permitted slavery, this inhumane practice was legal in the Portuguese territories. Shortly thereafter, the Spanish rulers ordered the Jesuit missions to be disbanded, and Pope Clement XIV (r. 1769–1774) suppressed the Jesuits, forcing the missionaries to abandon their work in approximately 100 Reductions in the Americas, including those in Paraguay. However, in 1754, the Guaraní Indians and a few dissident Jesuits refused to abide by the order to disband the missions and created a short-lived rebellion that was cruelly put down by the Spanish authorities.

The work of the Jesuits came into conflict with the growing desire of wealthy Spanish landowners to control Paraguay and this contributed to the expulsion of the Jesuits in 1767 by Spain's King Charles III (r. 1759–1788). Many of the Paraguayan Indians were captured and sold into slavery, where they were gradually absorbed into mestizo society; however, those who escaped usually returned to their indigenous way of life in remote areas. After 1767, the spiritual administration of the Jesuit Reductions was transferred to the Franciscans and other religious orders, while the public administration was given to Spanish and Portuguese civil officials.

The church suffered greatly through the 19th century. It lost half its members in the War of the Triple Alliance (1865–1870) and never had enough priests. Catholicism still dominates throughout the land, but the church remains relatively poor, and the folk Catholicism that has arisen in various parts of South America, mixing Catholic faith with traditional animistic religions, is widespread in Paraguay.

For much of the 19th century, church-state relations ranged from indifferent to hostile. The state assumed the prerogatives of royal patronage that the Vatican had granted to the Spanish rulers and sought to control both the bishops and the clergy. President José Gaspar Rodríguez de Francia (r. 1814–1840) was committed to a secular state; he was frugal and cruel beyond description; he hated all foreigners and was fearful of all foreign entanglements; and he was violently anticlerical. He suppressed monastic orders, eliminated the tithe, instituted civil marriage, and cut off communication with the Vatican. President Francisco Solano López (r. 1862–1870) used the church as if it were a branch of the government; he enlisted priests as secret agents to report on signs of disaffection and subversion among the populace.

Church-state relations worsened after the government executed the bishop of Asunción, Manuel Antonio Palacio, during the War of the Triple Alliance. When the war ended, there were only 55 priests left in the whole country, and the church was without a bishop for 11 years.

The modern Paraguayan Catholic Church was established largely under the direction of Monsignor Juan Sinforiano Bogarón, the archbishop of Asunción (r. 1930–1949), and his successor, Monsignor Aníbal Mena Porta (r. 1949–1969). Both envisioned a church whose role in Paraguay's political struggles was that of a neutral mediator among the various contenders for power. Monsignor Ismael Blas Roldán Silvero followed Porta as archbishop (r. 1970–1989) and was followed by Monsignor Felipe Santiago Benitez Avalos (r. 1989–2002). Contemporary archbishops have stressed the importance of respecting human rights, strengthening democracy, and encouraging political dialogue among all social sectors.

Beginning in the late 1950s, the bishops and priests were frequently at odds with the national government. Confrontations began with individual priests who preached sermons calling for political freedom and social justice. The political and human rights activities of the clergy and various lay groups, such as Catholic Action, pushed the church hierarchy to make increasingly critical statements about the regime of President Stroessner (beginning 1954), who was finally overthrown by a military coup in 1989.

Bible scholar José Luis Caravias has worked with the Christian Agrarian Leagues since the 1960s; he was the principal editor of *Vivir como Hermanos* (*Live as Brothers*), published in 1971, which is one of the most important documents produced in Paraguay by proponents of Liberation Theology, a socially and politically progressive Latin American Catholic movement.

Diverse tensions arose within the Paraguayan Catholic Church during the 1960s and following years, which resulted from challenges posed by the Second Vatican Council (1962–1965), the Conference of Latin American Bishops held in Medellín (Colombia) in 1968, Latin American Liberation Theology, and the Catholic Charismatic Renewal movement. These powerful new currents polarized Catholic bishops, priests (diocesan and religious), lay brothers and sisters (members of religious orders), and the laity in general into various factions. *Traditionalists* wanted the church to remain as it was prior to the reforms approved by the Second Vatican Council (mid-1960s), with an emphasis on apostolic authority, orthodox theology, the sacraments, and personal piety. *Reformers* generally supported the church's post–Second Vatican Council stance of modernization and toleration of diversity based on its official social doctrine. *Progressives*, inspired by reforms approved at the Second Vatican and Medellín conferences, sought to implement the new vision for "a preferential option for the poor" through social and political action aimed at transforming Paraguayan society and establishing social justice through peaceful democratic means. *Radicals* adopted the Marxist-inspired Liberation Theology and advocated violent revolution by the people as a means of overthrowing the right-wing military dictatorships and creating a Socialist state that would serve the poor marginalized masses. *Charismatic agents* sought to transform the spiritual and communal life of Catholics by means of the power and gifts of the Holy Spirit (including the "baptism of the Holy Spirit and speaking in tongues"), rather than by political and social activism.

Throughout the 1970s and 1980s, church authorities criticized the lack of political freedom in Paraguay and the government's dismal human rights record, and there were sporadic student demonstrations against the government and its repressive countermeasures. The government expelled foreign-born clergy and periodically closed the Catholic University of Our Lady of Asunción, the Catholic news magazine, and the Catholic radio station. In response, the archbishop of Asunción excommunicated several prominent government officials and refused, along with other clergy, to participate in major civic and religious celebrations.

In the early 1990s, the Catholic Bishops Conference of Paraguay, in a pronouncement entitled "One Constitution for our Nation" signed by 14 bishops, stated: "If at other times this nation completely identified itself with the Catholic religion, it was logical to talk about an official religion. Now pluralism better characterizes the civil society and it does not seem justified to have one Church joined to the State that, for this reason, reflects something imposed by force upon the people. The [Catholic] Church does not want to confuse the people or to confuse itself with the State."

In this way, the Catholic Church of Paraguay gave its unconditional support to establish a new era of religious liberty in the nation, which began with congressional approval of a new Constitution in February 1993.

Roman Catholicism still dominates the nation. About 5.3 million Paraguayans were Catholics in 2002 (or about 89.6 percent of the national population). The traditional animistic religions of the Paraguayan Amerindians have survived, although mixed with an overlay of Roman Catholicism during colonial times. This has created a Paraguayan "popular Catholicism" (syncretistic) among Amerindians and the Hispanic population. For many Paraguayans, affiliation with the Roman Catholic Church is more of a social obligation than a moral and spiritual commitment, with less than 20 percent of Catholics regularly attending Mass.

However, one of the main events in the Catholic calendar is the annual pilgrimage to the colonial city Caacupé (founded in 1770), the capital of the Province of Cordillera, in the southwestern region. There a major religious festival is held on December 8 in honor of the statuette of Our Lady of the Miracles. This statuette, carved in the 16th century by a devout convert, is believed to have curative powers (syncretism). An enormous basilica stands in the center of town, where an estimated 300,000 people gather annually for the festival.

In 2001, the Archdiocese of Asunción had only 774,000 Catholic adherents out of the city's total population of 1,602,173, or about 48 percent. However, the lowest percentage of Catholic adherents was registered in the Apostolic Vicariate of Polcomayo, with only 45.7 percent of the total population of 75,000 inhabitants. In the rest of the nation's dioceses, the Catholic population ranged in the 80 and 90 percentiles in 2001. Religious nominalism seems to be the dominant characteristic of Paraguayan Catholicism today.

In 2004, the Paraguayan Catholic Church reported one archdiocese (Asunción, established in 1929) and 13 dioceses with 358 parishes that were served by 355 secular priests and 428 religious priests (total of 783), assisted by 120 permanent deacons, 745 male religious and 2,132 female religious workers. The archbishop is Eustaquio Pastor Cuquejo Verga, C.Ss.R. (Congregation of the Most Holy Redeemer), appointed in 2002.

The Protestant Movement The first Protestant work began in Paraguay in the mid-19th century with the arrival of agents of the American Bible Society (1856), followed by missionaries of the Methodist Episcopal Church (1886), the Church of England (1886), and the German Lutherans (1893, Evangelical Church of the Plata River). It was a North American Methodist who became the first resident missionary in Paraguay in 1886. Two years later, the Church of England arrived when the South American Missionary Society (SAMS) shifted its focus from the indigenous Patagonians of southern Argentina to the Chaco region of Paraguay. Among the Society's accomplishments were the development of a written language for the Lengua people and the production of a Lengua Bible.

During the early 20th century, dozens of other Protestant groups appeared among the growing immigrant population or as the result of missionary endeavors from Europe and North America, and a variety of Pentecostal and other non-Pentecostal groups have been founded in more recent times, especially during the 1950s and 1960s.

Notable among the groups to establish work in Paraguay after 1900 were the U.S.-based Seventh-day Adventist Church (1900), which was the first to arrive, followed by the New Testament Missionary Fellowship (1902), the Inland South American Missionary Society (1902), Christian Missions in Many Lands (1909, Christian Brethren), and the Salvation Army (1910), with most of the later groups from Great Britain.

In 1917, the United Christian Missionary Society (Christian Church [Disciples of Christ]) arrived and eventually took over the Methodist work. In 1919, the Argentine Baptist Convention began work in Paraguay, and they later appealed to the Southern Baptist Convention for assistance (1945).

In 1927, the first Mennonite colony was established among Russian immigrants, which led to the involvement of the Mennonite Central Committee in 1930. The New Testament Missionary Union arrived in 1931, followed by the Mennonite Brethren Church of America in 1935 that began work among the Lengua Amerindians. The Lutheran Church–Missouri Synod sent their first missionaries in 1938 to work among German immigrants.

The arrival of the first Pentecostal missions among European immigrants in 1938 (the Filadelfia Church of Stockholm and the Swedish Free Mission) led to the introduction of Argentine Assemblies of God in 1943 and the U.S. Assemblies of God in 1945, who came to assist their Russian colleagues. Since then, Pentecostalism has grown very well in Paraguay, and a number of autochthonous Pentecostal churches have arisen in recent years.

The impact of World War II was a further catalyst for the development of religion in Paraguay. The Society of Brothers (now the Church Communities International), a German communal group modeled on the Hutterites, escaped Germany and settled in Paraguay in 1941. They were joined by Russian and Ukrainian immigrants who also found their way to Paraguay during the early 1940s. Paraguay became a magnet for Mennonites, the first being refugees from the newly established Soviet Union. After getting settled, they began missionary work among the people of the Chaco region and appealed for assistance from North American Mennonites. As a result an extensive work was developed among a group of agricultural colonies that eventually became the Evangelical Mennonite Church in Paraguay.

A few other denominations also arrived during the 1940s: Full Gospel Grace Fellowship (1940), the Free Methodist Church of North America (1948–1952), the fundamentalist New Tribes Mission (1946), General Conference Mennonite Church (1952), Evangelical Lu-

Paraguay

Religion	Followers in 1970	Followers in 2010	% of Population	Annual % growth 2000–2010	Followers in 2025	Followers in 2050
Christians	2,434,000	6,164,000	95.4	1.96	7,588,000	9,242,000
Roman Catholics	2,305,000	5,613,000	86.9	2.18	6,590,000	7,644,000
Independents	8,400	330,000	5.1	3.21	535,000	780,000
Protestants	41,600	240,000	3.7	2.87	440,000	710,000
Ethnoreligionists	32,200	125,000	1.9	2.03	150,000	180,000
Agnostics	9,800	120,000	1.9	4.00	200,000	300,000
Buddhists	2,000	16,300	0.3	1.99	30,000	50,000
Atheists	3,000	14,600	0.2	1.99	24,000	35,000
Baha'is	2,100	13,500	0.2	2.11	25,000	45,000
New religionists	200	3,900	0.1	1.99	6,000	12,000
Jews	1,200	3,200	0.0	2.00	3,500	4,000
Total population	**2,484,000**	**6,460,000**	**100.0**	**1.99**	**8,026,000**	**9,868,000**

theran Church (1949), the Mennonite Mission Network (1952), the Church of God World Missions (1954, from Cleveland, Tennessee), and the Evangelical Mennonite Conference (1957, from Canada).

Historically, only 5 Protestant missions and service agencies arrived prior to 1900; 12 more arrived between 1900 and 1939; 20 additional groups arrived between 1940 and 1979; and since 1980, at least 30 new groups have begun work in Paraguay.

Prior to the 1950s, the total Protestant population in Paraguay was less than 10,000, but by 2002 had grown to 364,839, or 6.2 percent of the total population (2002 census). The largest Protestant denominations in Paraguay were the Evangelical Baptist Convention (10,500 adherents; Southern Baptist-related); the Assemblies of God (U.S.-related) and the Assemblies of God Evangelical Mission (independent) with a combined total of 9,879 adherents; the Evangelical Church of the Plata River (Lutheran, with 8,850 adherents); all Mennonites (8,850 adherents); the Seventh-day Adventist Church (7,800 adherents); Anglicans (members of the Anglican Church of the Southern Cone of America, about 1,900 adherents); and the Church of God (Cleveland, Tennessee) (1,550 adherents). Also, there are 24 Mennonite denominations and service organizations that represent an estimated community of 70,000 (all ages), most of whom are found among the 17 agricultural colonies that are scattered across the northern and eastern regions of Paraguay.

There are no churches based in Paraguay that are members of the World Council of Churches. Conservative evangelical churches cooperate with the Asociación de Pastores del Paraguay, which in turn is affiliated with the World Evangelical Alliance.

Additional Groups An estimated 2.1 percent of the population represented adherents of other religious groups in 2002. One of these was the Ukrainian Orthodox Church with about 500 adherents and another 975 Orthodox believers (unspecified) were reported in 2002 (census). Also present are the following non-Protestant marginal Christian groups: the Church of Jesus Christ of Latter-day Saints (Mormons, 9,374 adherents in 2002), Jehovah's Witnesses (11,805 adherents in 2002), the independent quasi-Pentecostal People of God Church (with about 12,000 adherents in 2002, although church officials claim 150,000 adherents), the God Is Love Pentecostal Church (1,300 adherents), the Universal Church of the Kingdom of God (700 adherents), and the Voice of the Chief Cornerstone, among others.

Non-Christian Religions A variety of non-Christian religions have appeared, many since 1940, especially among immigrants from the Middle East (Judaism, Islam, and Baha'i) and Asia (Hindu, Buddhist, and Shinto sects). Animistic Amerindian religions continue to exist, especially in the western region of the

Chaco, with an estimated 25,000 adherents in 2002 (census).

By 1912 enough Jews had migrated to Paraguay, primarily from Germany, to justify the organization of the initial Jewish community. Today, there are an estimated 1,100 Jews in Paraguay, whose primary structure is the Consejo Representativo Israelita del Paraguay, headquartered in Asunción. The capital city has three Orthodox Jewish synagogues: one Ashkenazi, one Sephardi, and one Chabad (Lubavitcher).

There is a small Muslim community in Paraguay (872 adherents in 2002), mainly in the provinces of Asunción and Alto Paraná, as a result of Middle Eastern immigration from Syria, Lebanon, and Palestine. The Subud Association is also present. The Baha'i Faith established its first local spiritual assembly in Asunción in 1944. It has spread among the Yanaigua, Chulupi, and Maka indigenous peoples.

Immigrants from Korea and Japan introduced Buddhism (about 2,000 adherents in 2002) and Japanese religions, including Seicho-No-Ie, Shinto, Soka Gakkai International, Reiyukai America, Nichiren Shoshu, Tenrikyo, and the Foguangshan Buddhist Order.

Hinduism is represented by the International Society for Krishna Consciousness (ISKCON), the Transcendental Meditation (TM) movement (now organized as the Global Country of World Peace), and the Sathya Sai Baba movement.

Also present in Paraguay are religious movements representing the Western Esoteric tradition: Rosicrucians, the Grand Universal Fraternity (GFU; from Venezuela), the Center of Gnostic Studies of Anthropology and Sciences, New Acropolis Cultural Centers, and the Cafh Foundation; the Afro-Brazilian religions of Condomblé and Umbanda; and the Psychic-Spiritualist-New Age traditions: the Basilio Scientific School, Kardec Spiritualist Centers (Spiritism), the Paraguayan Center of Spiritualist Philosophy, and the Unification Church of Reverend Sun Myung Moon, among others. In 2000, officials of the Unification Church purchased 300,000 hectares of land in Paraguay for logging and timber exportation to Asia. The acquired land is the ancestral territory of the indigenous Chamacoco (Ishir) people, who live in the northern region of the country.

The population with no religion or no declared religious affiliation (includes atheists and agnostics) was 2.1 percent in 2002 (about 81,500 persons).

Clifton L. Holland

See also: Agnosticism; Anglican Province of the Southern Cone of America; Assemblies of God; Atheism; Baha'i Faith; Christian Brethren; Christian Church (Disciples of Christ); Church Communities International; Church of England; Church of Jesus Christ of Latter-day Saints; Church of God (Cleveland, Tennessee); Evangelical Church of the River Platte; Franciscans; Free Methodist Church of North America; Global Country of World Peace; Hutterites; International Society for Krishna Consciousness; Jehovah's Witnesses; Jesuits; Lubavitch Hassidism; Lutheran Church–Missouri Synod; Lutheranism; Mary, Blessed Virgin; Mennonite Church, USA; Mennonites; New Acropolis; Nichiren Shoshu; Paraguay, Mennonites in; Orthodox Judaism; People of God; Reiyukai; Roman Catholic Church; Salvation Army; Sathya Sai Baba Movement; Seicho-No-Ie; Seventh-day Adventist Church; Shinto; Soka Gakkai International; Southern Baptist Convention; Spiritism; Subud; Tenrikyo; Ukraine Eastern Orthodoxy in; Umbanda; Unification Movement; Universal Church of the Kingdom of God; World Council of Churches; World Evangelical Alliance.

References

Browning, W. E. *The River Plate Republics: A Survey of the Religious, Economic and Social Conditions in Argentina, Paraguay and Uruguay*. London: World Dominion Press, 1928.

Catholic Hierarchy website. http://www.catholic-hierarchy.org/country/scpy1.html.

Herring, Hubert. *A History of Latin America from the Beginnings to the Present*. 3rd ed. New York: Alfred A. Knopf, 1968.

Huonder, Anthony. "Reductions of Paraguay." In *The Catholic Encyclopedia*. Vol. 12. New York: Robert Appleton Company, 1911. http://www.newadvent.org/cathen/12688b.htm.

Introvigne, Massimo. "Controversial Pentecostalism: Paraguay's People of God." Center for Studies on

New Religions (CESNUR). http://www.cesnur.org/2004/mi_pueblo.htm.

Jaenike, William H. *Black Robes in Paraguay: The Success of the Guarani Missions Hastened the Abolition of the Jesuits*. Minneapolis, MN: Kirk House Publishers, 2008.

Jetter de Walker, Luisa. *Siembra y Cosecha: Reseña histórico de las Asambleas de Dios en Argentina, Bolivia, Chile, Paraguay, Perú y Uruguay.* Vol. 2. Deerfield, FL: Editorial Vida, 1992.

Moreno-Lacalle, Julian. "Paraguay." In *The Catholic Encyclopedia.* Vol. 11. New York: Robert Appleton Company, 1911. http://www.newadvent.org/cathen/11470b.htm.

Plett, R. *El protestantismo en el Paraguay: su aporte cultural económico y espiritual*. Asunción, Paraguay: Instituto Bíblico Asunción, 1987.

PROLADES-RITA (Religion-In-The-Americas) database on "Religion in Paraguay." http://www.prolades.com/cra/regions/sam/par/par-rd.htm.

PROLADES-RITA (Religion-In-The-Americas) website. "A Chronology of Protestant Beginnings in Paraguay." http://www.prolades.com/cra/regions/sam/par/par-chron.pdf.

Stoesz, Edgar. *Like a Mustard Seed: Mennonites in Paraguay*. Scottdale, PA: Herald Press, 2008.

U.S. Department of Commerce. *International Religious Freedom Report 2008.* http://www.state.gov/g/drl/rls/irf/2008/108535.htm.

U.S. Department of State, Bureau of Western Hemisphere Affairs. *Background Note: Paraguay* (August 2009). http://www.state.gov/r/pa/ei/bgn/1841.htm.

Paraguay, Mennonites in

The Mennonite community of Paraguay is both one of the largest Mennonite communities outside of North America in the world and one of the largest non-Catholic communities in Paraguay. The movement of Mennonites to Paraguay began in 1926, when the first group arrived from Manitoba, Canada. However, what was to become the numerically stronger group, Russian Mennonites who had fled to Germany in 1929, arrived in Paraguay in 1930. They were able to settle in the country after the provisions of a special law passed for the Canadian group were applied to them as well. They established an initial settlement in western Paraguay called Colony Fernheim. In 1937 a second colony, named Friesland, was established in eastern Paraguay. An additional group of Russian Mennonites arrived after World War II.

The Russian settlers brought with them some of the divisions that had splintered the Mennonite community in their previous homeland. Some were affiliated with the Mennonite Brethren, a group that dated from a Pietist revival that had swept through the community in the 1860s. Other groups had been influenced by the attempts of Baptists from Germany to convert the Mennonites, leading to a difference of opinion on baptism. Although few became Baptists, some Mennonites accepted the idea that baptism should be by immersion, as Baptists taught, while most Mennonites continued to baptize by pouring. Once in Paraguay, language differences would also appear as some continued to use German, others adopted Spanish, and still others chose to use one of the Native languages (primarily Guaraní, which is spoken by more Paraguayans than Spanish, or Lengua).

All of the colonies established by both the Canadian and Russian groups were agricultural settlements, which prospered with little modern farming equipment. The colonies also attempted to rebuild the movement's social, cultural, and religious life (which operated as a German-speaking enclave in Russia), and Sunday schools, Bible study programs, and efforts to evangelize the Native peoples were launched. Although the very conservative Canadian groups have remained somewhat aloof, those groups originating in Russia have continued to work together while maintaining separate ecclesiastical organizations.

Of the several groups, the Mennonite Brethren (Vereinigung der Mennonitengemeinden von Paragua, or Hermanos Menonitas) is possibly the largest, with some 8,000 people affiliated. Some 4,600 are associated with the Convención de las Iglesias Evangélicas Unitas, which has adopted Lengua as its primary language. Some 3,000 people worship with the Convención Evangélica de Iglesias Paraguayas Hermanos

Menonitas, who use Spanish and Guaraní. The remainder of the approximately 28,000 Mennonites (2008) in Paraguay is divided among more than a dozen smaller groups.

Mennonite Brethren
c/o Gerhard Ratzlaff
Casilla de Correo 1154
Asunción
Paraguay

Convención de las Iglesias Evangélicas Unitas
c/o Oficina ASCIM
Filadelfia, c.d.c. 984
Asunción
Paraguay

Convención Evangélica de Iglesias Paraguayas Hermanos Menonitas
Juan Diaz de Solis 2150
C.C. 1154
Asunción
Paraguay

J. Gordon Melton

See also: Mennonites.

References

Dyck, Cornelius J. *An Introduction to Mennonite History: A Popular History of the Anabaptists and the Mennonite*s. Scottdale, PA: Herald Press, 1967.

Fretz, J. W. *Pilgrims in Paraguay*. Scottdale, PA: Herald Press, 1953.

Klassen, Peter P. *Die Mennoniten in Paraguay: Reich Gottes und Reich dieser Welt*. Bolanden Weierhof, Germany: Mennonitischer Geschichtsverein, 1988.

Parham, Charles Fox

1873–1929

Charles Fox Parham, a Methodist local preacher and founder of a Bible school, is the founder of modern Pentecostalism. With his students, he developed the unique Pentecostal notion that speaking in tongues was the visible sign of the baptism of the Holy Spirit, which he tied to a belief that the gifts of the Holy Spirit were meant to operate in the contemporary Christian church.

Parham was born in Muscatine, Iowa, on June 4, 1873. He grew up as a Methodist in Kansas and became a Sunday school teacher. As a young man he was licensed to preach by the Methodist Episcopal Church (now an integral part of the United Methodist Church). After preaching for several years, he left the Methodists in 1894, and began life as an independent nondenominational Holiness evangelist. In 1896, with his wife Sarah Thistlewaite, he opened Bethel, a healing home, in Topeka, Kansas. He eventually lost control of his home, and in 1900 moved across town and opened a new Bethel, where students could reside and learn from his evangelistic experience.

In December 1900, on the eve of an evangelistic trip, he gave the Bethel students a new assignment. They were to study the New Testament for any references to the baptism of the Holy Spirit and anything associated with it. Methodist Holiness people generally associated the baptism of the Holy Spirit with the experience of sanctification, an act of grace that God worked on believers that made them perfect in love.

Upon Parham's return just as the year was ending, the students reviewed their findings. They had concluded that speaking in tongues seemed to be the sign of baptism with the Holy Spirit. Thus on New Year's Eve, the group gathered in Bethel's chapel and began to pray for the baptism. In the morning hours of January 1, 1900, one of the students, Agnes Oznam (1870–1937), became the first person in modern times to pray intentionally for the baptism and the accompanying speaking in tongues and to receive a positive answer to her prayer. The resultant uniting of the baptism of the Spirit with the accompanying phenomenon of speaking in tongues would become the distinguishing feature of a new movement among the Holiness people—Pentecostalism. As he remained an advocate of the Holiness movement, Parham presented the baptism of the Holy Spirit as a new work of grace available to those believers who had already experienced sanctification, the normative Holiness experience.

Parham initially presented this new teaching to Holiness revival meetings in Kansas and nearby states. Having raised the controversial issue, within a few years he relocated to Houston, Texas, where he opened another Bible school. While in Houston, he was, in 1905, approached by an African American preacher William J. Seymour (1870–1922), formerly with the Church of God (Anderson, Indiana), who asked permission to sit in on the classes. In the segregated south of the period, such would not be allowed, but Parham did give Seymour permission to sit just outside the classroom door and listen.

Some months later, early in 1906, Parham assisted Seymour's move to Los Angeles. He had been invited to become pastor of a small African American Baptist church. Almost immediately, Seymour tried to introduce the new teaching to his congregation. In response, he was locked out of the church, but not before he had gained the attention of a few. With the several who wished to hear, he continued to preach and on April 9, 1906, the first member of the group spoke in tongues. The growing group soon moved to a building in Azusa Street where the revival services would continue for the next three years. Seymour adopted Parham's name for the organization that oversaw and facilitated the revival services, Apostolic Faith.

With some desire to see what was happening, Parham came to Los Angeles. He rejected the spontaneous excitement of people speaking in tongues mixed with the general informal ways of African American worship. Parham split from Seymour and condemned Azusa and spiritualism and hypnotism. However, while the revival continued, Parham developed a more serious problem. He was arrested for approaching two boys for sexual favors, and though the charges were later dropped and those close to him claimed them to be without foundation, the rumors cost him and the movement in the Midwest dearly. The mainstream of the rapidly growing movement was alienated from him.

Parham eventually settled in Baxter Springs, Kansas, and spent his time teaching in a small Bible school and traveling to nearby communities and preaching. A set of congregations grew out of his ministry and associated together as the Apostolic Faith. Parham died on January 29, 1929, all but forgotten by the movement he initiated. Subsequently, his wife defended him in her biography of him. In recent decades, mainstream Pentecostal historians have developed a new appreciation for him and his role at the beginning of their movement.

J. Gordon Melton

See also: Church of God (Anderson, Indiana); Holiness Movement; Pentecostalism; Seymour, William J.

References

Goff, James. *Fields White Unto Harvest: Charles Fox Parham and the Missionary Origins of Pentecostalism.* Fayetteville: University of Arkansas Press, 1988.

Parham, Charles F. *The Everlasting Gospel.* Baxter Springs, KS: Charles F. Parham, 1911.

Parham, Charles F. *A Voice Crying in the Wilderness.* 1944; rpt.: N.p.: Charles F. Parham, 1902.

Parham, Robert L., ed. *Selected Sermons of the Late Charles F. Parham and Sarah E. Parham, Co-Founders of the Original Apostolic Faith Movement.* Baxter Springs, KS: Robert Parham, 1941.

Parham, Sarah. *The Life of Charles Fox Parham.* Baxter Springs, KS: Sarah Parham and Tri-State Printing, 1930.

Paris Mission

The Paris Mission, officially the Société des Missions Evangéliques chez les peuples non-chrétiens à Paris, was the missionary arm of French Protestantism through much of the 19th and 20th centuries. It began with a number of prayer groups that had been established among Protestants (primarily members of the Reformed Church of France) in support of the Basel Mission and the London Missionary Society, both products of the Pietism and the evangelical Awakening that had spread through European Protestantism in the late 18th century. As one component, that Awakening had spurred an interest in world missions, and as it was perpetuated would turn the Protestant movement into a worldwide phenomenon in the 19th. The Paris Mission was formally organized in 1822 and soon established branches in Holland, Italy, and French-speaking Switzerland. The Mission originally assumed an interdenominational stance, but in fact was largely supported by members of the Reformed churches.

The first missionaries supported by the Mission were sent to South Africa in 1829. From that original base, work expanded into Lesotho and Zambia. Through the remainder of the century, the Mission grew primarily by assuming control of older missions established in what had become French territories. Various Congregational and Presbyterians missions turned work over to the Paris Mission in order to quiet the fears and prejudices of French colonial authorities directed to non-Catholic foreigners working among new French subjects. By this manner, the Paris Mission acquired work in Tahiti (and other South Pacific islands) and in Africa (Madagascar, Gabon, Togo, and Cameroon).

Through the decades following World War II, the Paris Mission oversaw the maturing of most of its missions into independent churches. The end of this phase of its work contributed to its voting itself out of existence in 1971 and contributing its resources to two new organizations, the Départment Français d'Action Apostolique, a common mission board serving several French Protestant denominations, and the Communauté Evangélique d'Action Apostolique, an international communion of 47 churches working in French-speaking lands. Both organizations are based in Paris.

J. Gordon Melton

See also: Reformed Church of France.

Reference

Leonard, Jeanne-Marie. *Mémoires d'évangile: les archives de la Société des missions évangéliques de Paris, 1822–1949*. Paris, Défap, 2000.

Paryushana

Paryushana is a primary festival among the Jains of India. Its origin lies in the beginning of Jainism itself, which emerged as an order of monks. Practicing a form of nonattachment, the monks traveled about living from day to day on what was offered them. India has a rainy season (roughly June to September) in which travel is difficult, and it became common for monks to settle down in one place, usually at the edge of a city for the several months (a minimum of 70 days).

In the old Indian lunar calendar, Paryushana would begin on the fifth day of the waxing moon (*shukla-paksha*) half of the month of Bhadrapada. It would last from 8 to 10 days, depending upon which of the two main divisions of the Jains were holding it. The Swetambaras hold an 8-day festival and the Digambaras a 10-day event.

The festival is a time for reflection on one's life and actions during the past year, and a time to renew one's focus on what are considered the 10 cardinal virtues: forgiveness, charity, simplicity, contentment, truthfulness, self-restraint, fasting, detachment, humility, and continence. These virtues are embedded in a game that is played during the week called Gyanbazi, a game of chance in which morality is taught and the goal becomes enlightenment. The game was observed by the British and brought back to the West where it was secularized and marketed as "snakes-and-ladders" and in America as "Chutes and Ladders."

The festival is marked by several events, including recitation of the text of the Kalpa Sutra, the book that includes the earliest accounts of the Tirthankaras, the enlightened masters from whose teachings Jainism derives. Fasting is common among the monks during this time, and many laypeople, who already are vegetarians, deny themselves specific food items (much like Christians during Lent). The evening is spent in the practice of Pratikraman, a form of meditation that allows for stringent introspection, a review of one's life, a means of repentance for negative thoughts and actions, and a reminder not to repeat them. There are several types.

Pratikraman is practiced daily by devout Jains. Other forms are undertaken once every 15 days or once every 4 months. Samvatsari Pratikraman is done once per year—on the last day of the Paryushana festival. In a sense, the first days of the Paryushana are meant to lead up to the last, during which a most unique practice accompanies the Pratikraman. Those at the event ask forgiveness of every individual they may have offended during the past year. This becomes a time to forget old differences and renew the community. This act consists of folding one's hands before the person and requesting "Micchamidukadam" (May my bad deeds toward you be fruitless).

A form of Paryushana has been imported to the West though there are relatively few monks and the Indian rainy session does not exist. Westerners attending the event have been especially impressed by the acts of forgiveness on its final day.

J. Gordon Melton

See also: Jainism; Lent; Meditation; Vegetarianism.

References

Hynson, Colin. *Discover Jainism.* Ed. by Mehool Sanghrajka. London: Institute of Jainology, 2007.

Jain, Duli Chandra, ed. *Studies in Jainism.* 3 vols. New York: Jain Stucy Circle, 2004.

Rankin, Aidan. *The Jain Path: Ancient Wisdom for the West.* Washington, DC: O Books, 2006.

Pashupata Saivism

The Pashupatas (Sanskrit: "adherents of Pashupati's [that is, Siva's] teaching") are a sect of Saiva ascetics whose cult probably goes back to the second century CE. They trace their origin to Pashupati, who is said to have appeared on Earth as Lakulisha (b. ca. 150), the founder of the sect. According to this account, Lakulisha composed the Pashupata Sutra, the most authoritative work on this system. Together with the important commentary by Kaundinya (fifth century) and the Ganakarika, a text about the group's rituals and worship practices, the Pashupata Sutra seems to be the only internal source for our knowledge of this group. But although important works are lost, external sources like the Puranas, the Tantras, and epigraphical records show that it was once widespread on the Indian subcontinent.

The religious observance of the Pashupatas presupposed access to the Veda—its practice being centered on the Vedic Mantras of the five faces of Siva—and was restricted to Brahmin males. It aimed at liberation through several stages. In the first, the ascetic was to dwell near a Siva temple, with his body smeared with ashes. He would worship the deity by meditating on the five mantras but also by imitating Siva's boisterous laughter. The next phase served to purify the ascetic through a peculiar mechanism: leaving the temple without his sectarian marks, the Pashupata would pretend in public to be mentally deranged or play the lecher and thus invite the contempt of others. Through his initiation he was considered to have the power to transfer his bad karma to those who abused him. This he did until the purification was effected and he could devote the end of his life to meditation on the five mantras.

In a sense Pashupata Saivism stands between the Vedic and the Tantric Saiva religion, not only systematically but also chronologically. Using an older indigenous terminology, Alexis Sanderson (1990) has proposed to classify them as belonging to the *atimarga*, in contradistinction to the later Tantric Saivism (*mantramarga*) that built upon it. Within this atimarga would fall a further branch of the Pashupatas, namely, the Lakulas (also called Kalamukhas or Mahavratas), whose ascetic practice includes the "Observance of the Skull" (*kapalavrata*), by which practitioners imitate Siva's penance by begging with a human skull as an alms bowl and vessel and by living in the impure cremation ground.

The Pashupata tradition spread to Nepal in the eighth century. The Pashupatinath Mandira along the banks of the Bagmati River in Kathmandu remains a primary pilgrimage site to this day. Today the followers of Pashupata Saivism may be found in all parts of India, but most are concentrated in Gujarat and the foothills of the Himalayas.

Jürgen Hanneder

See also: Asceticism; Meditation; Tantrism.

References

Hara, M. "Materials for the Study of Pasupata Saivism." Ph.D. diss., Harvard University, 1966.

Sanderson, Alexis. "Saivism and the Tantric Traditions." In *The World's Religions: The Religions of Asia,* edited by Friedhelm Hardy, 32–135. London: Routledge, 1990.

Passover

Passover is the English name of Pesach, the Jewish Feast of Unleavened Bread. Pesach was commanded

An Ultra-Orthodox Jew collects matzahs (unleavened bread) at a bakery in Jerusalem for the Passover holiday. Passover celebrates the liberation of the Jewish people from slavery in Egypt. (AFP/Getty Images)

to be an annual memorial festival among the Jewish people in Exodus 12, recalling God's deliverance of the Jewish people from slavery in Egypt. A key event in that deliverance was the plague in which God killed the firstborn of each Egyptian household, while passing over the homes of the Hebrews that had been marked with the blood of a freshly slaughtered lamb. This event was celebrated by a meal that included a lamb slaughtered in the Jewish temple and unleavened bread, bread taken on the trip out of Egypt prepared in haste with no time for the leaven to act. Each year, Jews would make a pilgrimage to Jerusalem to celebrate Pesach.

The Christian appropriation began simultaneously with the formation of the Christian community. Among the early memories of the life of Jesus was a trip he made to Jerusalem with his parents to celebrate Pesach when he was but 12 years old. While in the city, he wandered from the family and was found in the temple speaking to the elders (Luke 2:40–52). Then, during his adult ministry, he would spend much of the year traveling through the countryside but always returned to Jerusalem for Passover. Traditionally, the length of his ministry was set at three years as the New Testament accounts of his life placed him at three different Passovers in Jerusalem (John 2, John 5, and Mark 7), prior to the one during which time he was arrested and executed.

On the last visit to Jerusalem, he celebrated the Passover meal with his disciples, the account of which became the basis of the future remembrances of that as the Eucharist or the Lord's Supper, regularly celebrated by Christians today (though in a variety of forms and occasions that range from daily to weekly to monthly to quarterly to annually). Following that last Passover supper, he was arrested, tried, and executed. As he died, it was reported that the veil separating the most holy space from the rest of the temple was rent in two.

That year, Passover was on Thursday. Christ was executed on Friday, and remained dead through the Sabbath. Christianity emerged after Jesus was reported to have risen from the dead on the first day of the new week, Sunday, and subsequently appeared to his disciples at various times and places.

The celebration of Easter (that is, Christ's resurrection) superseded Passover in the Christian church. However, it was tied to Passover in that the events of Christ's death and resurrection began with a Passover Seder (Luke 22:15–16) and were concluded during the Passover week. Jesus was likened to a Passover lamb sacrificed by God for the deliverance of humanity—the lamb of God who takes away the sins of the world. Jesus as the Passover lamb continues as one of the most central and powerful symbols within Christianity.

Beginning early in the fourth century, as the church moved from its outlaw status in the Roman Empire, and began to hold church councils for deciding basic questions, the question of dating Easter came to the fore. A method was adopted that followed the Jewish methods of determining the date of Passover, which, due to the use of the lunar calendar, fell on a different day each year on the Julian calendar used throughout the Roman Empire at the time. Easter was set as the first Sunday after the first full moon following the Spring Equinox (March 21). Passover/Pesach fell on Nissan 15, the first full moon after the Spring Equinox.

Because of the inaccuracy in the Julian calendar, the actual Spring Equinox began to drift away from March 21. A reformed Julian calendar continues to be used among Eastern Orthodox (a few even continuing to used the unreformed calendar), and their Easter celebration has become separated from that of the Western church, which adopted the Gregorian calendar that returned the Spring Equinox to March 21. That congruence remains in effect in the Common Era calendar.

Toward a Christian Passover In the 19th century, following the Great Disappointment, when Adventist Christians were questioning the non-appearance of Christ as William Miller (1782–1849) had proclaimed would occur in 1843–1844, some Adventist leaders turned to the Bible for new insights. Ellen G. White (1827–1915) was introduced to Sabbatarianism, which she accepted. The practice led to a new appreciation of Jewish law and undergirded her interest in health and diet reform. Among Adventist Sabbatarians not connected to White and the Seventh-day Adventist Church she founded, speculation led toward a new appreciation of the Jewish festivals, a celebration of which developed among some of the splinter groups of the Church of God (Seventh-day). The renewed interest in the Jewish festivals was also related to a critique of the celebration of Christmas and Easter as surviving Paganism.

From the Sabbatarian Church of God groups, the celebration of the Jewish festivals, especially the Passover and Feast of Unleavened Bread, passed to Herbert W. Armstrong (1892–1986), the founder of the Worldwide Church of God. He tied the celebration of the Jewish feasts to a broad critique of holidays in general, both the uniquely Christian holidays and a number of widely celebrated secular holidays (Valentine's Day, Halloween) along with the idea of celebrating birthdays. Armstrong also believed in the practice of tithing and suggested that along with tithing a tenth of one's income to the Worldwide Church of God, members tithe a second 10 percent to be dedicated to celebrating Passover.

Still other Adventist groups, most notably the Jehovah's Witnesses, recognizing the Lord's Supper as having originated in a Passover Seder, adopted the practice of an annual memorial meal, sometimes called the Lord's Evening Meal, which is held on the first evening of Passover/Pesach each year. Witnesses do not use the modern Jewish calendar, and their dating will on occasion correspond more with the same full moon as the Jewish festival of Purim, which is celebrated on the 14th day of the Hebrew month of Adar (and hence usually occurs in mid-March on the Common Era calendar).

Jewish Christians Over the centuries, many Jews have converted to Christianity, but in the 20th century, a number of Jews who became Christians consciously decided to keep much of their Jewish culture, some to the point of founding and maintaining synagogues in which worship resembles that in a Jewish synagogue, as much as is possible without directly denying basic Christian affirmations concerning Jesus' divinity and his actions that bring salvation. Most Messianic synagogues continue to celebrate Passover but have poured new content into it. While adhering to many of the forms of the traditional Pesach meal, the Messianic practice centers on the concept that Jesus (whom they call in Hebrew Yeshua) was the sacrificial Passover lamb.

The Jews for Jesus, a group of Christians of Jewish background that originated at the same time as the Messianic movement, but do not believe in separate Christian synagogues, have developed a program for informing congregations of Christian believers about the Jewish background of their practices, especially Passover. Each spring, representatives of the movement will visit Christian congregations and offer a program demonstrating and explaining the Pesach meal and its role as background for the Christian communion service.

J. Gordon Melton

See also: Calendars, Religious; Common Era Calendar; Great Disappointment; Jerusalem; Pesach; Sabbatarianism; Seventh-day Adventist Church; Spring Equinox; White, Ellen G.; Worldwide Church of God.

References

Boston, Stephen. *The Essential Teachings of Herbert W. Armstrong: His Teachings Focused on the Incredible Human Potential. Did He Solve the Mystery of the Ages?* Lincoln, NB: iUniverse, 2002.

Lipson, Eric. *Passover Haggadah: A Messianic Celebration*. San Francisco: Purple Pomegranate Productions, 1986.

Sampson, Robin, and Linda Pierce. *A Family Guide to the Biblical Holidays*. Stafford, VA: Heart of Wisdom Publishing, 2001.

Stallings, Joseph M. *Rediscovering Passover: A Complete Guide for Christians*. Searcy, AK: Resource Publications, 1994.

Pasundan Christian Church

The Pasundan Christian Church (Gereja Kristen Pasundan [GKP]) originated in missionary activity begun by the Nederlandsche Gereformeerde Zendingsvereeniging, an independent Reformed missionary agency in the Dutch East Indies (now Indonesia). The agency entered western Java in 1863 but made little progress, partially because of the missionaries' very negative attitudes toward Islam, the dominant religion in the area, and the local culture. In the meantime, a second independent effort was begun by a Dutch layman who was a member of the Supreme Court of the Dutch Indies. He had notable success using methods that were considered by many to be unorthodox. The two works merged in 1885. Work was still slow, and in 1834 there were still only 4,000 Sudanese members. That year the churches joined together in a synod.

Missionaries remained in charge and chaired the synod until the Japanese arrived in 1942. The end of the war did not lessen the synod's problems, as the war for independence and a West Java Islamic revolt followed soon thereafter. It was not until the 1950s that stability returned to the area. The church was able to reorganize and settle into a quiet life that includes the sponsoring of a hospital and school system.

In 2005, the Pasundan Christian Church reported 33,000 members. It is a member of the World Council of Churches and the World Alliance of Reformed Churches.

Pasundan Christian Church
Kompleks Bandung Textil Centre
Jin Kebonjsati No. 44-48
Bandung 40181
Indonesia
http://www.gkp.or.id/

J. Gordon Melton

See also: World Alliance of Reformed Churches; World Council of Churches.

References

Bauswein, Jean-Jacques, and Lukas Vischner, eds. *The Reformed Family Worldwide: A Survey of Reformed Churches, Theological Schools, and International Organizations*. Grand Rapids, MI: William B. Eerdmans Publishing Company, 1999.

Van Beek, Huibert. *A Handbook of the Churches and Councils: Profiles of Ecumenical Relationships*. Geneva: World Council of Churches, 2006.

Patanjali

Patanjali (ca. second century CE) is the name attached to the unknown author of the Yoga Sutras, one of the classics of Hindu and Indian literature. The whole practice of yoga is ultimately traced to the Yoga Sutras, now dated to around 200 CE. Patanjali's name is also associated with another text, the Mahabhashya, a commentary on grammar, but it is dated to around 200 BCE, and hence by another author. In the absence of biographical data, the story of Patanjali has been integrated into Hindu lore. According to some stories, his origin has been pushed into the mythological past as he is the son of Angiras, one of the 10 sons of Brahma, the Hindu Creator deity, and of Sati, one of the consorts of Siva.

Elsewhere, Patanjali is seen as an incarnation of Adisesa, the serpent upon whom the deity Vishnu is seated. At one point, Vishnu became enthralled with the dancing of Siva. As he moved to the dance, Adisesa experienced great discomfort. When the dance ceased, Adisesa inquired into the reason for Vishnu's agitation. When informed of the dance, he asked how he could learn so he could eventually dance for Vishnu. Vishnu predicted that Adisesa would incarnate, during which time he would both learn the art of dance and shower humanity with blessings.

He then became aware of a childless yet virtuous woman named Gonika. As she prayed for a son, Adisesa presented himself to her in human form. Patanjali is often pictured with a human head and torso and the lower body of a snake. A canopy of five serpent heads is above his head.

In the 20th century, the study of the Yoga Sutras again became widespread. Not only has the study of yoga postures and their benefit become popular in the West, but a number of international yoga fellowships have emerged. In the last generation, a variety of yoga teachers have written and published commentaries on the Yoga Sutras.

The system described in the Yoga Sutras is often referred to as Ashtanga yoga, or "eight-limbed yoga." Practice involves eight steps, divided into two groups. There are five outer practices: *yama* and *niyama* (behavioral dos and don'ts), *asanas* (postures), *pranayama* (breath control), and *pratyahara* (sense control). There are three inward oriented practices: *dharana* (concentration), *dhyana* (meditation), and *samadhi* (bliss). Ashtanga yoga leads to a more focused sitting practice called *raja* yoga, which centers upon breathing. As one watches the breath, the practitioner is led to the development of additional means to concentrate and then control the mind. Patanjali's yoga, as do most forms of Hinduism, has as its goal liberation from the cycle of birth and rebirth, though it is particularly concentrated upon freeing the self (*purusha*) from its false attachment to the phenomenal world.

In the modern West, the asanas or postures have been somewhat separated from the whole of Patanjali's system and elevated to an independent practice valuable in its own right. The current popularity of *hatha* yoga obscures the fact that in the Yoga Sutras asanas are simply one of the eight "limbs" of yoga. Also, many (if not most) of the postures known today are later additions to the practice or represent practices developed elsewhere that have been integrated into Patanjali's system. Indeed, many of the contemporary yoga schools market themselves as possessing a unique and improved yoga system.

Constance A. Jones

See also: Hinduism; Meditation; Yoga.

References

Feuerstein, Georg, trans. *The Yoga-Sutra of Patanjali.* Rochester, VT: Inner Traditions, 1990.

Iyengar, K. S. *Light on Yoga: Yoga Pradipika.* Boston: Unwin Paperbacks, 1979.

Jopis, Sri K. Pattabhi. *Yoga Mala.* New York: North Point Press, 2002.

Kielhorn, F. *Katyayana and Patanjali: Their Relation to Each Other and to Panini.* Varanasi: Indological Book House, 1963.

Puri, Baij Nath. *India in the Time of Patanjali.* Bombay: Bharatiya Vidya Bhavan, 1957.

Whicher, Ian. *The Integrity of the Yoga Darsana: A Reconsideration of Classical Yoga.* Albany: State University of New York Press, 1998.

Patotsav

Patotsav is a Hindu festival celebrating the anniversaries of the installation of the *murtis* (statues of the deities) at the temple. It is primarily a festival within the Swaminarayan movement. As murtis may be installed at various points during the year, the celebration for any given murtis may occur on any given day.

Swaminarayan devotees see Patotsav as a reconsecration ceremony. The practice was begun out of a widespread belief that murtis lose their divinity to some degree simply from the volume of *maya* (illusion) they must deal with in their assisting devotees. Swaminarayan leaders have emphasized that such is not the case; the divinity of the murtis is never dissipated. It is the devotion of followers that often decreases. Patotsav is intended to revive the sentiments that devotees have for the murtis and for their guru.

Besides the annual Patotsav festival for the murtis, in Swaminarayan temples there is a daily *bhakti* (devotional) observance that begins with washing the murtis, first with a mixture of milk, yogurt, ghee, honey, and saffon water (*abbishek*) and then with water. Then the deities are dressed in their appropriate clothing for public viewing. The *bahishek* is later made available to devotees for their consumption. A similar daily occurrence is found in Krishna temples of the Gaudaya Math tradition (including those of the International Society for Krishna Consciousness).

Constance A. Jones

See also: Devotion/Devotional Traditions.

Reference

Mukuncharandas, Sadhu. *Hindu Festivals (Origin Sentiments & Rituals).* Amdavad, India: Swaminarayan Aksharpith, 2005.

Paul

ca. 10–ca. 67 CE

Paul, the Christian Apostle most known for his pioneering work to carry Christianity to the Gentile world of the Mediterranean basin, is considered the major force in transforming the movement that had grown up around the belief that Jesus was the Christ (Messiah) and had been resurrected from the dead following his execution from another "way" within Judaism to a international movement that welcomed people of all ethnicities and backgrounds.

Statue of Saint Paul, first-century Christian convert credited with the spread of Christianity throughout the Roman Empire. (Corel)

Paul was born in Tarsus, Cilicia, a city on the southern coast of what is now Turkey sometime before 10 CE. His influential Jewish family named him Saul after the ancient Jewish king. His father was a Pharisee and he was brought up to strictly observe the Mosaic Law. He was also a free citizen of Rome. More than once his dual citizenship stood him in good stead as he faced harsh treatment at the hands of municipal authorities in Greece and Asia Minor. Anywhere in the empire, Roman citizens had the right to appeal directly to Rome when serious charges were laid against them.

Paul was also well educated and his schooling included some years of training in Jerusalem, where he studied with the noted teacher Gamaliel (d. ca. 50 CE), the grandson of Hillel (ca. 110 BCE–10 CE). He was taught the trade of tent making, which he pursued throughout his life as his means of support. Likely his father trained him, as was the custom. For Paul, tent making would prove to be a secure occupation that would provide well for him and give flexibility for his ministry. Made of either textiles or leather, tents were homes for many throughout the Mediterranean. Growing up in Cilicia, Paul may have worked particularly with cilicum, a goat's hair cloth woven in the district and favored by seamen and soldiers.

As a young man, Saul was given responsibility in the attempted suppression of the Christian community and he first appears on the scene when he witnessed the death of Stephen, the first Christian martyr, in Jerusalem, and he later assumed a leading role in the persecution of Christians. Subsequently, while traveling from Jerusalem to Damascus (ca. 35) he had a visionary experience in which Jesus appeared to him and spoke of his persecution work. Saul was converted to the faith he had once so strongly opposed and soon emerged as one of its most capable leaders. He began to call himself an Apostle (a leader who had seen Jesus in the flesh) out of season (1 Corinthians 15:8), a reference to his having seen Jesus in the flesh, but in his resurrected body. Three accounts of his conversion experience are recorded in the New Testament book of Acts (in chapters 9, 22, and 26).

Following his conversion, Saul began to refer to himself as Paul and engage in evangelistic efforts in Damascus. He made his first trip to Jerusalem three years later and went through a period of winning over the other Apostles, who hesitated to accept him because of his past. He began to preach among the Greek-speaking Jews and then focused his mission to the Gentiles. His real work awaited the developing consensus that Gentiles could become Christians without also becoming Jews, being circumcised, and following Jewish dietary laws.

Dates are notoriously difficult to fix for most of Paul's career because there are few allusions in Paul's letters to events in the contemporary political world. Still, we can date Paul's arrival in Corinth in 49. A year and a half later he appeared before the Corinthian proconsul Gallio and then left Corinth (Acts 18:12). An inscription discovered at Delphi dates Gallio's short tenure in 51.

Paul's letters show he responded to immediate opportunities, traveling as needs arose, instead of planning a campaign from start to finish. He found himself returning to Corinth and Ephesus more often than the supposed "headquarters" in Jerusalem. Still, many find it convenient to organize Paul's career around the scheme of three missionary journeys.

Around 47, Paul began the first of these missionary journeys. It was limited primarily to Asia Minor (Turkey), and culminated in Paul's return to Jerusalem for a council in which the issue of circumcision was discussed. It was decided that circumcision was not to be required of male Gentile converts. Returning to Asia Minor (ca. 49), Paul had a vision of a man beckoning him to Macedonia. In response, he subsequently carried the Christian message to Europe for the first time. His second missionary journey took him to the Greek peninsula, where strong centers would emerge in such places as Thessalonica and Corinth. In Athens, on the Areopagus (Mars Hill), Paul had his confrontation with the learned men of the city. Toward the end of his journey, he authored his first writings (that have survived), the two epistles to the Thessalonians.

After a period in Antioch, Paul began his third journey around 54. It included a three-year stay in Ephesus, during which time he wrote the several letters to the Corinthians concerning problems that had arisen in the church there. He would later arrive in Corinth (ca. winter 57–58), and while there write the lengthy letter to the church in Rome, which he had yet to visit. He then returned to Jerusalem by way of Philippi.

In Jerusalem, he became involved in a disturbance at the temple and was arrested. In the process of being examined, he asserted his Roman citizenship. However, facing a trial in Jerusalem, where those who opposed the Christian movement and him personally were strong, Paul used his prerogative as a citizen and appealed his case to Caesar (Acts 25:9–11). He was subsequently transported to Rome. He was imprisoned in Rome for two years (ca. 61–63), during which time he wrote several more of his letters—Ephesians, Colossians, Philippians, Philemon. The primary account of Paul's life, the book of Acts, closes with him a prisoner in Rome.

According to the major traditions, Paul was eventually released (ca. 63) but remained in the city only to be rearrested around 67. In the meantime, the great fire broke out in Rome, and the emperor Nero (r. 54–68) blamed it on the Christian community. A general persecution of Christians followed. The tentacles of the persecution finally reached Paul and following his arrest he was executed, most likely by being beheaded. Convicted Roman citizens were commonly beheaded at a spot on the Ostian Way. Other traditions suggest that Paul went on to Spain and lived out the last years of his life there. It was Paul`s stated purpose to move on to Spain by way of Rome (Romans 15:24–28), but after the Roman imprisonment recorded in Acts, we have no documentary evidence that he was able to fulfill these travel plans.

The martyrdom of Paul is believed by most to have occurred on the Ostian Way. He would afterwards be interred on the property of a lady named Lucina. This site was first marked by a simple shrine and then by a church constructed by the emperor Constantine. The emperor Theodosius I (r. 379–395) began and Pope Leo I (r. 440–461) completed the erection of the new church of St. Paul Outside-the-Walls, which most believe was constructed over the grave of the Apostle Paul. That church was destroyed by fire in 1823, but reconstructed. During the reconstruction a fourth-century tomb was discovered that carried the inscription in Latin, "To Paul, apostle and martyr." The new basilica was consecrated by Pope Pius IX (r. 1846–1878) on December 10, 1854.

In the second and third centuries, Paul's writings, his epistles sent to the various churches and to individuals he knew, were gathered and copied and became part of the normative literature of the Christian movement. As the New Testament canon was closed, he emerged as the author of more items (14) than any other of the Apostolic writers. Some contemporary biblical scholars have called Paul's authorship of several of the epistles traditionally attributed to him into question, noting the distinctive style, vocabulary, and doctrinal emphasis. They have suggested that the letters (to Timothy, Titus, and the Hebrews) were produced by one or more persons directly influenced by Paul in the decades following his death. These criticisms have not, however, affected the canonical nature of these works.

Paul's writings have repeatedly become the sources of revival and reform movement within the larger Christian movement. Protestants especially drew upon his letters for their emphasis upon the centrality of faith and grace in the Christian life. Other new movements have seen his standing up to Peter and the other Apostles on behalf of the Gentiles as a model for standing against entrenched and ossified church authority. Theologians have always seen him as the pioneering and model Christian thinker whom they hope to emulate.

Since the 1960s, many Protestant scholars have challenged the anti-Catholic context of the 16th-century Protestant writings on Paul and have begun to offer a "New Perspective on Paul," based upon a fresh look at the Jewish context of his writings.

J. Gordon Melton

See also: Constantine the Great; Damascus; Jerusalem; Martyrdom; Rome/Vatican City.

References

Dunn, James G. D., ed. *Paul and the Mosaic Law*. Grand Rapids, MI: William B. Eerdmans Publishing Company, 2001.

Durham-Tübingen Research Symposium on Earliest Christianity and Judaism, University of Durham, 1994.

Harrington, Daniel J. *Meeting St. Paul Today: Understanding the Man, His Mission, and His Message*. Chicago: Loyola Press, 2008.

Schnelle, Udo. *Apostle Paul: His Life and Theology*. Grand Rapids, MI: Baker Academic and Brazos Press, 2005.

Wright, N. T. *Paul: In Fresh Perspective*. Minneapolis, MN: Augsburg Fortress Press, 2006.

Pentecost

Pentecost is the festival that marks the birth of the Christian church by the power of the Holy Spirit as recorded in the biblical book of the Acts of the Apostles 2:1–41. The word "Pentecost" means "50th day" and is celebrated 50 days after Easter. Because the timing of Pentecost is tied to the moveable date of Easter, it can occur as early as May 10 and as late as June 13.

The Christian feast of Pentecost originated in the Jewish festival that began on the 50th day after the beginning of Passover (Pesach). It is called the Feast of Weeks (Shavuot) and was originally an agricultural festival celebrating and giving thanks for the "first fruits" of the early spring harvest (Leviticus 23; Exodus 23, 34). By the early New Testament period, it had gradually lost its association with agriculture and became associated with the celebration of God's creation of his people and their religious history. By the destruction of Jerusalem in 70 CE, the festival focused exclusively on God's gift of Torah (the "Law") on Mount Sinai.

According to the account in Acts, 10 days after Jesus ascended into heaven, the Apostles gathered together in Jerusalem for the Jewish harvest festival. The day has significance in the history of the Christian church, whose members began to see the events of the day as the time God sent the outpouring of the Holy Spirit promised through the prophet Joel (Joel 2:28–29).

Pentecost is also called "Whitsunday" or "White Sunday" because in ancient times it was customary to baptize adult converts on Pentecost. The catechumens would wear white robes on that day. Consequently, the present-day rite of confirmation is still often celebrated on Pentecost.

The feast of Pentecost is universally celebrated in the Christian church, though the liturgical practices are not as extensive and well known as the greater feasts of Easter and Christmas, for example. The church fathers Irenaeus and Tertullian attest to its celebration in apostolic times.

In Italy it is customary to scatter rose leaves from the ceiling of the churches to recall the miracle of the fiery tongues. In France celebrants blow trumpets during the service to recall the sound of the mighty wind that accompanied the giving of the Spirit. The Eastern Orthodox carry flowers and green branches in their hands to mark the day.

Red is the liturgical color for Pentecost. Red recalls the tongues of flame in which the Holy Spirit descended on the first Pentecost. The color red also signifies the blood of the martyrs who, by the power of the Holy Spirit, held firm to the true faith even at the cost of their lives.

Pentecost represents God's gracious, enabling presence actively at work among his people, calling and enabling them to live out in dynamic ways their witness. For Christians, Pentecost Sunday is a day to celebrate hope evoked by the knowledge that God through his Holy Spirit is at work among his people. It is a celebration of newness, of re-creation, of renewal of purpose, mission, and calling as God's people. It is a celebration of God's ongoing work in the world. Yet, it is also a recognition that his work is done through his people as he pours out his presence upon them.

Kevin Quast

See also: Christmas; Easter; Pesach; Roman Catholic Church; Shavuot.

References

Adam, Adolf. *The Liturgical Year: Its History and Its Meaning after the Reform of the Liturgy.* New York: Pueblo, 1981.

Harrington, Daniel J. "Pentecost Past and Present." *America*, May 29, 2006.

Holweck, Frederick. "Pentecost (Whitsunday)." *The Catholic Encyclopedia*. Vol. 15. New York: Robert Appleton Company, 1912.

Stookey, Laurence Hull. *Calendar: Christ's Time for the Church.* Nashville: Abingdon, 1996.

Talley, Thomas J. *The Origins of the Liturgical Year.* 2nd ed. Collegeville, MN: Liturgical Press, 1991.

Pentecostal Assemblies of Canada

In November 1918, a meeting was convened in Mille Roche, a small town outside of Cornwall, Ontario. Its purpose was to begin to organize a cooperative fellowship and to obtain a government charter for Pentecostals in Canada. This action followed similar discussions in Montreal in 1917 and a previously failed attempt at Pentecostal union in 1909. Soon after the meeting, on May 17, 1919, the secretary of state of Canada signed the charter giving official sanction to Pentecostal leaders. They wished to organize on the basis of "fellowship, not doctrine" but agreed that "the baptism in the Holy Spirit with tongues as the initial evidence" was central to their identity. Thus Pentecostal Assemblies of Canada (PAOC) was born.

Revival had characterized a number of sectarian movements from the beginning of the 20th century, a time of rapid urbanization and accelerated religious change. As in the United States, the Wesleyan Holiness denominations in Canada contributed significantly to the growth of Pentecostalism. So did the Salvation Army, with its appeal to the uprooted urban masses, as well as the Mennonite Brethren in Christ and the Christian and Missionary Alliance. The outpouring of the Holy Spirit in 1906 at the Hebden Mission in Toronto left its mark on Canadian Pentecostalism, just as the Azusa Street revival shaped Pentecostalism in the United States. Hebden was the first of six Pentecostal missions started before 1910. As people from different religious traditions experienced spiritual phenomena in a new way, they sought common fellowship and common structures.

In 1919 a group of western Canadian Pentecostal churches formed as a district of the Assemblies of God (AG). A year later the PAOC in the east voted to become the Assemblies Eastern Canada District Council. This structural arrangement continued until 1925, when the Canadian Pentecostals voted to become autonomous.

Because of doctrinal similarities, geographic proximity, and fraternal working agreements, the influence of the AG on the PAOC is unquestionable. The PAOC adopted the AG Statement of Fundamental Truths, a statement adhering to a finished work theory of sanctification. It also positioned the movement away from the Oneness tradition of Pentecostalism, reaffirming the Trinitarian view of the Godhead.

As the largest single group of Canadian Pentecostals, the PAOC grew rapidly after its formation in 1919. Two years after its inception it listed 23 assemblies in eastern Canada and 10 in western Canada. According to census figures, the Pentecostals and Apostolic Brethren accounted for approximately 8,000 believers and adherents in Canada at this time. In 1951 the total Pentecostal constituency in Canada numbered 95,000 compared to 57,742 10 years previously. In 1988 the PAOC General Conference reported 1,058 congregations with 189,753 church members and adherents in Canada. By 1994 that figure had risen to 231,000.

Identified with classical Pentecostals in the United States, the PAOC gained greater favor after the AG were accepted into the National Association of Evangelicals in the mid-1940s. Evangelicals extended further openness toward Pentecostals in the 1960s with the rise of the Charismatic movement. Today the PAOC is an active participant in the Evangelical Fellowship of Canada, taking a leading role among its evangelical counterparts.

Pentecostal Assemblies of Canada
2450 Milltower Ct.
Mississauga, ON L5N 5Z6
Canada
http://www.paoc.org/

Irving A. Whitt

See also: Charismatic Movement; Pentecostalism.

References

Atter, G. F. *The Third Force.* Peterborough, ON: College Press, 1965, 1970.

Holm, Randall. "A Paradigmatic Analysis of Authority Within Pentecostalism." Ph.D. diss., University of Lavel, 1995.

Kydd, R. A. N. "Pentecostal Assemblies of Canada." In *Dictionary of Pentecostal and Charismatic Movements,* edited by Stanley M. Burgess and Gary B. McGee. Grand Rapids, MI: Zondervan Publishing House, 1988.

Miller, Thomas W. "The Canadian 'Azusa': The Hebden Mission in Toronto." *Pneuma* 8, no. 1 (1986): 5–30.

Miller, Thomas W. *Canadian Pentecostals: A History of the Pentecostal Assemblies of Canada.* Mississauga, ON: Full Gospel Publishing House, 1994.

Pentecostal Assemblies of the World

Claiming to be the oldest of the "Apostolic" or "Jesus Only" churches, the Pentecostal Assemblies of the World were organized as a loose fellowship by several people who had experienced the Pentecostal blessing (with the accompanying phenomenon of "speaking in tongues") at the revival occurring at the Apostolic Faith Mission on Azusa Street in Los Angeles. In 1913, at a Pentecostal camp meeting in Los Angeles, a Canadian minister, R. E. McAlister (d. 1953), talked about the belief he had arrived at from his study of the Bible, namely, that the commonly used Trinitarian baptismal formula was unbiblical. He asserted that baptism should be in the name of Jesus. Two prominent ministers, Frank J. Ewart (1876–1947) and John C. Scheppe, immediately accepted the idea. Soon other leading ministers such as Garfield Thomas Hayward (1880–1931), E. N. Bell (1866–1923), Glenn A. Cook, and H. A. Goss, signaled their acceptance of it.

The new perspective on baptism led to the development of a new form of Pentecostalism, which denied the traditional Christian idea of the Trinity with an understanding of Jesus as identical with God the Father and the Holy Spirit as the power of God/Jesus. Baptism by immersion in the name of Jesus was considered essential for salvation.

In 1914, a number of unaffiliated Pentecost leaders gathered in Little Rock to form the Assemblies of God. In the meantime, those who had allied themselves with the Pentecostal Assemblies had been holding their annual meetings in Indianapolis, where Thomas G. Hayward, an African American, had emerged as the popular leader. Over the next year the two organizations would go their separate way as the Assemblies of God adopted a Trinitarian position and the Pentecostal Assemblies moved into the Apostolic camp. The Pentecostal Assemblies also differed from the Assemblies of God in its inter-racial makeup. The Assemblies of God was, in fact, a fellowship of white Americans distinguished from the earlier predominantly African American group, the Church of God in Christ.

Through the decades of the 20th century, in spite of significant pressure to split along racial lines, Assemblies remained committed to its inter-racial character. A major challenge came in 1924, when many of the white members withdrew to form what became the United Pentecostal Church International. The remaining members reorganized with an episcopal polity and elected Hayward as the first presiding bishop. A second period of unrest followed Hayward's death. However, in 1937, Samuel Grimes became the new presiding bishop. He would hold the office for the next three decades during which time the Assemblies experienced its greatest period of growth. It developed congregations across the United States and missions in Nigeria, Jamaica, the United Kingdom, Ghana, and Egypt.

The current presiding bishop is Reverend Horace E. Smith, who succeeded Norman L. Wagner in 2004. In 2005, the Assemblies reported 1.5 million members in 1,750 congregations. More than 1,000 affiliated congregations were located outside of the United States. Today work is now found in Germany, the United Kingdom, India, Togo, Nigeria, Liberia, Egypt, Sierra Leone, Zimbabwe, the Cook Islands, the Fiji Islands, Australia and New Zealand, Haiti, Jamaica, the Bahamas, and a number of the Caribbean islands. The church sponsors Aenon Bible School in Indianapolis, Indiana.

Pentecostal Assemblies of the World
3939 Meadows Dr.
Indianapolis, IN 46205
http://www.pawinc.org/

J. Gordon Melton

See also: Assemblies of God; Church of God in Christ; Pentecostalism.

References

Dugas, Paul P., comp. *The Life and Writings of Elder G. T. Haywood.* Portland, OR: Apostolic Book Publishers, 1968.

Golder, Morris E. *History of the Pentecostal Assemblies of the World.* Indianapolis, IN: the author, 1973.

Golder, Morris E. *The Life and World of Bishop Garfield Thomas Hayward.* Indianapolis, IN: the author, 1977.

Tyson, James L. *The Early Pentecostal Revival: History of the Twentieth-Century Pentecostals and the Pentecostal Assemblies of the World, 1901–30.* St. Louis, MO: Word Aflame Press, 1992.

Pentecostal Church of Chile

The Pentecostal Church of Chile (Iglesia Pentecostal de Chile) was founded in 1945 by former members of the Methodist Pentecostal Church of Chile under the leadership of Bishop Enrique Chavez Campos. The church's strongest early presence was in the city of Curicó, some 150 miles south of Santiago. Like its parent body, the church experienced significant growth in the last half of the 20th century through its intensive evangelistic efforts among the poorer people of the country. By the mid-1980s it reported 90,000 members.

The church resembles the Methodist Pentecostal Church in doctrine, but it has a commitment to Christian unity and in 1961 joined the World Council of Churches, which has been considered a very liberal body by many Pentecostal churches. The highest legislative body of the church is its general assembly. It elects the bishops and an executive committee who lead the church between assembly meetings. The bishops appoint the pastors to their posts.

The church is committed to dealing with the problems of poverty in Chile and with the educational needs of the nation's youth. It supports the work of Evangelical Christian Aid in promoting social action programs among the poor, including providing agricultural education, skills training for women, and free-lunch facilities for the children of the poor.

In 2005, the church reported 125,000 members in 340 congregations.

Pentecostal Church of Chile
Calle Rodriguez 1177
Casilla 775
Curicó
Chile

J. Gordon Melton

See also: Methodist Pentecostal Church of Chile; World Council of Churches.

References

Van Beek, Huibert. *A Handbook of the Churches and Councils: Profiles of Ecumenical Relationships*. Geneva: World Council of Churches, 2006.

Van der Bent, Ans J., ed. *Handbook/Member Churches/World Council of Churches*. Geneva: World Council of Churches, 1985.

Pentecostal Church of God

John C. Sinclair, a former Presbyterian originally from Scotland who pastored the "first Pentecostal church in Chicago," went to the gathering of Pentecostal leaders held at Hot Springs, Arkansas, in 1914 and was appointed to the Executive Presbytery of the Assemblies of God, as was George Brinkman. Five years later, on December 30, 1919, seven ministers and a few church delegates met in Chicago to organize as the Pentecostal Assemblies of the U.S.A. Sinclair emerged as general chairman, Brinkman as secretary, and J. A. Bell as treasurer.

Brinkman owned and operated the Herald Publishing Company, which beginning in 1913 published a monthly publication called the *Pentecostal Herald*. The *Pentecostal Herald* was accepted as the official publication of the Pentecostal Assemblies. In 1922 the name Pentecostal Church of God (PCG) replaced Pentecostal Assemblies of the U.S.A. In 1926 the Messenger Printing Company was established in Ottumwa, Iowa, by A. D. McClure, who now edited the *Pentecostal Messenger*, which in 1927 became the church's official organ. Sinclair did not continue to associate with the church after its headquarters were relocated to Ottumwa.

In 1933 the PCG adopted a doctrinal statement. It had been previously thought that the 1914 meeting compromised the sovereignty of the local congregation and that the 1916 Assemblies of God Statement of Fundamental Truths was a move toward conventional ecclesiasticism. In 1950 the headquarters were moved to Joplin, Missouri. Across the street from the headquarters now sits Messenger College, which had opened in 1958 in Houston as Southern Bible College.

The PCG grants ordination to women ministers. Early on, the church adopted a view of divorce that allowed remarried people to become ministers, a position that barred the PCG from the Pentecostal Fellowship of North America (now Pentecostal/Charismatic Churches of North America) and the Pentecostal World Conference. The PCG will give the full range of licenses—from exhorters to ordained ministers—to divorced and remarried people on three grounds: (1) the divorce occurred prior to the first conversion experi-

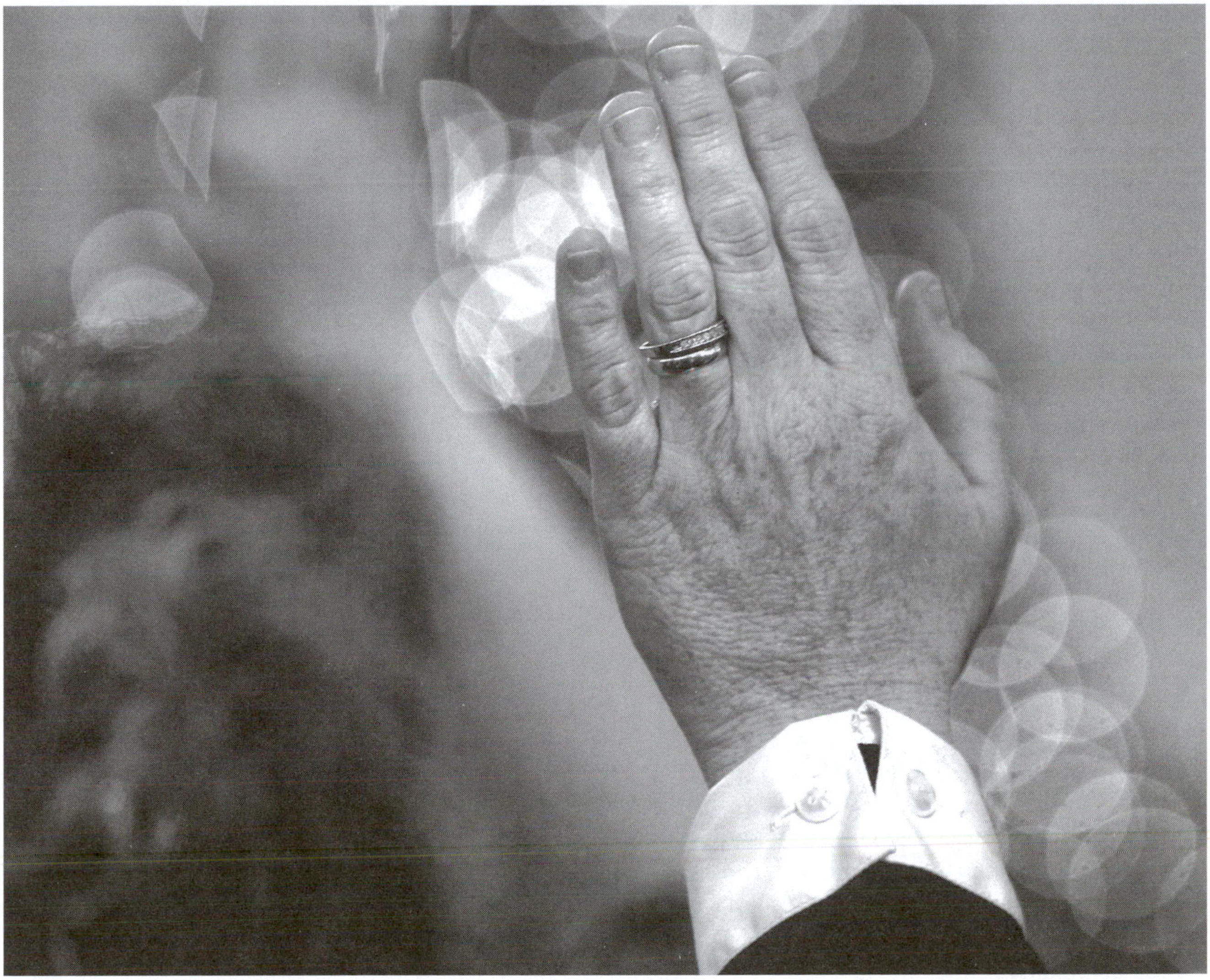

Worshippers raise their hands in prayer during a service at the Wilmington Pentecostal Church of God in Wilmington, Ohio, on December 21, 2008. (John Moore/Getty Images)

ence, (2) fornication was the grounds for divorce, or (3) desertion was the grounds for divorce. A 1997 review of this policy on credentialing ministers who are divorced and remarried suggested that naming desertion implies that the spouse was not a Christian. The first point was also debated because many people report their first conversion in childhood. The question was, should the adult conversion, after one "backslides," be definitive in such cases? And if only adult conversion matters, at what age is one an adult? In 1993 the denomination started naming apostles in their official list of ministers.

J. W. May, general superintendent of the PCG from June 1942 to June 1947, had been present in the meeting held by Charles Fox Parham (1875–1929), the original Pentecostal minister, in Topeka, Kansas, in 1901. R. Dennis Heard (1953–1975) was instrumental in leading the PCG into the National Association of Evangelicals, the Pentecostal Fellowship of North America, and the Pentecostal World Conference. The current general superintendent is James D. Gee.

In 2007 the PCG reported 608,000 constituents, 4,823 churches and preaching stations, and 6,750 ministers in 58 nations. In the United States, the church reported 88,627 constituents (of which 40,000 were formally members), 1,158 churches, and 2,796 ministers. Its strongest missionary activity is in East Africa, Europe (especially Russia), East Asia, Mexico, Argentina, and the Caribbean.

Pentecostal Church of God
4901 Pennsylvania
Joplin, MO 64801
http://www.pcg.org/

Harold D. Hunter

See also: Assemblies of God; Parham, Charles Fox; Pentecostalism; Pentecostal World Fellowship.

References

Martin, Larry. *In the Beginning*. Duncan, OK: Christian Life Books, 1994.
Moon, Elmer L. *The Pentecostal Church: A History and Popular Survey.* New York: Carlton Press, 1966.

Pentecostal Mission Church

The Pentecostal Mission Church (Misión Iglesia Pentecostal) is one of more than 100 independent churches that originated with the Methodist Pentecostal Church of Chile (MPCC), the largest of the Protestant/Free church communities in Chile. In 1933 the MPCC experienced its first schism, which led to the formation of the Evangelical Pentecostal Church. The Pentecostal Mission Church was formed in 1952 by 125 members of the Evangelical Pentecostal Church, second in Chile only to the MPCC.

The church manifested an immediate readiness to cooperate with other Christian groups in serving the needs of the poorer people of Chile, who formed its major constituency. It immediately began to work with Evangelical Christian Aid, best known for its food distribution program, but also branching out to provide a number of social services, from education to improving agriculture. The church was one of several Pentecostal churches in 1967 to cooperate with the Methodists and Anglicans to found the Evangelical Theological Community of Chile, an ecumenical training center.

Like the Pentecostal Church of Chile, the Pentecostal Mission Church placed an emphasis on Christian unity that led it in 1962 to affiliate with the World Council of Churches. The church has taken the lead in exploring innovative approaches to Christian education, theological reflection, and pastoral care. In 2005 it reported 9,000 members.

Pentecostal Mission Church
Santa Barbara 3613
Comuna of Recoleta
Santiago
Chile

J. Gordon Melton

See also: Methodist Pentecostal Church of Chile; Pentecostal Church of Chile; World Council of Churches.

References

Harmon, Nolan B. *Encyclopedia of World Methodism*. 2 vols. Nashville: United Methodist Publishing House, 1974.
Van Beek, Huibert. *A Handbook of the Churches and Councils: Profiles of Ecumenical Relationships*. Geneva: World Council of Churches, 2006.

Pentecostal Mission, The

The Pentecostal Mission (TPM) was founded by an Indian later known as Pastor Paul (his surname is not found in any documents), a Hindu convert from the Ezhava caste, while employed in Sri Lanka in 1921. It was incorporated by an act of the Parliament of Ceylon in 1970 and originally called the Ceylon Pentecostal Mission (CPM) in India and Sri Lanka. The name of the denomination in India was changed in 1984 to The Pentecostal Mission probably to avoid any charge of extraterritorial affinity in the light of Tamil-Singhalese problems in Sri Lanka.

The denomination may be the only one of Indian origin that has both spread to different countries and established churches among the native residents. (The Indian Pentecostal Church of God, whose origins parallel this movement, is also worldwide, but its membership is limited to the Indian diaspora.) The Pentecostal

Mission has centers/branches in Malaysia, Singapore, France, the United Kingdom, the United States, Canada, the West Indies (Puerto Rico, Dominican Republic), Sierra Leone, Australia, Papua New Guinea, Nepal, Fiji, Mexico, El Salvador, Costa Rica, Kenya, and Switzerland. In each of these countries, it is known by a different name (for example, in the United States it is known as the New Testament Church).

Unlike most of the classical Pentecostal denominations contemporaneous with it, the Mission is very conservative and takes a literal approach to the Bible, which it interprets from a dispensational perspective. The movement strongly advocates an ascetic life for its workers that includes a very strict dress code and strict obedience and submission to the elders. All workers are subject to the authority of the chief pastor.

The international headquarters of the denomination in Chennai (Madras) is also the office of the chief pastor, who is considered to be the "supreme spiritual head of the Mission throughout the world." The chief pastor "nominates a pastor to supervise the Church work in each country who shall carry out his function in consultation with the Chief Pastor." The international annual convention held in Chennai (Madras) draws thousands from all over India and representatives from all over the world.

Paulson Pulikottil

See also: Asceticism; Pentecostalism.

References

Martin, Paul C. "A Brief History of the Ceylon Pentecostal Church." In *Christianity Is Indian: The Emergence of an Indigenous Community,* edited by Roger E. Hedlund, 437–444. Delhi: ISPCK, 2000.

Pastor Paul. Chennai: Pentecostal Press Trust, 1986.

The Pentecostal Mission. *Rules and Regulations of the Church.* Chennai: Pentecostal Press Trust, n.d.

Pentecostal World Fellowship

After World War II many people wished to organize in some collective way the large amount of relief work and assistance being given to the suffering Pentecostal churches of Europe, and to carry out the further rehabilitation work still needed. Added to this were the continuing fight in some countries for full religious freedom for Pentecostal believers and the hope that a worldwide conference could speak and act with more authority and influence with the governments concerned.

In September 1946 it was decided to arrange a world Pentecostal conference in Zurich, Switzerland, from May 6 to 9, 1947. Leonard Steiner, the pastor of the Basel Church, acted as organizing secretary. Several European countries were represented.

Judging by the enthusiasm of the participants, the conference was a great success. Starting on May 5, large public meetings were held each evening in the Zurich city hall, which seated 2,000 and was packed night after night. On May 11, the closing meetings were held in the famous Congress Hall, and the crowd of about 3,000 was augmented by special trainloads of additional participants.

The work of the conference involved several key issues. First, it was agreed to appoint Leonard Steiner as the chairman, and he won quick approval because of his tact and unrivaled knowledge of the three official languages, English, German, and French. He was assisted by Donald Gee (1891–1966), Lewi Pethrus (1884–1974), K. Schneider, and Ernest S. Williams (1885–1981).

The conference was deeply moved by the reports from the needy European countries, but a serious division arose over the best method for helping. The large Scandinavian Pentecostal churches have always steadily opposed any organization beyond that of the local assembly. A compromise was found in recognizing the Basel Church as an international center for coordinating relief work. Leonard Steiner undertook supervision of this work. The Basel office eventually opened on December 1, 1947.

The conference participants also decided to establish a magazine. Donald Gee was asked to do the editing and publication. The first issue of the new world magazine appeared in September 1947 with the name *Pentecost*, which in 1970 became *World Pentecost.* The magazine was discontinued in 1998.

René Fauvel served as host for the second meeting, which met in Paris in 1949. The meeting was held in a building that had an upstairs hall to accommodate the business sessions and a downstairs hall with seating for 2,000 for public revival meetings. A key subject of discussion was the formation of some kind of world Pentecostal organization. The Scandinavians were there in force, and the Northern European bloc emphatically opposed any organizational steps such as a mutual declaration of faith, election of officers, or anything from the tradition of the old denominations. Yet with equal vigor, those from other parts of the world desired such steps.

It was a surprise, then, that when the proposals for organizing were brought forward they were accepted unanimously. These stipulated that a World Pentecostal Conference should be held every three years in different parts of the world. For each Conference, a secretary was to be elected, assisted by five advisors. It was emphasized that the committee should have no authority over individual movements or churches. South African minister David J. du Plessis (1905–1989) was unanimously elected as the first secretary.

At the London meeting of the Conference in 1952, the theme "Into All The World" welcomed, for the first time, participants from Asia and Africa. At the 1955 meeting in Stockholm, under the theme "The Pentecostal Movement: A Revaluation," Lewi Pethrus and the Swedish churches extended this welcome: "All accredited Pentecostal ministers will be members of the Conference by virtue of their personal status. The purposes of the Conference are not legislative but spiritual."

The theme "The Purpose of God in the Pentecostal Movement for This Hour" was used in the 1958 meeting in Toronto, which was hosted by W. E. McAlister. Demos Shakarian (1913–1993), founder of the Full Gospel Business Men's Fellowship International, was among the major speakers. The popular radio show *Revivaltime* was broadcast directly from the Conference by the program's host, C. M. Ward (1909–1996). About 5,000 took part in a breaking of bread service, when Lewi Pethrus gave an address on the work of the Holy Spirit in the church.

Now called the Pentecostal World Conference, the group assembled in Jerusalem over Whitsuntide in 1961. The emphasis three years later in Helsinki was on world evangelization. Meetings were held in a "tent-cathedral" with a seating capacity of 15,000. Speakers were asked to avoid reference to political issues, as it was stressed that the purpose of the Conference was to "Magnify the Lord Jesus Christ." A delicate matter occupying the minds of the leaders of the Pentecostal churches at the time was their relationship with the World Council of Churches (WCC). Two small Pentecostal groups in Chile had been received in the recent WCC meeting in New Delhi, but it was clear that the overwhelming sentiment of those present in Helsinki was against joining the WCC.

The keynote address at the Nairobi meeting in 1982 was brought by conference chair Thomas F. Zimmerman, who cited figures from David Barrett's newly published *World Christian Encyclopedia*. Zimmerman claimed that there were 62 to 100 million Pentecostals in the world, making them the largest single family of churches in world Protestantism. The theme was "Alive in the Spirit in Today's World." Reflecting upon the approaching end of the millennium, speakers offered little hope that the world could be changed before the Second Coming of Christ.

The most controversial message of the week was delivered by James A. Forbes, Jr., professor at New York's Union Theological Seminary, who chided the world Pentecostal movement for its "drift toward pride and institutionalism" while occasionally supporting the "status quo of oppression and exploitation." Forbes called on attendees to be "prophets" and further challenged Pentecostals to be "ecumenical." Forbes's message, though warmly applauded by the crowd, received a frosty reception from the platform.

Subsequent meetings have been held in Zürich (1985), Singapore (1989), Oslo (1992), Jerusalem (1995), and Seoul (1998). Zimmerman chaired the Conference until 1989, when he was succeeded by Ray H. Hughes, who in turn was succeeded by Thomas Trask in 1998. A theology program track emerged at the 1995 gathering, which was augmented by a more substantive academic track during the sessions in 1998, hosted by the Yoido Full Gospel Church in Seoul, Korea, reportedly the largest Christian congregation in the world. The 2001 Conference, planned as a celebration of the Pentecostal centennial, was hosted by

Frederick K. C. Price at the Crenshaw Christian Center in Los Angeles, the site of the revival that launched Pentecostalism as a world movement. Most recently the Pentecostal World Conference changed its name to Pentecostal World Fellowship.

Pentecostal World Fellowship
1445 Boonville Ave.
Springfield, MO 65804
http://www.pentecostalworldfellowship.org

Harold D. Hunter

See also: Pentecostalism; World Council of Churches.

References

Gee, Donald. *Wind and Flame*. Croydon, UK: Heath Press, 1967.

Robeck, Cecil M. "Pentecostal World Conference." In *Dictionary of Pentecostal and Charismatic Movements*, edited by Stanley M. Burgess and Gary B. McGee, 707–710. Grand Rapids, MI: Zondervan Publishing House, 1988.

Pentecostalism

The Pentecostal movement developed at the beginning of the 20th century, initially as a revitalization movement with the Holiness churches in the United States. The Holiness churches had placed a great emphasis upon the doctrine of perfection as derived from the teachings of John Wesley (1703–1791), the founder of Methodism. This doctrine teaches that it is possible for Christian believers to be made perfect in love by an act of God, often described as the baptism of the Holy Spirit. However, within the Holiness churches the living of the holy life and perfection in love were primarily the keeping of a strict set of moral and behavioral codes. Many complained that the Holiness movement had fallen into legalism.

The first event of importance in the founding of the Pentecostal movement occurred at a Bible school in Topeka, Kansas, under the direction of former Methodist minister Charles F. Parham (1873–1929). After assigning his students to research the baptism of the Holy Spirit in the New Testament, Parham accepted their findings: that the baptism of the Holy Spirit was always accompanied by the experience of speaking in an unknown tongue. He then led his students in prayer for such an experience, and speaking in tongues began to be experienced on January 1, 1901. Agnes Ozman (1870–1937) was the first to speak in tongues, but eventually Parham and the others also received the baptism.

Parham began to preach about the baptism of the Holy Spirit through the south-central states. Then in 1906, one of his students, an African American preacher named William J. Seymour (1870–1922), took the teachings to Los Angeles, where a revival took place at an independent mission on Azusa Street. From this mission, the Pentecostal movement would spread across North America, and within a decade it was found around the world.

The original Pentecostal teachings built directly upon Holiness teachings. Pentecostalism offered to Holiness believers—who had already experienced sanctification as a second work of God's grace (their initial experience of faith in Christ being considered the first experience)—the baptism of the Holy Spirit and the accompanying experience of speaking in tongues as a third experience with God. Among Holiness Pentecostals, the experience of Holiness was considered a prerequisite for experiencing the baptism of the Holy Spirit. This understanding continues among such groups as the Church of God (Cleveland, Tennessee), the Church of God in Christ, and the International Pentecostal Holiness Church.

Soon after the Pentecostal teachings emerged, a group of ministers dissented from the Holiness teachings and declared that the baptism of the Holy Spirit was available to every believer quite apart from the experience of sanctification. This perspective occasioned a split in the movement and resulted in new groups such as the Assemblies of God.

Several years later, still another dissenting opinion was developed by ministers who rejected the orthodox understanding of the Christian doctrine of the Trinity. They placed a renewed emphasis on the Oneness of God and baptism in the name of Jesus, rather than in the name of the Father, Son, and Holy Spirit, which most churches follow. The Oneness or Apostolic churches

A Nigerian man worships in a Pentecostal church in Port Harcourt, Nigeria. (Chris Hondros/Getty Images)

are represented by such groups as the United Pentecostal Church International, and the Pentecostal Assemblies of the World.

The Pentecostal movement would find notable response in Scandinavia, Africa, and Latin America, where numerous independent Pentecostal churches would emerge. The Danish, Finnish, Norwegian, and Swedish Pentecostals would come to form the largest segment of Christians in those countries, apart from the state churches. In Africa, the Zionist and Apostolic churches would take the lead in the spread of Pentecostalism from South Africa north to the Sahara. Mexican believers at the Azusa Street mission would take the movement to Mexico and Central America. In the last half of the 20th century, Pentecostalism would become the major movement contesting the hegemony of Roman Catholicism across South America.

Pentecostals have found some international fellowship through the Pentecostal World Conference. The largest Christian congregation in the world is the Yoido Full Gospel Church, a Pentecostal church in Seoul, South Korea. New life was given to Pentecostalism in the last decades of the 20th century by the Charismatic movement.

J. Gordon Melton

See also: Assemblies of God; Charismatic Movement; Church of God (Cleveland, Tennessee); Church of God in Christ; International Pentecostal Holiness Church; Methodism; Parham, Charles Fox; Pentecostal Assemblies of the World; Pentecostal World Fellowship; United Pentecostal Church International; Wesley, John; Yoido Full Gospel Church; Zionist and Apostolic Churches.

References

Anderson, Allan. *An Introduction to Pentecostalism*. Cambridge: Cambridge University Press, 2004.

Burgess, Stanley M., and Eduard M. van der Maas, eds. *The New International Dictionary of Pentecostal and Charismatic Movements*. Grand Rapids, MI: Zondervan, 2002.

Hollenweger, Walter J. *Pentecostalism: Origins and Developments Worldwide*. Eugene, OR: Hendrickson Publishers, 1997.
Hunter, Harold D. *Spirit Baptism: A Pentecostal Alternative*. Washington, DC: University Press of America, 1983.
Kalu, Ogbu. *African Pentecostalism: An Introduction*. New York: Oxford University Press, 2008.
Martin, David. *Pentecostalism: The World Their Parish*. New York: Wiley-Blackwell, 2008.
Miller, Donald E., and Tetsunao Yamamori. *Global Pentecostalism: The New Face of Christian Social Engagement*. Berkeley: University of California Press, 2007.
Studebaker, Stephen M. *Defining Issues in Pentecostalism: Classical and Emergent*. Eugene, OR: Pickwick Publications, 2008.
Synon, Vinson. *The Century of the Holy Spirit: 100 Years of Pentecostal and Charismatic Renewal, 1901–2001*. Nashville: Thomas Nelson, 2001.

Pentecostalism in Scandinavia

Pentecostalism, a Christian movement that emerged in the United States at the beginning of the 20th century, spread around the globe in its first decade and through the century became an important force within the larger Christian community. It was carried to Scandinavia in 1907, and its new home became an important launching point for its development not only throughout Europe, but in both Africa and Latin America.

In 1906 Thomas B. Barrett (1862–1940), a prominent minister in the Methodist Episcopal Church (now a constituent part of the United Methodist Church) in Norway, visited the United States, where he came in contact with the burgeoning Pentecostal revival that had begun in Los Angeles. When he returned to Oslo, he became the voice of the revival there and of its keynote experience, the baptism of the Holy Spirit as evidenced by speaking in tongues. Barrett operated as an independent evangelist for the next decade, before formally resigning from the Methodist Church and founding the Filadelfia Church in Oslo.

In 1907 a youthful pastor from Stockholm, Sweden, Petrus Lewi Pethrus (1884–1974), traveled to Oslo to meet Barrett. He experienced the baptism of the Holy Spirit and returned home to share the experience with the Baptist church he pastored. His church eventually accepted the new teachings, and from Stockholm the movement spread to other churches in Sweden. However, the Baptist Convention expelled Pethrus and the congregation in 1913, though the reason was ostensibly their practice of open Communion rather than Pentecostalism.

Pethrus's congregation, also called the Filadelfia Church, would be the largest Pentecostal church in the world until it was overtaken by several in the Third World, such as the Yoido Full Gospel Church in South Korea. Pethrus founded a number of publishing ventures and a Bible school, and he went on to become the most prominent Pentecostal leader in northern Europe. His Filadelfia Church became the center of the Pentecostal Revival movement (Pingstväckelsen), now the third largest religious group in Sweden. It commissioned missionaries who carried Pentecostalism to Africa and Latin America, where many churches developed under the name Assemblies of God (often confused with the American body of the same name). The Swedish Pentecostal assemblies have, like their American counterpart, evolved as a congregationally governed body.

Pentecostalism spread to Denmark as the result of the efforts of a prominent Danish actress, Anna Larssen (1879–1955). In 1908 she went to Oslo and under Barrett's preaching received the baptism of the Holy Spirit. Upon her return to Copenhagen, she began to hold Pentecostal meetings in her large home. She gave up her acting career in 1909 and in 1919 married Sigurd Bjorner, at the time the general secretary of the Danish YMCA. They traveled the country as evangelists, and congregations began to emerge out of their efforts. Then in 1919, while in Sweden, the couple submitted to rebaptism, which led to their exclusion from the Church of Denmark. In 1923 they brought the association of churches that they had raised up into fellowship with the Apostolic Church, headquartered in England. They broke relations with the Apostolic Church in the 1930s, and the fellowship continued as the Pentecostal movement in Denmark (Pinsebevaegelsen).

Pentecostalism would spread to Finland within a few years, and the original groups, called the Pentecostal Revival of Finland (Helluntal Ystvät), were founded in 1911. Finnish Pentecostalism has become distinguished by the large number of missionaries it has commissioned and the exemplary role of women, with more than 600 serving as evangelists. The Finnish annual summer gatherings are year by year the largest Pentecostal events in Scandinavia.

Thomas Barrett introduced Pentecostalism to Iceland in 1920, and additional Swedish and Norwegian evangelists targeted the island through the remainder of the decade. What would become the largest congregation in the country, the Filadefia Church, was founded in 1936 and has about 600 members. The Pentecostal movement is now the third largest religious group in Iceland.

Besides bringing Pentecostalism to Scandinavia, Thomas Barrett also influenced its emergence in other European countries. Among those who came to Oslo to meet Barrett was Alexander A. Boddy (1854–1930), a British Anglican priest who had been active in the Welsh Revival of 1904. After his 1907 visit, Boddy brought the Pentecostal experience to the United Kingdom and was later active in the formation of the Pentecostal Missionary Union, the first Pentecostal organization in the country. About the same time, two Norwegian women who had become Pentecostals traveled to Kassel, Germany, where they held meetings for the evangelical (Lutheran) congregation headed by Heinrich Dallmeyer. These meetings were widely reported in the press. Dallmeyer at first supported the revival that broke out but later renounced it. In spite of condemnation by Dallmeyer and other evangelical leaders, the revival spread and eventually led to the formation of a spectrum of German Pentecostal groups such as the Mülheim Association of Christian Fellowships.

Barrett stands out as the fountainhead of the Pentecostal World Conference. In 1911 he wrote "An Urgent Call for Charity and Unity," in which he sought a manifestation of the unity of the spreading Pentecostal movement. This call would lead to initial attempts at international fellowship gatherings that culminated in the European Pentecostal Conference held in Stockholm in 1939, on the eve of World War II. The effort led to the holding of the triennial gatherings of the World Pentecostal Conference, beginning in 1946. Scandinavian countries have regularly taken their turn in hosting the Conference.

J. Gordon Melton

See also: Apostolic Church; Mülheim Association of Christian Fellowships; Pentecostal World Fellowship; Pentecostalism; United Methodist Church.

References

Bloch-Hoell, Nils. *The Pentecostal Movement*. Oslo: Oslo University Press, 1964.

Bundy, David D. "Thomas B. Barrett and *Byposten*: An Early Pentecostal Leader and His Periodical." In *Pentecost, Mission and Ecumenism: Essays on Intercultural Theology,* edited by Jan A. B. Jongeneel, 115–122. Frankfurt am Main: Peter Lang, 1992.

Burgess, Stanley M., and Eduard M. van der Maas, eds. *The New International Dictionary of Pentecostal and Charismatic Movements*. Grand Rapids, MI: Zondervan, 2002.

Elbert, Paul, ed. *Essays on Apostolic Themes.* Peabody, MA: Hendrickson Publishers, 1985.

Hollenweger, Walter J. *Pentecostalism: Origins and Developments Worldwide.* Peabody, UK: Hendrickson, 1997.

Lindberg, Alf. "The Swedish Pentecostal Movement: Some Ideological Features." *European Pentecostal Theological Association Journal* 6, no. 2 (1987): 40–45.

Matre, Frank. "A Synopsis of Norwegian Pentecostal History." *European Pentecostal Theological Association Journal* 9, nos. 2–3 (1990): 53–62.

Synan, Vinson. *The Century of the Holy Spirit: 100 Years of Pentecostal and Charismatic Renewal.* Nashville: Thomas Nelson, 2001.

People of God

The People of God is an indigenous (and somewhat idiosyncratic) form of Pentecostalism born in Paraguay and now present in several countries. Leonor Paredes ("Brother José," 1898–1970) was born in Villarica, Paraguay, in 1898. He received the baptism of the Holy Spirit in 1940 and moved to Argentina, where he worked for 20 years as an independent Pentecostal preacher. Following a prophetic warning, in 1963 he returned to Paraguay, where he established the People of God (Pueblo de Dios) community in Repatriación, a village located some 150 miles from the capital city, Asunción. Initially, the community comprised 22 families. Brother José died in 1970; his successor as leading elder was Mariano Bobadilla ("Brother Luke," 1915–1991), who had converted following a miraculous cure attributed to Brother José's "key of prayer" in Laguna Blanca, Argentina, in 1946.

Brother Luke's administration fell during a difficult time for Paraguay, then ruled by dictator General Alfredo Stroessner (1912–2006). The regime regarded the People of God as a "cult," potentially "Communist" due to its communal structure. Persecution followed, and several leaders, including Brother Luke, were arrested. The group managed to survive, thanks particularly to Carlos Marcial Russo Cantero, a distinguished law professor at the National University in Asunción, lawyer, and politician who not only successfully represented Brother Luke and other leaders in court but was eventually so impressed by their message that he too converted to the People of God. He joined its Santo Domingo Libertador congregation in Lambaré (near Asunción), the largest in the country after the Central Congregation in Repatriación. It was in this same community of Lambaré that Brother Luke died in 1991.

His successor was Severiano Estigarribia ("Brother Elias," 1931–1995), who managed to obtain legal recognition for the community in Paraguay according to Presidential Decree No. 14336 of July 28, 1992. Brother Elias died unexpectedly in 1995, and Andrés Fretes ("Brother Juan," b. 1941) was recognized as leading elder in his place. Fretes had been a successful missionary to Brazil, which, together with Argentina, Uruguay, Colombia, and Italy, was the main missionary field for the People of God. In 1996 he supervised the establishment of COPROSA (Cooperativa Multiactiva de Producción, Servicios Públicos, Consumo, Ahorros y Crédito San Andres, Ltda.), a cooperative enterprise that oversees most economic activities of the People of God.

The People of God's theology is basically Pentecostal, although with some distinctive features. More than the insistence on demons and demonization (not uncommon in contemporary Pentecostalism), what is unique to the People of God is the practice of celibacy by a number of its members, although by no means all. The People of God emphasizes miracles, prophecy, the prophetic value of dreams, and the charismatic mission of Brother José and his successors. An important practice is the "key of prayer," whereby a prayer is repeated seven times while kneeling, followed by a spiritual conversation with God.

The daily life of the some 5,000 church members living in Repatriación's Central Congregation includes communal singing, prayer, and work within a strict and rather austere lifestyle, often denounced by critics as "cultic." The work is mostly agricultural; the congregation grows cotton, corn, sunflowers, and soy beans. The Central Congregation includes schools, from kindergarten to high school, artistic and cultural centers, hospitals, and sports facilities. The leading elder (also called the leading apostle) oversees a hierarchy including 12 elder apostles and 12 lesser apostles; "messengers," or itinerant teachers, are also sent to the congregations in Paraguay and abroad.

People of God
2a Linea
Irrazabal Norte
Repatriación, Caaguazú
Paraguay
http://congregacionpueblodedios.blogspot.com/

Massimo Introvigne and PierLuigi Zoccatelli

See also: Pentecostalism.

Reference

Cardozo Vera, Juan Diosnel. *La Verdad sobre el Pueblo de Dios: Su historia, organización y doctrina*. Asunción: Pueblo de Dios, 1999.

Peoples Temple

Peoples Temple was a multiracial utopian group that began in Indiana in the 1950s, flourished in California

Portrait of Jim Jones, charismatic leader of the Peoples Temple, a religious community he founded in 1960 in Indianapolis, Indiana. Facing intense controversy, Jones moved the group to a colony in Guyana, South America in 1977 and a year later the community committed mass suicide under his direction. (AP Photo)

in the early 1970s, and developed an agricultural project called Jonestown in Guyana, South America. Espousing a doctrine of "apostolic socialism," the inter-racial group sought to create an integrated society of justice and equality. It is most known for the 1978 assassination of a California congressman and three reporters on a jungle airstrip, and the murders and suicides of more than 900 persons by ingesting poison-laced fruit punch in their jungle commune.

Led by a charismatic preacher, James "Jim" Warren Jones (1931–1978), Peoples Temple was originally incorporated in 1955 as Wings of Deliverance in Indianapolis, Indiana. An active social outreach ministry and an integrationist message attracted a large interracial congregation. A vision of nuclear holocaust prompted Jones to move his family to Brazil in the early 1960s and then to relocate the congregation to northern California in 1965. About 80 members followed Jones to Redwood Valley, where they ran homes for youth with mental disabilities, convalescent centers, and senior care facilities. From there the group evangelized the urban poor in San Francisco, opening a church in the heart of the black ghetto in 1972 and starting a third branch in Los Angeles the same year. The group officially joined the Disciples of Christ (Christian Church) in 1960, and by 1978 it was the largest congregational contributor in the denomination. At its height, the temple claimed to have 20,000 members, but 5,000 is a more realistic estimate. Although Jones preached a social gospel message in a dynamic Pentecostal style that attracted black churchgoers, a small cadre of young white leaders adopted a socialistic philosophy of egalitarianism and communalism.

In 1976 Peoples Temple signed a lease with the government of Guyana, a former British colony on the north coast of South America, to develop 3,852 acres of jungle in the interior. A small group of pioneers had already begun clearing land in 1974 in Guyana's Northwest District, close to the Venezuelan border. Throughout 1977, large numbers of Peoples Temple members emigrated from the United States and resettled in the Peoples Temple Agricultural Project, which soon became known as Jonestown. The project boasted a school, a library, a furniture-making facility, and a basketball court, as well as a large farm and quarters for livestock. Despite the intensive investment of human labor and financial capital, however, the group was unable to become self-sufficient, and by 1978 it was importing rice and other food to supplement what it produced.

As the church grew in membership and influence in the 1970s, controversies began to grow along with it. Former members described all-night sessions of confession and punishment (called catharsis); gave accounts of phony faith healings and financial misdealing; and claimed that voter fraud, extortion, and even murder had occurred. Opposition to the temple was organized by a group of former members and relatives of members called the Concerned Relatives. This group focused its efforts on a custody battle over John Victor Stoen, the son of Grace Stoen and the presumptive son of Jim Jones, who was living in Jonestown. Throughout 1976, 1977, and 1978, the Concerned Relatives contacted state and federal government agencies, the news media, lawyers, and members of Congress with their fears about what was happening to relatives in Peoples Temple and in Jonestown. The most dramatic report came from former member Deborah Layton (Blakey) in June 1978, who said that residents of Jonestown were conducting suicide drills and planned to die in a collective ritual.

Layton's report prompted the visit of Congressman Leo J. Ryan to Jonestown in November 1978. Accompanied by news reporters and members of the Concerned Relatives, the congressman left Jonestown on November 18 with a generally favorable impression of the community. As he and a group of 15 defectors from Jonestown were preparing to depart from a nearby airstrip, however, a group of Jonestown residents opened fire, killing Ryan, 3 members of the media, and one defector. Back in Jonestown, Jones had assembled the community and, according to a tape made at the time, exhorted his followers to drink a mixture of cyanide, tranquilizers, and fruit punch. Although the tape reveals some opposition to the plan, there was a general consensus to go forward with the "revolutionary suicide," which would send the message that people would rather die than live in a capitalistic system. In all, 918 people died on November 18, 1978: 5 people at the airstrip, 909 in Jonestown, and 4 in Georgetown, Guyana, where a mother killed her 3 children and herself.

Questions remain about the deaths, including the extent to which coercion was involved and whether U.S. officials provoked the incident. A body of conspiracy theories has arisen to explain various gaps and discrepancies in the official story. The release of currently classified government documents may answer some questions, but the ultimate mystery will remain: How could people be persuaded to kill their parents and their children?

Rebecca Moore

See also: Christian Church (Disciples of Christ).

References

"Alternative Considerations of Jonestown and Peoples Temple." Website sponsored by the Religious Studies Department at San Diego State University. http://jonestown.sdsu.edu/. Accessed January 15, 2009.

Hall, John R. *Gone from the Promised Land: Jonestown in American Cultural History*. New Brunswick, NJ: Transaction Books, 1987, 2004.

Moore, Rebecca. *Understanding Jonestown and Peoples Temple*. Westport, CT: Praeger, 2009.

Reiterman, Tim, with John Jacobs. *Raven: The Untold Story of The Rev. Jim Jones and His People*. New York: Dutton, 1982, 2008.

Stephenson, Denice. *Dear People: Remembering Jonestown*. San Francisco and Berkeley: California Historical Society and Heyday Books, 2005.

Perennialism

Perennialism is a historically self-conscious perspective that emerged among modern exponents of Western Esoteric thought. It is most identified with thinkers from the Traditionalist school of thought, such as René Guenon (1886–1951), Frithjof Schuon (1907–1998), Julius (Giulio) Evola (1898–1974), and Seyyed Hosseyn Nasr (b. 1933).

The perennial philosophy emerged during the Renaissance period, although there is evidence that the thoughts associated with the philosophy existed prior to this period. The term "philosophia perennis" was first used in the work of Augustinus Steuchius (1497–1548), a theologian and librarian of the Vatican, by Gottfried Leibniz (1646–1716), a German mathematician and philosopher. The coining of the term "perennial philosophy," however, is often attributed to Leibniz, as he was the first to use the term to connote a universal set of underlying truths common to all religions and the mystical elements associated with them. The term has since surfaced among various schools of thought. Scholasticism, a form of Christian philosophy and theology that flourished during the medieval period of European history, experienced a revival in the 16th century after a period of dormancy following the Middle Ages. Proponents of Scholasticism asserted a system founded on the notion of the perennial philosophy that attempted to integrate ideas from classical Roman and Greek writings, Christian scripture, and the writings of the patristic fathers preceding the medieval period. Aristotle's and Plato's views were also important in the formation of the system of the Scholastics.

The Traditionalists, initiated by René Guenon (1886–1951), also ascribe to philosophy of perennialism. The Traditionalists, however, assert that only the major world religious traditions are pathways to attaining an understanding of the transcendent source of reality. It is only through these religions that unity with the transcendent source may be achieved. Further, the Traditionalists believe that it is not the external structure and dogmatism of the religions that enable unity with the transcendent source. Rather, they believe that it is the inner mystical core of the major religions that rare individuals are able to acknowledge and comprehend that enables this unity. The Traditionalists assert that while there are many religions, only the major traditions contain all of the necessary elements to attain unity with the transcendent source while many new religious movements lead away from the transcendent source. The notion that there are many paths that lead to the summit of a mountain is an analogy used to describe the major religions as paths to the transcendent source. Religions that do not contain the necessary elements to reach the summit are envisioned by the Traditionalists as leading followers around and around the base of the mountain in circles. Thus, the Traditionalists believe in an elitist hierarchical system that designates the ability to achieve this unity.

The central tenets upon which the perennial philosophy rests require the ability to acknowledge a force, a transcendent source, beyond our human presence. The major world religions vary in their approaches in acknowledging this transcendent source. In the Abrahamic religions (Judaism, Christianity, and Islam) the transcendent source is called God. Religions such as Buddhism and Daoism portray the transcendent source quite differently, as they are non-theistic. Hinduism encompasses a variety of deities depicting various aspects of the transcendent source.

The tenets central to perennialism are based on the notion that there are universal truths that most religions are founded upon. Proponents of the perennial philosophy posit that our understandings of reality, the world, and the meaning and purpose of existence reveal commonalities across cultures and time, despite cultural and social variations of the presentation and perceptions of these truths. These truths are believed to be revealed by a transcendent source of Reality that we will never fully be able to know. The social and cultural variations of each religion are believed to reflect the many variations of the elements of the transcendent source and our different perceptions of this source. The world and our understanding of the world are only partial reflections of the transcendent source. Proponents of perennialism believe that all humans have the capacity to intuit the transcendent source, excluding the Traditionalists who believe this ability is available only to an elite few. While perennialists believe the fullness of reality and the transcendent source to be incomprehensible to humankind, cultivating our understanding of reality, the world, and achieving unity with the transcendent source is believed to be the ultimate purpose of our existence.

Wendy Mason

See also: Buddhism; Evola, Giulio; Hinduism; Western Esoteric Tradition.

References

Guenon, René. *The Crisis of the Modern World.* Hillsdale, NY: Sophia Perennis, 2004.

Huxley, Aldous. *The Perennial Philosophy*. New York: Harper and Row, 1945.

Lings, Martin, and Clinton Minaar. *The Underlying Religion: An Introduction to the Perennial Philosophy*. World Wisdom, 2007.

Nasr, Seyyed Hosseyn. *Religion and the Order of Nature*. London: Oxford University Press, 1996.

Schuon, Frithjof. *The Transcendent Unity of Religions.* Rev. ed. Wheaton, IL: Theosophical Publishing House, 1993.

Smith, Huston. *The World's Religions: Our Great Wisdom Traditions*. HarperOne. 1991.

Toynton, G. *Primordial Traditions Compendium 2009*. Oxford: Twin Serpents Ltd., 2009.

Perfect Liberty Kyodan

Perfect Liberty Kyodan was founded in Japan in 1946, although its teachings reach back to 1912, when Tokumitsu Kanada (1863–1919) founded Shinto Tokumitsu-Ko (the Divine Way), drawing on elements from both Shinto and Shingon Buddhism. He incorporated an emphasis on art and nature as well as a healing ritual called Ofurikae (the power of temporarily curing illness). Among those who received the benefits of this healing work was Miki Tokuharu (1871–1938), who joined Kanada's movement and became a fervent disciple.

In the period immediately prior to his death in the early 1920s, Kanada urged Tokuharu to pray that the remaining precepts of the religion be revealed to him, and after receiving the revelation, to found a new organization that incorporated them. Tokuharu followed his teacher's urging and in 1924 founded Tokumitsu Kyokai (in 1931 changing the name to Hitonomichi Kyokai).

In 1937, as World War II began, the Japanese government ordered Tokuharu to disband his religion, which conflicted with official Shinto beliefs at several points. Shortly thereafter, both Tokuharu and his son Miki Tokuchita (1900–1983) were arrested. Upon their release they revived and reorganized the religion under the name of Perfect Liberty Kyodan, or Church of Perfect Liberty. Observers have noticed that of all the new Japanese religions to emerge after World War II, only this one chose to be known by an English name.

The basic perspective of the church is simple. It advises members to create a way of living that embodies the precept "life is art." The accomplishment of this way of living is a state of "perfect liberty," or total mental freedom. Such a life is characterized by creativity, balance, and aesthetic expression on both a personal and a social level. The way to freedom is summarized in the Twenty-One Precepts and Twenty-One Principles received by Kanada and Tokuharu. The artistic life finds expression in the *asamairi*, a morning service in which the pledge to the artistic life is renewed. August 1, Founder's Day, is the church's major annual holiday, celebrated with massive displays of art in its various forms.

Perfect Liberty headquarters are located in Osaka, Japan. Nearby in the Habikino Hills is the 590-foot Perfect Liberty Peace Tower, memorializing those who have died as a result of war. The movement reports some 500 centers and 1 million members in Japan. Churches are also found in the United States, Canada, Brazil, Paraguay, Argentina, Peru, France, and Australia. By far the largest overseas community (350,000) is found in Brazil.

Perfect Liberty Kyodan
2172-1 Shindou
Tondabayashi, Osaka 584-8651
Japan
http://web.perfect-liberty.or.jp/

J. Gordon Melton

References

Bach, Marcus. *The Power of Perfect Liberty*. Englewood Cliffs, NJ: Prentice-Hall, 1971.

Clarke, Peter. *A Bibliography of Japanese New Religious Movements with Annotations and an Introduction to Japanese New Religions at Home and Abroad*. Richmond, Surrey, UK: Japan Library, 1999.

Perfect Liberty: Guide to Perfect Liberty. Glendale, CA: PL North American Headquarters, 1975.

■ Peru

Peru is located in western South America, bordered by the Pacific Ocean to the west, Chile to the south, Ecuador to the north, and Colombia, Brazil, and Bolivia to the east. The former home of the pre-Columbian Inca Empire, modern Peru includes 494,000 square miles of territory. The country has a varied geography divided by the Andean highlands in the center, the dry western coastal lowlands, and the eastern tropical lowlands, which are headwaters of the Amazon River. The total population of Peru (2007 census) was 29 million, making it the fourth most populous country in South America.

Racially, the population was classified as 45 percent Amerindian, 37 percent *mestizo* (mixed Amerindian and European), 15 percent white, and 3 percent black, Japanese, Chinese, and other races. Peru's official languages are Spanish and, according to the Peruvian Constitution of 1993, the various Amerindian languages (such as Quechua, Aymara, and others) in areas where they are dominant. Spanish is spoken as the first language of 83.9 percent of Peruvians (over age 5) and Quechua is spoken by 13.2 percent of the population, followed by Aymara. Ninety-two languages are spoken in Peru, and in the Amazonian region alone there are 16 ethnolinguistic families and more than 65 distinct ethnic groups.

Peru is a multi-ethnic nation formed by a combination of different groups during the last five centuries. The Amerindian population decreased from an estimated 9 million in the 1520s to around 600,000 in 1620 due to warfare and infectious diseases. During Spanish colonial rule, Spaniards intermarried with Amerindian and African women, which produced new generations of mestizo and mulatto children. After independence on July 15, 1821, there was gradual immigration to Venezuela from England, France, Germany, Italy, and Spain, followed by Chinese contract-laborers beginning in the 1850s and Japanese farmers in the 1890s. The Chinese and Japanese minorities have become a major influence in Peruvian society.

The 1993 Constitution provides for freedom of religion, and other laws and policies contributed to the generally free practice of religion. The law at all levels protects this right in full against abuse, by either governmental or private actors.

Article 50 of the 1993 Constitution establishes separation of church and state but recognizes the Catholic Church's role as "an important element in the historical, cultural, and moral development of the nation." The government acts independently of Catholic Church policy; however, it maintains a close relationship with the Catholic Church, and an agreement signed with the Vatican in 1980 grants the Catholic Church special status.

According to the 2007 Peruvian national census, religious affiliation was determined to be Roman Catholic 81.3 percent, Protestant-evangelical 12.5 percent, other religions 3.3 percent, and unspecified or none 2.9 percent. By comparison, the 1993 census reported the following: Roman Catholic 89.0 percent; Protestant-evangelical 6.7 percent; other religions 2.8 percent; and unspecified or none 1.4 percent. The decline in Roman Catholic adherents by 7.7 percent, and the increase in Protestant-evangelical adherents by 5.8 percent, is a significant shift in religious affiliation; the number of Protestant adherents increased by 87 percent in 14 years.

The land now demarked as the nation of Peru has been inhabited for several millennia by various peoples; however, in the 12th century CE, a new empire arose out of the Peruvian highlands around Cuzco and began a process of unifying the inhabitants not only of Peru but also of neighboring regions in the Andes Mountains to the north (Ecuador and Colombia) and the south (Bolivia, Chile and Argentina). Similarities still shared by the Amerindian peoples of Peru are in part accounted for by the dominance of the Incan culture until the arrival of the Spanish Conquistadors in 1524.

When Francisco Pizarro (ca. 1475–1541) and his small army (just 180 men and 37 horses) reached Cajamarca, the capital of the Inca Empire located in the northern highlands, the Incas were in the midst of a leadership dispute, a fact that Pizarro utilized quickly to conquer the Incas during 1532–1537.

The Spanish Viceroyalty of Peru was established in 1542, but it took the next two centuries to completely pacify the lands due to Amerindian resistance. During the height of its importance, the Spanish Viceroyalty of Peru included much of South America apart from Brazil. It would be restructured by the creation of the Viceroyalty of New Granada (1717) in Bogotá (with jurisdiction over modern Panama, Colombia, Ecuador, and Venezuela) and the Viceroyalty of Rio de la Plata (1776) at Buenos Aires (with jurisdiction over present-day Argentina, Bolivia, Paraguay, and Uruguay). For nearly three centuries, Peru was ruled by viceroys, representatives of the king of Spain, who were vested with almost absolute power (including being the vice patron of the Catholic Church).

A parallel cultural development began in Peru as a result of the confrontation between the Spanish and the Amerindian inhabitants. The Inca language and cosmology were important elements of the Amerindian civilization in Peru when the Quechuas and other ethnolinguistic groups resisted colonization and Christianization by the Spaniards. The Quechua cultural strategy for survival in the aftermath of the Spanish conquest was based on adaptation, resistance, and exchange; it also led to the internal development of Quechua self-identity. In this process Spanish-European elements were incorporated into Quechua culture.

K'achampa dancers performing in the Fiesta Pentecostes in the Inca village of Ollantaytambo (Sacred Valley), Peru. (Rfoxphoto/Dreamstime.com)

The parallel development of Hispanic culture and society in Peru was initiated by the Spanish colonial government, which established its headquarters in Lima on the Pacific Coast, not in Cuzco in the central highlands in southern Peru where the capital of the Inca Empire was located. Citizens of Spanish descent (the colonizers) were considered to be members of the Spanish nation, while the population of Amerindian descent was considered part of the (colonized) indigenous nation. The members of these separate "nations" had different obligations to the Spanish Crown.

The country's first accurate census (1791) showed the impact of Hispanic dominance over the Amerindians: the total population had declined to slightly more than 1 million, including Europeans, people of mixed ancestry (mestizos and mulattos), and black slaves. After independence in 1821, the nation's population gradually increased, mainly as a result of high birth rates. By the mid-1960s, the population of Peru was about the same as at the height of the Incan civilization—in other words, it took more than 300 years to replace the population lost in the first century of Spanish domination.

The institution of slavery began in Peru in 1524. During the course of the slave trade, approximately 95,000 Africans were brought to Peru, with the last group arriving in 1850. Slaves were purchased in Panama or Colombia and transported to Peru.

The ruling Spanish and *criollo* (Peruvian-born of pure Spanish ancestry) elite resisted any changes that would affect their economic and political situation negatively, and only after Simón Bolívar (1783–1830) and José de San Martín (1778–1850) combined their armies (composed of Chileans, Argentines, and various soldiers of fortune) and marched on the country in 1824 were the Spanish colonial authorities driven out.

During 1810–1824, Peru achieved independence and created a new republican nation in which, at a theoretical level, the separate nations of Spanish and Amerindian would become integrated. In reality, the division between these two "nations" was maintained, but within a new social and political order. The population of Indians, mestizos, and descendants of African slaves constituted the marginalized sectors of Peruvian society, while the white Spanish population enjoyed all the privileges of higher status. At the same time, the several Constitutions adopted by Peru between 1824 and 1911 recognized Roman Catholicism as the official religion with the exclusion of any other.

The modern state of Peru was largely the product of Ramón Castilla y Marquesado (r. 1844–1863), the four-time president of Peru. Castilla's second presidency was marked by the liberation of slaves and indigenous Peruvians, a new postal system, and a new Constitution (1860), which concentrated power in the hands of the president.

The Peruvian census of 1876 estimated the total number of inhabitants at 2,676,000. In 1906, it was estimated that the population had increased to 3,547,829. Of this total, 50 percent were Amerindians; 15 percent were whites, mostly Spanish descendants; 3 percent were black; 1 percent was Chinese and Japanese; and the remaining 31 percent were the offspring of different races (mestizos and mulattos).

The War of the Pacific (aka the Saltpeter War, 1879–1884), an armed conflict between Chile and the joint forces of Bolivia and Peru, centered on controlling substantial mineral-rich deposits in the Atacama Desert. Chile's victory led to the annexation of the Peruvian territories of Tarapaca and Arica, and Bolivia became a landlocked country. The price of recovery for Peru was an influx of British financial investment and control.

After World War II (1939–1945), Peru's mineral industry blossomed under the Mining Code of 1950, due primarily to sizable foreign investments, but also due to the development of the local medium-sized mining industry. Extensive exploration led to the discovery and development of many ore deposits. However, Peru's mining development slowed drastically after 1968 as a consequence of the nationalization of foreign enterprises, more restrictive mining regulations, and the emergence of terrorism against foreign-owned companies.

The development of democratic government in Peru has been thwarted by the military on several occasions. The return to civilian government in 1978 was followed by regular democratic elections through 1990. However, President Alberto Ken'ya Fujimori (1990–2000), a Japanese Peruvian (b. 1938 in Lima) elected in 1990, abolished Congress in 1992, in what was termed a "self-coup," while announcing that he would return to more democratic rule after the country's economic conditions improved. During Fujimori's first term in office, more leftist parties remained in control of both chambers of Congress, which hampered his ability to enact economic reforms and became an obstacle to combating the Maoist guerrilla organization Shining Path (Sendero Luminoso). In April 1992, President Fujimori, with the support of the Peruvian military, carried out a presidential coup, called a *Fujigolpe*. He shut down Congress, suspended the Constitution, and purged the judiciary of his opponents. Not only was the coup itself marked by favorable public opinion in several independent polls, but also public approval of the Fujimori administration jumped significantly in the wake of the self-coup. On April 7, 2009, he was convicted of human rights violations and sentenced to 25 years in prison by a three-judge panel. On July 20, 2009, a Peruvian court sentenced him to an additional 7 years for embezzlement.

The Roman Catholic Church The Spanish introduced Catholicism to Peru when they arrived in the 1520s. The initial diocese was erected at Cuzco in 1536, and the Diocese of Lima was established five years later, in 1541. Both of these dioceses were under the jurisdiction of the Metropolitan See of Seville, Spain. In 1546, the Diocese of Lima was elevated by Pope Paul III (r. 1534–1549) to the controlling metropolitan see (archdiocese) for the Pacific Coast of the Americas, between Costa Rica to the north and Chile to the south, which was under the Viceroyalty of Lima.

After completing the conquest of Peru in 1534, Pizarro appointed Father Vincente Valverde (1490–1543) as bishop of Cuzco and his jurisdiction extended over the whole territory of the newly conquered domain. Valverde was one of five Dominicans who accompanied the conqueror from Spain. After taking Cuzco, the capital of the Inca Empire, Pizarro established a municipal government (*cabildo*) in Cuzco and encouraged its settlement by Spaniards by providing liberal land grants. In September 1538, Bishop Valverde laid the foundations of the cathedral in Cuzco, and later a Dominican monastery was erected on the site of the Inca Temple of the Sun. Also, a nunnery was established, and several churches and other monasteries built in Cuzco.

Besides the priests that Pizarro was required to take with him from Spain to Peru in his own vessels, the succeeding ships brought additional missionaries, who devoted themselves to the task of "converting the natives." The Dominicans, the Brothers of Mercy, and other missionary orders became actively engaged in propagating the Catholic faith among the Amerindians. The Franciscans were among the pioneer missionaries of Peru, and their labors reached to the remotest regions of South America. The Order of Saint Augustine is also prominent in the annals of Peruvian church history; the Church of Our Lady of Mercy is one of the most attractive Catholic churches constructed in Lima. In 1567, at the request of King Philip II, the first Jesuits were sent to Peru. The Jesuits built a convent, a seminary, and a church in Lima; and then they built churches and schools throughout Peru. However, the work of the Jesuits came to an abrupt end after King Charles III ordered their expulsion from the Spanish colonies in 1769.

Francisco de Toledo y Figueroa, the fifth viceroy of Peru (1569–1581), established in Lima the Permanent Tribunal of the Holy Office of the Inquisition in 1570, which was not abolished until 1820. The Inquisition, as an ecclesiastical tribunal, had jurisdiction only over baptized Christians. It was welcomed by conscientious bishops and viceroys who considered heresy a cardinal sin and the condoning of doctrinal error as an affront to God. This included those who practiced forms of Christianity other than Catholicism, and at the time were considered heretics by the Catholic Church in Spanish kingdoms. In general, the Spanish Inquisition sought to ensure the orthodoxy of recent converts, especially those Jews, Muslims, and others coerced on pain of death to adopt the Christian religion. In the Americas, the Inquisition became a sort of police court for tracking down bigamists, robbers, seducers of youth, and other undesirable people as well as heretics.

The Inquisition was mainly used to judge non-indigenous people who were accused of crimes against the church. These crimes included heresy, sorcery, witchcraft, and other superstitious practices. People accused of these crimes were generally from the lower status of Peruvian society. Among them were individuals of African descent, mestizos, and women, as well as Jewish or Protestant Europeans who were discovered in the Spanish colonies and considered heretics. However, during the 250 years of the Inquisition in South America, only 30 people were actually burned at the stake in Lima, although thousands of people were arrested and brought before the Tribunal. Torture was often used to extract confessions from the unfortunate ones who were imprisoned in the dungeons of the Inquisition in Lima.

Peru became an independent republic in 1824, but it was not until the 1867 Constitution that Roman Catholicism became the official state religion. The Catholic Church continued its hegemony over religion throughout the 20th century. It has been a conservative body, both religiously and politically, although amid the changes in the decades after World War II, it developed a noteworthy stance against a series of oppressive authoritarian governments that ruled Peru and neighboring countries.

Diverse tensions arose within the Peruvian Catholic Church during the 1960s and following years, resulting from challenges posed by the Second Vatican Council (1962–1965), the General Conference of Latin American Bishops in Medellín (Colombia) in 1968, Latin American Liberation Theology, and the Catholic Charismatic Renewal. These new movements polarized Catholic bishops, parish priests, religious workers, and the laity into various factions: *traditionalists,* who wanted the church to remain as it was prior to the reforms approved by the Second Vatican Council; *reformers,* who supported the church's modern stance; *progressives,* who sought to implement the new vision for "a preferential option for the poor" through social and political action aimed at transforming Peruvian society and establishing social justice through peaceful democratic means; *radicals,* who adopted Liberation

Peru

Tumbes
Talara
Sullana
Piura
Paita
Chachapoyas
Iquitos
Yurimaguas
Moyobamba
Tarapoto
Chiclayo
Cajamarca
Peru
Trujillo
Salaverry
Santa Lucia
Pucallpa
Chimbote
Huaraz
Huanuco
Goyllarisquizga
Cerro de Pasco
Huacho
Lima
Huancayo
Puerto Maldonado
Huancavelica
Quillabamba
Ayacucho
Abancay
Cusco
Pisco
Ica
Nazca
Juliaca
Puno
Arequipa
Desaguadero
Matarani
Moquegua
Ilo
Tacna
N

Theology, based on Marxist ideology, and advocated violent revolution by the people as a means of overthrowing the oligarchy and creating a socialist state that would serve the marginalized masses; and *charismatic agents* (priests, nuns, and lay members), who sought to transform the spiritual and communal life of Catholics by means of the power and gifts of the Holy Spirit (including the "baptism of the Holy Spirit and speaking in tongues").

The social and ecclesial context of Peru witnessed the emergence of the first clear articulation of Liberation Theology, as well as the backlash against that theology represented by the Catholic right-wing organization Sodalitium Vitae. All of this occurred in a broader political context disrupted by the violent tactics of the Maoist Shining Path guerrilla movement and the attempts of the Peruvian government to counter those tactics, to the point of violating the human rights of ordinary citizens not connected with the guerrilla movement. The so-called theology of reconciliation, developed by the founder of Sodalitium Vitae, was an attempt by conservatives to undermine the religious and political implications of Liberation Theology by linking it, falsely, with the Shining Path revolutionaries.

Among the many books and articles published on Liberation Theology in the 1970s, one of the most famous was written by a Peruvian Dominican priest, Gustavo Gutiérrez. In his groundbreaking book, *A Theology of Liberation: History, Politics, Salvation* (1971), Gutiérrez (b. 1928), now a professor at the University of Notre Dame in the United States, theorized that a combination of Marxist and Catholic social teachings had contributed to a socialist current within the Catholic Church. However, the Latin American bishops never supported Liberation Theology, which has also been frowned on by the Vatican. Top Catholic officials tried to slow its spread as it was considered antithetical to the Catholic Church's global teachings.

The Catholic Charismatic Renewal (CCR) movement, which began in Peru in 1970, is one of many ecclesiastical movements that form part of the Episcopal Commission of the Apostolic Laity of the Peruvian Episcopal Conference. The movement did not enjoy the same success it has had in other countries, however. According to a 2007 report, nationally, there were only 23,500 active participants.

During the 1990s, conservative Catholic priests, missionary brothers, and missionary sisters suffered persecution throughout Peru from the Shining Path, a Marxist guerrilla organization. Foreign-born priests and nuns were taking the brunt of the attacks against the Catholic Church. The Shining Path opposed the church's many benevolent social improvement activities, as they tended to lessen revolutionary fervor.

President Fujimori put harsh anti-terrorist legislation in place to curb the violence of several leftist guerrilla groups throughout the 1980s and 1990s. Action to suppress the terrorists, however, affected hundreds of innocent men and women who were arrested, tortured, and sentenced to lengthy prison terms. Only a decade later were these convictions reviewed and the innocent pardoned.

Although Peru is considered overwhelmingly Catholic (81.3 percent in 2007), the church has suffered from an inability to recruit Peruvian priests since the 1960s. For example, the Archdiocese of Lima reported a total of 817 priests in 1970 and 613 in 2004; although the number of religious brothers increased from 933 in 1970 to 1,136 in 2004, the number of female religious (nuns) declined from 2,435 in 1970 to 1,755 in 2004. This decline in pastoral leadership and services has had a direct impact on the vitality of the Peruvian Catholic Church, which currently has a very low level of participation of its nominal membership. The Episcopal Commission for Social Action, a Catholic NGO, estimated that only about 5 percent of Peruvian Catholics regularly attend Mass.

In 2004, the Peruvian Catholic Church reported 7 archdioceses and 37 dioceses with 1,426 parishes, which were served by 2,472 priests (1,401 diocesan and 1,071 religious) and assisted by 47 permanent deacons, 2,195 male religious workers, and 5,156 female religious workers. The current archbishop of Lima, Cardinal Juan Luis Cipriani Thorne (ordained a priest of Opus Dei in 1977), was appointed in 1999 and named cardinal in 2001.

The Protestant Movement Between 1822 and 1888, the British and Foreign Bible Society (BFBS) and the American Bible Society (ABS) engaged in sporadic pioneer efforts to distribute the scriptures in Peru. James Thomson (1788–1854), a Baptist pastor from Edinburgh, arrived in Lima in 1822 as a joint representative of the British and Foreign School Society (Lancastrian system of education) and the BFBS as a colporteur. He was invited to Peru by the Liberator José de San Martín for the purpose of establishing the first schools to provide general education for all classes with government sponsorship. Three schools were established by Thomson prior to September 1824 and 30 more were established before 1847 by Peruvians trained by Thomson.

Protestants were allowed to worship in Peru throughout the 19th century, but they were not allowed to proselytize. Members of the Church of England (now a part of the Anglican Province of the Southern Cone) began work in Peru in 1849 under these conditions by establishing chaplaincies among foreign residents in Lima and the port of Callao.

During 1859–1860, A. J. Duffield, an agent of the BFBS, operated out of Lima to supply Bibles, New Testaments, and scripture portions to colporteurs scattered among the nations on the Pacific Coast of South America. By July 1859, his sales in the capital and the interior reached 3,740 copies. Up to that date, the aggregate of scriptures provided to the agency amounted to 52,931 volumes.

In 1859, the American Seamen's Friend Society of New York City sent Methodist minister G. A. Swaney to Callao as a chaplain to merchant seamen and foreign residents, but he only stayed for a few years. In 1877, Methodist laymen William and Archibald Taylor arrived in Callao looking for opportunities to establish a self-supporting mission using the Lancastrian system of education, but both left the country after less than a year to seek better opportunities elsewhere.

Between 1884 and 1886, private religious services were held, in both English and Spanish, at the home of Mr. and Mrs. Peterson (Swedish Lutherans) in Callao for foreign residents and visitors who were non-Conformists (non-Anglicans). One of the leaders of this small congregation was a Christian Brethren layman.

In 1888, an Italian-Uruguayan Methodist layman, Francisco G. Penzotti, established the Peruvian Bible Society in Callao (affiliated with the ABS), aided by another Uruguayan ABS colporteur, J. B. Arancet. Penzotti actively engaged in preaching and evangelism wherever and whenever there was opportunity, such as in Callao at the Peterson home among foreign residents. However, Penzotti's activities were soon brought to the attention of the civil authorities, which led to his arrest and imprisonment for eight months during 1890–1891 for illegally conducting non-Catholic religious meetings.

When news of his plight reached the evangelical public in Europe and North America, there was a spontaneous response by some evangelical leaders to begin training and sending missionaries to Peru and other South American countries, which were perceived to be in "spiritual darkness" due to paganism among the Amerindians and idolatry among adherents to "popular Catholicism" among the Spanish-speaking population.

Penzotti's efforts resulted in the organization of a Methodist congregation in Callao with 31 members and 95 probationers in 1890. In 1891, the Methodist Episcopal Church Board of Foreign Missions sent the Reverend and Mrs. Thomas B. Wood to Peru to take over Penzotti's work in Lima-Callao so that he could continue his work elsewhere. Wood and his assistants were active in the distribution of the scriptures with assistance from the ABS. The Methodists also began establishing schools for Peruvians. The Woods remained in Peru until 1912. By 1914, there were 12 Methodist churches with 1,072 members and probationers in Peru.

In 1893, a congregation was established in barrio Chucuito de Callao by a Scottish Christian Brethren layman, Charles H. Bright, who built on the earlier work begun in the Petersons' home among non-Conformists. One of the first converts was Alfonso Muñoz, who later became an early leader in the Peruvian Evangelical Church (IEP).

In 1894, three young Englishmen arrived independently in Peru who had graduated from the Harley Bible and Missionary Training College in London, founded by Henry Grattan Guinness, who had also founded the Regions Beyond Missionary Union (RBMU) in 1898. Adam Robert Stark, John L. Jarrett, and Frederick J. Peters laid the foundations for RBMU's work in Lima, Cusco, and Trujillo; in 1911, the RBMU became part of the Evangelical Union of

South America (EUSA). The EUSA merged with World Team (formerly known as the West Indies Mission) in 1995.

In April 1896, Bright established a congregation on Calle Negreiros in Lima, which is considered the birthplace of the IEP. In 1906, John Ritchie, a Scottish Presbyterian, arrived in Peru under the sponsorship of the RBMU. Ritchie was assigned by the RBMU to work at the independent congregation on Calle Negreiros. At the beginning of 1920, at least 25 congregations had been formed in the highlands in connection with the Calle Negreiros church, and by the middle of 1924 the number of congregations had increased to 44.

In 1919, the first synod was held in Lima and a second synod was held at Muquiyauyo. The name Iglesia Evangélica Peruana (IEP) was approved at the later synod, along with a simple constitution based on Presbyterian polity. The IEP later became a cooperative venture between the EUSA, the Christian and Missionary Alliance, and the Presbyterians.

Additional Protestant groups arrived in the 1890s, including the Seventh-day Adventist Church, which was successful among the Aymara people in the Lake Titicaca region of southern Peru. In 1967, the Adventists reported almost 30,000 adherents among whom the Aymara people movement accounted for 50 percent. There have also been several schismatic movements among the Seventh-day Adventists. The largest of the independent groups is known as the Israelites of the New Universal Covenant, in both Peru and Bolivia, whose prophets wear long beards and white robes imitating the Aaronic priesthood of the Old Testament. Another group is called the Reformed Adventists.

Between 1900 and 1940, a host of additional denominations and mission agencies began to operate in Peru, including the Pilgrim Holiness Church (later affiliated with Wesleyan Church World Missions), the Church of the Nazarene (1914), the Free Church of Scotland (1915, Presbyterian), the Young Men's Christian Association (1921), the South American Mission (1921), the Association of Baptists for World Evangelization (1929), the Independent Board of Presbyterian Foreign Missions (1935), Baptist Faith Missions (1935), the Presbyterian Church in the United States of America (1936), and Baptist Mid-Missions. In October 1915, Congress modified the Constitution in a way that opened the door to allow freedom of religion and worship, with certain restrictions not removed until 1933.

Early independent Pentecostal work began in Callao and Lima by Mr. and Mrs. Hubert W. Cragin, who only stayed eight months. They worked in Ecuador and Bolivia until 1925, when, now affiliated with the Assemblies of God, they returned to Peru. The Assemblies of God had first entered Peru in 1919 with the arrival of Mr. and Mrs. Forrest Barker and J. Ramon Hurlburt who began missionary work in Macate de Ancash. In 1991, the Assemblies reported 1,511 churches with 75,833 members and 204,750 adherents, and at that time it was one of the largest Protestant and Free church groups in the country. Pentecostal growth was further accelerated in Peru by the arrival of a variety of other Pentecostal denominations.

In late 1940, facing the possibility that many missionaries might have to be withdrawn from Peru due to the hostilities of World War II, the National Evangelical Council of Peru (CONEP) was founded, composed of the following groups: the Christian and Missionary Alliance, the Church of the Nazarene, the Evangelical Union of South America, the Peruvian Evangelical Church, the Methodist Church, the Free Church of Scotland, the Peruvian Inland Mission, the Irish Baptist Church, the Assemblies of God, the American Bible Society, and the British and Foreign Bible Society. CONEP soon became the victim of a split, however, between evangelicals who were predominately focused on missionary activity, and members of older Protestant denominations who were interested in building stronger ecumenical relationships. The fundamentalist Independent Board of Presbyterian Foreign Missions (IBPFM), related to Dr. Carl McIntire (1906–2002) and the International Council of Christian Churches (ICCC), arrived in Peru in 1936 and cooperated with the IEP. It rejected CONEP, however, as it was strongly opposed to the ecumenical movement and the World Council of Churches. The IBPFM severed its ties to the IEP in 1944 and began to work independently. The Christian and Missionary Alliance withdrew from CONEP in 1954.

In spite of the loss of a few members, CONEP has steadily expanded its membership since its founding in 1940. In March 2009, it reported a total of 105

Peru

Religion	Followers in 1970	Followers in 2010	% of Population	Annual % growth 2000–2010	Followers in 2025	Followers in 2050
Christians	12,933,000	27,866,000	96.4	1.22	32,630,000	36,838,000
Roman Catholics	12,889,000	27,331,000	94.6	1.15	31,669,000	34,947,000
Protestants	295,000	2,250,000	7.8	4.82	3,300,000	4,300,000
Independents	68,400	1,300,000	4.5	2.93	1,800,000	2,300,000
Ethnoreligionists	160,000	385,000	1.3	1.24	400,000	380,000
Agnostics	39,000	350,000	1.2	1.23	700,000	1,250,000
New religionists	6,000	94,000	0.3	1.23	140,000	195,000
Buddhists	20,000	70,400	0.2	1.23	100,000	150,000
Atheists	12,800	55,300	0.2	5.00	75,000	100,000
Baha'is	13,500	42,800	0.1	1.23	65,000	90,000
Chinese folk	3,000	19,500	0.1	1.23	24,000	28,000
Jews	5,000	10,500	0.0	1.22	13,000	15,000
Muslims	300	800	0.0	1.21	1,500	2,500
Total population	**13,193,000**	**28,894,000**	**100.0**	**1.23**	**34,148,000**	**39,049,000**

member organizations. During the military regime of Velasco Alvarado (1968–1972), legislation was passed that required foreign missionaries and local congregations to be affiliated with a legally incorporated religious organization in Peru. As CONEP was able to provide this kind of legal status, many organizations affiliated with it. CONEP also assisted missionaries in obtaining legal residence to work in the country, exoneration from paying taxes on donations received from foreign sources, and letters of presentation that certified their membership in CONEP.

During the 1940s and 1950s, six additional mission boards began work in Peru. Seven North American mission agencies began work in Peru during the 1960s, 4 more during the 1970s, 10 more during the 1980s, and 7 more during the 1990s.

Overall, since 1960, the Protestant community has grown significantly. PROLADES (Programa Latinoamericano de Estudios Sociorreligiosos) estimated that the largest Protestant denominations in Peru in 2000 were the following, based on baptized church membership: (1) Assemblies of God, 265,000; (2) Seventh-day Adventist Church, 252,000; (3) Peruvian Evangelical Church (IEP), 80,200; (4) Evangelical Pentecostal Missionary Church, 31,600; (5) Christian and Missionary Alliance, 27,000; (6) Church of the Nazarene, 24,900; (7) Worldwide Missionary Movement, 18,500; (8) Evangelical Presbyterian-Reformed Church, 15,000; (9) Independent Evangelical Pentecostal Church, 12,700; and the (10) Southern Baptist Convention, 10,400.

In 2000, the largest 25 Protestant denominations in Peru represented 822,990 baptized church members and approximately 2.1 million Protestant adherents, while the total Protestant population was estimated at 3.1 million in 2000, or 12.0 percent of the total national population of 26.1 million.

Many pastors and lay leaders of organizations that are members of CONEP are also affiliated with the Latin American Confraternity of Evangelicals (CONELA), which is associated with the World Evangelical Fellowship. The Methodist Church of Peru is the only denomination headquartered in Peru that is a member of the World Council of Churches (WCC). However, the membership of the Latin American Council of Churches (CLAI), which is affiliated with the WCC, includes the following organizations in Peru: Iglesia Evangélica de los Peregrinos del Perú (Pilgrim Holiness), Diócesis Anglicana del Perú, Iglesia Evangélica Luterana de Habla Alemana, Iglesia Luterana Evangélica Peruana, and the Iglesia Metodista del Perú.

Other Christian Groups The only known Eastern Orthodox jurisdiction in Peru is the Greek Orthodox Church (Iglesia Ortodoxa de la Santísima Trinidad) in Pueblo Libre de Lima, affiliated with the Arquidiócesis

Ortodoxa Griega de Buenos Aires y Exarca de Sudamérica, with headquarters in Buenos Aires, Argentina, which is under the broader jurisdiction of the Ecumenical Patriarchate. This archdiocese covers Argentina, Bolivia, Brazil, Chile, Ecuador, Paraguay, Peru, and Uruguay. The Orthodox community in Peru includes immigrants from Greece, Russia, Romania, and Palestine, as well as Peruvian converts to Eastern Orthodoxy.

A variety of non-Protestant Christian groups exists in Peru today, including the following: the Church of Jesus Christ of Latter-day Saints (Mormons, founded in 1956; reported 1 temple and 751 churches with 462,353 adherents in 2008), Jehovah's Witnesses (1,136 churches with 105,422 members and 314,735 adherents in 2008), the Worldwide Church of God, the Philadelphia Church of God, the Light of the World Church (from Mexico), the Voice of the Corner Stone (from Puerto Rico), and Growing in Grace International Ministries (Miami, Florida).

In addition, the Evangelical Association of the Israelite Mission of the New Universal Covenant (AEMINPU) is considered a New Religious movement; it was officially founded in 1968 by Ezekiel Ataucusi Gamonal in Lima, and there was some initial influence on the founder while an active member of the Seventh-day Adventist Church, although the beliefs and practices of this new movement are more in harmony with Pentecostalism, with an emphasis on signs and wonders, speaking in tongues, prophecy, faith healing, and ecstatic experiences. In 1985, there were an estimated 80,000 AEMINPU adherents in Peru. Also, there are several offshoots of this movement in various parts of Peru and Bolivia.

Additional Religious Groups Non-Christian religions include Judaism, Baha'is, Muslims, Hindus, and Buddhism (especially among the Chinese and Japanese populations). The Jewish community of Peru can be traced to Marranos who immigrated to Peru from Spain, but only in the last century did a visible Jewish community come into existence. It includes both Sephardic and Ashkenazi traditions. Most of the approximately 5,000 Peruvian Jews live in Lima, where there are orthodox synagogues for the Ashkenazi, the Sephardic, and Lubavitch Hasidism. There is also a small Jewish population in Cuzco.

The Baha'i Faith found its early success in the Cuzco area and in the 1970s expanded rapidly among the Quechua people in the central highlands. The small Muslim community (about 400) gathers at the Islamic Association of Peru in Lima; the Muslim community in Lima is mostly of Palestinian origin, and in Tacna it is mostly of Pakistani origin. The Subud Association also exists in Peru.

Among Chinese immigrants and their descendants in Peru (an estimated 870,000 in 2008) are adherents of traditional Chinese religions (including Ancestor Worship, Daoism, and Buddhism). Also, there are Buddhist adherents among Japanese immigrants and their descendants (an estimated 90,000 in 2008). In addition, some Peruvians and people of other nationalities practice Buddhism: Diamond Way Buddhism, Reiyukai America, Kagyu Dak Shang Choling, the Buddhist Center of Lima, Sakya Tashi Ling Buddhist Retreat Center (Sakyapa Tibetan Tradition), and the Buddhist Community of Seita Jodo-Shinshu Honpa-Honganji. Japanese immigrants have also established Soka Gakkai International and Perfect Liberty Kyodan, both of which engage in proselytizing outside the Japanese community.

Hinduism is represented by the International Society of Krishna Consciousness (ISKON), the International Sri Sathya Sai Baba Organizations, the Suddha Dharma Mandalam, the Transcendental Meditation (TM, now organized as the Global Country of World Peace), and the Vaisnava Mission in Lima. The Sant Mat tradition is present through the Sant Thaker Singh movement, now led by Baljit Singh, and the Sawan Ruhani Mission-Science of Spirituality.

The Western Esoteric tradition is represented by numerous Freemasonry orders: La Gran Logia Occidental del Peru (Ancient and Acceptable Scottish Rite), founded in Callao in 1817, now with eight lodges; The Great Northern Lodge of Peru, founded in Trujillo in 1883; The Grand Lodge of Central Peru, founded in Huancayo in 1885 (four lodges); and The Grand Lodge of Southern Peru, founded in 1971 in Arequipa (seven lodges). Also present are the following groups: the Ancient and Mystical Order Rosae Crucis (AMORC); the Grand Universal Fraternity, Order of Aquarius (from Venezuela); and the Christian Gnostic movement (from Colombia and Mexico); and Illuminati

Order of Peru (Gran Oriente Illuminati), with headquarters in Lima, founded in 2009 by Víctor Flores Tantaleán; and followers of Wicca.

The Psychic-Spiritualist-New Age movements are represented by the St. Francis of Assisi Spiritist Brotherhood Center in Lima; the Spiritist Association; the Anthroposophical Society of Peru; New Acropolis Cultural Centers; Ishaya Techniques; the Silvan Method; Universal Life—the Inner Religion; and various UFO-related groups: Alfa and Omega Divine Revelation, the Peruvian Institute of Inter-Planetary Relations, the Rahma Mission, the Guimal Institute, and the Raelian Movement International.

The traditional Amerindian religions (animist) have survived in remote areas of Peru. Many of the Native communities practice various forms of their traditional systems, while others practice "popular Catholicism" (syncretistic) that blends Catholic and pre-Columbian beliefs, especially in the Andean highlands (Quechuas, Aymaras, and other groups), whereas the tribal peoples in the remote eastern tropical rainforests continue to practice traditional belief systems. Ninety indigenous languages are spoken in Peru. Mestizo folk healers (*curanderos*) and others have discovered the ritual use of hallucinogenic substances that some practitioners of traditional animistic religions have utilized for centuries in the Amazonian lowlands.

Those indigenous groups that want to resist efforts to convert them to Christianity have received massive support from Europeans and North Americans who have discovered and placed their own overlay of belief onto ancient Peruvian sites. In particular, the ruins of Machu Picchu near Cuzco have become a pilgrimage spot for New Age believers who see it as a power spot of great significance. The so-called Nasca lines in the Peruvian desert, along with a variety of other Peruvian archaeological sites and artifacts, are believed to be indicators of visitations to Earth by extraterrestrials, according to UFO enthusiasts who believe in regular contact with Earth by humanoid beings from outer space.

For a millennium, Lake Titicaca has held great religious and economic significance for the Amerindian peoples. The pre-Incan peoples believed the sun deity and the Sun itself had originally emerged from the lake; for the Sun-worshipping Incas, it was considered the birthplace of humankind, beginning with the mythical founder of the Inca Kingdom, Manco Cápac.

According to Incan mythology, Manco Cápac was a son of the sun god Inti and Mama Quilla (the moon goddess), the brother of Pacha Kamaq (the creator of the world) and the husband of Pacha Mama (mother earth). Manco Cápac himself was worshipped as a fire and a sun god. According to legend, Manco Cápac and his siblings were sent up to the Earth by the sun god and emerged from the cave of Pacaritambo carrying a golden staff, called "tapac-yauri." They were instructed to create a Temple of the Sun in the spot where the staff sank into the earth; they traveled to Cuzco via underground caves and there built a temple in honor of their father, the sun god Inti. The indigenous religion centered in Pachamama is practiced currently in parallel with Catholicism, to the point that many people are simultaneously Catholic and *pachamamistas* (syncretism).

Clifton L. Holland

See also: Ancient and Mystical Order Rosae Crucis; Anglican Province of the Southern Cone; Anthroposophical Society; Baha'i Faith; Christian and Missionary Alliance; Christian Brethren; Church of England; Church of Jesus Christ of Latter-day Saints; Church of the Nazarene; Diamond Way Buddhism; Dominicans; Ecumenical Patriarchate/Patriarchate of Constantinople; Franciscans; Global Country of World Peace; International Society for Krishna Consciousness; Jehovah's Witnesses; Jesuits; Lubavitch Hasidism; Methodist Church of Peru; Pentecostalism; Perfect Liberty Kyodan; Philadelphia Church of God; Raelian Movement International; Reiyukai; Roman Catholic Church; Seventh-day Adventist Church; Sikhism/Sant Mat; Soka Gakkai International; Southern Baptist Convention; Spiritism; UFO Religions; Universal Life; Wesleyan Church; World Council of Churches; World Evangelical Fellowship; Worldwide Church of God.

References

Barrera, Saúl. *Orígenes y Desarrollo de la Iglesia Evangélica Peruana: 100 Años de Misión*. Lima, Peru: Centro de Estudios Pastorales del Perú (CEDEPP), 1993.

Bauswein, Jean-Jacques, and Lukas Vischer, eds. *The Reformed Family Worldwide: A Survey of Reformed Churches, Theological Schools and International Organizations.* Grand Rapids, MI: William B. Eerdmans Publishing Company, 1999.

Brierly, Peter. *World Churches Handbook.* London: Christian Research, 1997.

Burgess, Stanley M., ed. "Peru." In the *International Dictionary of Pentecostal and Charismatic Movements.* Grand Rapids, MI: Zondervan, 2001–2002.

Catholic Hierarchy website. http://www.catholic-hierarchy.org/country/scpe1.html.

Consejo Nacional Evangélico del Perú. Directorio [de Denominaciones y Asociaciones de Iglesias Independientes del Perú]. Lima, Peru: PROMIES, 1993.

Cronehed, Johan. *Identity and Nationalism in Peru.* http://www.thegrammarofthehype.com/peru/Identity%20and%20Nationalism%20in%20Peru.htm.

Equipo de Investigación AMANECER-PERU. I Congreso Nacional Evangelístico-Misionero "Perú para Cristo." Lima, Perú: AMANECER-PERU, 1993.

Fleet, Michael, and Brian H. Smith. *The Catholic Church and Democracy in Chile and Peru.* Notre Dame, IN: University of Notre Dame Press, 2000.

Herring, Hubert, and Helen Baldwin Herring. *A History of Latin America, from the Beginnings to the Present.* 3rd ed. New York: Alfred A. Knopf, 1968.

Holland, Clifton L. "A Chronology of Protestant Beginnings in Peru: 1812–1995." http://www.prolades.com/cra/regions/sam/per/per-chron.pdf.

Holland, Clifton L. "National Census Data on Religious Affiliation in Peru: 1993–2007." http://www.prolades.com/cra/regions/sam/per/polls_2008.pdf.

Huertas, Pilar, Jesús de Miguel, and Antonio Sánchez. *La Inquisición: Tribunal Contra los Delitos de Fe.* Madrid, Spain: Editorial LIBSA, 2003.

Kessler, J. B. A., Jr. *A Study of the Older Protestant Missions and Churches in Peru and Chile.* Goes, The Netherlands: Oosterbaan le Cointre, 1967.

Lewis, M. Paul, ed. *Ethnologue: Languages of the World.* 16th ed. Dallas, TX: SIL International, 2009.

Moreno-Lacalle, Julian. "Peru." In *The Catholic Encyclopedia.* Vol. 11. New York: Robert Appleton Company, 1911. http://www.newadvent.org/cathen/11732b.htm.

Secretariado General de la CLAR. *Estudio sociográfico de los religiosos y las religiosas en América Latina.* Bogota, Colombia: Secretariado General de la CLAR (Confederación Latinoamericana de Religiosos), 1971.

Scott, Kenneth D. "La Asociación Evangélica de la Misión Israelita del Nuevo Pacto," ca. 1990. http://www.prolades.com/cra/regions/sam/per/israelitas-scott.pdf.

U.S. Central Intelligence Agency (CIA). *World Factbook on Peru, 2009.* https://www.cia.gov/library/publications/the-world-factbook/geos/pe.html.

U.S. Department of State. *International Religious Freedom Report, 2008: Peru.* http://www.state.gov/g/drl/rls/irf/2008/108536.htm.

Weber, Linda J., and Dotsy Welliver, eds. *Mission Handbook of U.S. and Canadian Christian Ministries Overseas (2007–2009).* Wheaton, IL: Evangelism and Missions Information Service, 2007.

Peruvian Evangelical Church

The Peruvian Evangelical Church (Iglesia Evangélica Peruana [IEP]) traces its beginnings to the late 1880s, when private religious services were held, in both English and Spanish, in the home of two Swedish Lutherans, Mr. and Mrs. Peterson, for foreign residents and visitors who were non-Conformists (non-Anglicans). One of the leaders of this small congregation was a Christian Brethren layman. In 1893, a congregation was established in barrio Chucuito de Callao by Charles H. Bright, a Scottish Christian Brethren layman who built on the earlier work begun in the Petersons' home. One of the first converts was Alfonso Muñoz, who would later become an early leader in the Peruvian Evangelical Church. Bright refused to cooperate with the

Methodists, the other Protestant group then working in Peru, because of the strong anti-denominational stance he possessed from his Christian Brethren background in Britain.

In 1894, three young Englishmen arrived independently in Peru who had graduated from the Harley Bible and Missionary Training College in London, founded by Henry Grattan Guinness (1835–1910), who also founded the Regions Beyond Missionary Union (RBMU) in 1898. Adam Robert Stark, John L. Jarrett, and Frederick J. Peters laid the foundations for RBMU's work in Lima, Cuzco, and Trujillo; in 1911, the RBMU became part of the Evangelical Union of South America (EUSA). The EUSA merged with World Team (formerly known as the West Indies Mission) in 1995.

In April 1896, Bright established a congregation on Calle Negreiros in Lima, which is considered the birth place of the Peruvian Evangelical Church; this congregation functioned at that location from 1896 to 1930. From this small congregation, unpaid lay evangelists traveled all over Peru to preach and teach the gospel in nearly 100 locations. In 1898, two Brethren missionaries from Scotland arrived, Thomas Cullen and James Watson, both for the purpose of assisting Bright at the church on Calle Negreiros in Lima. Cullen worked with Bright from 1898 until 1902, when Bright left to work in Ecuador, and in 1903 Cullen left Peru. Watson worked in Nazca until 1903, when he returned to Lima to pastor the church on Calle Negreiros after Cullen's departure; he remained there from 1903 to 1908. However, Watson had never fully mastered Spanish and his pastoral work in Lima was not prospering, so he requested help from the Regions Beyond Missionary Union (RBMU) in 1907. Watson left Peru in 1912.

In 1906, John Ritchie, a Scottish Presbyterian, arrived in Peru under the sponsorship of the RBMU. Ritchie was assigned by the RBMU to work with Watson at the independent congregation on Calle Negreiros in Lima from 1907 to 1912. After Watson's departure, Ritchie became the principal leader of the Calle Negreiros church, which further linked it with the RBMU-EUSA and later to the Peruvian Evangelical Church, founded by Ritchie and his Peruvian co-workers in 1919. In 1916, Alfonso Muñoz, who worked as an ABS agent in Lima, was called to pastor the Calle Negreiros church, which enabled Ritchie to give more attention to the expansion of the work in other regions of Peru.

By 1916, churches linked to the Calle Negreiros church had been established in Huantán, Morochocha, and Cedrro de Pasco. After 1918, many new groups of believers started springing up but few trained pastors were available to assist them. It became clear to Ritchie and his associated national leaders that some form of organizational structure was needed for mutual support to these new congregations and preaching points scattered across the country. At the beginning of 1920, at least 25 congregations had been formed in the highlands in connection with the Calle Negreiros church, and by the middle of 1924 the number of congregations had increased to 44.

In 1919, the first synod was held in Lima with the participation of 11 delegates from local congregations associated with the work of the Calle Negreiros church. The second synod was held at Muquiyauyo in the central highlands with 11 churches represented and 19 delegates in attendance. The name Iglesia Evangélica Peruana (IEP) was approved at the later synod, along with a simple constitution based on Presbyterian polity. The IEP later became a cooperative venture between the EUSA, the Christian and Missionary Alliance, and the Presbyterians.

In late 1940, IEP became a founding member of the National Evangelical Council of Peru (CONEP). By 2000, the IEP had grown to be the third largest non-Catholic church in Peru with an estimated 80,200 members.

Iglesia Evangélical Peruana
Jr. Luis Gonzaga No. 709
San Juan de Lurigancho
Lima
Peru

Clifton L. Holland

See also: Christian and Missionary Alliance; Christian Brethren; Evangelicalism.

References

Barrera, Saúl. *Orígenes y Desarrollo de la Iglesia Evangélica Peruana: 100 Años de Misión.* Lima, Peru: Centro de Estudios Pastorales del Perú (CEDEPP), 1993.

Holland, Clifton L. "A Chronology of Protestant Beginnings in Peru: 1812–1995." http://www.prolades.com/cra/regions/sam/per/per-chron.pdf.

Kessler, J. B. A., Jr. *A Study of the Older Protestant Missions and Churches in Peru and Chile*. Goes, The Netherlands: Oosterbaan le Cointre, 1967.

Pesach

Pesach, the Hebrew name of what in English is termed Passover, is a major festival in the Jewish ritual year. Pesach calls to memory major events in the Exodus of the Hebrew people from Egypt and the establishment Judaism. The events are recorded in the opening chapters of the book of Exodus in the Jewish Bible (the Christian Old Testament), but especially chapter 12. According to the story, Moses, who had escaped Egypt after killing a brutal Egyptian slave master, returned to Pharaoh's court with a demand that the Hebrews be allowed to leave Israel. When Pharaoh refused, he threatened calamities and successively a set of plagues hit the land.

Unmoved by the plagues, the still stubborn Pharaoh was struck with one final plague. God threatened to move among the Egyptians and kill the firstborn in each house, including the heir to the throne. Speaking on God's behalf, Moses then instructed the Hebrews to take a lamb free of blemishes and on the appointed day kill it. He then instructed that "they shall take of the blood, and put it on the two side-posts and on the lintel, upon the houses wherein they shall eat it. And they shall eat the flesh in that night, roast with fire, and unleavened bread; with bitter herbs they shall eat it. Eat not of it raw, nor sodden at all with water, but roast with fire; its head with its legs and with the inwards thereof. And ye shall let nothing of it remain until the morning; but that which remaineth of it until the morning ye shall burn with fire. And thus shall ye eat it: with your loins girded, your shoes on your feet, and your staff in your hand; and ye shall eat it in haste—it is the LORD'S passover. For I will go through the land of Egypt in that night, and will smite all the first-born in the land of Egypt, both man and beast; and against all the gods of Egypt I will execute judgments: I am the LORD. And the blood shall be to you for a token upon the houses where ye are; and when I see the blood, I will pass over you, and there shall no plague be upon you to destroy you, when I smite the land of Egypt" (Exodus 12:7–13).

In the wake of the deaths, Pharaoh relented and the Hebrews left Egypt, crossed the Red Sea, and found their way to Mount Sinai, where God gave them the law. Pharaoh's army being destroyed when it attempted to pursue the Hebrews, there was no attempt to return them to Egypt in the years ahead in the Sinai.

In the giving of the instructions for the Hebrews to kill the lamb, mark their homes with blood, cook the lamb, and consume it, Moses also underscored the importance of the events by telling the Hebrew to set up their calendar with these events marking the first month, to prepare to repeat the events annually forever as a means of remembering what had happened. After the Exodus had begun, the Hebrews were told that the annual remembrance of Pesach would be for seven days (Exodus 13:6). Further details would be added later.

And through the centuries, the events would be remembered. Throughout the Jewish Bible, God would be spoken of as the "the LORD your God, who brought you up out of Egypt." The events of the Exodus are recalled in the daily morning and evening prayers and tied to the prayer shawl and the *tefillin* worn on the Sabbath.

The celebration of Pesach carried with it the setting of the Jewish calendar to begin in the spring, in what is now termed the month of Nissan. However, in the sixth century BCE, during the Babylonia Exile, New Year's was moved to the fall. Today, some speak of the religious year beginning Nissan 1 and the civil year beginning Tishri 1. In either case, should Nissan 1 occur too early (before the Spring Equinox) an intercalary year is added immediately before the month of Nissan. Passover is a week-long festival (seven days for reform Jews and eight days for Conservative and Orthodox Jews) that begins on Nissan 14.

Pesach, along with Shavuot and Sukkot, was one of the three pilgrim festivals during which the entire Jewish community made a pilgrimage to Jerusalem, where access to the temple was available. The destruction of the temple and the scattering of the Jewish people thus have had a marked effect upon the way that the three festivals are celebrated. The Samaritans, a sect

Russian Jews celebrate Pesach, illustration from about 1900. (Jewish Chronical/StockphotoPro)

with Jewish origins, still make pilgrimages for these festivals to Mount Gerizim, though only males engage in public worship.

In celebrating Pesach, Jews attempt to both remember the events and symbolically reenact them, and thus come from the festival feeling as if they had just been delivered form bondage. In preparation for the Pesach, houses will be cleaned to make sure that no leaven is in the home. During the week only matzoh bread, unleavened bread made simply and quickly, is an acceptable form of grain product for consumption. When the Exodus began, there was no time to wait for the bread to rise. For this reason, Pesach is often called the Feast of Unleavened Bread. Orthodox Jews will have a separate set of dishes for use during Pesach. Products for Pesach will be especially designated in stores that serve or sell Jewish "kosher" foods.

On the first two evenings of Passover (Nissan 15 and 16), a special ritual feast, the Seder, is held in the home. Guests are invited and included in the celebration where possible. The ritual for the occasion consists primarily of retelling the Exodus deliverance story, especially for the children, recalling Exodus 12:26–27. "And it shall come to pass, when your children shall say unto you: What mean ye by this service? that ye shall say: It is the sacrifice of the Lord's passover, for that He passed over the houses of the children of Israel in Egypt, when He smote the Egyptians, and delivered our houses." At key points in the story, the children and youth take the lead in directing the story, and as it begins, the youngest child asks, "Why is this night different from all other nights of the year?"

The Seder service also includes the blessing and consumption of wine—four cups symbolic of the four-fold redemption recounted in Exodus 6:6: "I am the LORD, and I will *bring you out* from under the burdens of the Egyptians, and I will *deliver you* from their bondage, and I will *redeem you* with an outstretched arm, and with great judgments; and I will *take you to Me* for a people." Also a fifth cup is poured symbolizing that God's promise of returning his people to their homeland remains unfulfilled. Traditionally, the wine in this cup is not drunk. It is often called Elijah's cup, as the prophet Elijah is supposed to usher in the messianic age. Since the founding of the state of Israel, many Jews look upon the cup as symbolic of a promise that is beginning to be fulfilled, and will sip from Elijah's cup.

As recounted in the instructions instituting Pesach, bitter herbs are eaten with the meal, symbolic of the bitterness of slavery. A mixture of chopped nuts, apple, cinnamon, and wine symbolizes the mortar used in the building projects of the Pharaoh at which the Hebrews labored. A roasted shank bone is placed on the Seder table, but not eaten. It is a reminder of the temple, now destroyed, where the paschal lamb for the Passover meal was sacrificed. Since the destruction of the temple, no paschal lamb can be sacrificed. Thus the Seder thus ends with the proclamation, "Next year in Jerusalem!"

Contemporary Jews see the liberation from bondage theme of Pesach as having great relevance for the Jewish presence in the larger social realm. Jews were prominent through the 20th century in the struggles to free the Jewish community from the effects of prejudice and in the struggle generalized their condition to other groups with whom they share a history of slavery, persecution, and discrimination.

In Israel, Passover is observed as a seven-day holiday. The first and last days are recognized as legal holidays. Within the religious community, these days are considered holy days that should be marked by abstention from work and religious services, especially those surrounding the Seder meals. The middle days of Pesach are known as Chol HaMoed, or festival days.

Passover and Christianity Of all the Jewish holy days, Pesach has had the most effect on Christianity. Jesus' death was associated with Passover, and Christ was described as the paschal lamb. The setting of the dates of the Christian Holy Week culminating in Easter is based on the date of Passover. In the 20th century some Christian groups, primarily out of the Adventist tradition, began to celebrate the Feast of Unleavened Bread as a primary Christian festival. In a different vein, Messianic Jews, consisting of Jews and others who follow Jewish culture, have also instituted the practice of celebrating a Christian Passover.

J. Gordon Melton

See also: Calendars, Religious; Gerizim, Mount; Jerusalem; Moses; Passover; Pilgrimage; Shavuot; Sinai, Mount; Spring Equinox; Sukkot; Temples—Jewish.

References

Bloch, Abraham P. *The Biblical and Historical Background of Jewish Customs and Ceremonies.* New York: Ktav Publishing House, Inc., 1980.

Eckstein, Yecheil. *What You Should Know About Jews and Judaism.* Waco, TX: Word Books, 1984.

Greenberg, Irving. *The Jewish Way: Living the Holidays.* New York: Jason Aronson, 1998.

Posner, Raphael, Uri Kaploun, and Sherman Cohen, eds. *Jewish Liturgy: Prayer and Synagogue Service through the Ages.* New York: Leon Amiel Publisher; Jerusalem: Keter Publishing House, 1975.

Schauss, Hayyim. *The Jewish Festivals: A Guide to Their History and Observance.* New York: Schocken, 1996.

Philadelphia Church of God

The Philadelphia Church of God is one of the three largest offshoots of the Worldwide Church of God (WCOG), with an active television, magazine, book, and booklet outreach. The Philadelphia Church of God was founded in 1989 by Gerald Flurry (b. 1935), a pastor in the WCOG. Flurry was dismayed by the WCOG's movement away from the teachings of its founder, Herbert W. Armstrong (1892–1986), after Armstrong's death in 1986, and he was particularly worried by the decision of the new pastor general Joseph W. Tkach, Sr.

(1927–1995), to cease publication of Armstrong's last book, *Mystery of the Ages*, about which Armstrong had said, "It may be the most important book since the Bible." Tkach's son Joe, Jr. (b. 1951) (himself later to be pastor general of the WCOG) told Flurry that the book was "riddled with error."

Flurry left the WCOG to found the Philadelphia Church of God, which like most of the other offshoots of the WCOG, believes in seven Church Eras, of which the most faithful to God is the Philadelphia church, as described in the Bible: "for thou hast a little strength, and hast kept my word, and hast not denied my name" (Revelation 3:8b). The WCOG, according to Philadelphia and most other offshoots, has become the Laodicean Church: "because thou art lukewarm . . . I will spew thee out of my mouth" (Revelation 3:16).

Flurry distributed copies of *Mystery of the Ages* to inquirers, and when the church ran out in 1997, he had further copies printed. The WCOG challenged this as a violation of its copyright. A landmark district court judgment in favor of the Philadelphia Church of God in 1997, which distinguished between a religion as believers and a religion as a corporation, was overturned by a court of appeals in 2000. Philadelphia COG were determined to gain the right to distribute the book, which they regard as fundamental to their ministry. Following further legal exchanges the matter was finally settled out of court in 2003, with WCOG selling Philadelphia COG the copyright to *Mystery of the Ages* and 18 other books that WCOG would never have published again, for a sum variously stated as $2 million or $3 million.

Like most of the offshoots of the WCOG, Philadelphia COG, which is Sabbatarian and millenarian, claims that its teachings are those of the WCOG at the time of Armstrong's death. Unlike most of the other offshoots, it also claims new revelations that "prove" that it is the legitimate successor to the WCOG. The Philadelphia Church of God is the most hard-line of the three major offshoots of the Worldwide Church of God. It believes that Herbert W. Armstrong was the end-time Elijah as foretold in the Scriptures (Matthew 17:11), that the "apostasy" of the WCOG is also prophesied, and that so is the rise of the Philadelphia Church of God under Gerald Flurry, who claims that his own book about the "apostasy" of WCOG, *Malachi's Message*, is the "little book" mentioned in Revelation 10.

Although the church is happy to send its literature to any inquirers, it is not favorably disposed toward researchers and academics. It is believed to have had around 7,500 members at its height, and although this has been reduced by the secession of several senior ministers because of Flurry's perceived authoritarianism, with the subsequent formation of further offshoot churches, it is still possibly the second or more likely the third largest offshoot from the WCOG, with an estimated 4,000 to 5,000 members.

The church broadcasts the *Key of David* TV program.

Philadelphia Church of God
PO Box 3700
Edmond, OK 73083
www.pcog.org
www.keyofdavid.com

David V. Barrett

See also: Sabbatarianism; Philadelphia Church of God; Worldwide Church of God.

References

Barrett, David V. *The New Believers.* London: Cassell, 2001.

Flurry, Gerald. *Malachi's Message to God's Church Today.* Edmond, OK: Philadelphia Church of God, 1990, 1995.

Flurry, Gerald. *Worldwide Church of God Doctrinal Changes and the Tragic Results.* Edmond, OK: Philadelphia Church of God, 1994.

The Journal: News of the Churches of God. Big Sandy, TX: JMC Associates.

Tkach, Joseph. *Transformed by Truth.* Sisters, OR: Multnomah Books, 1997.

Philippine Independent Church

In 1898 the United States took control of the Philippines from Spain. Some Filipinos, wishing for their country's full independence, staged a revolt under the leadership of Emilio Aguinaldo (1869–1964). Aguinaldo in turn appointed Gregorio Aglipay (1860–1940) as a vicar general to head the Roman Catholic Church in the area of the country he controlled. In 1899 the archbishop of Manila excommunicated Aglipay, and he reorganized the church under his control as the Iglesia Filipina Independente (Philippine Independent Church [PIC]). Aglipay served as a leader in the rebel army and became a hero of the people in his failed endeavor to bring freedom to the country. After the revolt, he suffered another defeat when in 1906 the courts ordered most of the property being used by those loyal to him turned over to the Roman Catholic Church.

In spite of the loss of most of its property, the PIC survived in the atmosphere of religious freedom imposed on the islands by the Americans. In the meantime, Aglipay became influenced by Unitarian views, and the church opened itself to a rejection of its traditional Trinitarian theology. In 1939 Dr. Louis Cornish (1870–1950), president of the American Unitarian Association (now an integral part of the Unitarian Universalist Association), was named the honorary president of the PIC. Aglipay died in 1940 and was succeeded by Isebelo de los Reyes, who was unsympathetic to the drift into Unitarianism. When the church reorganized in 1947, he led it to adopt a new statement of faith that included a strong affirmation of the Trinity. The church also began to use the Apostles' Creed and the Nicene Creed.

Reyes also led the church into a relationship with the Episcopal Church, the American representative of the Anglican Communion, which had established an Episcopal mission in the Philippines at the beginning of the century. In 1948 Episcopal bishops consecrated Reyes and two other PIC bishops, thus passing to them the Anglican lineage of apostolic succession. In 1959 the church followed members to the United States and, with the permission of the Episcopal bishop of Hawaii, opened their first foreign mission in Honolulu. As the church spread, its congregations met in local Episcopal parish facilities.

The church soon came into full relationship with the Episcopal Church, accepting the 1931 Bonn Agreement, which brought the Church of England into communion with the Old Catholic churches in Europe. Through that action the PIC came into communion with the Episcopal Church in the Philippines and the other churches of the worldwide Anglican Communion. In 1999, the church signed a "covenant of partnership" with the United Church of Christ in the Philippines.

In 1985 the PIC reported 4.5 million members, most in the Philippines. More recent estimates acknowledge a far lower figure, approximately 2 million, with a constituency twice that number. The church is led by its supreme bishop, who is currently Most Reverend Godofredo J. David, elected in 2005. The church ordained its first female priest in 1997. The church is a member of the World Council of Churches.

In the 1970s, the church experienced problems growing out of the participation of its missionary bishop, Francisco Pagtakhan, and two other PIC bishops in the consecration of several individuals who had left the Episcopal Church to establish conservative Anglican churches in the United States. The first consecrations took place in 1978, and the new bishops went on to found the Anglican Catholic Church, the Diocese of Christ the King, and the United Episcopal Church of North America. The issues first raised by Pagtakhan's actions culminated with the refusal of the church to reelect Marcario V. Ga as the supreme bishop. As a result, Ga led his followers out of the church and reorganized as the autonomous Philippine Independent Catholic Church.

Philippine Independent Church
1500 Taft Avenue, Ermita
PO Box 2484
Manila
Philippines

J. Gordon Melton

See also: Anglican Communion/Anglican Consultative Council; Episcopal Church; Episcopal Church in the Philippines; Roman Catholic Church; United Church of Christ in the Philippines; Unitarian Universalist Association; World Council of Churches.

References

Anderson, Gerald H., ed. *Studies in Philippine Church History.* Ithaca, NY: Cornell University Press, 1969.

Deats, Richard L. *Nationalism and Christianity in the Philippines.* Dallas, TX: Southern Methodist University Press, 1967.

■ Philippines

The Philippines is a multi-island nation located in the Pacific Ocean north of Indonesia and west of Vietnam. The 7,000 islands of what is today the Philippines sprawl for approximately 1,000 miles from the north to the south. Of these 7,000 islands only about 1,000 are inhabited, and fewer than 500 are larger than one square mile. Its population of 92 million (2009) make it the 12th most populous country in the world.

Diversity is perhaps the Philippines' most striking characteristic; the variety found in the flora, fauna, and terrain of these islands hosts a cultural and ethnic mosaic, and the Philippines are seen as an exemplar of human diversity. Scholars generally hold that the archipelago was once connected to the Asian continent by land bridges that were submerged more than 7,000 years ago. It is believed that the proto-Malay people initially crossed over these bridges from Borneo. Although this is a matter of anthropological speculation, it is clear that successive migrations populated the islands as early as 15,000 years ago from the interior tribes of China.

Subsequent migrations from southern China and Vietnam brought stone and bronze tools and introduced rice farming and the water buffalo to the islands. These waves of early Chinese migrations settled in what is known today as Luzon, the northernmost island of the archipelago. Some 2,000 years ago, Malays from both Indonesia and the West Malaysian Peninsula made their way to the central islands known as the Visayans. They brought a fishing culture that was structured around a small clan led by the clan chief. The *barangay*, the boat that brought them, became the name of the extended family unit that forms the basic political structure of society today in the Philippines.

By the middle of the 14th century CE, Java, Sumatra, Malaya, Cambodia, Siam, and the Indochina states of Annam and Tonkin had entered into trade relations with the Philippines. The trade invariably left an imprint of Buddhist, Hindu, and Islamic religious

The Romanesque-style Cathedral of Manila in the Philippines was built in 1958. (iStockPhoto.com)

culture on the Philippines. These traces can be seen in the Sanskrit loan words, such as *dukkha* for suffering, *bodhi* for soul, and *katha* for legend or story, which have been absorbed into the Tagalog language world. Recent archaeological evidence dated to the 10th century CE gives some credence to the arrival at that time of yet another culture—the Srivijaya Kingdom, a maritime power from Sumatra that dominated the Strait of Malacca.

Today Roman Catholicism is the dominant religion in the Philippines; it is claimed by about 80 percent of the population. The Roman Catholic Church was introduced in the islands in 1521, when Ferdinand Magellan (ca. 1480–1521), a Portuguese explorer, led a Spanish expedition to the islands and planted the cross there, starting the Christianization of the Native population. The systematic propagation of Roman

Catholicism by missionaries from Spain eventually made the Philippines the only predominantly Catholic nation in Asia.

Well before Catholicism reached the Philippines, Arab missionaries had already introduced Islam among the inhabitants of the southern islands. It is claimed that Islam antedates Catholic Christianity by about three centuries, yet Islam remained principally confined to the Sulu Archipelago and some of the coastal areas of the island of Mindanao. After about seven centuries of existence in the Philippines, Muslims remain a numerically small portion of the religious population. Most Muslims follow the Sunni Shafiite School and are generally referred to as Moros (Spanish: Moors).

American Protestantism was brought to the country in 1898, when Spain ceded the Philippines to the United States in the Treaty of Paris. As the Americans began to assume dominance in the islands, they brought their new faith. The different Protestant churches divided the country among themselves to convert Catholics to Protestantism, just as the various Catholic orders had apportioned the territory during the 450 years of the Spanish regime. The difference, however, was that whereas the Catholic religious orders were converting the indigenous peoples to one church, Protestants wanted the Filipinos to choose among various denominations.

Among the more important denominations to arise from the Protestant effort are the United Church of Christ in the Philippines, the Convention of Philippine Baptist Churches, and the Evangelical Methodist Church in the Philippines. The Episcopal Church also began work in the country and over the years developed a relationship with a group that had left the Catholic Church to form a Philippine Independent Church (PIC). With more than 2.5 million members, the PIC is the largest non-Catholic church in the country. It claimed almost 4.5 million members before a split in the 1980s produced the Philippine Independent Catholic Church.

Despite the coming of the world's religions through colonial powers and the significant conversion of the population to a variety of forms of Christianity, some indigenous, pre-Magellan religious elements continue to thrive in the culture. Sixteenth-century Spanish missionary records provide the best clues to the religious substrata that influence the contemporary religious landscape in the Philippines. Most of these records are taken from the central islands of the archipelago, the Visayans.

When the Spanish arrived, Bisayans, native residents of the Visayan Islands, worshipped nature spirits, gods of particular localities, and their own ancestors. Religious practitioners were male or female mediums who contacted spirit patrons in a state of trance to determine the cause and cure of illness. Sacrifices included foodstuffs, beverages, and live fowl, hogs, or human beings. The ancestor spirits and deities were invoked at feasts in which these sacrifices were offered up. Ancestor spirits were also invited to partake of any meal, and their well-being in the next world depended on sacrifices offered by their descendants both before and after their death.

Bisayans considered themselves vastly outnumbered by a variety of invisible beings. Gods and goddesses were called *diwata*, a word still in use among Bisayans living in the remote mountains of Panay. "Diwata" is a Malay-Sanskrit term for gods or godhead, and in the Bisayan language a *maniwata* or *magdiwata* is a shaman or human intermediary who invokes or defies the spiritual realm. The diwata were generally neutral and could be approached ritually for good crops, health, and fortune, but they also caused illness or misfortune if not given due respect. They thus functioned to sanction approved social behavior. Naturally, malevolent beings, ranging from the mischievous to the demonic, had to be avoided or fended off by precautionary acts. These beings had no single name as a class—Spanish lexicographers simply called them witches—*brujas* or *hechiceros*. Today Bisayans have supplied modern Spanish terms such as *duende* (goblin) and *encanto* (enchantment).

In some cases the diwata actually constituted a pantheon, with a hierarchy arranged by the specific roles each divinity played. Some were specifically connected with basic rights of passages such as birth, naming, marriage, death, and afterlife. Others were the patrons of specific human conditions, such as the Dalikmata, a diwata with many eyes, who was invoked in the case of eye ailments, or Makabosog, who moved a person to gluttony. The Cebuanos, the Natives of the island of Cebu who first encountered Magellan's

PHILIPPINES

Philippines

Religion	Followers in 1970	Followers in 2010	% of Population	Annual % growth 2000–2010	Followers in 2025	Followers in 2050
Christians	34,354,000	83,151,000	89.4	2.09	103,588,000	125,252,000
Roman Catholics	30,860,000	72,065,000	77.5	1.25	84,595,000	95,103,000
Independents	7,053,000	19,500,000	21.0	1.38	25,400,000	31,500,000
Protestants	1,446,000	4,700,000	5.1	–0.42	7,000,000	9,000,000
Muslims	1,565,000	6,000,000	6.5	2.10	7,500,000	9,100,000
Ethnoreligionists	338,000	2,500,000	2.7	2.08	2,700,000	2,900,000
Agnostics	78,000	700,000	0.8	3.42	1,100,000	1,800,000
Baha'is	67,500	273,000	0.3	2.10	420,000	550,000
Atheists	20,000	175,000	0.2	2.10	280,000	450,000
Buddhists	50,000	111,000	0.1	2.10	160,000	250,000
Chinese folk	70,000	52,300	0.1	2.10	70,000	85,000
Sikhs	5,000	23,000	0.0	2.10	28,000	32,000
New religionists	2,000	9,000	0.0	2.10	20,000	30,000
Hindus	1,000	3,000	0.0	2.11	6,500	10,000
Confucianists	0	2,200	0.0	2.11	4,000	6,200
Jews	500	1,100	0.0	2.11	1,200	1,200
Total population	**36,551,000**	**93,001,000**	**100.0**	**2.10**	**115,878,000**	**140,466,000**

expedition, referred to the image of the Holy Christ Child as "the Spaniards' diwata." The Cebuanos supposedly rendered it homage after Magellan's death.

The earliest known records of the diwata were written by Miguel de in Panay in 1582. His records identified Si Dapa as a diwata who was said to mark out one's mortal lifespan on a tree trunk on Mount Madayaas at the time of birth. He also identified other beings, including Magwayen, who was said to ferry the souls of the deceased across to a kind of inferno, and Pandaki, a diwata who rescued the deserving for a more pleasant afterlife. Loarca showed the linkage between the diwata and natural phenomena by describing a fire-breathing goddess as Mayong, a diwata of the volcano in Ibalon that bears her name.

Later interpreters have classified the pre-Magellan gods into a three-tiered system. The first tier is composed of the gods of the heavens, such as Bathala, MayKapal, Kabunian, Maguayen, and Sidava. These deities were the source and creators of things in the world. Events in the world were ultimately traced to their agency. To reach the highest of the gods one had to go through channels or intermediaries—lesser gods. Thus, petitions and sacrifices were addressed to lesser gods.

A second tier of gods concerns those of the underworld, such as Sisiburnanen, Pandague, and Sumpay. These gods were connected with death. It was believed that when a person died, the soul, or élan vital, was brought to the underworld by one of the gods and would be kept there unless another minor underworld god would liberate it. The "liberator god" would act in response to sacrifices offered by the living for the dead. The liberated soul would then reside in the high mountains.

The third tier of gods, located between heaven and the underworld, consists of the deities and spirits of the Earth. The Spanish records refer to a goddess of harvest called Lalahon. Followers of Lalahon believed that as long as they pleased her, the fields would be fruitful and they would be assured of a bountiful harvest. If displeased, she would send swarms of locusts to destroy the crops. Hence, the people offered her sacrifices and invoked her blessings for a good harvest. The most widespread of the spirits in the middle tier is the *anitos*. Among the Tagalogs, natives of central Luzon, the anitos were considered agents of the high gods such as Bathala and could be found everywhere within the environment. The resources of nature thus belonged to the spirits, but humans might use them provided they made proper acknowledgment to the spirit owners.

Today, these Filipino indigenous religious beliefs and practices are incorporated into the world religions in a variety of regional folk practices. Once driven underground by colonial powers, these same beliefs and practices have re-emerged in the last 90 years in an environment of religious tolerance and nationalism.

Indigenous beliefs and practices have also contributed to the rise of many new religious communities in the Philippines. The rapid growth of the Iglesia ni Cristo (Church of Christ), established in 1914 by Felix Manalo (1886–1963), serves as the best illustration of the new indigenous communities. At the beginning of the 20th century the various factions of Christianity in the Philippines collided in the life of Felix Manalo. Baptized a Roman Catholic in 1886, he became a Methodist in 1904 and a Presbyterian in 1905. After years of disillusionment with a variety of Protestant churches and during a time when the nation hungered for political independence, Manalo established an independent church. The Iglesia Kristo reflected his particular charismatic teachings, which identify "true religion." The Iglesia is considered a truly Filipino organization, drawing many indigenous beliefs and practices into its polity.

The rise of many new religions, coupled with the assault on the country by numerous Christian missionary agencies since World War II, has made the Philippines one of the most religiously pluralistic countries in the world.

Graham B. Walker Jr.

See also: Convention of Philippine Baptist Churches; Episcopal Church; Evangelical Methodist Church in the Philippines; Philippine Independent Church; Roman Catholic Church; Shafiite School of Islam; United Church of Christ in the Philippines.

References

Anderson, Gerald H., ed. *Studies in Philippine Church History*. Ithaca, NY: Cornell University Press, 1969.

Blair, Emma, and James Robertson, eds. *The Philippine Islands, 1493–1898*. 55 vols. Cleveland: Arthur H. Clark, 1903–1909.

Demetrio, Francisco. *Myths and Symbols in the Philippines*. Manila: National Books, 1981.

Friend, Theodore, ed. *Religion and Religiosity in the Philippines and Indonesia: Essays in State, Society, and Public Creeds*. Baltimore: Southeast Asia Studies Program, Johns Hopkins University, 2006.

Scott, William H. *Barangay: Sixteenth-Century Philippine Culture and Society*. Manila: Ateneo de Manila University Press, 1994.

Shirley, Steven. *Guided by God: The Legacy of the Catholic Church in Philippine Politics*. Singapore: Marshall Cavendish Academic, 2004.

Silliman, Robert B. *Religious Beliefs and Life at the Beginning of the Spanish Regime in the Philippines*. Dumaguete City: Silliman University, 1964.

Pilgrimage

Although the English term "pilgrimage" derives from Latin and has close associations with Christianity, it represents universal themes relating to traveling to and performing acts of reverence at places with special resonance for the traveler. Normally this resonance is associated with notions of the sacred, with the site visited being the locus of some special event or events that mark it out from the ordinary world or a site where visitors can access some spiritual force. Thus places associated with seminal events in religious traditions (for example, places associated with the life of Jesus, with the Buddha's journey to enlightenment, or with Muhammad's final visit to Mecca) have become significant pilgrimage centers. Likewise, tales of miracle and apparition have helped make certain places into pilgrimage sites, as with the Marian apparitions and miracles that have sacralized Catholic sites such as Lourdes, Knock, Fatima, and Clearwater (in the United States), and similar phenomena associated with the Buddhist figure Kannon (Guan Yin), which have given rise to Japanese pilgrimage sites, such as the 33-temple Saikoku Kannon pilgrimage.

The traces of sacred figures, too, in reality or legend, also have been formative in the creation of pilgrimages. Santiago de Compostela, one of Catholi-

Pilgrims climbing to the Gateway to Heaven Temple atop Mount Tai Shan, China. (Corbis)

cism's great pilgrimage centers, attained prominence because it was the (legendary) locale of the relics of Saint James, while the tombs of Sufis in Islam, of Catholic saints, and of Buddhist sect founders such as Kukai, whose mausoleum at Mount Koya remains a major pilgrimage site in Japan, have developed as pilgrimage locations because they are seen as possessing special power due to those interred therein. Similarly, places associated with important myths and legends relating to the deities of traditions and to important landscape features significant to religious traditions—for instance, Hindu sites such as Kedarnath in the Himalayas and Varanasi (Benares) on the River Ganges, both associated with Hindu myths and legends—are a recurrent feature of pilgrimage sites globally.

Ubiquity and the Secular Pilgrimage is ubiquitous, a prominent feature not just of older religious traditions but of the new as well. New religions frequently create their own sacred geographies and pilgrimages as part of their development process and to affirm the new spiritual frameworks and worldviews they propound. Thus Tenri, the birthplace of Miki Nakayama, the 19th-century founder of the Japanese new religion Tenrikyo, and which she taught was where humanity originated and where the divine and human worlds intersect, has become the sacred center for Tenrikyo. Pilgrimages there are a key Tenrikyo practice, one that asserts Tenrikyo's vision of the world. The New Age movement, too, has developed its own pilgrimage centers—such as Sedona in Arizona and Glastonbury in the United Kingdom, both geographically striking sites that were sacred to other traditions in earlier times, the former for Native Americans, the latter in medieval Christianity, and that have been appropriated as modern pilgrimage centers of the New Age.

In recent times, too, many places with no specific religious affiliation but often combining aspects of the factors cited above and holding special emotional significance for their visitors, have attracted visitors whose reverential behavior indicates that they, too, can be seen as modern manifestations of pilgrimage. War grave sites in Europe are the focus of organized pilgrimage tours for those who wish to commemorate the dead, while the Vietnam War Memorial Wall in Washington, D.C., receives visits from those who lost kin or comrades in the war and those seeking to commemorate the nation's loss. Vietnam veterans also perform an annual motorbike journey (which they view as a pilgrimage) from California to the memorial, involving commemorative rituals along the way. Furthermore, places associated with figures of popular culture, such as Graceland (home and burial place of Elvis Presley), receive numerous visitors whose demeanor and rituals resemble those of pilgrims at sacred places, especially during the annual Elvis Presley Memorial Week around his death anniversary, which includes candlelight vigils and prayers. As such, pilgrimage goes beyond the boundaries of the formally religious and is manifest in secular contexts as well.

Symbolism and Sacred Traces Pilgrimages may vary across different religions but there are a number of themes that are found widely enough to be regarded as normative. While pilgrimage usually involves a physical journey, this often is also symbolically a spiritual one, with the outer journey a physical manifestation of inner teachings. Buddhism's teachings about renunciation, for example, were enacted by the Buddha when he left home in search of enlightenment; his wanderings represented both a physical and a spiritual pilgrimage through life, and those who followed in his footsteps and renounced the world did likewise. Early Buddhist pilgrimages involved visiting sites in the Indian subcontinent associated with the founder's journey (his birthplace, Lumbini; Bodh Gaya, where he attained enlightenment; Sarnath, where he preached the first sermon; and Kushinagara, where he died); it was thus a journey that symbolically traced the Buddha's journey through life, and served as a template for the spiritual progress of his followers.

This symbolism of pilgrimage as a spiritual journey is often linked to the idea of following in the footsteps of founders and holy figures. Pilgrims in the Christian holy land thus walk in the places where Jesus was, while pilgrims on the Shikoku pilgrimage—an 88-temple Buddhist pilgrimage around the Japanese island of Shikoku—follow in the footsteps of the Buddhist holy figure Kobo Daishi (Kukai) who, according to legend, founded the pilgrimage. The pilgrimage is also symbolically a journey to enlightenment, and this motif also frames the pilgrim's path. A recurrent theme in pilgrimages—and evident in the above-mentioned Buddhist pilgrimages—is they enable the ordinary person to step outside the everyday world and enter into a special sacred realm; in Buddhist terms, the pilgrim temporarily becomes like a monk or nun, and may don special clothing to indicate this separation from the world. Indeed, wearing special clothes and insignia to indicate one stands apart from the mundane is widely found in pilgrimages, from the Muslims on the *hajj,* who wear special pilgrimage clothing denoting purity, to Shikoku pilgrims, whose white clothing both signifies purity and indicates that they are "dead to the world" during their pilgrimage.

The death symbolism of Shikoku pilgrims' clothes also implies rebirth and renewal—a common pilgrimage motif and a potent motivation for pilgrims, who believe that completing the journey implies being cleansed of sins and being reborn or renewed. For Japanese pilgrims, this incorporates also a motif of rebirth and salvation, with the widespread belief that performing pilgrimages such as Saikoku and Shikoku means that pilgrims will pass safely into the Pure Land at death. Such themes—the pilgrimage as journey to higher spiritual states, as a life journey, as encounter with the world beyond this, and as means of renewal—are found in numerous pilgrimage cultures beyond Japan. Thus the Christian pilgrimage to Jerusalem has traditionally been seen not merely as a physical journey following Jesus' footsteps, but as a spiritual journey to another realm, while Hindu pilgrimages to sacred crossing places such as rivers (a common location of pilgrimage sites) may be full of images and symbolic themes of transition from one realm to another and of renewal and reinvigoration for those who return home afterward.

The extraordinary and the miraculous are also recurrent themes in the formation of pilgrimage sites and in motivating pilgrims. The rumored apparition of a sacred figure such as the Virgin Mary or the occurrence of a miracle (for example, a cure for illness) may draw people to particular places and foment pilgrimage cults. Lourdes in France, for instance, developed as a pilgrimage center because of stories associated with the visions of Bernadette and the apparitions of Mary there and the belief that Mary's presence enabled miracles of healing to occur there.

Pilgrimage sites, in such contexts, are often seen as locales where sacred and human realms intersect and where humans can directly access the sacred and derive benefits from it. Although symbolically pilgrimages may be associated with journeys to higher realms, it is commonly such worldly concerns as healing and other practical benefits that most motivate pilgrims and make pilgrimage sites popular. Lourdes pilgrims travel in the hope of cures and other blessings, as do Japanese pilgrims in Shikoku, Hindu pilgrims in India who may travel to holy pilgrimage temples to seek boons from their deities, and Muslims who visit the graves of Sufis and other holy figures in their tradition for similar purposes.

Buildings and Landscape Pilgrimage sites often produce major physical constructions—temples, shrines, churches, statues, tombs—signifying the physical presence of the sacred and intended to inspire visitors. This is as true for the vast shrine buildings of Tenrikyo as for Catholic pilgrimage cathedrals at Chartres and Santiago and the Buddhist Mahabodhi temple at Bodh Gaya, all of which speak of a grandeur that articulates in physical form the spiritual power they are believed to hold. Yet grandeur is not a necessary component of pilgrimage. Many of the Shikoku temples, for example, are not particularly striking; their significance relates to their legendary association with the footsteps of Kobo Daishi. Often more important is the landscape: the New Age sites of Sedona and Glastonbury owe much to their dramatic scenery, while features such as rivers and mountains are prominent in many pilgrimage contexts. In Hinduism, important life-giving rivers such as the Ganges (and crossing places on it such as Varanasi) are prominent as pilgrimage sites, while awe-inspiring mountains such as the Himalayas, often symbolically considered as the abode of gods, may become the focus of pilgrimage practices and sites. Elsewhere, too, mountains have become pilgrimage centers, such as Croagh Patrick in Ireland, Mount Athos in Greece, Mount Kailas in Tibet, sacred for Hindus and Buddhists, and Japanese peaks such as Fuji and Ontake.

Places and Routes There is often a tension in pilgrimage between movement and place, and between route and site. Some pilgrimages (Santiago and Shikoku are good examples) focus on a special route that brings the pilgrim to one or more sacred sites. In such cases emphasis might be placed on the activities and practices engaged in while journeying to and between the sites. In other cases, however, the main emphasis is on activities at or around the site itself; Lourdes and Mecca are examples of such pilgrimages. However, this does not mean that the journey to these places is not important; pilgrims have provided rich accounts of the emotional feelings acquired through traveling from their homes to Lourdes with a group of fellow pilgrims, while for Muslims the processes of preparing for the hajj via their journey to Mecca, help heighten their sense of expectation as they approach the holy region itself. While different pilgrimages may emphasize different aspects of the process, both journey and place form parts of a wider whole and should be considered as parts of a unitary pilgrimage process.

Replication and Localization The notion that pilgrimage only involves journeys to distant places is erroneous; pilgrimages may also have highly localized dimensions. Many Shikoku pilgrims are local people, and the pilgrimage is very much part of regional folk belief. Likewise Saudi Arabians living close to Mecca also make pilgrimages there. Pilgrimages may also be replicated and copied, often in localized forms. In earlier times, making replicas of distant pilgrimage sites for the benefit of those who could not travel afar was common; Walsingham, in England, developed in the 11th century as a replica of the Christian Holy Land, while throughout Japan smaller-scale regional copies of the Saikoku and Shikoku routes flourished from the 17th century on. In more recent times, numerous copies of the Lourdes grotto have been built in Japan, in the United States, and in the United Kingdom; the English Catholic diocese of Lancaster, for example, has its own Lourdes replica, which is the focus of an annual diocesan pilgrimage. Diaspora communities often make replicas of sacred pilgrimage sites as a way of helping them settle in and create a new identity in their new homelands; Hindus in the United Kingdom and the United States, for example, have built replicas of prominent Hindu pilgrimage sites in these countries.

Tourism, Travel, and Modernity Pilgrimages are deeply associated with entertainment, escape, travel, and, especially in modern times, tourism. Always a way of stepping outside one's normal environment, they offered people in pre-modern times perhaps the only means of escape from the confines of feudal societies; it was often the only way they could gain permission to travel with any legitimacy. In pre-modern Japan, for example, travel permits were usually only granted for making pilgrimages to major sites, which meant that those wanting to travel dressed up their journeys in a religious guise as a result. It also meant that pilgrimage centers developed into tourist as well as religious locations. The same was true for medieval Europe. In both contexts it is clear that the earliest package tours (the staple of the modern tourist industry) grew out of pilgrimage. In medieval Europe, for example, as the overland journey to the Holy Land became increasingly difficult, the seafarers of Venice who controlled the Mediterranean sea lanes offered all-inclusive tours to the Holy Land for aspirant pilgrims. In Japan, similarly, guides from Ise, the country's main Shinto pilgrimage center, provided all-inclusive package tours from far villages to Ise, including lodging and religious services at the shrines. Pilgrimage centers generally provided the means for pilgrims to let off steam after performing their religious activities and provided entertainment to attract potential clients; it was a rare site that did not (like Ise) have plentiful bars and entertainment quarters to service those who had completed their religious devotions. Likewise, because many pilgrimage sites were also endowed with great architecture and were important cultural sites in their own right, they attracted visitors who came both as pilgrims and as tourists.

The links of pilgrimage and tourism have grown in the modern era, as mass transportation, modern infrastructures, and a moneyed economy have made it increasingly easy for greater numbers of people to travel. Modern transport, in making once distant places accessible, has stimulated a huge growth in pilgrimage; Lourdes, for example, benefited from the opening, not long after the 1858 apparitions, of a railway line that made it accessible to people from distant cities such as Paris. In the latter half of the 20th century, the advent of mass air travel made journeys to Mecca far quicker and less dangerous for people across the Muslim world and led to a huge rise in pilgrim numbers. In Japan, the rise of bus package tours in Shikoku pilgrimage—which until the mid-20th century could only be accomplished by foot—led to huge growth in pilgrim numbers. Pilgrims have always made use of whatever transport systems are available, and pilgrimages have commonly been boosted by economic advances and developments, so it is unsurprising that the modern day has seen immense growth in the numbers making pilgrimages; Lourdes gets more than 6 million pilgrims a year, while the hajj now gets 2.5 million pilgrims (compared to around 30,000 in the 1930s). Modernity has also expanded the pilgrimage clientele immensely. In earlier eras, the long and arduous journey to Mecca or to Shikoku would have defeated all but the hardiest, and few older people could have managed it. Nowadays even age and infirmity are no longer barriers to long distance pilgrimage.

All this has enhanced the tourist dimensions of pilgrimage. In Shikoku, for example, contemporary pilgrimage literature frequently emphasizes the cultural treasures and sights associated with the temples and route, along with the comforts available along the way. The huge growth in pilgrims has enhanced the commercial surroundings of many pilgrimage locations. While shops selling goods and souvenirs have been found at pilgrimage sites from the outset, the intertwining of marketplace and pilgrimage places has been pronounced in modern terms; one Muslim pilgrim, for example, commented that while on the hajj he felt that pilgrims oscillated between the mosque and the marketplace. Often, too, the commodities sold at sacred sites form a key motivation for visitors; pilgrims in Japan have reported in surveys that obtaining the scroll that signifies their completion of the pilgrimage is a prime reason for doing it in the first place, while pilgrims to Marian sites such as Lourdes are often motivated by the wish to acquire holy water and other such talismans from these sites.

However, while modernity has led to increasing numbers of pilgrims using motorized transport, the numbers of walkers on long-distance pilgrimage routes such as Shikoku and Santiago, have also increased. For such people, these pilgrimages offer a challenge and an alternative to the travails and rush of modern life; many, too, see these pilgrimages as offering a new way of self-development unconnected to organized religious traditions. Indeed, many such modern pilgrims appear to eschew religious faith altogether. Studies show that many walking the Santiago route do so not because of Catholic faith but as a challenge, and as a journey of self-discovery driven by individual spiritual motivations. The same is true in Shikoku, where the growing numbers of foot pilgrims in recent years are more motivated by challenge than by Buddhist faith. Even those on organized bus tours in Shikoku tend to cite searching for Japanese cultural heritage and identity as a key motivation, rather than religious faith. Likewise, now that modern medicine offers health solutions unavailable in earlier ages, there may be less emphasis on doing pilgrimages to seek miraculous healing and more on seeing it as a way of exercise that enables one to remain fit and healthy. Many Shikoku pilgrims, for example, cite fitness and health as motivations for doing it—including those on organized tours, who report that the activity keeps them mentally as well as physically healthy.

These patterns are evident also in the growing numbers of "non-religious" pilgrimages and sites with no particular religious associations, such as the aforementioned war grave pilgrimages in Europe and sites with resonances of remembrance for the dead such as the Vietnam Wall in Washington. Places such as Glastonbury or Graceland, or, indeed, places such as Disneyland in the United States (whose construction of an idealized image of "traditional main street America," has caused some scholars to depict it as a form of American secular pilgrimage) have flourished in part because they offer people the means to engage in pilgrim activity combined with visiting interesting places, while not being tied to specific religious traditions. As such, pilgrimage—a practice deeply associated with the origins of religious traditions and with the miraculous—continues to flourish in modern contexts; it remains a basic and central feature in many traditions, while new places of pilgrimage, often of a modern secularized nature, continue to emerge to attract the interest of new clienteles.

Ian Reader

See also: Athos, Mount; Benares; Bodh-Gaya; Devotion/Devotional Traditions; Enlightenment; Fatima; Guan Yin's Birthday; Ise Shrine, The; Jerusalem; Kedarnath; Koya, Mount; Kukai (Kobo Daishi); Kusinagara; Lourdes; Lumbini; Mary, Blessed Virgin; Mecca; Modernity; Muhammad; Saigoku Kannon Pilgrimage; Sarnath; Shikoku Pilgrimage; Sufism; Tenri City; Tenrikyo.

References

Coleman, Simon, and John Elsner. *Pilgrimage: Past and Present in the World Religions*. Cambridge: Harvard University Press, 1995.

Dubisch, Jill. "'Heartland of America': Memory, Motion and the (re)Construction of History on a Motorcycle Pilgrimage." In *Reframing Pilgrimage: Cultures in Motion*, edited by Simon Coleman and John Eade, 105–132. London: Routledge, 2004.

Frey, Nancy Louise. *Pilgrim Stories: On and Off the Road to Santiago*. Berkeley: University of California Press, 1998.

Gitlitz, David, and Linda Davidson. *Pilgrimage: An Encyclopedia*. 2 vols. Santa Barbara, CA: ABC-Clio, 2002.

Hammoudi, Abdellah. *A Season in Mecca: Narrative of a Pilgrimage*. Cambridge: Polity Press, 2005.

Harris, Ruth. *Lourdes: Body and Spirit in the Secular Age*. London: Allen Lane, 1999.

Kaufman, Suzanne K. *Consuming Visions: Mass Culture and the Lourdes Shrine*. Ithaca, NY: Cornell University Press, 2004.

Moore, Alexander. "Walt Disney World: Bounded Ritual Space and the Playful Pilgrimage Center." *Anthropological Quarterly* 53, no. 4 (1980): 207–217.

Reader, Ian. *Making Pilgrimages: Meaning and Practice in Shikoku*. Honolulu: University of Hawaii Press, 2005.

Reader, Ian, and Tony Walter, eds. *Pilgrimage in Popular Culture*. Basingstoke, UK: Palgrave, 1993.

■ Pitcairn Island

The Pitcairn Islands group consists of four volcanic islands that are now a dependency of New Zealand. The islands are located in the South Pacific, halfway between Australia and the coast of Chile. The four islands have a total land area of but 16 square miles. The population has decreased markedly in recent decades, and today stands at less than 50 (2008).

Pitcairn, the only inhabited island of the four, became world famous as the site chosen as a refuge by the mutineers of the HMS *Bounty,* made famous in the novel by Charles Nordhoff (1887–1947) and James Hall (1887–1951) and later turned into several movies. Following the mutiny in 1790, the crew settled briefly in Tahiti. From there, most of them took wives from among the Natives and sailed to Pitcairn before the British could catch up with them. Though it had been discovered and named by Robert Pitcairn in 1767, at the time of the mutiny the island was not on the maps of the British navy.

Until the 20th century, the island's entire population (which peaked at 200 in 1937) consisted entirely of descendants of the *Bounty* crew. One of the *Bounty* mutineers, a devout member of the Church of England, organized an Anglican parish. However, in 1877 some literature from the Seventh-day Adventist Church arrived on the island. As a result, in 1887 the population converted to Adventism and the Seventh-day

PITCAIRN ISLAND

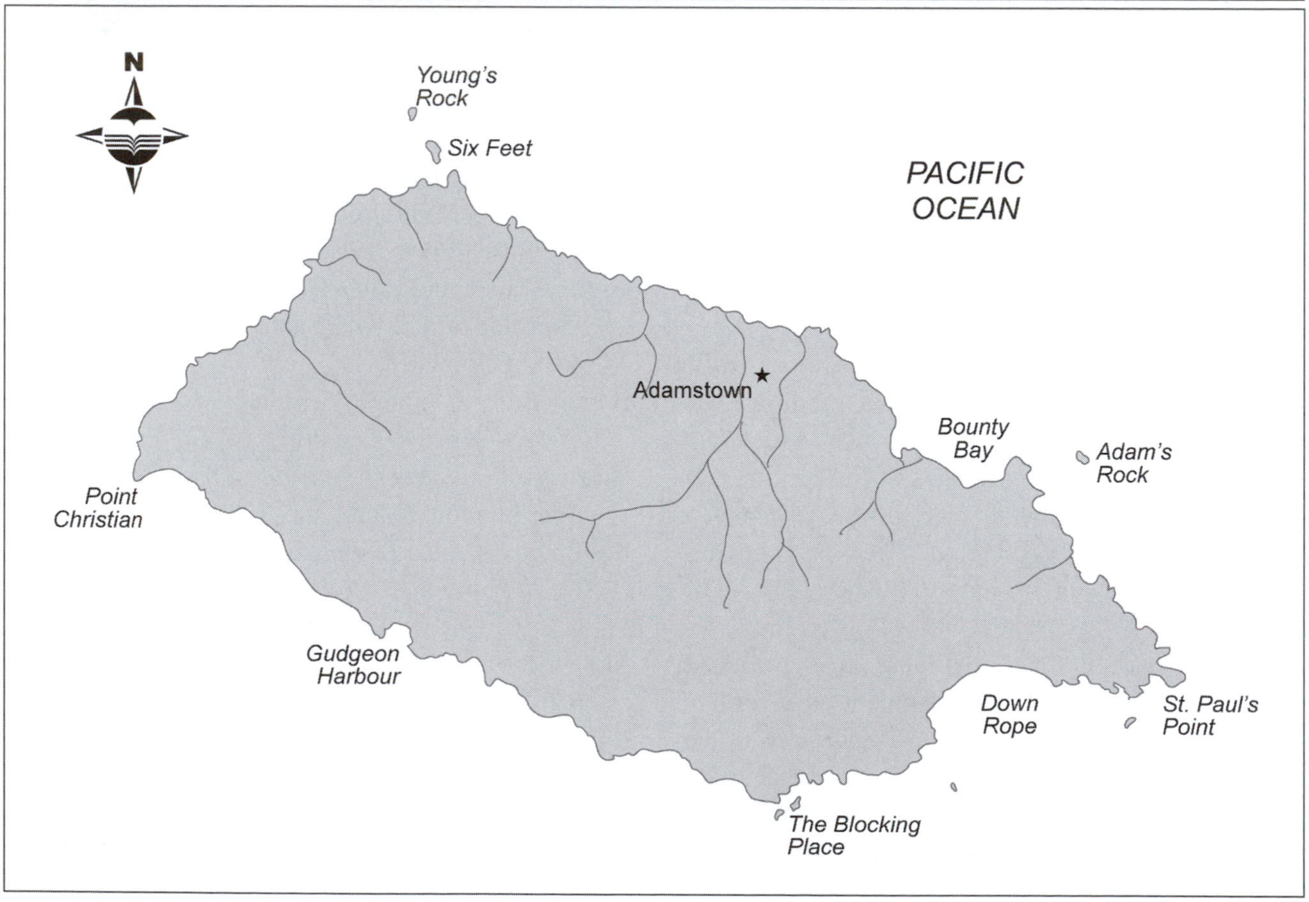

Pitcairn Island

Religion	Followers in 1970	Followers in 2010	% of Population	Annual % growth 2000–2010	Followers in 2025	Followers in 2050
Christians	90	50	92.0	–2.79	50	50
Protestants	90	50	92.0	–2.79	50	50
Agnostics	0	10	8.0	–4.36	10	10
Total population	**90**	**60**	**100.0**	**–2.92**	**60**	**60**

Adventist Pitcairn Island Mission was formally organized in 1895. It is currently the only religion practiced on the island.

J. Gordon Melton

See also: Church of England; Seventh-day Adventist Church.

References

Barrett, David, ed. *The Encyclopedia of World Christianity*. 2nd ed. New York: Oxford University Press, 2001.

Forman, Charles H. *The Island Churches of the South Pacific: Emergence in the Twentieth Century*. Maryknoll, NY: Orbis, 1982.

Kirk, Robert W. *Pitcairn Island, the Bounty Mutineers and Their Descendants: A History*. Jeffersonville, NC: McFarland & Company, 2008.

Plymouth Brethren (Exclusive)

See Christian Brethren.

■ Poland

Poland is an Eastern European nation on the Baltic Sea between Germany and the isolated enclave of Russian, Kaliningrad Oblast. It additionally shares borders with Lithuania, Belarus, Ukraine, Slovakia, and the Czech Republic. Its territory includes 117,600 square miles of land and a population of 38,500,000.

Christianized in the 10th century, Poland has had a long tradition of religious pluralism that existed even before the Reformation. Besides Catholics, there were a number of Orthodox, Jews, Pagans (in some remote regions of the country), and, later, Protestants and Muslims. The degree of religious and ethnic pluralism gradually declined after the 16th century due to migrations, changes of borders, and the Holocaust, and the proportion of the population being both Roman Catholic and ethnically Polish approached 100 percent after World War II.

As a result, the role of the Roman Catholic Church, with more than 90 percent of the Polish population as members, has become greater than before. The fact that Catholicism has been viewed as an antidote to Communism and as a defender of national identity against the danger of Sovietization also contributed to its growing importance. As a result, since the mid-1970s the surveys reveal a growing rate of participation in Catholic practices and a growing number of persons identifying themselves as believers and as firm believers. The election of Karol Wojtyla (1920–2005), a Polish national, as Pope John Paul II (r. 1978–2005), the appearance of the Solidarity movement, and the role of the church during the martial law period further contributed to the Catholic revival that continued to the end of the 1980s. At the beginning of the 21st century, this dominant form of religiosity is still widespread, and during the last decade it has remained almost at the same level as before, which places Poland among the most religious Christian countries (together with Ireland and the United States).

Other religions, either traditional or new, comprise about 2 percent of the population. The biggest groups are the Orthodox Church of Poland, concentrated mainly in the eastern parts of the country, the Jehovah's Witnesses, and the Evangelical Church of the Augsburg Confession, concentrated mainly in the southwest part of Poland.

An Orthodox celebration of the Feast of Jordan (Theophany) in St. Onuphrius Monastery in Jableczna, Poland. (Dariusz Majgier/Dreamstime.com)

The appearance of new religions in Poland provides some interesting patterns pertinent to theories of secularization. New religious movements (NRMs) seem to have emerged in Poland not on the ruins of a dominant religious tradition but parallel to it. The appearance of new religions in Poland in the 1970s may be seen as the reintroduction of religious pluralism, which had to a large extent vanished from Poland as an effect of World War II. The scale and character of the NRMs that began to appear at that time were, however, totally new. They usually represent more exotic and less established religious traditions, being often new not only in Poland but also throughout the West. Important changes in regulations concerning the freedom of religion were issued in 1989 that made the official registration relatively easy, but some groups still prefer informal ways of activity, being too small to be registered (initially, the law required a minimum of 15 persons for registration, and now it requires 100).

The largest proportion of membership in NRMs can be observed among movements growing inside the Catholic Church. Their number grew from about 20 in the early 1980s to more than 180 by 1994. Movements like the Apostles of Sobriety (present in 35.8 percent of the 7,579 Catholic parishes surveyed in 1988), Light-Life or Oases (present in 31.5 percent of parishes), God's Mercy Votaries (18.3 percent), Life and Family Apostles (9.4 percent), Family of Families (9.3 percent), Charismatic Renewal in the Holy Spirit (5.3 percent), Eucharist-Marian Crusade (4.1 percent), Maitri (2.1 percent), Neo-Catechumenal Community (1.9 percent), and others stress particular aspects of religious renewal and contribute to the growing endogenous pluralism of the Catholic Church (Firlit et al. 1990). The majority are of Polish origin but some international Catholic religious movements are also present.

The development of the intrachurch Catholic movements is one of the most significant factors of change

POLAND

in the Polish religious context in recent years. Some spectacular conversions of popular journalists and rock musicians have garnered much publicity in the media. Therefore, the growing number of movements and their members (now more than 1 million) constitutes, both quantitatively and qualitatively, perhaps the most effective alternative to the secularization trend mentioned earlier. These "small churches" inside "the big church" create possibilities for pluralism within the Catholic Church, which may be conducive to better fulfillment of individual religious needs and the higher commitment of its members. These groups are not negatively stigmatized as are some sects and cults, but they are to some extent, and contribute to better mobilization of resources within the church. According to some estimations, a large proportion (about 60 percent) of priestly vocations come from these movements. However, much of any group's success depends on the

Poland

Religion	Followers in 1970	Followers in 2010	% of Population	Annual % growth 2000–2010	Followers in 2025	Followers in 2050
Christians	29,633,000	36,523,000	96.4	–0.10	35,222,000	29,513,000
Roman Catholics	28,783,000	34,730,000	91.6	–0.21	33,500,000	28,000,000
Orthodox	532,000	578,000	1.5	0.01	600,000	550,000
Marginals	22,500	219,000	0.6	0.71	270,000	270,000
Agnostics	2,033,000	1,250,000	3.3	–0.67	1,000,000	650,000
Atheists	969,000	92,800	0.2	–0.12	70,000	45,000
Jews	8,000	9,600	0.0	0.65	9,600	9,600
Muslims	100	8,900	0.0	–0.12	12,500	15,000
Spiritists	0	7,600	0.0	–0.12	9,000	10,000
New religionists	20,000	7,400	0.0	–0.12	8,000	9,000
Buddhists	0	2,100	0.0	–0.13	4,000	6,000
Baha'is	100	1,000	0.0	–0.12	1,500	2,500
Total population	**32,664,000**	**37,902,000**	**100.0**	**–0.12**	**36,337,000**	**30,260,000**

attitude of the church hierarchy toward it. As a whole, the groups were supported by Pope John Paul II, who in a letter to the participants of the Congress of the Catholic Movements in 1994 stressed their significant role in religious renewal and compared them to the "spring in the Church." His support may have changed the reservations of some bishops toward these movements.

Some of these Catholic communities, however, become too radical to remain within the Roman Catholic Church, either due to their own decisions or due to the decisions of the local bishop. After the bonds with the institutional church have been broken, they often register as separate religious bodies and define themselves within the Protestant tradition.

The largest group of newly registered religious bodies belong to the Protestant tradition, both mainline and marginal. They constitute a variety of movements that often cluster in distinct families (Baptist, Adventist, Pentecostal, and so on). At least one of the reasons for their growth is their tendency to organize themselves on the basis of locality and to register as separate religious unions. Many of the local religious unions belong to this category of "congregational revival" and represent various evangelical groups that are not significantly differentiated in doctrinal terms.

Among the most dynamically growing Protestant families are those emphasizing Pentecostal forms of piety. Although not all of them are quite new, in the 1990s their rates of growth were the most visible and contrasted with those of the major Protestant churches (Lutheran, Reformed, and Methodist), which were experiencing a period of decline. Doctrinal differentiation among the Pentecostals is usually greater than among other groups, manifested in Trinitarian or Unitarian theologies while also emphasizing different theological formulations such as "prosperity theology" or "eternal security." The Pentecostal movement in Poland also includes some formerly Catholic Charismatic, or "Oases," groups.

Possibly the most spectacular case of a marginal Protestant movement is the Jehovah's Witnesses. Despite persecutions in former decades, it now constitutes the third largest denominational group in Poland. Although their appearance in Poland dates back to the beginning of the 20th century, the Jehovah's Witnesses were officially registered in 1989, which has given the movement the principal impetus for growth (about 5 percent annually in the first years of the 1990s), most of the new converts having a Catholic background.

New Religious movements related to other traditions are much smaller. The International Society for Krishna Consciousness is perhaps the biggest among Hindu groups, and Karma-Kagyupa Tibetan Buddhism is the largest among Buddhist groups. There are also a few NRMs of Polish origin. Together with movements that were born earlier and are now more respected denominations (such as the Polish Catholic Church and two Old Catholic Church of Mariavites), they are examples of religious creativity, which seems in Poland somewhat less vigorous than in neighboring countries like Russia and Germany, perhaps due to the strength of the dominant Catholic religious tradition. The most numerous among these are neo-Pagan groups, which have emerged as an attempt to reconstruct and revive old Slavonic religion from pre-Christian times. As part of the neo-Pagan revival in the region, groups such as the Clan of Ausrans have close relations with other neo-Pagan movements in neighboring countries, especially the Baltic countries and Ukraine.

The number of officially registered religious communities in Poland increased about 4 times in the last decade of the 20th century, now numbering more than 150, and a few have shown dynamic growth in membership. Recently, however, this growth has significantly decreased, due in large part to the growing social perception of religious minorities as a "sect problem" and to the resulting changes in legislation. The data on membership of particular movements that are registered as religious unions are gathered by the Main Statistical Office on the basis of annual reports presented by the movements themselves.

Thadeus Doktor

See also: Clan of Ausrans; Evangelical Church of the Augsburg Confession; International Society for Krishna Consciousness; Jehovah's Witnesses; Karma-Kagyupa Tibetan Buddhism; Old Catholic Church of Mariavites/Catholic Church of Mariavites.

References

Abramsky, Chimen. *The Jews in Poland.* New York: Wiley-Blackwell, 1991.

Adamczuk, L., P. Ciecielag, M. Chmielewski, T. Doktór, and G. Gudaszewski. *Wyznania religijne. Stowarzyszenia narodowosciowe i etniczne w Polsce, 1997–1999.* Warsaw: GUS, 2000.

Braun, J. *Poland in Christian Civilization.* London: Veritas Foundation, 1985.

Doktór, Tadeusz. "Buddhism in Poland." In *New Religions and New Religiosity,* edited by Eileen Barker and Margit Warburg, 83–94. Aarhus, Denmark: Aarhus University Press, 1998.

Doktór, Tadeusz. *State, Church and New Religious Movements in Poland.* Krakow: Nomos, 1999.

Kloczowski, Jerry. *A History of Polish Christianity.* Cambridge: Cambridge University Press, 2000.

Korbonski, A. *The Church and State in Poland after World War II.* Washington, DC: Council for Soviet and East European Research, 1994.

Teter, Magda. *Jews and Heretics in Catholic Poland: A Beleaguered Church in the Post-Reformation Era.* Cambridge: Cambridge University Press, 2005.

Zdaniewiez, W., and T. Zembrzuski, eds. *Kosciól i religijnosc Polaków 1945–1999.* Warsaw: Pallotinum, 2000.

Polish National Catholic Church/Polish Catholic Church

The Polish National Catholic Church (PNCC; Kosciol Polskokatolicki) was founded by former Roman Catholic clergyman Franciszek (Francis) Hodur (1866–1953) in Scranton, Pennsylvania, in 1897. The immediate reason for the formation of a national church among Poles in America was a conflict about non-Polish priests assigned to predominantly Polish American parishes. The Polish immigrant members of the parishes resented the fact that the priests made use of parish funds without consulting the members. The reaction to the felt discrimination against Polish Catholics was addressed mainly to the predominantly Irish/German hierarchy in the United States. However, beginning in 1919, the church started to spread in Poland as well. In the early 1950s, the former missionary diocese of the PNCC in Poland became a separate denomination called the Polish Catholic Church (PCC).

The PNCC had a somewhat conflictual beginning, and the missionary church in Poland also encountered notable obstacles. Its petitions to be recognized as a full-fledged denomination were ignored by the government. The church was harassed by the local authorities, being charged with unauthorized use of Catholic liturgical vestments and furnishings and refused access to burial grounds that were under control of Roman Catholic parishes. Some local offices even refused to register births, marriages, and deaths of some Polish National Catholics.

Many years prior to Vatican II (1962–1965), the PNCC introduced the Polish tongue, as opposed to Latin, into rituals, catechism classes, and sermons. The General Synod in 1954 finally decided that Polish would be the sole language of the liturgy. However, English is now in more frequent use in worship in the United States. In doctrine, the PNCC is closest to the various Old Catholic churches with whom it has fraternal relationships. The church's major departure from the Roman Catholic Church, aside from breaking from its jurisdiction, has been discarding the dogma of papal infallibility. The PNCC recognizes Catholic teaching on the Highest Being, the salvation of the world, the work of the Holy Spirit, the responsibility of individuals for their actions before God, divine grace, and the need for a sacramental priesthood. Since 1909, however, the church has rejected the belief that people can eternally disappear or suffer in hell forever. More recently, the doctrines of original sin and the devil have been rejected as well. The year 1909 also marked the addition of a new sacrament, the Hearing and Announcing of the Word of God. In 1921 communal confession was introduced, and baptism and confirmation were joined into one sacrament. Celibacy was abolished in 1921.

In 1904 the church was given a synodal character, the Church Council was elected to exercise authority in the periods between synods, and the position of the elected bishop was introduced. The first bishop was consecrated in 1906. Since 1914, parishes cannot sell any of their estate without the consent of their bishop. They also cannot choose their pastor, though the bishop makes pastoral appointments only after consultation with the parish. In Poland, the parish council has less power than in the United States. Polish lay members have tended to be more subordinate to the clergy, as is the custom in the Roman Catholic parishes.

The highest authority in the PNCC is given to the Universal Synod (ordinary or extraordinary). The legislative authority in the diocese, limited by the requirements of the church constitution, belongs to the provincial synod, and in the parish it belongs to the parish assembly. When the synod is not in session, the responsible authority rests with the Church Council, chosen by the synod from among the priests and laymen. The executive authority covers church responsibilities as follows: the prime bishop with the Church Council has executive authority over the whole church, the diocesan bishop with the diocesan council has authority in dioceses, and parish committees have authority in parishes.

As of 2004, there were approximately 60,000 members in the PNCC. They were divided among 126 parishes and 37 missions, served by approximately 137 priests. There are four dioceses: Central, Eastern, Buffalo-Pittsburgh, and Western. Offspring of the church are the PNCC of Canada (previously an independent diocese consisting of six parishes and three missions) and the parishes in Brazil that remain a part of the church in the United States. The priests are trained in the Savonarola Theological Seminary in Scranton, Pennsylvania.

In Poland, the highest authority of jurisdiction and supervision rests with the General Polish Synod, which gathers every four years. The main executive body is the Council of Synod together with its president, who is both a bishop and the superior of the PCC. There are three dioceses in Poland: Warsaw, Wrocław, and Krakow. They cover 11 decanates. The PCC oversees 80 parishes. Some 20,000 members are served by 82 priests. The largest parishes and the largest number of parishes are to be found in the Province of Lublin and the area around Rzeszów. Both the PNCC and the PCC are members of the World Council of Churches. and maintain strong ties to the larger Old Catholic movement.

Polish National Catholic Church (U.S.A.)
1002 Pittston Ave.
Scranton, PA 18505
http://www.pncc.org

Polish Catholic Church (Poland)
Kosciol Polskokatolicki w RP
ul. Balonowa 7
02-635 Warszawa
Poland

Leslaw Borowski

See also: Roman Catholic Church; World Council of Churches.

References

Anson, Peter. *Bishops at Large*. London: Faber and Faber, 1964.

Darczewska-Adamus, Krystyna. *Kosciol Polskokatolicki*. Warsaw: Instytut Filozofii i Socjologii PAN, 1968.

Fox, Paul. *The Polish National Catholic Church*. Scranton, PA: School of Christian Living, 1955.

Kubiak, Hieronim. *The Polish National Catholic Church in the United States of America from 1897 to 1980*. Warsaw and Krakow: Panstwowe Wydawnictwo Naukowe, 1982.

Wlodarski, Stephen. *The Origin and Growth of the Polish National Catholic Church*: Scranton, PA: The Polish National Catholic Church, 1974.

Polygamy-Practicing Mormons

When Wilford Woodruff (1807–1898) announced the Manifesto of 1890 it began the end of official sanctioned polygamy within the Church of Jesus Christ of Latter-day Saints. With that he drew a line that would be debated from that point forward about whether there was still authority to perform plural marriage. Within two decades those who continued in the principle and those who followed the Mormon church prophet's admonition to discontinue the practice of the polygamy became deeply divided. These were decades of significant confusion, as church-sanctioned marriages continued in some locations including in the Mexican colonies. Nevertheless, by 1904 and what was called the Second Manifesto, church policy was to excommunicate those who married additional women.

Many believed that the Manifesto was an accommodation to the government, a gesture designed to pave the way for statehood, and certainly not based on a revelation from God. The ambiguous language of the document seemed to prove this belief—leaving room for continuing polygamy outside the confines of the United States in Mexico or Canada.

Fundamentalism (a popular designation of those continuing to practice polygamy) as a movement began in the 1920s when some polygamists gathered around the charismatic personalities of Loren C. Woolley (1856–1934), John Y. Barlow (1874–1949), and Joseph W. Musser (1872–1954), among others. Excommunicated after 1904 for their disobedience to the Mormon prophet's Manifesto, fundamentalists settled in a small southern Utah town—Short Creek—and in various places around the Great Basin.

During the 1920s, Loren C. Woolley claimed that he had received the special commission to continue plural marriage in Centerville, Utah, in 1886. There he allegedly witnessed a visit of Jesus Christ and Joseph Smith, Jr. (1805–1844), to John Taylor (1808–1887), then prophet of the church in hiding from the federal marshals. Although many rejected this claim, the division between the official church organization and those who chose to continue in the doctrine was distinct—sealed by both official church policy and informal social division.

Distinguished first by the practice of plural marriage, the fundamentalists follow the teachings of the 19th-century presidents of the church, and some groups have established themselves communally in such organizations as the United Effort Firm of Short Creek. Separated from the Mormon church by excommunication, the fundamentalists believe they have continued priesthood to perform sacred marriage ceremonies, which they believe are binding through eternity.

It is estimated by the Utah attorney general's office that there are as many as 50,000 fundamentalists in Utah. While many of these belong to groups and live and worship together, there are also thousands of independent polygamists who practice the principle in isolation. What unites them is their continued belief that plurality is essential to their salvation, that it is a teaching of God, and that it is the best way to organize their family life.

In the 1940s and again in 1953, the government attempted to end polygamy in Utah and Arizona by arresting many of the men in the groups on a variety of charges other than polygamy. Typically these charges included cohabitation, violations of the Mann and Lindbergh statutes (designed to prohibit slavery and kidnapping), and statutory rape. More difficult to prove, polygamy was deemed justification for a community-wide roundup in 1953 under the auspices of the governor of Arizona, Howard Pyle. Since the 1950s Utah

A Mormon family of the 1870s, with a husband, two wives, and nine children. (Bettmann/Corbis)

had an unofficial policy of leaving the polygamists alone until 2001, when independent polygamist Tom Green was tried for bigamy. Convicted because of his marriages to underage girls and problems in supporting his very large family of more than 20 children, Green became a self-designated spokesperson for the movement—appearing on numerous national television talk shows advocating his unusual lifestyle. More typically fundamentalists practice polygamy in private, separated from the mainstream, and avoid both publicity and public knowledge of the specifics of their family life.

Popular estimates suggest that polygamists may be 20,000 to 30,000 in number. Among the larger groups are the Apostolic United Apostolic Brethren, led by Owen Allred. They may be reached at 3139 W. 14700 S., No. A, Bluffsville, UT 84065. They report approximately 6,000 members. The United Order Effort, also known as the Fundamentalist LDS Church, is led by Rulon Jeffs and may be reached c/o Dan Barlow, Colorado City, AZ 86021. There are approximately 8,000 associated members. There are a variety of smaller groups located in Utah and adjacent states. One group, the Church of the First Born of the Fullness of Times, was decimated by violence when Ervil LeBaron (d. 1981), brother of founder Joel LeBaron (d. 1972), left the church, founded a rival group, and then masterminded a spree of violence at the church and other polygamy-practicing groups.

Leroy S. Johnson (1888–1986) led the group until his death in 1986. As the group's spiritual and temporal leader, he managed the financial affairs of the United Effort Firm and the Fundamentalist Church of Jesus Christ of Latter-day Saints (FLDS). Before his successor, Rulon K. Jeffs (1909–2002), died in 2002, he turned much of the control over the church to his son Warren Jeffs (b. 1955). Under his administration the FLDS retrenched and became more exclusive and closed off from the world outside at the same time Utah Attorney General Mark Shurtleff began a period of increased prosecution of cases of alleged child abuse in the group. The principal focus was underaged marriages. In perhaps the most notorious case since the 19th century concerning polygamy, Warren Jeffs was indicted by the state of Utah for his alleged involvement in the arrangement of underage marriages and on eight additional charges by Arizona. In May 2006, he was placed on the FBI's Ten Most Wanted List because of his "unlawful flight to avoid prosecution" in Utah. He was arrested in August 2006 outside Las Vegas and tried in Utah in two separate cases in September 2007. He was found guilty on two counts of rape as an accomplice. In November 2007 he began serving a sentence of 10 years to life in the Utah State Prison.

Under Warren Jeffs the FLDS began building complexes of buildings in remote locations for members of the group. The most well known was the Yearning for Zion Ranch in Eldorado, Texas. The 1,700-member YFZ Ranch is found in Schleicher Co., in West Texas. On April 3, 2008, the Child Protective Services (CPS) Agency of Texas initiated a raid against the community in response to a phone call from an alleged 16-year-old girl, "Sarah," who said she was being held against her will. CPS considered the children to be the residents of a single household where they were exposed to polygamy and pressured into underaged marriages. Judge Barbara Walther of the 51st District Court issued the order for the removal of all the community's children—462—under the age of 17 years. They were held at Fort Concho and at the Wells Fargo Pavilion in San Angelo, Texas. In May, the Third Court of Appeals ruled that the state had insufficient evidence that the children were in immediate danger. Within the year all the children were returned to their families, though litigation continues.

Martha Sonntag Bradley

See also: Church of Jesus Christ of Latter-day Saints; Smith, Joseph, Jr.

References

Allred, Rulon C. *Treasures of Knowledge*. 2 vols. Hamilton, MT: Bitterroot Publishing Co., 1982.

Bennion, Janet. *Women of the Principle.* New York: Oxford University Press, 1998.

Bradley, Martha Sonntag. *Kidnapped from That Land: The Government Raids on the Short Creek Polygamists.* Salt Lake City: University of Utah Press, 1993.

Hardy, B. Carmon. *Doing the Works of Abraham. Mormon Polygamy: Its Origin, Practice, and Demise*. Norman, OK: Arthur H. Clark Company, 2007.

Musser, Joseph W. *Celestial or Plural Marriage*. Salt Lake City, UT: Truth Publishing Co., 1944.

Pomun Order of Korean Buddhism

Although the vast majority of Buddhist laity in the Republic of Korea are women, the largest and most influential Buddhist orders, the Chogye Order and the T'aego Order, are controlled by monks. The Pomun Order of Korean Buddhism is significant because it is the first organization in the Republic of Korea to be directed by and oriented toward Buddhist women. One of the primary purposes of the Pomun Order is to provide its members with ample opportunities to obtain merit that can be directed toward their ancestors and family members. So, aside from the traditional Buddhist observances of the day of the Buddha's birth, his leaving home, and his nirvana, the Pomun Order annually celebrates the Ghost Festival and commemorates their founder and monthly holds ritual services invoking the bodhisattvas Ksitigarbha and Avalokitesvara.

The origin of the Pomun Order of Korean Buddhist nuns is found in the establishment of the Yuji Chaedan Taehan Pulgyo Pomunwon, a Korean Buddhist foundation and support center, on August 5, 1971, by the nun Unyong. The next year, on April 20, 1972, the Pomun Order was officially organized, with Pomunsa, located in Seoul, Korea, as its headquarters. The nun Kungt'an (1885–1980) was named head of the order, and Unyong became the director of general affairs. By June 16 of that same year the nuns re-created the interior of the ancient Buddhist grotto of Sokkuram at Pomun Nunnery; by July 6 they were officially registered with the government as the Pomun Order.

The chapter titled "The Gateway to Everywhere of the Bodhisattva, He Who Observes the Sounds of the World" (Pomunp'um) of the Lotus Sutra, also known as the Avalokitesvara Sutra (Kwanum kyong), is the most important teaching of this religious group, suggesting that the nuns' activities are focused on developing compassion like that of Avalokitesvara, the Bodhisattva of Compassion. Other teachings and doctrines of the order are essentially the same as those of traditional mainstream East Asian Mahayana Buddhism and the Korean Chogye Order: they revere the Buddha Sakyamuni and encourage meditation and the study of the Diamond Sutra and Huineng's Platform Sutra of the Sixth Patriarch. Special attention is given to the personal development of the three wisdoms (*samhye*): the wisdom that comes from hearing the Buddha's teaching (*munhye*), contemplating and reflecting upon it (*sahye*), and directly experiencing it in meditation (*suhye*).

As of 2008, the order reported a membership of 57,251 lay followers (18,801 males and 38,450 females), who are served by 204 religious specialists. The order operates a main nunnery and 35 branch nunneries, a nursing home, an orphanage, and 3 kindergartens.

Pomun Order of Korean Buddhism
Songbuk-ku Pomun-dong 3-ga 168
Seoul, 136-083
Republic of Korea

Richard D. McBride II

See also: Bodhisattva; Chogye Order; Korean Buddhism; Mahayana Buddhism; Wesak; Women, Status and Role of.

References

Samu Sunim. "Euyeong Sunim and the Founding of Pomun-jong, the First Independent Bhikshumi Order." *Spring Wind Buddhist Cultural Forum* 6, nos. 1–3 (1986): 129–162.

Taehan Pulgyo Chinhungwon, ed. *Han'guk Pulgyo ch'ongnam*. 3rd ed. Seoul: Taehan Pulgyo Chinhungwon, 2008. s.v. Taehan Pulgyo Pomun-jong, 55–56.

Popocatepetl, Mount/Mount Iztaccihuatl

Mount Popocatepetl and Mount Iztaccihuatl are two volcanic mountains that were sacred to the Aztec people of Mexico. They are located some 45 miles southeast of Mexico City and what was the capital of the Aztec Empire, Tenochtitlan. Popocatepetl, the "Smoking Mountain," reaches upward some 17,800 feet. It has been active in recent history and frequently releases clouds of smoke from its summit. Iztaccihuatl, the "Sleeping Lady," is an extinct volcano some 17,400 feet in height. Historical records of the mountains and activity around them date to the arrival at the city of Cholula in 1519 by the Spanish conquistador Hernando Cortes (1485–1547) though evidence of human habitation in the area goes back to 700 BCE.

One pre-Spanish tale related to the mountains recounts the relation of the warrior Popocatepetl and his great love Iztaccihuatl. Their marriage depended on Popocatepetl winning an upcoming battle. He won, but while away, a rival spread a false rumor that he had died. Iztaccihuatl died of grief before he returned. Upon his return, Popocatepetl placed her body atop the mountain range west of the mountain named for his love, which now has the shape of a sleeping woman. Popocatepetl then climbed the mountain named for him where, torch in hand, he keeps vigil.

Both the height and the activity of Popocatepetl made it a object of attention. Bernardino de Sahagun, a Franciscan friar who observed and recorded the activities of Native Mexicans at the time of the Spanish conquest, noted that Popocatepetl and Iztaccihuatl derived some of their sacred status because rain clouds tended to gather around them. Believers would climb the mountains to venerate the water deities. Unfortunately, Sahagun failed to identify either the deities associated with the mountains or the mythology that surrounded them. At Chocula is a pyramid, Tlachihualtepetl (Man-made Hill), the largest in the Americas. It appears to have been constructed as a smaller Popocatepetl, possibly in reaction to the major eruption of 90 CE.

Volcanic eruptions have driven people away, while the rich soil around the mountain attracts people back. Traditional rituals designed to keep Popocatepetl calm were still being observed as late as the 1980s, but seemed to have disappeared as the 21st century began.

J. Gordon Melton

See also: Franciscans; Mountains.

The snow-covered Popocatepetl volcano stands behind Los Remedios Church in the valley region of Puebla, Mexico. Popocatepetl, which means Smoking Mountain in Aztec, is located 34 miles east of Mexico City and is North America's second highest volcano and one of the most active in the Aztec territory. (Ulises Ruiz/epa/Corbis)

References

Gruzinski, Serge. *The Aztecs: Rise and Fall of an Empire*. New York: Harry N. Abrams, 1992.

Plunket, Patricia, and Gabriela Uruñuela. "Appeasing the Volcano Gods." *Archeology* 51, no. 4 (July–August 1998). http://www.archaeology.org/9807/abstracts/volcano.html.

Pohl, John. *Aztecs and Conquistadores: The Spanish Invasion and the Collapse of the Aztec Empire*. Oxford: Osprey Publishing, 2005.

■ Portugal

Portugal, the westernmost country of continental Europe, has a lengthy western coast on the North Atlantic Ocean. It otherwise shares the Iberian Peninsula with Spain. Its 35,672 square miles of territory are home to its 10,707,924 people.

Portugal was imagined by the propaganda of the fascist regime (1926–1974) as a profoundly Catholic nation. The results of the 2001 census validate this notion inasmuch as 93 percent of the people who answered the question regarding religion declared themselves Catholics. This represented a 2 percent decrease since 1991, benefiting evenly the "irreligious" and "other Christians" categories. By 2001, the latter two represented, respectively, 4 percent and 2 percent of the population. Official statistics estimated the overall population in December 2007 at 10,617,575 people. Twenty-six percent of these lived on or, mostly, around the capital city of Lisbon. The former metropolis of the Portuguese Empire has witnessed many peoples come and go throughout the ages: pre-Roman Iberians, Phoenicians, Romans, Jews, Suebi, Vandals, Visigoths, Moors, and sub-Saharan Africans. All these were blended into the ethnic makeup of the Portuguese people. Still, the Roma constitute a centuries-old

Worshippers attend an international pilgrimage at Fatima Sanctuary in Fatima, Portugal, 2009. (Ruigouveia/Dreamstime .com)

unassimilated ethnic minority. Recent migratory influxes originate in areas of the globe that were part of the former empire—Goa, several African countries, and Brazil, among others—and Eastern Europe. Portuguese idiom, a Romance language spoken by more than 240 million people in Portugal, its former colonies, and respective diasporas, binds most of these peoples.

Despite imperial expansion overseas, the frontiers of mainland Portugal have remained remarkably stable over time. The frontier municipality of Olivença/Olivenza—historically disputed with Spain, which exerts de facto control over the territory—is the sole contentious boundary in the last few centuries of Portuguese history. However, notwithstanding this overall picture of a homogeneous country, the scholars of the democratic period discovered several strata of religious syncretism. For instance, the extensive 1998 ISSP survey on religious beliefs and attitudes seems to corroborate that canonical and non-canonical beliefs and practices coexist effortlessly in Portuguese society. In this encyclopedia entry, we will mention both these strands but will give a special focus to those ideas and movements that belong to the Portuguese religious heterodoxy (for a recent history of the Roman Catholic Church in Portugal, see Azevedo, 2000–2002).

Prior to the founding of the Portuguese state in 1139 CE, the territory that corresponds to present-day mainland Portugal had already been subjected to a cross-pollination of religious influences by the ways of conquest, trade, and migration. However, the history of the region before the first Iron Age, which began as the Phoenician colonization of the Iberian Peninsula advanced, is shrouded because of the absence of thorough archaeological research. The Phoenicians brought not only the technology of iron and the first form of writing known in the peninsula but also new rites, gods, and ways of worship. Contemporary scholarship emphasizes the survival of these practices in Christian garb. An infernal god named Endovellicus, the most documented indigenous deity (with 70 inscriptions extant), provides an example of the survival of this ancient religious stratum; his cult not only thrived under the Roman Empire but is believed to have taken a later Christian shape in the cult of Saint Michael.

The story of Priscillianism, a fourth-century Christian heresy that emerged in the northwest part of the peninsula, also demonstrates that almost anything could happen religiously in Portugal. In the second half of the fourth century, an Egyptian named Marcus arrived in the peninsula preaching Gnostic and Manichean ideas. Several well-off laymen and laywomen paid him attention, and a religious movement began. Priscillian (ca. 340–385), a landowner, took leadership of the movement and used his rhetorical gifts in proselytizing. In 380, 12 Catholic bishops met in Saragossa to write 8 canons condemning Priscillianism. By 385 Priscillian and four of his followers were executed by decapitation in Treveros under accusations of maleficium, or malevolent magic. Their remains were carried back home and revered by their followers. The movement continued, stronger if anything, and dwindled only in the sixth century. Historian José Mattoso has suggested that the main characteristic of the movement was a certain doctrinal formlessness that facilitated its trickling down from the upper stratum of society and its blending with popular Paganism.

Arab Muslims, or Moors, invaded Portugal in the eighth century as part of their spread across the Iberian Peninsula, and Islam continued to dominate the region for the next three centuries. Beginning in the 11th century, a decades-long effort led to the expulsion of the Arabs and the virtual elimination of Islam from the country. Today, there is a small Muslim community, the Comunidade Islámica de Lisbon, that originated in the 20th century around expatriates from former Portuguese colonies.

The Knights Templar helped the first king of Portugal, Afonso Henriques (ca. 1109–1185), to conquer the southwestern part of the peninsula from the Moors, who had controlled it since 711. After the suppression of the order by Pope Clement V in 1312, King Dinis (1261–1325) renamed its Portuguese branch the Order of Christ and left it to go about its business as usual. Henry the Navigator (1394–1460), mastermind of the 15th-century discoveries, was himself leader of this order, and the ships that sailed off from Lisbon were flagged with the cross of the Order of Christ. These facts are the cornerstones of a vast literature of mystic nationalism that speculates about the real aim of the Portuguese discoveries.

In the beginning of the 14th century, Joachim de Fiore's (ca. 1132–1202) theory of the Three Ages began to permeate Portugal. Cistercian and Franciscan monks were the first to succumb to its charms, but the royal family itself would not be unmoved. This theory proclaimed the imminent rise of an Age of the Holy Ghost, following the Ages of the Father and the Son. In this new aeon, humanity would receive a Fifth Gospel by a ceaseless and direct dispensation of the Holy Ghost, and the ideal of universal brotherhood would finally become a reality.

The Festivities of the Holy Ghost began during the reign of King Dinis (1261–1325) and Queen Saint Isabel (1270–1336), circa 1305, and the massive popular adherence that followed quickly spread the festivities throughout the mainland and, later on, into Portugal's overseas possessions, thus constituting a phenomenon unparalleled in other Christian countries. The main features of these festivities were the coronation of a child or man of low social standing, symbolizing that the Empire of the Spirit belongs to the "simple and naive ones"; a collective banquet, symbolizing fraternity among men; and the unchaining of a prisoner, symbolizing the liberation of humanity.

The Counter-Reformation and, later, 19th-century liberalism contributed to the progressive deterioration of these festivities, which eventually almost disappeared from mainland Portugal. They are still very much alive in the Azores, in some parts of Brazil, and in some Azorean emigrant communities in the United States. The Empire of the Holy Ghost, as a concept, would re-emerge throughout the history of Portuguese mystic thought, under the guise of the Fifth Empire proclaimed by Sebastianism.

The Inquisition was established in 1536 and remained active until 1821, when it was abolished as a result of the liberal revolution of 1820. The estimates of the number of victims, mainly Jews, vary widely,

Portugal

Valenca
Braganca
Chaves
Viana do Castelo
Braga
Fafe
Guimaraes
Vila Real
Porto
Barca d'Alva
Viseu
Vilar Formoso
Aveiro
Guarda
Coimbra
Covilha
Figueira da Foz
Castelo Branco
Leiria
Tomar
Abrantes
Caldas da Rainha
Santarem
Portalegre
Portugal
Mora
Estremoz
Lisbon
Vendas Novas
Almada
Barreiro
Evora
Setubal
Alcacer do Sal
Grandola
Moura
Beja
Serpa
Sines
Vila Real de Santo Antonio
Portimao
Lagos
Faro
Tavira
Sagres
N

but the national archive is reported to hold registers of 40,000 inquisitorial processes. Many scholars track Portugal's decadence, a recurrent theme in discussions of national identity, to this source. The persecution focusing on witchcraft happened later and was milder (12 casualties) than in the rest of Europe.

In 1578 the disappearance of King Sebastião (1554–1578) at the catastrophic Battle of Alcácer-Quibir, in Morocco, created one of the most serious succession crises in the history of the country, resulting in the appropriation of the Portuguese throne by King Philip II of Spain. During this national eclipse, a belief spread among the population that King Sebastião had not died in North Africa and would return to claim his throne and to restitute Portugal's independence and grandeur. This period constituted the so-called first stage of Sebastianism, when the still reasonable belief in the physical return of the monarch fostered the emergence of diviners, fake King Sebastiãos, and prophets, many of them newly converted Jews who saw in this new form of messianism a desperate solution for their miserable condition. Before the king's disappearance, Bandarra (1500–ca. 1556), a village shoemaker, had composed a set of prophetic verses that after the battle was readily spread around the country and interpreted within a Sebastianistic context. This enthusiasm was severely repressed by the Inquisition, which, in the following centuries, would continue to look at Sebastianism as an undesirable popular belief and, in its later configurations, as a dangerous Christian heterodoxy.

As time went by, dwindling hope in the king's comeback led to the second phase of Sebastianism, which was no longer the simple belief in the return of a particular savior. Instead, Sebastianism was now a political philosophy, of which the most influential figure is the Jesuit priest António Vieira (1608–1697). According to Vieira's comparative analysis of biblical texts and Bandarra's prophecies, the return of D. Sebastião, the Concealed One, will coincide with the advent of the Fifth Empire, a kingdom, both spiritual and temporal, that will establish a new ecumenical order upon Earth. From this point on, Sebastianism and Fifth Empirealism became, for many, a foundation of national identity, presenting Portugal with the role of future redeemer of the world, a chosen but yet unfulfilled nation.

As Sebastianistic theories were built, their antitheses inevitably arose as well. In the 18th and 19th centuries, bitter disputes were fought between Sebastianistic and anti-Sebastianistic politicians and scholars. Although popular belief in Sebastianism decreased until it disappeared, philosophy and literature continued to drink from this spring. In the 20th century, poets such as Fernando Pessoa (1888–1935) and Teixeira de Pascoaes (1877–1952), and philosophical movements such as Renascença Portuguesa, Integralismo Lusitano, and Filosofia Portuguesa, used Sebastianism in conceptualizing philosophical and aesthetic systems that were meant to reflect an idiosyncratically Portuguese vision and sensibility.

The hegemony of the Roman Catholic Church was severely disrupted by the rise of the liberal movement in the 19th century. Thus, 1834 saw the extinction of all male religious orders and the nationalization and auction of convents, monasteries, and colleges. Many holy days and religious processions were also abolished. This was not a mere action of secularization but a strong blow against the main pillar of absolutist rule, which relied on the male religious orders for the planning and development of the country's natural resources, the colonization of overseas possessions, and the management of education and culture. The Masonically inspired First Republic (1910) separated state from church, no longer recognizing Catholic Christianity as the nation's official religion.

It was in this context that Theosophy and Kardecian Spiritism rose and enjoyed some popularity among intellectuals, artists, and the military. The Portuguese Theosophical Society was founded in 1921 and the Portuguese Spiritist Federation in 1926. While the Theosophical movement never showed significant adhesion or social impact, the Spiritist movement gathered important public figures and physical resources. All this ended in 1953, when the then fascist regime's Ministry of Education ordered the Spiritist Federation to cease all activities. Portuguese Spiritists were thus driven underground up to the revolution in 1974. The same happened with other religious minorities, such as Jehovah's Witnesses. The Spiritist movement, which

Portugal

Religion	Followers in 1970	Followers in 2010	% of Population	Annual % growth 2000–2010	Followers in 2025	Followers in 2050
Christians	8,371,000	9,645,000	89.9	0.12	9,386,000	8,539,000
Roman Catholics	7,979,000	9,175,000	85.5	–0.05	8,800,000	7,846,000
Independents	10,900	240,000	2.2	2.18	320,000	400,000
Marginals	19,500	135,000	1.3	0.60	200,000	250,000
Agnostics	275,000	823,000	7.7	7.01	1,021,000	1,088,000
Atheists	30,000	134,000	1.2	2.16	150,000	160,000
Buddhists	0	60,000	0.6	0.58	70,000	90,000
Muslims	800	26,200	0.2	0.58	40,000	53,000
Chinese folk	0	22,000	0.2	0.58	25,000	26,000
Hindus	0	6,500	0.1	0.58	9,000	12,000
Spiritists	0	4,000	0.0	0.58	5,000	6,500
Baha'is	1,800	2,100	0.0	0.58	3,000	4,000
Ethnoreligionists	0	1,600	0.0	0.59	2,000	2,200
Jews	1,300	460	0.0	0.57	460	460
Sikhs	0	450	0.0	0.58	600	800
Total population	**8,680,000**	**10,725,000**	**100.0**	**0.58**	**10,712,000**	**9,982,000**

began as an elite group and integrated a society of psychical research in Oporto, never regained its original splendor, but the term *espiritismo* was appropriated by a wide array of healers and mediums, and evolved into a very popular form of religiousness revolving around the non-corporeal figures of Sousa Martins, a famous Portuguese medical doctor, and Padre Cruz, a pious Catholic priest.

Theosophy, on the other hand, has played an interesting if subtle role. Fernando Pessoa, whose monumental oeuvre also dwells on occult and Gnostic themes, acknowledged the influence of Helena Blavatsky and Annie Besant and was one of the first translators of their works. Much more recently, in 1988, the Centro Lusitano de Unificação Cultural, one of the most international of Portuguese New Religious movements (NRMs), was founded under Theosophical inspiration. Their books, usually "channeled" by figures of all times and cultures, explicitly utilize Theosophical terms and concepts.

By 1926 a military coup brought in 48 years of dictatorship. During this period the Roman Catholic Church would regain its hegemony. Thus, by 1929 the religious orders were allowed to return and in 1940 the Holy See celebrated a Concordat with the Portuguese state. This document, which would only be revised late in the new democratic period, gave the Roman Catholic Church exclusive privileges, including the right to celebrate marriages (which could not be terminated by a legal action of divorce); it also returned control over confiscated assets to the Roman Catholic Church and reintroduced Catholic religious education in public schools, which had been abolished by the First Republic. Although most of the non-Catholic denominations established prior to the military coup were not forbidden by the new regime, public visibility and proselytism were strongly discouraged and even repressed. Consequently, most religious minorities adopted a low profile during the dictatorship that, for some of them, proved hard to surpass even in the democratic period.

The 1974 revolution brought in a new Constitution that granted the right of religious association and freedom of religious choice, thus allowing foreign NRMs to establish themselves in Portugal. However, only in 1996 did a Law of Religious Freedom begin to be discussed in Parliament, a slow process that culminated in its approval in 2001. The new law enhances equality of rights for all faiths and creates the legal entity of Established Church, for which any religious community legally extant in Portugal for more than 30 years (or 60 years abroad) can apply. Despite this equalitarian and globally more favorable context for religious minorities, in 2004 a new Concordat was celebrated between Portugal and the Holy See, privileging the Roman Catholic Church in its relationship with the Portuguese state.

The total of individuals belonging to NRMs may be lower than 2 percent of the population, including older movements such as Jehovah's Witnesses and Seventh-day Adventists. NRMs have not raised much interest at the political or social level, with the exception of two Pentecostal movements, the Brazilian Universal Church of the Kingdom of God and the Portuguese Igreja Maná, which has had a significant expansion to African Portuguese-speaking countries.

Finally, one of the most polychromatic aspects of Portuguese religiosity lies in the seasonal religious festivities, most of them celebrated locally with particular variants. Many of these, blending religious-magical motifs, still present remains of ancient pre-Christian traditions while manifesting a creative syncretism with Catholic ceremonies and the cult of saints. In terms of popular religiosity, however, the pilgrimage to the Marian shrine of Fatima is the main seasonal event. The apparitions and other alleged miracles that occurred from May to October 1917, amid a period of social and political turmoil, not only helped the Roman Catholic Church to regain its local power but turned into an international religious phenomenon moving hundreds of thousands of pilgrims each year in search of healing or the payment of promises.

Tiago Santos, Pedro Soares, and Miguel Farias

See also: Jehovah's Witnesses; Roman Catholic Church; Seventh-day Adventist Church; Spiritism; Theosophical Society (America); Universal Church of the Kingdom of God.

References

Azevedo, Carlos Moreira, ed. *História Religiosa de Portugal*. Lisbon: Círculo de Leitores, 2000–2002.

Mattoso, José, ed. *História de Portugal*. Vols. 1–8. Lisbon: Círculo de Leitores, 1993–1994.

Pais, José Machado, ed. *Atitudes Sociais dos Portugueses 2. Religião e Bioética*. Lisbon: Instituto de Ciências Sociais da Universidade de Lisboa, 2001.

Vasconcellos, José Leite de. *Religiões da Lusitânia*. Vols. 1–3. Lisbon: Imprensa Nacional, 1878, 1905, 1913.

Vilaça, Helena. *Da Torre de Babel às terras prometidas: pluralismo religioso em Portugal*. Oporto: Afrontamento, 2006.

Possession

Possessive phenomena are recognized broadly across all of the world's religions and also among the multitude of popular or folk religions on every continent (Holmberg 1993). Religious explanations of possessive phenomena include the idea that a spirit or spiritual being controls the body of a person or animal (the host) to the extent that it is the spirit being that determines some or all of the host's behavior. Alternate terms include "trance," "dissociation," and "ecstatic state." Because the central idea is that of control rather than ownership, the English term "possession" is somewhat of a misnomer. The type of control seen ranges from localized physical phenomena (uncontrolled limb movements) to complete control, in which case possession is an appropriate term.

Religious beliefs about the beings that possess people vary widely. They may be seen as gods, angels (good or evil), the dead who have returned to this world in some way, nature spirits, ghosts, or other spirit beings (Katz 1987). These beings may be perceived to be essentially good, in which case possession is a gift to be sought after (Pentecostal Christians being baptized by the Holy Spirit). They may be seen as neutral or having the same foibles as humans, depending on the circumstances in which they reveal themselves. In these cases possession can be a mixed blessing for the host—depending on the mood of the possessing being (African "living dead" possessing a descendant because they are being ignored). They may be understood to be vengeful, punishing individuals or whole communities for reasons not fully known (spirits causing epidemics among Chinese migrants who settled in Taiwan; Katz 1987). In the worst cases, the possessing beings are malevolent and their purpose is to torment—possibly even kill—their hosts. In such

A Haitian woman is possessed by spirits while dancing during a Vodou ceremony in Soukri, Haiti. (AP Photo/Daniel Morel)

cases religious specialists are brought in to perform an exorcism if possible.

While possession of animals is always involuntary, people can become possessed through *voluntary* and *involuntary* means. Those who choose to become possessed do so through a variety of means. Typically this comes through specific ritual activity. Some engage in ceremonies that incorporate rhythmic dancing or other bodily movement, usually accompanied by percussive music and chanting (Walker 1972). Others pray special prayers while engaging in magical activities (blood-letting or sacrifices), designed to attract or bind the possessing being. This may also include endurance trials (sun dancing), self-mortification (Sutton 1990), intake of hallucinogenic drugs (such as peyote), and putting on or wearing spiritually powerful items (clothing, masks, rings, amulets, or accessories; Merrill 2004). People may seek possession out of devotion to the possessing spirit (McDaniel 1988), to help them face or overcome social tensions (reversing social bias, Kraemer 1979; witch hunts, Jones 1989), or to become specialized religious practitioners (Kawamura 2003).

A person or animal may also be involuntarily possessed. It may be manifest through certain disorders (epilepsy, certain types of schizophrenia), though the diagnosis is left to specialists (*zar* possession in Ethiopia, Natvig 1988). In some cases the reason for such possession is looked for in the community of the possessed since the possessed themselves may not have done anything to bring about the condition. They may be victims on behalf of the community for reasons that require the discernment of specialized religious practitioners. This is more often seen among certain types of vulnerable people (young children, pregnant women, those perceived to be mentally disturbed; Karim 1989, 287–288).

Because the beings that do the possessing are not physically seen, the sole evidence of possession comes through observation of the host: manifestations of anomalous states of being (trance, catatonic stupor or excitement, seizures), physical abnormalities (change of voice, agitation, facial expressions), unusual actions (self-mutilation, fainting, extraordinary strength or endurance), atypical verbal expressions (singing, glossolalia, prophesying, cursing, extreme vulgarity), and other peculiar phenomena (automatic drawing or writing, inexplicable knowledge, environmental changes around the host).

Wherever possessive phenomena are found, religious teachings give local practitioners a variety of means to deal with possession. In many traditional African settings possession is one type of sign that the host is to be set apart to become a religious practitioner such as a medium, shaman, or diviner. By way of contrast, African Christians believe that the possessed are to be set free through prayer (Laurent 2001). Religions in a variety of Asian settings teach that a person can be possessed because the spirits want to disclose a message or warning, and possessing a person is understood as an appropriate means of conveyance (McDaniel 1988). In Latin American settings, newer religious traditions incorporate spirit possession as integral to religious expression (Candomblé in Brazil; Van de Port 2007). It should be noted that many traditional religious adherents understand possession as evidence of sound—even exemplary—social, psychological, and spiritual health of the host. In contrast, secular social and psychological typologies almost universally cast possession as pathological (Smith 2001, 211).

In those societies most impacted by modernism and subsequent secularized orientations to life, newer and more secular sets of explanations for possession phenomena were developed, especially by those in social science and health-related fields. Anthropologists, sociologists, psychologists, and medical professionals generated explanations for possession phenomena framed in terms of social (ritual and culturally approved responses to social stress or lack of social power, Newell 2007), psychological (wish-fulfillment, dissociation resulting from trauma, hysteria, paranoia, or schizophrenia; Lietaer and Corveleyn 1995; Ward and Beaubrun 1980), and biological (asthma, epilepsy, hypnotic states, chemical or hormonal imbalance, shock) (Marayam 2001) sources.

Religious practitioners exposed to these more contemporary perspectives have been adept at incorporating the newer frames of reference into their own taxonomies without necessarily discarding religious explanations. For example, many Africans distinguish "Western" diseases—treatable through secular means—from "local" diseases, which are treatable only through traditional means (Oosthuizen 1988). They may also develop criteria to distinguish possessive phenomena that are fully explainable by secular approaches from those that are only explainable by spiritual causes. In such cases, the former are recognized as possessive-like behavior while the latter are still seen as genuine possession. For example, it is not unusual to find Christians in Western societies who incorporate sophisticated medical and psychological evaluations in their assessment and treatment of those who exhibit symptoms of possession (Augsburger 1988; Oger 1996; Peck 2005).

It appears that the extent of observable possessive phenomena does not lessen with the rise of antireligious worldviews or secular education (Paper 1996). Traditional religious explanations, together with traditional approaches to ameliorate negative possessive behavior, will continue to serve in societies that rely on them. It is likely that newer syncretistic practices will arise as well (Mary 2001; Rich 2006). While in general the academic world has tended to treat such phenomena in secular ways, the ontological puzzle that possession phenomena provide has yet to be fully explained through such methods.

The rich variety of phenomena, the contrasting and ever-changing explanations, and the continuing stresses of societies around the world will continue to provide invaluable resources for ongoing religious study of the fascinating (and frightening) phenomena known as possession.

A. Scott Moreau

See also: Ancestors; Exorcism; Nepal, Indigenous Religions in; Pentecostalism.

References

Augsburger, David. *Pastoral Counseling across Cultures.* Philadelphia: Westminster, 1986.

Caulder, Sharon. *African Vodu: The Spirituality of a People.* Carpinteria, CA: Pacifica Graduate Institute, 2000.

Chajes, Jeffrey H. *Between Worlds: Dybbuks, Exorcists, and Early Modern Judaism.* Philadelphia: University of Pennsylvania Press, 2003.

Cohen, Emma. *The Mind Possessed: The Cognition of Spirit Possession in an Afro-Brazilian Religious Tradition.* Oxford and New York: Oxford University Press, 2007.

Filan, Kenaz, and Raven Kaldera. *Drawing Down the Spirits: The Traditions and Techniques of Spirit Possession.* Rochester, VT: Destiny Books, 2009.

Fjelstad, Karen, and Thi H. Nguyen. *Possessed by the Spirits: Mediumship in Contemporary Vietnamese Communities.* Ithaca, NY: Southeast Asia Program Publications, Southeast Asia Program, Cornell University, 2006.

Heredero, J. M. *The Dead Rescue the Living: Spirit Possession in a Gujarati Christian Community.* Anand, Gujarat: Gujarat Sahitya Prakash, 2001.

Holmberg, David. "The Shamanic Illusion." *Journal of Ritual Studies* 7, no. 1 (1993): 163–175.

Jones, Gwilym I. "Recollections of the Spirit Movement in the Ibibio Area of Calabar Province." *Africa (London, England: 1928)* 59, no. 4 (1989): 517–527.

Karim, Anwarul. "Shamanism in Bangladesh." *Asian Folklore Studies* 47, no. 2 (1988): 277–309.

Katz, Paul R. "Demons or Deities: The *Wangye* of Taiwan." *Asian Folklore Studies* 46, no. 2 (1987): 197–215.

Kawamura, Kunimitsu. "A Female Shaman's Mind and Body, and Possession." *Asian Folklore Studies* 62, no. 2 (2003): 257–289.

Klass, Morton. *Mind over Mind: The Anthropology and Psychology of Spirit Possession.* Lanham, MD: Rowman & Littlefield, 2003.

Kraemer, Ross S. "Ecstasy and Possession: The Attraction of Women to the Cult of Dionysus." *Harvard Theological Review* 72, nos. 1–2 (1979): 55–80.

Laurent, Pierre J. "The Faith-Healers of the Assemblies of God in Burkina Faso: Taking Responsibility for Diseases Related to 'Living Together.'" *Social Compass* 48, no. 3 (2001): 333–351.

Lewis, I. M. *Ecstatic Religion: A Study of Shamanism and Spirit Possession.* London; New York: Routledge, 2003.

Lietaer, Hugo, and Jozef Corveleyn. "Psychoanalytical Interpretation of the Demoniacal Possession and the Mystical Development of Sister Jeanne Des Anges from Loudun (1605–1665)." *International Journal for the Psychology of Religion* 5, no. 4 (1995): 259–276.

Makris, G. P. *Changing Masters: Spirit Possession and Identity Construction among Slave Descendants and Other Subordinates in the Sudan.* Evanston, IL: Northwestern University Press, 2000.

Mary, André. "From One Syncretism to Another: Culture of Trance and Charisma of Deliverance." *Social Compass* 48, no. 3 (2001): 315–331.

Mayaram, Shail. "Recent Anthropological Works on Spirit Possession." *Religious Studies Review* 27, no. 3 (2001): 213–222.

McDaniel, June. "Possession States among the Śaktas of West Bengal." *Journal of Ritual Studies* 2, no. 1 (1988): 87–99.

Merrill, Michael S. "Masks, Metaphor and Transformation: The Communication of Belief in Ritual Performance." *Journal of Ritual Studies* 18, no. 1 (2004): 16–33.

Natvig, Richard. "Liminal Rites and Female Symbolism in the Egyptian Zār Possession Cult." *Numen* 35, no. 1 (1988): 57–68.

Newell, Sasha. "Pentecostal Witchcraft: Neoliberal Possession and Demonic Discourse in Ivoirian Pentecostal Churches." *Journal of Religion in Africa* 37, no. 4 (2007): 461–490.

Oesterreich, Traugott K. *Possession: Demonical and Other: Among Primitive Races in Antiquity, the Middle Ages and Modern Times*. London: Kegan Paul, 2002.

Oger, Louis. "The Pastoral Approach to Spirit Possession: A Zambian Case." *AFER* 38, no. 5 (1996): 274–290.

Oosthuizen, Gerhardus C. "Interpretation of Demonic Powers in Southern African Independent Churches." *Missiology* 16, no. 1 (1988): 3–22.

Paper, Jordan D. "Mediums and Modernity: The Institutionalization of Ecstatic Religious Functionaries in Taiwan." *Journal of Chinese Religions*, no. 24 (Fall 1996): 105–129.

Patil, S. R. *Phenomenon of Possession: Psycho-Social Clinical Study of Spirits*. New Delhi: Reliance, 2006.

Peck, M. Scott. *Glimpses of the Devil: A Psychiatrist's Personal Accounts of Possession, Exorcism, and Redemption*. New York: The Free Press, 2005.

Rich, Cynthia H. "Spirits and the Spirit: The Ministry of Madagascar's Healing Shepherds." *Religion & Theology* 13, no. 1 (2006): 54–71.

Smith, Frederick M. "The Current State of Possession Studies as a Cross-Disciplinary Project." *Religious Studies Review* 27, no. 3 (2001): 203–212.

Stoller, Paul. *Fusion of the Worlds: An Ethnography of Possession among the Songhay of Niger*. Chicago: University of Chicago Press, 2003.

Sutton, Donald S. "Rituals of Self-Mortification: Taiwanese Spirit-Mediums in Comparative Perspective." *Journal of Ritual Studies* 4, no. 1 (1990): 99–125.

Van der Port, Mattijs. "Bahian White: The Dispersion of Candomblé Imagery in the Public Sphere of Bahia." *Material Religion* 3, no. 2 (2007): 242–272.

Walker, Sheila. *Ceremonial Spirit Possession in Africa and Afro-America: Forms, Meanings, and Functional Significance for Individuals and Social Groups*. Leiden: Brill, 1972.

Ward, Colleen A., and Michael H. Beaubrun. "The Psychodynamics of Demon Possession." *Journal for the Scientific Study of Religion* 19, no. 2 (1980): 201–207.

Prambanan

Prambanan (Lorojonggrang) is the largest Hindu temple complex in Indonesia. It is located in the small Indonesian province of Yogyakarta in south-central Java. It was built following the rise of the Hindu Sanjaya dynasty, which replaced the Buddhist Sailendra dynasty that had controlled the southern half of the island of Java. Buddhists had constructed a large stupa complex at Borobudur north of Yogyakarta City. The Prambanan temple complex is only 25 miles from Yogyakarta City and about 12 miles from Borobudur.

Initial construction on Prambanan was begun by Rakai Pikatan (who had a Buddhist wife) about 850 CE. After he constructed the main temple, various groups of Hindu believers added additional buildings. The main temple was surrounded by a wall that both separated it from the other temples and allowed a nearby river to be diverted so it flowed along the temple's edge.

Saivism dominated Javanese Hinduism, and the Sanjaya dynasty closely aligned itself with the deity Shiva. Worship at Prambanan mixed the worship of Shiva and the other deities with acts of veneration to the ruler. At the same time, the lesser temples were built by lower-level royalty who attempted to assert their position in the emerging system that combined the creation of a new religious and a new political order.

Prambanan, like nearby Borobudur, was fated to pass from the scene. Java was conquered by Islam and the new rulers suppressed Hinduism. Any acknowledgment of previous rulers at Prambanan especially irritated the Islam leadership, as its smacked of idolatry. In a relatively brief time, the complex was abandoned and the jungle allowed to overrun it, Like Borobudur, its very existence was forgotten, and news of its existence came in 1733, at which time a Dutch explorer, C. A. Lons, rediscovered it. For various reasons, clearing of the site was delayed for more than a century and meaningful excavation only began in 1885. Real restoration waited until after World War I and then had to be abandoned by the advent of World War II. Today, restoration continues on the hundreds of temples at the complex, though in the meantime believers (firmly entrenched in the nearby island of Bali) have begun to utilize the site. The main Siva temple was rededicated in 1953.

Prambanan Temple Complex, Java, Indonesia. Built in the ninth century, it is the largest Hindu temple in Indonesia. (Yai/Dreamstime.com)

The focus at Prambanan is on the main Siva temple and 15 nearby slightly smaller temples dedicated to other important Hindu deities including Vishnu and Brahma, all located within the center square. Then outside the wall are 224 smaller temples. These temples are arranged in four rows with the temples shrinking in size (and status) the further from the main temple they are located. There is also a second wall that encompasses these smaller temples, and gates admit people to the various sections of the complex. The complex is now the primary temple complex for Java's Hindu minority and increasingly draws believers from the other islands. In 1991, Prambanan was named to the list of World Heritage Sites by the United Nations.

J. Gordon Melton

See also: Borobudur; Devotion/Devotional Traditions; Pilgrimage; Temples, Hindu.

References

Bunce, Frederick W. *The Iconography of Architectural Plans: A Study of the Influence of Buddhism and Hinduism on Plans of South and Southeast Asia*. New Delhi: D. K. Printworld, 2002.

Iyer, Alessandra. *Prambanan: Sculpture and Dance in Ancient Java. A Study in Dance Iconography*. Bangkok: White Lotus Press, 1998.

Jipto, Moert, and Bambang Prasetyo. *The Siwa Temple of Prambanan*. Yogyakarta, Indonesia: Penerbit Kanisius, 1992.

Jordaan, Roy E. *In Praise of Prambanan: Dutch Essays on the Lord Jonggrang Temple Complex*. Leiden: KITLV Press, 1996.

Prana

See Energy.

Presbyterian Church in Cameroon

The Presbyterian Church in Cameroon (Église presbytérienne camérounaise) shares its early history with several churches, including the Evangelical Church of Cameroon, which have their roots in the original Baptist mission begun in 1845. The Baptists were forced out in 1884 when Germany gained hegemony over the region, and they were replaced with missionaries from the Basel Mission, most of whom were of the Swiss Reformed tradition. The Baptist members were upset with the very different system of church discipline introduced by the Basel missionaries and by their introduction of infant baptism (Baptists believe in the baptism only of adults who have made a profession of the Christian faith). Many left, but the missionaries continued to work with the remaining members and initiated their own new mission stations.

With the outbreak of World War I in 1914, the British and French moved into the region and divided the territory. The Basel missionaries turned over their 15 stations in French Cameroon to the Paris Mission. These eventually became the core from which the Evangelical Church of Cameroon would emerge. The remaining work was turned over to African leaders who headed the church for the next decade. Finally, in 1925, the missionaries from the Basel Mission were allowed to return to the British-controlled part of Cameroon. They continued to work with the church that they had nurtured through World War I but soon realized that it was time for the mission to become independent.

In 1957 the Presbyterian Church in Cameroon was constituted. It is organized with a presbyterial polity, with a synod as the highest legislative body. The Mission continues to support the schools and medical facilities, with both financial aid and staff. In 1968 the schools were turned over to the church. Among the schools now sponsored by the church is the Theological Seminary at Kumba.

In 2005, the Presbyterian Church in Cameroon reported 700,000 members in its 1,306 congregations. It is a member of the World Alliance of Reformed Churches and the World Council of Churches.

Presbyterian Church in Cameroon
PO Box 19
Buea
Cameroon

J. Gordon Melton

See also: Evangelical Church of Cameroon; Paris Mission; World Alliance of Reformed Churches; World Council of Churches.

References

Bauswein, Jean-Jacques, and Lukas Vischner, eds. *The Reformed Family Worldwide: A Survey of Reformed Churches, Theological Schools, and International Organizations*. Grand Rapids, MI: William B. Eerdmans Publishing Company, 1999.

Lukunze, Edward Focrcha. *Evangelistic Strategies for the Year 2000 and Beyond: Ruby Jubilee Historical Reflections of the Presbyterian Church in Cameroon*. N.p., 1999.

Matute, Daniel Lyonga. *A Brief History of the Presbyterian Church in Cameroon, 1886–1986: A Centenary Souvenir*. N.p.: the author, 1986.

Nku, Nyansako-ni. *Journey in Faith: The Story of the Presbyterian Church in Cameroon*. Buea, Cameroon: Presbyterian Church in Cameroon, 1982.

Presbyterian Church in Canada

The Presbyterian Church in Canada (PCC) has its origins in the 16th-century Protestant Reformation in Europe and in the teachings of Reformers John Calvin (1509–1564) and John Knox (ca. 1514–1572). The Presbyterian presence in Canada began with the arrival of Scottish Presbyterians in the Maritime

Interior of St. Andrew's Presbyterian Church in Toronto, Canada. (iStockphoto.com)

Provinces and Ontario in the late 18th century. The various locations and organizations of Presbyterians in Canada followed trends in immigration from Scotland, as well as mirroring the doctrinal disputes occurring in Scotland.

The 19th century, however, saw a slow unification of the various diverse Presbyterian denominations. In 1875 these unions culminated in the formation of the Presbyterian Church in Canada. By the end of the 19th century the PCC was "neck and neck" with the Methodists in the race to be the largest Protestant denomination in Canada. In 1925 about one-third of the PCC membership refused to join with the Methodists and the Congregationalists in the formation of the United Church of Canada, instead remaining autonomous as the PCC. The PCC experienced a significant decrease in membership at the end of the 20th century, with membership standing at around 135,000 in 1,000 congregations.

Many famous Canadians have been Presbyterians, including George M. Grant (1835–1902), principal at Queens University; Prime Minister William Mackenzie King (1874–1950); and Charles W. Gordon, known as a novelist by the name Ralph Connor (1860–1937).

The word "presbyterian" comes from the Greek word *presbyteros*, meaning "elder." The PCC is governed by elders elected from each congregation. These elders, along with the ordained clergy, provide leadership in the church and at the various levels of church government: the session; the presbytery; the synod; and the general assembly, the highest court of the church, which meets once a year. The PCC teaches that the Bible is the most authoritative source for faith and practice, and its subordinate standards are expressed in the Westminster Confession of Faith and the statement of belief entitled "Living Faith." Two sacraments are practiced: infant baptism and the Lord's Supper, which is celebrated weekly, monthly, or quarterly.

Recent trends in the PCC include a growing ethnic diversity in the churches. Although still retaining much of its Scottish heritage, the modern PCC includes growing Korean, Chinese, Ghanaian, and other "ethnic" congregations. The church's head office is in Toronto, Ontario. The PCC actively participates with the Canadian Council of Churches, the World Council of Churches, and the World Alliance of Reformed Churches.

Presbyterian Church in Canada
50 Wynford Dr.
Toronto, ON M3C 1J7
Canada
http://www.presbyterian.ca

Gordon L. Heath

See also: United Church of Canada; World Alliance of Reformed Churches; World Council of Churches.

References

Congram, John. *This Presbyterian Church of Ours.* Winfield, BC: Wood Lake Books, Inc., 1995.
Moir, John. *Enduring Witness: A History of the Presbyterian Church in Canada* Hamilton, ON: Presbyterian Press, 1987.

Presbyterian Church in Taiwan

The Presbyterian Church in Taiwan dates to the arrival of British Presbyterians in 1865. They were joined by their colleagues from Canada in 1872. The British started their mission work on the southern part of the island and the Canadians in the north. Both added medical work to their missionary enterprise.

In 1895 the Japanese invaded and occupied the island. After that date no new missions were allowed

A young Paiwan aboriginal boy prays in a Presbyterian church during an evening youth service in Laolauran, southeastern Taiwan. (AP Photo/Wally Santana)

to enter, and thus the Presbyterian work developed without the competition that had characterized many early-20th-century settings. The mission continued to progress normally into the 1930s, but as war loomed and the authorities assumed a more militant stance, the missionaries withdrew and turned the church over to the Taiwanese leadership.

The missionaries returned after World War II. They picked up their work and in 1951 led in the uniting of the two missions under a single general assembly of what became the Presbyterian Church in Taiwan. The church now found itself in a radically changed environment. The population exploded, with thousands of refugees coming to Taiwan from mainland China. Not only did they bring new Christian movements with them, but a variety of missionaries from across the Protestant/Free church spectrum also founded new missionary efforts on the island. The church doubled its membership in the decade from 1955 to 1965. It has since focused on evangelism and continued to grow through the last half of the 20th century, though it is still very much a minority religion in a largely Buddhist country.

In 2005 the church reported 217,612 members in a country of 23 million. It has a presbyterial polity with a biennial general assembly as the highest lawmaking body. It adheres to the Heidelberg Confession and the Westminster Confession as its standards of doctrine.

The church has shown a self-conscious desire to become an indigenous body and has continually expressed its concern for the Republic of China and the future of the people of Taiwan. Beginning in the 1970s it has issued a number of official statements on Taiwan, beginning with "Our National Fate" in 1971. It followed with "Our Appeal" (1975); "On Human Rights" (1977); "Recommendations Concerning the Present Situation" (1990); and "On the Sovereignty of Taiwan" (1991). It has worked on a variety of social issues concerning the working classes and the plight of prostitutes. Continuing the early medical work of the missions, it now sponsors a set of hospitals. The church is a member of the World Alliance of Reformed Churches and the World Council of Churches.

Presbyterian Church in Taiwan
3, Lane 269
Roosevelt Rd., Sec. 3
Taipei 106
Taiwan
http://www.pct.org.tw/

J. Gordon Melton

See also: World Alliance of Reformed Churches; World Council of Churches.

References

Bauswein, Jean-Jacques, and Lukas Vischner, eds. *The Reformed Family Worldwide: A Survey of Reformed Churches, Theological Schools, and International Organizations*. Grand Rapids, MI: William B. Eerdmans Publishing Company, 1999.

Lin, Christian Louise. *The Presbyterian Church in Taiwan and the Advocacy of Local Autonomy*. Philadelphia: Department of Asian and Middle Eastern Studies, University of Pennsylvania, 1999.

Van Beek, Huibert. *A Handbook of the Churches and Councils: Profiles of Ecumenical Relationships*. Geneva: World Council of Churches, 2006.

Presbyterian Church in the Republic of Korea

The most liberal of the various Presbyterian churches in Korea, the Presbyterian Church in the Republic of [South] Korea originated in a controversy involving the Presbyterian Church in Korea in the years immediately following World War II. In 1938 the students and faculty of Chosun Seminary, then located in Pyongyang, Korea, refused to worship as ordered at the emperor's shrine. The seminary was closed down, and those associated with it scattered. A year later, they reopened the seminary in southern Korea. Its faculty adopted a liberal Protestant theological perspective.

In 1946 the reorganized Presbyterian Church of Korea recognized Chosun Seminary as its seminary. However, shortly thereafter, an intense theological debate developed over a document released by the president. Conservative members of the church accused the seminary of teaching heresy. One professor left and founded a new seminary, which the general assembly of the church also recognized.

In order to resolve its stance relative to the two seminaries, the assembly next withdrew its support from both schools and asked the leadership to resolve their differences. During the succeeding negotiations, however, it became obvious that the positions taken by the representatives of Chosun Seminary did not represent the stance of the church. In 1952 the seminary president, Dr. Kim Jae-Joon (1901–1984), was expelled from the church.

In 1953 the supporters of the seminary formed the Presbyterian Church in the Republic of Korea. Its appearance came just a few years before the Presbyterian Church of Korea would split into two factions—the Presbyterian Church of Korea (TongHap) and the Presbyterian Church of Korea (HapDong). The Presbyterian Church in the Republic of Korea has aligned itself with the most liberal elements in Presbyterianism worldwide. It was the first of the Korean churches to invite females into the ordained ministry. In 1987 it adopted a new confession, similar in tone to the Confession of 1967 of the Presbyterian Church (U.S.A.). It has backed efforts toward the reunification of North and South Korea.

In 2005 the church reported more than 334,000 members. The general assembly is the highest legislative body in the church. It supports Theological Seminary, Seoul, and HanShin University, Suwon. It is a member of the World Alliance of Reformed Churches and the World Council of Churches.

Presbyterian Church in the Republic of Korea
#1501 Korean Ecumenical Building
136-56 YunJi-Dong
ChongRo-Gu
Seoul 110-470
Republic of Korea

J. Gordon Melton

See also: Presbyterian Church of Korea (HapDong); Presbyterian Church of Korea (TongHap); Presbyterian Church (U.S.A.); World Alliance of Reformed Churches; World Council of Churches.

References

Bauswein, Jean-Jacques, and Lukas Vischner, eds. *The Reformed Family Worldwide: A Survey of Reformed Churches, Theological Schools, and International Organizations*. Grand Rapids, MI: William B. Eerdmans Publishing Company, 1999.

Van Beek, Huibert. *A Handbook of the Churches and Councils: Profiles of Ecumenical Relationships*. Geneva: World Council of Churches, 2006.

Presbyterian Church in Trinidad

The Presbyterian Church of Trinidad emerged from the United Church of Canada in 1960. Nearly a century of mission work by Canadian Presbyterians in the community of indentured laborers from India resulted in the strong association between Indians and the church in the Caribbean today. Even though Presbyterians are only about 3 percent of Trinidad and Tobago's population today, the significance of the church lies in its unique role as the primary educator of ethnic Indians in Trinidad's colonial period.

The contemporary presence of the Presbyterian Church in Trinidad has its origins in the intertwined histories of the 19th-century British colonial economy and the evangelism of two Canadian missionaries: John (1839–1911) and Sarah Morton. Presbyterian churches in Trinidad are also called East Indian churches because of the close association between Canadian mission work and migrants from South Asia who were imported by the British to work on sugarcane plantations. Despite the fact that less than half of all Christian Indians are Presbyterian, Christian Indians and Presbyterianism have a strong association in Trinidad. Certainly this is the impression given by the preponderance of literature on Presbyterian (East) Indians, and the fact that 95 percent of the Presbyterian population is ethnically Indian. According to the 2000 census 36,710 people identified themselves as Presbyterian. Since the vast majority of Presbyterians are Indian, this would represent about 8 percent of the Indian population and 3.3 percent of the total 2000 population.

The Canadian mission began in the small village of Iere in south-central Trinidad. At the time, the village of Iere was surrounded by cane fields, and southern Trinidad had the highest concentration of South Asian Indians on the island. Most laborers were Hindu, and a smaller proportion were Muslim. Early in the 1860s,

Canadians John and Sarah Morton visited Trinidad when their Barbados-bound ship was blown off course. They were distraught over the lack of mission work among the Indian laborers and decided to make this their life's work. After several failed attempts to gain support in Canada for their mission, they arrived in Iere, Trinidad, in 1868 in order to serve a small African population left by a failed American Presbyterian mission. As the Mortons did not have their own resources, the abandonment of the Presbyterian church in the southern sugar district proved to be serendipitous. Rev. Morton would make excursions into the village and to surrounding estate barracks, but he had little success at first. The Indians did not trust him, and they also were hesitant to mix with Africans, mainly for ritual and linguistic reasons.

Since Morton's goal was to evangelize among Indians and they were resisting his invitations to visit the church, he established a school on the church's doorstep within three months of arriving in Trinidad. The lessons were especially designed for the Indians and given in what was still broken Hindi. During his visits to Indians in their homes, shops, and estate barracks, Morton employed a number of techniques. These included learning Hindi, observing Indian religious life in order to converse freely with Indians, providing simple medical and legal assistance, denying caste, making a Hindi hymnal, and going anywhere to help Indians—the latter a practice that earned him both trust and respect. Sarah Morton gained the confidence of women and opened an orphanage for girls. The Mortons trained new converts as Native evangelists and teachers, and they took advantage of the East Indians' great pride in their ethnic cohesiveness by providing them with their own East Indian Church.

Finally, the Mortons provided the single most important means for Indians to gain an education. The Mortons' Hindi would improve and the number of schools would increase, eventually becoming the trademarks of the mission. Thus, the Iere village doorstep school was only the beginning of a process that would last for more than a century under Canadian leadership. By 1915 there were 97 preaching stations, of which 89 had a separate church structure. Over the years the number of preaching stations/schools varied, with a peak of 129 by 1967, when the Canadian missionaries began the process of creating the Presbyterian Church of Trinidad. During this period Trinidad and Tobago had achieved independence (1962), and all schools were subsumed under the central government, although they retained their sectarian identities.

To this day, small Indian communities who wish to hold Presbyterian services, yet are not formally recognized as a congregation, will meet in someone's home with a minister, just as John Morton visited barracks on estates to hold the first services. As the community is able to build a structure, the congregation becomes formalized. An active promotion of incipient congregations throughout Trinidad, some of them very small, means that the number of congregations tends to fluctuate between 90 and 100. The church is a member of the Caribbean Conference of Churches, the World Alliance of Reformed Churches, and the World Council of Churches. It supports St. Andrew's Theological College, also located in San Fernando.

The dual function of the Presbyterian church as school and the Presbyterian school as church is as much a part of the contemporary identity of the East Indian Church in Trinidad as are its ethnic association and sectarian philosophy. Yet despite the success of the mission, as evidenced by the very existence of so many Presbyterian churches in Trinidad's landscape, it is also important to note that the missionaries converted only a small proportion of the Indian population, and the number of congregations has declined. Most Native ministers are responsible for several congregations each, and new missionaries (mainly American Pentecostals) have targeted Indian Christians, so the number of congregations continues to decline. Presbyterian schools continue to be highly regarded by Indians, but today few choose to convert to the faith. Thus, one must conclude that the mission was of limited success.

Presbyterian Church in Trinidad
Box 92
Paradise Hill
San Fernando
Trinidad

Carolyn V. Prorok

See also: United Church of Canada; World Alliance of Reformed Churches; World Council of Churches.

References

Doodnath, S. *A Short History of the Early Presbyterian Church and the Indian Immigrant, 1845–1945.* Trinidad, 1983.

Hamid, I. *A History of the Presbyterian Church in Trinidad, 1868–1968: The Struggles of a Church in Colonial Captivity.* Trinidad: Privately published, 1980.

Morton, S. E. *John Morton of Trinidad.* Toronto, 1916.

Prorok, Carolyn V. "The Significance of Historical Geography: A Case Study of the Church as School in the Diffusion of the Presbyterian Mission to Trinidad." *Historical Reflections/ Reflexions Historiques* 23, no. 3 (1997): 371–388.

Presbyterian Church of Africa

The Free Church of Scotland began missionary work in South Africa soon after its formation in the 1840s. In 1898, on the eve of its merger with the United Presbyterian Church (now a constituent part of the Church of Scotland), six Free church African ministers under the leadership of Panibani Mzimba left the South African mission in a dispute that revolved around the use of the mission's financial resources. With a number of lay supporters they organized congregations and continued their ministry. A century later the church had become one of the largest in South Africa, with a reported 3,381,000 members (2005).

The Presbyterian Church of Africa is a member of the World Alliance of Reformed Churches and the World Council of Churches, and it led in the founding of the African Independent Churches Association. Its membership is concentrated among the African Native peoples of the Eastern Cape and Natal, with a significant following also in Malawi. The church has accepted the Westminster Confession as its doctrinal statement. It began admitting females to the ordained ministry in the 1980s.

Presbyterian Church of Africa
PO Box 3939
Durham 4000
South Africa

J. Gordon Melton

See also: World Alliance of Reformed Churches; World Council of Churches.

References

Bauswein, Jean-Jacques, and Lukas Vischner, eds. *The Reformed Family Worldwide: A Survey of Reformed Churches, Theological Schools, and International Organizations*. Grand Rapids, MI: William B. Eerdmans Publishing Company, 1999.

Van Beek, Huibert. *A Handbook of the Churches and Councils: Profiles of Ecumenical Relationships*. Geneva: World Council of Churches, 2006.

Presbyterian Church of Aotearoa New Zealand

Settlers who had been members of the Church of Scotland in their homeland arrived in New Zealand in the 1830s. Their first church was founded in 1840 in Wellington. Meanwhile, back in Scotland, the church underwent a disruption that led many ministers and congregations to leave and found the Free church of Scotland, and it was from the Free church that ministers arrived to provide leadership for the New Zealand Presbyterians. The Free church prospered in New Zealand, with two separate churches developing, one on the north island and one on the south island. The two churches merged in 1901 to form the present Presbyterian Church of Aotearoa New Zealand.

The church continues the doctrine and practice of the Church of Scotland. It affirms the Westminster Catechism and the Westminster Confession of Faith, but it has more recently composed its own contemporary statement, the "Faith We Affirm Together." The church is headed by a general assembly, which meets annually. Within the church, there are a Maori Synod (Te Aka Puaho) that oversees ministry to the Maori people and a Pacific Islanders' Synod. The church also admits women fully to every level of ministry and service.

In 2005, the church reported some 44,000 members. The church sponsors Knox Theological Hall (founded in 1876) and the Center for Advanced Ministry Studies. It is a member of the World Alliance of Reformed Churches and the World Council of Churches.

Presbyterian Church of Aotearoa New Zealand, General Assembly
PO Box 9049
Wellington
Aotearoa
New Zealand
http://www.presbyterian.org.nz/

J. Gordon Melton

See also: Church of Scotland; World Alliance of Reformed Churches; World Council of Churches.

References

Elder, John Rawson. *The History of the Presbyterian Church of New Zealand, 1840–1940.* Christchurch, New Zealand: Presbyterian Bookroom, 1940.

McEldowney, Dennis, ed. *Presbyterians in Aotearoa New Zealand, 1840–1990*. Wellington, New Zealand: The Presbyterian Church of New Zealand, 1990.

Presbyterian Church of Australia (Continuing)

In 1977, the majority of the Presbyterian Church of Australia merged into the Uniting Church in Australia. Approximately 30 percent of the church, the more conservative wing, refused to join in the merger and reorganized to continue as a strictly Presbyterian church. The Westminster Confession was reaffirmed as the church's doctrinal standard and congregations were regrouped in new presbyteries, and nationally a General Assembly was organized to meet every three years.

The church has taken a number of steps to reaffirm its role as a traditional Presbyterian body, not the least being its withdrawal from the World Alliance of Reformed Churches and its joining the Reformed Ecumenical Council in 1982. A renewed interest in Reformed theology has been noticed and an emphasis on world missions has led to the sponsoring of missionaries in more than 20 countries in the South Pacific and around the Indian Ocean.

As the new century begins, the church has some 70,000 members in more than 400 congregations. In 1991, the General Assembly rescinded its approval of the ordination of women, though some parts of the church still recognize them. It supports 11 colleges, including 3 theological schools.

Presbyterian Church of Australia (Continuing)
PO Box 100
420 Elizabeth St.
Surry Hills, Sydney
NSW 2001
Australia
http://www.presbyterian.org.au/

J. Gordon Melton

See also: Reformed Ecumenical Council; World Alliance of Reformed Churches.

References

Breward, I. *A History of the Australian Churches.* St. Leonards, Australia: Allen & Unwin, 1993.

Humphries, R. A., and R. S. Ward, eds. *Religious Bodies in Australia: A Comprehensive Guide.* Wantirna, Australia: New Melbourne Press, 1995.

Ward, Rowland S. *The Bush Still Burns: The Presbyterian and Reformed Faith in Australia, 1788–1988*. N.p.: the author, 1989.

Ward, Rowland S. *A Witness for Christ: The Presbyterian Church of Eastern Australia: 1846–1996.* N.p.: Presbyterian Church of Eastern Australia, 1996.

Presbyterian Church of Brazil

Reformed efforts to establish a presence in Brazil were initiated briefly in the 1550s and again in the mid-1600s, but it was not until the early 19th century and the introduction of a degree of religious liberty in the 1820s that permanent work could be established. In 1855, Robert Reid Kalley (1809–1888), a physician, settled in Rio de Janeiro. Out of his efforts the Igreja Evangelica Fluininense was founded. That congregation became the beginning of Congregationalism in Brazil. Asbel Green Simonton (1831–1867), a missionary from the American Presbyterian Church (now the Presbyterian Church [U.S.A.]) arrived in 1859 and four years later organized the first Presbyterian church in

Rio. He and Kalley worked closely together, the latter supporting Green as he founded a Protestant periodical and opened a seminary to train church workers.

After the American Civil War (1861–1865), American Presbyterians from the two large Presbyterian churches in the United States supported Green's work and contributed both finances and personnel. The Presbyterian movement in Brazil became the largest of the several Protestant missions. The work prospered through the 19th century, but as the new century began it was hit with a major controversy over local autonomy, which many Brazilian leaders began to demand. That controversy expanded as one group began to denounce Freemasonry. The dissenting faction left to form the Independent Presbyterian Church.

The church that continued under the guidance of the missionaries weathered the storm and continued to grow. After World War II, the process of creating the Presbyterian Church of Brazil was formally completed. The church adopted the Westminster Confession of Faith as its doctrinal standard.

The church was hit with another controversy in the 1970s, when the more liberal wing of the church protested a set of doctrinal positions and the church's social stance. They joined with some ministers and congregations that had already left the Independent Presbyterian Church to form the United Presbyterian Church of Brazil. However, with some 40,000 members, the Presbyterian Church of Brazil remains the largest of the several churches of the Reformed tradition in the country, though its place as the largest of the non-Catholic bodies has been eclipsed by a number of Free church and Pentecostal movements. The church is a member of neither the World Council of Churches nor the World Alliance of Reformed Churches.

Presbyterian Church of Brazil
Caixa Postal 17
Rua Silva Jardin 23
Centro, 20050-060
Rio de Janeiro RJ
Brazil

J. Gordon Melton

See also: Presbyterian Church (U.S.A.); United Presbyterian Church of Brazil; World Alliance of Reformed Churches; World Council of Churches.

Reference

Bauswein, Jean-Jacques, and Lukas Vischner, eds. *The Reformed Family Worldwide: A Survey of Reformed Churches, Theological Schools, and International Organizations*. Grand Rapids, MI: William B. Eerdmans Publishing Company, 1999.

Presbyterian Church of Cameroon

The Presbyterian Church of Cameroon grew out of the mission of the U.S. Presbyterians in Gabon. In 1875 a new missionary station was opened in Batanga, in southern Cameroon. A decade later Cameroon came under German hegemony. Subsequently, an agreement was reached to extend the Presbyterian work, including the formation of primary schools for the residents, farther into Cameroon. The government demanded that Gennan be used as a primary language.

In 1892 work was launched among the Bulu people that prospered through the rest of the decade. The first works in the Bulu language, the Bible and some hymns, were published in 1894. However, in 1898 a revolt developed among the Bulu directed at the German authorities who were interfering with the trade between Yaoundé and the port city of Kribi. In their effort to quell the uprising, the Germans seized the mission station that had been opened at Lolodorf in 1897. The Presbyterians demanded compensation, at which point the U.S. government became involved. The Presbyterians received compensation, but their relations with the German authorities were ruined. Although the church-sponsored schools employed German teachers, the students were denied the privilege of sitting for the German examination that was necessary for admittance to European universities.

German control in Cameroon ended during World War I. The Paris Mission came into Cameroon and took over the work of the Basel Mission. In 1902 it released that work, consisting of some 94 congregations, to the Presbyterian mission. It subsequently grew into one of the largest missionary enterprises in the country. In the 1950s the mission began the translation of the Bible (published in 1960) into the Bassa language used by many who had come to it from the Paris Mission.

In 1956 the mission was granted autonomy as the Presbyterian Church of Cameroon (Église presbytérienne camérounaise). It is organized with a presbyterial order, with congregations associated in five synods. Doctrinally, the church recognizes the Heidelberg Catechism and the Westminster Confession as its doctrinal standards.

In 2005 the church reported 1,800,000 members in 300 congregations. It sponsors Dager Theological School in Bibia and the Faculty of Protestant Theology at Yaoundé. It is a member of the World Council of Churches and the World Alliance of Reformed Churches.

Presbyterian Church of Cameroon
BP 519
Yaoundé
Cameroon

J. Gordon Melton

See also: Basel Mission; Paris Mission; World Alliance of Reformed Churches; World Council of Churches.

References

Bauswein, Jean-Jacques, and Lukas Vischner, eds. *The Reformed Family Worldwide: A Survey of Reformed Churches, Theological Schools, and International Organizations*. Grand Rapids, MI: William B. Eerdmans Publishing Company, 1999.

Nku, Nyansako-ni. *Journey in Faith: The Story of the Presbyterian Church in Cameroon*. Buea, Cameroon: Presbyterian Church in Cameroon, 1982.

Van Beek, Huibert. *A Handbook of the Churches and Councils: Profiles of Ecumenical Relationships*. Geneva: World Council of Churches, 2006.

Presbyterian Church of Colombia

Henry Barrington Post, a missionary with the Presbyterian Church in the United States (now a constituent part of the Presbyterian Church [U.S.A.]), arrived in Colombia in 1856 and settled in Santa Fe de Bogatá. Five years later he was able to open a church and begin a Protestant mission, which included a program of public education. He was assisted in this educational enterprise by Kate McFarren, who joined him in 1868. She founded a girls' school that later became known as the Colegio Americano. Additional schools were opened in Barranquilla, Bucaramanga, Ibagué, and Girardot. The mission grew slowly, the dominant Roman Catholic Church viewing it as an unwanted intrusion into its territory. Conditions changed only after the Second Vatican Council and the general improvement of Protestant-Catholic relations in the 1960s.

In the 1980s the mission, which had now become the independent Presbyterian Church of Colombia, experienced some internal turmoil over leadership. The issues were finally resolved by dividing the church and its properties between two jurisdictions. One, called the Presbyterian Synod, retained approximately one-third of the members in three presbyteries. The other, called the Reformed Synod, has four presbyteries. Apart from leadership personnel, the two synods are largely the same. Both have the Westminster Confession as their standard of faith. Both retain a presbyterial organization with a synod as the highest legislative body. Both recognize each other as parts of the same church.

In the mid-1990s, the Presbyterian Synod reported some 4,500 members in 35 congregations. It supports the Presbyterian Theological Seminary in Barranquilla, originally set up to train ministers in Colombia, Venezuela, and Ecuador. In 2005, the church reported 12,000 members in 45 congregations. It is a member of the World Alliance of Reformed Churches and in 2005 joined the World Council of Churches.

In the mid-1990s the Reformed Synod reported 5,700 members in 15 congregations. It supports three schools: the Biblical Institute at Monteria, the Presbyterian Theological Faculty at Ibagué, and the Corporate Theological Faculty at Bogatá. In addition, the synod supports an extensive primary and secondary school system.

The Presbyterian Synod
AA 562 Carrera 46
No. 48-50
Barranquilla, Atlco
Colombia

The Reformed Synod
Carrera 4a #4-11
Ibangué, Tolima
Colombia

J. Gordon Melton

See also: Presbyterian Church (U.S.A.); World Alliance of Reformed Churches; World Council of Churches.

References

Bauswein, Jean-Jacques, and Lukas Vischner, eds. *The Reformed Family Worldwide: A Survey of Reformed Churches, Theological Schools, and International Organizations*. Grand Rapids, MI: William B. Eerdmans Publishing Company, 1999.

Van Beek, Huibert. *A Handbook of the Churches and Councils: Profiles of Ecumenical Relationships*. Geneva: World Council of Churches, 2006.

Presbyterian Church of East Africa

The Presbyterian Church of East Africa began in 1891, when a small group of independent Presbyterian missionaries initiated work at Kibwezi. Later in the decade they opened a second station at Kikuyu, the Kikuyu being the largest single group among Kenya's indigenous peoples. Through the Scottish Missionary Society, the Church of Scotland took responsibility for the mission in 1901. The Kikuyu proved a challenge, and only in 1907 was an initial baptism recorded. Only a few hundred became Christians in the first decades of the new century. In 1920 a presbytery was finally established, combining the mission with the church serving Scottish expatriates residing in what was then a British colony. Some progress was noted in 1926, when the first class of Kenyan pastors was ordained.

The upward trajectory recorded through the 1920s came to an abrupt end in 1929, when a controversy broke out in Kikuyu country over the practice of female circumcision. The presbytery issued a statement declaring the practice incompatible with Christian faith. The Kikuyu leaders declared that the church was against their culture and tradition. Only slowly, as the church passed to African leadership and the controversy died, did the church regain its initiative.

A new growth phase began in 1945, when the work of the Gospel Missionary Society, an independent U.S.-based missionary organization, merged into the presbytery. The Presbyterian Church of East Africa, as the mission had become known, became independent in 1956. At that time, the Overseas Presbytery of Kenya, a predominantly white body, including one congregation each in Tanzania and Uganda that had been constituted separately in 1936, merged into the new church. The first Kenyan general secretary, John Gatu, took office. The church admitted women to ordination in 1976.

In 2005 the Presbyterian Church of East Africa reported 4 million members. It supports the Reformed College of East Africa and, with the Methodist, Anglican, and Reformed churches, St. Paul's United Theological College. It is a member of the World Alliance of Reformed Churches and the World Council of Churches.

Presbyterian Church of East Africa
PO Box 48268
00 100 Nairobi
Kenya

J. Gordon Melton

See also: World Alliance of Reformed Churches; World Council of Churches.

References

Bauswein, Jean-Jacques, and Lukas Vischner, eds. *The Reformed Family Worldwide: A Survey of Reformed Churches, Theological Schools, and International Organizations*. Grand Rapids, MI: William B. Eerdmans Publishing Company, 1999.

Macphearson, R. *The Presbyterian Church in Kenya: An Account of the Origins and Growth of the Presbyterian Church of East Africa*. Nairobi: Presbyterian Church of East Africa, 1970.

Ogot, Bethwell A. *My Footprints in the Sands of Time: An Autobiography*. Victoria, BC: Trafford Publishing, 2006.

Presbyterian Church of Ghana

In the 1820s, the Basel Mission, supported by Reformed and Lutheran churches in Germany and Switzerland, began one of its first Christian missionary efforts in what was then the Gold Coast among the Ga- and Twi-speaking peoples in the eastern part of the region. Stations were subsequently opened in other parts of the country. Some of the converts who showed promise were sent to Europe for training. One of these students, David Asante (1834–1892), who was trained at Basel, was in 1864 the first African ordained by the missionaries.

During World War I, German and Swiss missionaries had to leave the Gold Coast. In 1920 the Basel Mission turned its work over to the Scottish Mission. The mission matured into the Presbyterian Church of the Gold Coast in 1926. The Gold Coast became the independent nation of Ghana in 1957, and subsequently the Presbyterian Church changed its name.

The church has subsequently spread to all parts of the nation and has become one of the larger religious bodies in the country. Its 565,637 members (2005) are divided into 14 presbyteries. A synod serves as the church's highest legislative body. The church has also developed an extensive educational and medical program. Worship is now conducted in a variety of languages. Most recently, the church has experienced both the new life and the disturbances that have come as the Charismatic movement has spread through its ranks. The church is a member of the World Alliance of Reformed Churches and the World Council of Churches.

Presbyterian Church of Ghana
PO Box 1800
Thorpe Rd.
Accra
Ghana

J. Gordon Melton

See also: Basel Mission; World Alliance of Reformed Churches; World Council of Churches.

References

Bauswein, Jean-Jacques, and Lukas Vischner, eds. *The Reformed Family Worldwide: A Survey of Reformed Churches, Theological Schools, and International Organizations*. Grand Rapids, MI: William B. Eerdmans Publishing Company, 1999.

Beeko, Anthony A. *The Trail Blazers. Fruits of 175 Years of the Presbyterian Church of Ghana (1828–2003)*. Accra, Ghana: Afram Publications, 2005.

Hall, Peter. *Autobiography of Rev. Peter Hall: First Moderator of the Presbyterian Church of Ghana*. Accra, Ghana: Waterville Pub. House, 1965.

Kpobi, David Nii Anum. *Triple Heritage: Facts and Figures about the Presbyterian Church of Ghana*. Accra, Ghana: Asempa Publishers, 1995.

Nkanse-Kyeremateng, K. *The Presbyterian Church of Ghana and National Development*. Accra, Ghana: Sebewie Publishers, 1995.

Presbyterian Church of India

The Presbyterian Church of India has its roots in the original Baptist mission that in 1813 had opened work in the area of the Kasai Hills, in the easternmost part of Bengal. Although there was some response to this work over the next two decades, in 1938 the mission was abandoned. In 1841 Thomas Jones (d. 1849) and his wife Anne (d. 1846), Presbyterians from Wales, arrived and started evangelistic work in the same area. They worked alone until they were joined by William Pryse. Their work had success over the next two decades, and in 1867 the first presbytery was formed. As the work continued to grow through the last half of the century, in 1895 it was divided into five presbyteries, and the following year a synod called the Assembly created.

At the same time, work began in Sylhet and Cachar in what is now Bangladesh, where in the early 20th century a second assembly developed. In 1894 missionary activity was extended to Mizoram in northeast India, growing rapidly through several mass movements of people into the church. Today the region is largely Christian. Early in the 20th century, the work extended into the area around the North Cachar Hills, leading in 1930 to the creation of another assembly.

In 1926 the various segments of the work that had been developed for almost a century were brought together as the Presbyterian Church of North India, and an assembly for the entire church created. The various geographic regions were reorganized as synods. The church had been extended to a number of Indian peoples speaking a variety of languages, and as the church continued to grow more than over 20 languages were in regular use.

The post–World War II era brought a number of changes. A significant part of the church operated in what became Pakistan in 1947, and the partition separated this group from the main body of the church. In 1959 a number of Christians in Manipur of different denominational and linguistic backgrounds were organized as Presbyterians and in 1959 were included in the church. The Manipur Synod was created in 1978.

In the late 1990s the Presbyterian Church of India reported 797,700 members. The church has been part of the larger Protestant community of northern India, but it stayed out of the several mergers that led to the formation of the Church of North India in 1970. It is not a member of the World Council of Churches, but it is a member of the World Alliance of Reformed Churches and the National Council of Churches in India, and is a partner with the Council on World Mission.

Presbyterian Assembly House
Central Ward, OPP
State Library
Shillong Meghalaya, 793 001
India

J. Gordon Melton

See also: Church of North India; World Alliance of Reformed Churches; World Council of Churches.

Reference

Bauswein, Jean-Jacques, and Lukas Vischner, eds. *The Reformed Family Worldwide: A Survey of Reformed Churches, Theological Schools, and International Organizations*. Grand Rapids, MI: William B. Eerdmans Publishing Company, 1999.

Presbyterian Church of Korea (HapDong)

The Presbyterian Church in Korea was a united body until 1959, when a major split created the Presbyterian Church in Korea (HapDong) and the Presbyterian Church of Korea (TongHap). Disrupted by the Japanese occupation and World War II, the Presbyterian movement was reconstituted as the Presbyterian Church of Korea (PCK) in 1949. During the 1950s the Korean War overshadowed a theological war that raged within the church, as some leaders associated with the newly founded International Council of Christian Churches, a fundamentalist body founded by associates of U.S. minister Carl McIntire (1906–2002), wooed the conservative leadership of the PCK. At issue were ecumenism, membership in the World Council of Churches, and the theological perspective of the church's seminaries.

Unable to arrive at an amicable solution, the church split into two bodies in 1959. The more conservative group aligned with the International Council of Christian Churches as the Presbyterian Church in Korea (HapDong). In subsequent years, it has had spectacular growth and is now the largest Presbyterian church in the country, with more than 2.1 million members.

Although the church has experienced growth, its history has had a tumultuous course. In 1961 a group withdrew to found the Bible Presbyterian Church (now the Presbyterian Church of Korea [Dae Shin]). In 1979 another fracture began when Kim Hee Bo, the president of ChongShin Seminary, became an advocate of the historical-critical approach to the Pentateuch, the first five books of the Bible. As the controversy raged, some attempted to find a way to heal the breach. Eventually both the group supporting the seminary and the group that had attempted to make peace broke with the larger body of the church.

The Presbyterian Church in Korea (HapDong) is organized presbyterially. The assembly is its highest legislative body. It adheres to the Westminster Confession of Faith. Though it retains its conservative theological stance, it is no longer associated with the International Council of Christian Churches.

Presbyterian Church in Korea (HapDong)
1007-3 DaeChi-Dong
KangNam-GU
Seoul
Republic of Korea

J. Gordon Melton

See also: International Council of Christian Churches; Presbyterian Church of Korea (TongHap); World Council of Churches.

References

Bauswein, Jean-Jacques, and Lukas Vischner, eds. *The Reformed Family Worldwide: A Survey of Reformed Churches, Theological Schools, and International Organizations*. Grand Rapids, MI: William B. Eerdmans Publishing Company, 1999.

Ho, Sun-gil. *The Church Preserved Through Fires: A History of the Presbyterian Church in Korea*. Alberta, Canada: Inheritance Publications, 2006.

Presbyterian Church of Korea (TongHap)

The more liberal of the two large Presbyterian churches in the Republic of Korea, the Presbyterian Church of Korea (TongHap) is generally seen as carrying on the missionary tradition. The story of Presbyterianism in Korea begins in Manchuria, where a Korean, Suh Sang-Yoon, was converted in 1876 by missionaries of the Scottish Missionary Society (related to the Church of Scotland) and in turn assisted in the translation of the New Testament into Korean. Upon his return to his homeland in 1883, he gathered the first Protestant community. American Presbyterian missionaries of the United Presbyterian Church in North America (now an integral part of the Presbyterian Church [U.S.A.]) arrived in 1884, and Horace N. Allen (1858–1932) opened the first church-supported medical facility. The Americans were soon joined by colleagues from Australia and Canada. In 1893 the several Presbyterian groups organized a mission council for Presbyterian churches, the first product of their cooperation being the theological seminary located at Pyongyang.

The progress of the church was interrupted by the Japanese invasion of the country in 1910 and the subsequent invasion that lasted through World War II. Initially, the Presbyterian movement continued to grow, and in 1912 the missionaries and the Korean pastors established the General Assembly of the Presbyterian Church in Chosun. In the 1930s, however, the church was continually faced with the issue of shrine worship. The Occupation authorities demanded that everyone, especially the Christians, acknowledge the Shinto shrine. In 1938, under extreme pressure, the general assembly approved worship of the shrine. Some Korean pastors and laypeople started a resistance movement, which led to their arrest and imprisonment. In 1941, as the war began, most of the missionaries were expelled. The general assembly was dissolved and its membership transferred to the newly founded Chosun Presbyterian Church of Christ in Japan.

After the war, momentous change ensued. The Japanese were expelled, but the country was divided. The People's Republic of Korea closed the Presbyterian Church and established an antireligious regime. In southern Korea, the Presbyterian Church was reconstituted at assemblies in 1946 and 1947, taking the name Presbyterian Church of Korea in 1949. A period of rapid growth followed. That growth has been attributed to the fact that people did not identify Christianity with the colonial government and to the lay-oriented evangelism that characterized the church.

During the period of reconstituting the church, many called for a cleansing from the church of those who had worshipped at the Shinto shrine. Resistance leaders organized a presbytery in 1945 and called for full repentance by those who did not resist. They founded a seminary in Pusan, but the new Presbyterian Church refused to recognize it. The core of the resistance movement refused to join with the larger body and now exists as the Presbyterian Church in Korea (KoShin).

Through the 1950s, the church faced the issue of participation in the ecumenical movement. One group favored membership in the World Council of Churches. The other leaned toward the fundamentalist International Council of Christian Churches. The issue came to culmination in 1959, when the church divided into two somewhat equal factions, both carrying the name Presbyterian Church of Korea (PCK). The PCK (TongHap) affiliated with the World Council of Churches and the World Alliance of Reformed Churches.

Today, the PCK (TongHap) represents the more liberal wing of Korean Presbyterianism. In 2005 it reported 334,520 million members in 998 congregations. In 1984, in celebration of the 100th anniversary of Korean Presbyterianism, the church opened a new headquarters building in Seoul. Two years later it adopted a new confession of faith as a modern restatement of the Reformed theological position. It accepted the ordination of women in 1995. The church is led by its general assembly. It is one of the partner churches of the Council for World Mission (United Reformed Church in the United Kingdom) and the Global Ministries of the Christian Church (Disciples of Christ) and the United Church of Christ. The church supports a number of institutions of higher learning, and it now has a worldwide ministry among Koreans who left the country during and after the Korean War.

Presbyterian Church of Korea (TongHap)
PO Box 1125
135 YunChi-Dong
ChongRo-ku, Seoul 100-611
Republic of Korea

J. Gordon Melton

See also: Christian Church (Disciples of Christ); Church of Scotland; International Council of Christian Churches; Presbyterian Church (U.S.A.); United Church of Christ; United Reformed Church of the United Kingdom; World Alliance of Reformed Churches; World Council of Churches.

References

Bauswein, Jean-Jacques, and Lukas Vischner, eds. *The Reformed Family Worldwide: A Survey of Reformed Churches, Theological Schools, and International Organizations*. Grand Rapids, MI: William B. Eerdmans Publishing Company, 1999.

Park, Chung-Shin. *Protestantism and Politics in Korea*. Seattle: University of Washington Press, 2003.

Van Beek, Huibert. *A Handbook of the Churches and Councils: Profiles of Ecumenical Relationships*. Geneva: World Council of Churches, 2006.

Presbyterian Church of Liberia

The Presbyterian Church in Liberia originated in the American Presbyterian support for the American Colonization Society (ACS) and its efforts to resettle free African Americans in Africa. Modern Liberia was founded as a homeland for the ACS program. Presbyterian work in Liberia began in 1833 and over the next 50 years, the Mission Board of the Presbyterian Church in the U.S.A. (now an integral part of the Presbyterian Church [U.S.A.]) recruited African Americans as missionaries.

Members of the Presbyterian church pose in front of their banner for the "Stranger Mission" in Liberia, about 1900. (Corbis)

In 1928, the presbytery of Liberia (now the Presbyterian Church of Liberia) became independent and over the next decades relations waned between it and its former American supporters. In 1980, the church developed a primary relationship with the continuing Cumberland Presbyterian Church. Most recently, in the wake of the Liberian civil war and subsequent period of unrest, the Liberian church moved to re-establish relationships with its parent body.

In 2005, the church reported 1,083 members in 13 congregations. It is a member of the World Council of Churches and the World Alliance of Reformed Churches.

Presbyterian Church of Liberia
c/o City Hall
PO Box 3350
Monrovia
Liberia

J. Gordon Melton

See also: Presbyterian Church (U.S.A.); World Alliance of Reformed Churches; World Council of Churches.

Reference

Van Beek, Huibert. *A Handbook of the Churches and Councils: Profiles of Ecumenical Relationships*. Geneva: World Council of Churches, 2006.

Presbyterian Church of Mozambique

Reformed Christianity entered Mozambique through the preaching of Josefa Mhalamkala, who had discovered Christianity while visiting South Africa. In 1887 his work was picked up by Swiss Reformed missionary Paul Berthoud (1847–1930). The work concentrated in the southern provinces of Mozambique through the first half of the 20th century. In subsequent decades, the church started the process of becoming an independent body, and it also began to spread to other parts of the country.

In 1961 Eduardo Mondlane (d. 1969), an official with the United Nations and a member of the Presbyterian Church of Mozambique, came back to his native land and organized FRELIMO (Frente de Liberta Vão de Mozambique), the united front against colonialism. He led the group until his assassination in 1969. In 1972 the Portuguese colonial authorities moved against the church and arrested a number of its leaders. Synod President Zedekias Manganhela was tortured and killed in prison. Pressure on the church was relieved only by the end of colonial rule in 1975.

In 2005 the church reported 24,000 members. It is a member of the World Council of Churches and the World Alliance of Reformed Churches. It supports two theological schools, the Theological Institute of Ricatla and the Theological School of Khovo. The highest legislative body in the church is the general assembly. Doctrinally it adheres to the teachings in the Heidelburg Catechism. It has a continuing close relationship with the Federation of Swiss Protestant Churches.

Presbyterian Church of Mozambique
Caixa Postal 21
Av. Ahmed Sekou Touré 1822
Maputo
Mozambique

J. Gordon Melton

See also: Federation of Swiss Protestant Churches; World Alliance of Reformed Churches; World Council of Churches.

References

Bauswein, Jean-Jacques, and Lukas Vischner, eds. *The Reformed Family Worldwide: A Survey of Reformed Churches, Theological Schools, and International Organizations*. Grand Rapids, MI: William B. Eerdmans Publishing Company, 1999.

Van Beek, Huibert. *A Handbook of the Churches and Councils: Profiles of Ecumenical Relationships*. Geneva: World Council of Churches, 2006.

Presbyterian Church of Nigeria

The Presbyterian Church of Nigeria has its origins in the Scottish Missionary Society's work in Jamaica. The church worked among the Africans living in Jamaica and participated in the movement for the abolition of slavery during the 1830s. After abolition, the Presbyterians experienced an influx of members, and in the 1840s the first ministers graduated from the presbytery's school. The church developed a missionary perspective and in 1846 commissioned the first of its ministers as missionaries to Calabar on the Gulf of Guinea in present-day Nigeria. The first stations were established at Duke Town and Creek Town. A third station began at Old Town Calabar in 1847. The mission work gradually moved inland.

The Church of Scotland assumed responsibility for the work even before the British established their hegemony over the area. Work has concentrated among the Efik, Ibo, and Tiv peoples.

The church gained autonomy in 1954. It has a presbyterian polity and admits women to ordination. It is a member of both the World Alliance of Reformed Churches and the Reformed Ecumenical Council. Numerous Presbyterian and Reformed churches, primarily in the early 20th century, began missions among one or more of Nigeria's 500 peoples/language groups. No less than 11 different Reformed/Presbyterian churches are now operating there; the Presbyterian Church of Nigeria is the oldest but by no means the largest. It is a member of the Reformed Ecumenical Council of Nigeria, which provides fellowship and coordination among the different churches.

The Presbyterian Church of Nigeria reported 500,000 members in 2005. It joined the World Council of Churches in 1961.

The Presbyterian Church of Nigeria
PO Box 2635
26-29 Ehere Rd.
Ogbor Hill, ABA Abia State
Nigeria

J. Gordon Melton

See also: Church of Scotland; Reformed Ecumenical Council; World Alliance of Reformed Churches; World Council of Churches.

References

Bauswein, Jean-Jacques, and Lukas Vischner, eds. *The Reformed Family Worldwide: A Survey of Reformed Churches, Theological Schools, and International Organizations*. Grand Rapids, MI: William B. Eerdmans Publishing Company, 1999.

Johnston, Geoffrey. *Of God and Maxim Guns: Presbyterianism in Nigeria, 1846–1966*. Waterloo, ON: Wilfrid Laurier University Press, 1988.

Palmer, Timothy. *The Reformed and Presbyterian Faith: A View from Nigeria*. Bukuru, Nigeria: TCNN Publications, 1996.

Van Beek, Huibert. *A Handbook of the Churches and Councils: Profiles of Ecumenical Relationships*. Geneva: World Council of Churches, 2006.

Presbyterian Church of Pakistan

The Presbyterian Church of Pakistan grew out of the original Protestant Christian work in that part of India that is now Pakistan. Missionaries initially arrived in the 1830s from the Punjab. The first appears to have been John C. Lowrie (1808–1900), who settled in Lahore in 1834, though he soon had to retire. Then in 1849 Charles W. Forman (1821–1894) opened the first permanent missionary station and went on to develop the impressive educational program that led to the founding of a string of elementary and secondary schools, several colleges, and a seminary. Forman led in the founding of the Lahore Church Council. In 1904 the Lahore Church Council joined the United Church of Northern India (a union of Congregational and Presbyterian missions that would later become part of the Church of North India).

A second missionary thrust began in 1855 under Andrew Gordon (1828–1887) of the United Presbyterian Church in the U.S.A. (now a part of the Presbyterian Church [U.S.A.]). He began in Lahore and then expanded to Sialkot. Four years later the Presbytery of Sialkot was organized. In 1893 the Sialkot work incorporated as one presbytery in the Synod of the Punjab of the United Presbyterian Church in the U.S.A. In 1961 the synod became independent as the United Presbyterian Church of Pakistan. Seven years later the church experienced a severe split when representatives of the International Council of Christian Churches attempted to woo support to its fundamentalist position. Over the subsequent decades, the schism was largely healed.

In 1993 the Lahore Church Council and the United Presbyterian Church of Pakistan merged to become the Presbyterian Church of Pakistan. In the later 1990s it reported 400,000 members in 200 congregations. It sponsors the Gujranwala Theological Seminary. Though it stayed out of the merger that created the Church of Pakistan, it remains in close relationship with the latter and is also a member of both the World Alliance of Reformed Churches and the World Council of Churches. In 2005, the church reported 400,000 members.

Presbyterian Church of Pakistan
PO Box 13
2 Empress Rd.
Lahore 54000
Pakistan

J. Gordon Melton

See also: Church of North India; International Council of Christian Churches; World Alliance of Reformed Churches; World Council of Churches.

References

Bauswein, Jean-Jacques, and Lukas Vischner, eds. *The Reformed Family Worldwide: A Survey of Reformed Churches, Theological Schools, and International Organizations*. Grand Rapids, MI: William B. Eerdmans Publishing Company, 1999.

Van Beek, Huibert. *A Handbook of the Churches and Councils: Profiles of Ecumenical Relationships*. Geneva: World Council of Churches, 2006.

Presbyterian Church of Rwanda

The Presbyterian Church of Rwanda grew out of the work of the Bethel Mission, a German society created especially to evangelize the lands of the expanding German colonial empire. Germany was given hegemony over Rwanda by the Berlin Conference of 1885, and the Bethel Mission established its work in 1907. The Mission had hardly established itself when World War I began, and following Germany's defeat, the missionaries were forced out. Rwanda was reassigned as a Belgian protectorate, and the Bethel Mission's work was taken over by the Belgian Protestant Missionary Society. The missionary society remained in control until 1959, when the mission became independent as the Presbyterian Church of Rwanda.

For more than a generation the church experienced equal growth among the several major groups of Rwanda, Hutu, Tutsi, and Twa peoples. It created a system of primary and secondary schools and several professional schools and medical facilities. However, in 1994 when the tribal war began, the church faced severe disruption, as it had members among both the persecuted Tutsi and the persecutor Hutu. It lost 16 pastors and an uncounted number of members in the massacres. In the years since, the major work of the church has focused upon the necessary reconciliation, healing, and restitution for all of the killing that took place.

In 2005, the church reported 300,000 members. It is organized with a presbyterian polity, and the general assembly is the highest lawmaking body in the church. The church is a member of the World Council of Churches and the World Alliance of Reformed Churches.

Presbyterian Church of Rwanda
BP 56
Kigali
Rwanda

J. Gordon Melton

See also: World Alliance of Reformed Churches; World Council of Churches.

References

Bauswein, Jean-Jacques, and Lukas Vischner, eds. *The Reformed Family Worldwide: A Survey of Reformed Churches, Theological Schools, and International Organizations*. Grand Rapids, MI: William B. Eerdmans Publishing Company, 1999.

Van Beek, Huibert. *A Handbook of the Churches and Councils: Profiles of Ecumenical Relationships*. Geneva: World Council of Churches, 2006.

Presbyterian Church of Southern Africa

See Uniting Presbyterian Church in Southern Africa.

Presbyterian Church of the Sudan

American Presbyterians entered the Sudan in 1901 and established their initial station at Omdurman in the southern part of the country. The north was not open to them at the time, and evangelization was directed toward people living in the province of the Upper Nile. There was a small educational effort in the north based in a community of expatriate Egyptians. It was connected with the Evangelical Church–Synod of the Nile, but it now exists as the independent Sudan Presbyterian Evangelical Church.

The work in the south spread among various peoples: the Shilluk, Nuer, Dinka, Anuak, and Murle. The work progressed slowly, but the first Sudanese pastor was ordained in 1942. Plans to unite the Presbyterian work with both the work in the north and the Anglican work were pursued but produced no positive results.

Since the time of national independence in 1956, the work of what became the Presbyterian Church of the Sudan has proceeded only under the most difficult of conditions. The country's Constitution failed to give the non-Muslim area in the south, consisting primarily of Africans, any guarantees against encroachment from the Arab north. A civil war began that lasted until 1972. Peace lasted 11 years, and then the government declared its intention of making Muslim law the law of the land. In 1983 war was renewed, and a state of hostility has continued to the present.

The Presbyterian Church is headed by a general assembly that meets quadrennially. The congregations are divided into two presbyteries, one serving the area controlled by the government and the other, the area controlled by the rebel forces. All growth is in the latter area. The church has experienced one major schism, in 1986, when the members among the Dinka people left to found the independent Trinity Presbyterian Church of Sudan.

In 2005, the Presbyterian Church of the Sudan reported approximately 1 million members in 500 congregations. It is a member of the World Council of Churches and the World Alliance of Reformed Churches and operates the Nile Theological College in Khartoum.

Presbyterian Church of the Sudan
PO Box 3421
Khartoum
Sudan

J. Gordon Melton

See also: Evangelical Church–Synod of the Nile; World Alliance of Reformed Churches; World Council of Churches.

References

Bauswein, Jean-Jacques, and Lukas Vischner, eds. *The Reformed Family Worldwide: A Survey of Reformed Churches, Theological Schools, and International Organizations*. Grand Rapids, MI: William B. Eerdmans Publishing Company, 1999.

Van Beek, Huibert. *A Handbook of the Churches and Councils: Profiles of Ecumenical Relationships*. Geneva: World Council of Churches, 2006.

Presbyterian Church of Vanuatu

The Presbyterian Church of Vanuatu continues the missionary efforts established by the London Missionary Society (LMS) in 1938 on the South Sea islands of the New Hebrides, now the independent nation of Vanuatu. In 1838 the pioneer South Sea missionary John Williams (1796–1839) decided to expand the work of the LMS into the New Hebrides from his base on Samoa. Accompanied by three Samoan teachers and fellow LMS missionary James Harris (d. 1839), he arrived on Tanna Island, where he left the three Samoans while he and Harris moved on to Erromanga. Unfortunately, they were both killed.

On two occasions, in 1840 and 1845, missionaries had to leave Tanna when the locals blamed them for outbreaks of disease. This targeting of missionaries would continue as British and French slavers operated the islands—the residents blaming the missionaries, whom they identified with European authorities, for the loss of neighbors and loved ones. A significant number of missionaries were murdered.

At the end of the 1840s, the LMS work was superseded by the arrival of Presbyterians, most notably John Geddie (1815–1872) from Canada and John G. Paton (1824–1907), and a team of missionaries affiliated with the Church of Scotland. Their work was supplemented by William Witt and Peter Milne (1834–1908), who arrived in 1869–1870 from the Presbyterian Church of New Zealand. Finally, after the British and French decided to stop fighting over the islands and began to work out their unique cooperative administration, the Reformed Church of France began a small work.

All of the Presbyterian missionary activity was eventually united and reorganized as the Presbyterian Church of Vanuatu. At this time the church was transferred to local leadership from the foreign missionaries, by this time primarily from Australia and New Zealand. The church has had a significant role in the development of Bislama, a neo-Melanesian language that has subsequently become the official language of the new nation of Vanuatu. It promoted it as a common language through the development of a Bible translation that is used in worship throughout the islands. (Earlier, the church had supported the work of translating the Bible into more than 21 other languages that are still spoken throughout the islands.)

In 2005, the church reported 78,000 members. The largest religious group in Vanuatu, it is a member of the World Council of Churches and the Vanuatu Christian Council.

Presbyterian Church of Vanuatu
Presbiterian Jyos Blong Venuatu
PO Box 150
Port Vila
Vanuatu

J. Gordon Melton

See also: Church of Scotland; London Missionary Society; Reformed Church of France; World Council of Churches.

References

Bauswein, Jean-Jacques, and Lukas Vischner, eds. *The Reformed Family Worldwide: A Survey of Reformed Churches, Theological Schools, and International Organizations*. Grand Rapids, MI: William B. Eerdmans Publishing Company, 1999.

Forman, Charles H. *The Island Churches of the South Pacific: Emergence in the Twentieth Century*. Maryknoll, NY: Orbis, 1982.

Van Beek, Huibert. *A Handbook of the Churches and Councils: Profiles of Ecumenical Relationships*. Geneva: World Council of Churches, 2006.

Presbyterian Church of Wales

The Presbyterian Church of Wales (Egiwys Bresbyteraidd Cynirn) grew out of the evangelical Awakening of the 17th century in Great Britain. The primary organizational expression of the awakening was the Methodist Church (U.K.), which developed under the leadership of John Wesley (1703–1791). Closely associated with Wesley was George Whitefield (1714–1770), a classmate at Oxford, who had encouraged Wesley to expand his work beyond London and had introduced the High Church–oriented Wesley to outdoor preaching. Although they were friends, Wesley and Whitefield had deep doctrinal differences, Whitefield leaning toward Calvinism and its emphasis on predestination while Wesley adhered to the theology of Jacob Arminius (1560–1609) and an emphasis on free grace and human response.

Around 1735 Whitefield became acquainted with Howel Harris (1714–1773), a Welshman who had begun an independent teaching mission following a deep conversion experience. Harris began to preach throughout Wales, and at times Wesley traveled through the country with him. In the 1740s Wesley and Whitefield parted over their doctrinal differences. About this same time, Harris introduced Whitefield to Selina Hastings, the countess of Huntington (1707–1791), who tried unsuccessfully to bring about a reconciliation. When that proved impossible, she sided with Whitefield, having already contributed generously to his orphanage project in the American colonies.

As a member of the royalty, the countess of Huntington also had the ability to appoint "chaplains," ministers who had no Church of England parish but who could function as ministers of the established church. She encouraged the erection of chapels in various locations where her chaplains could preach. She also endowed a training college for young preachers at Trevecca in Wales. This informal network of preachers and chapels became known informally as the Countess of Huntington Connection. In 1779 a parish minister brought suit against the countess, and the authorities ruled against the growing work. It had to be reorganized as a dissenting movement, the Calvinist Methodist Connection.

The Presbyterian Church of Wales continues the Welsh branch of the Calvinist Methodist Connection. As an independent body, it held its first general assembly in 1864. In the 20th century it became known as the Calvinist/Methodist Church of Wales and then assumed its present name. In 1933 it adopted its present constitution and received the assent of Parliament for its promulgation.

In the 1990s, the Presbyterian Church of Wales reported 54,000 members. Its Confession of Faith places it in the Reformed theological tradition. The general assembly is the highest legislative body. The church is a member of both the World Council of Churches and the World Alliance of Reformed Churches.

The Presbyterian Church of Wales
53 Richmond Rd.
Cardiff/Cymru
Wales CF2 3UP
United Kingdom
http://www.ebcpcw.org.uk/

J. Gordon Melton

See also: Wesley, John; World Alliance of Reformed Churches; World Council of Churches.

References

Bauswein, Jean-Jacques, and Lukas Vischner, eds. *The Reformed Family Worldwide: A Survey of Reformed Churches, Theological Schools, and International Organizations*. Grand Rapids, MI: William B. Eerdmans Publishing Company, 1999.

Van Beek, Huibert. *A Handbook of the Churches and Councils: Profiles of Ecumenical Relationships*. Geneva: World Council of Churches, 2006.

Presbyterian Church (U.S.A.)

The Presbyterian Church (U.S.A.), formed in 1983 by a merger of the United Presbyterian Church in the U.S.A. and the Presbyterian Church in the United States, is the primary body continuing the British and Scottish Presbyterian traditions in the United States. The United Presbyterian Church was itself the product of a variety of mergers, and its constituent parts include the very first Presbyterian synods founded during the American colonial era.

Presbyterians, who constituted one segment of the larger Puritan movement in Great Britain, began to move to the American colonies in the 17th century, especially after the end of the Commonwealth (1648–1660). Congregations were formed, especially in Connecticut, New York, Pennsylvania, and New Jersey. The first synod was formed in 1706. In the middle of the 18th century, the movement was split between those who supported the new revivalism, as proposed by the likes of independent Anglican George Whitefield (1714–1770) and Congregationalist Jonathan Edwards (1703–1758), and those who rejected it. Revivalism would be a continuing issue dividing Presbyterians through the 19th century. The main body of American Presbyterians held together until the end of the American Civil War, but then it split into two factions. The northern faction emerged as the Presbyterian Church in the United States of America; the southern group as the Presbyterian Church in the United States.

After the American Revolution, the church had spread westward. During the early part of the 19th century, it made common cause with the Congregationalists, and the two groups developed a plan of union to cut down on competition as the two churches developed on the frontier. However, on the frontier, revivalism again divided Presbyterians as a new issue arose: the camp meeting. Those who supported camp meetings and revivalism on the frontier departed to form the Cumberland Presbyterian Church.

In the decades prior to the American Revolution, Scottish Covenanters found their way to the colonies. Covenanters in Scotland had formed their own church in 1733 in protest against the authority of the established Church of Scotland. By 1773, several Covenanter ministers had arrived in the colonies and formed the Reformed Presbyterian Church. A second secession occurred in the 1700s among people who protested the patronage system of the Church of Scotland and its lack of spiritual fervor. Still a third schism occurred in protest of the burghers who took the oath of loyalty that allowed them to hold public office in Scotland. The anti-burgher faction opposed the oath and charged that taking it supported the episcopacy. People associated with the Covenanter and anti-burgher factions came to the colonies in the middle of the 18th century and in 1753 formed the Associate Presbyterian Church. In 1782, the Reformed Presbyterian Church and the Associate Presbyterian Church united to form the Associate Reformed Presbyterian Church.

But some members of the Associate Presbyterian Church declined to join the merger and continued to exist under that name. In 1822, the Associate Reformed Presbyterian Church split into two factions, one in the North and one in the southern part of the country. In 1858, the continuing Associate Presbyterian Church and the northern faction of the Associate Reformed

Interior of the Second Presbyterian Church in Chicago, a congregation established in 1842. (iStockPhoto.com)

Church merged to constitute the United Presbyterian Church of North America.

In 1906, the Presbyterian Church in the United States of America and the Cumberland Presbyterian Church merged and continued under the name of the former body. Then, in 1958, that body merged with the United Presbyterian Church in North America to become the United Presbyterian Church in the U.S.A. That merger brought most American Presbyterians into two organizations. These two groups, the United Presbyterian Church in the U.S.A. and the Presbyterian Church in the United States, merged in 1983 to constitute the Presbyterian Church (U.S.A.).

In 2000 the Presbyterian Church (U.S.A.) reported 2.56 million members. The church is organized on a presbyterial model. Its highest legislative body is the general assembly. Congregations are grouped into presbyteries and synods across the country. The church supports a number of colleges and theological seminaries. The constituent bodies forming the Presbyterian Church (U.S.A.) began ordaining women to the ministry in 1956.

In 1967 the United Presbyterian Church caused considerable controversy when it adopted a new Confession of Faith, which the church saw as a contemporary restatement of the Presbyterian tradition but which many conservatives saw as a marked departure from traditional standards. The church subsequently published a book containing the Apostles' Creed, the Nicene Creed, several Reformed confessions, the Westminster documents, and the new 1967 confession. It is generally understood that these statements of the Christian and Reformed tradition are to be understood both in the light of history and contemporary theology. Some church members and leaders, primarily from the Presbyterian Church in the United States, who rejected what they saw as the liberal theological tendencies in the church implied by the new confession, stayed out of the proposed merger and in the 1970s formed the conservative Presbyterian Church in America.

The Presbyterian Church (U.S.A.) is ecumenically oriented, and its constituent bodies produced some of the outstanding ecumenical leaders of the 20th century. The church is a leading member of the World Alliance of Reformed Churches and the World Council of Churches. In 2006, the church reported an inclusive membership of 3,025,740 members in 11,903 churches.

The Presbyterian Church (U.S.A.)
100 Witherspoon St.
Louisville, KY 40202
http://www.pcusa.org

J. Gordon Melton

See also: World Alliance of Reformed Churches; World Council of Churches.

References

Balmer, Randall, and Gerald L. Fitzmier. *The Presbyterians*. Westmont, CT: Praeger, 1994.

Hart, D. G., and Mark A. Noll, eds. *Dictionary of the Presbyterian and Reformed Tradition in America*. Des Plaines, IL: InterVarsity Press, 1999.

Lucas, Sean Michael. *On Being Presbyterian: Our Beliefs, Practices, and Stories*. Phillipsburg, NJ: P & R Publishing, 2006.

Patton, Jacob Harris. *A Popular History of the Presbyterian Church in the United States of America*. Amsterdam: Fredonia Books, 2003.

Weeks, Louis B. *To Be a Presbyterian*. Philadelphia: Westminster John Knox Press, 1987.

Weston, William J. *Presbyterian Pluralism: Competition in a Protestant House*. Knoxville: University of Tennessee Press, 1997.

Presbyterian Reformed Church in Cuba

During the last decades of the 19th century, many Cubans found their way to Florida, where they encountered Protestant churches for the first time. In 1890 Evaristo Collazo, who in the 1880s had resided in Tampa, Florida, returned to Cuba and began to gather small groups in Havana, Santa Clara, and Placetas. He also came to Cuba to support the revolutionary struggle to free Cuba from Spain. Collazo later was ordained as a Presbyterian missionary and became a lieutenant in the revolutionary army in the Spanish-American War.

After the war, in 1902, Collazo reopened the church and was assisted by American Presbyterian missionaries. The communities they founded eventually constituted themselves as a presbytery of the Synod of New Jersey of the Presbyterian Church in the U.S.A. (now a constituent part of the Presbyterian Church [U.S.A.]). The church experienced steady growth through World War II, and in 1945 it joined with the Methodists and Episcopalians in forming the Seminary of Matanzas.

In 1967 the Presbyterian mission became an autonomous body as the Presbyterian Reformed Church in Cuba (Iglesia Presbiteriana-Reformada en Cuba). In 1969 Fidel Castro overthrew the government and established the regime he still heads. The government adopted an antireligious policy, but the church survived through the next quarter of a century and then experienced a spurt of growth, as regulations on religion were loosened in the 1990s.

The church is organized presbyterially. Its highest legislative body is the national synod. It published its own confession of faith in 1968. It is a member of both the World Alliance of Reformed Churches and the World Council of Churches. In 2005 it reported 15,000 members in 53 congregations.

Presbyterian Reformed Church in Cuba
Salud 222 E/Lealtad y Campanario
La Habana 10200
Cuba

J. Gordon Melton

See also: Presbyterian Church (U.S.A.); World Alliance of Reformed Churches; World Council of Churches.

References

Bauswein, Jean-Jacques, and Lukas Vischner, eds. *The Reformed Family Worldwide: A Survey of Reformed Churches, Theological Schools, and International Organizations*. Grand Rapids, MI: William B. Eerdmans Publishing Company, 1999.

Young, David P. *Cuba and the Presbyterian Church: More than One Hundred Years of Faithful Witness*. Louisville, KY: Presbyterian Church (U.S.A.), Global Mission Ministry Unit, 1991.

Presbytery of Liberia

Missionaries from the Presbyterian Church in the U.S.A. (now an integral part of the Presbyterian Church [U.S.A.]) arrived in Liberia in 1833. As mission work proceeded, they discovered that personnel, one by one, were falling victim to malaria. They instituted a policy of sending only African American personnel but soon discovered that these workers were just as susceptible to the disease. In spite of their problems, the missionaries were able to play an important role in the developing country, and one of their number signed the country's Declaration of Independence in 1847. Support in the form of missionary personnel continued through the 1880s.

The Liberian Presbytery was among the earliest of the Christian missions in Africa to move entirely under local control and then attain status as an independent church. It was also unusual in the African context in that it had been originally constituted by repatriated Africans who had been returned to Africa after their sojourn in the United States. The presbytery became independent in 1928. It also became one of the first churches to ordain women—as deacons in the 1940s and as elders in the 1950s.

In the late 1990s the presbytery reported 1,083 members in 13 congregations. It is a member of both the World Council of Churches and the World Alliance of Reformed Churches. In the 1970s it developed a new relationship with the Cumberland Presbyterian Church and in 1980s became a provisional presbytery in that church.

Presbytery of Liberia
PO Box 3350
Broad and Johnson St.
Monrovia
Liberia

J. Gordon Melton

See also: Cumberland Presbyterian Church; Presbyterian Church (U.S.A.); World Alliance of Reformed Churches; World Council of Churches.

References

Bauswein, Jean-Jacques, and Lukas Vischner, eds. *The Reformed Family Worldwide: A Survey of Reformed Churches, Theological Schools, and International Organizations*. Grand Rapids, MI: William B. Eerdmans Publishing Company, 1999.

Van Beek, Huibert. *A Handbook of the Churches and Councils: Profiles of Ecumenical Relationships*. Geneva: World Council of Churches, 2006.

Priory of Sion

The Priory of Sion is a secret society legally established in France in 1972 by Pierre Plantard (1920–2000), yet claiming great antiquity. Legends connected with the Priory of Sion have generated great interest through the years, particularly as a result of the publication in 1982 of *The Holy Blood and the Holy Grail* by British journalists Michael Baigent, Richard Leigh, and Henry Lincoln, a nonfictional book that is the basis for the international best-selling novel *The Da Vinci Code* (2003) by American novelist Dan Brown. The story starts with Father Berenger Saunière (1852–1917), who in 1885 became the parish priest of Rennes-le-Château, a small village in the French region of Aude, near the Pyrenees Mountains. Saunière, it seems, was a rather strange character, deeply interested in symbolism; he also had a penchant for building a number of constructions around his parish church, including a bizarre neo-Gothic "Tower of Magdala." These construction projects obviously cost a good deal of money, while Saunière was known to come from a poor family, and one did not normally become rich in 19th-century France by being a parish priest in a mountain hamlet.

Rennes-le-Château lies at the heart of the area once inhabited by the Cathars, and rumors spread that Saunière had found a treasure buried in the Middle Ages by the persecuted heretics. The fact that Saunière

The gothic "Tower of Magdala," built by Berenger Saunière, the eccentric parish priest of Rennes-le-Château, a small village in southwest France. (Andreas Stecher/StockphotoPro)

was also an archaeology buff, and had found some old artifacts while digging in the vicinity of the parish church, added fuel to the fire of rumors. The priest did his excavations at night, in order to remain the sole owner of his findings (which, according to French law, he should have given to the state). This obviously did not endear Saunière to the municipality, and some villagers also suspected him of having an affair with his servant, Marie Denarnaud (1868–1953), who was undoubtedly fiercely loyal to the controversial priest.

These rumors could not have failed to attract the attention of the local Catholic bishop, and having investigated the matter he concluded that, rather than having found a Cathar treasure, Saunière had made his money from "trafficking in Masses," a not uncommon wrongdoing among 19th- and early-20th-century priests. In the Roman Catholic Church, Masses can be celebrated for the benefit of a specific soul, in the hope of helping a deceased loved one to ascend from purgatory into heaven. Masses can also be said for a specific aim for the benefit of living persons (for instance, for healing purposes). Prior to Vatican II, priests received a stipend, that is, a fixed amount of money for each Mass they said. "Trafficking in Masses" meant, in practice, that priests advertised their willingness to celebrate a great number of Masses for both the dead and the living. Advertising in this way was regarded as a kind of unfair competition toward other priests, and was condemned by the Church as illicit. The matter became even worse, of course, when priests failed to celebrate the Masses requested, despite having received the appropriate stipend. The bishop traced advertisements placed by Saunière in Catholic magazines throughout France, and even abroad, and quickly determined that he could not possibly have celebrated all the Masses he had received payments for, thus in fact defrauding his "clients." In 1909, the bishop asked Saunière to leave Rennes-le-Château; the priest refused and was suspended from his priestly duties and privileges (a lesser sanction than excommunication, but a painful sanction nonetheless, which ended Saunière's ecclesiastical career). He decided to remain in Rennes-le-Château, however, and the ownership of his buildings (Tower of Magdala included) did not pass to the diocese, because Saunière had taken the precaution of transferring their ownership to Marie Denarnaud.

Although the bishop had concluded that trafficking in Masses was enough to explain Saunière's suspicious wealth, rumors about buried treasures (and alleged contacts with the Paris esoteric milieu) continued until his death in 1917, and even in the years that followed. The rumors resurfaced again in the early 1950s, when Marie Denarnaud, who was still the owner of all the properties, in her old age, was trying to sell them. She probably thought that rumors of buried treasures would raise the value of the properties. One buyer was Noel Corbu (1912–1968), who in 1956 started spreading the Saunière treasure legend through the local press, in the hope of attracting clients to the restaurant he had opened in one of the buildings. The rumors did spread largely, thanks to friendly contacts between Corbu, some local reporters, and members of the Paris esoteric milieu.

Pierre Plantard, who had been the leader of a minor occult-political organization known as Alpha Galates, told an even taller story about Rennes-le-Château, firstly to selected friends from the late 1950s, then to the esoteric author Gérard De Sède (1921–2004), who in 1967 published a book entitled *L'Or de Rennes* (*Rennes' Gold*). It was De Sède who in turn interested the three British journalists, Baigent, Leigh, and Lincoln, in the story, and they jointly saw to it that Rennes-le-Château became a household name throughout the English-speaking world, thanks to a BBC TV series based on their reports, as well as several popular books. In short, the story told by Plantard to De Sède, and later popularized by the British journalists, was that Saunière did indeed discover a buried treasure, and that it included much more than valuable antiquities. Buried in Rennes-le-Château were documents confirming the old southern French legends that Jesus Christ, rather than ascending into heaven, had come to live in France with his wife, Mary Magdalene. Plantard added that the divine couple did indeed have children in France and that they initiated a dynasty, which eventually became known as the Merovingian dynasty of France. This, Plantard suggested, was the true meaning of the Grail legends: the Holy Grail, in French *Saint Graal*, was in fact the *Sang Réal*, which in medieval French means "Holy Blood," that is, the blood of Jesus Christ himself flowing in the veins of the Merovingians. When the Merovingian dynasty fell from power, Plantard continued, their descendants went underground and a secret organization, the Priory of Sion, has preserved their holy blood even since. Cathars and Knights Templar, as well as early Freemasons and various literary and artistic figures (prominent among them being the painter Nicholas Poussin, 1594–1655), were all said to be connected to the secretive Priory. Plantard gradually started to imply that he was himself not only the current Grand Master of the elusive Priory, but also the last descendant of the Merovingians and the current vessel of Christ's holy blood.

Plantard's tale, if true, would of course have turned Christianity on its head, and inspired a whole new interpretation of world history. Historians remain understandably skeptical, regarding the Priory of Sion as nothing more than a figment of Plantard's imagination (although a Catholic order known as the Priory of Sion did exist in the Middle Ages, they note, it had nothing to do with the Merovingians, the blood of Jesus Christ, or Rennes-le-Château). Millions of readers of popular books about Rennes-le-Château, and more recently of *The Da Vinci Code*, took the story quite seriously, however, and many in the esoteric milieu were happy to join the Priory of Sion after Plantard legally established it in 1972. It is also not impossible (as reported by several journalists) that some people in the political, financial, and intelligence worlds also took a genuine interest in the Priory's activities, seeing it almost as a more secretive and elite brand of Freemasonry, and some may even have joined it. Be that as it may be, the Rennes-le-Château saga became an integral part of international popular culture even before *The Da Vinci Code* through novels and movies; *Preacher* and *The Magdalena* (recently joined by *Rex Mundi*) were among the popular comic book series that also focused interest on the subject. The Priory remains an interesting organization, combining themes from several pre-existing occult orders, which even those who doubt that the Rennes-le-Château legends are factually true, may nevertheless be tempted to join. As a secret society, the Priory's address (in the Paris region) remains confidential, and the organization does not maintain a website. A number of organizations calling themselves "Priory of Sion" were established after 2003 by fans of *The Da Vinci Code* and occasionally surface on the Web, but they have no connection with Plantard's original French group.

Massimo Introvigne and J. Gordon Melton

See also: Roman Catholic Church.

References

Baigent, Michael, Richard Leigh, and Henry Lincoln. *The Holy Blood and the Holy Grail*. London: Jonathan Cape, 1982.

De Sède, Gérard. *L'Or de Rennes, ou la vie insolite de Bérenger Saunière, curé de Rennes-le-Château*. 2nd ed. Paris: Julliard, 1967.

Introvigne, Massimo. *Gli Illuminati e il Priorato di Sion. La verità sulle due società segrete del "Codice da Vinci" e di "Angeli e demoni."* Casale Monferrato (Alessandria): Piemme, 2005.

Saul, John M., and Janice A. Glaholm. *Rennes-le-Château: A Bibliography*. London: Mercurius Press, 1985.

Progressive National Baptist Convention of America

Among the least known of the organizational remnants of the 1960s civil rights movement in the United States, the Progressive National Baptist Convention of America was formed in 1961 by Baptist pastors who supported Martin Luther King, Jr.'s nonviolent protests against laws and social patterns that allowed racial discrimination to persist in American life. The Convention grew out of the National Baptist Convention, U.S.A., which at the time was the largest institution in the United States led and supported by African Americans.

Formed late in the 19th century, the National Baptist Convention represented a new attempt by African Americans to control their own religious organizations. Prior to its founding, most black Baptists were affiliated with the American Baptists (now the American Baptist Churches in the U.S.A.), many serving in its employ as writers, missionaries, and denominational agency workers. However, African Americans were largely excluded from the higher levels of control and decision making within the denomination. Soon after the formation of the National Baptist Convention, however, the African American community was confronted with a series of new laws that mandated a segregated society in the American South (where most African Americans resided).

Through the early 20th century, a long struggle for social equality took place, and many black leaders were prepared to continue that struggle long into the future. Observing the repressive responses to the occasional race riots that broke out in some U.S. cities, they concluded that attempts to change the situation by taking to the streets were counterproductive. Among those who believed it was futile to try to change racial patterns suddenly was Joseph H. Jackson (d. 1990), the pastor of a large Baptist congregation in the heart of Chicago's African American community and the powerful president of the National Baptist Convention.

Into this setting came Martin Luther King, Jr. (1929–1968), the pastor of a relatively small congregation in Montgomery, Alabama. King had been inspired by the example of Mahatma Gandhi and his successful efforts to free India from colonial rule. Utilizing the opportunity presented initially by the rude treatment of a black woman on a public bus in December 1955, he organized the African American community across the South in a protest against segregation laws. He impressed the example of Gandhi upon the protesters, giving a uniquely Christian twist to the idea of nonviolent moral challenge to the authorities. The idea caught the imagination of the younger generation, and a mass movement ensued.

In 1961 King's supporters in the National Baptist Convention demanded that the Convention, the most prestigious African American religious organization in the country, declare its support of King and the movement. They immediately faced opposition from

President Jackson and others who feared that repercussions would be dire if King took to the streets. They refused the support. The demand for support of the civil rights movement was also tied to a challenge of Jackson's leadership of the Convention. He had been president for nine years in 1961. However, Jackson's commitment to the gradual elimination of racial discrimination still had the majority support of the Convention, and the challenge to his continued presidency by Gardner C. Taylor (b. 1918) in 1961 was defeated.

Following their defeat, Taylor and his supporters in the Convention decided that the best way to lead African American Baptists in a new direction was to issue a call to form a new association. In November 1961, 23 pastors answered and with the messengers (representatives) from their churches formed the Progressive National Baptist Convention. The news of the formation of the Convention was largely lost outside the African American community, as the nation's attention was on King and the Southern Christian Leadership Conference, which provided the direct guidance to the civil rights movement at the time. Among the bylaws accepted by the new Convention the following year was a provision limiting the length of the term of the president. The Convention grew quickly over the next years, as the movement culminated in the passing of the comprehensive Civil Rights Act in 1964.

In 2005 the Progressive National Baptist Convention reported a membership of 2.5 million in some 2,000 congregations. It cooperates with the other National Baptist conventions in the support of two theological schools. Cooperative action with other Baptist bodies has been a keynote of its national program. Among its earliest efforts was the Fund for Renewal, a program jointly sponsored with the American Baptists and designed to give new life to black Baptist schools. King and Ralph Abernathy (1926–1990), the American Baptist who succeeded King as leader of the Southern Christian Leadership Conference following King's assassination, lent their support to the fund. The Progressive National Baptist Convention is also a member of the Baptist World Alliance and the World Council of Churches.

Progressive National Baptist Convention of America
601 50th St., N.E.
Washington, DC 20019
http://www.pnbc.org

J. Gordon Melton

See also: American Baptist Churches in the U.S.A.; Baptist World Alliance; National Baptist Convention, U.S.A.; World Council of Churches.

References

Avant, Albert A., Jr. *The Social Teaching of the Progressive National Baptist Convention, Inc. Since 1961: A Critical Analysis of the Least, the Lost and the Left-Out*. New York: Routledge, 2003.

Booth, William D. *A Call to Greatness: The Story of the Founding of the Progressive National Baptist Convention*. Richmond, VA: Brunswick Publishing Corporation, 2001.

Fitts, Leroy. *A History of Black Baptists*. Nashville: Broadman Press, 1985.

Payne, Wardell J. *Directory of African-American Religious Bodies*. 2nd ed. Washington, DC: Howard University Press, 1996.

Protestant Christian Batak Church

The Protestant Christian Batak Church (Huria Kristen Batak Protestan [HKBP]) dates to the arrival on Sumatra of Ludwig Ingwer Nommensen (1834–1918) as a representative of the German Rhenish Mission, a missionary agency associated with the German Lutheran Church. Nommensen initiated work among the Batak people who had settled on Sumatra in the ancient past. The Batak prospered, and over the centuries various Batak subdivisions appeared. Nommensen moved into the heart of Batak country and established a mission, and colleagues soon followed. The mission's work spread across the island.

In the 1920s the Sumatran Lutherans began to manifest signs of desiring independence. For example, they asked the German missionaries to relinquish control of the church. Formal independence was granted in 1930, though the German missionaries remained in place with a slightly altered status. The new church took the name Huria Kristen Batak Protestan, or Protestant Christian Batak Church, and is generally known by the initials of its Indonesian name (HKBP).

A Protestant Christian Batak church on Samosir Island, Lake Toba, Sumatra. (Valery Shanin/Dreamstime.com)

Then in 1940 Germany invaded the Netherlands. In response, the Dutch government on Sumatra interned all the German missionaries and did not allow anyone to use their homes or offices. The church was suddenly cut off from its financial resources. While the church was still trying to cope with this crisis, the Japanese invaded and tried to force some Shinto practices on the Christian community.

In the face of the wartime problems, the HKBP elected its first Indonesian *endorus* (bishop). In 1951 it issued a confession of faith that acknowledged the authority of the ancient ecumenical creeds, the Reformation confessions, and the Barmen Declaration (a statement against some of the religious claims of Nazism), but it also went on to create its own restatement of Christianity that spoke against a number of views that it opposed, such as Pentecostalism and nationalistic Christianity. The new confession did not choose between Lutheran and Reformed doctrine, but the newly autonomous church decided to continue its Lutheran associations and applied for membership in the Lutheran World Federation. It has subsequently become a member of the World Council of Churches and the Community of Churches in Indonesia.

In 1954 the church opened Nommensen University, currently with two campuses. The university's former theological school now exists as a separate institution. The church also maintains an extensive school system of elementary and secondary schools. Other ministries include a farming project, a youth center, an orphanage, and a center to assist the blind and crippled. The church also works with many of its poorer members to improve their skills as farmers and tradespeople. Deaconesses from Germany were introduced very early into the Sumatran mission, and the church has since developed its own deaconess program. Deaconesses work in the church-sponsored hospital and as community workers.

The HKBP has developed a modern denominational organization to facilitate its mission. It is led by its bishop and a general secretary. The major legislative body is the biennial synodical convention. Parishes are organized into resorts, and resorts into districts. Each district is led by a superintendent. Women have been admitted to the ordained ministry since 1982.

The church uses Toba Batak as its official language, but it has faced a severe problem concerning language because several other languages, including Bahasa Indonesia, compete as the primary language of its members. Many congregations, especially those located in urban areas, now conduct services in Indonesian.

The HKBP is the oldest and largest of the several bodies that have grown from the original Rhenish Mission. These several churches, which separated over the years either from the older Batak mission or from the HKBP after World War II, include the Batak Christian Community Church (GPKB), the Christian Protestant Church in Indonesia (GKPI), the Indonesian Christian Church (HKI), and the Simalungun Protestant Christian Church (GKPS).

In 2005, the HKBP reported 3.5 million members. It carries on missionary programs among modern

Indonesia's three thousand islands and its many distinct ethnic and language groups.

Protestant Christian Batak Church
Pearaja Tarutung 22413
Tapanuli Utara
Sumatra
Indonesia

J. Gordon Melton

See also: Lutheran World Federation; Pentecostalism; Rhenish Mission; World Council of Churches.

References

Bachmann, E. Theodore, and Mercia Brenne Bachmann. *Lutheran Churches in the World: A Handbook*. Minneapolis, MN: Augsburg Press, 1989.

Van Beek, Huibert. *A Handbook of the Churches and Councils: Profiles of Ecumenical Relationships*. Geneva: World Council of Churches, 2006.

Protestant Christian Church–Angkola

The Protestant Christian Church–Angkola (Gereja Kristen Protestan Angkola [GKPA]) developed as the work of the Protestant Christian Batak Church (HKBP) spread among the Angkola people of Indonesia, one of the Batak subgroups. The HKBP began in 1861 at Sipirok, Sumatra, where the Rhenish Mission originally established a mission station. However, the Angkola language was distinctive enough that Angkola church leaders requested separation so they could pursue the development of an Angkola church. The HKBP acted favorably on that request in 1974, and the new church was set up. The formation of the GKPA motivated the completion of the translation of the Bible into Angkola.

Except for one parish in Jakarta, the parishes of the church are all in northern Sumatra. They are grouped into districts that operate under the synod, the highest legislative body in the church. The church opened a training center to facilitate the self-help and independence of people in the rural villages, where most of the church's congregations are located. The church is also ecumenically oriented and is a member of both the Lutheran World Federation and the World Council of Churches. It also carries on a program of Christian-Muslim dialogue. In 2005 the church reported 28,000 members.

Protestant Christian Church–Angkola
Jalan Teuku Umar 102
22722 Padangsidimouan
South Tapanuli, North Sumatra
Indonesia

J. Gordon Melton

See also: Lutheran World Federation; Protestant Christian Batak Church; Rhenish Mission; World Council of Churches.

References

Bachmann, E. Theodore, and Mercia Brenne Bachmann. *Lutheran Churches in the World: A Handbook*. Minneapolis, MN: Augsburg Press, 1989.

Van Beek, Huibert. *A Handbook of the Churches and Councils: Profiles of Ecumenical Relationships*. Geneva: World Council of Churches, 2006.

Protestant Christian Church of Bali

The Protestant Christian Church of Bali (Gereja Kristen Protestan di Bali [GKPB]) began in 1929 with the arrival on Bali of Tsang To Hang, a Chinese missionary with the Christian and Missionary Alliance. Bali was unusual among the Indonesian islands in that it had resisted the earlier incursion of Islam and had remained predominantly Hindu. In 1864 a representative of the Netherlands Reformed Church had established a mission. He had baptized only one convert as a result of his work. He was murdered in 1881 and as a result of his death, the Dutch authorities did not allow other missionaries to work on the island.

Tsang To Hang had better results. By 1931 he had baptized a group of Balinese and had established a church. However, he was banished in 1933. After a time, the Christian Church in East Java was permitted to assume the care of the small Christian community on Bali. Growth was slow and by 1949 when the church became independent, there were still fewer than 2,000 Balinese Christians. During the period since its independence, the church has been assisted by the movement of many Balinese throughout Indonesia, where they have encountered other Christian churches before returning to Bali to join the Christian church there.

The church has presbyterian polity and has adopted the ancient Christian creeds as its doctrinal standard. It operates a school system, a hospital, and several clinics. In the 1990s it reported 12,000 members in 72 congregations. It is a member of the World Council of Churches.

Protestant Church of Bali
PO Box 72
Jalan Dr. Sutomo 101A
Denpasir 80118
Bali
Indonesia

J. Gordon Melton

See also: Christian and Missionary Alliance; Netherlands Reformed Church; World Council of Churches.

References

Bauswein, Jean-Jacques, and Lukas Vischner, eds. *The Reformed Family Worldwide: A Survey of Reformed Churches, Theological Schools, and International Organizations*. Grand Rapids, MI: William B. Eerdmans Publishing Company, 1999.

Van Beek, Huibert. *A Handbook of the Churches and Councils: Profiles of Ecumenical Relationships*. Geneva: World Council of Churches, 2006.

Protestant Christian Church of Nias

The Protestant Christian Church of Nias (Banua Niha Keriso Protestan [BNKP]) dates to the arrival of missionaries from the Rhenish Mission, a German missionary society with roots in both Lutheran and Reformed traditions. The missionaries came to Nias, an island east of Sumatra that is now a part of Indonesia, because they had been expelled from Kalimantan (Borneo), another Indonesian island. They began to work among the various people of the island, each of whom spoke their own local languages. It was not until 1874 that a process of communication was established and the first convert was received and baptized. Some 20,000 Niassans had become Christians by the beginning of World War I.

In the years immediately after the war, the mission entered an unexpected growth phase, tripling in size within a few years. In 1936 the first synod of what became the Protestant Christian Church of Nias was convened. The present presbyterial church order was adopted in 1938, which is considered the church's official beginning. One of the German missionaries chaired the church meetings until 1940. The church continued to grow through the decades after World War II, but it also experienced a set of schisms related to traditional Niassan power structures. The church would eventually become the religion of the majority of the island's residents and would be credited with bringing a sense of unity to the island as it was thrust into the modern world. The Nias language spoken in the northern half of the island was chosen for a translation of the Bible, which was printed in 1913. It subsequently became the common language of the island.

In the late 1990s, the church reported 326,000 members, approximately 60 percent of the population. It was a member of the World Council of Churches, but in recent years has withdrawn.

Protestant Christian Church of Nias
Gunungsitoli 22813
Nias Sumatera Utara
Indonesia

J. Gordon Melton

See also: Rhenish Mission; World Council of Churches.

Reference

Bauswein, Jean-Jacques, and Lukas Vischner, eds. *The Reformed Family Worldwide: A Survey of Reformed Churches, Theological Schools, and International Organizations*. Grand Rapids, MI: William B. Eerdmans Publishing Company, 1999.

Protestant Church in Indonesia

The Protestant Church in Indonesia is a unique body within the larger Indonesian Christian community, and dates to the years of the Dutch East Indies Company (established in 1602). During the two centuries that the company managed the economic and political affairs of the Indonesian islands, various Reformed and Lutheran churches had established congregations, primarily in Minahasa (northern Sulavesi), the Moluccas, and the Timor archipelago. Through the years, members of these three churches moved to western Indonesia; congregations were established to accommodate them. The Dutch East India Company went bankrupt in the 1790s; following its dissolution in 1800, the government of the Netherlands nationalized Indonesia as the Dutch East Indies. The government took responsibility for the Christian churches and organized them into the Protestant Church of the Netherlands Indies. It was led by a church board located in Batavia (now Jakarta). The government largely paid the church's bills.

As an institution of a religiously neutral government, the Protestant Church of the Netherlands Indies was supposed to care for its members, but not proselytize non-Christians. It grew in some places by incorporating the congregations that had been developed by the independent missionary agencies then operating in the country.

In 1935, the relationship between the church and the state was severed, a change that resulted in a variety of adjustments throughout the country. The church developed a presbyterian polity and adopted the Apostles' Creed as its doctrinal standard. The congregations in Minahasa and the Moluccas reorganized as autonomous bodies almost immediately and those on Timor and in western Indonesia soon after the end of World War II. Thus the Protestant Church of the Netherlands Indies (which became the Protestant Church in Indonesia) emerged as an ecumenical body through which its former congregations, now reorganized as four autonomous bodies, related to each other and cooperated on various issues. The church subsequently offered itself as the ecumenical organ for all of the Indonesian Protestant church to come together. That offer was, however, rejected in favor of a new Indonesian council of churches.

By the mid-1950s, the Protestant Church in Indonesia had largely lost its function and for a period virtually ceased to exist. In recent years, however, it has been revived as a structure through which a dozen autonomous churches, including the four original churches, now cooperate with each other and seek to manifest a sense of unity in the multi-island national state.

The Protestant Church in Indonesia is a member of the World Council of Churches. Four of its member bodies are also independently members of the World Council—the Evangelical Christian Church in Minahasa, the Protestant Church in the Moluccas, the Protestant Evangelical Church in Timor, and the Protestant Church in Western Indonesia.

As of 2006, the Protestant Church in Indonesia represented some 4 million Protestant Christians in its 12 member churches, about half of whom are in the church in Timor.

Protestant Church in Indonesia
Jion Medan Merdeka Timur 10
Jakarta 10110
Indonesia

J. Gordon Melton

See also: Protestant Church in the Moluccas; Protestant Church in Western Indonesia; Protestant Evangelical Church in Timor; World Council of Churches.

References

Bauswein, Jean-Jacques, and Lukas Vischner, eds. *The Reformed Family Worldwide: A Survey of Reformed Churches, Theological Schools, and International Organizations*. Grand Rapids, MI: William B. Eerdmans Publishing Company, 1999.

Van Beek, Huibert. *A Handbook of the Churches and Councils: Profiles of Ecumenical Relationships*. Geneva: World Council of Churches, 2006.

Protestant Church in Sabah (Malaysia)

Soon after World War II, the Seventh-day Adventist Church began a mission on the Kudat Peninsula in the state of Sabah in the Malaysian part of Borneo. Many who were ready to become Christian were not ready to accept some of the prohibitions demanded by the Adventists, including refraining from pork and alcohol. In 1951 the Rungus people approached the Basel Mission (now the Evangelical Missionary Society), requesting it to send missionaries to them. Heinrich Honegger arrived two years later. Along with his evangelistic work, he led in the foundation of an agricultural school. Growth was relatively quick and the church became independent in 1965, although it still utilized Basel Mission personnel. Four years later it faced a crisis when the country's Islamic government expelled all of the foreign missionaries and began a campaign to convert the Christians of Sabah to Islam.

Once the Islamization campaign ended in 1976, the church entered a new growth phase. It adopted a congregational form of church government, but it has a synod that is headed by a bishop or head pastor. The church ordains women.

In 2005 the Protestant Church in Sabah reported approximately 30,000 members in 307 churches. It has grown among the various groups indigenous to Sabah, extending also to mainland Malaysia as people from Sabah have moved around the country. The church now works among various Bornean people and in the Chinese community, and it is a member of the World Council of Churches. It has emphasized the Lutheran tradition of the Basel Mission (which represents both Lutheran and Reformed congregations in Germany and Switzerland) and has joined the Lutheran World Federation.

Protestant Church in Sabah
PO Box 69
Kudat, Sabah
Malaysia

J. Gordon Melton

See also: Basel Mission; Lutheran World Federation; Seventh-day Adventist Church.

References

Bachmann, E. Theodore, and Mercia Brenne Bachmann. *Lutheran Churches in the World: A Handbook*. Minneapolis, MN: Augsburg Press, 1989.

Van Beek, Huibert. *A Handbook of the Churches and Councils: Profiles of Ecumenical Relationships*. Geneva: World Council of Churches, 2006.

Protestant Church in Southeast Sulawesi

The Protestant Church in Southeast Sulawesi (Gereja Protestan di Sulawesi Tenggara [GEPSULTRA]) originated when a Protestant church was established for government and military officials residing on the island of Sulawesi, now a part of Indonesia. In 1916 a missionary began to expand this work into the countryside, where Islam was dominant. The first Native baptism occurred in 1918. Congregations of Sulawesians were formed over the next two decades, but no ministers were ordained and the church property was not registered. This neglect caused the church severe problems when the Japanese invaded and the missionaries were no longer available. Attempts to reorganize after the war were slowed by unrest among Muslims, who were unhappy with the new Indonesian central government. In 1950 Muslim guerrillas killed a missionary and several church workers who had been traveling around the country to survey the church's situation.

Only in 1957 did the situation in the region stabilize enough for the church to meet and constitute itself as an independent body. It adopted a presbyterial government, with a synod as the highest legislative body. In the late 1960s the government began to move workers into southeast Sulawesi, a sparsely populated region, and the church began to grow among the new residents. Its membership currently includes more than 25 ethnic/language groups. Church membership has grown to more than 30,000 (2005), though it still constitutes a small minority in the predominantly Muslim culture.

The immigrants to Sulawesi brought with them a form of agriculture that threatened the local ecosystem. In the 1970s the church responded with a program in agricultural education that attempted to build a progressive view of farming combined with a spiritual worldview.

This small church supports a limited set of social programs, including two orphanages, an elementary school, and four secondary schools. The church is a member of the World Alliance of Reformed Churches and the World Council of Churches.

Protestant Church in Southeast Sulawesi
PO Box 3
Jalan Dr. Ratulangi 121
Kendari 93121
Sulawesi Tenggari
Indonesia

J. Gordon Melton

See also: World Alliance of Reformed Churches; World Council of Churches.

References

Bauswein, Jean-Jacques, and Lukas Vischner, eds. *The Reformed Family Worldwide: A Survey of Reformed Churches, Theological Schools, and International Organizations*. Grand Rapids, MI: William B. Eerdmans Publishing Company, 1999.

Van Beek, Huibert. *A Handbook of the Churches and Councils: Profiles of Ecumenical Relationships*. Geneva: World Council of Churches, 2006.

Protestant Church in the Moluccas

The history of the Protestant Church in the Moluccas (Gereja Protestan Moluccas [GPM]) goes back to the arrival of the Portuguese into the East Indies in the 16th century. A Catholic mission established in the Moluccas, or Spice Islands, baptized its first convert in 1538. Francis Xavier (1506–1552) visited the Christian community there in 1546. After more than 60 years of work, the Portuguese were driven out by the Dutch, who installed Reformed church ministers in place of the priests. The community went through a process of Protestantization. The first Protestant church service in Asia was held in the Moluccas on February 27, 1605.

A vital church was built throughout the islands from its center in Ambon. The Heidelberg Catechism was translated into Malay and published in 1625. The New Testament followed in 1668. The complete Bible (1733) was followed by a Psalm book (1735). Sermons in Dutch were translated and given to lay ministers for presentation in Malay worship services. Over the next century an indigenous Christianity was created in the Moluccas.

A wave of Pietistic fervor that had come to the church in Holland was imported to the Moluccas by a new missionary society, the Nederlandsche Gereformeerde Zendingsvereenining (NZG). Missionaries from this society arrived in Indonesia in 1815, among them Joseph Kam (1769–1833), who settled in Ambon, where he had a vital ministry for the next 18 years. He recruited numerous lay teachers, who were then deployed in missions throughout the Dutch East Indies.

After World War I the church was readied for autonomy, which occurred in 1935 when the GPM was established as a branch of what was called the Protestant Church in Indonesia, headquartered in Jakarta. Though the church was locally autonomous, important decisions were referred to Jakarta for final approval. This arrangement became increasingly dysfunctional, and after World War II the attempt to keep the churches in the different island groups united faded. The Protestant Church in Indonesia was transformed into an ecumenical council and then faded into obscurity.

The Protestant Church in the Moluccas suffered greatly during the Japanese occupation. No fewer than 54 church leaders were killed. In 1944 the church's archives, located in Ambon, were destroyed during Allied bombing of the city. In 1950 Ambon was also the site of heavy fighting when the government put down an insurrection by some who opposed the new government of Indonesia.

In the immediate aftermath of the founding of Indonesia in 1948, the church went through a period of self-reflection. It adopted a new church order with a presbyterian polity. It reflected on its relationship with Islam, an increasing factor in the religious life of the Moluccas and the dominant religion in Indonesia. A new emphasis was placed on ministerial education, and the church now supports a theological faculty at the Maluku Christian University in Ambon. The church is a member of both the World Council of Churches and the World Alliance of Reformed Churches.

In 2005 the Protestant Church in the Moluccas reported 575,000 members. Once the majority religion on the island, it has been challenged by the movement of so many Indonesians to the Moluccas. A branch of the church was established in the Netherlands by some 4,000 Moluccans who moved to Holland after World War II at the expense of the Dutch government.

Protestant Church in the Moluccas
Jalan Mayjend
DI Panjaitan 2
Ambon 97124
Maluku
Indonesia

J. Gordon Melton

See also: World Alliance of Reformed Churches; World Council of Churches.

References

Bauswein, Jean-Jacques, and Lukas Vischner, eds. *The Reformed Family Worldwide: A Survey of Reformed Churches, Theological Schools, and International Organizations*. Grand Rapids, MI: William B. Eerdmans Publishing Company, 1999.

Enklaar, I. H. and Joseph Kam. "Apostel der." In *Molukken*. s'Gravenhage, 1963.

Van Beek, Huibert. *A Handbook of the Churches and Councils: Profiles of Ecumenical Relationships*. Geneva: World Council of Churches, 2006.

Protestant Church in the Netherlands

The Protestant Church in the Netherlands (Protestantse Kerk in Nederland [PKN]) is the second largest Protestant church in the Netherlands with approximately 1.8 million members served by about 1,700 ministries in about 1,800 local communities (2006). The PKN is the combination of the Netherlands Reformed Church (De Nederlandse Hervormde Kerk [NHK]), the Reformed Churches in the Netherlands (De Gereformeerde Kerken in Nederland [GKN]) and the Evangelical Lutheran Churches in the Kingdom of the Netherlands (ELK). The PKN was grounded on May 1, 2004, after many difficult years of fundamental discussions. A part of the right wing of the NHK, the Reformed Federation (Gerefomeerde Bond) refused this combination and founded The Restored Reformed Church (De Hersteld Hervormde Kerk). A part of the GKN founded The Continued Reformed Churches in the Netherlands (De Voortgezette Gereformeerde Kerken in Nederland [VGKN]).

The Netherlands Reformed Church (Nederlandse Hervormde Kerk) was at the beginning of the 21st century the oldest and largest Protestant church in the Netherlands with approximately 2 million members served by 1,750 ministers in 1,340 local communities. The church originated as the Dutch phase of the Reformation in the 16th century, and the history of Protestantism in the Netherlands was almost fully synonymous with the history of the church. In 1816 King William I (1772–1843) reorganized the church and gave it its present name. It was the national church until 1951. The Dutch Reformed Church has left its imprint on Dutch civilization and as an internationally influential body is the source for a number of contemporary Reformed churches, especially in Indonesia, South Africa, and the United States. An inclusive church, it includes a spectrum of theological perspectives, from very liberal to very strict and traditional.

The beginning of the Reformation in the northern Netherlands (the later Dutch Republic) is somewhat complicated. Sacramentalism, biblical Humanism, Anabaptism, and Lutheranism all played their part, but eventually Calvinism (Reformed Protestantism) found the largest constituency. Swiss Reformers Huldrych (Ulrich) Zwingli (1484–1531) and Heinrich Bullinger (1504–1575) influenced several Dutch theologians, including Cornelis Hoen (d. 1524), Johannes Anastasius Veluanus (1500–1575), and Hendrik van Bommel (ca. 1490–1570). At the beginning of the 17th century, the life of the church was marked by the conflict between the liberal theologian Jacob Arminius (1560–1609), the "grounding father" of the Remonstrant Brotherhood, and Franciscus Gomarus (1563–1641), a strict Calvinist. Arminius proclaimed that the practice of confession and the catechism should be revised. He taught that all people are included in God's reconciling act in Christ (though God ultimately chooses only those who turn in faith to him), that humans are not totally perverted by sin (that a part of God's image remains undistorted by sin), and that perseverance in belief is a matter of free will. The Synod of Dordrecht condemned these beliefs in its five articles against the Remonstrants (*Canones synodi Dordracenae*), which, together with the Dutch Confession of Faith and the Heidelberg Catechism, remain the doctrinal standard of the church. At the Synod of Dordrecht it was also decided to translate the Bible into Dutch. The Dutch Bible, called the Statenvertaling, became very important for the development of the Dutch language and is still used in a revised form in some of the more strict Reformed churches.

The Netherlands Reformed Church includes several recognizable movements or wings: a strictly orthodox one, a liberal one, and a moderate one. The strictly orthodox wing has several origins, the most important

Netherlands Reformed church in Den Hoorn, Netherlands, built in the early fifteenth century. (iStockPhoto.com)

being the Nearer Reformation, which looks for the radical reformation of doctrine and life in a manner similar to the Puritanism of the Anglo-Saxon countries and the Pietism of Germany. This wing teaches that believers should seek a mystical experience of God and avoid worldliness. Believers affirm the need for a spiritual rebirth, the visible marks of faith, and the practice of a God-fearing life. They also believe in the strictest form of predestination. They look to the government to promote the Reformed religion and to banish every false religion. The Nearer Reformation supporters have also been the strongest critics of the move toward unity, called the Samen op Weg (Together on the Way), with the Reformed Church in the Netherlands (GKN), and the Evangelical Lutheran Church in the Kingdom of the Netherlands. The perspective of the Nearer Reformation continues within the church through the Reformed Federation (Gereformeerde Bond), supported by some 400 ministers, 312 local churches, and 450 local parishes.

The Nearer Reformation perspective also underlies a small, very strict orthodox denomination founded in 1962 around the periodical *Het gekrookte riet,* a title borrowed from one of the important books of 145 sermons of Bernardus Smijtegelt (1665–1739). This group rejects television and radio and other forms of enjoyment and culture. Only those chosen by God are believed to come to real conversion. All believers must therefore doubt their eternal salvation. The denomination counts some 10 ministers. Finally, the Confessional Unity (Confessionele Vereniging), founded in 1864, emphasizes obedience to the holy scriptures and strict community within the confession of the church, and looks to the restoration of the church along biblical standards. It counts 165 active ministers and around 4,000 members.

The more progressive wing of the church has its origins in 19th-century theological liberalism. It also draws upon the tradition of free thinking in the Dutch Republic in the 16th and 17th centuries associated with the biblical Humanism of Erasmus (1467–1536), Sebastian Franck (ca. 1499–ca. 1542), Dirck Volkertszoon Coornhert (1522–1590), Baruch de Spinoza (1632–1677), and others. The most prominent representative of this wing is the Unity of Liberal Protestants (Vereniging van Vrijzinnig Hervormden), officially founded in 1913. The Unity advocates freedom of belief and confession and argues against the infallible authority of church and scriptures. The Unity was most significant in the decades prior to World War II. As the 21st century begins, it counts some 6,000 members.

The Zwingli-Unity (Zwingli Bond), founded in 1948, is the more radical modernist wing of the Netherlands Reformed Church. It advocates a Unitarian perspective that rejects the Trinity of God and therefore denies the divinity of Jesus and the Holy Spirit. It teaches that God is too great to be known and that Jesus is the ideal human being and our example in faith. The scriptures are not inspired by God but are only a collection of human writings that include all the aspects of human desire and passion. The Zwingli-Unity is a small group inside the church, with only 300 members.

The moderate wing of the church, called Midden-Orthodox, stands between the strict orthodox and the free-thinking wing. It advocates biblical preaching about subjects bearing on the problems of the modern society, such as homosexuality, abortion, euthanasia (active and passive), and racial questions.

The Walloon Churches (Églises Wallones) have had a special place in the Netherlands Reformed Church. They originated after the fall of Antwerp in 1585, when many Flemish- and French-speaking Protestants from the southern Netherlands (Belgium) fled to the northern Netherlands. The French-speaking believers organized their own denomination. Additionally, after the revocation of the Edict of Nantes in 1685, some 100,000 French Huguenots (Protestants) also fled to the Northern Netherlands. The denomination flourished through the 19th century, with 82 local parishes. In 2000 the French-speaking Églises Wallones, now one of the 54 classes of the Dutch Reformed Church, count 13 parishes, 12 ministers, and around 2,000 believers.

The Reformed Churches in the Netherlands (called the GKN for its Dutch name, De Gereformeerde Kerken in Nederland), not to be confused with the GKN (Liberated), founded in 1892, is the third largest Protestant church in the Netherlands. At the beginning of the 21st century, it had approximately 650,000 believers in 840 parishes served by 320 ministers. Though officially founded in 1892, its origins can be traced to the Separation movement in 1832 and the Dutch Nonconformism movement in 1886, both of which were separation movements from the Netherlands Reformed Church. The primary issue leading to the separations was the growing adherence to liberal theological thinking within the Netherlands Reformed Church, which had assumed an increasingly important role.

The father of the unity of the two separations was Abraham Kuyper (1837–1920), also the founder of the Free University (Vrije Uniiversiteit) in Amsterdam (1880) and of the former Anti Revolutionaire Partij, an important Protestant party (now a constituent part of the Christian Party, the CDA). This kind of political activism remains significant in the GKN, and for many years, it has had an influence in the Netherlands beyond its direct religious influence upon its members. Doctrinally, however, the GKN is much like other Reformed church bodies in accepting the Heidelberg Catechism, the Canons of the Synod of Dort, and the Dutch Confession as its standards of faith and practice.

Through the mid-1920s, the GKN developed its organized life, with many active believers founding Reformed schools, newspapers, political parties, clubs, and other groups. At the same time, it experienced a variety of theological disagreements, especially over the role of the government in answering questions of belief. Then an initial rupture came in 1926. Dr. Johannes G. Geelkerken (1879–1960) was condemned for his belief that the holy scriptures are not inspired by God. A second very important rupture occurred during the German occupation of World War II, with criticism of the teachings of Kuyper, the church's revered founder. Dr. Klass Schilder (1890–1952), a professor at Kampen, one of the church's ministerial training centers, criticized Kuyper's views on common grace, the nature of the soul, the covenant of grace, and rebirth. Schilder was condemned in 1944, and he left with many followers to found the Reformed Churches in the Netherlands (Liberated).

In the late 20th century, the GKN experienced a new set of theological tensions. Important theologians such as Drs. Herman Wiersinga, H. M. Kuitert, and C. J. Den Heijer offered variant perspectives on the traditional Reformed teachings. Among other ideas, they have directly questioned belief in the divine inspiration of the Bible, the divine character of Jesus, and the nature of human reconciliation. Although the majority of the GKN has aligned itself with these theologians, an important part rejects them. The last-named group is united in the Society of Worried (Vereniging van Verontrusten) and in Reformed Churches in the Netherlands (affliction communities).

The Evangelical Lutheran Church in the Kingdom of the Netherlands (Evangelisch-Lutherse in het Koninkrijk der Nederlanden) began with the arrival of Lutheran refugees in Amsterdam from the southern Netherlands (now Belgium), where Roman Catholic authorities had been unappreciative of attempts to spread Protestantism. Amsterdam was at the time (1566) the most religiously tolerant city in Europe. Continuing to worship in members' homes, the group adopted a confession and church order in 1588 at the time a church was formally organized. In 1600, Holland, which had become a Reformed Calvinist country, formally granted religious tolerance to both Roman Catholics and Lutherans. By 1605, no less than five congregations had emerged in Holland, and a synod was formed.

The toleration act allowed the Lutherans to own houses of worship, provided they did not look like churches. In 1633 the group purchased a former warehouse, which they converted into their main church building. Known as the "Old Church at the Spui," it remains the home of an active congregation today. During the century the group spread to England, and became the source of the first Lutheran congregation in New York.

The Dutch Lutheran community experienced one major schism, the result of a growing rationalist approach to theology in the 18th century. The more orthodox confessional wing of the church broke away in 1793 to form the Restored Evangelical Lutheran Church. It was 1952 before the two branches reunited. By that time, both had been changed by a new era of research on Lutheran roots and a new commitment to Lutheran theological basics. Three years after the union, a new hymnal and liturgy were published.

In 1986 the synods of the Netherlands Reformed Church and the Reformed Church in the Netherlands (GKN) declared that they were in a "state of union." They were soon joined by the Evangelical Lutheran Church of the kingdom of the Netherlands in what was termed the "Together on the Way" process. Early in the process, it was decided that a new church order was necessary, based on an ecclesiological vision rather than a collection of pragmatic arrangements. This church order was adopted in 2003. It declared that the church shares in the expectation of the people of Israel and therefore, as a Christ-confessing community of faith, seeks dialogue with Israel. It also expressed the church's place in the larger Christian fellowship or "oikoumene." It adopted the three ecumenical creeds (Apostles', Nicene, Chalcedonian), the Belgic Confession, the Heidelberg Catechism, the Canons of Dordt, the Unaltered Augsburg Confession, and Luther's Catechism as the doctrinal standards of the church.

The PCN adopted a presbyterian-synodal model of church governance with a board and a moderator and general secretary. It established its national office and service center in Utrecht. Its missionary and diaconal work is pursued in cooperation with several smaller churches in the Netherlands, under the banner of "Kerkinactie" (churches acting together). At the local level, the congregations have been invited to explore the options available to them, and some congregations have united while others have maintained a separate existence, often to keep alive the specific theological tradition they belonged to prior to the national union. The new church order grants space for local diversity while inviting the congregations to engage in discussions between different traditions and spiritualities, and thus discover what the Lutheran identity (now a distinct minority position in the united body) can offer to the larger church, and what the Reformed tradition can mean for the Lutherans.

The PCN is a member of the World Council of Churches, World Alliance of Reformed Churches, Lutheran World Federation, the Reformed Ecumenical Council, and the Community of Protestant Churches in Europe. The church maintains international relationships with many partner churches (products of the

19th-century missionary program of the church) in all parts of the world (including more than 30 denominations in Indonesia).

At the forefront of the agenda for the PCN has been a recognition of the extent of secularization in the Netherlands, which has led many to withdraw from organized religious life. At the same time, the church is challenged by the seemingly vibrant life of the congregations made up of migrants from the former Dutch colonies. They model a life of activity in mission and service. At the very first synod meeting of the PCN (May 2004), the representatives recognized their responsibility to work for renewal in culture, society, and nation. They believed that Dutch society cannot exist without a source of inspiration. They also saw a need to join the struggle against poverty and injustice.

Also, at present, an important work is being carried on by the Evangelic Work Organisation inside the Protestant Church in the Netherlands (Evangelisch Werkverband binnen de Protestantse Kerk in Nederland, EW). The EW, a movement to revive the whole church in its religious life, is a reaction to the evangelical movement outside the church. Since 1995 some ministers have developed models for renewing the life of the communities, and their plans have received many enthusiastic reactions. The EW has thus gained the support of many ministers and lay believers.

Protestant Church in the Netherlands
Synodsecretariaat
Postbus 8399
NL-3503 Utrecht
The Netherlands

E. G. Hoekstra

See also: Anabaptism; Arminius, Jacob; Calvinism; Community of Protestant Churches in Europe; Lutheran World Federation; Lutheranism; Reformed Churches in the Netherlands (Liberated); Reformed Ecumenical Council; Reformed/Presbyterian Tradition; Remonstrant Brotherhood; Roman Catholic Church; World Alliance of Reformed Churches; World Council of Churches.

References

Augustijn, C., et al., eds., *Reformatorica. Teksten uit de geschiedenis van het Nederlandse protestantisme.* Zoetermeer: Boekencentruim, 1996.

Bachmann, E. Theodore, and Mercia Brenne Bachmann. *Lutheran Churches in the World: A Handbook.* Minneapolis, MN: Augsburg Press, 1989.

Bakhuizen van den Brink, J. N., et al. *Documenta reformatoria. Teksten uit de geschiedenis van kerk en theologie sedert de Hervorming.* 2 vols. Kampen: Kok, 1960–1962.

Blei, Karel. *De Nederlandse Hervormde Kerk. Haar geschiedenis en identiteit, series Wegwijs.* Kampen: Kok, 2000.

Crom, A. P., ed. *Anderhalve eeuw gereformeerden in stad en land.* 12 vols. Kampen: Kok, 1984–1985.

de Jong, O. J. *Nederlandse kerkgeschiedenis.* Nijkerk: Callenbach, 1985.

Endedijk, H. C. *De Gereformeerde Kerken in Nederland.* 2 vols. Kampen: Kok, 1990–1992.

Jaarboek van de Gereformeerde Kerken in Nederland. Issued annually.

Hoekstra, E. G., and M. H. Ipenburg. *Handboek christelijk Nederland. Kerken, gemeenten, samenkomsten en vergaderingen.* Kampen: Kok, 2008.

Hoekstra, E. G., and M. H. Ipenburg. *Wegwijs in religieus en levensbeschouwelijk Nederland. Handboek religies, kerken, stromingen en organisaties.* Kampen: Uitgeverij Kok, 2000.

Post, J. E. *Gereformeerd zijn en blijven, een wankel evenwich.* Kampen: Kok, 1998.

Rasker, A. J. *De Nederlandse Hervormde Kerk vanaf.* Kampen: Kok, 1795, 1986.

Van Beek, Huibert. *A Handbook of the Churches and Councils: Profiles of Ecumenical Relationships.* Geneva: World Council of Churches, 2006.

Van der Bent, Ans J., ed. *Handbook/Member Churches/World Council of Churches.* Geneva: World Council of Churches, 1985.

Protestant Church in Timor Lorosa'e

The Roman Catholic Church arrived on Timor around 1660, in the form of priests of the Dominican Order who came to the East Indies with the Portuguese. When

A Christian church in East Timor. Christianity is the majority religion in East Timor. (INSADCO Photography/ StockphotoPro)

the Dutch took over in 1613, they did not in fact take over nearly as completely as in much of the rest of their territory; they allowed the Portuguese to retain control of Timor and the Catholic Church to keep its mission on Timor. The Portuguese suppressed any attempt of Protestants to organize, and Roman Catholicism remains the dominant religious group. In East Timor Protestant churches began to appear only in the 20th century.

Protestantism had gained a following by 1975, when Portugal abandoned East Timor and it was annexed to Indonesia. There were some Protestants among the government officials who moved to the island in 1975, and they took the lead in forming congregations. Also, a number of nominal Roman Catholics identified with the new church. In 1979, the Protestant Church in Indonesia established the Coordinating Agency of Protestant Christian Congregations in East Timor. This agency moved to establish a regional church of the kind that operated on other Indonesian islands. The first synod of what became the Christian Church in East Timor (Gereja Kristen di Timor Timur [GKTT]) met in 1988.

The church adopted a presbyterian form of church order and followed other Protestant bodies in the country by making the ancient Christian creeds its standards of doctrine and not adding any of the 16th-century Protestant confessions. The church adopted an ecumenical stance, and in 1989 it identified with the World Alliance of Reformed Churches. It joined the World Council of Churches in 1993.

The church has grown rapidly. It had less than 7,000 members when organized in 1979. In 1996 it reported 34,625 members in its 67 congregations. It oversees four maternity schools and one clinic as part of its commitment to the larger community in East Timor.

Protestant Church in Timor Lorosa'e
PO Box 1186
Jalan Martires de Patria
Dili 88110 Timor Timur
Indonesia

J. Gordon Melton

See also: Dominicans; Protestant Church in Indonesia; Roman Catholic Church; World Alliance of Reformed Churches; World Council of Churches.

Reference

Bauswein, Jean-Jacques, and Lukas Vischner, eds. *The Reformed Family Worldwide: A Survey of Reformed Churches, Theological Schools, and International Organizations*. Grand Rapids, MI: William B. Eerdmans Publishing Company, 1999.

Protestant Church in Western Indonesia

As early as the 17th century, during the time that the Dutch East Indies Company controlled what is now

Indonesia, Protestant Christian churches were established on Timor, the Moluccas, and Minahasa (northern Sulavesi). These congregations were eventually organized as the Protestant Church of the Netherlands Indies following the Dutch government's takeover of the islands in 1800 after the company went bankrupt.

Through the 19th century, church members moved to the towns in the westernmost island of the East Indies. As churches were built to accommodate these members, the congregations were incorporated into the Protestant Church of the Netherlands Indies. The church served as the state church of the Dutch East Indies until the 1930s. In 1935, church and state were separated and the money that had been given the church annually was gradually withdrawn. After World War II, the Protestant Church of the Netherlands Indies became the Protestant Church in Indonesia. Simultaneously, the various segments of the church were organized into four autonomous churches. In 1948, the congregations in the west were organized into the Protestant Church in Western Indonesia. The Protestant Church in Indonesia, with whom the Protestant Church in Western Indonesia shares its national headquarters, has remained as a national structure through which the four widely separated churches have remained in relation to each other.

The Protestant Church in Western Indonesia is spread out over 25 of the 32 provinces of Indonesia, with congregations located in both the big cities and the remote rural countryside. As of 2006, it had some 600,000 members in its 280 congregations. It joined the World Council of Churches in 1991. The church's synod meets every five years.

Protestant Church in Western Indonesia
Jion Medan Merdeka Timur 10
Jakarta 10110
Indonesia

J. Gordon Melton

See also: Protestant Church in Indonesia; World Council of Churches.

References

Bauswein, Jean-Jacques, and Lukas Vischner, eds. *The Reformed Family Worldwide: A Survey of Reformed Churches, Theological Schools, and International Organizations*. Grand Rapids, MI: William B. Eerdmans Publishing Company, 1999.

Van Beek, Huibert. *A Handbook of the Churches and Councils: Profiles of Ecumenical Relationships*. Geneva: World Council of Churches, 2006.

Protestant Church of Algeria

The Protestant Church of Algeria has inherited the traditions of 19th-century Protestant/Free church missionary activity in Algeria. After the call for French settlers to come to Algeria in 1873, Protestantism was offered an opening. The Reformed Church of France came to Algeria and established work there, primarily among French Protestants because the government frowned upon proselytizing within the Muslim community. Through the early 20th century, as the French expatriate community grew, the Reformed Church became the largest of the many non-Catholic church bodies in the country.

In 1908 two women who had been conducting an independent mission in Algiers since 1893 affiliated themselves with the Methodist Episcopal Church (now a constituent part of the United Methodist Church), and in 1909 the Methodist Episcopal Church's Woman's Foreign Missionary Society assumed their support. Other women were accepted to extend the work, though the first U.S. worker did not arrive until 1922. Work spread among the coastal cities and was based in medical and social services. In 1966 the Methodists opened a hospital in the northeastern city of Il Maten.

The independence of Algeria in 1962 deeply affected the Protestant community. The exodus of 500,000 people with French passports depleted many Christian groups of their support, especially the Reformed Church. Then the Methodist Church was hit by charges that their missionaries were agents of the U.S. Central Intelligence Agency in 1969, and 10 percent (a significant percentage) were expelled from the country. The church's missionaries in Oran had withdrawn the year before for other reasons, and the church was left with 215 members.

In 1970 the French Reformed Church, the Methodists, and several other groups that had also lost significant resources since 1962 merged to become the

Protestant Church of Algeria. The church is a member of the World Council of Churches and the World Alliance of Reformed Churches. The church acknowledges both Methodist and Reformed doctrinal positions. It also cooperates with the Roman Catholic Church in various social programs.

The actual membership of the church has always been difficult to count. There are some 5,000 core members with that many more constituent members, including some people who have never reported their conversion from Islam. In 2005, the church reported 14 "communities," or parishes.

In March 2008, the government acted on a law passed in February 2006, which mandated non-Muslim religious centers to obtain a permit for gathering for worship from their regional prefecture and banned the production of any media intended to "shake the faith of a Muslim." Thirteen chapels were ordered closed, including 11 in Tizi Ouzou, one in Bejaia, and one in Bouira (towns in the coastal region east of Algiers).

Protestant Church of Algeria
31 rue Reda Houhou
16000 Algiers
Algeria

J. Gordon Melton

See also: Reformed Church of France; Roman Catholic Church; United Methodist Church; World Alliance of Reformed Churches; World Council of Churches.

References

Bauswein, Jean-Jacques, and Lukas Vischner, eds. *The Reformed Family Worldwide: A Survey of Reformed Churches, Theological Schools, and International Organizations*. Grand Rapids, MI: William B. Eerdmans Publishing Company, 1999.

Van Beek, Huibert. *A Handbook of the Churches and Councils: Profiles of Ecumenical Relationships*. Geneva: World Council of Churches, 2006.

Protestant Church of Senegal

One of the world's smaller Christian denominations, the Protestant Church of Senegal began in the 19th-century attempts of the Paris Mission (affiliated with the Reformed Church of France) to build a mission among the Native people of Senegal. They had little success from their beginning in 1862 until after François Villegier translated a portion of the Bible into Wolof, one of the local languages, and Walter Taylor, a former slave who resided in Sierra Leone, joined the effort. Taylor concentrated his evangelistic activity among freed slaves residing in Khor, a small community near St. Louis.

A second church was opened in Dakar after it became the capital in 1904. However, the missionaries found the largely Muslim population unresponsive to their attempts to convert them. The church became independent in 1972 and is now completely in Senegalese hands, but the membership largely consists of expatriates. In the mid-1990s, the church reported 250 members in 2 congregations. It is a member of the World Alliance of Reformed Churches. It had been a member of the World Council of Churches in the 1990s, but has since withdrawn.

Protestant Church of Senegal
BP 22390
Dakar Ponty
Senegal

J. Gordon Melton

See also: Paris Mission; Reformed Church of France; World Alliance of Reformed Churches; World Council of Churches.

Reference

Bauswein, Jean-Jacques, and Lukas Vischner, eds. *The Reformed Family Worldwide: A Survey of Reformed Churches, Theological Schools, and International Organizations*. Grand Rapids, MI: William B. Eerdmans Publishing Company, 1999.

Protestant Evangelical Church in Timor

The Protestant Evangelical Church in Timor (Gereja Masehi Injili Timor [GMIT]) dates from the coming of the Dutch into Indonesia and specifically to the Timor archipelago in the second decade of the 17th century.

The Roman Catholic Church had previously established work, and in this area, unlike other islands, the Dutch allowed them to remain. Thus the Reformed Church mission developed beside that of the Catholic Church. The mission was centered on Kupang, and it grew slowly, except on the island of Rote, where a large number of people became Christian in the 1740s. Attempts to build a more effective mission in the 19th century failed.

Then early in the 20th century, after the Dutch government had finally established an effective administrative system, the Reformed Church missionaries launched a comprehensive program that utilized all they had learned from work on the other Indonesian islands. The year 1912 marked the beginning of a quarter century of growth, during which time the church grew ten-fold. The first steps toward an autonomous church were made in the 1930s, but interrupted by World War II. The church's synod met for the first time in 1947. After a period of stagnation, the church experienced a revival in the late 1960s, when in a few years' time the membership doubled. In the 1990s it reported 850,000 members in 1,500 congregations.

The church oversees a number of institutions, including kindergartens, hospitals, homes for the elderly, and orphanages. Ministerial education is handled through the theological faculty at the Artha Wacan Christian University in Kupang. The church is a member of the World Council of Churches and the World Alliance of Reformed Churches.

Protestant Evangelical Church in Timor
PO Box 85228
Jalan Perintis Kemerdekaan Walikota Baru
Kupang 85228 NTT
Indonesia

J. Gordon Melton

See also: Roman Catholic Church; World Alliance of Reformed Churches; World Council of Churches.

Reference

Bauswein, Jean-Jacques, and Lukas Vischner, eds. *The Reformed Family Worldwide: A Survey of Reformed Churches, Theological Schools, and International Organizations*. Grand Rapids, MI: William B. Eerdmans Publishing Company, 1999.

Protestant Evangelical Church of Guinea

The Protestant Evangelical Church of Guinea is an evangelical Christian church that grew out of the efforts in West Africa of the Christian and Missionary Church (CMA). CMA missionaries entered Guinea early in the 20th century and founded the church in 1918. It was granted autonomy in 1962. It has subsequently been under local leadership and become self-supporting. Its first years of autonomy coincided with the rise of the country's president Ahmed Sékou Touré (1922–1984) to a position of dictator, operating from a Marxist perspective. In 1967, the government expelled almost all the Western missionaries from the country. It appears that in his younger years, Sekou Touré had positive contact with the CMA, and thus allowed eight CMA personnel to remain in Guinea, though their activity was severely restricted.

The church operates from an evangelical Protestant perspective and strongly affirms the authority of the Bible, the Trinity, salvation through Jesus Christ, and the necessity of personal conversion to faith in Christ. The church also limits baptism to those who make a personal confession of faith in Christ, and hence only about half of its members have been baptized.

The church has developed an expansive program in elementary education, medical clinics, and rural development projects. It also has promoted efforts to arrive at a deeper consciousness of its role in the post-Touré Guinea.

The church's highest legislative authority is its general assembly. It supports the church's biblical institute, at which ministers are trained. It has developed an ecumenical consciousness and works collegially with other Protestant bodies and the Roman Catholic Church on different concerns and projects. In 2005, it joined the World Council of Churches, and is one of the three groups that came together in 2001 to form the Christian Council of Guinea. Earlier, it joined the Christian Reformed Church, the French Assemblies of God, the World Evangelistic Crusade, SIM International and Mission Philafricaine in forming the Association of Evangelical Churches and Missions in Guinea (which is in turn affiliated with the World Evangelical Alliance).

In 2005, the church reported 65,000 members and 550 congregations.

J. Gordon Melton

See also: Roman Catholic Church; World Council of Churches; World Evangelical Alliance.

Reference

Van Beek, Huibert. *A Handbook of the Churches and Councils: Profiles of Ecumenical Relationships.* Geneva: World Council of Churches, 2006.

Protestant Methodist Church in Cote d'Ivoire

See United Methodist Church in Ivory Coast.

Protestant Methodist Church of Benin

The largest non-Catholic church in the African nation of Benin, the Protestant Methodist Church was founded by missionary Thomas Birch Freeman (1809–1890), the son of an English mother and an African father. In 1838 Freeman returned to Africa from England as a representative of the Wesleyan Methodist Connection (now an integral part of the Methodist Church) in Great Britain. He began work in Ghana, then known as the Gold Coast, before moving on to Benin, then known as Dahomey, in 1843. Freeman and his wife settled in Quidab on the Benin Coast and shortly thereafter traveled inland to Abomey to interview the king of the region, but they were unable to obtain his cooperation for the missionary work. The king was still involved in the slave trade, and Freeman had begun a program of employing freed slaves from the Americas to assist in the mission's leadership.

The work did not begin to grow until after the French protectorate was declared in 1851 and pacification occurred over the next decades. Noteworthy leadership was supplied later in the century by the Methodist African superintendent, Thomas Joseph Marshall. Along with the work in neighboring Togo, the mission remained a district in the British Methodist Conference until after Benin became independent in 1974 as a Marxist state. The Methodist mission subsequently became an independent body as the Protestant Methodist Church of Benin.

The church has continued to grow and by 2005 reported approximately 90,000 members. At the same time it has been an ecumenical church, supporting cooperative educational endeavors with several other churches. In 1965 it initiated a cooperative evangelistic endeavor that targeted the Fon people and included the production of a Bible in the Fon language. The church is a member of the World Council of Churches. Following the British lead, the church is led by a president rather than a bishop.

Protestant Methodist Church of Benin
01 BP 34
Cotonou
Benin

J. Gordon Melton

See also: World Council of Churches.

References

Harmon, Nolan B. *Encyclopedia of World Methodism.* 2 vols. Nashville: United Methodist Publishing House, 1974.

Van Beek, Huibert. *A Handbook of the Churches and Councils: Profiles of Ecumenical Relationships.* Geneva: World Council of Churches, 2006.

World Methodist Council, Handbook of Information, 2002–2006. Lake Junaluska, NC: World Methodist Council, 2003.

Province of the Episcopal Church in Rwanda

Anglican work in Rwanda was launched in 1926 by the Rwanda General and Medical Mission, a group representing the most theologically conservative wing of the Church Missionary Society. Its early growth was spurred by a revival that swept through Rwanda in the later 1920s, and growth was remarkable through the 1930s, continuing for several decades. In 1968, the church reported 85,000 members.

The church also stepped into a unique situation relative to the indigenous population. The population was divided between two groups, the Tutsi (Watusi)

Pilgrims from Kenya, Tanzania, Sudan, Rwanda, and other African countries pray at the Catholic Basilica Church of the Uganda Martyrs a day before the Ugandan national Martyrs Day holiday on June 2, 2005, in Namugongo, Uganda. (AFP/Getty Images)

and the Hutu, the latter constituting approximately 85 percent of the population. Though a distinct minority, the Tutsi were the ruling elite and remained so after colonization. In 1963, a year after the country gained its independence, a civil war broke out. Some 160,000 Tutsi were expelled, most relocating to Burundi. Relative peace followed for the next three decades, but in 1994, the president of Rwanda (a Hutu) died under mysterious circumstance in a plane crash. Subsequently, death squads were released throughout the country, and hundreds of thousands, the majority of the Tutsi, were killed. When a Tutsi army countered and took control of the government, some 200,000 Hutu fled the country. One Anglican Bishop Samuel Musabyimana (d. 2005) was among several church leaders from different denominations arrested for his reputed role in the genocide, but he died before his trial could take place.

Through the 1950s, the work of the church in Rwanda was under the direct jurisdiction of the archbishop of Canterbury. In 1961 he led in the formation of the Church of the Province of Uganda, Rwanda, and Burundi. The first bishop for Rwanda was appointed in 1965. In 1980, the Province of Uganda was set apart as an independent jurisdiction, and the new Church of the Province of Burundi, Rwanda, and Zaire constructed. This province was divided into three new provinces in 1992, and the present Province of the Episcopal Church in Rwanda emerged.

The Church of Rwanda is headed by its archbishop. That post, then held by Most Reverend Augustin Nshamihogo, was vacated in 1994, and remained vacant until 2000, when a new archbishop, the Most Reverend Emmanuel Mbona-Kolini (b. 1945), was selected to assume the post. Archbishop Kolini has become one of the more controversial bishops in the Anglican Communion for his effort to establish the Anglican Mission in America, a missionary diocese that aimed at competing for the allegiance of American Anglicans with the Episcopal Church. In 2000, he joined his fellow Rwandan, Bishop John Rucyahana, in consecrating two American Episcopalian priests as bishops who were to lead the Anglican Mission. He subsequently supported the movement of the mission into the new Anglican Church of North America.

In 2005, the Church in Rwanda reported 1 million members in its nine dioceses. It is a member of the worldwide Anglican Communion and since 1961 the World Council of Churches. Since 1994, the church has reoriented its program to deal with the trauma of 1994 and the poverty into which the country has been plunged. The church lost many clergy during the period of genocide and currently continues the effort to recruit and train replacements. It supports eight primary schools, Stanley Smith College, and United Theological College of Butare.

Province of the Episcopal Church in Rwanda
PB 2487
Kigali
Rwanda

J. Gordon Melton

See also: Anglican Church of North America; Anglican Communion/Anglican Consultative Council; Church Missionary Society; World Council of Churches.

References

The Church of England Yearbook. London: Church Publishing House, published annually.

Hassett, Miranda K. *Anglican Communion in Crisis: How Episcopal Dissidents and Their African Allies Are Reshaping Anglicanism*. Princeton, NJ: Princeton University Press, 2007.

Norman, Edward. *Anglican Difficulties: A New Syllabus of Errors*. New York: Morehouse Publishing, 2004.

Van Beek, Huibert. *A Handbook of the Churches and Councils: Profiles of Ecumenical Relationships*. Geneva: World Council of Churches, 2006.

Van der Bent, Ans J., ed. *Handbook/Member Churches/World Council of Churches*. Geneva: World Council of Churches, 1985.

■ Puerto Rico

The Commonwealth of Puerto Rico is located in the Caribbean Sea, east of the Dominican Republic and west of the Virgin Islands. Geographically, Puerto Rico is an archipelago that includes the main island of Puerto Rico and a number of smaller islands and keys, the largest of which are Vieques, Culebra, and Mona. Puerto Rico has a land area of 3,425 square miles and 1,900 square miles is marine area. It has a population of 3,994,259 (July 2007 estimate), mostly of European and African heritage. The main island of Borinquen is about 100 miles long by 35 miles wide.

San Juan is the capital and most populous municipality in Puerto Rico. The population of the San Juan Metropolitan Statistical Area (SJMSA) is about 2 million inhabitants. Today about half the country's population lives and works in the SJMSA.

According to the U.S. Census of 2000, 84 percent of Puerto Ricans described themselves as "White"; 10.9 percent as "Black or African American"; 8.3 percent as "some other race," 0.7 percent as "American Indian," and 0.5 percent as "Asian" (the total is more

Cathedral of San Juan Bautista, a Roman Catholic cathedral in San Juan, Puerto Rico. (Jose Oquendo)

than 100 percent because individuals may have reported more than one race). Other ethnographical studies have found that 74 percent of the population is a mixture (*mestizo*) of white, black, and Amerindian (Taíno), and only 10 percent is white and about 16 percent is black.

The official languages are Spanish and English, with Spanish being primary. English is taught as a second language in public and private elementary and high schools, and in the universities.

Emigration has been a major part of Puerto Rico's recent history. Starting soon after World War II, a combination of poverty, inexpensive airfare, and hope for better economic conditions caused waves of Puerto Ricans to move to the continental United States. In 2003, the U.S. Census Bureau estimated that more people of Puerto Rican birth or ancestry lived in the United States than in Puerto Rico.

In addition, Puerto Rico has become the permanent home of more than 100,000 legal residents who immigrated from Spain and Latin America, mainly from Cuba (20,000 in 2000), the Dominican Republic, Colombia, Venezuela, and Argentina. An influx of Chinese immigrants began to arrive in Puerto Rico after the Chinese Exclusion Act was repealed in 1943, and in the 1960s when hundreds of Chinese fled Cuba after Fidel Castro came to power. However, in 2000, there were only 45,684 non-Hispanic residents in Puerto Rico, of which only 1,873 were Chinese and 4,789 were Asian Indian.

No information is currently available about religious affiliation in Puerto Rico based on recent census data or public opinion polls. However, the *World Christian Encyclopedia* (Barrett 2001) estimated that Roman Catholics represented 75 percent of the total population, Protestants and Independents 19.5 percent, Marginal Christians 2.5 percent, other religions 1.4 percent, and non-religious 1.6 percent in 2000.

In 1980, *World Christianity: Central America and the Caribbean* (Holland 1981) estimated that 90 percent of the total population was Catholic, 8 percent Protestant, and 2 percent other/none. However, it was reported that 15 percent of those who lived in San Juan claimed to be Protestant, which indicates a higher percentage of Protestants in cities than in other areas of the country.

When Christopher Columbus (1451–1506) arrived in Puerto Rico on his second voyage to the Americas on November 19, 1493, the island was inhabited by a group of Arawak Indians, known as Taínos. They called the island Borikén or, in Spanish, Borinquen. Columbus named the island San Juan Bautista in honor of Saint John the Baptist. Later, the island took the name of Porto Rico (Spanish: Rich Port), while the capital was named San Juan. In 1508, Spanish conquistador Juan Ponce de León (1460–1521) became the island's first governor. Various forts and walls, such as La Fortaleza (the oldest executive mansion in continuous use in the Americas), El Castillo San Felipe del Morro and El Castillo de San Cristóbal, were built to protect the port of San Juan from European enemies.

The Taíno tribe was largely killed off by the combination of disease, violent warfare, and a high incidence of suicide caused by harsh conditions imposed by the Spanish colonial system. After the decline of the Amerindian population in the early 16th century, African slaves were brought to Puerto Rico to work on sugarcane plantations, which became the island's main industry. The number of slaves in Puerto Rico rose from 1,500 in 1530 to 15,000 by 1555. The vast majority of the slaves imported by the Spanish were Yorubas and Igbos from Nigeria. The slaves were stamped with a hot iron on the forehead, a branding that meant that they were brought to the country legally and prevented their kidnapping. During the 19th century, slave revolts attempted unsuccessfully to overthrow Spanish rule.

The French, Dutch, and English made several attempts to capture Puerto Rico but failed to achieve long-term occupancy. During the late 17th and early 18th centuries, Spain's colonial emphasis was on the more prosperous mainland territories, which left Puerto Rico impoverished of settlers. The island became primarily a garrison for Spanish ships on their way to or from richer Spanish colonies. In 1570, there were an estimated 1,000 whites and 10,300 black slaves and Amerindians. A Spanish edict of 1664 offered freedom and land to African people from non-Spanish colonies, such as Jamaica and St. Dominique (Haiti), who immigrated to Puerto Rico and provided a population base to support the Puerto Rican garrison and its forts. The freemen who settled the western and southern parts of the island soon adopted the language and customs of the Spaniards. However, in 1673, the estimated total population of Puerto Rico was only 820 whites, 667 black slaves, and 304 free nonwhites (included Amerindians).

During the 1800s, thousands of immigrants arrived from Spain (mainly from Catalonia, Asturias, Galicia, the Balearic Islands, Andalusia, and the Canary Islands), along with numerous Spanish loyalists from Spain's former colonies in South America. In addition, hundreds arrived from Corsica, France, and Portugal, along with settlers from Ireland, Scotland, Germany, Italy, and others who were granted land by Spain during the Real Cédula de Gracias de 1815 (Royal Decree of Graces of 1815), which allowed European Catholics to settle in Puerto Rico with a certain amount of free land. This mass immigration during the 19th century helped the population grow from 155,000 in 1800 to almost a million at the close of the century. The census of 1858 reported that the population included 300,430 identified as whites; 341,015 as free colored;

and 41,736 as black slaves. Slavery was finally abolished in Puerto Rico on March 22, 1873.

French immigration to Puerto Rico came about as a result of the economic and political situations that occurred in various places, such as Louisiana (United States), Saint-Domingue (Haiti), and parts of Europe. Also, in 1815, the Spanish Crown decided that one of the ways to end the pro-independence movement in Puerto Rico was to allow Europeans of non-Hispanic origin who swore loyalty to the Spanish Crown to settle on the island. The decree encouraged slave labor to revive agriculture and attract new settlers. Therefore, the Royal Decree of Graces of 1815 was printed in three languages: Spanish, English, and French. The French who immigrated to Puerto Rico intermarried with the locals and settled in various places on the island. They were instrumental in the development of Puerto Rico's tobacco, cotton, and sugar industries and distinguished themselves as business people, politicians, and writers.

Contemporary Puerto Ricans date their independence from Spain to the unsuccessful revolt of 1868 led by Ramón Emeterio Betances (1827–1893), who proclaimed the island's independence prior to his defeat by Spanish military forces. The institution of slavery was finally abolished in 1873. Cuba and Puerto Rico were Spain's last colonies in the Americas in 1898 when, as a result of the defeat of Spanish forces by the U.S. military in the Spanish-American War, control of Puerto Rico passed to the U.S. government that year. English was imposed as the official language, and in 1917 Puerto Ricans became U.S. citizens but with limited control over local government. The governor and other key officials were not elected but appointed by the U.S. president, and the governor could veto any legislation.

After World War II, local rule was turned over to the island's residents. The new government, elected in 1948, moved to transform Puerto Rico into a commonwealth. The U.S. government retained power in foreign relations, defense, and some financial affairs; Puerto Ricans retained their U.S. citizenship. An ongoing debate over the island's status has been held in Puerto Rico, with some favoring statehood and others desiring full independence, but the commonwealth status continued to be supported by the majority of the population.

Today, Puerto Rico has a republican form of government, subject to U.S. jurisdiction and sovereignty. Its current powers are all delegated by the U.S. Congress and lack full protection under the U.S. Constitution. Puerto Rico's head of state is the president of the United States of America.

Luis Guillermo Fortuño-Burset (b. 1960) is the ninth and current governor of the Commonwealth of Puerto Rico. Fortuño is also the president of the pro-statehood New Progressive Party of Puerto Rico (NPP) and a member of the U.S. Republican Party. Fortuño holds the distinction of being the first Republican to be elected governor of Puerto Rico since 1969, and only the second Republican governor since 1949. He began his term in office on January 2, 2009.

The Roman Catholic Church Historically, the Roman Catholic Church has been the dominant religion in Puerto Rico. The first ecclesiastical province was established in 1511 by Pope Julius II (r. 1503–1513) with three dioceses: two in Hispaniola (Santo Domingo and Concepción de la Vega); the third was in the island of San Juan (modern Puerto Rico). The new dioceses were made suffragans of the Province of Seville, Spain.

Father Alonso Manso (1460–1539), canon of the cathedral of Salamanca, was transferred to the newly erected See of San Juan, of which he took possession two years later. When he arrived in 1513, the island had only 2 European settlements, which were inhabited by approximately 200 Spaniards and about 500 native "Christians." According to a letter that this prelate addressed later to the Spanish monarch, he was the first bishop to reach the New World.

Bishop Manso became the first inquisitor general of the Indies, appointed in 1519 by Cardinal Adrian de Utrecht, who later became Pope Adrian VI (r. 1522–1523). The vice provincial of the Dominicans, Pedro de Cordoba, resided in Santo Domingo until the establishment in 1522 of the Convent of St. Thomas Aquinas, the first religious community in Puerto Rico.

The first Catholic church (building) was erected in 1511 at Caparra and dedicated to Saint John the Baptist. The edifice was a temporary structure, which fell into ruin after the capital was transferred to another location. In 1512 another structure was erected for the inhabitants on the southern coast at a point known as

San German, some distance from the actual site of the town of that name. For many years the Diocese of Porto Rico had only these two centers of worship, with little increase in population.

The location of the actual cathedral of San Juan marks the site of the first church erected in 1520 or 1521 by Bishop Manso. This wooden structure was replaced by Bishop Bastidas, who began the work in 1543, and in the year following informed the king that the building was still unfinished for lack of funds; the same was true in 1549. Successive structures were destroyed by hurricanes, earthquakes, and foreign invaders, and were replaced by others.

The present cathedral, which is comparatively modern in its principal part, dates back to the early part of the 18th century. The rear portion, however, reveals a distinct style of architecture from a much more remote period. On August 12, 1908, the remains of Don Juan Ponce de Leon were solemnly conveyed from the Church of San José to the cathedral, where a suitable monument now marks the resting place of this "intrepid soldier and Christian cavalier."

Iberian popular Catholicism was brought to Puerto Rico by the first Spanish settlers and inhabitants of the Island of Borinquen. Everyday life was governed by the church's liturgical calendar and was organized in cycles or periods, namely, Advent, Nativity, Epiphany, Lent, and Easter.

When Africans were forcibly transported to the New World as slaves, they brought with them their ancient religious beliefs and practices. The Catholic Church, which had as its mission the evangelization and Christianization of indigenous communities since the beginning of Spanish colonialism, also proceeded to force African slaves to convert immediately to Christianity.

The effort of converting black slaves to Christianity commenced at the moment they came ashore on Borinquen. As soon as church authorities learned about the arrival of a slave ship, priests were assigned to visit the ship and screen the passengers to determine their religious traditions. Immediately after coming ashore, priests began teaching the Catechism to the newly arrived African slaves, educating them in the foundations of Catholic doctrine, which is the first step toward receiving the sacrament of baptism.

However, many black slaves resisted conversion to Roman Catholicism and devised diverse ways of hiding their allegiance to their traditional belief systems. Some of the African slaves brought to the New World had embraced Islam in their countries of origin, but most of them conserved elements of their ancient animistic beliefs and practices. Moreover, the language barrier hindered communication between Catholic evangelists and their potential converts.

Consequently, the black slaves had no choice but to go along with the outward expressions of the Catholic faith while secretly observing their African traditions. The rosaries were sung as promises to the saints or as pledges of gratefulness for the soul of the sick or the dead in the family, and this practice was used to conceal the chanting of prayers and promises to their ancient gods and goddesses when sung in their ancestral languages.

Although Catholicism grew in Puerto Rico, its leadership was all but wiped out late in the 17th century by a smallpox epidemic; only four priests survived and they were given little additional assistance during the early part of the next century. The Catholic Church was greatly strengthened in the early 19th century, when additional priests came to Puerto Rico from other regions in Latin America where wars of independence had put their lives in danger. Their loyalty to Spain did not go unnoticed when the various slave revolts began to occur.

In 1833, Bishop Pedro Gutierrez de Cos (1750–1833) died, leaving the diocese vacant until the nomination in 1846 of Bishop Francisco de La Puente (1779–1854). During this interval the Catholic Church was subjected to violent measures on the part of the governors of the island, who confiscated a great deal of the church's property and disbanded the only two communities of religious men, the Dominicans and Franciscans, appropriating to the state their convents and other properties.

During the Spanish domination of the island the Catholic Church was under royal patronage and the civil and religious authorities were intimately associated. On the assumption by the U.S. of control over Puerto Rico in 1898, full justice and every consideration was granted by the new government, which even went to the extent of paying $300,000 for the church property previously confiscated by Spain.

Puerto Rico

Puerto Rico
Fajardo
Maguabo
Rio Grande
Loiza Aldea
Humacao
Caguas
Maunabo
San Lorenzo
San Juan
Bayamon
Cayey
Comerio
Guayama
Corozal
Vega Baja
Coamo
Santa Isabel
Orocovis
Barceloneta
Ponce
Arecibo
Utuado
Castaner
Yauco
Quebradillas
San Sebastian
Ensenada
San German
Mayaguez
Centro Puntas
N

Under the U.S. occupation, the Catholic Church struggled to retain its traditional role and self-image as a Latin American institution while trying to remain relevant in the new U.S.-oriented world. The Catholic Church of Puerto Rico entered the 20th century without a single bishop, but new dioceses were created in 1924, 1960, and 1964. San Juan was elevated to archiepiscopal status in 1960.

In 1903, the Diocese of Porto Rico was severed from the province of Santiago de Cuba, and administered directly by the Holy See. All municipalities in Puerto Rico had at least one Catholic church (building), most of which are located at the town center or main plaza.

In 1910, the Diocese of Porto Rico was comprised of 78 parishes, which were mainly served by members of the religious bodies: the Lazarists, Augustinians, and Capuchins from Spain; the Dominicans from Holland; and the Redemptorists from Baltimore, Maryland. About 300 women belonging to the different religious communities were chiefly at work in the schools and hospitals. The Carmelites, Sisters of Charity, Religious of the Sacred Heart, and Servants of Mary were established in Spanish colonial times. Since the U.S. occupation, additional religious communities have arrived: the Mission Helpers of the Sacred Heart; the Sisters of Saint Francis from Buffalo, New York; and the Sisters of Saint Dominic from Brooklyn, New York.

Diverse tensions arose within the Puerto Rican Catholic Church during the 1960s and following years, which resulted from challenges posed by the Second Vatican Council (1962–1965), the Conference of Latin American Bishops held in Medellín (Colombia) in 1968, Latin American Liberation Theology, and the Catholic Charismatic Renewal movement. These powerful new currents polarized Catholic bishops, priests (diocesan and religious), lay brothers and sisters (members of religious orders), and the laity in general into various factions. *Traditionalists* wanted the church to remain as it was prior to the reforms approved by the Second Vatican Council (mid-1960s), with an emphasis on apostolic authority, orthodox theology, the sacraments, and personal piety. *Reformers* generally supported the church's post–Second Vatican Council stance of modernization and toleration of diversity based on its official social doctrine. *Progressives*, inspired by reforms approved at the Second Vatican and Medellín conferences, sought to implement the new vision for "a preferential option for the poor" through social and political action aimed at transforming Puerto Rican society and establishing greater social justice through peaceful democratic means. *Radicals* adopted the Marxist-inspired Liberation Theology and advocated violent revolution by the people as a means of overthrowing the right-wing military dictatorships in Latin America and creating a socialist state that would serve the poor marginalized masses. *Charismatic agents* sought to transform the spiritual and communal life of Catholics by means of the power and gifts of the Holy Spirit (including the "baptism of the Holy Spirit and speaking in tongues"), rather than by political and social activism.

The Catholic Charismatic Renewal found strong support in Puerto Rico in the 1970s and has continued to attract a large number of participants. The majority of Puerto Ricans are still Roman Catholics despite the growth and development of the Protestant movement after 1898, and especially since the 1960s.

In 2002, the Puerto Rican Catholic Church consisted of one archdiocese, the Metropolitan See of San Juan de Puerto Rico, 5 dioceses (Ponce, Arecibo, Mayagüez, Caguas, and Fajardo-Humacao) and 354 parishes that were served by 365 diocesan priests and 367 religious priests (total of 752); 418 permanent deacons; 498 male religious and 1,152 female religious. The current archbishop of San Juan is Roberto Octavio González Nieves, who was appointed and installed in 1999. The previous archbishop, Cardinal Luis Aponte Martínez (b. 1922), served from 1964 until his retirement in 1999. He had the honor of being the first Puerto Rican to be appointed bishop in 157 years.

The patron saints of Puerto Rico are Saint John the Baptist (feast day celebrated on June 24) and Our Lady of Divine Providence (feast day celebrated on Saturday before the third Sunday of November). Our Lady of Guadalupe is the patron saint of the Diocese of Ponce, which holds a special celebration on December 12.

The Protestant Movement Protestantism was suppressed under the Spanish regime but was encouraged under U.S. occupancy and governance, making modern

Puerto Rico interconfessional. The establishment of the Episcopal Church in Puerto Rico in 1872 heralded the arrival of missionaries from a number of other U.S. denominations between 1898 and 1900, beginning with the Northern Baptists, the Congregational Christian Church, the Christian Church–Disciples of Christ, the Evangelical United Brethren, the Evangelical Lutherans, the Presbyterian Church in the U.S.A., the Methodist Episcopal Church and the Christian and Missionary Alliance, followed by the Seventh-day Adventist Church in 1901.

William Sloan, a minister in the Northern Baptist Convention (now the American Baptist Churches in the U.S.A.), made an initial tour of the island and made recommendations that led to the founding of Baptist work there. Following an agreement among the several denominations, the Northern Baptists focused their work in the north, between Ponce and San Juan. The first congregation was opened in Rio Piedras, a suburb of San Juan. The Convention of Baptist Churches of Puerto Rico was formed in 1902.

Lutheran work was initiated in 1898 by the Augustana Synod (now a constituent part of the Evangelical Lutheran Church in America) in San Juan. Five churches were founded during the first decade, and eventually responsibility for the work passed to the United Lutheran Church in America.

The first Presbyterian missionaries arrived (J. M. Greene and Milton E. Cadwell) in 1899 and concentrated their work in the area of Aguadilla and Mayagüez. The first church was organized in 1900 and a presbytery was established in 1902. In January 1973, the Boriquén Synod of the Presbyterian Church in the U.S.A. was officially founded, which reported 71 congregations and 8,385 members in 1998.

The Methodist Episcopal Church (now a constituent part of the United Methodist Church) responded to the new situation in Puerto Rico by sending Charles W. Drees (1851–1926) to the island in 1900. Drees, who had previously been working in Uruguay, initiated both Spanish and English services in San Juan. The work remained attached to the United Methodist Church until 1992, when it was set apart as the semiautonomous Methodist Church of Puerto Rico. It became fully autonomous in 2000.

Adventist work began in 1901 with the arrival of missionary A. M. Fischer in Mayagüez. The work was organized in 1909 into the East Puerto Rico Conference and the West Puerto Rico Conference, both of which are part of the Antillian Union Conference, which also includes work in the Dominican Republic. The Puerto Rican Union Conference reported 290 churches in 2007 with 36,442 members; in 1997, there were 256 churches with 30,087 members.

In 1931, the United Evangelical Church (UEC) was formed in Fajardo, Puerto Rico, by a merger of the United Brethren in Christ, the Christian Church–Disciples of Christ, and the Congregational Christian Church. In 1990, this denomination officially became part of the United Church of Christ in the U.S.A. In 1995, the UEC reported 61 churches, 42 preaching points, and 4,591 members.

The Evangelical Congregational Church of Puerto Rico (Iglesia Evangélica Congregacional de Puerto Rico) was founded in 1948 in Humacao, Puerto Rico. The original name of this denomination in Puerto Rico was the United Brethren in Christ (Los Hermanos Unidos en Cristo).

Throughout the 20th century, a variety of traditional Protestant and Free churches and service agencies initiated work in Puerto Rico: the Church of the Nazarene (1944), the Mennonite Board of Missions (1945), Child Evangelism Fellowship (1946), International Gospel League (1949), Wesleyan World Missions (1952), Baptist Bible Fellowship International (1955), Home Mission Society of the Southern Baptist Convention (1956), Baptist Mid-Missions (1959), Grace Ministries International (1963), Wisconsin Evangelical Lutheran Church (1963), Baptist International Missions (1965), Biblical Ministries Worldwide (1968), independent Christian Churches and Churches of Christ (1976), Macedonian World Baptist Missions (1981), Maranatha Baptist Mission (1983), UFM International (1986, formerly known as Unevangelized Fields Mission), Apostolic Christian Church (1989), InterVarsity Mission (1992), Lutheran Church–Missouri Synod (1993), Open Door Baptist Missions (1995), and World Indigenous Missions (1996).

Pentecostalism, especially, had a significant role in the development of a variety of new Puerto Rican–

initiated churches, many of which have spread throughout the Spanish-speaking world, including Hispanic communities in the United States.

The Pentecostal Church of God, International Mission (Iglesia de Dios Pentecostal, Misión Internacional [IDPMI]), was founded in 1916 by Juan L. Lugo and other Puerto Rican leaders in Arecibo, Puerto Rico. It was affiliated with the Assemblies of God in the United States from 1918 until 1956, when the two church bodies went their separate ways. In 1999, this denomination reported 2,123 congregations in 32 countries, with approximately 221,000 members. The current PCOG president is the Reverend William Hernánez Ortiz, with offices in San Juan. Missionary work is conducted in many Latin American countries.

The Defenders of the Faith (Defensores de la Fe) was founded in 1925 in Kansas City, Missouri, by the Reverend Gerald B. Winrod. It began as a Fundamentalist denomination and became part of the Pentecostal movement in Puerto Rico through the ministry of Juan Francisco Rodríguez Rivera in 1934, with headquarters in Bayamón. This denomination has affiliated churches in Latin America and the Caribbean.

The Soldiers of the Cross of Christ International Evangelical Church (Iglesia Evangélica Internacional Soldados de la Cruz de Cristo) is a sabbatical Pentecostal denomination, founded between 1922 and 1925 in Havana, Cuba, by Ernest William Sellers (1869–1953), a Methodist layman and businessman from Wisconsin, who was known by his followers as "Apostle Daddy John." Since the 1960s, missionary work has been conducted in many Latin American countries and Hispanic communities in the United States, from its international headquarters in Miami, Florida.

The Church of Christ in the Antilles (Iglesia de Cristo en Las Antillas) was founded in 1935 in Los Dolores del Río Grande, Puerto Rico, by Reverend Pablo Rodríguez García in 1934–1935 following evangelistic campaigns conducted by the Reverend Francisco Olazábal in the Caribbean. In 1938, when the name of the denomination was changed to Council of Missionary Churches of Christ (Concilio de Iglesias de Cristo Misionera), a small group of pastors retained the original name but later changed it to the Universal Church of Christ (Iglesia de Cristo Universal). The churches affiliated with this denomination are mainly located in Puerto Rico and the eastern United States.

The Council of Missionary Churches of Christ (Concilio de Iglesias de Cristo Misionera) was founded in 1938 in Los Dolores del Río Grande, Puerto Rico by Florentino Figueroa Rosa. This denomination resulted from a reorganization of the Church of Christ in the Antilles (Iglesia de Cristo en Las Antillas). The current name was adopted in 1987. Today there are affiliated churches in the United States, Canada, Mexico, the Caribbean (Puerto Rico, the Dominican Republic, and Cuba), all of the Central American countries, Venezuela, Colombia, Ecuador, Peru, Bolivia, Argentina, Chile, Uruguay, and Paraguay. In December 2007, this denomination reported 771 organized churches and 274 missions, with an estimated total membership of 45,400. Whereas this denomination reported 96 organized churches in Puerto Rico, there were 309 affiliated churches in Honduras, 101 in the United States, 38 in the Dominican Republic, and 35 in Venezuela.

The International Council of Pentecostal Churches of Jesus Christ (Concilio Internacional de Iglesias Pentecostales de Jesucristo) was founded in Puerto Rico in 1938 by the Reverend Félix Rivera Cardona, who previously was a pastor with the Pentecostal Church of God in Mayagüez. In 1947, missionary work was begun in New York City by Juana Rivera, Félix's sister. The international headquarters are located in Ponce, Puerto Rico. There are 110 churches in Puerto Rico and 10 in New York City, and missionary work is conducted in about 10 other Latin American countries.

The Church of God, Inc. (La Iglesia de Dios, Inc.) was founded in 1938 in Fajardo and Las Piedras, Puerto Rico, by Aurelio Tiburcio and Benito Cintrón, among others, in response to "a great Pentecostal revival within the traditional churches, especially among sugar plantation workers." The central offices are now located in Caguas. As a result of emigration, affiliated churches were established in the United States (mainly in Chicago, Illinois, and East Chicago, Indiana), the Dominican Republic, Mexico, Honduras, El Salvador, and Panama.

The Assembly of Christian Churches (Asamblea de Iglesias Cristianas) was founded in 1939 in New York City by a group of Puerto Rican pastors—Carlos

Sepúlveda, Felipe G. Sabater, Pedro Serrano, and Frank Hernández—who were marginalized by the Mexican-American leadership of CLADIC (Concilio Latino Americano de Iglesias Cristianas) in 1938, after the death of the famous Mexican Pentecostal evangelist Francisco Olazábal in Texas. Sepúlveda and his associates wanted to continue the legacy of Olazábal among Puerto Ricans. Today there are affiliated churches in the Caribbean and Latin America, principally in Puerto Rico.

The Samaria Evangelical Church (Iglesia Evangélica Samaria) was founded in 1941 in Puerto Rico by Pentecostal pastor Julio Guzmán Silva. It has affiliated churches in many Latin American countries.

The Worldwide Missionary Movement, Inc. (Movimiento Misionero Mundial, Inc. [MMM]), was founded in 1963 in Puerto Rico by the Reverend Luis M. Ortiz Marrero and his wife, Rebecca de Ortiz, who had served in the Dominican Republic and Cuba as missionaries with the Assemblies of God from 1944 to 1960. They returned to Puerto Rico in 1959 and organized the Worldwide Missionary Movement with headquarters in Trujillo Alto in 1963. After Ortiz's death in 1996, the Reverend Rubén Rosas Salcedo was named president of the association. In January 2003, this denomination reported 4,980 churches, 4,400 preaching points, and 3,949 pastors in 52 countries. Missionary work is conducted in most Latin American countries, in the United States and Canada, in Europe (England, Germany, Holland, Italy, and Spain), Africa, Australia, and Asia.

The famous Puerto Rican Pentecostal evangelist José Juaquín (Yiye) Avila founded the "Christ Is Coming Ministry" in 1967 in Camuy, Puerto Rico. Avila has celebrated divine healing and liberation campaigns throughout the Americas and in Spain. In 1988, he founded a television network called The Miracle Network ("La Cadena del Milagro"), which includes five channels that cover all of Puerto Rico and the Caribbean.

The International Council of Churches Freed by Jesus Christ, Inc. (Concilio Internacional de Iglesias Libres por Jesucristo, Inc.) was founded in 1974 in the Bronx, New York, by the Reverend Valentín Cruz Canales, who was born in Santurce, Puerto Rico. He also founded the Instituto Evangélico Elim in 1974 with extension programs in Puerto Rico and the Dominican Republic. This Pentecostal denominational has affiliated churches in the United States, Puerto Rico, the Dominican Republic, Haiti, and Colombia.

The Missionary Association of Pentecostal Churches, Inc. (Asociación Misionera de Iglesias Pentecostales, Inc. [AMIP]) was founded in 2003 by the Reverend José D. Muñoz in San Juan. The AMIP operates the Berea Bible Institute in San Juan and has extension programs in other countries via the Internet. There are affiliated churches in Cuba, the Dominican Republic, Panama, Colombia, Ecuador, Chile, and the United States.

In addition, Pentecostal denominations from the United States began work in Puerto Rico: the International Church of the Foursquare Gospel (1930), the Church of God of Prophecy (1938), the Church of God (Cleveland, Tennessee) (1944, known as the Church of God Mission Board [Iglesia de Dios Mission Board], with headquarters in Saint Just), the Assemblies of God (1957), Open Bible Standard Churches (1958), the United Pentecostal Church International (1962), and the Pentecostal Free Will Baptist Church (founding date unknown).

Other Protestant denominations include the Sociedad Misionera Internacional of the Seventh-day Adventist Church Reform Movement, General Conference, which has its Puerto Rican headquarters in San Juan; the Brethren Assemblies (Christian Brethren); the Church of the Brethren; the Christian Reformed Church; Fellowship of Grace Brethren Churches; Free Methodist Church; National Association of Free Will Baptists; Southwide Baptist Fellowship; the Quakers; and The Salvation Army. Also, the Berachah Church (an independent fundamentalist church founded in 1935 in Houston, Texas, by C. W. Colgan and Robert B. Thieme, Jr.) claims to have mission work in Puerto Rico. The Maranatha World Revival Church (Iglesia de Avivamiento Mundial Maranatha) was founded in 1974 in Chicago, Illinois, by Nahum y Minerva Rosario. It now has more than 300 affiliated churches in the United States, Mexico, Costa Rica, Panama, Puerto Rico, Cuba, the Dominican Republic, Argentina, Chile, Venezuela, Europe, and Africa.

In 1908, the Federation of Evangelical Churches of Puerto Rico was established, which was later known

Puerto Rico

Religion	Followers in 1970	Followers in 2010	% of Population	Annual % growth 2000–2010	Followers in 2025	Followers in 2050
Christians	2,673,000	3,918,000	96.6	0.56	4,139,000	4,182,000
Roman Catholics	2,586,000	2,865,000	70.6	0.63	2,888,000	2,800,000
Protestants	228,000	620,000	15.3	1.73	700,000	750,000
Independents	80,000	377,000	9.3	2.30	450,000	500,000
Agnostics	29,000	79,500	2.0	1.75	120,000	160,000
Spiritists	4,000	28,800	0.7	0.58	31,000	32,000
Atheists	5,000	15,800	0.4	0.58	18,000	20,000
Hindus	1,000	3,600	0.1	0.58	6,000	8,000
Baha'is	1,200	3,000	0.1	0.58	6,000	10,000
Jews	2,000	2,800	0.1	0.58	2,800	3,000
New religionists	1,000	1,500	0.0	0.57	1,800	1,800
Muslims	0	1,200	0.0	0.59	2,000	3,000
Chinese folk	0	730	0.0	0.57	800	1,000
Buddhists	0	600	0.0	0.60	1,000	1,500
Total population	**2,716,000**	**4,056,000**	**100.0**	**0.58**	**4,328,000**	**4,422,000**

as The Evangelical Union of Puerto Rico in 1916, the Association of Evangelical Churches of Puerto Rico in 1934, and the Evangelical Council of Puerto Rico (ECPR) in 1954. Current members of the ECPR are the Presbyterian Synod of Borinquen, the Christian Church–Disciples of Christ, the American Baptist Association, the Methodist Church, the Church of the Brethren, the United Evangelical Church, the First Union Church, and the Second Union Church.

Member organizations of the Latin American Council of Churches (CLAI), which is affiliated with the World Council of Churches (WCC), in Puerto Rico include the entire ECPR membership. Additional associate members include: Caribbean Synod of the Evangelical Lutheran Church and the Episcopal Church Diocese of Puerto Rico.

The Latin American Confraternity of Evangelicals (CONELA) is not associated with an interdenominational evangelical fellowship organization in Puerto Rico, but the CONELA representative was listed as David Casillas.

Other Religions The Puerto Rican National Catholic Church (independent of the Vatican) was founded in Puerto Rico in 1926 by Monsignor Héctor Gonzáles, loosely affiliated with the Polish National Catholic Church in the United States. In 1961, the former changed its name to the Holy Orthodox Catholic Apostolic Church of Puerto Rico and became affiliated with the Russian Orthodox Church in the Americas. In 1968 González withdrew from the latter and formed the Western Rite Vicariate with parishes in Puerto Rico, the Dominican Republic, Brazil, and the United States. The name was later changed to the United Hispanic Old Catholic Episcopate, but after several years of controversy the official name was changed again to that used today: Hispanic-Brazilian Confraternity of Christian Doctrine, Saint Pius X (headquarters in Brooklyn, New York).

Non-Protestant marginal Christian groups in Puerto Rico are: the Church of Christ, Scientist (Mary Baker Eddy, 1892; Boston, Massachusetts), Christadelphian Bible Mission, Growing in Grace International Ministries, Jehovah's Witnesses, Light of the World Church (Mexico), Mormons, Mita Congregation, People of Amos Church, Philadelphia Church of God, Unity Church, Voice of the Cornerstone, and Universal Church of the Kingdom of God (also known as Oración Fuerte al Espíritu Santo, founded in Brazil in 1977 by Bishop Edir Macedo and arriving in Puerto Rico in 1993).

Gardner H. Russell began meetings affiliated with the Church of Jesus Christ of Latter-day Saints (LDS) in 1947 among U.S. military personnel stationed at Guajataca. He later opened a mission in San Juan. By

1987, membership had increased to 12,000. Despite the move of several military church members from Puerto Rico in 1993, membership had reached 19,700 throughout the island. In 1996, the number of LDS congregations had grown to the point that the San Juan Mission was formally recognized, with headquarters in Rio Piedras. In 2005, the LDS reported 43 congregations and 29,064 members. The Jehovah's Witnesses entered the country in the early 1930s. By 2005, there were 323 Witness congregations in Puerto Rico with 24,601 adherents.

Mita Congregation (Congregación Mita), established in 1940 in San Juan, was founded by Juanita García Peraza, who is known as "Mita" ("Spirit of Life"); her followers are called "los Mitas." She is believed by her followers to be the embodiment of the Holy Spirit and the "voice of God on Earth." After Juanita's death in 1970 at age 72, the new head of this movement became Teófilo Vargas Seín, who is called Aarón by his followers. There are affiliated churches in many countries of the Caribbean Basin, including the Dominican Republic, Costa Rica, and Colombia. The original San Juan community serves as a developmental model for the newer congregations abroad which, in turn, communicate with the center through all modern media. Active members have swollen to more than 30,000 worldwide. The new San Juan temple alone seats 6,000, but actually the largest following is in Colombia, which has now surpassed Puerto Rico as a whole; the Dominican Republic ranks third, with 65 congregations.

After the death of Mita Congregation founder Juanita García Peraza in 1970, there was a power struggle between Teófio Vargas and Nicolás Tosado Aviles (1919–2007) over who would be the leader of Mita Congregation, which resulted in Vargas winning that leadership position and Tosado being expelled from the movement. In 1972, Tosado left with a small group of followers and formed the People of Amos Church (Iglesia Pueblo de Amós), with "Amos" being Tosado's new spiritual name. Since 1991 its headquarters have been in Barrio Guzmán Abajo de Río Grande, Puerto Rico. From Puerto Rico this new movement spread to the United States (mainly in Texas, Georgia, and California), El Salvador (now with more than 20 congregations), Spain, Guatemala, Honduras, Nicaragua, Costa Rica, and Mexico. Tosado, who was considered by his followers to be "a Prophet and Intercessor between God and men" and in whose body dwelt "The Divine Trinity," died at age 88 in December 2007 in Puerto Rico.

The Voice of the Cornerstone (Voz de la Piedra Angular) was founded in 1974 in Cayey, Puerto Rico, by William Soto Santiago, a disciple of the Pentecostal evangelist and faith-healer William Branham who founded a similar movement in Jeffersonville, Indiana, in 1955. Although there is no evidence that the two ever met, Soto borrowed much of the teachings of Branham and launched his own movement, calling himself the "Voice of the Chief Cornerstone" and the "Angel who opens the Seventh Seal" in the book of Revelation. There are affiliated groups in many countries of Latin America.

Non-Christian religions in Puerto Rico include Baha'i Faith, Judaism, Islam, Buddhism, Hinduism, Ancient Wisdom, and Psychic-Spiritualist-New Age traditions.

Today, Puerto Rico is home to the largest and wealthiest Jewish community in the Caribbean, with more than 3,000 Jewish inhabitants, and is also the only Caribbean island in which all three major Jewish denominations are represented. Most of the Jewish community lives in San Juan, but there are also Jewish families in Ponce and Mayagüez. San Juan has three synagogues: Reform Congregation Temple Beth Shalom, established in 1967; Conservative Congregation Shaare Zedeck, established in 1953; and Chabad Lubavitch of Puerto Rico, established in 1997. In addition, there are a Satmar Community in the western part of the island in Mayagüez, known as Toiras Jesed; and a Reform synagogue and a Conservative synagogue in the city of Santruce.

In 2007, there were 5,119 Muslims in Puerto Rico, with 8 mosques spread throughout the island, with most Muslims living in the San Juan suburb of Rio Piedras.

Buddhism is represented in Puerto Rico by Mahikari de America, Centro Soto Zen de Puerto Rico, Rinzai-Ji, Centro de Meditación y Estudios Budistas del Caribe (Theravada and Mahayana traditions), and the Padmasambhava Buddhist Center (Tibetan Buddhism).

Hinduism is represented by the Krishnamurti Foundation (Hato Rey), International Society of Divine Love, International Society for Krishna Consciousness (ISKCON), Sri Sathya Sai Baba International Organization, Sri Chinmoy centers, and the Transcendental Meditation (TM) movement (now known as the Global Country of World Peace).

Traditional Chinese religions include Daoism, Confucianism, and Buddhism; the only Japanese-origin religions are Mahikari ("Divine True Light") and Sekai Mahikari Bunmei Kyodan.

The Western Esoteric tradition is represented by the Ancient Mystical Order of the Rosae Crucis (AMORC), which has lodges in Mayagüez (Font de la Jara Chapter), Ponce (Ponce Lodge) and San Juan (Luz de AMORC Lodge); Freemasonry; Gran Fraternidad Universal, Misión de Acuarius (GFU, founded in Venezuela by Dr. Serge Raynaud de la Ferrière); and the Christian Gnostic Movement (founded by Samael Aun Weor in Mexico).

The Psychic-Spiritualist-New Age traditions include the Celicia Temple (also known as Las Profetas, founded in a slum area of Caguas, Puerto Rico, in 1953), the Spiritist Confederation of Puerto Rico (founded in 1903), the Movement for Inner Peace, the New Thought Development Foundation (founded in 1987 in San Juan), and the Church of Scientology.

Puerto Rico is one of several island nations where Afro-Caribbean religions have been very successful. Various African religious beliefs and practices have been present since the arrival of black slaves in Puerto Rico. In particular, the belief systems of Ifa from Nigeria (among the Yoruba people) and Palo Mayombe from the Congo River basin (among Bantu peoples) find adherence among those who practice some form of African traditional religion. In addition, Taíno religious beliefs and practices have been rediscovered or reinvented to a degree by a handful of advocates who practice Amerindian spirituality.

Santeria, also known as Regla de Ocha, derived from Yoruban religion with an overlay of Spanish Catholicism, is very strong in Puerto Rico today. According to scholars, modern Santeria was introduced into Puerto Rico by Cuban immigrants during the 1940s, 1950s, and 1960s. The popular Afro-Cuban-Puerto Rican religious tradition honors its deities and the dead with offerings of flowers, food dishes, the burning candles, ritual cleansing with rum, and other animistic practices. Also, Regla Arará, a variation of Haitian Vodou, is practiced in Cuba and Puerto Rico.

The belief in magic spells, male and female witches, disembodied spirits, the devil, and occult practices was neither in the past nor is today an exclusive patrimony of black Puerto Ricans. Because Santeria identified Yoruban deities with Roman Catholic saints, initially as a means of retaining the African belief system while outwardly practicing Roman Catholicism, many Puerto Ricans identify with both religions.

Many Puerto Rican Catholics practice religious syncretism, which combines ancient animistic beliefs and practices of Amerindian and African-roots with a Roman Catholicism imposed on Native Americans and African slaves by civil and religious authorities during the Spanish colonial period. The result is a "popular Catholicism" that retains significant elements of African and Amerindian spirituality, which includes animistic beliefs and practices such as magic (white and black, good and evil), witchcraft (*bujería*), herbal healing (*curanderismo*) and shamanism (the shaman is an intermediary with the spirit world).

Clifton L. Holland and J. Gordon Melton

See also: Advent; American Baptist Churches in the U.S.A.; Ancient and Mystical Order Rosae Crucis; Assemblies of God; Augustinians; Baha'i Faith; Baptist Bible Fellowship International; Capuchins; Cathedrals—Christian; Christadelphians; Christian and Missionary Alliance; Christian Brethren; Christian Church (Disciples of Christ); Christian Reformed Church in North America; Christmas; Church of Christ, Scientist; Church of God (Cleveland, Tennessee); Church of God of Prophecy; Church of Jesus Christ of Latter-day Saints; Church of Scientology; Church of the Brethren; Church of the Nazarene; Congregationalism; Dominicans; Easter; Eddy, Mary Baker; Epiphany; Episcopal Church; Evangelical Lutheran Church in America; Franciscans; Freemasonry; Global Country of World Peace; Gnostic Movement; Ife; International Church of the Foursquare Gospel; International Society for Krishna Consciousness; Jehovah's Witnesses; Krishnamurti Foundations; Latin American Council of Churches; Lent; Light of the World Church; Lubavitch Hasidism; Lutheran Church–Missouri Synod; Methodist Church of Puerto Rico; Mita Congregation; Palo Mayombe; Pentecostalism; Philadelphia Church of God; Reform Judaism; Roman Catholic Church; Salvation Army; Santeria; Satmar Hasidism; Seventh-day Adventist Church; Seventh-Day Adventist Reform Movements; Southern Baptist Convention; Sri Chinmoy Centre; United Methodist Church; United Pentecostal Church International; Universal Church of the Kingdom of God; Vodou; Western Esoteric Tradition; Wisconsin Evangelical Lutheran Synod; Witchcraft; World Council of Churches.

References

Carver, E. Earl. "Showcase for God: A Study of Evangelical Church Growth in Puerto Rico." Unpublished master's thesis, Fuller Theological Seminary, 1972.

Cook, Scott. "The Prophets: A Revivalistic Folk Religious Movement in Puerto Rico." In *Peoples and Cultures of the Caribbean: An Anthropological Reader*, edited by Michael M. Horowitz. Garden City, NY: The Natural History Press, 1971.

Cruz, Samuel. *Masked Africanisms: Puerto Rican Pentecostalism*. Dubuque, IA: Kendall/Hunt Publishing Company, 2005.

De La Torre, Miguel A. *Santería: The Beliefs and Rituals of a Growing Religion in America.* Grand Rapids, MI: William B. Eerdmans Publishing Company, 2004.

Fernández Olmos, Margarite, and Lizabeth Paravisini-Gebert, eds. *Sacred Possessions: Vodou, Santería, Obeah and the Caribbean.* New Brunswick, NJ: Rutgers University Press, 1997.

Fundación Puerto Rico Evangélico. "100 años de protestantismo en Puerto Rico." *Presencia* 1 (1998).

Gutiérrez, Ángel L. *Evangélicos en Puerto Rico en la época Española*. Río Piedras, Puerto Rico: Editorial Chari; Puerto Rico Evangélico, Inc.; and Seminario Evangélico de Puerto Rico.

Holland, Clifton L., ed. *World Christianity: Central America and the Caribbean*. Monrovia, CA: MARC–World Vision International, 1981.

Icken Safa, Helen. *The Urban Poor of Puerto Rico: A Study in Development and Inequality.* New York: Holt, Rinehart and Winston, Inc., 1974.

Jones, William. "Porto Rico." In *The Catholic Encyclopedia*. Vol. 12. New York: Robert Appleton Company, 1911. http://www.newadvent.org/cathen/12291b.htm.

Middledyk, R. A. *The History of Puerto Rico: From the Spanish Discovery to the American Occupation*. Charleston, SC: BiblioBazaar, 2006.

Moore, Donald T. *Puerto Rico para Cristo: A History of the Progress of the Evangelical Missions on the Island of Puerto Rico*. Cuernavaca, México: Centro Intercultural de Documentación (Sondeos, Número 43), 1969.

PROLADES. *A Chronology of Protestant Beginnings in Puerto Rico, 1598–2003.* http://www.prolades.com/cra/regions/caribe/pri/pri-rd.htm.

PROLADES. *A Table of the Estimated Size of the Protestant Movement in Puerto Rico, 2000.* http://www.prolades.com/cra/regions/caribe/pri/pri-rd.htm.

Roman, Reinaldo L. *Governing Spirits: Religion, Miracles, and Spectacles in Cuba and Puerto Rico, 1898–1956*. Chapel Hill: University of North Carolina Press, 2007.

Weber, Linda J., and Dotsey Welliver, eds. *Mission Handbook of U.S. and Canadian Protestant Ministries Overseas, 2007–2009.* Wheaton, IL: Evangelism and Missions Information Service (EMIS) and the Billy Graham Center at Wheaton College, 2007.

Ziegler, M. O. *The Origins and Growth of the Methodist Church in Puerto Rico, 1900–1970*. Immaculate, PA: Immaculata College, 1988.

Pure Brightness Festival

The Pure Brightness Festival is one of the few Chinese festivals tied to the solar year rather than the lunar calendar. It is held 107 days after the Winter Solstice (and 15 days after the Spring Equinox); hence it is always April 4 or 5 on the Western or Common Era calendar. It is preceded by what is designated Cold Food Day.

As practiced, it has become another day to especially honor one's ancestors.

As the story told of Pure Brightness Day goes, a prince of the state of Jin, a power province in the feudal world of northern China's Spring and Autumn Period (722–403 BCE), neglected to reward one of the men who had stood by him in a time of exile prior to his attaining the throne. The man, Jie Zitui, had retired to live quietly on Mian Mountain. Realizing his lack of gratitude, the prince sought out his former companion, but was unable to locate him. A courtier suggested burning the mountainside to force him out, but no Jie Zitui appeared. Further searching found him, and his mother, dead beneath a willow tree. To commemorate his former companion, the prince ordered that the day would henceforth be remembered as the Hanshi Festival and ordered that no fires be kindled on that day—hence the eating of cold food. The tree under which Jie Zitui was found was named Pure Bright Willow and the day after the Hanshi Festival named the Pure Bright Day.

In China, including Taiwan, the Hanshi Festival has largely been neglected, but the Pure Bright Festival is widely celebrated and acknowledged as the first day of the year when one can leave the confinement of the house during the winter and enjoy the out-of-doors. It is also a popular time to acknowledge one's ancestors by going to their tombs, making necessary repairs, and cleaning them of any clutter or trash accumulated through the winter. Thus, Pure Brightness Day is often termed "Tomb Sweeping Day." Before leaving, people will also commonly burn what is called spirit money. Such money is printed especially for burning, hence sending into the spirit world, for the use of the spirits of the dead. It is also a day to think about willow trees. Some plant new willow trees. Others decorate them with model birds made of flour and dates, and called Zitui swallows.

J. Gordon Melton

See also: Ancestors; Winter Solstice.

References

Kaulbach, B., and B. Proksch. *Arts and Culture in Taiwan*. Taipei: Southern Materials Center, 1984.

Latsch, Marie-Luise. *Traditional Chinese Festivals*. Singapore: Greaham Brash, 1984.

Liming, Wei. *Chinese Festivals: Traditions, Customs, and Rituals*. Hong Kong: China International Press, 2005.

Pure Land Buddhism

The Pure Land mythos, which eventually came to center upon the popular practice of invoking Buddha Amida's name with the intention of being born in his Pure Land of Bliss, the Western Paradise, was one of the most important variations of Mahayana Buddhism, and flourished in China, Korea, Japan, and Vietnam.

In the case of China, it was imported from northern India as early as the second or third century CE, as indicated by sutra translations. Subsequently, beginning at least with the monk Lu-shan Hui-yuan (344–416) its practices were adopted and spread widely in Chinese monasteries. Pure Land ideas never really formed an independent teaching lineage, however, and they instead coexisted with normal monastic lineages, especially the T'ien-t'ai founded by Chih-i (aka, Zhi Yi) (538–597). A key Chinese addition to the canon in the early period was the Kuan-ching (Visualization Sutra), which described nine detailed statuses of potential rebirth in the Pure Land realm.

Pure Land doctrine and practice have remained up to the present a standard aspect of the repertoire of Chinese Buddhism, whether in monastic practice or in monastically influenced lay practice. In the Tang period (618–907) Pure Land became subordinated to the authority claims of Chan lineages. Nevertheless, all later monastic Buddhism was normally characterized by the "dual practice" of both Chan and Pure Land, as represented by the teaching of Chu-hung (1535–1615). Indeed, up to the present, apparently more Buddhist practitioners have put their hopes in rebirth in the Western paradise than in the attainment of success in pursuing the official bodhisattva path.

Much of Pure Land tradition in China went outside official monasticism. The Kuan-ching text in particular opened the way to popularization because it appeared to promote the efficacy of religious routines as simple as the recitation of the Buddha's name, which alone might lead to the Pure Land at its lowest level. A key teacher who was regarded as having emphasized

Temple of the Pure Land monastery in Buryatia, Russia. (Mikhail Markovskiy/Dreamstime.com)

this aspect of the teaching was Shan-tao (or Shan Dao) (613–681). (His presentation of the Pure Land perspective would later influence the Japanese monk Honen [1133–1212], who altered the Japanese tradition by his unique emphasis on the vocal invocation of Amida's name as the sole possible practice for his times.) Throughout the later Chinese imperial period (ca. 1200–1900), influential lay Pure Land movements flourished, sometimes supervised by the official monastic system and sometimes separate from it.

Chinese religious traditions including Buddhism were severely damaged by 20th-century political disorder and by post–World War II Maoism. However, vigorous revival has been underway, stimulated significantly by developments in Taiwan. The revival has remanifested earlier relationships of complementarity and tension between Pure Land and Chan and between monastic and lay forms of organization. Nonetheless, the Pure Land "language" of Buddhism continues to be preferred to the Chan by more Chinese practitioners, as it was in the past.

In comparative context it is noteworthy that no version of Chinese Pure Land has ever taken root that has been philosophically rigorous but also fundamentally non-monastic in conception (as in the Japanese Jodoshinshu school). Whether monastic or lay, Chinese followers have remained oriented to an approach that strongly valorizes ritual asceticism and precept-keeping.

Galen Amstutz

See also: Honen; Jodo-shinshu; Mahayana Buddhism; Shan Dao; Tian Tai/Tendai Buddhism; Zhi Yi.

References

Beginnings

Chappell, David W. "Chinese Buddhist Interpretations of the Pure Lands." In *Buddhist and Taoist*

Studies, edited by David W. Chappell and Michael Saso, 22–53. Honolulu: University of Hawaii Press, 1977.

Chappell, David W. "From Dispute to Dual Cultivation: Pure Land Responses to Ch'an Critics." In *Traditions of Meditation in Chinese Buddhism,* edited by Peter N. Gregory, 163–198. Honolulu: University of Hawaii Press, 1986.

Ch'ên, Kenneth Kuan Shêng. *Buddhism in China, a Historical Survey*. Princeton, NJ: Princeton University Press, 1964.

Pas, Julian F. *Visions of Sukhāvatī: Shan-tao's Commentary on the Kuan Wu-liang shou-fo ching*. Albany: State University of New York Press, 1995.

Tanaka, Kenneth K. *The Dawn of Chinese Pure Land Buddhist Doctrine: Ching-ying Hui-yuan's Commentary on the Visualization Sutra*. Albany: State University of New York Press, 1990.

Zürcher, E. *The Buddhist Conquest of China; the Spread and Adaptation of Buddhism in Early Medieval China*. Leiden: Brill, 1959.

Pre-modern Mature

Amstutz, Galen. "The Politics of Independent Pure Land in China." *Journal of Chinese Religions* 26 (1998): 21–50.

Getz, Daniel A. "Popular Religion and Pure Land in Song-Dynasty Tiantai Bodhisattva Precept Ordination Ceremonies." In *Going Forth: Visions of Buddhist Vinaya: Essays Presented in Honor of Professor Stanley Weinstein*, 161–184. Honolulu: University of Hawaii Press, 2005.

Getz, Daniel A. "Shengchang's Pure Conduct Society and the Chinese Pure Land Patriarchate." In *Approaching the Land of Bliss: Religious Praxis in the Cult of Amitābha,* edited by Richard K. Payne and Kenneth K. Payne, 52–76. Honolulu: University of Hawaii Press, 2004.

Gregory, Peter N., and Daniel A. Getz, Jr. *Buddhism in the Sung*. A Kuroda Institute Book. Honolulu: University of Hawaii Press, 1999.

Hsu, Sung-peng. *A Buddhist Leader in Ming China: The Life and Thought of Han-Shan Te-Ch'ing*. University Park and London: Pennsylvania State University Press, 1979.

Jones, Charles B. "Apologetic Strategies in Late Imperial Chinese Pure Land Buddhism." *Journal of Chinese Religions* 29 (2001): 69–90.

Sharf, Robert H. "On Pure Land Buddhism and Ch'an: Pure Land Syncretism in Medieval China." *T'oung Pao* (Leiden) 88, nos. 4–5 (2002): 282–331.

Shih, Heng-ching. *The Syncretism of Ch'an and Pure Land Buddhism.* New York: Peter Lang, 1992.

Stevenson, Daniel B. "Death-Bed Testimonials of the Pure Land Faithful." In *Buddhism in Practice*, edited by Donald S. Lopez, 592–602. Princeton: Princeton University Press, 1995.

Stevenson, Daniel B. "Pure Land Buddhist Worship and Meditation in China." In *Buddhism in Practice*, edited by Donald S. Lopez, 359–379. Princeton: Princeton University Press, 1995.

Yü, Chung-fang. *The Renewal of Buddhism in China: Chu-Hung and the Late Ming Synthesis*. New York: Columbia University Press, 1981.

Modern

Chandler, Stuart. *Establishing a Pure Land on Earth: The Foguang Buddhist Perspective on Modernization and Globalization.* Honolulu: University of Hawaii Press, 2004.

Jones, Charles Brewer. *Buddhism in Taiwan: Religion and the State, 1660–1990*. Honolulu: University of Hawaii Press, 1999.

Jones, Charles Brewer. "Foundations of Ethics and Practice in Chinese Pure Land Buddhism." *Journal of Buddhist Ethics* 10 (2003): 2–20.

Jones, Charles Brewer. "Transitions in the Practice and Defense of Chinese Pure Land Buddhism." In *Buddhism in the Modern World: Adaptations of an Ancient Tradition*, edited by Steven Heine and Charles S. Prebish, 125–142. Oxford and New York: Oxford University Press, 2003.

Laliberté, André. *The Politics of Buddhist Organizations in Taiwan: 1989–2003: Safeguarding the Faith, Building a Pure Land, Helping the Poor*. London: RoutledgeCurzon, 2004.

Pittman, Don A. *Toward a Modern Chinese Buddhism: Taixu's Reforms*. Honolulu: University of Hawaii Press, 2001.

Welch, Holmes. *The Practice of Chinese Buddhism, 1900–1950.* Cambridge: Harvard University Press, 1967.

Purim

Purim is an annual Jewish festival that celebrates the deliverance of the Jewish people of the ancient Persian Empire from a plot to annihilate them. The story is recorded in the Hebrew Bible (the Christian Old Testament) in the book of Esther. In the past, the king Ahasuerus described in the story was believed to be either Artaxerxes I (r. 465–424 BCE) or Artaxerxes II (r. 404–358). More recently, scholars have been more skeptical of the historicity of the story and seen it more as a legendary tale.

The book of Esther begins with the account of a feast given by King Ahasuerus at which alcohol flowed freely. In a drunken state, the king ordered his wife Vashti, wearing her crown, to "display her beauty" before those in attendance. Her refusal to do so caused Ahasuerus to put her away and to choose a new wife and queen. He chose a young woman at the court named Esther, unaware that she was, in fact, a Jewish orphan named Hadassah now in the care of her cousin Mordecai, Soon afterward, Mordecai discovered a plot by several courtiers to kill Ahasuerus. He made the plot public.

Haman, the king's highest official, came to despise Mordecai, for he refused to bow down to Haman. Haman discovered that Mordecai was Jewish and hatched a plot to kill not only him but the entire Jewish minority in the Persian Empire. After obtaining Ahasuerus's permission to go ahead with his plan, Haman cast lots (purim) to choose the date for executing it. The lot fell on the 13th day of the month of Adar. When Mordecai discovered Haman's plan, he informed Esther. She asked the Jewish community to engage in three days of fasting and prayer, and then requested an audience with Ahasuerus, even though to do so, without the king having summoned her, could have caused her death. But Esther found favor when the king saw her, and she invited the king and Haman to a feast. At this feast, she invited them to a second feast the next day.

Costumed players celebrate Purim, about 1657. Purim is a celebratory Jewish holiday in which plays and parodies are performed to commemorate the time when the Jewish people living in Persia were saved from extermination. (*The Jewish Encyclopedia,* ed. Isadore Singer, 1901)

On the night between the two feasts, Ahasuerus had trouble sleeping, and he asked that the annals be read to him. Learning that Mordecai had foiled a plot against him and that he had received no honor in return, the king asked Haman how properly to reward a man the king wished to honor. Thinking it was he himself of whom the king spoke, Haman replied that the man should be dressed in a kingly fashion and paraded on the king's horse. Haman, to his great despair, had then to do these things for Mordecai.

That evening, at the feast, Esther revealed that she was a Jew and informed the king of Haman's plot. She pointed out that if his plot were carried out, she would be executed. Ahasuerus then turned on Haman and ordered him hung. But a problem remained. The decree allowing Haman's action against the Jews had been signed; thus it could not be simply annulled—but it could be countered. Ahasuerus gave Esther and Mordecai leave to write a new decree allowing the Jews to defend themselves. When attacked on Adar 13, the Jewish community fought and triumphed over its enemies. Mordecai subsequently was given a prominent position in Ahasuerus's court. He initiated the annual commemoration of the Jewish people's deliverance.

Purim is celebrated on the 14th day of the Hebrew month of Adar (usually in mid-March on the Common Era calendar). In leap years, when a second month of Adar is added to the Hebrew lunar calendar (7 times in a 19-year cycle), so that holidays stay in their appointed seasons, Purim is celebrated during Adar II. This is the most unequivocally joyous of Jewish festivals, though it begins on Adar 13 with Taanit Esther, a fast (as Esther had asked the Jews to fast before she went to the king). If Adar 13 falls on a Sabbath, there will be further adjustment of the date.

Ritually, the service at the synagogue will feature a reading of the biblical book of Esther. This occurs twice, first after sunset when the new day begins on the Hebrew calendar, and a second time the next morning. In contrast to the quiet demeanor during the scripture readings at Sabbath services, during the reading of the book of Esther the congregation shouts and makes noise whenever Haman's name is read so as to blot out the sound of his name. Central to the day is a feast, which has been preceded by the sharing of gifts of food with others and the giving of money to the poor, with the understanding that joy is complete only when shared with the less fortunate. Additional customs have also developed above and beyond the guidelines of the biblical story, including the making of a particular dessert called *hamantaschen* (or "Haman's pockets"), a fruit-filled pastry. Purim is one day in which the drinking of alcohol in excess is acceptable.

The story of Esther is also commemorated as a teaching event. It reminds believers of the capricious nature of evil in the world and the need for action when it arises. It also builds confidence that God does not neglect his people.

From the Middle Ages to the present, Purim has, on occasion, been used, usually as part of a larger anti-Semitic attack, to charge the Jews with, on the one hand, the excessive use of violence, and, on the other, with the inability to respond to violence directed at them (as occurred in the Holocaust). Historic persecutions of the Jews and ongoing tensions with the Arab world since the founding of the state of Israel continue to provide occasions for Jews to construe anew the meaning of Purim and the tyranny of new Hamans who seek their destruction.

Purim is an official holiday in Israel.

J. Gordon Melton

See also: Calendars, Religious; Judaism.

References

Eckstein, Yecheil. *What You Should Know About Jews and Judaism*. Waco, TX: Word Books, 1984.

Greenberg, Irving. *The Jewish Way: Living the Holidays*. New York: Jason Aronson, 1998.

Horowitz, Elliott. *Reckless Rites: Purim and the Legacy of Jewish Violence*. Princeton, NJ: Princeton University Press, 2008.

Posner, Raphael, Uri Kaploun, and Sherman Cohen, eds. *Jewish Liturgy: Prayer and Synagogue Service through the Ages*. New York: Leon Amiel Publisher/Jerusalem: Keter Publishing House, 1975.

Schauss, Hayyim. *The Jewish Festivals: A Guide to Their History and Observance*. New York: Schocken, 1996.

Putuo Shan

Putuo Shan is an island off the coast of Zhejiang Province in China, east of Ningpo and south of Shanghai. Mount Putuo, though rising only a few hundred feet above the surrounding sea, is one of the four sacred mountains of Chinese Buddhism, the mountain of the south.

The island was identified as the home of Guan Yin (Avalokitesvara, Kuan Yin, Kwan Yin, or in Japan, Kannon, and in Tibet, Chenrezig), the bodhisattva or goddess of compassion/mercy, toward the end of the first millennium CE. To this end, a story was related about a princess named Miao Shan who was an emanation of the bodhisattva, and who lived on the island in the seventh century.

Among the early stories that have accumulated about the island, one tells of an Indian monk who

Puji Temple, built in 916, is a Buddhist temple located on the island of Putuo Shan in Zhejiang Province, China. (Chen Kehai/Dreamstime.com)

arrived on the island during the reign of Tang dynasty Emperor Xuanxong (847–860). According to the account, the monk not only attended lectures given by the Bodhisattva Avalokitesvara, but was given a seven-hued stone. A half century later, an eminent Japanese monk named Huie was stranded on Putuo Shan while attempting to deliver a statue of Guan Yin to Japan from Wu Tai Shan. In his stress, he prayed to the goddess, who relieved his situation. Rather than continue his journey, he stayed on the island and saw to the construction of a temple in which he placed the statue he was carrying. This temple is now known as the Bukenqu (or Reluctant to Go) Guan Yin Temple (now evolved to become Puji Temple, the largest on the island).

Additional temples would be constructed over the succeeding centuries, of which some 20 remain today. Of the 20, 3 stand out. Puji, Fayu and Huiji are each large temple complexes and known for their impressive architecture.

Puji Temple originated in 1080 and now covers some 45,932 square feet. In Great Yuantiong Hall, there are a 21-foot-high statue of the goddess of mercy and small ones of her reputed 32 incarnations. The Fayu Temple's Yuantong Hall is known for the many dragons, a reminder of its origins as a gift from the emperor. Inside a large ball hangs from the ceiling. On each of eight surrounding vertical pillars is carved a dragon that rears its head as if in a scramble for the ball. A ninth dragon comes out of the ceiling. At the highest point in the Fayu complex one finds the Treasured Pearl Guan Yin Hall, dominated by a large Guan Yin statue made of pure gold with a large pearl shining in the middle of her chest.

The Huiji Temple is located at the crest of Mount Putuo and provides a broad view of the vast stretch of the sea. It is unique on the island as it is a temple focused on Gautama Buddha as the main object of worship rather than Guan Yin.

The main additional attraction on Putuo Shan is the Guan Yin mega-statue. The statue is 108 feet tall and weighs more than 77 tons. When erected it was the largest bronze Guan Yin statue in the world and has become the symbol of Putuo Shan. Its base is a museum; Gongde Hall houses one room with 500 small bronze statues of Guan Yin, each with a distinct posture, and another room with various relief sculptures on wood and jade.

Three days are celebrated most seriously at Putuo Shan—Guan Yin's birthday, the 19th day of the 2nd lunar month (March); her enlightenment day on the 19th day of the 6th lunar month (June); and her renunciation day—when she become a nun—on the 19th day of the 9th lunar month (September). On these days tens of thousands of pilgrims will arrive for celebrations at the main temples that generally last three days.

A more recent event added to the Putuo Shan calendar is the annual Guan Yin Cultural Festival each November, designed to celebrate and make known the Guan Yin culture of China's Buddhism. Events begin on the festival eve when the monks of Puji Temple light up 1,000 lotus-shaped lamps from the ever-lit lamp inside Yuantong Hall. Worshipers will pass the lamps from one to another symbolizing the Buddhist light spreading to every corner on Earth. The lamp-passing ceremony leads into a display of fireworks. On the second day of the festival, worship is focused at Huiji Temple. The path to Huiji Temple consists of 1,087 stone steps, and worshippers will follow the head priest to the top of the mountain. Every nine steps they will pause to bow toward the top of the mountain

J. Gordon Melton

See also: Bodhisattva; Guan Yin's Birthday; Mahayana Buddhism.

References

Blofeld, John. *Bodhissatva of Compassion: The Mystical Tradition of Kuan Yin*. Boulder, CO: Shambhala, 1978

Isle of Mount Putuo. http://www.mtputuo.com/. Accessed May 15, 2009.

Karcher, Stephen. *Kuan Yin*. London: Time Warner, 2003.

Palmer, Ramsey Kwok. *Kuan Yin: Myths and Prophecies of the Chinese Goddess of Compassion*. San Francisco: Thorsons, 1995.

Yu, Chun-Fang. *Kuan Yin*. New York: Colombia University Press, 2000.

Q

Qadiriyya Rifa'i Sufi Order

The original Sufi teacher who established the Rifa'i Sufi Order was Ahmad al-Rifa'i (1118–1181), who was born in Basra, Iraq. Sheikh al-Rifa'i was a contemporary of Sheikh 'Abd al-Qadir Jilani in Baghdad, from whose teachings the Qadiriyya Sufi Order developed. Much of their theosophy focused upon the different stages (*maqamat*) and states (*awhal*) one needs to experience to touch God's beauty (*jamal*). "Love is fire" is a common phrase among the Rifa'i Sufis, who assert that love piety is essential for the mystical experience.

Egyptian Rifa'i Sufis have an intense veneration of the Prophet and his family; Central Asian Rifa'is are distinguished by the practice of piercing their skin with swords and eating glass during *dhikr* ("remembrance of Allah" devotional) sessions. The dhikr sessions include *verd* (spiritual readings) and practicing *tesbih* (repeating the names of God with the aid of a rosary). Today, the Rifa'i Sufis are located in Iraq, Turkey, Egypt, Syria, Palestine, Lebanon, Central Asia, and Southeastern Europe.

A new lineage of the Rifaiyya began early in the 20th century. It grew from the ruins of a prayer house (*tekke*) located in Kasimpasha, now a suburb of Istanbul, and the work of Sheikh Muhammad Ansari, an Iraqi who moved to Erzincan in northeastern Turkey in the early 1900s. A descendant of both 'Abd al-Qadir Jilani and Ahmad al-Rifa'i, he had become sheikh of the Rifa'i Order. In Turkey he met Sheikh Abdullah Hashimi, a Qadiri, and they worked together for many years. Eventually Sheikh Hashimi sent Ansari to Istanbul to establish the Qadiri Rifa'i Tariqa Order and revive the prayer house.

Sheikh Ansari headed the Qadiriyya Rifa'i Tariqa in Istanbul from 1915 until his death. His son, Sheikh Muhyiddin Ansari, succeeded him and spread the Order throughout Turkey, Germany, and the former Yugoslavia. He was succeeded in 1978 by Sheikh Nureddin Ozal. In May 1993, Sheikh Ozal passed away and Sheikh Taner Ansari became the new leader. Soon afterward, Sheikh Taner moved to the United States, where the center of the order is now located.

Qadiriyya Rifa'i Order
PO Box 833
Nassau, NY 12123
http://www.qadiri-rifai.org/

Qamar-ul Huda

See also: Devotion/Devotional Traditions; Qadiriyya Sufi Order; Sufism.

References

Blakney, Richard, trans. *The Eye of the Heart.* Istanbul: Redhouse Press, 1988.

De Jong, Frederick. *Turuq and Turuq-Linked Institutions in Nineteenth-Century Egypt.* Leiden: Brill, 1978.

Tanner Ansari er Rafai el Qadiri, Es-Seyyid Es-Shaykh. *The Sun Will Rise in the West: The Holy Trail.* Ansari Publications, 2000.

Trimingham, Spencer. *The Sufi Orders in Islam.* Oxford: Clarendon Press, 1971.

Qadiriyya Sufi Order

The Qadiriyya Sufi Order, named after 'Abd al-Qadir al-Jilani (d. 1166), was founded in Mesopotamia approximately 800 years ago. It is one of the oldest Sufi orders in existence. Al-Jilani is considered to be one of the greatest Sufi teachers of his time, referred to as "sheikh of sheikhs." The development of the Order and of its teachings is credited to his sons, 'Abd al-'Aziz and 'Abd al-Razzaq.

The Qadiri tradition includes philanthropic activities, meditative prayers to God called *dhikr*, specialized prayers, invocations, the use of music and poetry for spirituality, and special attention to studies in the Koran, law, and philosophy. The Sufi Order adheres to hierarchies of a Sufi society, where the elder Qadiri sheikh stands as the primary teacher and supervisor of all the disciples. Al-Jilani originally came from the Persian province of Gilan and settled in Baghdad. The Qadiriyya Order eventually spread to most major centers in the Islamic regions: Iran, Syria, Egypt, Spain, Lebanon, North and West Africa, South Asia, China, Turkey, Central Asia, eastern Africa, Bosnia, Macedonia, and Indonesia. Recently, the Order has established centers in many major cities in the Western world as well.

There is no central headquarters for the Order, but it may be contacted through Al-Baz Publishing, Incorporated.

Al-Baz Publishing, Inc.
1516 NW 38th Street
Oakland Park, FL 33334
http://www.al-baz.com/ (Al-Baz Publishing website)
http://www.al-baz.com/shaikhjilani.shtml (information about al-Jilani)

Qamar-ul Huda

See also: Qadiriyya Rifa'i Sufi Order; Sufism.

References

Aini, Mehmet Ali. *Un grand saint de l'Islam, 'Abd al-Qadir Guilani, 1077–1166.* Paris: Paul Geuthner, 1967.

Chabbi, Jacqueline. "Abd al-Kadir al-Djilani, personnage historique." *Studia Islamica* 38 (1973): 75–106.

Petrushevsky, I. P. *Islam in Iran.* Albany: State University of New York Press, 1985.

al-Tadifi, Muhammad ibn Yahya. *Qala'id al-Jawahir, or Necklaces of Gems.* N.p., n.d.

■ Qatar

Dawlat Qatar (the state of Qatar) is a small country of some 4,416 square miles, located on a peninsula that juts out from Arabia into the Persian Gulf. To the west is the island nation of Bahrain and to the south is Saudi Arabia. Long-standing border disputes with its neighbors were finally resolved in 2001. The original Arab population of the region received Islam in the seventh century CE and in successive centuries has also received significant numbers of immigrants, especially from Yemen, Palestine, Egypt, Pakistan, India, and Iran. Only 40 percent of the present population of 825,000 are native Qataris. Qataris are now the wealthiest per capita population in the world.

Qatar was conquered in 1076 by Bahrain and remained under Bahrain's hegemony until the 19th century, when the al-Tani family rose to power and led the fight for independence, which was finally obtained in 1868. The wealth of the country was traditionally built on the very fine pearls that came from the coastal waters, but demand for Qatari pearls collapsed in the 1930s because of Japanese competition. Qatar switched to oil, which has made it a wealthy nation. It is currently headed by Sheikh Hamad bin Khalifa th-Thani (b. 1950), to whom power passed in 1995.

Islam is the official religion of the country and any form of proselytization of Muslims is prohibited by law. Also, other religions are not allowed to construct and use church buildings. The majority of Qataris are Muslims and follow the strict Wahhabi School, which also dominates neighboring Saudi Arabia. However, the many immigrant groups that have moved into the country have brought other forms of Islam with them (for example, the Muslims from Iran tend to be Shias).

Christianity had spread across the Arabian Peninsula in the second and third centuries CE, but it was completely obliterated after the rise of Islam. The Roman Catholic Church attempted to rebuild a Christian presence in the area, beginning in 1841 in Aden. A vicariate was created in 1889, but it is now headquartered in Abu Dhabi, United Arab Emirates. There has been little response to the church in Qatar. A single priest resides in Doha.

Mosque outside the Khalifa sports stadium, Doha, Qatar. (Paul Cowan/Dreamstime.com)

Qatar

Religion	Followers in 1970	Followers in 2010	% of Population	Annual % growth 2000–2010	Followers in 2025	Followers in 2050
Muslims	106,000	738,000	83.4	5.70	909,000	1,091,000
Christians	4,800	84,700	9.6	1.87	110,000	136,000
Roman Catholics	680	62,000	7.0	2.25	80,000	100,000
Anglicans	700	7,000	0.8	0.00	8,000	9,000
Independents	450	4,900	0.6	−1.90	7,500	9,500
Hindus	0	22,500	2.5	5.24	28,000	34,000
Agnostics	100	20,800	2.4	4.87	30,000	40,000
Buddhists	0	17,000	1.9	5.24	22,000	27,000
Baha'is	300	1,400	0.2	5.93	2,400	3,700
Atheists	0	600	0.1	5.24	1,000	1,500
Total population	**111,000**	**885,000**	**100.0**	**5.24**	**1,102,000**	**1,333,000**

Protestant and Orthodox Christians are represented among the expatriates working in the oil field. The Arab American Oil Company employs chaplains who hold services. The Christian Brethren, one branch of the Plymouth Brethren movement, has organized several congregations. An Anglican chaplain from the Episcopal Church in Jerusalem and the Middle East resides in Abu Dhabi and also visits Qatar to conduct services.

QATAR

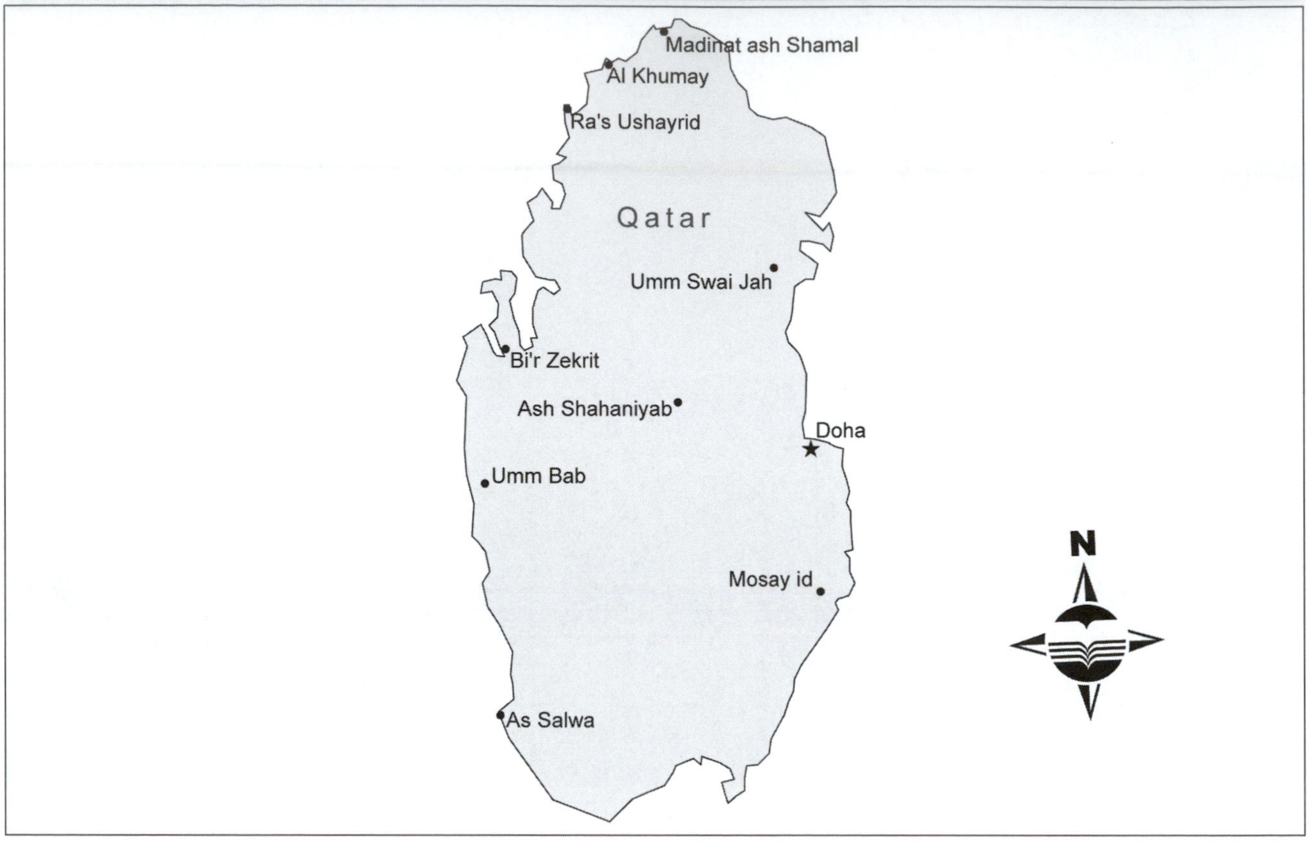

Since World War II, the Baha'i Faith has emerged in Qatar. It originated in nearby Iran, just across the Persian Gulf.

J. Gordon Melton

See also: Baha'i Faith; Christian Brethren; Episcopal Church in Jerusalem and the Middle East; Roman Catholic Church; Wahhabi Islam.

References

Anscombe, Frederick F. *The Ottoman Gulf: The Creation of Kuwait, Saudi Arabia, and Qatar.* New York: Columbia University Press, 1997.

Horner, N. A. "Present-day Christianity in the Gulf States of the Arabian Peninsula." *Occasional Bulletin of Missionary Research* 2 (April 1978): 53–63.

Rahman, Habibur. *The Emergence of Qatar*. New York: Taylor and Francis, 2006.

Vine, P., and P. Casey. *The Heritage of Qatar.* London: IMMEL Publishing, 1992.

Qigong

Qigong (also spelled Qi Gong and Chi-kung) is a Chinese tradition of mind-body training combining breath control, slow-motion gymnastics, and meditation. The term combines the Chinese characters *qi* (literally, "breath"; can also mean "vital breath" or "cosmic energy") and *gong* (literally "effort"; often understood as "discipline," "virtuosity," "spiritual power"). Techniques now known as qigong are mentioned in ancient Chinese texts from the sixth century BCE and earlier, including the *Laozi* and *Zhuangzi*, and became integral components of Chinese medicine, martial arts, and religion, notably Daoism and Chinese Mahayana Buddhism. A wide range of breathing, gymnastic, meditation, and visualization techniques, joined in an infinitely extensible array of combinations, could be used for the healing of illnesses, for nurturing health and longevity, or for spiritual transcendence and immortality.

The use of the term "qigong" as a single category covering all such techniques can be traced to the mid-20th century, and is the result of modernizing attempts to secularize useful Chinese traditions by extracting them from religion and superstition and reorganizing them into a scientific system. This project was carried out in the 1950s by the health authorities of the newly established People's Republic of China. Qigong was applied in modern clinical settings, and disseminated on a wide scale following the model of mass calisthenics. Banned during the Cultural Revolution (1966–1976), qigong reappeared in the late 1970s. Reports of healing through "external *qi*" (emission of qi without physical contact between a healer and a patient) caused a sensation in the Chinese press, while thousands of charismatic qigong healers attracted followings in the millions, and qigong became almost synonymous in popular discourse with paranormal phenomena and psychic powers. Some of China's leading scientists and senior Communist Party leaders supported the movement and facilitated its expansion.

In the 1980s and 1990s, a time when most forms of religion had been destroyed or strictly controlled in mainland China for decades, qigong became the main legal outlet for a rediscovery of China's spiritual traditions, and a mass movement within which hundreds of popular groups appeared. Many of these were full-fledged new religious movements with sophisticated China-wide or even global organizations—the largest of which, with tens of millions of practitioners, were Zhong Gong, founded by Zhang Hongbao in 1987, and Falun Gong, founded by Li Hongzhi in 1992. By the mid-1990s, the Chinese authorities, sensitive to accusations of quackery and pseudo-science being leveled at qigong by critics, and concerned about the growing influence of charismatic qigong masters, attempted to impose stricter regulations on qigong. Li Hongzhi immigrated to the United States in 1996 and Zhang Hongbao went into hiding (he reappeared on the American island of Guam in 2000). Most qigong groups declined or adopted a low profile. But Falun Gong, which, in addition to qigong exercises, had strongly moralistic teachings and a messianic, apocalyptic eschatology, continued to grow rapidly. Rejecting state regulations and criticisms from the official media, Falun Gong practitioners often staged protests and sit-ins. After 10,000 followers surrounded Zhongnanhai (the headquarters of the Chinese Communist leadership) in a silent protest on April 25, 1999, the government banned Falun Gong as an "evil cult" on July 22, 1999. Although other forms of qigong remained legal, in practice most other popular groups were dismantled, and only five sets of exercises, derived from the medical *daoyin* tradition, were authorized. Qigong ceased to exist as a mass movement in China, although the techniques continued to be practiced, under different names, in other contexts such as Daoism or Chinese medical health cultivation.

Most of the leading qigong masters of the 1980s and 1990s immigrated to North America, Europe, and Australia, contributing to the spread of qigong in Western countries. One of the first to introduce qigong to a Western audience, in 1979 as "Taoist esoteric yoga," was Mantak Chia (b. 1944), a Chinese born in Thailand, who had settled in New York and founded an organization known as Healing Tao. His disciple Michael Winn became one of the leading advocates of qigong in the United States. In Western countries, qigong found a welcoming niche in the diverse milieu of New Age spirituality, alternative healing, and Chinese medicine/martial arts/Tai chi and Daoism.

David A. Palmer

See also: Daoism; Energy; Falun Gong; Healing Tao; Mahayana Buddhism; Meditation; New Age Movement; Zhong Gong.

References

Palmer, David A. *Qigong Fever. Body, Science and Utopia in China*. New York: Columbia University Press, 2007.

Komjathy, Louis. "Qigong in America." In *Daoist Body Cultivation*, edited by Livia Kohn. Cambridge: Three Pines Press, 2006.

Quanzhen Daoism

Quanzhen, which translates as "Complete Realization," or "Complete Perfection," is one of two schools that today represent the Daoist alchemical tradition, in contrast to the liturgical tradition of Zhengyi Daoism. Quanzhen is also sometimes erroneously known as

Daoist monks look after a shrine where Chinese faithful pray and burn incense at the White Cloud Temple in Beijing. (AP Photo/Elizabeth Dalziel)

Northern Daoism, and Zhengyi is called Southern Daoism. About 80 percent of organized Daoism in mainland China belongs to this sect, which also prevails in Hong Kong.

For all its importance, Quanzhen is almost completely unknown in the West, where there has been little academic study of it. Many of the newer Western Daoist groups (Taoist Chi Society, Healing Tao Centers) have some relation to Quanzhen, though the exact nature of these ties remains unclear.

Emerging out of the ashes of war-torn 12th-century China, Quanzhen became the most important religious movement in China during the Yuan dynasty. Quanzhen was founded by Wang Zhe, who was also known by his religious name as Wang Chongyang (1113–1170). After living in seclusion on Mount Zhongnan in Shaanxi Province, he received seven disciples, who spread the new teaching. The most famous of these disciples was Qiu Chuji (1148–1227), who in a celebrated account in Chinese history accepted an invitation in 1219 to teach the Mongol Emperor Genghis Khan (ca. 1162–1227) about longevity. Because of this, many early khans showered patronage on Quanzhen Daoism. Indeed, Quanzhen Daoists were tax exempt and became semiofficial government representatives.

In the Qing dynasty, Qiu Chuji was retroactively given credit for founding the Longmen Pai (Dragon Gate Branch) of Quanzhen Daoism, the dominant sect today. Actually, Longmen Pai can only be definitively traced to the founding of the famous Baiyunguan (White Cloud Temple) in Beijing in 1656. In the Qing dynasty, Baiyunguan became the center for all Daoist schools, overseeing ordination, and many schools officially subsumed themselves into Longmen Pai. Today, Baiyunguan is the headquarters for both Quanzhen Daoism and the Chinese Taoist Association.

Quanzhen is a monastic and celibate tradition. Monks and nuns wear blue robes and topknots. The main altars of Quanzhen temples traditionally enshrine the Three Pure Ones, the high gods of Daoism, emanations of Dao. They are seated in meditation, rather like Buddhas. Indeed, Quanzhen owes not only its iconography but its architecture and philosophy to Buddhism. It ascetically rejects daily comforts, and it believes in rebirth and *karma*. Its emphasis on quiet sitting (*jingzuo*) was influenced by Chan Buddhism. Quanzhen is based on spiritual and moral cultivation, rather than on philosophical, scriptural, or ritual traditions.

That cultivation also incorporates much of "Inner Alchemy," a tradition concerning personal transformation that has been preserved largely due to the efforts of Quanzhen. The patron saint of Quanzhen Inner Alchemy is Lu Dongbin, a Tang dynasty sage. Lu Dongbin is head of the eight immortals. Depicted as a scholar with a fly whisk and a demon-slaying sword, he is a common subject in Yuan dynasty drama and popular art.

One of Wang Chongyang's aims was to bring the Three Teachings of China, Daoism, Confucianism, and Buddhism, into a single great system once more. Quanzhen borrowed not only from Buddhism but also from neo-Confucianism. In the 19th century, Quanzhen movements were popularized, particularly those involving the new divinatory craze of spirit writing, in which a sharp stick attached to a frame moved automatically over a planchette of sand. Many of these sects make up the current Hong Kong Daoist scene. Many temples there have a truly combinatory pantheon: Lu Dongbin, representing Daoism; the Jade Emperor, representing the celestial bureaucracy, hence Confucianism; and Guanyin, the Sinicized, feminized form of Avalokiteshvara, the bodhisattva of compassion, representing Buddhism.

Baiyunguan
6 Baiyunguan Jie
Xibianmenwai, Xuanwu District
Beijing
China

Elijah Siegler

See also: Alchemy, Daoist; Daoism; Healing Tao; Monasticism; Taoist Tai Chi Society; Wang Chongyang; Zhengyi Daoism.

References

Tsui, Bartholomew P. M. *Taoist Tradition and Change: The Story of the Complete Perfection Sect in Hong Kong*. Hong Kong: Christian Study Centre on Chinese Religion and Culture, 1991.

Wong, Eva. *Seven Taoist Masters*. Boston: Shambhala, 1990.

R

Rada Religion

The Rada religion (variously referred to as Alladah, Arara, or Arada) is a Caribbean religion derived from the name of an African city located along the Mina coast on the Bight of Benin. The city of Arada served as an important religious and political center during the 17th and 18th centuries, and Rada spirits (*lwa*) occupy a central place in African-derived religions throughout the Caribbean. Rada spirits are especially prominent in Haiti, where all African spirits are grouped into families, pantheons, and/or *nachon*s, and every lwa (whether a member of the Petro, Ibo, or Kongo nachon) is believed to have a Rada counterpart (Desmangles 1992, 94). Rada spirits are also present in the African-derived religions of Cuba, the Dominican Republic, Jamaica, Barbados, St. Kitts, Grenada, Carriacou (the Grenadines), and St. Vincent.

The major Rada spirits include Dada Segbo (the creator), Daugbwe (the serpent), Elegba (spirit of the crossroads), Sakpata (an Earth spirit), and Ogou (the spirit of iron). Some observers associate Rada lwa with benevolent forces and contrast them with Petro lwa, who are seen as bitter and aggressive. This is an oversimplification. As Desmangles (1992) points out, the distinction is not one between good and evil. Rada lwa are often conceived as gentle guardians of the universe, but they too can be unpredictable and vindictive. For example, Elegba, who directs the course of human destiny, can also cause accidents altering that destiny. All lwa have complex personalities.

The purest form of Rada ritual was on the Caribbean island of Trinidad during the late 19th century (Carr 1953). In the 1860s a free Rada population from Dahomey (now Benin) settled in the Belmont section of Port of Spain, and Abojevi Zalwenu, an African-trained diviner and herbalist, came to Trinidad to meet the religious needs of this immigrant community. Zalwenu (also known by his Creole name Robert Antoine and more popularly as "Papa Nanee") purchased acreage in Belmont, where he established a residential compound that remained a center of Rada ceremonial life until his death in 1899. In 1886, a local court convicted Zalwenu of practicing black magic (Obeah), but the conviction was overturned because Zalwenu's lawyer successfully argued that the Rada leader did not perform Obeah for money and functioned as a religious leader according to the beliefs of his followers. This case established a much-cited precedent for the cause of religious freedom in Trinidad.

Under Zalwenu, Rada ceremonies were carried out in strict accordance with African calendar cycles, and new *vodunsi* (priests) were initiated on a regular basis. Unlike other Rada ceremonies in the Caribbean, Zalwenu's Trinidad rituals closely followed 19th-century African practice. Elsewhere, however, Rada rituals contained a mixture of practices from a variety of African traditions (Petro, Kongo, and so on). These "mixed" ceremonies have preserved elements of 17th- and 18th-century Rada ritual that were lost in Africa and unknown to Zalwenu.

The Belmont place of worship, called a *vodunkwe* (house of the gods), survives, but Rada rituals have been greatly modified and the number of services, especially those involving animal sacrifices, have declined in recent years. (The author visited the compound with the late Andrew Carr in 1976, and again visited in 1985 and 1999.) In 1999 the site was used primarily as a *panyard* (musical shrine) and a center for Orisha devotees, but a number of vodunsi were in residence. In the 19th century, Zalwenu established different shrines (and stools) to the lwa at various locations around the vodunkwe. Devotees continue to make fresh blood offerings at these stools.

Rada is one of the few African-derived religions in the Caribbean where men constitute the majority of adherents. But as older members have died, they have not been replaced by younger adherents. Many Trinidadians do not distinguish the Rada lwa from other African-derived deities. Hucks (2001) suggested that Trinidadian Rada may eventually be absorbed into the more active Trinidad Orisha movement. This has not occurred. Interest in "pure" Rada continues, and Andrew Carr's 1989 study is still widely consulted, suggestive of a possible resurgence of the Rada tradition in Trinidad.

The Belmont Vodunkwe
127-129 Belmont Circular Rd.
Port of Spain
Trinidad

Stephen D. Glazier

See also: African Traditional Religions.

References

Adderley, Rosanne Marion. *"New Negroes from Africa": Slave Trade Abolition and Free African Settlement in the Nineteenth-Century Caribbean.* Bloomington: Indiana University Press, 2006.

Burton, Richard D. E. *Afro-Creole Power: Opposition and Play in the Caribbean*. Ithaca, NY: Cornell University Press, 1997.

Carr, Andrew T. *A Rada Community in Trinidad*. 1953; rpt.: Port of Spain: Paria Publishing, 1989.

Desmangles, Leslie G. *The Faces of the Gods: Vodu and Roman Catholicism in Haiti.* Chapel Hill: University of North Carolina Press, 1992.

Glazier, Stephen D. *Marchin' the Pilgrims Home: A Study of the Spiritual Baptists of Trinidad.* Salem, WI: Sheffield, 1991.

Hucks, Tracey. "Trinidad, African-Derived Religions." In *The Encyclopedia of African and African-American Religions,* edited by Stephen D. Glazier, 338–343. New York: Routledge, 2001.

Warner-Lewis, Maureen. *Trinidad Yoruba: From Mother Tongue to Memory*. Tuscaloosa: University of Alabama Press, 1996.

Radhasoami

The Radhasoami tradition was formally founded in 1861 in Agra, Uttar Pradesh, India, by Shiv Dayal Singh (1818–1878), who was associated with two Sant Mat gurus, Tulsi Sahib (1764–1848) in Hathras and Girdhari Das (d. 1861) in Agra. Shiv Dayal Singh, more popularly known as Soamiji Maharaj, advocated the practice of *surat shabd* yoga (union of the soul with the divine sound), a strict lacto-vegetarian diet, and devotion to a living guru who would guide initiates to higher regions of consciousness. The name Radhasoami (usually spelled as one word, with the variation Radhaswami) was apparently coined by one of Shiv Dayal Singh's chief disciples, Rai Salig Ram (1839–1898), who elevated his guru to the highest divine status. In Salig Ram's theology, Radha stands for soul and Soami for lord, and thus Radhasoami means "Lord of the Soul." This interpretation has been shared by almost all practitioners of the faith. The phrase is also used as a greeting between members.

After Shiv Dayal Singh's death in 1878, several disciples worked as his spiritual successors. This eventually led to a number of schisms, and it is now estimated that there are well over 100 different branches of the Radhasoami tradition worldwide. The most popular Radhasoami group in the world is the Radhasoami Satsang, Beas (Punjab), which has more than 4 million followers and centers in Europe, Africa, Asia, and North America.

Founded by Jaimal Singh (1838–1903) in 1891, the Beas Satsang (spiritual gathering) lineage of gurus have all been born Sikh. Since Radhasoami advocates devotion to a living human guru, this has naturally led to political and religious tension among orthodox Sikh groups in the Punjab.

The Radhasoamis are not a sub-sect of Sikhism, but they do share much of the Sant philosophy in common. The current leader of the Beas Satsang is Gurinder Singh Dhillon (b. 1954), who has been instrumental in expanding the property holdings of the group worldwide, including large estates in California, North Carolina, Hawaii, England, and South Africa.

Other important Radhasoami branches, each with their own unique guru lineages, include three founded in the city of Agra, India: Soami Bagh, Dayal Bagh, and Peepal Mandi. Each of these branches traces its lineage back to Shiv Dayal Singh through Rai Salig Ram (otherwise known as Huzur Maharaj). Unlike the Beas-related *satsangs* that advocate repeating the spiritual mantra of five holy names (*panch nam*), the Agra-related groups teach repetition of one holy name, Radhasoami. In addition, unlike the Beas satsangs, which argue that Radhasoami is simply a modern manifestation of Sant Mat, the "doctrine of the saints," the Agra groups also believe that their founder, Shiv Dayal Singh, was a unique and supreme incarnation of the highest lord, Anami Purush, and presented a new and higher path to God.

There are at least 100,000 followers in each of the Agra schools, though most of the disciples are Indian-born.

Arguably the most controversial guru in Radhasoami history was Faqir Chand (1886–1981), founder of the Manvta Mandir branch in Hoshiarpur, Punjab, and disciple of Shiv Brat Lal (1860–1939), who taught that all gurus are "unknowing" and that whatever miracles or visions occur in a devotee's life are directly due to his or her faith and devotion. The guru, in sum, has no paranormal powers whatsoever. Faqir's views are generally viewed in Radhasoami circles as heretical and heterodox. However, Faqir's writings have become increasingly more popular since his death.

The Radhasoami tradition has also influenced other new religious movements, including Ruhani Satsang (founded by Kirpal Singh [1894–1974], disciple of the Beas guru, Sawan Singh); ECKANKAR (founded by Paul Twitchell [ca. 1909–1971], former disciple of Kirpal Singh); Master Ching Hai Meditation Association, also known as God's Direct Contact (founded by Ching Hai [b. 1929], one-time disciple of Thakar Singh); the eclectic Movement of Spiritual Inner Awareness, founded by John-Roger Hinkins (b. 1934); Elan Vital (formerly the Divine Light Mission); and MasterPath. founded by Gary Olsen, who claims spiritual allegiance with Sawan Singh and was a former follower of ECKANKAR.

Because there are so many different gurus and branches in the Radhasoami tradition, there have been a significant number of succession disputes within the movement's history. The most contentious fight was between Soami Bagh and Dayal Bagh and resulted in a decades-long legal battle over the worship and property rights at Shiv Dayal Singh's *samadh* (burial site).

Despite these squabbles, Radhasoami is one of the fastest growing of the newer religious traditions in the world. The total number of followers worldwide (among all branches) is estimated to be well over 5 million.

David Christopher Lane

See also: ECKANKAR; Elan Vital/Divine Light Mission; Master Ching Hai Meditation Association; Movement of Spiritual Inner Awareness; Satsang Network; Sikhism/Sant Mat.

References

Juergensmeyer, Mark. *Radhasoami Reality*. Princeton, NJ: Princeton University Press, 1991.

Lane, David Christopher. *The Radhasoami Tradition*. New York: Garland Publishers, 1994.

The Unknowing Sage: The Life and Work of Baba Faqir Chand. Walnut, CA: MSAC Philosophy Group, 1993.

Raelian Movement International

The Raelian Movement International is the largest UFO religion in the world, currently claiming 80,000 members, or those who have undergone the "baptism," called the "transmission of the cellular plan," in which initiates acknowledge the extraterrestrials, the Elohim, as their Creator. The movement was founded in 1976 by Claude Vorilhon, known to his followers as Rael. He was born in Vichy, France, in 1946. He was a pop singer, a journalist, and for many years a race car driver, but has recently retired.

Rael's charismatic claim is that he is a prophet chosen by the Elohim, extraterrestrials from another planet in our galaxy. His alleged encounter with the Elohim took place on December 13, 1973 (the day of Saint Lucie, whose name means "light"), in the mountains near Clermont-Ferrand in France. A green, childlike being emerged from their ship and invited Rael

Claude Vorilhon, a former French journalist, is the spiritual leader of the Raelians. (Christopher J. Morris/ Corbis)

aboard for Bible instruction. During this time, it was revealed that Genesis was a starship's log account of the Earth colonization project of the Elohim scientists. Vorilhon learned that these scientists created the first humans in laboratories out of their own DNA. The Fall of Humanity was the consequence of forbidden science lessons taught to the little "Adams and Eves" born out of test tubes, and the casting out of Eden was the "grounding" of the original team of extraterrestrials as a punitive action, the result of a struggle between rival political factions on the home planet over the issue of whether or not earthlings should be given scientific knowledge.

The Elohim gave Vorilhon the title Rael (from Is-Rael, meaning "bearer of light") and told him that he had been chosen to found a movement that would spread globally and would demystify the world's religions with the literal truth: the message of humankind's true origins and destiny. His mission is to arrange the construction of an embassy on neutral territory in Jerusalem, where the extraterrestrials could land and meet the representatives of all the nations and be filmed by television crews.

Rael founded MADECH (Mouvement pour l'Accueil des Elohim Créateurs de l'Humanité), the forerunner of the Raelian Movement, in 1974. MADECH published Rael's account of his extraterrestrial encounter: *Le Livre qui dit la vérité: J'ai rencontré un extraterrestre* (1974). The founding of the Raelian Movement International in 1976 made the transition from ufologist club to a distinct new religious movement.

Rael encountered the extraterrestrials again on October 7, 1975, a meeting described in *They Took Me to Their Planet* (*Les Extra-terrestres m'ont emmené sur leur planète,* 1997). While on their planet, he received the hospitality of six female biological robots, with whom he spent a night of lovemaking and who taught him the sensual awareness technique to activate his psychic potential and grow new neural pathways. Sensual meditation, described in his third book, *Sensual Meditation*, involves a relaxation exercise called *harmonization avec l'infini*, a mental-anatomical tour of the body that arrives eventually at the brain, a visualization of the planet of the Elohim, and an exercise in telepathic rapport.

On this same trip, he was introduced to the mysteries of cloning and watched his own double being formed in a vat. For Raelians, the hope of immortality will be fulfilled by regeneration through science. Hence, Rael established an initiation called "the transmission of the cellular plan," which formalizes members' recognition of the Elohim as their creators. They are also encouraged to sign a contract giving a local mortuary permission, upon their decease, to remove 0.39 square inch of the "frontal bone" to be stored in a bank in Switzerland, awaiting collection by the Elohim and future cloning.

In the 21st century, the movement has received considerable publicity due to Rael's support of human cloning. On March 9, 1997, Rael announced the creation of Valiant Venture, Ltd., a company that offers Clonaid to parents who wish to clone a child, for the fee of $200,000. Another service offered by the company is Insuraclone; for $50,000, the cell of a child can be stored to be cloned in the event of an untimely death. On Boxing Day, 2002, Dr. Brigitte Boisellier, a Raelian bishop, announced in a press conference the successful birth of the first human clone. This event was an international media event, allowing Rael to fulfill his divine mandate to "spread the message"—but the cloned baby never materialized.

Raelian membership is divided into two levels: the committed core group of Guides, who make up the group's hierarchy, called the Structure, and the most recently joined members or loosely affiliated Raelians, who after baptism received the bulletin *Apocalypse*. The six levels in the pyramidal Structure are, from low to high, assistant animator, animator, assistant guide, priest guide, bishop guide, and finally, the planetary guide or Guide of Guides (Rael).The priest and bishop guides are empowered to transmit the cellular codes, or "baptize," new members. The Guide of guides (Rael) is re-elected by the bishops every seven years. There is also a Council of Discipline with the power to excommunicate errant members, as well as an administrative body, the Council of the Wise.

Rael, called the "Last of Forty Prophets," was born soon after the first atomic explosion in Hiroshima in 1945, when humanity entered the "Age of Apocalypse." Raelians believe that during this age of scientific revelation, humanity will come to understand its true origins. "With the Elohim's guidance and humanity's right choices, this age holds marvelous potentialities: liberation, power, quasi-immortality, once the Elohim arrive and bequeath to their creations scientific knowledge that will enable humans to travel through space and colonize virgin planets in our own image."

The group is known as the Raelian Religion in the United States, where it has won tax-exempt status. It is known as the Raelian Church in Canada, where it is seeking recognition as a religion. The Raelian movement was established in Quebec in 1976. The Canadian movement was the second of the international movements after France. By March 1995, the movement had acquired religious corporation status from the Quebec government. When the Raelian Church of Quebec applied for tax-exempt status, it was denied on the grounds that "the Raelian 'gods' did not meet the standards (as material rather than transcendent beings) of the *loi d'impôt*."

The central headquarters of the international movement is in Quebec, at UFOland in Valcourt, where Rael resides, though the address of the international headquarters is formally listed Geneva, Switzerland. There is also a retreat, called Eden, in Alby, France. There are more than 5,000 Raelians in Canada, nearly all of them in Quebec. The movement has branches in 84 countries, though most members are found in French-speaking Europe, Quebec, and Japan.

The Raelians have four large gatherings annually on dates that commemorate Rael's encounters with the Elohim. Members also participate in an annual one-week *stage d'éveil* in a rural setting, featuring daily lectures, sensual meditation, fasting, non-mandatory nudity, sensory awareness exercises, and sexual experimentation—the ultimate goal being to experience the "cosmic orgasm."

Raelian Movement, International
PO Box 225
CH-1211 Geneva 8
Switzerland
http://www.rael.org/ (multilingual)

Susan Palmer

See also: UFO Religions.

References

Bouchard, Alain. "Mouvement Raelien." In *Nouvel Age . . . Nouvelles Croyances*. Written under the direction of the Centre d'Information sur les Nouvelles Religions. Montreal: Editions Paulines & Mediaspaul, 1989.

Palmer, Susan J. *Aliens Adored: Rael's Ufo Religion*. New Brunswick, NJ: Rutgers University Press, 2004.

Palmer, Susan J. *Il Movimiento raelieni*. Torino, Italy: Editions Elle DiCi, 2000.

Palmer, Susan J. "The Raelians Are Coming: The Future of a UFO Religion." In *Religion in a Changing World,* edited by Madeleine Cousineau, 136–146. Westport, CT: Praeger, 1998.

Vorilhon, Claude. *Le Livre qui dit la vérité*. Vaduz, Liechtenstein: Fondation Raelienne, 1974.

Vorilhon, Claude. *Les Extra-terrestres m'ont emmené sur leur planète*. Brantome, France: L'Edition du Message, 1977.
Vorilhon, Claude. *La Meditation Sensuelle.* Vaduz, Liechtenstein: Fondation Raelienne, 1980.

Ramadan

According to numerous accounts of the Prophet Muhammad, fasting was a regular part of his practice and he admonished his followers to follow his example as they were able. For him, a normal routine was to fast during the daylight hours and pray during the evening (his prayer time taking from his sleeping hours). For followers, these days of fasting through the years were seen as supererogatory acts, above and beyond the basic requirements of the faith. The fasting done by Muhammad, though not required of the faithful, set the pattern to be followed in the required month of fasting known as Ramadan.

One of the five pillars of Islam, Ramadan is an annual fast named for the ninth month of the Islamic calendar when it occurs. As the Islamic calendar is a strictly lunar calendar, Ramadan occurs at a different point in the Common Era calendar each year. Ramadan recalls the beginning of Muhammad's writing down the Koran. It is a requirement of all, and those who because of illness cannot fast, are required to make up the days once they again attain their health.

Fasting begins at daybreak, defined as the moment one can discern the first streak of dawn against the black horizon (usually an hour and a half before sunrise). The fast continues until sunset. The day of fasting begins with a predawn meal (*sahur*) and ends with a light fast-breaking meal (*iftar*) that is followed by a time of prayer. People may gather at the mosque at the end of the day to share the iftar and hold communal

Thousands of devout Muslims congregate at the Jama Mosque in New Delhi, India, for prayers on the first day of the Eid celebration marking the end of Ramadan. (AP/Wide World Photos)

prayers (*tarawih*). Muhammad advised people to break the fast each day quickly; thus it became common to prepare food ahead of time and have it ready as soon as the sun descended beyond the horizon.

The practice of fasting is seen as one of the ways, if not the best way, to please God, though it is meant as a means of teaching self-discipline, not only about food and the body, but about life in general and relationships with others. Thus, during the fast, one takes pains not to use questionable language or show anger, and one responds to any screaming or shouting with the simple observation that she or he is fasting. Those who have taken up bad habits (such as the consumption of tobacco or alcohol) have Ramadan as a time to drop such practices.

Ramadan is also a time for additional prayer, the reading of the Koran, and the showing of generosity. Muslims are also required to pay a percentage of their income for the care of the poor (another pillar of the faith), and Ramadan is often chosen as the time to fulfill that obligation.

While Ramadan as a whole is considered a remembrance of the giving of the Koran, one night in particular, called Laylat al-Qadir, the Night of Power, is commemorated as the anniversary of the actual day that the Koran first began to be revealed to Muhammad by the angel Gabriel.

The Night of Power is usually observed on the 27th day of Ramadan, but it also carries with it a certain element of mystery. It is a night marked by the descent of angels from the heavens to the earthly realm. For those engaged in prayer it is a time to receive mercy and protection from every bad thing. Muhammad requested his followers to search for it and attempt to discern when it occurred, noting only that it was one night in the last 10 of the 30-day month. He noted that it was only one night and that the time of receiving its benefits lasted until dawn. Appropriate actions for the night include prayer, self-examination, the asking of forgiveness for oneself and all Muslims, listening to sermons and engaging in discussion concerning the Night of Power, and remembering Allah.

Ramadan is immediately followed by Eid ul-Fitr, the Festival of Breaking the Fast, a feast day that marks the end of the fasting period. It is the first day of the 10th month in the Islamic calendar (months being marked from new moon to new moon). The day is a truly festive occasion, being seen as a sign of God's blessing following the time of testing and discipline, and is marked by donning fresh (and/or new) clothes, donating food to the poor (Zakat al-Fitr), and visiting family, friends, and neighbors. The day begins early in the morning with prayers in the local mosque.

In countries in which Islam is the predominant religion, the society is organized to accommodate Ramadan. Muslims living in other countries have imported the practice and accommodate their lives so as to participate fully in the fast and other activities.

J. Gordon Melton

See also: Devotion/Devotional Traditions; Islam; Mosques; Muhammad.

References

Algül, Hüseyin. *The Blessed Days and Nights of the Islamic Year*. Somerset, NJ: Light, 2005.

al-Jibouri, Yasin T. *Fast of the Month of Ramadan: Philosophy and Ahkam*. Falls Church, VA: International Islamic Society of Virginia, 1994.

Budak, Ali. *Fasting in Islam and the Month of Ramadan*. Somerset, NJ: The Light, 2005.

Robinson, Neal. *Islam; A Concise Introduction*. London: Curzon Press, 1999.

Ramtha's School of Enlightenment

Ramtha's School of Enlightenment was founded in the late 1980s in Yelm, Washington, by JZ Knight (b. 1946), who was the most popular of a new wave of channelers that had emerged in the West along with the New Age movement. In 1977 the spiritual entity Ramtha appeared to Knight, then a housewife in Tacoma, Washington, and introduced himself as the Enlightened One. The next year, Knight began to channel Ramtha publicly. She initially held weekend sessions called Dialogues, where she would channel Ramtha. The Dialogues were held around the United States and increasingly in several foreign countries, and many of these sessions were later transcribed and published as books or made available on videotape. However, in 1988 the decision was made to discontinue the Dialogues and to concentrate on developing a body of students who wished to go more deeply into the process of actualizing the enlightenment about which Ramtha had spoken.

According to the channeled messages, Ramtha is a 35,000-year-old warrior who at the height of his power was almost killed. He found enlightenment during his time of recovery and eventually ascended to a spiritual realm. Once Ramtha's School of Enlightenment was formed, Ramtha began to teach a set of practices that would allow students to access and become directly aware of the spiritual realms. The basic practice, termed "energy and consciousness," involves controlled breathing and *kundalini* yoga, in which latent energy believed to be located at the base of the spine is allowed to rise up the spine and bring its energy and enlightenment to the self.

Ramtha describes the universe as divided into seven levels, at the center of which is the Void (Pure Potentiality) out of which the other levels are derived. The seventh level is the visible world, into which individuals as spiritual entities have come. The spiritual entities created this world, but then they became trapped in it and forgetful of their spiritual origin. Enlightenment comes as one is able to remember and experience one's spiritual origin and can freely navigate the several levels.

The school is organized as an Esoteric mystery school. Students initially pass through a graded curriculum before being admitted to the larger student body of those who continually work on their self-awareness as spiritual beings. The larger student body gathers at the headquarters twice each year for advanced retreats, at which time new teachings and perspectives are released by Ramtha.

Some 3,000 students are active in the school. During the 1990s, all events were held at Yelm, but at the close of the decade Knight began to travel again and introductory sessions concerning Ramtha are now being held annually by senior students at locations in Europe, South Africa, and Australia. Literature is published in Spanish, German, Italian, French, Japanese, and Norwegian.

During the early 1990s, Knight and the school passed through a period of intense controversy, much of which was related to the secretive Esoteric nature of the school's work. In the mid-1990s Knight opened up the school to a group of scholars, including several psychologists who ran a set of tests on Knight and some of her leading students. Their positive reports concerning her psychological health and the extraordinary nature of her channeling activity largely ended the attacks she had previously experienced.

At the beginning of the new century, one of Ramtha's students who was a filmmaker produced what became an award-winning movie, *What the Bleep Do We Know*, initially released in 2004. The movie, which stars Oscar-winning actress Marlee Matlin, explored the relationship between quantum physics, neurology, and molecular biology and the world of spirituality and Esoteric teachings, especially privileging Ramtha's teachings. JZ Knight (channeling Ramtha) and several of her students appeared in the movie and it quickly gained a following beyond the school's membership. The response prompted an expanded version with additional material dealing with questions raised by the original movie; it was released as *Down the Rabbit Hole*. The movie became a vital factor in the continued growth of the school.

Beginning in the 1990s, Ramtha began to train a set of teachers who now have assumed responsibilities for most of the introductory course for the school and have aided the global expansion that annually includes events at locations around the world. Coordinators for local activities have been appointed in some 35 countries.

Ramtha School of Enlightenment
PO Box 579
Yelm, WA 98597
http://www.ramtha.com/

J. Gordon Melton

See also: New Age Movement; Western Esoteric Tradition; Yoga.

References

Knight, JZ. *A State of Mind*. New York: Warner Books, 1997.

Melton, J. Gordon. *Finding Enlightenment: Ramtha's School of Ancient Wisdom*. Hillsboro, OR: Beyond Worlds Publishing, 1998.

Ramtha (through JZ Knight). *A Beginner's Guide to Creating Reality*. Yelm, WA: JZK Publishing, 2000.

Ramtha (through JZ Knight). *A Master's Reflections on the History of Humanity*. 2 vols. Yelm, WA: JZK Publishing, 2001–2002.

Ramtha (through JZ Knight). *Ramtha*. Ed. by Steven Weinberg. Eastsound, WA: Sovereignty, 1986.

Ramtha (through JZ Knight). *That Elixir Called Love*. Yelm, WA: JZK Publishing, 2003.

Simmon, Greg. *These Things You Shall Do . . . And Greater: The Physics of Change*. Rainier, WA: Mulai de Guise Publishing, 2006.

Rastafarians

Rastafarianism is a social, political, and religious movement that began on the Caribbean island of Jamaica in the late 1920s. Followers of the movement, sometimes called Rastas or Dreads, are best known as the originators of the popular musical style reggae, for their extensive ritual use of *ganja* (marijuana), and for wearing their hair in long, rope-like braids called dreadlocks. Since its emergence in the ghettos of West Kingston, the Rastafarian movement has transformed itself from an obscure religion of the oppressed into a dominant cultural force. Music has played a significant role in this transformation. Ganja has also played a significant and changing role. Following slavery, black Jamaicans used ganja as a palliative, but it is only in the 20th century that ganja assumed symbolic importance and began to be identified as a "holy herb."

The name Rastafarianism is borrowed from Ras Tafari, a name for former Emperor Haile Selassie I of Ethiopia (1892–1975), who reigned from 1916 to 1974. Although a number of the founders of Rastafarianism (notably Leonard Howell [1898–1981] and Archibald Dunckley) preached that Haile Selassie was a Living God, Emperor Selassie himself remained a devout leader within the Ethiopian Orthodox Tewahedo

Rastafari men play drums, Jamaica. Rastafari is a religious and political movement that began in Jamaica in the 1930s. (Bojan Brecelj/Corbis)

Church. When Selassie visited Jamaica in 1966, he was greatly puzzled by Rastafarians, who seemed to be worshipping him.

Although there are many variants within Rastafarianism, the 1983 Rastafari Theocratic Assembly passed a resolution declaring a single variant—that associated with the House of Nyahbinghi—as the orthodox faith. The House of Nyahbinghi creed proclaims Haile Selassie a Living God and states that all African peoples are one and that the descendants of those who were taken from Africa to be slaves in Babylon will be repatriated. It is contended that all African people are descendants of the ancient Hebrews and that the reason Africans now live outside Africa is that their descendants disobeyed Ja (short for Jehovah, the God of the Hebrews), who then punished them by making them slaves to whites. Haile Selassie I was expected to arrange for the return of all people of African descent to Africa, but following his death in 1975, there has been less emphasis on a physical return to Africa and greater emphasis on a spiritual return.

Rastafarianism today is a worldwide movement with membership in Jamaica, other Caribbean islands, the United States, Canada, Australia, New Zealand (the Maori), South Africa, Ghana, Ethiopia, islands of the South Pacific, and parts of Western Europe (especially England, Holland, and Germany). Native Americans (the Hopi) have also been influenced by the group's theology. Although contemporary Rastas represent many races and nationalities, the religion began as an African American nationalist movement. Contemporary adherents stress that it is much more than a nationalist movement. It is a way of life. Many Rastas prefer to describe their religious involvement in terms of *livity,* the adoption of a lifestyle informed by strict theocratic principles.

One central Rastafarian ritual, called "reasoning," is a group discussion and debate about the interpretation of biblical texts, local politics, predictions about the future, and commentary on world events. During these ceremonies Rastas also smoke ganja, which, many believe, brings them closer to Ja. For a majority of Rastas, smoking ganja is believed to have medicinal as well as spiritual benefits. But an increasing number of Trinidad Rastas no longer smoke ganja on a regular basis.

Rastafarianism is a highly successful religious movement that has persisted for more than 70 years. It continues to play a major part in the struggles of people of African descent for freedom and equality throughout the world. It is a very decentralized movement with a variety of organizations (mostly local), diverse publications, and self-initiated activities. In addition, the religion has a lively presence on the Internet.

Stephen D. Glazier and J. Gordon Melton

See also: Ethiopian Orthodox Tewahedo Church

References

Bernard, Akeia A. "The Material Roots of Rastafarian Marijuana Symbolism." *History and Anthropology* 18, no. 1 (2007): 89–99.

Chevannes, Barry. *Rastafari: Roots and Ideology*. Syracuse, NY: Syracuse University Press, 1994.

Edmonds, Ennis Barrington. *Rastafari: From Outcasts to Culture Bearers.* New York: Oxford University Press, 2003.

Erskine, Noel Leo. *From Garvey to Marley: Rastafari Theology.* Gainesville: University Press of Florida, 2005.

Mulvaney, Rebekah Michele. *Rastafari and Reggae: A Dictionary and Sourcebook*. Westport, CT: Greenwood, 1990.

Murrell, Nathaniel Samuel, William David Spencer, and Adrian Anthony McFarlane, eds. *Chanting Down Babylon: The Rastafari Reader*. Philadelphia: Temple University Press, 1998.

Rawze-e-Sharif

The story of Rawze-e-Sharif (the Blue Mosque) located in Mazari Sharif, Afghanistan, begins with the assassination of Ali ibn Abi Talib (ca. 597–661), the fourth caliph of the Muslim community. Ali had become the focus of the community's division, and his followers were at this time in the minority. He was buried in a secret location. In the eighth century, the leader of what became the Shia Islam community, Al-Shaykh Al-Mufid (the sixth Imam), claimed that he knew the location and that it was at Najaf. There a shrine and mosque would be built and a city emerged.

Some contend, however, that the story does not end with the Najaf burial. Rather they say, some of Ali's followers, concerned about the possible discovery and desecration of the body, removed it, placed it on a camel, and headed east. After several weeks, the camel dropped from exhaustion, and the men buried the body at that spot. In the following years, that location was lost.

However, early in the 12th century, a man living in the area had a dream in which Ali appeared to him and revealed the reburial site near the city of Balkh, in northern Afghanistan. The truth of the claim was investigated and after being confirmed, the local sultan ordered that a shrine be built and a city founded. Around 1220 that mosque and city were destroyed by Genghis Khan (ca. 1162–1227). Some rebuilding had occurred by the time Tamerlane (1336–1405) again laid waste to the region and annexed it to his regime based in Bukhara (Uzbekistan). A new mosque was finally built in the 15th century.

The present mosque has undergone various refurbishings and expansions over the intervening centuries. Many of the alterations were for the addition of tombs of various Afghan political and religious leaders whose bodies now rest within the mosque. Also within the mosque is the tomb chamber of Zarathustra (Zoroaster, the founder of the Zoroastrian religion, who was killed at Balkh by invading forces).

The region remained under the control of Bukhara until 1850, when it was returned to Afghanistan. In 1866, following a malaria outbreak, the regional capital was moved from Balkh to Mazar Sharif. In the late 1990s, Mazar Sharif became a battleground between the local Shia militia and the Taliban, who are Sunni Muslims. Several battles were fought over control of the city and several massacres are said to have occurred. It is currently (2009) occupied by NATO peacekeeping forces as the post 9/11 war in Afghanistan continues.

J. Gordon Melton

See also: Ali ibn Abi Talib; Bukhara; Mosques; Taliban; Zoroastrianism.

References

Ball, Warwick. *The Monuments of Afghanistan: History, Archaeology and Architecture*. London: I. B. Tauris, 2008.

Ewans, Martin. *Afghanistan: A Short History of Its People and Politics*. New York: Harper Perennial, 2002.

Reconstructionist Judaism

Reconstructionist Judaism developed in the United States, largely the product of the fertile mind of Mordecai M. Kaplan (1881–1983). Born in Lithuania, Kaplan came to the United States with his parents, attended the Jewish Theological Seminary, and subsequently became the rabbi of an Orthodox synagogue in New York. While there he became one of the founders of the youth movement that later matured as Young Israel.

Although Kaplan spent the vast part of his long career as a professor at the Jewish Theological Seminary, which trained rabbis for the growing movement of Conservative Judaism, and although he had also originally served as a rabbi in Orthodox synagogues, in 1922 he founded his own synagogue, the Society for the Advancement of Judaism. This became one of the settings in which Kaplan evolved his Reconstructionist Judaism, a very different approach to adapting Judaism to the modern world. His classic text, *Judaism as a Civilization* (1934), argues that Jews must make radical changes to their own social and organizational life in order to accommodate to each culture in which they reside. For Kaplan, Judaism constituted an evolving religious civilization, one that must be reconciled with contemporary forces. Kaplan's reconstruction of Judaism led him to reject the notion of a supernatural God and to redefine God as the power in the universe that makes for salvation. He rejected authoritarianism and supernaturalism in every aspect of Jewish religious life, abandoning the notion of the commandments and God's laws in favor of celebrating Jewish traditions as folkways, which the people could and should modify to meet their changed circumstances of contemporary life.

Kaplan's pragmatic approach to Jewish life centered on the community. His rejection of the divine origin of the Torah (the Jewish Bible) was but one issue that made for tense relations between Kaplan and his colleagues both in the Conservative movement and

Portrait of Rabbi Mordecai Kaplan, founder of Reconstructionist Judaism, the youngest and smallest of the four denominations of American Judaism. (American Jewish Archives)

among the Orthodox, and eventually led to the development of Reconstructionism as a separate branch of American Judaism. As Kaplan and his colleagues concretized his ideas in a series of new prayer books, a group of Orthodox rabbis, in 1945, burned his Sabbath prayer book and formally excommunicated him..

The Reconstructionist movement evolved organizationally in stages. In 1935 Kaplan founded a periodical called the *Reconstructionist.* In 1940 the Jewish Reconstructionist Foundation was founded, and soon thereafter the first Reconstructionist synagogues opened their doors. The foundation was superseded in 1955 by a synagogue association, which went through several name changes before emerging in 1996 as the Jewish Reconstructionist Federation. Along the way it had absorbed many Jews who had participated in the *harvurot* movement, a communal movement that developed in the 1960s. Rabbi Ira Eisenstein (1907–2001), Kaplan's son-in-law and the second prominent leader of the movement, took the lead in founding the Reconstructionist Rabbinical College in 1968. The Reconstructionist Rabbinical Association was founded in 1974.

Reconstructionism is largely limited to the United States. It has steadily moved toward alliances with Liberal and Reform Judaism, with which it has now identified through its affiliation with the World Union for Progressive Judaism. As the 21st century begins, there are approximately 100 Reconstructionist congregations, including 3 in Canada, and some 50,000 members in North America. There is a single congregation in Curaçao.

Jewish Reconstructionist Federation
Beit Devora
101 Greenwood Ave. Suite 430
Jenkintown, PA 19046
http://www.jrf.org

Pamela S. Nadell and J. Gordon Melton

See also: Conservative Judaism; Kaplan, Mordecai Menahem; Orthodox Judaism; Reform Judaism; Satmar Hasidism; Young Israel.

References

Alpert, Rebecca T., and Jacob J. Staub. *Exploring Judaism: A Reconstructionist Approach*. Elkins Park, PA: Reconstructionist Press, 2000.

Eisenstein, Ira. *Reconstructing Judaism: An Autobiography*. Elkins Park, PA: Reconstructionist Press, 1986.

Kaplan, Mordecai M. *Basic Values in Jewish Religion*. New York: Reconstructionist Press, 1948.

Kaplan, Mordecai M. *Judaism as a Civilization.* New York: Macmillan Company, 1934.

Scult, Mel. *Judaism Faces the Twentieth Century: A Biography of Mordecai Kaplan*. Elkins Park, PA : Reconstructionist Press, 1993.

Reform Baptists (Russia)

The Reform Baptists emerged in 1961 as a major schism in the All-Union Council of Evangelical Christians–

Baptists of Russia in what was then the Soviet Union. In 1960 the union, which represented Baptists and Pentecostals in the Soviet Union, had been forced by the Khrushchev government to issue a letter of instruction to its member congregations. The letter ordered the congregations to hold back on their evangelistic efforts. Some leaders in the union rejected the letter and saw it as indicative of an unacceptable intimacy between the union and the state.

In 1961 a group left the union and formed an Organizing Committee, officially organizing in 1965 as the Council of Churches of Evangelical Christians–Baptists, commonly referred to as Reform Baptists. They chose as their first president Gennadii K. Kryuchkov. He was soon arrested and served time in prison. He then disappeared into the underground. The secretary, Georgi P. Vins (1928–1998), served two prison terms before being allowed to come to the United States, which became his base of operations for the continued advocacy for Russian Christians.

The schism between the union and the Reform Baptists continues. Only in 1988 with the beginning of reforms under Soviet president Mikhail Gorbachev (b. 1931) did the Reform Baptists get some relief. By the end of the year, all the Reform Baptists in prison were released and the church launched a new evangelism campaign. In 1989 the Reform Baptists held their first congress unmolested by the authorities, with delegates representing its 42,000 members. By 1993 they had some 50,000 members.

J. Gordon Melton

See also: Baptists.

Reference

Wardin, Albert W., ed. *Baptists around the World.* Nashville: Holman Publishers, 1995.

Reform Judaism

In the 18th century, Jewish scholars, most notably Moses Mendelssohn (1729–1786), began to advocate an acculturation of traditional Jewish life to modern European life. This advocacy also coincided with the integration of many Jews, especially in Germany, into the emerging post-Enlightenment secular culture. That integration was encouraged by the changes brought to Europe by the Napoleonic conquests.

Portrait of Moses Mendelssohn, eighteenth-century Jewish philosopher and the founder of modern German Judaism. (Library of Congress)

In the 19th century, the dialogue with non-Jewish culture would contribute to the development of a new movement within the Jewish community to develop a liberal and even rationalistic form of Jewish existence. Taking the lead would be German-speaking Jews in Central Europe and North America. The reforms began with the introduction of organ music, sermons delivered in German, and prayers in German rather than Hebrew. What began as simply an attempt to make the synagogue more appealing to "modern" Jews led to a new way of viewing Judaism. In Germany, the lead was taken by Abraham Geiger (1810–1874), who was chief rabbi of Breslau. Geiger argued that Judaism was always in a state of change and that God might demand at one time what at another time was inappropriate. Given the changes of the past, the rabbis of the present have leave to make changes as demanded by the times.

In the 1820s, younger members of a synagogue in Charleston, South Carolina, one of the early Jewish worship centers in the United States, also sought to implement reforms. When the congregation refused, some members left to found the Reformed Society of Israelites. However, Reform Judaism really developed in the United States in the last half of the century. Isaac Mayer Wise (1819–1900) emerged as Geiger's American counterpart, and in America the program of Reform led to the creation of a set of structures to embody the movement's ideals—the Union of American Hebrew Congregations (1873; today the Union for Reform Judaism), Hebrew Union College (1875), and the Central Conference of American Rabbis (1889). Cincinnati, Ohio, became the center of Reform Jewish life. (A Reform synagogue was opened in Canada, but until the last half of the 20th century the movement did not take hold there.)

The Reform movement's challenge to traditional Judaism was qualitatively different from Jewish movements during the previous millennium. It questioned the necessity of a host of practices that had been considered normative for Jewish religious life. Kosher food practices were discarded, as was peculiar dress. All laws from the Jewish Bible and the Talmud (later writings of the rabbis that developed Jewish law) were examined in the light of modern needs and discarded if judged nonessential. Reform Jews were distinct from non-practicing traditional Jews in that they did not simply ignore the law but argued that in following the Reform path, one could be a complete religious Jew. This idea directly challenged traditional Judaism and the authority of traditional rabbis.

As the movement developed, most, but not all, Reform Jewish leaders initially opposed Zionism, although this opposition was thoroughly reversed after World War II. Reform Judaism has broken down the barriers between men and women in the synagogue, recognized Jewish lineage through both the father and the mother (whereas traditional Judaism is matrilineal), expressed a willingness to accept converts to the faith, and most recently accepted gay and lesbian Jews into the rabbinate.

The Reform movement spread to Jewish communities worldwide through the 20th century, moving in the 1930s to the Jewish community in Palestine. After several unsuccessful starts, Liberal Judaism in Israel experienced a new beginning in 1958, when the Harel Synagogue opened in Jerusalem. As other synagogues opened, they associated together as the Israel Movement for Progressive Judaism (incorporated in 1971), and their leadership formed the Council of Progressive Rabbis. The Israeli movement has differed from American Reform Jews in its retention of various Orthodox practices in recognition of their important role in Israeli life.

In Israel, Orthodox Jews challenged the status of Reform (and Conservative) Jews, and moves were made to prevent their spread and the construction of Reform synagogues. Many Orthodox Jewish rabbis consider Reform Judaism as a separate religion. As a result, marriages performed in Israel by Reform rabbis (and any non-Orthodox rabbis) are still not recognized by the civil authorities, and Reform couples must undergo a second wedding service to meet legal demands. The lack of official recognition has had an impact on the movement's perceived lack of authenticity, has altered its relationship to the Israeli government, and has led many to treat it much like one of the various non-Jewish religious communities in Israel.

The Reform movement globally is represented by the World Union for Progressive Judaism. Approximately two-thirds of the world's 1.5 million Reform and Progressive Jews reside in the United States. Other important Reform organizations include the Union for Reform Judaism and the Israel Movement for Progressive Judaism, which shares headquarters with the World Union for Progressive Judaism.

World Union for Progressive Judaism, International Headquarters
13 King David St.
Jerusalem, 94101
Israel
http://wupj.org/

World Union for Progressive Judaism, North American Headquarters
633 Third Ave.

New York, NY 10017-6778
http://wupj.org/

Pamela S. Nadell and J. Gordon Melton

See also: Conservative Judaism; Orthodox Judaism; Zionism.

References

An Intimate Portrait of the Union of American Hebrew Congregations—A Centennial Documentary. Cincinnati, OH: American Jewish Archives, 1973.

Kaplan, Dana Evan. *American Reform Judaism: An Introduction*. New Brunswick, NJ: Rutgers University Press, 2003.

Meyer, Michael A. *Response to Modernity: A History of the Reform Movement in Judaism*. Detroit: Wayne State University Press, 1995.

Plaut, W. Gunther. *The Rise of Reform Judaism*. New York: World Union for Progressive Judaism, 1963.

Tabory, Ephraim. *Progressive Judaism in Israel: Progress and Prospects*. New York: American Jewish Committee, 1998.

Warshofsky, Mark. *Jewish Living: A Guide to Contemporary Reform Practice*. New York: Union of Reform Judaism Press, 2000.

Reformed Christian Church in Slovakia

The Reformed phase of the Protestant Reformation reached Slovakia in the 16th century and found some immediate support from people already affected by the reforms attempted by Jan Hus (ca. 1373–1415) a century earlier. By 1564 enough congregations had been formed to designate four presbyteries. After the Hungarian takeover of the region, the presbyteries were incorporated into the Reformed Church of Hungary.

Although Hungary was primarily a Roman Catholic country, there were powerful Protestant royalty, especially among the Transylvanian princes, who used their influence to protect the Reformed faith. Repression in the mid-17th century led to what became known as the "Bloody Tribunal" at Bratislava in 1673. Pastors who refused to realign with the Roman Catholic Church were forced into exile, and a few were even sold into slavery. The repression was not relaxed until the Edict of Toleration in 1781, and Protestants were finally granted basic civil rights in 1791.

The church tended to be Hungarian in leadership, and especially after the country's constitutional changes enacted in 1881, Slovak cultural peculiarities were largely eliminated from church life. Following World War I and the separation of Czechoslovakia from the Austro-Hungarian Empire, the Reformed Church of Slovakia was set apart as an independent body. It originally included some 235,000 members, approximately 20,000 of whom lived in nearby Ukraine. The next decades were filled with tensions, as the Hungarian minority objected to the changes in church life introduced by the new Slovak leaders.

World War II brought additional changes. During the Nazi regime, the church was once again merged into the Reformed Church of Hungary, though its independence was re-established soon after the war ended. The Ukrainian members were lost as the Ukraine was integrated into the Soviet Union. Then in 1951, the church adopted a new constitution. The synod was named the highest legislative body in the church, and a synodal council was organized as the synod's executive arm. Further changes came in 1993 when Slovakia was separated from what is now the Czech Republic.

The Reformed Christian Church of Slovakia has approximately 120,000 members in more than 325 congregations. It supports the Theological Seminary located at Komárno. A Hungarian-speaking minority remains an important component of the church's life. It is a member of the World Council of Churches, the World Alliance of Reformed Churches, and the International Conference of Reformed Churches.

Reformed Christian Church of Slovakia
Jókaiho 34
94 501 Komárno
Slovakia

J. Gordon Melton

See also: International Conference of Reformed Churches; Reformed Church of Hungary; Roman Catholic Church; World Alliance of Reformed Churches; World Council of Churches.

References

Bauswein, Jean-Jacques, and Lukas Vischner, eds. *The Reformed Family Worldwide: A Survey of Reformed Churches, Theological Schools, and International Organizations*. Grand Rapids, MI: William B. Eerdmans Publishing Company, 1999.

Capek, D., ed. *Fellowship of Service: Life and Work of Protestant Churches in Czechoslovakia*. Prague: Ecumenical Council of Churches,

Van Beek, Huibert. *A Handbook of the Churches and Councils: Profiles of Ecumenical Relationships*. Geneva: World Council of Churches, 2006.

Reformed Christian Church in Yugoslavia

In the 16th century, the Reformed Church spread throughout Hungary and Hungarian-speaking converts formed the Reformed Church of Hungary. In 1920, as a result of settlements following World War I and the breakup of the Austro-Hungarian Empire, a section in the southern portion of the empire adjacent to Serbia was transferred to Serbian control. In 1933, those members of the Reformed Church who found themselves in a new country formed the Reformed Christian Church in Yugoslavia.

The new church also included several German-speaking Reformed congregations that had originated in the 18th century among people who had moved into the area from Germany. The Germans were forced out of the area following World War II. Atrocities committed by occupying German troops had made people of German background unwelcome in the new nation of Yugoslavia that was being formed.

The surviving church suffered suppression under the Marxist regime during the generation after World War II, and many members immigrated to Hungary. However, the church continued into the post-Marxist era. It experienced a major loss when Croatia separated from Yugoslavia as an independent country and the members residing there organized separately in 1993 as the Reformed Christian Church in Croatia.

The church has a Reformed theological stance, having adopted the Heidelberg Catechism and the Helvetic Confession as doctrinal standards. It has a presbyterial organization, with a synod as its highest legislative body. Worship is primarily in Hungarian and Czech. In 2002 the church reported approximately 17,000 members in 19 congregations, but it has been losing Hungarian-speaking members, as many have left the country seeking a more hospitable environment. The church is a member of the World Alliance of Reformed Churches, World Council of Churches, and the Ecumenical Council of Churches in Serbia and Montenegro.

Reformed Christian Church in Yugoslavia
Ul. Bratstva 26
YU-24, 323 Feketic
Yugoslavia
http://www.netministries.org/see/churches.exe/ch01797

J. Gordon Melton

See also: World Alliance of Reformed Churches; World Council of Churches.

References

Bauswein, Jean-Jacques, and Lukas Vischner, eds. *The Reformed Family Worldwide: A Survey of Reformed Churches, Theological Schools, and International Organizations*. Grand Rapids, MI: William B. Eerdmans Publishing Company, 1999.

Van Beek, Huibert. *A Handbook of the Churches and Councils: Profiles of Ecumenical Relationships*. Geneva: World Council of Churches, 2006.

Reformed Church in America

The Reformed Church in America is the primary bearer of the Dutch Reformed Christian tradition in the United States. The church traces its origin to the establishment of a colony on the eastern coast of North America at the beginning of the 17th century on Manhattan Island, today the heart of New York City. The first congregation was established in 1628 by Reverend Jonas Michaelius (1577–ca. 1633). Through the next century, the church spread through the Hudson River valley and then into the colony of New Jersey. Its growth was somewhat blunted by the British takeover of New Amsterdam (New York) in 1664, but Dutch migration to the colonies continued. As church members moved westward, the church established congregations in different parts of the country, though the strength remained in the East. Queens College (now Rutgers University) was established to provide college and theological training.

As the colonies' break with England became a possibility, in 1770 John Livingston (1746–1825), who had been in Holland completing his education, arrived back in New York with a plan of union for the scattered Reformed congregations. It was not until 1792 that a constitution was adopted. In 1819 the church incorporated under the name Reformed Protestant Dutch Church. It followed the beliefs and practices of the Reformed Churches in the Netherlands (now the Protestant Church in the Netherlands).

The church had a spurt of growth in the middle of the 19th century, when a new wave of immigration from Holland brought many Dutch settlers to Michigan, Iowa, and neighboring states as far west as South Dakota. A few congregations were founded in Canada. As it Americanized, the church adopted its present name in 1867. Through the late 19th and early 20th centuries, the church developed an extensive missionary program. It continues to sponsor work in Japan, Taiwan, Hong Kong, the Philippines, Venezuela, Ecuador, Honduras, Nicaragua, and India. The church sponsored the Arabic Mission, founded in the 1880s by Samuel Zwemer (1867–1952), which was dedicated to spreading Christianity in the Muslim lands of the Middle East. The church continues to support the small congregations and social institutions the mission initiated in Bahrain, Saudi Arabia, Kuwait, and Oman.

The church's headquarters are located in New York, in a building that also houses the offices of the National Council of Churches in the U.S.A. and a variety of organizations representing the various concerns of the more ecumenically minded churches in the United States. It is organized presbyterially. In 1999 it reported 299,000 members in the United States and 6,500 members in Canada. The highest legislative body is the annual general assembly. Its decisions are implemented by a 62-member executive committee. The church is divided into eight regional synods and further divided into two classes, or presbyteries. The church supports three colleges and two seminaries. The first women were admitted to the ordained ministry in the church in 1981. It is a member of the World Alliance of Reformed Churches and the World Council of Churches.

Reformed Churches in America
247 Riverside Dr.
New York, NY 10015
http://www.rca.org/

J. Gordon Melton

See also: Protestant Church in the Netherlands; World Alliance of Reformed Churches; World Council of Churches; Zwemer, Samuel Marinus.

References

Hart, D. G., and Mark Noll. *Dictionary of the Presbyterian and Reformed Tradition in America.* Downers Grove, IL: InterVarsity Press, 1999.

Hood, F. J. *Reformed America.* Tuscaloosa: University of Alabama Press, 1980.

Van Beek, Huibert. *A Handbook of the Churches and Councils: Profiles of Ecumenical Relationships.* Geneva: World Council of Churches, 2006.

Van Hoeven, J. W., ed. *Piety and Patriotism: Bicentennial Studies of the Reformed Church in America.* Grand Rapids, MI: William B. Eerdmans Publishing Company, 1976.

Reformed Church in Romania

In the middle of the 16th century the ideas of John Calvin (1509–1564) were introduced into Transylvania (then connected with Hungary) and found their greatest acceptance among the Hungarian-speaking population, most of whom were formerly adherents of the Roman Catholic Church. Within a short time, as Calvin's perspective spread, a large number of Catholic monasteries would disappear.

Around 1530 Protestant preachers (both Calvinist and Lutheran) were active in the area of Satmar, Transylvania, where they operated under the protection of a powerful Romanian nobleman, Gaspar Dragfl. Later, Calvinism spread in the neighboring districts. By 1566 it had spread to Oradea and throughout the northern half of Transylvania. The synods of Abrud (1545),

A Romanian Reformed church in Sibiu, Romania. (Constantin Sava/Dreamstime.com)

Debrecen (1567), Oradea (1567), and Satu Mare (1646) were held in order to determine the organization of mission and of religious life. Catholicism was a shadow of its former self in the region, with many deserted churches and a shortage of priests; indeed, no Catholic priests remained in the district by 1598. By 1609 the Catholic cathedral in Oradea, though not yet destroyed, no longer held the altar with the relics of Saint Ladislas (1040–1095). The cathedral was finally pulled down in 1618, and the stones were used to rebuild the city. At the same time, the statues of the canonized kings were melted, and the bronze was used for casting cannons.

The Calvinists separated completely from the Lutherans in 1564, and two subsequent synods in 1564 and 1567 set the organizational foundations for the Reformed Church in Transylvania. The church accepted the Second Helvetic Confession as its doctrinal standard at the synod in 1567. Somewhat of an anomaly in the Reformed tradition, the leaders retained the title of bishop, and the church's primary organizational units are termed dioceses. The Diet of Turda (1564) recognized the Calvinist church, and the Catholic monks and priests were banished from the areas inhabited by the Magyars. Protestantism became dominant in the region, and the conflict between Protestants and Catholics continued as the Protestant princes supported the conversion of the remaining Catholic element of the population to the new faith, sometimes even with the help of the military.

The Diet of 1572 slowed down the spread of the Reformed movement by granting freedom of expression to the Catholic Church. Under these circumstances, Catholicism survived and regained momentum in areas like Ciuc, Sfântu Gheorghe, Odorheiu, and Trei Scaune. During Michael the Brave's (Michael II Apafi, r. 1690–1697) short regime in Transylvania, attempts were made to consolidate the traditional churches. He restored the Orthodox bishop to his former rights, but this measure was ephemeral. Then, as soon as Transylvania became an archduchy under Austrian domination, Catholicism resumed its missionary activity. In 1691 the Leopoldine Diploma officially recognized and strengthened the rights of the Catholic Church. The Calvinists were obliged to return several places of worship to the Catholics, Catholic schools were re-established, and some landed properties of the former monasteries were restored. In 1697 the king of Austria, Leopold I (1640–1705, r. 1658–1705), appointed a Catholic bishop for Transylvania, but due to Calvinist opposition, he would not be installed until 1716.

As Transylvania was under foreign dominion, churches in this territory were subject to the general regulations concerning denominations. The Geley Canons, instituted in 1646, included the main rules of the Reformed Church and was in effect until 1949, when the new statutes of the Calvinist church were approved. The unification of Transylvania with Romania after World War I brought about several changes in the organization of the Reformed Church—most important, the separation of the work in Romania from the Reformed Church of Hungary. Dioceses, though disproportionate with respect to each other (as the Diocese of Cluj has almost twice as many members as the Diocese of Oradea), are organized in a similar manner and are autonomous. Each diocese is led by a general assembly (made up of 50 percent priests and 50 percent laypeople) and a consistory that includes the bishop, the primcurator, the church notary, the mission advisor, and the councilors.

The present organization retains the tradition of parish autonomy instituted by the Diet of Turda in 1564, in which the priest must be appointed by the believers of the parish. The Calvinist believers are organized in parishes, which are linked in districts under an archpriest for administrative reasons. The districts are included in the two dioceses (Oradea and Cluj).

The Reformed Church is found throughout Romania's most widely spread denominations. In 1930, 3.9 percent of the population declared themselves to be Calvinists (710,706 believers). At the end of the 1990s, the church reported 802,454 members. The church is a member of the World Council of Churches and the World Alliance of Reformed Churches.

Reformed Church in Romania
Diocese of Cluj
Str. C. Bratianu Nr. 51
Transylvanian District
3400 Cluj
Romania

Reformed Church in Romania
Diocese of Oradea
Str. Craiovei I Nagyvarad
3700 Oradea
Romania

Constantin Cuciuc

See also: Calvin, John; Reformed Church of Hungary; Roman Catholic Church; World Alliance of Reformed Churches; World Council of Churches.

References

Branzea, Nicolae I., and Stefan Ionita. *Religious Life in Romania.* Bucharest: Editura Paideia, 1999.

Cuciuc, Constantin. *Atlasul Religiilor şi al Monumentelor Istorice Religioase din Romania.* Bucharest: Editura Gnosis, 1996.

Van Beek, Huibert. *A Handbook of the Churches and Councils: Profiles of Ecumenical Relationships.* Geneva: World Council of Churches, 2006.

Reformed Church in Zambia

The Reformed Church in Zambia originated in the preaching of a 19th-century Native evangelist among the Ngoni people who lived in what is now eastern Zambia near the present-day city of Chipata. Chief Mpezeni of the Ngoni (ca. 1830–1900) was impressed and invited missionaries into his territory. Thus, in 1899 representatives from the Dutch Reformed Church (NKG), based in South Africa, arrived and founded their first mission. After a generation of activity, in 1929 the first Zambian national, Justo Mwale, was ordained.

In 1943 the mission was reorganized as the African Reformed Church, but white missionaries from South Africa continued to control the work. It was not until 1961 that a Zambian was elected as moderator. Zambia became an independent country in 1964, and two years later the African Reformed Church became independent. The church assumed its present name in 1968.

In the 1980s, as the policy of apartheid became an international issue and the Dutch Reformed Church identified itself with that policy, the Zambian church called the relationship to its parent body into question. In 1989 it threatened to sever ties to South Africa unless the church rejected apartheid. That did not occur, and in 1991 the Reformed Church of Zambia suspended all relationships with the Dutch Reformed Church.

In the mid-1990s the Reformed Church in Zambia reported 250,000 members in 131 congregations. The church is headed by a general synod that meets quadrennially and two regional synods, each of which meet biennially. The seminary at Lusaka is named for Justo Mwale. The church is a member of the World Council of Churches and both the Reformed Ecumenical Council and the World Alliance of Reformed Churches.

Reformed Church in Zambia
Synod Office
Box 550100

Katete
Zambia

J. Gordon Melton

See also: Dutch Reformed Church; Reformed Ecumenical Council; World Alliance of Reformed Churches; World Council of Churches.

References

Bauswein, Jean-Jacques, and Lukas Vischner, eds. *The Reformed Family Worldwide: A Survey of Reformed Churches, Theological Schools, and International Organizations*. Grand Rapids, MI: William B. Eerdmans Publishing Company, 1999.

Van Beek, Huibert. *A Handbook of the Churches and Councils: Profiles of Ecumenical Relationships*. Geneva: World Council of Churches, 2006.

Reformed Church in Zimbabwe

The Reformed Church in Zimbabwe began in 1891, when Andrew A. Louw (1862–1956), a missionary with the Dutch Reformed Church in South Africa, assisted by several African workers, established an initial missionary station in the land traditionally inhabited by the Shona people. In the next century, work was extended to the Nyanja people and most recently among the Tonga.

Today, as an independent body, the 80,000-member church is organized with a mixed congregational and presbyterian polity. The synod is the highest legislative structure. The church recognizes the traditional Reformed doctrinal statements in the Heidelberg Catechism and the Canons of the Synod of Dort. It is a member of the World Alliance of Reformed Churches and the World Council of Churches, and it supports Murray Theological College.

Reformed Church in Zimbabwe
PO Box 670
62 Hughe St.
Masvingo
Zimbabwe

J. Gordon Melton

See also: Dutch Reformed Church; World Alliance of Reformed Churches; World Council of Churches.

References

Bauswein, Jean-Jacques, and Lukas Vischner, eds. *The Reformed Family Worldwide: A Survey of Reformed Churches, Theological Schools, and International Organizations*. Grand Rapids, MI: William B. Eerdmans Publishing Company, 1999.

Van Beek, Huibert. *A Handbook of the Churches and Councils: Profiles of Ecumenical Relationships*. Geneva: World Council of Churches, 2006.

Reformed Church of Alsace and Lorraine

The Reformed Church of Alsace and Lorraine (a section of France bordering Germany) shares much of the history of the Reformed Church of France. As in the rest of France, the Protestant Reformed movement spread through Alsace and Lorraine in the 16th century, endured persecution in the decades prior to the Edict of Nantes (1598), and enjoyed toleration until Louis XIV (r. 1643–1715) revoked the edict in 1685. The church was almost destroyed by the migration of its members or their conversion to the Roman Catholic Church during the 18th century. After the French Revolution and Napoleon's rise to power, the Reformed Church was again allowed to operate openly, though Napoleonic restrictions limited church life, including the development of a representative national organization.

The Napoleonic structure regulating church life in France stayed in place until separation of church and state was adopted in 1906. However, by that time Alsace and Lorraine had been lost to France as a result of the Franco-Prussian War. They were returned to France at the end of World War II. Once back in relation to the French government, the churches of the region chose to retain the relationship they had had under the Napoleonic regulations. The church also decided to stay out of the merger that created the Reformed Church of France in 1938.

Although it maintains a close working relationship with the French Reformed Church, the Reformed

Church in Alsace and Lorraine is administratively separate. It is represented in the National Assembly of the Reformed Church of France and has a close working relationship with the (Lutheran) Church of the Augsburg Confession in Alsace and Lorraine, the two churches sharing the same headquarters building in Strasbourg.

The Reformed Church of Alsace and Lorraine has a membership of approximately 33,000. It is a member of the World Council of Churches and the Protestant Federation of France.

Reformed Church of Alsace and Lorraine
1 quai St. Thomas
F-67081 Strassbourg Cédex
France

J. Gordon Melton

See also: Church of the Augsburg Confession of Alsace and Lorraine; Reformed Church of France; World Council of Churches.

References

Annuaire de la France Protestante. Paris: Fédération Protestante de France, issued annually.

Bauswein, Jean-Jacques, and Lukas Vischner, eds. *The Reformed Family Worldwide: A Survey of Reformed Churches, Theological Schools, and International Organizations*. Grand Rapids, MI: William B. Eerdmans Publishing Company, 1999.

Van Beek, Huibert. *A Handbook of the Churches and Councils: Profiles of Ecumenical Relationships*. Geneva: World Council of Churches, 2006.

Reformed Church of Christ in Nigeria

The Reformed Church of Christ in Nigeria was formed in 1973 as the Church of Christ in Nigeria by former members of the Christian Reformed Church in Nigeria ("Reformed" was added to the name in 1993). The majority of people originally constituting the new church were Kuteb people, but in succeeding years people from several other neighboring groups have affiliated.

There being little of a doctrinal element in the church's split with the Christian Reformed Church, the new church continued the parent body's commitments to the basic Reformed statements of faith, including the Heidelberg Catechism and the Canons of Dort. It also continued a Reformed polity in its organization. Congregations are organized into classes, and the 10 classes constitute the synod.

The church has experienced several decades of rapid growth and now reports 277,000 members in its 41 churches. It is a member of the Reformed Ecumenical Council, the World Alliance of Reformed Churches, and the World Council of Churches.

Reformed Church of Christ in Nigeria
PO Box 42
Lupwe Road n 2 ussa, Takum
Taraba State
Nigeria

J. Gordon Melton

See also: Reformed Ecumenical Council; World Alliance of Reformed Churches; World Council of Churches.

References

Bauswein, Jean-Jacques, and Lukas Vischner, eds. *The Reformed Family Worldwide: A Survey of Reformed Churches, Theological Schools, and International Organizations*. Grand Rapids, MI: William B. Eerdmans Publishing Company, 1999.

Van Beek, Huibert. *A Handbook of the Churches and Councils: Profiles of Ecumenical Relationships*. Geneva: World Council of Churches, 2006.

Reformed Church of France

The Reformed Church of France traces its origin to the spread of the Calvinist phase of the Protestant Reformation in France in the 1540s. Best estimates set the adherents of reform at approximately 10 percent of the population by the time of the church's first national assembly in 1559. Representatives at that assembly established the Gallican Confession as the doctrinal standard. Through the rest of the century, the Reformers experienced periods of persecution, highlighted by the Saint Bartholomew's Day Massacre in 1572.

Finally, in 1598, via the Edict of Nantes, the French government granted religious toleration. Then in 1685, Louis XIV (1638–1715) revoked the Edict of Nantes and asserted his right as ruler to name the religion of the people and demand uniformity. As a result, many Protestants (known as Huguenots) fled the country, and many others joined the Roman Catholic Church.

However, the Reformation survived in France as an underground movement. In 1789 King Louis XVI (r. 1774–1792) recognized its existence by allowing Protestants to register their births, marriages, and deaths apart from the Roman Catholic Church. The church was finally able to come out of hiding following the French Revolution. Napoleon Bonaparte (1769–1821) established a system that recognized both Lutheran and Reformed churches and governed their existence in France. Although not fully free, they were able to operate openly. In 1820, the Reformed Church manifested its openness to the growing world missionary movement by sponsoring a new missionary organization, the Paris Mission, which gradually established work in most French colonies (now overseas departments) around the world.

In 1906 the French government adopted a system of separation of church and state. Although churches no longer received government financial support, they were now free to operate as corporate entities and grow. Two new Reformed churches emerged, one more liberal and one more conservative. The more liberal church became intimately involved with the various ecumenical efforts that were leading to the formation of the World Council of Churches. In 1938 these two branches of Reformed life, along with the French Methodists and some Free churches, merged to create the present-day Reformed Church of France. A new Declaration of Faith was promulgated at this time.

The Reformed Church has congregations across France, though it is weakest in one part of eastern France, where Lutheranism has dominated. Also, following World War I, when France recovered Alsace and Lorraine, the Reformed Church of Alsace and Lorraine chose to remain corporately separate though in close communion with the Reformed Church of France.

The Reformed Church of France reports approximately 182,000 members in a population of 58 million. It is a member of the World Council of Churches and the Protestant Federation of France.

Reformed Church of France
47, rue de Clichy
F-75311 Paris
France

J. Gordon Melton

See also: Lutheranism; Paris Mission; Reformed Church of Alsace and Lorraine; Roman Catholic Church; World Council of Churches.

References

Annuaire de la France Protestante. Paris: Fédération Protestante de France, issued annually.

Bauswein, Jean-Jacques, and Lukas Vischner, eds. *The Reformed Family Worldwide: A Survey of Reformed Churches, Theological Schools, and International Organizations*. Grand Rapids, MI: William B. Eerdmans Publishing Company, 1999.

Leonard, E. G. *A History of Protestantism*. Trans. by M. H. Joyce. London: Nelson, 1965.

Van Beek, Huibert. *A Handbook of the Churches and Councils: Profiles of Ecumenical Relationships*. Geneva: World Council of Churches, 2006.

Reformed Church of Hungary

It did not take long for the Reformation to spread from Germany and Switzerland to Hungary in the 16th century. The first wave was Lutheran, but a second wave of Reformed teachings also took hold, especially in Transylvania. During the 17th century authorities of the Roman Catholic Church throughout the Hapsburg Empire attempted various measures to repress Reformed congregations. These efforts culminated in what became known as the Bloody Tribunal, held at Bratislava in 1673. Pastors who refused to return to the Roman Catholic Church were banished, imprisoned, or in some cases sold as galley slaves. Protestants in the region did not receive toleration until 1791, although the church survived in spite of the persecution. A presbyterian system of church order was developed, and the office of bishop was retained as an administrative position.

Through the 19th century, Hungary was much larger than it is today. After World War I and again after World War II, significant segments of Hungary were separated and incorporated into neighboring states. Transylvania, for example, was transferred to Romania. As these lands were separated, Reformed churches in those lands were also separated from the parent body.

Following World War II, Hungary came under a Marxist regime that had an anti-religious bias. Although officially proclaiming religious freedom, the government imposed tight controls on religious organizations and confiscated much church property. The church survived until the end of Communist rule in 1989. Since that time, religious freedom has returned. The church has experienced a new burst of growth and has received back some of the property it had lost.

In the midst of its rebuilding, the Reformed Church of Hungary attempted in the 1990s to re-establish contact with Hungarian-speaking Reformed churches in other countries. In 1995 it hosted a consultative synod of Hungarian-speaking churches. Such churches can now be found in the Czech Republic, Slovakia, the Ukraine, Romania, Serbia, and Croatia. There are also Reformed churches of Hungarian heritage in the United States and several South American countries, although for the most part these abandoned the Hungarian language in the 20th century.

In the late 1990s the church reported 1.6 million members in 1,100 churches. It is a member of the World Alliance of Reformed Churches and the World Council of Churches. It oversees three theological schools.

Reformed Church of Hungary
PO Box 5
Abonyi-u 21
H-Budapest 1146
Hungary
http://www.reformatus.hu/ (in Hungarian)
http://www.reformatus.hu/english/english.htm (in English)

J. Gordon Melton

See also: Roman Catholic Church; World Alliance of Reformed Churches; World Council of Churches.

References

Bauswein, Jean-Jacques, and Lukas Vischner, eds. *The Reformed Family Worldwide: A Survey of Reformed Churches, Theological Schools, and International Organizations*. Grand Rapids, MI: William B. Eerdmans Publishing Company, 1999.

Van Beek, Huibert. *A Handbook of the Churches and Councils: Profiles of Ecumenical Relationships*. Geneva: World Council of Churches, 2006.

Reformed Churches in the Netherlands (GKN)

See Protestant Church in the Netherlands.

Reformed Churches in the Netherlands (Liberated)

The Reformed Churches in the Netherlands (Liberated) (Gereformeerde Kerken in Nederland [Vrijgemaakt]) has its origins in the separation of a number of ministers and members from the Reformed Churches in the Netherlands (GKN) (now an integral part of the Protestant Church in the Netherlands). Several professors, most notably Drs. Klass Schilder (1890–1952) and S. Greydanus, both of the Theological University of Kampen, expressed misgivings about the views associated with Abraham Kuyper (1837–1920), the founding father of the Reformed Churches in the Netherlands. They rejected his teachings on common grace, the nature of the soul, the covenant of grace, rebirth, and baptism, among others. The 1944 General Synod condemned Schilder and his associates. Some 77,000 Reformed believers left the mother church and founded a new one, with the same name, adding the word "liberated" for postal reasons.

The Liberated Churches, as they are also known, consider themselves to be the real continuation of the churches grounded in earlier movements of 1832 (the

Separation movement) and 1886 (Dutch Nonconformism). As the 21st century begins, the denomination includes some 124,000 believers, with 260 parishes and 290 ministers. It has its own university in Kampen (Broederweg) and is active in foreign missions. It is a member of the International Conference of Reformed Churches and also has particular affiliations with the Free Reformed Churches of Australia, the Presbyterian Church of Eastern Australia, the Canadian and American Reformed Churches, the Free Reformed Churches of the Philippines, Eglise Réformée Evangélique, the Evangelical Presbyterian Church of Ireland, Gereja Gereja Reformasi di Indonesia N.T.T., the Korean Presbyterian Church, the Free Church of Scotland, the Reformed Church in the United States, Eglise Reformée Confessante au Zaire, and Die vrije Gereformeerde Kerk in Suid-Afrika.

In the 1960s, the Liberated Churches experienced a serious problem. Some ministers wanted to establish formal communications with the Reformed Churches in the Netherlands (GKN), for which they were condemned by the synod. Around 20 percent of the members and 30 percent of the ministers subsequently left the church. First they gathered in what were termed Home-Communities, and then in 1979 they became the Netherlands Reformed Churches.

Today the church has many internal problems, including the discussions about the arrangement of the Sunday services, the use of the new songbook of the churches, the new form of the wedding service, the Sunday's rest, and yes or no to cooperation with the Christian Reformed Churches in the Netherlands.

Reformed Churches in the Netherlands
(Liberated)
Burgmeester Vos de Waelstraat 2
8011 AT Zwolle
The Netherlands
http://www.gkv.nl/ (in Dutch)

E. G. Hoekstra

See also: International Conference of Reformed Churches; Netherlands Reformed Churches; Protestant Church in the Netherlands.

References

de Roon, L. H., ed. *Waar zijn wij en waar gaan wij heen? Kroniek van een verandering in de Gereformeerde Kerken (vrijgemaakt).* Rotterdam, 1993.

Deddens, D., and M. te Velde. *Vrijmaking-wederkeer. Vijftig jaar vrijmaking in beeld gebracht 1944–1994.* Barneveld, 1994.

Hoekstra, E. G., and M. H. Ipenburg. *Handboek christelijk Nederland. Kerken, gemeenten, samenkomsten en vergaderingen.* Kampen: Kok, 2008.

Hoekstra, E. G., and M. H. Ipenburg. *Wegwijs in religieus en levensbeschouwelijk Nederland. Handboek religies, kerken, stromingen en organisaties.* Kampen: Uitgeverij Kok, 2000.

Reformed Denomination

The Reformed Denomination is a collective of small networks of congregations and many individual local congregations that make up the most conservative wing of Reformed Protestantism in the Netherlands. They are found in the so-called Bible Belt of the Netherlands—Zeeland, the isles of South Holland, along the great Dutch rivers and the Veluwe hills—and as the 21st century begins they count some 250,000 believers. The approximately 50 local congregations are the result of various schisms due to differences in belief, problems with ministers, and other organizational concerns.

The perspective of the Reformed Denomination is also found in the right wing of the Netherlands Reformed Church (now part of the Protestant Church of the Netherlands) (the Reformed Unity/de Gereformeerde Bond), the Reformed Congregations (Gereformeerde Gemeenten), the Reformed Congregations in the Netherlands (Gereformeerde Gemeenten in Nederland), the Old Reformed Churches (Oud Gereformeerde Gemeenten), the Old Reformed Churches in the Netherlands (Oud Gereformeerde Gemeenten in Nederland), and a small part of the Christian Reformed Churches in the Netherlands (De Christelijk Gereformeerde Kerken in Nederland). The local churches, most originating in the late 19th century, have different names. Believers support their own political party, the Political Reformed Party (Staatkundig Gereformeerde Partij, SGP), which has three of the 150 seats in the Dutch Parliament.

The beliefs of the Reformed Denomination include (1) the doctrine of election, which states that before one's birth, God destined one's eternal salvation or damnation; (2) an emphasis on the need for personal conversion as a token of God's election; (3) a distinction between persons who are converted and those who are not; (4) a pietistic experience of God, with a strictly personal experience being the result of the personal conversion; (5) the popularity of the theologians of the 17th and 18th centuries, who emphasized the analysis of the soul and the essentials of truth belief; (6) the recognition that humans are unable to do anything to be saved; (7) resignation to the power of God's providence in the life of the believer; (8) the assertion that the holy scriptures are inspired by God; (9) the singing of the psalms in the rhymed version of Datheen and those of 1773; and (10) confidence that the Holy Spirit uses the Word of God in one's heart. Generally, the Bible is read in the Dutch translation of 1637.

The Reformed Denomination is served by several periodicals, including *Reformatorisch Dagblad* (newspaper), *Standvastig*, and *Terdege*.

E. G. Hoekstra

See also: Protestant Church in the Netherlands.

References

Brienen, T., et al. *De Nadere Reformatie. Beschrijving van haar voornaamste vertegenwoordigers.* s'Gravenhage: Uitgeverij Boekensentrum B.V., 1986.

Hoekstra, E. G., and M. H. Ipenburg. *Handboek christelijk Nederland. Kerken, gemeenten, samenkomsten en vergaderingen.* Kampen: Kok, 2008.

Hoekstra, E. G., and M. H. Ipenburg. *Wegwijs in religieus en levensbeschouwelijk Nederland. Handboek religies, kerken, stromingen en organisaties.* Kampen: Uitgeverij, 2000.

Jonkers, J. B. G. *De gereformeerden.* Kampen: Kok, 1997.

Meiden, A. van der. *De zwarte kousen kerken. Bevindelijk heroverwogen portret.* Utrecht: Amboboeken, 1993.

Zwemer, J. P. *De bevindelijk gereformeerden.* Kampen: Kok, 2001.

Reformed Ecumenical Council

The Reformed Ecumenical Council (REC) was founded in 1946 as the Reformed Ecumenical Synod. It adopted its present name in 1988. It includes in its membership a number of more conservative Reformed bodies, the most prominent being the Christian Reformed Church in North America. Many of the member churches were formed as missions of the Christian Reformed Church or in relation to the Reformed Churches in the Netherlands, the Dutch counterpart of the Christian Reformed Church.

Membership in the REC is based on doctrinal agreement, a shared confession of faith being a basis of the union. The member churches seek to present a unified witness to the world of the historic Christian faith. Member churches may adopt any one of the several historical statements of the Reformed faith as a basis of their doctrinal confession.

The churches of the REC meet in an assembly quadrennially. A permanent secretariat and an interim committee carry on the affairs of the REC between assemblies. The program is focused in theology, mission services, and youth activities.

The REC has 42 member churches from 26 countries (2009). As this encyclopedia goes to press, the REC has announced its intention to merge with the World Alliance of Reformed Churches, the resulting organization to be known as the World Communion of Reformed Churches. The two bodies have made significant progress on a constitution and resolved most of the issues between them, and could merge as early as 2010. The Council has, in the past, provided a conservative alternative to the World Alliance of Reformed Churches. Currently, only one of its member churches, the Greek Evangelical Church, is also a member of the World Alliance and/or the World Council of Churches.

Reformed Ecumenical Council
2050 Breton Rd., SE, Ste. 102
Grand Rapids, MI 49546–5547
http://www.recweb.org

J. Gordon Melton

See also: Christian Reformed Church in North America; Greek Evangelical Church; Reformed Churches in the Netherlands; World Alliance of

Reformed Churches; World Communion of Reformed Churches; World Council of Churches.

References

Bauswein, Jean-Jacques, and Lukas Vischner, eds. *The Reformed Family Worldwide: A Survey of Reformed Churches, Theological Schools, and International Organizations*. Grand Rapids, MI: William B. Eerdmans Publishing Company, 1999.

Handbook. Grand Rapids, MI: Reformed Ecumenical Synod, 1997.

Reformed Presbyterian Church of Equatorial Guinea

The Reformed Presbyterian Church of Equatorial Guinea (Iglesia Reformada de Guinea Equatorial) can be traced to the work initiated by American Presbyterian missionaries on Corisco, an island off the coast of Guinea, in 1840. In 1865 the work moved to the mainland, which was then under the control of the French. It moved quickly to develop indigenous leadership, ordaining the first native minister in 1870. In 1901 Spain took control of the mainland territory and periodically generally acted so as to suppress Protestant work.

In the period immediately after the founding of the Spanish Republic (1932–1936), the government's activity became less suppressive. In 1933 the World Evangelical Crusade (WEC), an independent evangelical missionary agency, opened work among the Okak people. In 1952 all Protestant churches in the region were closed and pastors were stopped from any religious activity. In spite of the suppression, both the WEC and the Presbyterian work continued to grow. In 1969, the year after the country became an independent nation, the two churches merged to become the Evangelical Church.

Independence did little to relieve the Protestants' situation. Spanish rule was followed by dictatorial regimes, first under the leadership of Macias Nguema (r. 1968–1979) and then his nephew Obiang Nguema (r. 1979–). Meanwhile, beginning in 1970, the Primitive Methodist Church in Great Britain (now a constituent part of the Methodist Church of Great Britain) had built the largest Protestant following of the several churches active in Equatorial Guinea. Much of its strength was on the island of Fernando Pó (now called Bioko). In 1973 the Evangelical Church and the Methodist Church united to form the Reformed Church of Equatorial Guinea.

The merger turned out to be an ill-advised enterprise, as there was no clear understanding as to how the new church would function and what authority it would have over its respective member bodies. Through the 1990s, it came to be seen as a federation of churches that functioned loosely while the two churches worked on the issues that blocked their merger. In the meantime, the former Evangelical Church has assumed a new existence as the Presbyterian Reformed Church of Equatorial Guinea.

In the 1990s the Reformed Presbyterian Church of Equatorial Guinea reported 8,000 members in a country that is predominantly Roman Catholic. Its membership is drawn primarily from the Fang, Ntumu, and Okak peoples. The church is a member of the World Alliance of Reformed Churches and the World Council of Churches.

Reformed Presbyterian Church of Equatorial Guinea
Apdo Postal 22y
Bata
Equatorial Guinea

J. Gordon Melton

See also: World Alliance of Reformed Churches; World Council of Churches.

References

Bauswein, Jean-Jacques, and Lukas Vischner, eds. *The Reformed Family Worldwide: A Survey of Reformed Churches, Theological Schools, and International Organizations*. Grand Rapids, MI: William B. Eerdmans Publishing Company, 1999.

Van Beek, Huibert. *A Handbook of the Churches and Councils: Profiles of Ecumenical Relationships*. Geneva: World Council of Churches, 2006.

Reformed/Presbyterian Tradition

The Reformed and Presbyterian churches trace their common history to the thought and ministry of John Calvin (1509–1564) and the Protestant Reformation of the 16th century. Calvin assumed a leadership position among French-speaking Protestants following the publication of his systematic theology, *Institutes of the Christian Religion* (1536), and then took control of the Protestant cause in the Canton of Geneva in Switzerland, first for two years (1536–1538) and then more permanently in 1541.

In the *Institutes,* Calvin proposed the Reformed theology and a presbyterian organization. Theologically, Calvin was close to Martin Luther (1483–1546), their primary disagreement being about the nature of Christ's presence in the Eucharistic sacrament. Luther's view, termed "consubstantiation," held that Christ is truly present in the substance of the elements. Calvin's view was that Christ is present in the sacrament both symbolically and by the spiritual power that is imparted to the faithful by their faith. This basic theological difference also gave the Reformed church a distinctive stance toward reform. Lutherans tended to discard only those parts of the traditional Western Christian practice that were found to be in opposition to the Bible. The Reformed churches tended to discard anything that was not actually biblical. This more radical approach had concrete implications, making most Reformed church buildings more austere than their Lutheran counterparts, for example.

As the Reformed movement spread to the British Isles, first to Scotland and then to England, the issue of church organization came to the fore. Those who followed Calvin's lead tended to emphasize the presbyterian polity, which called for leadership by elders (presbyters) rather than bishops. Thus they became designated as Presbyterian churches rather than as Reformed churches, as those in continental Europe were generally called. In the British (and American) context, arguments over questions of polity in the 17th century tended to split the churches of the Reformed theological tradition, and both the Congregationalists and Baptists, who accepted a congregational form of church governance, dissented from the Presbyterian consensus.

In the 19th century, Congregationalists and Presbyterians cooperated to a significant extent in their world mission enterprise, especially through the work of the American Board of Commissioners for Foreign Missions and the London Missionary Society, though in each case the Congregationalists emerged as the dominant force. In the 20th century, the Presbyterians and Congregationalists formed several international cooperative agencies, especially the World Alliance of Reformed Churches, which includes Reformed, Presbyterian, and Congregational church bodies and has its headquarters in the same building that houses the World Council of Churches.

The Reformed/Presbyterian tradition found definitional expression in a set of confessions issued through the 16th and 17th centuries, most important, the Gallican (1559), Belgic (1561), Second Helvetic (1566), and Westminster (1647–1648) confessions and the Heidelberg (1563) and Westminster (1647–1648) catechisms. These documents affirmed the Reformed emphasis on God's sovereignty, an important element of which is his work of electing his people to salvation. Implicit in this emphasis is a belief in predestination. This element of Reformed theology was challenged by Dutch theologian Jacob Arminius (1560–1609), whose critique led to the writing of the other widely accepted Reformed doctrinal text, the Canons of the Synod of Dort (1619), which affirmed the traditional doctrines related to predestination.

In the 20th century, the Reformed tradition was challenged by the new historical-critical approach to the Bible and the scientific critique of biblical literalism. The Presbyterians were among the major bodies split by the Fundamentalist-Modernist debates in the 1920s and 1930s, with the Modernists taking control of the larger Presbyterian churches, especially what is now known as the Presbyterian Church (U.S.A.). That church accepts the Confession of 1967, promulgated by one of its constituent bodies, and has tended to see the other confessions as relativized by their historical context. More conservative Reformed and Presbyterian churches accept the authority of the older creeds as a valid contemporary interpretation of biblical teachings.

J. Gordon Melton

See also: Calvin, John; London Missionary Society; Presbyterian Church (U.S.A.); World Alliance of Reformed Churches; World Council of Churches.

References

Bauswein, Jean-Jacques, and Lukas Vischner, eds. *The Reformed Family Worldwide: A Survey of Reformed Churches, Theological Schools, and International Organizations*. Grand Rapids, MI: William B. Eerdmans Publishing Company, 1999.

Calvin, John. *Institutes of the Christian Religion*. 2 vols. Philadelphia: Westminster Press, 1960.

Cochrane, Arthur C., ed. *The Reformed Confessions of the Sixteenth Century*. Philadelphia: Westminster Press, 1966.

Hart, D. C., and Mark A. Noll. *Dictionary of the Presbyterian and Reformed Tradition in America*. Phillipsburg, NJ: P & R Publishing, 2005.

Leith, John H. *An Introduction to the Reformed Tradition*. Atlanta, GA: John Knox Press, 1977.

Lucas, Sean Michael. *On Being Presbyterian: Our Beliefs, Practices, and Stories*. Phillipsburg, NJ: P & R Publishing, 2006.

McKim, Donald K., ed. *Encyclopedia of the Reformed Faith*. Louisville: Westminster/John Knox Press/Edinburgh: Saint Andrew Press, 1992.

McKim, Donald K., ed. *Introducing the Reformed Faith: Biblical Revelation, Christian Tradition, Contemporary Significance*. Louisville: Westminster/John Knox Press, 2001.

Nichols, James Hastings. *Corporate Worship in the Reformed Tradition*. Philadelphia: Westminster Press, 1968.

Sproul, R. C. *What Is Reformed Theology? Understanding the Basics*. Grand Rapids, MI: Baker Books, 2005.

Reiha-no-Hikari

Reiha-no-Hikari, a Japanese new religion, was founded by Hase Yoshio (1914–1984) in 1954 under the name Reiha-no-Hikari Sangyo Kai. Suffering from illness, Hase undertook a religious pilgrimage at the age of 24. At Mount Goken in Kagawa Prefecture he heard the voice of Kami (the divine) and miraculously recovered. He continued the religious pilgrimage. In 1954 he received a revelation from Kami, telling him to become the messenger of Kami at the top of Mount Goken. It is believed that Hase is a messiah, born to save human beings through the divine power of *reiha* (spirit waves) sent from Kami through Hase's body.

Over the next few years Hase surrounded himself with a small group, of some 40 people, who had been saved by his spirit waves. He founded the Hase Sensei Sankokai (Master Hase Adoration Association). Three years later the group was incorporated, and in 1969 the headquarters was moved to its present location in Noda. March 7, the day the founder realized his relationship as a child of the great cosmic god, is commemorated annually with a festival. After his death in 1984, its members came to believe that Hase became an eternal wave of spiritual energy.

In response to their beliefs about their founder, Reiha-no-Hikari's members recite the prayer "Goshugojin-sam [Guardian God of Humanity: the founder], Nidai-sama [the second and current leader], please help us follow the path to the salvation of humankind" to receive reiha. That text is printed on the Gosintai Ofuda (Divine Emblem Plaque) that is installed in the altar in each member's home. Reiha-no-Hikari's main scriptures are the Gosho (Writings) and the Seikun (Oath Instructions), written by the founder.

The current leader of Reiha-no-Hikari is Hase Keiji (b. 1948), the founder's son. As the 21st century began, the group claimed approximately 825,636 members.

Reiha-no-Hikari
2683-1, Yamasaki
Noda-shi, Chiba Prefecture 278-0022
Japan
ttp://www.rhk.or.jp/ (in Japanese)

Keishin Inaba

See also: Devotion/Devotional Traditions.

References

Inoue, Nobutaka, et al., eds. *Shinshûkyo Kyodan Jinbutsu Jiten*. Tokyo: Kobundo, 1996.

Watanabe, Masako, and Midori Igeta. "Healing in the New Religions: Charisma and 'Holy Water.'"

Contemporary Papers on Japanese Religion, 2: *New Religions*, 1991. http://www.kokugakuin.ac.jp/ijcc/wp/cpjr/newreligions/igeta.html. Accessed January 10, 2002.

Reincarnation

Reincarnation denotes the passage of a spiritual or non-material soul or life-force from a human body to a new body—usually human but not necessarily so. Many terms are employed to represent this process, among them metempsychosis, metensomatosis, palingenesis, and transmigration. Etymologically, reincarnation (*re-*, "again"; *incarnare,* "make flesh"), metensomatosis (*meta-* [in conjunction with verbs], "change"; *soma,* "body"], and palingenesis (*palin-*, "again"; *genesis,* "birth") refer to the act of re-embodiment, taking a (new) body, or rebirth; transmigration (*trans-,* "across," "over," "beyond"; *migrare,* "move" [from one place or condition to another]) and metempsychosis (*meta-,* "change"; *psyche,* "soul") refer to the passage or change (from one body to another) by the soul. What distinguishes reincarnation from resurrection is the inhabiting of different bodies by the soul as opposed to the invigoration of the same body in the act of resurrection. More important, however, is the question of personal identity: *Is the newly reincarnated entity the same or different from the previous entity?* This question will be discussed along with other questions that are pertinent to this subject: What reincarnates? What are the vehicles for the reincarnating principle? Is the process immediate, or is there an intermediate existence between death and rebirth? Do actions in the previous life have consequences in the future life? What evidence is there that reincarnation is a provable fact?

The acceptance of the teaching of reincarnation, as either a certainty or a possibility, is found throughout the world. It is accepted among many non-literate and tribal cultures, the South Asian religions, and a number of ancient cultures, including the Greeks, and mentioned and even accepted in elements of the Abrahamic religions. The literature on the subject of reincarnation is extensive, with Joel Bjorling citing 1,612 selected titles in his *Reincarnation: A Bibliography*, published in 1996. Gananath Obeyesekere (*Imagining Karma*) provides informative accounts of different types of reincarnation, emphasizing the Amerindian, Greek, and Buddhist types as do Antonia Mills and Richard Slobodin, who edited the book *Amerindian Rebirth.* The importance of these works indicates that reincarnation is not localized, nor is it necessarily derived from one culture, one people, or one region of the world.

Reincarnation is usually premised on the assumption that the reincarnating element is a non-material entity, thereby establishing a fundamental dualistic stance in the makeup of the individual. This is discussed especially in Greek and Hindu sources, examples being Aristotle (*De Anima* II.1: "the body cannot be soul") and *Upadeasahasri* 12 ("I am different from the body"). Since the soul is separate from the body, it cannot be destroyed. Plato states that the soul existed before birth and will exist after (*Phaedo*) and that human rebirth comes about for the purpose of discipline, which in turn purifies the soul (*Phaedrus*). This establishes the immortality of the soul, which is discussed in Plato's *Phaedrus*. If immortality signifies no end, eternality signifies neither a beginning nor an end. Furthermore, eternality implies pre-existence, for in the *Phaedo,* the teaching of knowledge as recollection implies a previous time in which we learn what we later recollect. Eternality and immortality of the soul also are discussed in India. The reincarnating entity (*atman*) was "one alone, in the beginning" (Aitareya Upanishad 1.1.1). That is, the atman is one with Brahman, the Supreme entity (Chandogya Upanishad 3.14.1).

The one notable exception to the teaching that the soul reincarnates is Buddhism. According to the Buddhist teaching, the individual is made up only of mental and material aggregates. What in fact reincarnates is the conditioned consciousness process impelled by *karma*, the force that leads to results for all actions (mental, physical, verbal) previously performed.

A question that often arises is whether only human bodies are subject to reincarnation. In this regard there are differences of opinion. Indeed, even the terms above are sometimes associated with one or the other point of view. R. W. Lowrie (*Life and Afterlife,* 92–93), for instance, distinguishes transmigration and reincarnation by asserting that transmigration refers to the re-entrance of "the soul into an animal body instead of human" (93) whereas reincarnation (and metempsychosis, 92) limits the process to a human body. The view that the soul can inhabit animal bodies may be traced to Pythagoras in the West, as noted by the Greek historian and traveler Diodorus Siculus (first century BCE), who records Pythagoras's notion of "the transmigration of the soul into every living thing" (*The Library of History,* 1.98). The teaching that a human can reincarnate as an animal or insect is abundantly clear in the *Book of Manu,* the Hindu law book, especially chapter 12, verses 54f., and also among the Amerindians. Other forms of reincarnation exist: cross-sex reincarnation and multiple simultaneous reincarnation (that is, reincarnating as several people at once), the former among the Amerindians such as the Inuit, Kwakiutl, and Hopi and the latter among the Haida, Tlingit, Gitksan, and Kwakiutl.

The teaching on the intermediate existence, the period between death and rebirth, is an important topic in Tibetan Buddhism. This is a later development, however, since the early Buddhist attitude was that of an instantaneous rebirth of an entity that was neither identical with nor unrelated to the dying person. Differing accounts appear in the later Buddhist schools and traditions, but the teachings on the *bardo,* or intermediate state, in the *Bardo Thodol* ("The Great Book of the Liberation through Understanding in the Intermediate State"; popularly known as the *Book of the Dead*) give extensive descriptions of the reincarnating consciousness or life stream impelled by karma that will lead to a rebirth in one of the five or six realms of worldly existence (human, divine or heavenly, titan, animal, hellish, or sometimes the world of the hungry ghosts) or, if one keeps the bodhisattva or savior Kuan-yin or the Buddha Amitabha in mind, the Pure Land or the Heaven of Delight (*tushita).* An important factor in determining the quality of the rebirth is karma. In the religions of South India, karma plays an important role in determining the rebirth of the individual. It is viewed as a force that connects intended actions (verbal, mental, and bodily) to their consequences. Karma is intimately connected with the cycle of existence (*samsara*). As early as the Upanishads (4.4.5), karma is viewed as exhibiting not only causal powers but also ethical qualities associated with the consequences of actions. It is in this context that the quality of the rebirth is based upon one's previous actions. Whether this ethical element in reincarnation is limited to Hinduism, Buddhism, and Jainism is a matter of interpretation (on which, see Mills and Obeyesekere), but there is no doubt that these South Asian religions introduce individual salvation as a consequence of destroying any karmic activity. Karma, therefore, depending upon the quality of action, leads to a better or worse rebirth by commensurate actions. Paradoxically, certain actions, usually equivalent to those that make up a spiritual path (yoga or the Middle Path, for instance), will lead to the destruction of karma and any form of rebirth.

The one exception to the dependency on karma for a continuance of the transmigratory cycle is the teaching of the so-called Living Buddhas, that is, bodhisattvas or beings who achieve enlightenment, thereby allowing them to enter *nirvana,* but who, out of a sense of compassion, instead decide to be reborn in order to aid all sentient beings gain emancipation. This is a rebirth, therefore, that is not fueled by intended actions or karma but rather through the impulse of compassion.

Although the teaching of reincarnation in the West is viewed as an exotic teaching, it has gained in awareness through the efforts of the Theosophical Society and its various offshoots and successors. Theosophists were cognizant of the Greek, Kabbalistic, and Hindu teachings and so devised a teaching that became an integral part of Theosophical teaching from the 1880s on. One modification was advanced by Theosophists that contradicts the Hindu and Buddhist progressive nature of reincarnation. Based upon this teaching, no human can be reborn as an animal or as any being lower than human. This teaching may be based upon Allan Kardec's *Le Livre des Esprits*, considering reincarnation to be a progressive improvement of the soul until it reaches perfection and purification, illustrated in Annie Besant's "Reincarnation": "the object of reincarnation is to train the animal-man until it becomes the perfect instrument of the Divine" (45).

A collateral teaching that was popularized, if not invented, by Theosophists is the notion of "collective karma." Karma may therefore apply to families, castes, nations, and races as well. No clear reference on collective karma in the literature of South Asian religions exists, so it is most likely that this is a Theosophical innovation. The implication for such a teaching is that the type and quality of reincarnation are based at least in part on external factors, not simply on the actions of the previously existent being.

After all is said and done, is there evidence that suggests reincarnation is a fact? This is a hotly contested issue with evidence presented on both sides. Ducasse offers a series of arguments pro and con, with the strongest evidence based upon the assumption and proof that "the mind of a now living person is *the same mind* as that of a person whose body died some time before" (304). If the surviving component is neither body nor soul (that is, if the soul is regarded as neither physical nor mental) but rather "psychological," then it is possible that dispositions might retain life on the analogy of a person in deep sleep or in a faint, or some form of mental activity (Ducasse 1961, 127–128). Explanations are conjectural, but what is more compelling is the evidence that is being collected that however the phenomena are explained, there is something to explain. The work of the late Professor Ian Stevenson of the University of Virginia has provided considerable evidence that reincarnation should be seriously investigated. His earlier books, *Twenty Cases Suggestive of Reincarnation* and *Cases of the Reincarnation Type* (4 vols.), as also his later work (*Reincarnation and Biology, Children Who Remember Previous Lives: A Question of Reincarnation,* and *European Cases of the Reincarnation Type)* collectively make up the most impressive evidence as also the publication *Parapsychology: Research on Exceptional Experiences.* For a general overview, the Division of Perceptual Studies (University of Virginia Health System) offers an overview of the investigations that have gone on over the past half-century.

James A. Santucci

See also: Besant, Annie; Bodhisattva; Theosophical Society (Adyar); Yoga.

References

Aristotle, *On the Soul*. Trans. by J. A. Smith. http://classics.mit.edu/Aristotle/soul.1.i.html.

Besant, Annie. *Karma*. London: Theosophical Publishing House, 1895.

Bjorling, Joel. *Reincarnation: A Bibliography*. New York: Garland Publishing, Inc., 1996.

Ducasse, C. J. *A Critical Examination of the Belief in a Life after Death*. Springfield, IL: Charles C. Thomas, 1961.

Henry, Jane, ed. *Parapsychology: Research on Exceptional Experiences.* London and New York: Routledge, 2005.

Judge, W. Q. *The Ocean of Theosophy*. 1893; rpt.: Los Angeles: The Theosophy Company, 1987.

Kardec, Allan. *Le Livre des Esprits*, translated as *The Spirits' Book.* Sao Paulo, Brazil: Lake-Livraria Allan Kardec Editora Lta., 1972.

Lowrie, R. W. *Life and Afterlife.* Dade City, FL: Island Press Publishers, 2002.

Mills, Antonia, and Richard Slobodin, eds. *Amerindian Rebirth: Reincarnation Belief among North American Indians and Inuit.* Toronto and Buffalo: University of Toronto Press, 1994.

Obeyesekere, Gananath. *Imagining Karma: Ethical Transformation in Amerindian, Buddhist, and Greek Rebirth.* Berkeley: University of California Press, 2002.

Olivelle, Patrick. *The Early Upanishads: Annotated Text and Translation.* New York: Oxford University Press, 1998.

Plato. *Phaedo.* Trans. by Benjamin Jowett. http://classics.mit.edu/Plato/phaedo.html.

Plato. *Phaedrus.* Trans. by Benjamin Jowett. http://classics.mit.edu/Plato/phaedrus.html.

Sankarâchârya, Srî. *Upadeasahasri: A Thousand Teachings*. Trans. by Swâmi Jagadânanda. Mylapore, Madras: Sri Ramakrishna Math, 1961.

Stevenson, Ian. *Cases of the Reincarnation Type.* 4 vols. Charlottesville: University Press of Virginia, 1975–1983.

Stevenson, Ian. *Children Who Remember Previous Lives: A Question of Reincarnation.* Rev. ed. Jefferson, NC: McFarland, 2001.

Stevenson, Ian. *European Cases of the Reincarnation Type.* Jefferson, NC: McFarland, 2003.

Stevenson, Ian. *Reincarnation and Biology.* Westport, CT: Praeger, 1997.

Stevenson, Ian. *Twenty Cases Suggestive of Reincarnation.* 2nd ed. Charlottesville: University Press of Virginia, 1974.

Reiyukai

Reiyukai (Society of the Friends of the Spirit), a Japanese lay organization, derived from the tradition of Nichiren Buddhism and was founded between 1919 and 1925 in Tokyo by Kakutaro Kubo (1890–1944) and his sister-in-law Kimi Kotani (1901–1971). It arose out of Kubo's sense of apocalypse, which originated from the social and intellectual transformation of Japan during the Taisho period (1912–1926), combined with his understanding of Nichiren Buddhism and finally accentuated by the Great Tokyo Earthquake of 1923.

Kubo had received instruction in the nationalistic ideas of Nichiren Buddhism, but he was more interested in formulating a religious way for the laity to respond to the crisis of modern society. Kubo saw the sociopolitical upheavals of his time as evidence of ancestral distress caused by the neglect of ancestor worship by the laity, who had entrusted it to the Buddhist clergy. Therefore, he formulated lay rites of ancestral worship. In Reiyukai, the rite for ancestral worship is the twice daily recital of Aokyokan, or the Blue Sutra, which is an abridged version of Lotus Sutra, the doctrine of Nichiren Buddhism. The rite also involves the practice of venerating the *sokaimyo*, a tablet in which the posthumous names of all the ancestors of the husband and the wife are inscribed and enshrined in the domestic altar.

Although Kubo provided the doctrinal foundation for this lay movement, it was the organizational skill and charismatic healing powers of Kimi Kotani that drew the initial followers into Reiyukai. She proselytized by combining faith healing with teachings that claimed to improve living conditions as well as instill self-esteem in her converts, who were initially the urban proletariat but later small business owners and the self-employed.

The proselytization activity in Reiyukai is called *michibiki*. The proselytizer is called the "guide parent" (*michibiki no oya*) and the convert is the "guide child" (*michibiki no ko*). This "parent-child" link of proselytization is the organizational principle of Reiyukai. Another notable feature of Reiyukai is the *hoza*, a kind of group counseling circle, which is also the smallest unit of organization, formed by these links of proselytization.

In 1945 Reiyukai was one of the fastest growing new religions in Japan, but it suffered several setbacks, including financial scandals involving Kimi Kotani and the secessions of several groups, such as Rissho Kosei-kai, now the second largest new religion in Japan, Myochikai, and others. These problems have led to a decline in its membership. In 1999, Reiyukai had a membership of about 2 million in Japan and centers in 17 foreign countries. Since Kotani's death in 1971, faith healing-related practices have declined considerably. The emphasis has shifted to social welfare programs, youth activities, and overseas missions in North and South America and Asia.

Reiyukai has three major religious centers: Shakaden, the Tokyo headquarters of Reiyukai, enshrining the statue of Shakyamuni Buddha; Mirokusan, the youth training center dedicated to the Future Buddha Maitreya; and Shichimenzan, where pilgrimages are undertaken during equinox days. Reiyukai advocates traditional ethics in familial relationships and in politics, and it supports conservative political parties and causes.

Reiyukai
1-7-8 Azabudai, Minato-ku
Tokyo 106-8644
Japan
http://www.reiyukai-usa.org/ (United States)
http://www.reiyukai.org/ (Canada)

Ranjana Mukhopadhyaya

See also: Nichiren; Rissho Kosei-kai.

References

Hardacre, Helen, *Lay Buddhism in Contemporary Japan: Reiyukai Kyodan.* Princeton, NJ: Princeton University Press, 1984.
Kotani, Kimi. *A Guide to Reiyukai.* Tokyo: Reiyukai, 1958, 1972.
Reiyukai: Awareness, Action and Development. Tokyo: Reiyukai, 1997.

Relics

Strictly speaking, relics are the material remains of holy persons, most notably their bones, which are preserved in a sacred context for religious purposes. More

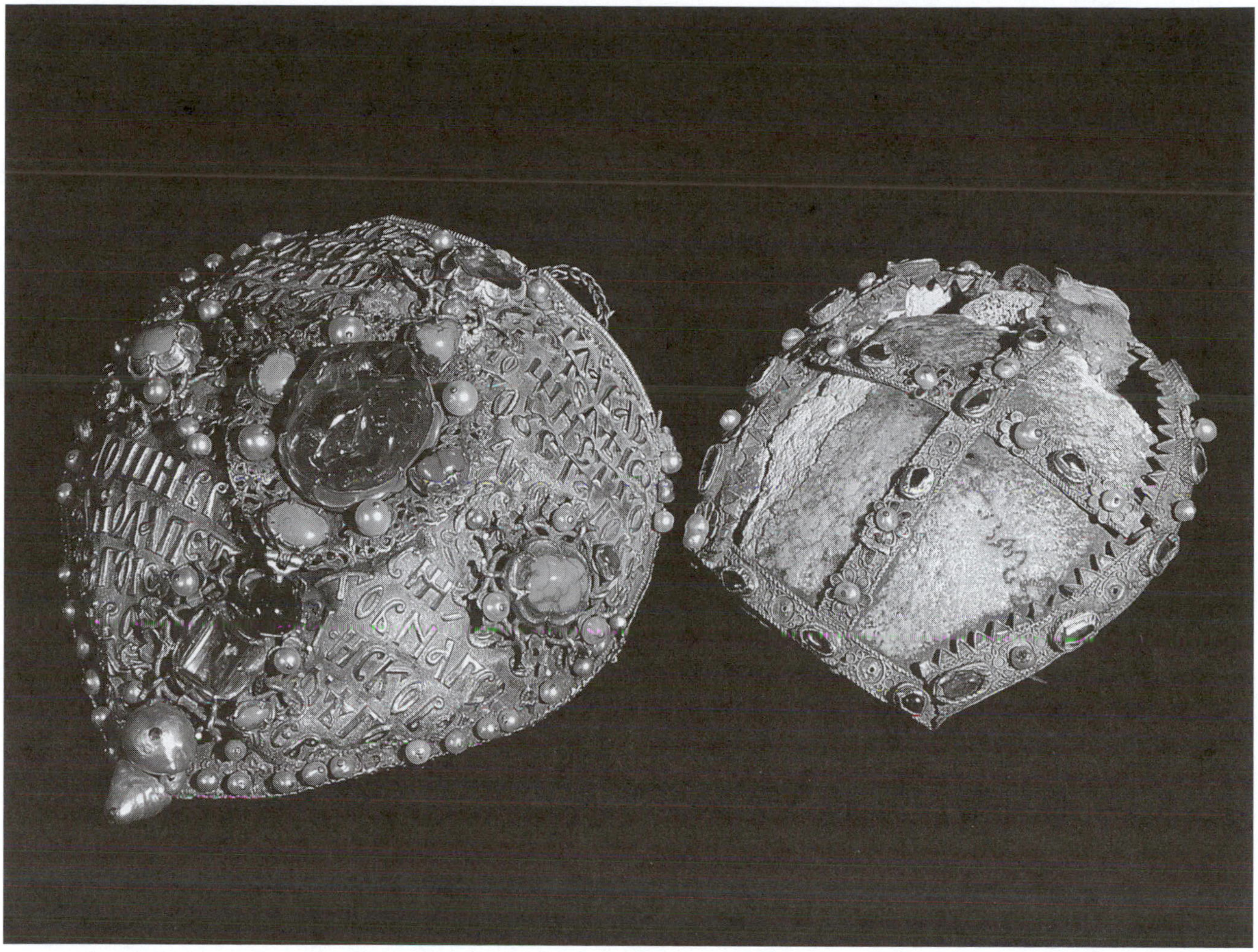

Relic of part of the skull of Saint John the Baptist, decorated with gold and semiprecious stones. The inscription shows that the work is Bulgarian. (Werner Forman/Art Resource, NY)

broadly, the term "relic" may refer to clothing or other objects closely associated with them, items they used in their daily life such as a writing instrument or ritual object, or items associated with a particularly important event. Relics appear to have been an element in a wide spectrum of religions, but have emerged as an especially important part of Buddhism and Roman Catholicism.

Buddhist Relics The Buddhist interest in relics began soon after the death of Gautama, the historical Buddha, in 480 BCE. His body was cremated, and the remaining ashes contained pieces of bone and teeth. At this point several people of royal status expressed their desire to have the Buddha's remains. A Brahmin priest named Drona stepped forward and divided the relics into eight equal portions. These were sent to the eight rulers desirous of having them. Each of the rulers had a stupa built to house the relics. The stupas were located in the cities of Kapilavastu, Bodhgaya, Mrigadava, Jetavananatha, Pindadarama, Vaisali, Rajagriha, Kanyakubja, and Kushinagara. It was later discovered that Drona had secretly set aside a ninth set for himself, but these were stone. He retained the vase in which the relics had been originally stored. At a later date, King Ashoka (ca. 304–232 BCE) brought all the lands where the relics had been sent into his kingdom. He regathered the relics and redistributed them to a variety of places throughout southern Asia from Sri Lanka to China, though details on the process and locations are scant.

Ashoka's kingdom stretched from southern India to what is now Afghanistan. While he does not seem to have ever left his kingdom, he sent missionaries far and wide. His two children were responsible for the first conversions in Sri Lanka. Missionaries went as far as Mongolia, Vietnam, and the Mediterranean basin. In the case of Southeast Asia, they began the conversion of Myanmar, Thailand, Cambodia, and Vietnam, and set the stage for stories tying places in those countries to the early history of Buddhism elsewhere.

At the time of Buddha's death and the initial distribution of the Buddha's relics and even of Ashoka's redistribution of them several centuries later, Buddhism had yet to become a literary faith. It was not until the first century BCE that the teachings of the Buddha began to be written down, and with them the stories of his life and adventures with his companions committed to paper. There would be a further gap between the move to documenting the Buddha's life and the first accounts of the emergence of items that claim to be relics of the Buddha. Thus, the locations of where Ashoka distributed the relics he possessed remains unknown, and the obscurity that covers the fate of the relics provides fertile ground for a variety of stories of relics lost and found and carried by various personages to different parts of Asia. And items presented as relics are usually beyond the ability of modern researchers directly to study and evaluate; however, devout Buddhists believe them to be exactly what they claim to be, notwithstanding the obscurity of their origin and the gap between those items presently claimed to be genuine relics of the Buddha and the events reputed to have occurred immediately following his death and during the reign of Ashoka. Many Buddhists also believe that the relics had an ability to reproduce themselves.

For Buddhists, relics have primarily been those of the historical Buddha himself. Most of the Buddhas and bodhisattvas of Mahayana Buddhism are believed to have had earthly lives (and their birthdays are celebrated), but those lives were lived in times and places difficult to document and the earthly bodies of the future bodhisattvas were never available to the Buddhist community. One notable exception to that lack of access concerns Manjushri. In the seventh century, the Korean monk Chajang spent a period of time at Wutai Shan, one of the Chinese mountains sacred to Buddhism. It is believed to be the home of Manjushri. According to the story, one day after chanting to Manjushri, Chajang was given a cryptic poem in a dream. Unable to understand the poem, he consulted a local monk who gave him several relics that he claimed to be those of Manjushri. A short time later, Chajang had a vision that informed him that the monk was in fact Manjushri. After his return to Korea, he built T'ongdo-sa Temple and placed the relics in a stupa behind the Great Hall, where they remain to this day.

As Vajrayana Buddhism developed, especially in Tibet, leadership was assumed by men assumed to be emanations of various Buddhas and bodhisattvas, who came to be described as Living Buddhas. Of these, the heads of the main branches of Tibetan Buddhism stand out. When they passed away, their relics also came to be venerated and would be installed in stupas in or near the temples over which they presided. The Potala Palace, in Lhasa, Tibet, for example, has eight stupa chapels that house the relics of a number of the Dalai Lamas.

Vajrayana practitioners also believe that when the body of a spiritually enlightened person is cremated, beautiful pearl-like crystals are often found alongside the unconsumed bone fragments among the ashes. These crystals are termed *ringsel,* and Vajrayana Buddhists believe that those crystals manifest the person's inner purity and hold his or her living essence. In addition, they are thought to emit spiritual energy and even on rare occasions to multiply.

While almost all countries in which Buddhism maintains a significant presence have at least one relic of the Buddha, several countries have notable sets of relics.

Buddhism spread to Sri Lanka when Ashoka sent his son Mahinda to the island. After his conversion, the king donated land for the first Buddhist temple, the Mahavihara, at what was then the capital, Anuradhapura. Mahinda's sister Sanghamita then arrived with a cutting from the Bodhi tree, the fig tree under which Buddha was believed to have found enlightenment at Bodhgaya (India), which was planted at Anuradhapura.

Planted in 288 BCE, it is the oldest living human-planted tree in the world with a known planting date. Sri Lanka's Bodhi tree has been the ultimate source of all the many Bodhi tree leaves as well as the several existing Bodhi trees now found around the world, including the one presently at Bodhgaya, which replaced the original one that was destroyed in the second century BCE by a Hindu king.

Thuparama Dagabawhich, a stupa at Anuradhapura, houses what is said to be Buddha's alms bowl and his right collarbone. In Kandy, at the center of the island nation, one may visit the Buddha's tooth, now housed in a golden stupa, known as Malagawa Vihara (or Dalada Maligawa). In 1986, the president of Sri Lanka donated a true relic of the Buddha to the leader of the Japanese Buddhist group Agon Shu, for enshrinement in their temple near Kyoto.

The arrival of Buddha's relics in Myanmar is part of the legend of the famous Shwedagon Pagoda in Yangon. While archaeologists have dated the building of the monument to around the 10th century, possibly as early as the sixth century, many believers place its origins during the lifetime of Gautama Buddha. According to the story, two brothers, Taphussa and Bhallika, merchants from what is now Myanmar met with the Buddha, from whom they received eight of the Buddha's hairs to be enshrined in their homeland. The two brothers found the local ruler, King Okkalapa, and discovered Singuttara Hill, now in the midst of Yangon, where relics of other Buddhas preceding Gautama Buddha had already been enshrined. Here the hairs were enshrined in what became the Shwedagon Pagoda.

A second collection of Buddha's relics, each with its own story of how it was recovered at different times, is gathered in the Buddha Relics Chamber in Myingyan, in north-central Myanmar.

One of the more interesting relic stories from Myanmar begins in the 11th century when King Anawrahta of Bagan (1044–1077 CE), who founded the First Myanmar Empire, became desirous of worshipping Buddha's relics. He first asked the emperor of China for the Buddha's tooth he owned. He was given, instead, a jade image of the Buddha. He then asked for the tooth kept at Kandy, Sri Lanka. The king of Sri Lanka would not give up the tooth, but honored the request with a replica of it, which Anawrahta enshrined in the Shwezigon Pagoda he built at Nyaung Oo, near Bagan, Burma, in 1059. He also had four additional duplicates of this tooth made and placed in four pagodas in other parts of his kingdom. Another duplicate from Sri Lanka was sent in 1574 to King Bayint Naung (1551–1581 CE), the founder of the Second Myanmar Empire, who enshrined it in the Maha Zedi Pagoda in Bago. These duplicate relics remain important objects of veneration in the country.

In still another story, two monks, Gawunpadi and Kuthlayone, delivered one of Buddha's teeth (of which there were 40) to a monk named Buhala who brought it to Rakhine State (Arakan), now part of Myanmar. Here the Bagan Pagoda was built some 2,300 years ago near Mrauk-U. That pagoda collapsed in 1980 and an abbot of a nearby monastery discovered the Buddha tooth relic. That relic was subsequently given as a gift to the Golden Pagoda Buddhist Temple in Singapore. That temple's abbot, Venerable Shi Fazhao, had been in Bagan assisting in the rebuilding of Buddhist temples at the time of the find. He has most recently overseen the construction of a new temple just to house the tooth.

China is home to two of the most famous relics of the Buddha. In the present capital of China, Beijing, Ling Guang Si Monastery is home to one of Buddha's teeth, the same one the Burmese ruler attempted to obtain in the 11th century. Meanwhile, the medieval capital, Xian, had been the home to Buddha's finger bone, housed in Famen Si Monastery. According to the story told at Famen, Ashoka's emissaries ventured into China and left the emperor with four little bones, said to be finger bones of the Buddha. The emperor and his successors had vaguely heard of Buddhism, but knew little of it and were not impressed. Little notice of the relics was taken in the following centuries.

Only during the Tang dynasty (618–907 CE) did the issue of the bones arise. The government built an underground crypt beneath a high tower to house the bones. Once each 30 years the bones would be brought out for public viewing. Then, when the Tang dynasty fell, the crypt was closed up and over the next centuries the treasure it contained again forgotten. Only a local rumor of the crypt's existence persisted. Then in 1981, when a reconstruction of the collapsed tower was initiated, the underground crypt was rediscovered, its importance recognized, and the finger once again put on display.

Thailand traces its relic story to King Asoka, who sent two missionaries, Sona Dhera and Uttara Dhera, to Nakhon Pathom, which appears to have been the capital of Suwannaphumi (ca. 139 BCE–457 CE), a nation in what is today Thailand. Stories of the arrival of relics of the Buddha into Thailand generally begin with that event and the large stupa that is now one of the attractions of Nakhon Pathom. Over the centuries, additional stupas, called *chendis* in Thailand, have been erected across Thailand, many claiming to hold relics of the Buddha.

Through the last half of the 20th century, Thailand proved generous with its many relics. In 1994, for example, Thailand initiated a project at Kushinagar, where Buddha died, as part of a larger movement to re-establish Buddhism in the land of its origin. The Maha Chetiya, a shrine designed by the Thai King Bhumibhol Adulyadej, was included within the impressive monastic complex and here some of Buddha's relics formerly kept in Thailand were placed. Again, in 2008, Somdet Phra Nyanasaam Vara, the supreme Buddhist patriarch of Thailand, presented Sikkim with some relics on the occasion of their erecting a 130-foot statue of Buddha at Karma Thekchenling monastery in Rabong, Sikkim.

At the beginning of the 21st century, the Foundation for the Preservation of the Mahayana Tradition moved forward with the Maitreya Project, an effort to create a 500-foot statue of the Buddha Maitreya in the mountains of northern India. As part of this effort, Lama Zopa Rinpoche has assembled a huge collection of Buddhist relics, mostly those of various Buddhist holy men, but some from Gautama Buddha. In 2007, he conducted a world tour with the relics, designed to both publicize the project and raise financial support. Subsequently, he has made the collection available to groups who wish to sponsor a display of the relics in their community.

Christian Relics The Christian attention to relics was generated in three stages. It initially emerged during the persecutions of the church within the Roman Empire. Among the early mentions of the use of relics are the reflections on the death of Polycarp in 156 CE. Polycarp was the bishop of Smyrna (in what today is Turkey), and some who knew him circulated a letter concerning the aftermath of his death in which they note, "We afterwards took up his bones which are more valuable than precious stones and finer than refined gold, and laid them in a suitable place; where the Lord will permit us to gather ourselves together, as we are able, in gladness and joy, and to celebrate the birth-day of his martyrdom for the commemoration of those that have already fought in the contest, and for the training and preparation of those that shall do so hereafter."

The first relics of the Christian movement thus became the bones of those who died as martyrs. They became increasingly important as an element in worship, and eventually a rule would be made that relics of martyrs should be incorporated into church altars where the Eucharist was celebrated. This notion evolved to the point where it was (and remains) forbidden for Roman Catholic priests to celebrate the Mass at an altar devoid of relics. The increasing emphasis on the relics of the martyrs was quite consistent with the worship gatherings of what remained a marginalized and sporadically persecuted minority, which at times had to meet in the catacombs amid the bodies of the dead.

In the fourth century, beginning with the victory of Constantine at Milvian Bridge (312 CE), the church went from being an outlawed and persecuted religion to legal religion to privileged religion in little more than a decade. Among the changes wrought by Constantine's conversion was the new access it gave to Palestine and the locations at which the seminal events in the founding of the faith occurred. Suddenly, it was possible to think about Jesus and the events and objects related to his life, death, and resurrection. While his bones had long since disappeared (and it was believed that following his resurrection, his body ascended into heaven), the list of objects possibly associated with him was lengthy. It could include any clothes he wore, pieces of the True Cross on which he was crucified, the crown of thorns he wore, the spear used to pierce his side, the cup from which he drank at the Last Supper, and other objects related to the biblical story. Toward the end of her life and her son's reign, Constantine's mother Helena visited Palestine and while there was presented with a spectrum of items that she believed to be true relics. Among the many items she had sent back to Constantinople was the True Cross. Many of the relics unearthed by Helena subsequently found their way to Rome.

Along with the relics of Jesus, and second only to them, were the relics of the Virgin Mary and the Twelve Apostles. As with Jesus, since the Virgin Mother was reputedly translated to heaven, no bodily remains were believed extant. The bodies of several of the Apostles, however, were claimed to have survived. Most notable among these were the bodies of Peter and Paul, believed to be in Rome, and that of James, which was believed to have been transported to Santiago de Compostela in northwest Spain. St. Peter's Cathedral is believed to have been built over the burial site of Peter.

Relics of various biblical characters would find their way to churches across Europe. Helena is, for example, supposed to have discovered the bones of the Three Magi who visited Jesus shortly after his birth. These bones were taken to Constantinople, but later found their way to Milan. From Milan, they were given to the cathedral at Cologne in 1154. Helena is also credited with finding the tunic worn by Jesus when he was crucified. That tunic, like the bones of the Three Magi, made its way initially to Constantinople and then to Trier, Germany, in the 12th century.

The more famous but less documented relics reputedly collected by Helena emerged at the end of the 11th century, a result of the new level of popularity given to them by the Crusades. Crusaders returned from the Holy Land with a host of new and exciting relics (from the blood of Jesus to the milk from the Virgin Mary). This new supply of relics from Palestine also paralleled a seeming multiplication of miracle stories centered on saintly people, from healings to the unusual preservation of their bodies. The rich and powerful emerged as collectors of relics or with public shows of piety in the form of endowing local churches with prominent relics.

Through the 16th century, the building of St. Peter's Cathedral occasioned the assembling of possibly the largest and most impressive collection of relics ever assembled within Christianity. Among the many treasures claimed to be found there are Veronica's veil, the cloth used to wipe the sweat from Jesus as he carried the cross, at which time an image of Jesus was transferred to it; the Spear of Longinus, with which Jesus was pierced while on the cross; and a piece of the True Cross. There are several rivals to both the Veronica's veil and the spear of Longinus now at St. Peter's.

At the same time that relics were being assembled for and installed at St. Peter's, Protestants launched a critique of relics. They challenged both their efficacy and the biblical basis of their use. The effect of Protestantism on the cult of relics is clearly seen in the life of Frederick, the elector of Saxony. An early defender of Reformer Martin Luther, the pious Frederick also owned one of the larger collections of relics in Germany. He would in the end give up his collection as incompatible with his Reformed faith.

Luther's initial attack on relics in the church evolved into broad attack upon relics in general. Protestants attacked the superstitious nature of beliefs in relics and publicized the problems that arose because of the gap between the time of Jesus and the Apostles and the initial appearance of any individual relic. The use of relics was largely abandoned in the various Protestant churches. Toward the end of the 16th century, the Council of Trent, called to respond to the losses suffered by the Catholic Church due to the Protestant movement, reaffirmed the legitimacy and role of relics in the church, but offered some criticism of the excesses of relic veneration.

In the 20th century, the growing body of knowledge relative to Western history and the new abilities of science to evaluate objects created a new historical criticism of relics. A number of relics have been tested using the techniques of modern chemistry, biology, and physics, in the context of critical historical examination of stories concerning their origin. The mass of evidence has found them, in many cases, to have originated at the time when they "reappeared" on the historical stage after a period of being lost. The critique of the historicity of many prominent relics, such as the Shroud of Turin or the crown of thorns now housed in Paris, France, has also been joined by the scientific critique of many extraordinary occurrences associated with different artifacts, such as the "supernatural" noncorruptibility of the body of different saints.

The Roman Catholic Church does not commonly attempt to speak officially relative to the authentication of relics, but does offer its general approval of some relics in its allowing the veneration of some objects, its inclusion of relics in prominent locations, and the necessity of relics to the celebration of the Eucharist. At the same time, it does make the acceptance of a particular relic a matter of compulsion, and maintains a conversation with scholars of the church on the issue.

Christianity, especially the Roman Catholic Church, more than Buddhism, draws a sharp distinction between the *veneration* appropriate to saints and the *worship* that is only offered to God. Further, it makes a distinction between the worship of God, during which the assistance of the saints is sought, and the honor paid to saintly individuals as exemplars of the faith. These distinctions can be obscured in practice in the case of relics, especially where supernatural powers and miraculous claims are attached to them.

Eastern Orthodoxy has a history of and belief in relics similar to Roman Catholicism. For example, the relics of martyrs and saints are included in the altar where the Eucharist is celebrated. When a new church building is consecrated, it is common for the local bishop to present a relic of a saint, which is then placed in or on the altar where the Eucharist is celebrated. In the Eastern church, there is also a piece of silk cloth, the *antimins*, used during the Eucharist which usually also contains one or more relics of a saint. There is likewise a sharp distinction between veneration toward relics and worship toward God. There are some differences in Orthodoxy, however, many deriving from the slightly different definition of who is a saint, others deriving from the differences in burial practices in Eastern and Western Europe.

The church believes all Christians who have made it to heaven are saints. At the same time, some people have been recognized as saintly persons during their earthly life, and the church has through an archbishop patriarch recognized that fact. The veneration of a saint usually begins locally and then spreads nationally and internationally. At some point, the veneration might lead to a worship service in which a particular person is formally recognized as a saint—a process called glorification. Prominent saints might have their stylized image placed on an icon. The ecumenical patriarch, who resides in Istanbul, on occasion distributes letters in which he names a saint and assigns a day on the church's calendar when they are especially honored. Relics, to which miraculous powers have been ascribed, may support that person's being formally glorified.

Relics in Islam Given its concern to avoid anything that hints of idolatry, Islam places less emphasis on relics than does Christianity, but nevertheless, the relics associated with Muhammad and his companions are highly valued. No better collection of such relics is to be found than the one assembled in Istanbul at Topkapi Palace. The initial relics in the collection appear to have been acquired by Sultan Selim I (1465–1520). Following his incorporation of Egypt into the Ottoman Empire, his representative in Mecca sent him some relics of Muhammad.

As the collection in Istanbul grew, it came to include some hair from Muhammad's beard, a chip from one of his teeth, and a footprint preserved in porphyry. He is believed to have used other items—a cloak, a seal, and a bow. Muhammad's cloak, called Hirka-i Saadet, is kept in a solid gold box. There is also a letter he wrote. Among additional prized possessions at the palace museum are the oldest known copy of the Koran, two pieces of cloth formerly used to cover the Kaaba in Mecca, and a sword used by the first four caliphs, who have a special place in secular and sacred Muslim history. The sword is a symbol of the authority that each of the four caliphs exercised and passed on to their successors, and that was eventually assumed by the Ottoman emperors. This extensive collection of relics has made Topkapi not just a tourist destination, but a pilgrimage site.

It is to be noted that Muhammad's body was buried in a secret location, unknown today, and was neither cremated nor dismembered. Remains were limited to hair and fingernail clippings, but a number of examples are found around the Middle East, while footprints are found built into a number of mosques.

Relics and Unbelief The community of Unbelief, which includes atheists and a wide spectrum of religious skeptics, has been among the most vocal critics of relics, which they have seen as relics of a superstitious belief and an untenable supernaturalism, neither of which has a place in a modern scientific work. Some, such as scholar of the supernatural, Joe Nickel, have seen relics as a glowing symbol of religion's weak foundation. Such critics have marshaled the scientific critiques of popular relics, especially those now displayed in European churches, while conducting original research on contemporary objects with the potential of becoming relics, as part of a campaign both to refute and ridicule them. In this regard they have aligned themselves with the larger number of religious believers who have also done research that has led to negative observations on different relics.

The campaign against relics is part of a larger effort to deal with what skeptics have termed pseudoscience. Individual scholars and others, such as stage magicians, have attacked what they consider to be claims of "supernatural" phenomena, since the rise of materialization séances in 19th-century spiritualism. Their effort led to the formation of the Committee for the Scientific Investigation of the Claims of the Paranormal (CSICOP) by a group of Humanists in the 1970s. CSICOP has more recently evolved into the Committee of Skeptical Inquiry (CSI). CSI is a member of the International Humanist and Ethical Union and ascribes to the Amsterdam Declaration, a manifesto on Humanism. Through the Center for Inquiry, the Committee is related to the Council for Secular Humanism.

J. Gordon Melton

See also: Ashoka; Atheism; Buddhism; Constantine the Great; Council for Secular Humanism; Eastern Orthodoxy; Ecumenical Patriarchate/Patriarchate of Constantinople; Foundation for the Preservation of the Mahayana Tradition; Helena, Flavia Iulia; Humanism; Luther, Martin; Mecca; Muhammad; Roman Catholic Church; Rome/Vatican City; Saints; Tibetan Buddhism; Unbelief.

References

Bentley, James. *Restless Bones: The Story of Relics.* London: Constable, 1985.

Fleet, J. F. "The Tradition about the Corporeal Relics of Buddha." *Journal of the Royal Asiatic Society* (1907): 341–363. http://www.lightwatcher.com/old_lightbytes/buddha_on_tour.html. Accessed May 15, 2009.

Gauthier, Marie-Madeleine. *Highways of the Faith: Relics and Reliquaries from Jerusalem to Compostela*. Trans. by J. A. Underwood. London: Alpine Fine Arts, 1983.

Landes, Richard. *Relics, Apocalypse, and the Deceits of History: Ademar of Chabannes, 989–1034.* Cambridge: Harvard University Press, 1995.

Nickell, Joe. *Looking for a Miracle.* Amherst, NY: Prometheus Books, 1998.

Nickell, Joe. *Relics of the Christ*. Lexington: University Press of Kentucky, 2007.

Rhys Davids, T. W. "Asoka and the Buddha-Relics." *Journal of the Royal Asiatic Society* (1901): 397–410.

Rufus, Anneli. *Magnificent Corpses: Searching Through Europe for St. Peter's Head, St. Claire's Heart, St. Stephen's Hand, and Other Saints' Relics.* Cambridge: Da Capo Press, 1999

Sora, Steven. *Treasures from Heaven: Relics from Noah's Ark to the Shroud of Turin*. New York: Wiley, 2005.

Standish, Russell R., and Colin D. Standish. *Holy Relics or Revelation: Recent Astounding Archaeological Claims Evaluated.* Rapidan, VA: Hartland Publications, 1999.

Strong, John. *Relics of the Buddha*. Princeton, NJ: Princeton University Press, 2004.

Wheeler, Brannon M. *Mecca and Eden: Rituals, Relics and Territory in Islam.* Chicago: University of Chicago Press, 2006.

Religion-Government Relations

Across the globe there are a variety of relationships between religious groups and the governments of the states in which they are located—frequently for historical and cultural reasons—and these interactions are often underpinned by law (Robbers 2005). At a very general level four different types of relationships can be distinguished (Cranmer and Oliva 2009). The first two are characterized by the very close connection between the state and one or more religious communities. Such a relationship may be characterized by the control of religious matters by the state (Erastianism) or by the control of the state by a religious group (theocracy). The third is the converse situation: separation between the state and religion, typically in the form of a constitutional barrier forbidding financial support or the establishment of any particular religious

American flag waves in front of a small church. (James Martin/Dreamstime.com)

group. The fourth, known variously as hybrid, cooperationist, or concordatarian systems, comprises those countries that fall between the extremes: a clear differentiation between religious communities and secular government, coupled with clear evidence of cooperation between the two.

The Erastian model is characterized by a close association between one or more religious groups and the state under which the secular authorities exercise supremacy over religion. Historically, this has been a common model in Europe (Cranmer and Oliva 2009), perhaps epitomized by the Henrician Reformation in England: an argument—to put it simply—over whether the pope or the king was going to make policy for the church. Although no modern state in Europe is Erastian in the full sense of that term, some churches are subject to a much greater degree of state supervision than others. Many Constitutions (such as those of the United Kingdom, Denmark, Greece, Finland, Malta and Bulgaria) continue to give a special status to one or more religious communities, which may be styled as a state, national, established, or folk church.

Perhaps the most striking modern example of quasi-Erastianism is the Church of Denmark. Its dignitaries are appointed by the Crown on the recommendation of the minister of ecclesiastical affairs, it has no synod or legal personality and it is not a corporate body. The Ministry of Ecclesiastical Affairs determines rules concerning membership and the creation of new parishes and approves the appointment and dismissal of clergy—who have the status of civil servants and who act as civil registrars for births. Though Denmark is the extreme case, there are many less overt instances of governmental involvement in church affairs. An obvious example is the United Kingdom, where bishops of the Church of England sit in the legislature and where church measures are part of the law of the land, requiring parliamentary approval before they can become law (Hill 2007, para 1.25; Hill 2009a).

The converse is theocracy, where the secular authorities are subordinate to the religious—the de facto situation in Geneva during Calvin's ascendancy. Iran under Ayatollah Khomeini exemplifies this approach, while several Islamic states have introduced overtly religious elements such as the *sharia* into their legal and political systems.

Both quasi-Erastian and theocratic religion-state relationships are extremely heterogeneous. For instance, although there are close ties between church and state in both Denmark and Greece, the high degree of state control over the Church of Denmark is not paralleled in Greece, where the Orthodox Church has its own status as a legal entity and where its self-governance is guaranteed by the Greek Constitution.

Moreover, close ties between religion and the state often have more to do with theory than with practice (Sandberg and Doe 2007). In many countries historically significant connections with religious communities have lessened. In some, such as Sweden and Wales, legislation has resulted in the disestablishment of a particular religious community. Moreover, even in those countries where one or more churches are established by law, to describe the situation as quasi-Erastian does not necessarily paint an accurate picture of the full interaction between religion and government, focusing as it does upon the relationship between one religious group and the state (Hill 2009b). Even in Finland (where there are two state churches—the Evangelical Lutheran Church and the Orthodox Church) other religious communities benefit from tax exemptions once they are registered under the Freedom of Religion Act 2003.

The third type of relationship is separation between the state and religion, usually in the form of a constitutional prohibition forbidding government intervention in religious affairs. Separation is the American solution: the "Jefferson Wall." Famously, the First Amendment to the U.S. Constitution provides that "Congress shall make no law respecting an establishment of religion, or prohibiting the free exercise thereof" and, in principle, the secular and the religious are completely removed from one another. However, in practice separation between the two is not absolute. For example, the Supreme Court has allowed tax deductions for parental expenditure on tuition, textbooks and transport for those whose children attend church schools on the same basis as for those with children at the public schools thereby according to faith schools (and the parents of children attending them) federal fiscal advantages on like terms as non-sectarian public schools.

The same is true in the case of France, the European country seen as the separation system par excellence. Although the Constitution states that "The Republic does not recognize, remunerate, or subsidize any religious denomination" and "France shall be an indivisible, secular, democratic and social Republic," there is much regulation of religion—and some special treatment of it. The Bureau des Cultes of the Ministry of the Interior plays an active role in ensuring religious freedom; religious groups enjoy special status as religious associations, diocesan associations, charitable and educational associations, religious orders, and new religious movements and sects; state subsidies are given to activities that have a general character despite having a religious setting, to religious ministers when they render services to the general public, and to fund repairs to Roman Catholic places of worship built before 1905. A similar picture can be found in Ireland (Colton 2006): though the Constitution provides that "The State guarantees not to endow any religion," schools are organized predominantly on denominational lines and extensively supported by state funding. A recent amendment to the Irish criminal law will re-introduce the offense of blasphemy and accord protection from religious hate speech. In contrast, in Turkey the rhetoric of the Constitution declaring that Turkey "is a democratic, secular and social state governed by the rule of law" has led the Constitutional Court to close down two political parties on the grounds that their existence breached the principle of secularism—bans that were subsequently upheld by the European Court of Human Rights.

The separationist model, like the others, is characterized by diversity. However, in most countries in this category, separation is seen not as the pre-eminent goal but rather as the means toward a larger end of protecting religious freedom. This requires from the state not indifference, but positive action to facilitate religious freedom. In practice, therefore, in many separationist systems there is little to distinguish the relationship between the government and all religious groups from the relationship between the government and all religious groups other than the specially protected religion(s) in quasi-Erastian systems.

The cooperationist model is, on the face of it, the most problematic, comprising those relationships that cannot be fitted into the other categories—broad and imprecisely-defined though they may be. In theory, this type is characterized by even-handedness toward religious groups and the recognition of pluralism and cooperation on the part of the state. Legally, the state may recognize the value of religion in the form of an agreement, a treaty, or (as in the case of Spain and Italy) a Concordat. Alternatively, the state may regulate religious groups as voluntary associations in the same way as other voluntary bodies but, nevertheless, give a measure of direct or indirect financial support to some of their social and educational activities or may treat them on the same basis, as is the case in Belgium.

However, many of the apparent characteristics of countries in the fourth category—equality, cooperation, and recognition of pluralism—are characteristics of democracies generally (Sandberg 2008). The European Court of Human Rights has spoken of the state's role as "the neutral and impartial organiser of the exercise of various religions, faiths and beliefs" (*Leyla Şahin v. Turkey* [2005], No. 44774/98 para 107) and stressed the state's duty of neutrality and impartiality. Many countries operate a system under which, in return for registering with the state, faith communities qualify for a range of benefits, such as the right to hold property as juridical persons, civil recognition of their marriages, and tax concessions as charitable institutions. However, these countries are not all to be found in the fourth type; examples can be found within all of them. Moreover, even within the third type, it is clear that states cooperate more with some religious groups than others, creating a closer connection with some of them that is not dissimilar from that found in the first type. Italy, Spain, and Belgium operate a three-tier distinction between the Roman Catholic Church, other religious communities with whom the state has made agreements, and all other religious groups with whom no agreement has been made. These countries seem to favor one religious denomination to the same extent (if not to a greater one) as do the countries found in the first type.

In conclusion, it is possible at a general level to categorize forms of religion-government relations into four different models in order to provide a convenient starting-point for comparative analysis. That said, however, such relationships differ from country to country and from religious group to religious group. Four important qualifications need to be kept in mind. First, it should be recognized that a great number of different laws affect the manifestation of religion; and it is important, therefore, not to confine discussion of religion-government relations solely to issues of constitutional law. Second, the regulation of religious manifestation is increasingly affected by international laws and norms, not least by human rights provisions; the result is a degree of homogeneity, particularly in relation to minimum standards, that should not be overlooked (Doe 2009). Third, though religious manifestation is undoubtedly affected by the governmental system of the nation-state, governance at the sub-national level is also important. Governmental relations with religious groups are not the sole preserve of central government (Oliva and Lambert 2009): for example, under Article 72 of the Swiss Constitution "the regulation of the relationship between church and state is a cantonal matter"—and different cantons have different arrangements. Fourth, the focus of any study should not merely be upon religious groups; secular policy and laws also impact upon individuals and many of the legal protections for religious activity are concerned with individual religious freedoms as well as belief systems (whether collective or individualistic) that fall outside of the traditional understanding of religion.

Russell Sandberg, Frank Cranmer, Javier García Oliva, Mark Hill, and Norman Doe

See also: Calvin, John; Church of England; Evangelical Lutheran Church in Denmark; Evangelical Lutheran Church of Finland; Finnish Orthodox Church; Roman Catholic Church.

References

Colton, Paul. "Religion and Law in Dialogue: Covenantal and Non-Covenantal Cooperation of State and Religions in Ireland." In *Religion and Law in Dialogue: Covenantal and Non-Covenantal Cooperation between State and Religion in Europe*, edited by R. Puza and N. Doe, 93–114. Leuven: Peeters, 2006.

Cranmer, Frank, and Javier Oliva. "Church-State Relationships: An Overview." *Law and Justice* 162 (2009): 4–17.

Doe, Norman. "Towards a 'Common Law' on Religion in the European Union." *Religion, State and Society* 37, nos. 1–2 (2009): 147–166.

Hill, Mark. *Ecclesiastical Law.* 3rd ed. Oxford: Oxford University Press, 2007.

Hill, Mark. "Voices in the Wilderness: the Established Church of England and the European Union." *Religion, State and Society* 37, nos. 1–2 (2009a): 167–180.

Hill, Mark. "Church and State in the United Kingdom: Anachronism or Microcosm?" *ICLARS* (2009b).

Oliva, Javier, and David Lambert. "Regional Ecclesiastical Law: Religion and Devolution in Spain and Wales." In *Law and Religion: New Horizons,* edited by Norman Doe and Russell Sandberg, 219–243. Leuven: Peeters, 2009.

Robbers, Gerhard. "State and Church in the European Union." In *State and Church in the European Union,* edited by Gerhard Robbers, 577–589. Baden-Baden: Nomos, 2005.

Sandberg, Russell, and Norman Doe. "Church-State Relations in Europe." *Religion Compass* 1, no. 5 (2007): 561–578.

Sandberg, Russell, and Norman Doe. "Church-State Relations in Europe: From Legal Models to an Interdisciplinary Approach." *Journal of Religion in Europe* 1, no. 3 (2008): 329–352.

Religious Freedom: Contemporary

The 21st century has inherited numerous public declarations supporting religious freedom as a fundamental human right; however, these declarations are frequently contradicted by government policies and social actions related to religious protectionism, extremism, and terrorism. Despite the many problems and challenges, the data indicate that religious freedom, when actually protected and practiced, is not only a benefit to religions themselves but is associated with better socioeconomic outcomes for societies and is instrumental in lowering the level of religious violence.

Responding to genocidal atrocities such as the Holocaust of World War II, the General Assembly of the United Nations adopted and proclaimed the Universal Declaration of Human Rights on December 10, 1948. Article 18 of the Declaration states that "Everyone has the right to freedom of thought, conscience and religion; this right includes freedom to change his religion or belief, and freedom, either alone or in community with others and in public or private, to manifest his religion or belief in teaching, practice, worship and observance." The Declaration has been distributed in more than 330 languages and serves as the basis for numerous other international human rights declarations. The United Nations also appoints a Special Rapporteur

Two women pray at a government-approved Catholic church in Beijing. The communist Beijing government ordered Chinese Catholics to break ties with the Vatican in 1951 and allows people to worship only in government-approved churches which do not recognize the Pope's authority. (AP Photo)

on Freedom of Religion or Belief to continually monitor grievances and bring them to the attention of governments. Religious freedom also was positively impacted by the change in the official position of the Roman Catholic Church, the world's largest single religious body. As part of the Second Vatican Council reforms, Pope Paul VI (r. 1963–1978) promulgated the Declaration on Religions Freedom, *Dignitatis humanae,* on December 7, 1965. *Dignitatis humanae* specifically states that "the human person has a right to religious freedom. This freedom means that all men are to be immune from coercion on the part of individuals or of social groups and of any human power, in such wise that no one is to be forced to act in a manner contrary to his own beliefs, whether privately or publicly, whether alone or in association with others, within due limits. . . . This right of the human person to religious freedom is to be recognized in the constitutional law whereby society is governed and thus it is to become a civil right."

The advance of religious freedom's promise is also seen by the protections that now exist for religious freedom in many countries' Constitutions (or basic law). Recent research by the Pew Forum (2009) shows that 76 percent of the countries surveyed, large and small, promise religious freedom in their Constitutions, and an additional 20 percent protect at least some religious practices. Only 4 percent of Constitutions provide no protections for religious freedom or the freedom to engage in certain religious practices. This seemingly strong level of constitutional protection can be, however, misleading. In only 22 percent of countries does the Constitution of the country not go on to qualify or contradict religious freedom. In 26 percent of the Constitutions, there is some qualification placed on religious freedom, such as stipulating that religious freedom is subject to law and order. In an additional 48 percent of the Constitutions, only some religious practices are protected.

Constitutional promises of religious freedom do not, however, automatically translate into guaranteed protection or practice of religious freedom. In the closing years of the 20th century and first years of the 21st century, hundreds of thousands of people have been abused or displaced specifically due to their religious identity, and tens of millions more have been killed or displaced due to religion-related conflicts. While many of these deaths have occurred in religion-related violence such as the sectarian conflict in Iraq, the abuse and displacement are much more widespread, occurring at least to some degree in more than one in two countries. While religion-related abuse and displacement (or religious violence) occur across all major religious traditions and in all regions of the globe, there is important variation depending on the perpetrator of the violence (government versus social actors), the level of violence, and the majority religion of the country.

New research has indicated that the presence of religious freedom in a country not only reduces religion-related violence and physical persecution, but it mathematically correlates with the presence of other fundamental freedoms, including civil and political liberty, press freedom, economic freedom, and the longevity of democracy. This means that wherever religious freedom is found, these other freedoms tend to be found as well. Harvard Economist and Nobel Laureate Amartya Sen argues, however, that human freedom is not just the *general* opportunity for such freedoms, but also the *specific* processes within a country that result in better lives. Thus, if religious freedom is considered an integral part of the bundled commodity of human freedoms, religious freedom should be closely associated with the betterment of people's lives. The data show that wherever religious freedom is high, there tend to be fewer incidents of armed conflict, better health outcomes, better educational opportunities for women, and higher levels of earned income for women as well as for men. Moreover, religious freedom is associated with higher overall human development. The close statistical correlation between religious freedom and other positive socioeconomic and political outcomes suggests that religious freedom is an inseparable part of the bundled commodity of fundamental human freedoms. Thus, religious freedom cannot be peeled off without adversely affecting the entire bundle.

The association between religious freedom and human development can be seen, for example, by comparing the work experiences of many in the Kingdom of Saudi Arabia with its immediate neighbor, the United Arab Emirates. In the Emirates, where many faiths are legal, people have many ways to contribute to society through religious associations as well as through other avenues. People tend to work hard and be involved in society. In Saudi Arabia, however, where all faiths but one faith are illegal, there is much less enthusiasm for work and many people express no real desire to contribute to society outside of work. These experiences, reported by many in both countries, suggest a connection between the level of religious freedom in each and the economic life of people in each. For instance, the 2007 per capita gross domestic product in U.S. purchasing power parity dollars (GDP-PPP) in the Emirates is $55,200, nearly triple the per capita GDP-PPP in Saudi Arabia, which is only $20,700.

The connection between religious freedom and human development can also be seen in China. During the Cultural Revolution, China repressed all public religious expression. From the early 1980s China left those dismal years of complete religious repression behind. Since then, China's economy has boomed, making it the rival of the West and the envy of many. Though the Chinese government continues to forcefully restrict religious groups operating without government approval, the comparative increase in religious freedom following the Cultural Revolution seems to have played a part in China's phenomenal development. It is reasonable to suggest that religious freedom's further expansion can help the Chinese make even greater social progress.

A growing body of research supports the proposition that the religious competition inherent in religious freedom results in increased and broad religious participation; concomitantly, religious participation can lead to a wide range of positive social and political outcomes. Furthermore, as a broad range of religious groups make contributions to society and become an accepted part of the fabric of society, religious freedom is consolidated. This can be conceptualized as a religious freedom cycle.

In recent years, many studies have looked at the benefits of the social and spiritual capital generated through civic and religious involvement. As more people actively participate in religion, religious groups engage in "processes," to use Amartya Sen's term, that bring tangible benefits ranging from literacy, vocational and health training, to marital and bereavement counseling, to feeding the hungry, clothing the poor, and caring for the sick. Research has found that faith-based organizations, for example, are the major providers of care and support services to people living with HIV/AIDS in the developing world, and there is growing scientific evidence of the health benefits associated with religious participation itself. Some studies suggest that the advent of new religious forms can help improve the lives of women and activate greater civic participation.

Sociologist Peter Berger, once a proponent of secularization theory, observes that we are in an age of explosive, pervasive religiosity. Berger and Anton Zijderveld further argue that the world is becoming increasingly pluralistic, and that when states try to impose limits on religious liberty, the growth of pluralism directly challenges state attempts to curtail religious freedom. Another eminent sociologist, N. J. Demerath, concludes that, given the global religious dynamics of today, the challenge for governments is to better understand cultural conflict and the impact of religious diversity. Thus, it is critical to understand how the affairs of nations and peoples are affected by religious freedom—in both its social and governmental aspects. The empirical data are clear on two points. First, religious freedom is part of the bundled commodity of fundamental and responsible human freedoms that energize broader *productive* participation in civil society by all religious groups, which arguably helps to stimulate the socioeconomic progress of women *and* men. Second, religious freedom reduces religion-related conflict and increases security by, among other things, removing grievances religious groups have toward governments and their fellow citizens. Furthermore, over the past 100 years, promises of religious freedom have been included in international declarations, country Constitutions, and laws. Despite the widespread religion-related violence that has marked the start of the 21st century, it is possible that the years ahead may see further advances of religious freedom in practice.

Brian J. Grim

See also: Roman Catholic Church; Violence, Religious.

Bibliography

Bates, M. Searle. *Religious Liberty: An Inquiry.* New York: International Missionary Council, 1945.

Berger, Peter, and Anton Zijderveld. *In Praise of Doubt: How to Have Convictions Without Becoming a Fanatic.* New York: HarperOne.

Demerath, N. J., III. *Crossing the Gods: Worldly Religions and Worldly Politics.* New Brunswick, NJ: Rutgers University, 2002.

Grim, Brian J. "Religious Freedom: Good for What Ails Us?" *The Review of Faith and International Affairs* 6, no. 2 (2008).

Grim, Brian J. "Religious Freedom in the World." In *Atlas of Global Christianity,* edited by Todd M. Johnson and Kenneth R. Ross, 37–43. Edinburgh: Edinburgh University Press, 2009.

Grim, Brian J., and Roger Finke. *The Price of Freedom Denied: Religious Persecution and Conflict in the 21st Century.* Cambridge: Cambridge University Press, forthcoming.

Grim, Brian J., and Roger Finke. "Religious Persecution in Cross-National Context: Clashing Civilizations or Regulated Religious Economies?" *American Sociological Review* 72, no. 4 (2007): 633–658.

Marshall, Paul, ed. *Religious Freedom in the World.* Lanham, MD: Rowman and Littlefield, 2008.

Religious Science

Religious Science is the youngest major tradition in the New Thought movement. It is also the second largest, with its two major groups, the United Church of Religious Science (UCRS) and Religious Science International (RSI), ranking second and third in size, respectively, behind the Unity School of Christianity/Association of Unity Churches. Both groups trace their origin to Ernest Shurtleff Holmes (1887–1960), one of the last students to study with the founder of New Thought, Emma Curtis Hopkins (1849–1925). Holmes's classic New Thought text, *The Science of Mind* (1926), supplies the basis for the tradition's primary beliefs and healing practices. It is also widely studied in other New Thought communities and serves as the primary religious text for many independent groups, most notably the non-affiliated Science of Mind churches. Holmes began his work in Los Angeles, California, and although Religious Science is an international movement today, the largest concentration of its churches is still in that state.

Holmes, together with his brother Fenwick, was active in the mental healing movement even before his studies with Hopkins. His early influences were diverse, including Ralph Waldo Emerson (1803–1882), Mary Baker Eddy (1821–1910), Henry Drummond (1851–1897), and especially Thomas Troward (1847–1916). The system he eventually developed is a synthesis of Christian Science and Troward's theories. He was ordained in Divine Science by Agnes J. Galer in 1917, when he was already attracting large crowds to his lectures on mental healing and a growing number of clients for his services as a practitioner. In 1925, the year after Ernest's studies with Hopkins, he parted from Fenwick on friendly terms; Fenwick went East, where he enjoyed considerable success as a New Thought author and lecturer, and Ernest settled in Los Angeles, where he began the work that grew into Religious Science.

The relationship of Hopkins to the formation of Religious Science is significant. It is notable that *The Science of Mind* was published two years after Holmes had studied with her. The following year (1927) he established the Institute of Religious Science and Philosophy, Inc., and began publishing *Religious Science Monthly* (by 1929 retitled *Science of Mind*). Holmes had previously written a book, established a religious Institute, and published a magazine, none of which had been particularly successful. After his studies with Hopkins, however, the same component elements came together to form the foundation of a religious movement. Holmes credited Hopkins with supplying what had been missing from his earlier endeavors—mysticism. Although Hopkins's mysticism is certainly a celebrated part of New Thought lore, her capacity to inspire persons to develop fully functional religious movements is probably more significant. She seems to have had provided some sort of inspiration to Holmes.

The emergence of Religious Science from Holmes's work in the late 1920s was gradual and can be measured in terms of several decisive turning points. In 1932 Robert H. Bitzer (1896–1994), who would later have a long tenure as president of International New Thought Alliance, started the Institute's second congregation. Others followed. In 1939 the Institute began

The founding Church of Religious Science in Los Angeles, California. (J. Gordon Melton)

to ordain ministers, and in the mid-1940s one of them, Carmelita Trowbridge, formed the first Religious Science church in Alhambra, California. She successfully resisted the Institute's efforts to prevent her from referring to her group as a "church." The church movement in Religious Science quickly gained momentum, and by 1949 the International Association of Religious Science Churches was formed.

Tensions between the Institute and the Association led the Institute to establish an ecclesiastical organization in 1953—the Church of Religious Science. In 1954 Holmes proposed eliminating the Association and replacing it with the newly formed Church of Religious Science. Forty-six churches joined the church, but 19 refused. Churches that affiliated with the church went on to become the United Church of Religious Science (UCRS), adopting that name in 1967; those staying with the Association became Religious Science International (RSI), adopting that name in 1972.

Both groups accept Holmes's teachings as normative, follow *Science of Mind* as their primary religious text, and recognize two classes of religious professionals: ministers and practitioners. Practitioners in Religious Science have a function similar to that of Christian Science practitioners; they facilitate mental healing and administer "spiritual mind treatment" to individuals on a one-to-one basis. Of all New Thought groups, Religious Science has most faithfully maintained the tradition of mental healing and the role of professional mental healer. This is further revealed in the recognition of practitioner status as a prerequisite for ministerial training in UCRS and RSI.

The chief differences between the groups lie in their organizational structures and in their educational systems. Organizationally, both groups are governed by elected boards and presided over by presidents, who are elected by the boards. UCRS is more centralized and hierarchical, but both groups allow churches significant autonomy, and members of the governing boards are elected by representatives selected by the churches. Educational curricula are largely the same in both groups, although UCRS requires education of its ministers at regional schools, of which there are four, and RSI allows for training at local churches.

Each group publishes a representative periodical. *Science of Mind* (UCRS) has 44,000 subscribers and *Creative Thought* (RSI) has 11,000. In recent years the groups have had a good relationship, establishing policies for accepting each other's ministers and practitioners and working to develop stronger ties through a Committee of Cooperation, established in the late 1980s. The relationship between the two seems to be growing even closer at present. As of 2008, RSI legally changed its name to International Centers for Spiritual Living. UCRS is undergoing a similar name change, currently referring to itself as the United Centers for Spiritual Living. The shared name change is the result of official merger negotiations between RSI (now ICSL) and UCRS and is reflected in the websites of both groups. The push toward a closer integration is also mirrored in both UCRS's and ICSL's collaboration with the larger New Thought movement. Together with other movements under the New Thought banner (such as the Unity organizations), UCRS and ICSL organized themselves under the Association of Global New Thought to form a single cohesive delegation at the Parliament of the World's Religions (December 2009 in Melbourne, Australia).

As of 2008, UCRS had 190 churches, 60 study groups, and 24 teaching chapters. ICSL had 140 churches. The vast majority of centers for both groups are in the United States, with highest concentrations in California. UCRS has representative groups in 20 countries, and ICSL in 35. UCRS operates a Ministry of Prayer that averages about 100,000 contacts annually. In the early 1990s a small number of ICSL (then RSI) ministers left the organization and formed Global Religious Science Ministries (incorporated in 1993). This group has experienced a similar name change, now referring to themselves as the Alliance for Spiritual Understanding. The group has 20 member churches and is headquartered in Richmond, Virginia.

As a branch of New Thought, Religious Science is an expression of popular religious idealism; as such it affirms that the basis of reality is mental, not material, and that mental states determine material conditions. As is characteristic of New Thought as a whole, Religious Science recognizes Mind as the Ultimate Reality, but unlike other New Thought groups its concept of God is far less anthropomorphic, with terms like Principle, Law, and Mind being more commonly used. It is also the least Christian of the groups, neither identifying itself with Christianity nor making any particular effort to retain elements of Christian doctrine. It accepts the perfection and omnipresence of the one Divine Mind and recognizes humanity's link with Mind through the "subjective" minds of individuals. "Spiritual mind treatment" consists of realizing the reality of the perfection of Divine Mind rather than an undesired condition. A typical treatment would include an affirmation, such as: "There is One Life, that Life is God, that Life is Perfect, that Life is my Life now."

United Centers for Spiritual Living/United Church of Religious Science
573 Park Point Dr.
Golden, CO 80401
http://www.religiousscience.org

Religious Science International
International Centers for Spiritual Living
PO Box 2152
Spokane, WA 99210
http://www.rsintl.org

Global Religious Science Ministries
Alliance for Spiritual Understanding
12594 Patterson Ave.
Richmond, VA 23238-6415
http://www.as-u.org/

Dell deChant, Natalie Hobbs, and J. Gordon Melton

See also: Eddy, Mary Baker; International New Thought Alliance; Unity School of Christianity/Association of Unity Churches.

References

Albanese, Catherine L. *A Republic of Mind and Spirit*. New Haven, CT: Yale University Press, 2007.

Braden, Charles. *Spirits in Rebellion: The Rise and Development of New Thought*. Dallas, TX: SMU Press, 1963.

deChant, Dell. "New Thought." In *World Religions in America*, edited by Jacob Neusner. 4th ed. Louisville: Westminster John Knox, 2009.

Holmes, Ernest. *The Science of Mind*. New York: Dodd, Mead and Company, 1944.

Holmes, Fenwick L. *Ernest Holmes: His Life and Times*. New York: Dodd, Mead and Company, 1970.

Remonstrant Brotherhood

The Remonstrant Brotherhood (Remonstrantse Broederschap), a liberal Protestant denomination, has its origins in the condemnation of the Remonstrants at the Synod of Dordrecht (1618–1619). This turn of events had been brought on by a theological struggle about the doctrine of predestination between Jacob Arminius (1560–1609) and Franciscus Gomarus (1563–1641), both professors at the University of Leiden. About 200 ministers supportive of Arminius were dismissed and removed from the Reformed Church of the Netherlands (the Nederduytsche of Gereformeerde Kerk, now an integral part of the Protestant Church of the Netherlands), at that time the privileged church. The Synod of Dordrecht issued the so-called Vijf Artikelen tegen de Remonstranten (the Five Articles against the Remonstrants, also known as the Confession of Dort), which today is still an element in Drie Formulieren van Enigheid (the Three Orders of Unity), the confession of faith in most of the orthodox Protestant Reformed Churches in the Netherlands.

The dismissed ministers fled to Antwerp and hoped that their condemnation would be repealed. The Remonstrant Brotherhood was founded in 1619, when their hope proved vain. A short time later, they returned to the Dutch Republic and created their first conventicle in 1631 in Amsterdam. Three years later, they founded a ministerial training college in Leiden, known since 1873 as the Remonstrant Seminary.

In the second part of the 19th century, the Remonstrant Brotherhood had its Golden Age. Its membership tripled because of the rise of modernism and the movement of more liberal church members into its ranks. In more recent decades, however, the Brotherhood has experienced a period of decline. Between 1966 and 1988, the number of believers sunk by approximately 50 percent. As the 21st century begins, the number of believers is about 7,000, in 46 communities served by 40 ministers. An additional community of about 3,000 is also served by the church. Individuals join the church on the basis of a personal confession. Local congregations identify themselves as Remonstrant Church or as Remonstrant-Reformed.

The Remonstrants' first confession was formulated by Arminius's student Simon Episcopius (1583–1643), and a more contemporary statement appeared in 1940. The Brotherhood believes that the phrasing of confessions is not perpetually valid, and their authority is not to be compared with that of the Bible and the Gospels. The confession is only "a token of time" and can be changed if the modern time makes it necessary; every time has its own needs and therefore its own answers.

The Brotherhood intends to be a community of faith, "rooted in the gospel of Christ and faithful to her principle of freedom and forbearance, and willing to adore God and to serve Him." It is not a confessional church, but an affirming church. The Brotherhood rejects the idea that its members are a "chosen" group, as is believed in most Reformed churches. Hence, everyone can take the holy Communion as long as they live in community with Christ.

Since 1989, every congregation in the Brotherhood has been independent, free to arrange its own spiritual and material affairs. Each congregation calls its own minister and has the right to represent itself at the Algemene Vergadering van de Remonstrantse Broederschap, the coordinating organization. Ongoing executive decisions are left to the Commissie tot de Zaken der Remonstrantse Broederschap (the Committee on the Affairs of the Remonstrant Brotherhood).

Laypeople play an important role in the direction of the Brotherhood. All offices are open to men as well as women. The Remonstrant Brotherhood was also the first church (1989) in the Netherlands to allow the blessing of non-marital communities and also homosexual and lesbian relationships.

The Remonstrant Brotherhood is active ecumenically and a member of the World Council of Churches, although it is critical of the Council's basic statement: "The World Council of Churches is a fellowship of churches that accept our Lord Jesus Christ as God and Saviour." It is also a member of the Council of Churches (in the Netherlands); thc Conference of European Churches (since 1959); the International Congregational Council (beginning in 1949); and since 1970, the World Alliance of Reformed Churches, because of its acceptance of the same spirit of freedom and tolerance, and the same aversion to church discipline in matters of faith. In 1973 the Brotherhood signed the Declaration of Leuenberg, an agreement between Reformed and Lutheran churches. The Brotherhood is also active in several international liberal councils.

The Brotherhood welcomes ministers from the Protestant Church of the Netherlands, the Fellowship of Liberal Reformed Protestants (Verenging van Vrijzinnig Hervormden), the Liberal Communion of Faith NPB (Vrijzinnige Geloofsgemeenschap NPB), and the Mennonite Church in the Netherlands (Algemene Doopsgezinde Sociëteit) to lead worship in Brotherhood congregations.

Remonstrant Brotherhood
Nieuwegracht 27a
3512 LC Utrecht
The Netherlands
http://www.remonstranten.org/ (in Dutch)

E. G. Hoekstra

See also: Arminius, Jacob; Community of Protestant Churches in Europe; Mennonite Church in the Netherlands; Protestant Church in the Netherlands; World Alliance of Reformed Churches.

References

Cossee, E. H., Th. M. van Leeuwen, and M.A. Bosman-Huizinga. *De remonstranten*. 2nd ed. Published in the series *Wegwijs. Kerken en groeperingen.* Kampen: Kok, 2001.

Drees, W. B., ed. *Een beetje geloven. Actualiteit en achtergronden van het vrijzinnig protestantisme*. Amsterdam: Balans, 1999.

Hoenderdaal, G. J., and P. M. Luca, ed. *Staat in de vrijheid. De geschiedenis van de remonstranten.* Zutphen, the Netherlands: De Walburg Pers, 1982.

Kuiper, J., and Th. M. van Leeuwen, eds. *Als een vuurbaken. Teksten over de functie van belij-denissen naar remonstrants inzicht.* Zoetermeer, the Netherlands: Meinema, 1994.

van Leeuwen, Th. M. *Van horen zeggen. Geschiedenis en uitleg van de bijbel.* 2nd ed. Amsterdam: Balans, 1999.

Reorganized Church of Jesus Christ of Latter Day Saints

See Community of Christ.

Restored Church of God

See Living Church of God (plus Global Church of God, and Restored Church of God).

Restored Reformed Church

The Restored Reformed Church (Hersteld Hervormde Kerk) has its origins in the right wing of the former Netherlands Reformed Church, which in 2004 merged with two other churches to form the Protestant Church in the Netherlands. Rather than enter the merger, many members and some ministers objected to this fusion because of their fear that the traditional fundamental doctrinal points would get lost in the new church. Also, they disagreed with the new rules governing church life, principally those that differed from the traditional rules of the Dutch Reformed Church of 1951, based on those from the Synod of Dordrecht (1618–1619). Also they disagreed with the possibility of the solemnization of homosexual relations in the new church. Finally, they especially disagreed with the membership of the Evangelical Lutheran Church in the Kingdom of the Netherlands in the new church, as it had a totally different doctrinal position.

The Restored Reformed Church reported 126 parishes with 53 active and 18 retired ministers and about 60,000 members (2007).

Restored Reformed Church
Postbox 116
3930 EC Woudenberg
The Netherlands

E. G. Hoekstra

See also: Protestant Church in the Netherlands.

References

Kerkelijk Jaarboek. Veenendaal, 2008–.

Hoekstra, E. G., and M. H. Ipenburg. *Handboek christelijk Nederland. Kerken, gemeenten, samenkomsten en vergaderingen*. Kampen: Kok, 2008.

Reuchlin, Johannes

1455–1522

Johannes Reuchlin was an influential leader of the German phase of the Humanist movement that arose in the 15th century with a new appreciation of classical languages, especially those in which the biblical text was originally penned. A Hebrew scholar, he would work for understanding between Christians and Jews, and in the end emerge as an advocate of the mystical appropriation of the Jewish Kabbalah.

Reuchlin was born on February 22, 1455, in Pforzheim, Baden, Germany. He attended the universities at Freiburg, Paris, and Basel, and after completing his master's degree, he taught Greek and Latin at Basel. He later turned his attention to mastering legal studies and received his bachelor's degree at Orléans. He later received a licentiate of law at Poitiers in 1481.

In 1482 and 1490 he made trips to Italy, where he met various Italian scholars known for their support of the new intellectual currents grouped under the general label of Humanism, and found himself well accepted as a colleague. Following the initial trip, he put his legal knowledge to work in the court of Count Eberhard of Württemburg. During these years he began his study of Hebrew. When the count died, he left the court somewhat fearful of the count's successor, but was able to find a new home in Heidelberg, where he became the counsel to the elector.

Johannes Reuchlin, German humanist and theologian. (Archive Photos/Getty Images)

His study of Hebrew culminated in 1498, when he visited Italy and had an extended visit with some learned Jews. His knowledge would be put to work after his becoming the imperial judge of the Swabian Confederation (1502–1512) at Stuttgart. He involved himself in a bitter controversy with the semi-literate Johannes Pfefferkorn (1469–ca. 1521). Pfefferkorn had been raised Jewish but converted to Catholicism, He subsequently published an anti-Semitic work and continued the crusade against his former community in 1509 by asking the Holy Roman Emperor to have all Jewish books burned. As a counselor to the elector, Reuchlin was among the persons from whom the emperor sought counsel. Though aware that the power of the Dominican Order that ran the Inquisition was backing Pfefferkorn, Reuchlin ventured into the debate. By this time he had used his influence to introduce Hebrew into Germany, and in 1506 had published a Hebrew lexicon and grammar. He defended Jewish literature and argued that only the few books that were directly against Catholic faith should be destroyed. Destruction should only follow judicial review and assessment.

The Dominican leader in Cologne called for Reuchlin to appear before the court of the Inquisition to defend his position. Reuchlin utilized his legal skills (and his position) to appeal directly to the pope. The pope, in turn, bypassed the Dominicans and established a special commission to examine the charges and found Reuchlin not guilty (1514). While his case was being adjudicated, Reuchlin published a Hebrew text of the Psalms with an accompanying Latin translation (1512).

After the public battle, Reuchlin assumed a semi-retired life for a few years, but in 1520 finished his outstanding career at Ingolstadt (1520–1521) and Tübingen (1521–1522) as a professor of Greek and Hebrew. In the meantime, as he mastered Hebrew he had been drawn to the Kabbalah, the Jewish mystical system often associated with the Hasidic movement. During his last years he wrote extensively on it, developing a Christianized version usually termed "Cabala" that could be accessed without also adopting Judaism. While finding few others who shared his interest during his lifetime, his writings would become important in later centuries as Christian Cabala found an audience among Western Esotericists.

Reuchlin also inadvertently contributed to the Protestant Reformation. His publications had made the Hebrew text of the Jewish Bible more generally available, at least in scholarly circles, and Martin Luther (1483–1546) would draw upon them as he bypassed the Latin Bible to create a new German translation. He would also find his greatest support from a young biblical scholar who joined him on the staff at the University of Wittenburg, Reuchlin's nephew Philipp Melanchthon (1497–1560). Unfortunately for Reuchlin, as the Reformation gathered steam, the pope's commission reversed its decision on him and ordered him silenced. The order had little effect, however, as Reuchlin died at Liebenzell on June 30, 1522.

J. Gordon Melton

See also: Dominicans; Hasidism; Humanism; Luther, Martin; Roman Catholic Church; Western Esoteric Tradition.

References :

Reuchlin, Johannes. *On the Art of the Kabbalah (De Arte Cabalistica).* Trans. by Martin Goodman and Sarah Goodman. Lincoln: University of Nebraska Press, 1993.

Reuchlin, Johannes. *Recommendation Whether to Confiscate, Destroy and Burn All Jewish Books: A Classic Treatise against Anti-Semitism.* Studies in Judaism and Christianity. New York: Paulist Press, 2000.

Rummel, Erika. *The Case Against Johann Reuchlin: Social and Religious Controversy in Sixteenth-Century Germany.* Toronto: University of Toronto Press, 2002.

Spitz, Lewis. "Reuchlin's Philosophy: Pythagoras and Cabala for Christ." *Archiv für Reformationsgeschichte* 47 (1956): 1–20.

■ Réunion

Réunion, an island and a French overseas department in the Indian Ocean west of Madagascar, proved a strategic part of France's colonial empire through the mid-19th century. Its 968 square miles provided an important stopping point for ships traveling around Africa to India and points east. Its value was diminished considerably after the opening of the Suez Canal in 1869. Over the last two centuries the population expanded considerably, from the first settlement to its present 766,000 (2004).

Réunion was uninhabited when Arab merchants discovered it in the 17th century, and remained as such when the Portuguese visited it at a later date. Finally, in the 18th century, the French established a settlement there and were able to assert their hegemony in the face of other European claims upon it. The French imported slaves to work the sugarcane and coffee plantations that the settlers created, and their descendants now form some 80 percent of the current population. The descendants of Chinese, Malaysian, and Indian laborers also reside on the island. Réunion's colonial status was altered into that of a department in 1946. There has been continual unrest since 1978, when the United Nations pronounced its favor of the island's independence.

Catholic church on the island of Réunion. (Yann Guichaoua/StockphotoPro.com)

Réunion

Religion	Followers in 1970	Followers in 2010	% of Population	Annual % growth 2000–2010	Followers in 2025	Followers in 2050
Christians	445,000	731,000	87.4	1.59	822,000	892,000
Roman Catholics	427,000	670,000	80.1	1.15	735,000	786,000
Protestants	2,200	48,300	5.8	2.45	70,000	90,000
Marginals	1,000	6,500	0.8	–0.59	14,000	19,000
Hindus	1,000	38,000	4.5	1.63	50,000	60,000
Muslims	10,900	35,000	4.2	1.63	41,000	50,000
Agnostics	1,000	16,400	2.0	3.55	30,000	40,000
Baha'is	1,200	7,200	0.9	1.93	10,000	14,000
Ethnoreligionists	1,000	3,500	0.4	1.63	4,000	4,000
Buddhists	0	1,600	0.2	1.63	2,400	3,600
Atheists	500	1,300	0.2	1.63	2,400	3,500
Jains	0	1,100	0.1	1.63	1,600	2,200
Sikhs	0	700	0.1	1.64	1,000	1,500
New religionists	100	300	0.0	1.57	500	800
Total population	**461,000**	**836,000**	**100.0**	**1.63**	**965,000**	**1,072,000**

Réunion

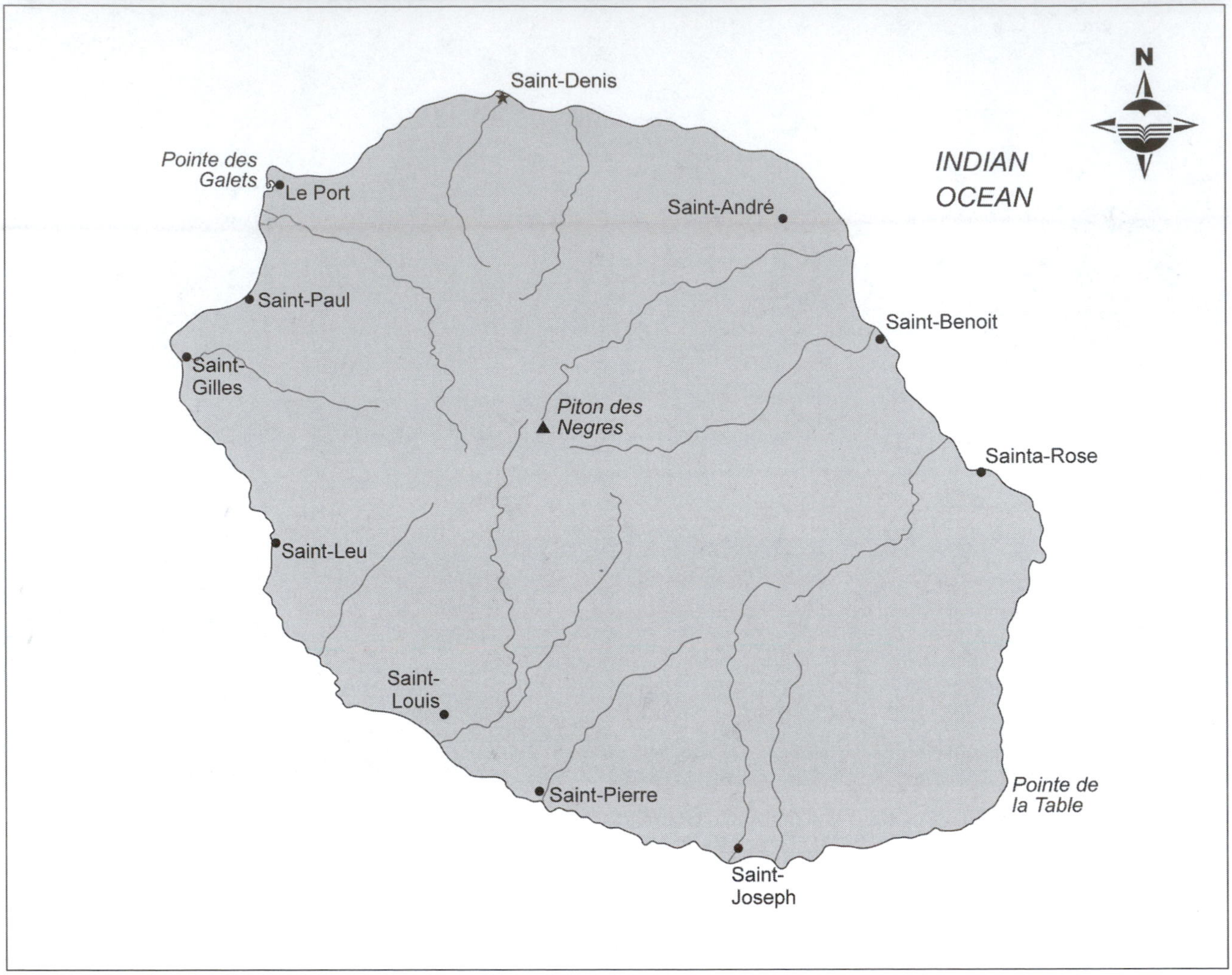

The great majority of Réunion's residents are members of the Roman Catholic Church, which arrived with settlers in 1653. The first resident priest arrived in 1712. A new era began in 1817 with the arrival of the sisters of the congregation of Saint Joseph of Cluny, who used Réunion as the headquarters for efforts to evangelize East Africa. The Holy Ghost Fathers assumed control of the island in 1917. The Diocese of Saint Denis was established in 1966. It includes a Chinese mission that had been founded in 1951.

The Roman Catholic Church enjoyed a religious monopoly on Réunion until 1936, when the Seventh-day Adventist Church established work. The church's Réunion Conference, formally organized in 1947, is part of the Indian Ocean Union Mission. There is also some work by the Assemblies of God, the Jehovah's Witnesses, and the Evangelical Church of Réunion, which grew out of the missionary efforts of the African Evangelical Fellowship.

Of religions other than Christianity, the Muslim community is the largest, though it is divided ethnically among Pakistani and Indian Muslims (mostly Shias) and East Africans (mostly Sunnis). There is a growing community of the Baha'i Faith, and a small Rosicrucian presence is supplied by the Ancient and Mystical Order Rosae Crucis. Officially, Réunion guarantees freedom of religion.

J. Gordon Melton

See also: Ancient and Mystical Order Rosae Crucis; Assemblies of God; Baha'i Faith; Holy Ghost Fathers; Jehovah's Witnesses; Roman Catholic Church; Seventh-day Adventist Church.

References

Eve, P. *La religion populaire à la Réunion*. 2 vols. Sainte-Clotilde, Réunion: Université de la Réunion, Institut de linguistique et d'anthropologie, 1985.

Foulon, A. *Les religions à la Réunion*. Livry-Gargan, France: Editions Orphie, 1989.

Ghasarian, Christian. "We Have the Best Gods! The Encounter between Hinduism and Christianity in La Réunion." *Journal of Asian and African Studies* 23, nos. 3–4 (1966): 286–295.

Vaxelaire, Daniel. *Le grand livre de l'histoire de la Réunion*. Sainte Clotilde, Réunion: Orphie, 2003.

Rhenish Mission

The United Rhenish Missionary Society, now the United Evangelical Mission, headquartered in Barmen, Germany, and popularly known as simply the Rhenish Mission, was one of the most important Protestant Christian missionary sending agencies of the 19th century. Most of its missions matured into independent Lutheran churches. The society began with the effort of 12 German laymen who in 1799 met at Elberfield, Germany, where they founded the Bergische Bible Society and the Wupperthal Tract Society. These two organizations merged with the Barmen Missionary Society (founded in 1815) to form the Rhenish Mission.

By the time of its creation, a new generation of leadership had recognized the opportunity for Protestantism on the world scene and had joined in what would become the movement's global expansion through the next century. The first commissioned missionary of the Rhenish Mission was sent to South Africa, though the center of the work became Namibia, where eventually 50 missionaries were supported. This work later matured into the Evangelical Lutheran Church in Southern Africa.

While building the African work, the Rhenish Mission developed a second focus in Southeast Asia, and it opened work in the 1830s in Borneo. In 1846 its concentration shifted to China, where a large mission developed, though much of it was lost in 1951. The Chinese Rhenish Church–Hong Kong Synod (with congregations in Taiwan) is the primary surviving remnant of the Chinese mission, though some of the work survives through the congregations of the China Christian Council. One of the most successful missions was launched in 1861 in Sumatra, where the church continues today as the Batak Protestant Christian Church. The Rhenish Mission expanded further with the entrance of Germany into the world colonial enterprise in the 1880s and suffered exceedingly from the destruction of that enterprise at the end of World War I; its work in Asia was changed completely by the events of World War II.

Through the 20th century, the Rhenish Mission began the process of developing indigenous leadership and overseeing the transfer of power to local ministers and lay personnel. At the same time it watched the development of the Evangelical Church in Germany, whose members supplied most of its financial resources. In 1971 it merged with the Bethel Society, another German missionary organization, to form the United Evangelical Mission–Community of Churches on Three Continents. The new society became more closely affiliated with the Evangelical Church, and a new emphasis on social service ministries has developed.

Today, the Mission sees itself as an international communion of 34 churches in Africa, Asia, and Germany, and the von Bodelschwingh [Charitable] Institutions Bethel. Its administrative office is at the mission house in Wuppertal, Germany, with additional regional offices in Africa (Dar-es-Salaam), Asia (Medan), and Germany (Wuppertal).

United Evangelical Mission
Rudolfstr. 137
D-42285 Wuppertal
Germany
http://www.vemission.org/ (in German and English)

J. Gordon Melton

See also: Evangelical Church in Germany; Evangelical Lutheran Church in Southern Africa; Lutheranism.

Reference

Bachmann, E. Theodore, and Mercia Brenne Bachmann. *Lutheran Churches in the World: A Handbook*. Minneapolis, MN: Augsburg Press, 1989.

Ridván, Festival of

Members of the Baha'i Faith consider the 12-day Festival of Ridván (Paradise) as pre-eminent among its various Holy Days. Ridván marks the inception of the Baha'i Faith as a distinct religion. It is observed from sunset on April 20 (marking the onset of April 21 in the Baha'i calendar) to sunset on May 2 but is punctuated with three Holy Days. On the 1st (April 21), 9th (April 29) and 12th (May 2) days of Ridván, work is suspended, as local Baha'i communities gather to commemorate the signal events of that historic occasion.

The Baha'i Faith was founded by Mírzá Husayn-'Alí Núrí (1817–1892), more popularly known by his spiritual title, Bahá'u'lláh ("Glory/Splendor of God"). It is also regarded as having been co-founded by Bahá'u'lláh's predecessor, Sayyid 'Alí-Muhammad of Shíráz (1819–1850), known as the Báb (the "Gate").

The "Festival of Paradise" commemorates Bahá'u'lláh's private disclosure of his eschatological identity to a handful of his companions—around four years prior to his public proclamation to the rulers and religious leaders of the world (ca. 1867–1873). The unfolding of Bahá'u'lláh's prophetic mission was progressively revealed in a series of disclosures. To a select few Bábís, Bahá'u'lláh announced that he was the "Promised One" foretold by the Báb. Several years later (ca. 1867–1870), Bahá'u'lláh sent open epistles (called Tablets) to a select group of the world's most powerful potentates and clerics, proclaiming himself to be the "Promised One" foretold by the prophets of all past religions. In these Tablets, together with general Tablets addressed to kings and religious leaders collectively, Bahá'u'lláh stated that he was, inter alia, the long-awaited "World Reformer" who came to unify the world—a transformation that would, in the course of time, come about through the power of his universal principles and laws adapted to the needs of this day and age.

The history of Ridván begins during the afternoon of April 21, 1863 (around 3:00 p.m.), when Bahá'u'lláh arrived in the Najíbíyyih Garden, subsequently designated as the Garden of Ridván. Located on the east bank of the Tigris in Baghdad, Najíbiyyih was once a wooded garden, where Muhammad-Najíb Páshá (Turkish: Mehmed Necib; d. May 1851), governor of Baghdad between 1842 and 1847, had built a palace and placed a wall around the garden. It is now the site of Baghdad Medical City (formerly known as Saddam Medical City), a large modern teaching hospital in Baghdad.

Bahá'u'lláh's entrance to the gardens signaled the commencement of his messianic announcement, first to his companions, and eventually to the world at large. Exactly what transpired, however, is shrouded in mystery, and accounts vary. Through the previous decade (1853–1863), Bahá'u'lláh had concealed his mission. This period of "messianic secrecy" has been referred to as the "Days of Concealment" (*ayyám-i-butun*—a term that connotes the image of embryonic development), although Bahá'u'lláh's writings in Baghdad during this period were rife with hints about his prophetic mission, especially in his pre-eminent doctrinal text, the *Book of Certitude* (*Kitáb-i-Íqán*), which was revealed in two days and two nights in January 1861.

Beyond the basic revelation that he was "He Whom God will make manifest," Bahá'u'lláh also proclaimed three additional matters of great import to Baha'is. He (1) abrogated holy war (*jihad*); (2) asserted that no independent Messenger of God (literally, "Manifestation of God") would appear for at least a full 1,000 years; and (3) dispensed entirely with the Islamic category of ritual impurity, or "uncleanness" (*najis*). Bahá'u'lláh later recounted this sweeping pronouncement in the Most Holy Book (the *Kitáb-i-Aqdas*): "God hath, likewise, as a bounty from His presence, abolished the concept of 'uncleanness,' whereby divers things and peoples have been held to be impure. He, of a certainty, is the Ever-Forgiving, the Most Generous. Verily, all created things were immersed in the sea of purification when, on that first day of Ridván, We shed upon the whole of creation the splendours of Our most excellent Names and Our most exalted Attributes."

In 1869, as part of the subsequent public proclamation of his mission to the world's political and religious leaders, Bahá'u'lláh dispatched his second epistle (ca. 1869) to Napoleon III (d. 1873). In this Tablet (spirited out of Bahá'u'lláh's prison cell by a Baha'i pilgrim, who concealed the letter in the brim of his hat) to the emperor of France, Bahá'u'lláh announced: "All feasts have attained their consummation in the two Most Great Festivals, and in two other Festivals that fall on the twin days." Here, the two "Most Great Festivals" are the Festival of Ridván and the Declaration of the Báb (evening of May 22, 1844). The "twin days" refer to the Birth of the Báb (October 20, 1819) and the Birth of Bahá'u'lláh (November 12, 1817).

The Festival of Ridván is important for yet another reason: most Baha'i elections take place at this time. On the first day of Ridván (April 21), all local Baha'i councils, each known as a Local Spiritual Assembly, are democratically elected, in a "spiritual election" conducted prayerfully and meditatively.

The system of Baha'i elections is unique, both religiously and politically. Arash Abizadeh, assistant professor of political science at McGill University in Canada, notes that Baha'i elections are governed by formal institutional rules and informal norms that specifically prohibit such familiar features of the political landscape as nominations, competitive campaigns, voting coalitions, or parties. As an alternative model of democratic elections, Baha'i elections incorporate three core values at the individual, interpersonal, and institutional levels: (1) the inherent dignity of each person; (2) the unity and solidarity of persons collectively; and (3) the inherent justice, fairness, and transparency of elected Baha'i institutions. Baha'i elections thus serve four primary functions: (1) selection (electing representatives); (2) legitimation (authorizing Baha'i governing bodies in the eyes of the community at large); (3) education (cultivating the spirit of responsibility in each Baha'i voter); and (4) integration (fostering solidarity within the community as a whole).

National Baha'i conventions are also held during the 12-day Festival of Ridván for the purpose of electing national councils, each of which is called a National Spiritual Assembly. An exception to the timing of these conventions occurs once every five years, when the Universal House of Justice, the international governing council of the Baha'i Faith, is elected during the Festival of Ridván. The next is scheduled for Ridván 2013, with national Baha'i elections rescheduled for May.

The Festival of Ridván marks the inchoative establishment of the Baha'i religion as a distinct faith community through Bahá'u'lláh's disclosure of his divine authority. The Festival of Ridván also marks the progressive advancement of the Baha'i Faith as a distinct administrative order through the process of electing the faith community's governing authorities.

Baha'is believe that in a future Golden Age—in which a self-governing world commonwealth emerges as the fruit of social evolution enlightened by Baha'i socio-moral principles—the Festival of Ridván is destined to become the greatest celebratory event in the world, according to the teleological Baha'i vision of the inevitable course of human history.

Christopher Buck

See also: Baha'i Faith; Bahá'u'lláh; Birth/Ascension of Bahá'u'lláh; Birth of the Báb; Calendars, Religious; Temples—Baha'i Faith; World Religion Day.

References

Abizadeh, Arash. "Democratic Elections without Campaigns? Normative Foundations of National Baha'i Elections." *World Order* 37, no. 1 (2005): 7–49.

Bahá'u'lláh. *The Summons of the Lord of Hosts.* Haifa: Baha'i World Centre, 2002.

Buck, Christopher. "The Eschatology of Globalization: Bahá'u'lláh's Multiple-Messiahship Revisited." In *Studies in Modern Religions, Religious Movements and the Babi-Baha'i Faiths*, edited by Moshe Sharon, 143–178. Leiden: Brill Academic Publishers, 2004.

Buck, Christopher. *Symbol and Secret: Qur'an Commentary in Bahá'u'lláh's Kitáb-i Íqán.* Los Angeles: Kalimát Press, 1995, 2004.

Keil, Gerald. *Time and the Baha'i Era: A Study of the Badí' Calendar*. Oxford: George Ronald, 2008.

Phelps, Myron H. *The Master in 'Akká*. Los Angeles: Kalimát Press, 1985. Reprint of *A Study of the Religion of the Babis, or Beha'is Founded by the Persian Bab and by His Successors, Beha Ullah and Abbas Effendi*. New York & London: G. P. Putnam's Sons, 1903.

Walbridge, John. "Festival of Ridván." In *Sacred Acts, Sacred Space, Sacred Time*, 232–241. Oxford: George Ronald, 1996.

Rigpa Fellowship

Among the most popular books on Buddhism to be published in the West in recent years is Sogyal Rinpoche's work, *The Tibetan Book of Living and Dying*. When it was published in 1992, it introduced the author and his relatively new Tibetan Buddhist organization, Rigpa, to many people.

The Rigpa Fellowship was established in the United Kingdom in 1979 under the spiritual direction of Sogyal Rinpoche (b. ca. 1949). Born in Tibet in the late 1940s, Sogyal Rinpoche was brought up from an early age by his master, Jamyang Khyentse Chokyi Lodro, who recognized him as the incarnation of Terton Sogyal (1856–1926), a teacher to the 13th Dalai Lama. In 1971 Sogyal Rinpoche moved to the United Kingdom in order to study comparative religion at Trinity College, Cambridge. Soon after, he moved to London, where he built up a small following of students and began to give teachings. In 1991 the present Rigpa Centre in north London was opened.

Sogyal Rinpoche, founder of the Rigpa Fellowship, a Tibetan Buddhist organization. (Corbis Sygma)

Eight international Rigpa retreats are held annually in various countries, drawing up to 3,000 participants overall. There are now 11 national centers around the world, in addition to retreat centers at Lerab Ling in the south of France and Dzogchen Beara in the southwest of Ireland. Buddhist teachers from a variety of traditions are invited to teach, as from the outset Rigpa has not relied exclusively on the teachings of Sogyal Rinpoche but has followed an ecumenical approach. International coordination takes place within three departments: finance and administration, teaching services, and executive directors. Though in each country there is a team responsible for running activities, the international staff offer support and are responsible for key strategic decisions in consultation with Sogyal Rinpoche and other lamas.

Rigpa has developed a graduated "study and practice" program that is delivered internationally, and that can take seven years to complete. It begins by introducing basic meditation practice, using *samatha* methods such as resting the mind on an object (usually a picture of Padmasambhava), mantra recitation, and watching the breath. Then the Mahayana compassion teachings of Lojong (Tibetan) are presented, together with the *tonglen* practice (giving and receiving). Next, students are introduced to the Vajrayana preliminaries, including "Going for Refuge" and *bodhicitta* (Sanskrit: "mind of awakening"). The main practice followed by committed students is the Longchen Nyingtik, which is based on the Dzogchen tradition of Tibetan Buddhism. In common with many other Buddhist groups, Rigpa does not rely on one sacred text but rather refers to a variety of Indian and Tibetan Buddhist texts.

In 1994 Sogyal Rinpoche was accused of fraud and assault. However these allegations were never proven. In response, senior students of Sogyal Rinpoche have said that they fear the lawsuit was part of a deliberate campaign to undermine the lama and his organization (Brown 1995). Sogyal Rinpoche, being from the Yogic tradition of the Nyingma School of Tibetan Buddhism, is not a monk and is therefore not bound by the monk's rules. He is not celibate; indeed, he has a partner and a son.

In 2009, Rigpa reported 130 centers in 41 countries around the world.

Rigpa International
8 Rue de la Bouquerie
Lodeve 34700
France
http://www.rigpa.org

Rigpa USA, National Office
9540 Waples Street, Ste. A
San Diego, CA 92121
www.rigpaus.org

Jamie Cresswell and J. Gordon Melton

See also: Nyingma Tibetan Buddhism; Padmasambhava; Tibetan Buddhism.

References

Brown, Mick. "Scandal and the Living Buddha." *Telegraph Magazine* (London). February 25, 1995.

Rinpoche, Sogyal. *Glimpse after Glimpse.* London: Rider, 1995.

Rinpoche, Sogyal. *The Spirit of Buddhism: The Future of Dharma in the West.* New York: HarperOne, 2003.

Rinpoche, Sogyal. *The Tibetan Book of Living and Dying.* London: Rider, 1992.

Rinzai (Japan), Lin-Chi (China), Imje (Korea), Lam-Te (Vietnam)

Rinzai, one of the five sects of Chinese Chan/Zen flourishing during the Sung period (960–1279), has survived until our times. It claims Lin-chi I-hsuan (Japanese: Rinzai Gigen; d. 866) for its founder, although it appeared as a distinct school a few generations after him. The pedagogical use of shouting that Lin-chi is credited for imprinted the sect with its roughness. After it split into two sub-sects, called Yang-chi (Japanese: Yogi) and Huang-lung (Japanese: Oryo), it became predominant when Chan/Zen was institutionalized during the Sung period.

Two figures stand out: Yuan-wu K'o-ch'in (Japanese: Engo Kokugon; 1063–1135) and his disciple Ta-hui Tsung-kao (Japanese: Daie Soko; 1089–1163). Yuan-wu, a fine representative of a learned Chan, compiled the "Blue Cliff Record" (Chinese: Pi-yen lu; Japanese: Hekiganroku), still an essential textbook for the sect. The Blue Cliff Record is composed of 100 "cases" or koan (Chinese: *kung-an*; Japanese: *koan*)—dialogues or blunt quotes—with commentary in prose and in verse.

With Ta-hui, the Lin-chi sect identifies with the method of "meditation that contemplates words" (Chinese: *k'an-hua ch'an*; Japanese: *kannazen*), in which the meditator concentrates on a key word (Chinese: *hua-t'ou*; Japanese: *wato*) taken from a kung-an (koan), in order to induce enlightenment (Japanese: *satori*). With the introduction of the koan, a new literature developed. Wu-men Hui-k'ai (Japanese: Mumon Ekai; 1183–1260) wrote a short compilation of 48 such kung-an called The Gateless Door (Chinese: Wu-men kuan; Japanese: Mumonkan), which had tremendous success in Japan.

The sect was introduced to Japan in the 13th century by a few Japanese and Chinese monks. Myoan Eisai (1141–1215), a Japanese monk who was made a Chan Master when visiting China, foreshadowed the interest in this tradition in Japan. He wrote a "Treaty on the Spreading of Zen for the Defense of the Country" (Japanese: Kozen Gokokuron), although he never tried to found a separate sect from Tendai Buddhism, to which he belonged. However, soon after it appeared in Japan, Rinzai experienced some success and quickly was institutionalized on the Chinese model. Its monasteries of Kyoto and Kamakura, known collectively as the Five-Mountains (Japanese: *gozan*), became important cultural, literary, and political centers in the 14th century, though lineages more intent on Buddhist practice remained somewhat independent of these more scholarly centers. Ikkyu Sojun (1394–1481) remains a popular figure of the sect. This uncompromising monk, close to the humble, embodied the saintly figure that mingles with the crowd of ordinary people. Like so many Japanese sects, Rinzai Zen knew a period of decline in the 16th and 17th centuries. It found its great reformer with Hakuin Ekaku (1685–1768), a sturdy and unconventional character.

Reikanji Temple in Kyoto, Japan, a nunnery of the Rinzai sect. (Jojobob/Dreamstime.com)

In Japan, Rinzai now exists through some 15 branches, which together include a few thousand monks and some 2.5 million followers. The majority of these developed from the primary lineage of Zen masters centered at the Myoshin-ji Monastery, established in the 14th century.

The Lin-chi sect has survived in China, where it crossed with elements of Pure Land Buddhism. In Japan, the Obaku sect, strictly separate from Rinzai, is a representative of this later form. Lin-chi Ch'an has also survived in Vietnam and Korea, although in syncretic forms. The Korean Chogye sect is thus a synthesis of the Lin-chi and Huayen sects. The work of Daisetsu T. Suzuki (1870–1966) introduced the Japanese sect to the West at the beginning of the 20th century. It has now settled in most continents, but compared to other Buddhist traditions, its impact remains relatively meager.

Eric Rommeluère
(English translation by Michel Proulx)

See also: Eisai; Kamakura; Pure Land Buddhism; Tian Tai/Tendai Buddhism; Zen Buddhism.

References

Collcutt, Martin. *Five Mountains: The Rinzai Zen Monastic Institution in Medieval Japan.* Cambridge: Harvard University Press, 1981.

Dumoulin, Heinrich. *Zen Buddhism: A History.* 2 vols. Trans. by James W. Heisig and Paul Knitter. New York: Macmillan Publishing Company, 1988, 1990.

The International Research Institute for Zen Buddhism. http://www.iijnet.or.jp/iriz (Japanese and English). Accessed January 11, 2002.

Two Zen Classics: Mumonkan and Hekiganroku. Trans. with commentaries by Katsuki Sekida. New York: Weatherhill, 1977.

The Zen Master Hakuin: Selected Writings. Trans. by Philip B. Yampolsky. New York: Columbia University Press. 1971.

Rishikesh

Rishikesh, one of the most revered of India's religious sites, is located along the Ganges River as it flows through the Himalayan Mountains in the northern Indian state of Uttaranchal. The city is home to a spectrum of temples and an aura of sanctity sets the environment that attracts different Hindu religious functionaries and thousands of pilgrims. A variety of new religious movements have established their headquarters in or near Rishikesh.

Legends tie Rishikesh's origins to Lord Siva, a key Hindu deity. According to the *Shrimad Bhaagvad*, in the timeless past, the gods of the universe began a quest through the ocean of consciousness in search of *amrit*, the nectar of immortality. However, before the nectar could be found, a wave of deadly venom swept toward the gods. They were in a crucial situation as they came to understand that drinking the venom was a necessary step to get to the amrit. As the gods contemplated their dilemma, Siva volunteered to consume the venom. As it hit his throat, it stayed there and turned it blue. The Nilkanth Mahadeo Temple located about eight miles from Rishikesh is the traditional spot identified as the place where Siva stood to drink the venom.

Hindu temple along the Ganges River in Rishikesh, India. (Federico Donatini/Dreamstime.com)

In spite of the Siva tales, Bharat Mandir, built in the 12th century and Rishikesh's oldest temple, points people in a different direction. It is named after Bharat, the brother of Rama, an incarnation of Lord Vishnu, to whom the temple is dedicated. The original temple was destroyed by Tamerlane (1336–1405), the Turkish conqueror who invaded the region in 1398, but was later rebuilt. Over the centuries, a number of famous sages lingered here to venerate Vishnu, some claiming to have been granted a vision of him.

Swami Sivananda (1887–1963) created Shiva Nanda Ashram, among the newer sites in Rishikesh; it is home to one of the most famous yoga schools in the world and the headquarters of the international Divine Life Society. Sivananda, who had wanted to be a physician in his younger years, transformed the image of Hindu monks (*sannyasins*) by advocating their adopting a life of service to the larger community. The original clinic founded by Sivananda evolved into one of India's largest charitable hospitals.

Equal in fame to Sivananda is Maharishi Mehesh Yogi (1918–2008), who brought Transcendental Meditation to the West. Ved Niketan remains the main Indian center of the movement he founded (embodied by the World Plan Executive Council), though its importance has decreased from the 1960s, when, for example, it was the site for the meeting of the British musical group the Beatles with their guru. Today the ashram sponsors a large Ayurveda medical center and joins the other ashrams in the city to participate in the annual celebration of international yoga week (the first week of February).

Today, while pilgrims flock to Rishikesh's many temples, *sadhus* (ascetics) also gather there. These holy men will spend most of their days alone in the nearby forests but come to town periodically. Most often they head for the Triveni Ghat, a place along the river where pilgrims gather to gain the blessings available from bathing in the river, when they come to town.

The Ghat is the site for a ceremony called the Maha Aarti, which is performed each evening and includes the floating of flames on the river.

Rishikesh is only 15 miles from the equally holy city of Hardwar. Just across the river from Rishikesh is Tapovan, the site of additional temples worthy of the pilgrims' attentions, among the most famous being one dedicated to Lakshmana, who purportedly carried out penances there. In fact, the whole region is filled with temples and sacred sites. Within that larger environment, Rishikesh has functioned as the starting point for pilgrims wishing to gain access to the Char Dham and its four holy centers of Badrinath, Kedarnath, Gangotri, and Yamunotri, where they hope to achieve peace and harmony and rid themselves of their worldly pain and sorrows.

J. Gordon Melton

See also: Asceticism; Devotion/Devotional Traditions; Divine Life Society; Pilgrimage; Temples—Hindu; Yoga.

References

Keemattam, Augusthy. *The Hermits of Rishikesh: A Sociological Study*. New Delhi: Intercultural Publications, 1997.

Khullar, Reeta, and Rupinder Khullar. *Gateway to the Gods: Haridwar Rishikesh; Yamunotri Gangotri Kedarnath Badrinath*. New Delhi: UBS, 2004.

Saltzman, Paul. *The Beatles in Rishikesh*. New York: Viking, 2000.

Venkatesananda, Swami. *Sivananda: Biography of a Modern Sage*. Sivanandanagar: Divine Life Society, 1985.

Rissho Kosei-kai

Rissho Kosei-kai (Society for the Establishment of Righteousness and Friendly Intercourse) is a lay Buddhist new religion of Japan. It was founded on March 5, 1938, in Tokyo by Nikkyo Niwano (1906–1999) and Myoko Naganuma (1889–1957)—the result of a secession from another new religion called Reiyukai, a group in the tradition of Nichirenshu.

Rissho Kosei-kai, claiming a membership of about 6 million in 1999, is the second largest new religion in Japan. Its phenomenal growth, especially during the 1950s and early 1960s, is credited to its emphasis on traditional social values like filial piety and ancestor worship combined with faith in the Lotus Sutra. However, this movement faced a major crisis in 1956, when a Japanese newspaper, *Yomiuri Shinbun,* carried out a prolonged attack on its proselytization activities and financial deals.

In its initial phase, the movement greatly relied on shamanistic practices such as "bodily reading" (*shikidoku*) of the Lotus Sutra by Naganuma and its interpretation by Niwano. After Naganuma's death in 1957, the shamanistic practices ceased and the emphasis shifted to a more doctrinal approach. Although the doctrinal basis of Rissho Kosei-kai is the Lotus Sutra, what is original about its teachings is that it combines the emphasis on helping others achieve salvation, which is characteristic of the Lotus Sutra and Mahayana Buddhism, with the principle of the Four Noble Truths (*shitai*) of early Buddhism that emphasizes one's own salvation. Rissho Kosei-kai preaches the practice of the Bodhisattva Way—that is, perfecting one's personality through the realization and cultivation of the Buddha nature and saving others by leading them to the faith. One of the prominent features of Rissho Kosei-kai is its group counseling session, called the *hoza*. In hoza, members try to find solutions to their personal problems by applying the teachings of the organization. Since 1964, the Eternal Buddha Shakyamuni, whose image is enshrined in the Great Sacred Hall, has been declared as its focus of worship.

The proselytization activity of Rissho Kosei-kai is called the *o-michibiki,* which means "to guide." In Rissho Kosei-kai, the leader-follower relationship is modeled after the parent-child (*oya-ko*) relationship; the senior member is referred as *michibiki no oya* (guide parent) and the new member is referred as *michibiki no ko* (guide child). Earlier this oya-ko relationship formed the basis of the branch organization, but since 1959 the parent-child branch system has been changed to a locality or diocese (*kyoku*)-based branch system. At present there are 239 branches in Japan and 6 branches overseas, mainly in the United States, Brazil, and Taiwan. In recent years Rissho Kosei-kai has distinguished itself in sponsoring inter-religious dialogue and international peace movements. Its social activities include sending blankets to the refugees in Africa and sponsoring the Donate One Meal Campaign. In 1969 it launched the Brighter Society movement for fostering community-based voluntary activities. It is also active in politics by supporting the candidates of conservative political parties.

Rissho Kosei-kai Headquarters
2-11-1 Wada, Suginami-ku
Tokyo 166-0012
Japan
http://www.kosei-kai.or.jp (in Japanese)

Ranjana Mukhopadhyaya

See also: Mahayana Buddhism; Nichirenshu; Reiyukai.

References

Dale, Kenneth J., and Akahoshi Susumu. *Circle of Harmony: A Case Study in Popular Japanese Buddhism with Implications for Christian Mission.* Tokyo: Seibunsha, 1975.

Morioka, Kiyomi. "The Institutionalization of a New Religious Movement." *Japanese Journal of Religious Studies* 6, nos. 1–2 (1979): 239–280.

Niwano, Nikkyo. *Lifetime Beginner, An Autobiography*. Trans. by Richard L. Gage. Tokyo: Kosei Publishing Co., 1978.

Rissho Kosei-kai. Tokyo: Kosei Publishing Co., 1966.

Rodzima Wiara (Poland)

Rodzima Wiara (the Indigenous Faith Association, formerly Zrzeszenie Rodzimej) is a continuation of a neo-Pagan association called Zadruga, which was active in Poland before World War II and emphasized political more than religious goals. Rodzima Wiara was founded by Stanisław Potrzebowski and Maciej Czarnowski, a member of the original Zadruga, at the beginning of the 1990s and registered as a religious union in 1996. In contrast to its predecessor, the Rodzima Wiara offers not only right-wing politics, nationalism, and anti-Catholicism, but also a theology and some religious practices that are based on scarce remnants of Slavonic neo-Paganism.

The theology is polytheistic and related to the pantheon of Slavonic gods, with the Sun, Mother Earth, and the Universal Power of Nature mentioned as gods in the theological credo of the movement. The Sun is the principal god and the main object of religious ceremonies such as the Welcoming the Sun rite at dawn. The liturgical calendar is based on a solar rhythm, and collective rituals that take the form of a Greeting of the Sun are performed at the beginning of the astronomical spring, summer, and autumn. The most important of them is the Noc Kupały ceremony, celebrated at the beginning of the astronomical summer, during the shortest night of the year.

The membership of the movement had grown from 68 in 1996 to 143 in 1999, and it remains the most numerous in the western part of Poland. The five regional branches of the movement are relatively independent, and there are also informal groupings across the regional branches. One of them, perhaps the most nationalistic, is associated with the skinhead movement, and another, more individualistic, is associated with the Pagan Folk Music movement.

The movement has been active in the Union of Baltic and Slavic faiths and the World Congress of Ethnic Religions (the latter founded during the World Pagan Congress in Vilnius, Latvia, in 1998).

Rodzima Wiara
Pocztowa 16 / 15
53-313 Wroclaw
Poland

Thadeus Doktor

Reference

Simpson, S. *Native Faith: Polish Neo-Paganism at the Brink of the Twenty-first Century*. Krakow: Nomos, 2000.

Roman Catholic Church

The term "catholic," from the Greek words meaning universal (*katholikos*), and according to the whole (*kath'holou*), was used in early Christianity to describe the nature of the church. The word "church" is also derived from Greek roots (*ek kaleo; ekklesia*), meaning "those who are called." "Catholic" implied being "orthodox"—that is, possessing the fullness of truth and holding correct doctrines—and the term was used in opposition to those movements that were considered heretical or schismatic. Catholicity also includes an openness to or appropriation of all truth in all cultures, languages, theological traditions, and expressions of spirituality.

In early statements of the faith, especially in the Nicene-Constantinopolitan Creed (ca. 381 CE), a creed recited during the liturgy today, catholicity was noted as one of the marks of the church, along with unity, holiness, and apostolicity. After the growing divisions between the Eastern and Western churches, the term "catholic" began to be increasingly used as a title of the Western church, while the Eastern churches appropriated the name Orthodox Church. During the period of the Protestant Reformation, the additional title of "Roman" to Catholic was used to demarcate those in communion with Rome. Today the Catholic Church numbers approximately one billion faithful, with churches spread throughout the world, and it encompasses a number of distinct ecclesial traditions, which include the largest, the Roman, in addition to the Byzantine, Armenian, Maronite, East and West Syrian, Coptic, and Ethiopian rites. The name Roman Catholic specifically describes those in the Catholic Church who belong to the Roman tradition, while the other churches in this communion (Armenian Catholic Church, Bulgarian Catholic Church, Chaldean Catholic Church, Coptic Catholic Church, Ethiopian Catholic Church, Greek Catholic Church, Italo-Albanian Catholic Church, Maronite Catholic Church, Melkite Catholic Church, Romanian Greek Catholic Church, Ruthenian Catholic Church, Syrian Catholic Church, Syro-Malabar Catholic Church, and Ukrainian Catholic Church) have their own respective nomenclature and distinct liturgical and theological traditions.

The Roman Catholic Church traces its origins to the time of the Apostles, to those who were commissioned by Jesus Christ to preach his message of salvation (or eternal life). The church believes that it is a faithful and authoritative transmitter of the message of Christ. Of special importance in defining its apostolic character is the pre-eminence of its major see in Rome, the city in which the Apostles Peter and Paul preached and were martyred. From the early beginnings of the church, Rome has affirmed its special importance in being an ancient and authentic guarantor of the faith, a claim that developed over time into a theology that saw the pope (also called the Roman pontiff or the bishop of Rome) as primate of the universal church. Rome's formulation of a universal primacy, however, has never been fully accepted by the other early Christian tradition of the church—namely, the Orthodox Church, and churches that emerged out of the Protestant Reformation.

Pope John Paul II, head of the Roman Catholic Church, conducts the New Year's Day mass in St. Peter's Basilica at the Vatican, January 1, 1999. (AP Photo/Plinio Lepri)

The Second Vatican Council (1962–1965) has been the major defining moment for modern Catholicism, an event that moved the church beyond some of the more intransigent theological categories of the Council of Trent (1545–1563) and the First Vatican Council (1869–1870). This recent Council had a significant influence on the modern theology of the church, the laity, evangelization, and relations with other Christians and other faiths, as well as on issues of social, political, and economic justice, secular society and the sciences, and the role of the human conscience in moral decision making, to name a few.

Theological Emphases Catholic theology, and Christian theology for that matter, is rooted in the revelation of God in the Hebrew scriptures (the Old Testament), in the New Testament, and in the tradition of the church. Scripture and tradition form a unified common source for Roman Catholic theology. Continuity with tradition in worship and theology is an important characteristic of Catholicism.

Faith in God is based on the self-disclosure of God in history, through various events and persons, preeminently as transmitted in the church's canon of holy scripture. The scriptures are considered to be inspired by God, and thus are a normative and authoritative expression of the faith. In this approach, the New Testament, conveying the life and words of Christ and his Apostles, is seen as the fulfillment of the Old Testament prophecies. A fuller knowledge of God was given through the revelation of the Son of God, or Jesus Christ, while the Spirit of God completes this transmission by making this revelation a continually living reality in the church throughout time. The public revelation of God is fulfilled in Christ and is concluded with the death of the last Apostle.

One may approach the knowledge of God through the use of reason, but only through revelation, and the corresponding response in faith, may one more fully apprehend the divine mystery. "Reason informed by faith" or "faith seeking understanding" implies the dialogue that occurs between faith (theology) and reason (the latter of which includes the modern sciences). All of humanity is called to respond to this revelation through the act of faith. The Second Vatican Council's Dogmatic Constitution on Divine Revelation (*Dei verbum*) reflects such a conception of revelation.

One should also note that three other texts of the Second Vatican Council—the Dogmatic Constitution on the Church (*Lumen gentium*), the Declaration on the Relationship of the Church to Non-Christian Religions (*Nostra aetate*), and the Decree on the Church's Missionary Activity (*Ad gentes divinitus*)—also provide additional themes on the notion of revelation. These texts address more explicitly the Catholic conception of the nature of revelation in the world religions, and they speak of Christ as the one who ultimately enlightens all nations. The mission of the church also includes mediating revelation for present times and cultures, where the official teaching body of the church, the magisterium, along with bishops and theologians, has a specific role in teaching and transmitting the faith. Doctrines are formal teachings of the church, and among them are included dogmas, which are teachings regarded as solemnly proclaimed and irreformable.

The Catholic Church holds a faith in one God, and so is monotheistic, but this monotheism is expressed in terms of a Trinitarian God, who is Father, Son, and Holy Spirit. Traditional Trinitarian theology has expressed such a God as three divine persons united by a common nature or essence. These divine persons are conceived of as analogically akin to human persons, with the qualification that human persons exist as individual centers of consciousness, while divine persons are defined in terms of persons-in-relation. This doctrine of the Trinity, although not explicitly contained in the scriptures, was developed in the early tradition in its reaction to various heresies, and it affirms that the three persons are distinct by saying that the Father is unbegotten, the Son is begotten, and the Holy Spirit proceeds from the Father (and/or through the Son). However, by virtue of their eternal communion or relationships, the three are simultaneously one. Perichoresis, or mutual indwelling, is the term used to express this inner-Trinitarian relationship. Sometimes their activity in the history of salvation is described as being Creator, Redeemer, and Sanctifier, for Father, Son, and Holy Spirit, respectively. A number of theologians have used psychological analogies, which are not without their limits, to describe the unity and diversity of the three, and they speak of God as being the Mind, Word, and Will, or they use the analogy of love, speaking of

God as Lover, Beloved, and Mutual Love. Language about the Trinitarian God is always qualified with the notion that created persons may not attain a full knowledge of the divine mystery by virtue of their created and finite natures, and so they rely on divine revelation in understanding how God is one, yet three. In Trinitarian theology, a methodological distinction is made between the immanent Trinity (God as mysteriously existing in the godhead) and the economic Trinity (God as active in the history of salvation), with the understanding that both ways of speaking about God refer to the same Triune God.

Very early in the tradition of the church, the notion emerged that God created the universe out of nothing (*creatio ex nihilo*) and that creation was good. These beliefs counteracted ideas that held that God created out of some pre-existent matter, a position that threatened the transcendence of God over created matter, or that creation was somehow accidental, which threatened the belief that God willed creation and had the absolute freedom to create. Creation in the book of Genesis is seen as good, willed by God, and a gift of God's love. There is linked to this protology (theology of first things) a rejection of any sort of dualism between good and evil in the material and spiritual realms. Such a God is Creator through the Son, who with the Spirit continually sustains and sanctifies creation. Of particular importance in such a cosmology is Jesus Christ, the Savior, through whom all of creation and humanity is renewed. Today's church seeks to correlate its fundamental theology of creation in the light of modern scientific discoveries, and it has become more sensitive to the crises existing in ecology.

Jesus Christ, as the second person of the Trinity, is seen as God who became incarnate in order for a fallen (sinful) humanity to attain salvation and in order for creation to be renewed. The incarnation is described by Saint Paul as a kenosis, which is literally a self-emptying or condescension of God's becoming human without thereby ceasing to be God. The name Christ means the anointed one—hence the related names of Messiah or Savior.

The classical doctrine in Christology (theology of Christ) is that Jesus Christ has two natures, both divine and human, which are united, without change, confusion, separation, or admixture, into one person. This doctrine, formulated very early on in the ecumenical councils, accounts for how Christ is Savior or Redeemer. As being fully God he is able to save, yet as also being fully human (of body and soul), he is able to freely accept the offer of salvation on behalf of humanity. Christ was like human persons in all things, except sin.

The Christ event, his incarnation, death, resurrection, and ascension to heaven, are the components that form the basis of the theology of salvation (soteriology) wrought by Christ. The universal significance of this event is that Christ is the sole mediator between God and humanity. He is seen as mediator to God and as the head of the body (the church). In the latter aspect, the participation and life of the person and community occur in and along with Christ. This ongoing presence in the community comes through the Spirit of Christ, who forms the link between the Jesus of history and the Christ of faith. In this latter aspect, Christ becomes existentially relevant to each person's, and the church's, life—that is, in their personal and communal worship, prayer, and experience.

The theology of Christ is related to the theology of the Spirit (pneumatology), and one cannot be understood without the other. The Spirit is the one who descends upon Christ (at his baptism), anointing him for his mission to spread the gospel. Christ also sends the Spirit to be the ongoing life-giver and sustainer for the church (at Pentecost). This Spirit endows the church and persons with many charisms, or gifts of grace, allowing them to continue to spread the good news of salvation and to participate sacramentally in the life of Christ. This same Spirit is the one who inspires the prophets, ensures that the church will not falter in its faith, and is the principle of communion (unity) among persons and churches.

The Church, Ministry, and Magisterium Much of the modern theology of the church (ecclesiology) is contained in the Second Vatican Council's statements on the church, ecumenism, the church in the modern world, and the church's missionary activity. The Second Vatican Council variously described the church as the body of Christ, the people of God, and the temple of the Spirit. In its earliest beginnings, Christians saw themselves as being in continuity with the temple worship of Judaism. Only later, as the two faith traditions grew apart, did separate churches, in homes and designated buildings, begin to emerge.

The church is described as both an invisible and a visible reality. The visible church is the institutional and hierarchically structured community that exists in the created realm, while the invisible aspect accounts for the fact that the church is also a heavenly reality, in that it is a community that is the body of Christ that exists in communion with God. Both of these aspects refer to the sacramentality of the church—that is, its being a means of a life of grace or holiness. The term "communion of saints" expresses the holiness of the earthly and heavenly church. The church is also described as being both a universal and a local reality. The local church is the community of faithful in a given place (a parish, city, or region), while the universal church is the unity or communion of these local churches. There has been a tendency in Catholic theology sometimes to see each local church as a part of the universal church. Theologians such as Jean-Marie Tillard, building upon the insights of the Second Vatican Council's description of communion ecclesiology, have emphasized that each local church has to be seen as fully a church in order to affirm the fullness of life in Christ in each community, and that each local church simultaneously forms part of the universal communion of churches.

The church has from earliest times been characterized as having four marks: unity, holiness, catholicity, and apostolicity. Unity is the oneness of life and doctrine in Christ and the Spirit. In modern times, there has been a concern for ecumenism, which is the dialogue that seeks unity between churches not in communion (or union) with each other. Major statements of agreement have come from dialogues with, for example, the Eastern Orthodox, Anglican, and Lutheran churches. Today's churches realize that disunity is contrary to the will of God and threatens the effective witness of the church. As for the church's holiness, it is primarily predicated on the notion that the church is essentially holy and lives a life of grace, despite its members at times being sinful. The previously mentioned etymology of the word "catholic" implies both a universality, but more important, a wholeness—the fullness of salvation is given in the church. The Second Vatican Council extended the notion of catholicity in its recognition that there are churches and ecclesial communities outside the Catholic Church that possess degrees of catholicity. The notion of apostolicity implies a continuity in the faith and ministry of the Apostles, and the authentic transmission of such faith in all times.

This mark of apostolicity is in part related to the institutional ministry, the latter of which is often described as safeguarding and transmitting Catholic doctrine, and as existing as servants to the faithful. The institutional church consists of a threefold ministerial structure of bishop, priest/presbyter, and deacon. The bishop is one who oversees each local community (diocese) but who is also entrusted with responsibility for the whole church. Each bishop is part of an episcopal college, whose head is the pope. This episcopal college formally meets either in conferences (of regions, countries) or in international bodies, such as in a council or synod. Priests and deacons are united to the bishop and pastorally minister to their respective local churches. Priests generally preside at the Eucharistic celebration, and when present, so do the bishops.

The notion of the Petrine ministry, the special commissioning of Peter to be the "rock" (foundation) upon which the church was to be built (Matthew 16:17–19), forms the basis of the claim of a universal primacy of the bishop of Rome, though each bishop in the church also shares this same Petrine vocation. Pope John Paul II (r. 1978–2005) in his encyclical *Ut unum sint* (1995), called for a re-envisioning of the role of the papacy in order for it to be more ecumenically acceptable to other Christian churches.

Each pastor of the church and each member of the church are called to spread the gospel; however, a special responsibility to teach is entrusted to the bishops. Formal teaching authority in matters of the faith and morals was entrusted to the successors of the Apostles—namely, the bishops, who are to guard and explain the faith fully. The word "magisterium" (Latin: *magister*: master) refers to the teaching authority of the church, and it is generally used to describe two types of teaching: extraordinary and ordinary. One type of the exercise of extraordinary magisterium is a universal (ecumenical) council when it proclaims a doctrine to be definitively held—hence, to be infallible. The First

Vatican Council (1869–1870) also decreed that the pope, as the one speaking from the chair of the bishop of Rome (*ex cathedra*), when he teaches on matters of faith and morals a doctrine to be universally held by the entire church, can teach infallibly. There has been only one such explicit exercise of papal infallibility in the history of Catholicism (Mary's Assumption, 1950). Ecumenical councils and infallible definitions of the pope as such are regarded as teachings of the extraordinary magisterium.

Another distinction to the teaching authority in the church is that exercised by each bishop, the entire episcopal college, or the pope in teaching on faith and morals in their "ordinary" teaching. Papal encyclicals, letters, statements of the various curial offices of the church (for example, the Congregation for the Doctrine of the Faith), or the bishops when teaching as individuals or as a collegial body, are examples of this aspect. Such a teaching function does not enjoy the charism of infallibility, but it is seen as authoritative and it does call for respect for the teaching (although infallible teachings may be contained in such an exercise of magisterium). According to canon law, dissent from ordinary magisterial teachings is theoretically possible, provided a number of strict conditions are met; however, dissent from infallible teachings is not permissible. The term "creeping infallibility" is used to describe the misconceived belief that all papal teachings are infallible. Another question in contemporary ecclesiology is to what extent the various curial offices can exercise magisterium outside of the college of bishops.

The distinction between extraordinary and ordinary magisterium is based on the theology of the development of doctrine. This notion of development essentially means that the church may explicitly teach a truth not explicitly contained in the Apostolic deposit of faith, or that the church may grow in its understanding of a doctrine, or that the expression of a doctrine may change in order to adapt to different languages and times, without the content of the doctrine changing. A further distinction is that the content of an infallible doctrine may not change, but doctrines not considered infallible may change. Changes in formal teaching in Catholicism have included the prohibition of slavery, religious liberty for all persons, and that there is the possibility of salvation outside the church. Another important doctrine is the *sensus fidelium* (sense of the faithful), which affirms that the Spirit of God has been bestowed upon the entire church, and not simply on the institutional ministries. The supernatural sense of the faithful can manifest an unerring quality when they reflect a universal consensus on faith and morals. The theological notion of reception is related to sense of the faithful when doctrines of faith and morals are received by the church as correct and authoritative, while non-reception would imply an ecclesial rejection of a teaching.

The College of Cardinals has a duty in assisting the papacy as a consultative body in governance of the universal church or in electing a new pope. The Roman curia is the formal ecclesial bureaucracy that assists in papal government through various congregations, councils, and commissions.

The ministry of the church is extended through various religious orders, special societies in the church whose members commit themselves to public vows of poverty, chastity, and obedience, and life in community with fellow members. Such societies are generally dedicated to specialized service in the church, whether education (Marist Brothers, Jesuits), evangelism (Dominicans), publishing (Society of Saint Paul), service to the poor or ill (such as the Missionaries of Charity, Sisters of Saint Joseph), or a life of prayer and contemplation (Carmelites). A number of these orders have assumed a particular role in foreign missions and the spread of the church internationally, including the Benedictines, Dominicans, Franciscans, Holy Ghost Fathers, Jesuits, Salesians, Ursulines, and White Fathers. There are also many local and international lay communities or associations who share in the life and mission of the church. One can number among these the Catholic Worker Movement (committed to social justice and peace), L'Arche (communities for those with disabilities), and Covenant House (providing shelter for homeless youth).

Theological Anthropology, Nature, and Grace

Theological anthropology deals with issues of human nature, creation, the relationship with God, free will, sin, and redemption. Catholic theology sees the person as created in the image and likeness of God, and thus possessing freedom of determination. All persons are called to live in a relationship with God, through Christ and in the Spirit, and the ultimate destiny to which each person is called is eternal life in the Trinitarian God.

The relationship between God and humans is expressed in the classic Catholic formulation of nature and grace. Nature in the nature-grace categories refers to our human condition and innate capacity to desire and receive grace, grace being the gratuitous divine self-communication or divine presence. This formulation is meant to bring to light two important points. The first is that grace is a free gift of God to human beings, and that the person is called to freely accept this gift. This doctrinal area implies a relationship with God and a transformation, or sanctification, of the person that results from that relationship. The other part of the equation is that grace cannot be attained by our own actions, or, in other words, one cannot attain salvation through one's own efforts. The scriptural formulation of this relationship is best expressed by contrasting a life lived in grace with a life lived in sin. The Western Christian tradition has tended to see grace as healing one from sin, while the Eastern Christian tradition has generally seen grace as leading to a process of sanctification or divinization, and despite the different emphases, both aspects exist in each tradition. The sanctifying and transformative power of grace is also now being incorporated into a theology of grace that includes all of creation, and not just humanity.

A distinction is drawn between uncreated grace and created grace. Uncreated grace refers to the inner Trinitarian life of God, while created grace refers to the gift and effects of being sanctified and brought into communion with God. This grace is also a universal gift that allows for the possibility of those who do not explicitly know Christ or God to authentically respond to God's offer of grace. Theologian Karl Rahner (1904–1984) has characterized this as "anonymous Christianity." This position still affirms that Christ is the unique or sole mediator of that divine grace. The Second Vatican Council's Declaration on Non-Christian Religions (*Nostra aetate*) addresses the church's relationship to Judaism, Islam, and other world religions. The text acknowledges the unity of humanity because of the creative work of God, and does not reject things that are true and holy in these religions. Dialogue and collaboration, as in the realm of ecumenism, is encouraged. The Second Vatican Council's Constitution on the Church recognized that non-Christians may achieve salvation, despite not being members of the visible Church.

Man and woman are also seen as being affected by original sin and the sins of humankind. Modern theology of sin has moved beyond some of the problems associated with holding a doctrine of biological transmission of sin or the sins of the first humans, and has viewed original sin in terms of a primordial (first) sin and personal responsibility. In a literal interpretation of the Genesis creation account, sin could be envisioned in categories of biological transmission. However, in the light of modern anthropology, psychology, and biblical criticism, Adam and Eve can be seen as symbols of the whole human race, which would emphasize each person's individual responsibility for sin. Catholicism has spoken of the corporate nature of sin, and that such sin can be manifested in a distortion of certain relationships (whether these be ecclesial or social, for example).

The theology of sin also addresses two basic types of sin: venial or mortal. Venial sins are spoken of as immoral because of their matter or because of a defect in the knowledge and freedom of the one sinning. Mortal sins are more severe in their subject matter and because there is the added notion that those committing them manifested sufficient thought and consent. Mortal sins destroy communion with God, while venial sins mar, but do not completely destroy, this communion.

Saints and Mary The term "saint," in common usage, refers to one who has been canonized by the church—that is, one who has been formally recognized to have lived a life of holiness or a life of grace. The numerous recognized saints witness to the diversity of lives and approaches to spirituality. An important part of ecclesiology and the theology of grace, though, is that all those who have attained salvation have become holy, or saints (both those canonized and those not). The communion of saints means that after death there still exist relationships between all Christians, both dead and alive. In Roman Catholicism, there is a formal process of recognition of sainthood that involves a number of criteria. A person is recognized by the church as blessed, then is beatified, and finally, is canonized. This process involves formal investigation of the person's life and attribution of miracles to a particular saint. Beatification allows a public veneration of the person, while canonization is a definitive belief that the person in question has indeed attained eternal life. Saints are not prayed to as if they are God, but rather, they are prayed to for their intercessory prayers—the grace and blessings always come from God. A distinction is made between the veneration of a saint and the worship (adoration) that is due to God alone. Veneration of saints, their images, statues, relics, or icons always leads to a worship of God.

Mary holds a special place of veneration among the saints, followed by the Apostles and early martyrs. Mary's particular importance within the cult of the saints stems from her sanctity of life and her accepting to be the mother of Jesus Christ. Mary is sometimes spoken of as the mother of God (Greek: *Theotokos*)—not of the divine nature of God, but of the incarnate Son of God. The theological understanding of Mary emerged alongside the early church's formal declarations on the nature of Christ. Mary is seen as being a virgin who conceived by the Holy Spirit, not by human procreation. Two other doctrines about Mary are important in Catholic theology—namely, the Immaculate Conception and the Assumption. The Immaculate Conception, a doctrine formalized in 1854, teaches that Mary, from the moment of her conception, by the grace of God and the merits of Christ's saving work, was free from original sin. The Assumption holds that Mary was taken up to heaven in body and soul. The Assumption witnesses to the fact that Christ's saving work will ultimately triumph over sin and death, and that all may hope for eternal life. The church does not require assent to apparitions of Mary (such as at Fatima and Lourdes).

Sacraments Sacraments, or mysteries, are means of the mediation of divine grace, signs of faith and acts of worship that are rooted in the ultimate mystery of the church being like a sacrament. Participants experience the grace and power of God, which is bestowed upon them gratuitously by virtue of Christ's suffering, death, and resurrection. The Christ event is thus the foundation for sacramental theology. The term in Greek, *mysterion*, connotes a broader understanding of God's grace to humanity, which is not limited to the number of sacraments. A trait of Catholicism is that it envisions itself as being sacramental—that is, as mediating communion with God. Modern theology after the Second Vatican Council has also emphasized the importance of the Christ event, as Christ being the first or primordial sacrament, and as the church also being like a sacrament. The number of formal sacraments, though, is seven: baptism, confirmation, Eucharist, reconciliation (penance), anointing of the sick, matrimony (marriage), and holy orders (ordination).

There are three sacraments of Christian initiation: baptism, confirmation, and Eucharist. Baptism is the incorporation of a person into the church, the body of Christ, and leads to the restoration of the imageness in Christ of the one being baptized. The forgiveness of sins also forms part of the theology of baptism. Christian churches generally recognize the unrepeatable character of baptism, provided that the act is done with a Trinitarian formula—that is, in the name of the Father, Son, and Holy Spirit—and the use of blessed water. As an incorporation into the church, each person thus also enters into the "priesthood of all believers." Baptism is thus seen as an ordination into the community, where the one baptized now forms part of the Eucharistic celebration.

Confirmation (chrismation) is an anointing with the holy oil of chrism whereby the initiate is sealed with the gift of the Spirit. Confirmation was initially practiced within the context of baptism, but it has become separated from this rite of initiation. Confirmation is celebrated as a second sacrament for baptized children who have reached the age of reason, and have thus undergone further catechesis, or it forms part of the rite of Christian initiation of adults. The Catholic Church, though, has in ecumenical dialogue with the Orthodox churches recognized the unity of the ancient rite of baptism, confirmation, and Eucharist, which proffered all three upon the one being initiated.

The Eucharist is seen as the culminating point of the initiation process, preceded by baptism and confirmation. Eucharist is literally a sacramental "thanksgiving" and praise of God, and a remembrance of the past and recollection of what God will do in the future. In the Eucharist, through participation in the mystical Body and Blood of Christ, sacramentally represented by the bread and wine, the faithful are brought into communion (union) in the body of Christ through the descent of the Spirit.

The sacrament of reconciliation is a ritual in which sins of the baptized are forgiven, thus leading to a reconciliation between the person and God. In reconciliation, the church recognizes that sin has a social dimension that affects the community. This sacrament, echoing the New Testament's universal call to reconciliation, also includes a penitential act, of either prayer or good works. Prayer, as a reconciliation with God, forms an important part of this ritual. A number of rituals exist with regard to reconciliation, whether it be a communal act or private act, or a combination of the two, with reconciliation before imminent death another ritual.

Anointing of the sick is also part of the church's prayer services, and has since medieval times been largely administered to those who are gravely ill or dying. Extreme unction is a synonym for this sacrament. In recent times there has been a renewal of this sacrament also to include all who are ill or those in old age.

Marriage is seen as an indissoluble covenant between a man and a woman that is geared to the expression of love between the two, and is also naturally ordered to the procreation of children. This marriage covenant echoes the fidelity of the covenant of God to the people. The church does not dissolve marriages that are sacramentally valid and consummated. Marriages, though, are dissolvable under very specific conditions set out by church canon law and that are adjudicated by local diocesan marriage tribunals.

Holy orders are basically a sacrament of ordination into the institutional priesthood, diaconate, or episcopate. The church teaches that through ordination, one becomes united in the ministry of Christ and the Apostles. Ordained ministers serve the church in various ways and in various degrees, from safeguarding the deposit of faith, governing, and administering the sacraments, to sanctifying. Generally, ordained ministers are celibate men. The primary justification for this is based upon the prototype of the high priesthood of Christ. There has since the last century been a movement in the church to extend ordination to women, especially in view of the increase in their roles in areas traditionally exercised by men, such as chaplaincy, spiritual direction, and pastoral associateship.

The Kingdom of God and Eschatology Eschatology (theology of last things) addresses questions such as death (or the end of the world), judgment, heaven, purgatory, hell, the resurrection of the body, and the coming of the kingdom of God. As mentioned, the goal of human existence is eternal life in God, which is expressed in Catholic theology as the beatific vision, and through the notion of the coming of the kingdom of God, or the end times (the *eschaton* or *parousia*). The kingdom of God theologically means the rule or reign of God. The end of the world does not necessarily imply the end of created matter, however, for the cosmos could be mysteriously transfigured. In the church's vision, the kingdom of God is already mysteriously upon us, yet this eternal kingdom is still awaiting its final consummation. This is antinomically described as the "already but not yet." Eternal life is a vision of God, and living in an eternal relationship of love and knowledge of God.

The church has never formally taught that anyone is in hell, or that it is a place of punishment by God; rather, hell is the place of total absence from God for those who would reject the gift of eternal life. Purgatory is seen as an intermediary place of purification from one's sins in preparation for the beatific vision. Purgatory has been spoken of in terms of a penal process, but some modern theologians have tended to focus on this intermediate state as a place of preparation and sanctification for eternal life. The church's magisterium has generally held that the resurrection of the dead takes place at the end of time, but some theologians have left open the possibility of an individual resurrection immediately after death. The destiny of each Christian thus includes purgatory, the resurrection of the body and soul, and the beatific vision (eternal life).

The Roman Catholic Church has its headquarters in Vatican City, a five-acre sovereign nation (the smallest of all the world's countries). In stark contrast, the

Roman Catholic Church is the world's largest religious organization, with slightly more than one billion members, or approximately 16 percent of the world's population. The Roman Catholic presence on the Internet is massive. The church has an official website at http://www.vatican.va/. In addition, many dioceses and religious orders also have web pages, and numerous sites of both a supportive and critical nature. http://www.catholic.net/ is particularly helpful, with links to a variety of Catholic periodicals, papal encyclicals, and other church documents.

Jaroslav Z. Skira

See also: Armenian Catholic Church; Bulgarian Catholic Church; Chaldean Catholic Church; Coptic Catholic Church; Death; Devotion/Devotional Traditions; Dominicans; Eastern Orthodoxy; Ethiopian Catholic Church; Franciscans; Greek Catholic Church; Holy Ghost Fathers; Italo-Albanian Catholic Church; Italy; Jesuits; Maronite Catholic Church; Martyrdom; Mary, Blessed Virgin; Melkite Catholic Church; Paul; Relics; Romanian Greek Catholic Church; Rome/Vatican City; Ruthenian Catholic Church; Saints; Salesians; Syrian Catholic Church; Syro-Malabar Catholic Church; Theology; Ukrainian Catholic Church; Ursulines; White Fathers.

References

Annuario Pontificio. Città del Vaticano: Libreria Editrice Vaticana, issued annually.

Bokenkotter, Thomas A. *A Concise History of the Catholic Church*. Rev. ed. Garden City, NY: Image, 1990.

Fiorenza, Francis Schüssler, and John P. Galvin, eds. *Systematic Theology: Roman Catholic Perspectives*. 2 vols. Minneapolis, MN: Fortress, 1991.

Flannery, Austin, ed. *Vatican Council II: The Conciliar and Post Conciliar Documents*. Rev. ed. Boston: St. Paul, 1992.

Foley, Leonard. *Believing in Jesus: A Popular Overview of the Catholic Church*. 4th ed. Cincinnati, OH: St. Anthony's Messenger, 2001.

Foy, Felician A., and Rose M. Avato. *A Concise Guide to the Catholic Church*. Huntington, IN: Our Sunday Visitor, 1984.

Hellwig, Monika K., ed. *The HarperCollins Encyclopedia of Catholicism*. New York: HarperCollins, 1995.

Hellwig, Monika K. *Understanding Catholicism*. New York: Paulist, 1981.

McBrien, Richard P. *Catholicism*. Rev. ed. New York: HarperSanFrancisco, 1994.

Rahner, Karl. *The Content of Faith: The Best of Karl Rahner's Theological Writings*. Ed. by Karl Lehmann and Albert Raffelt. Trans. by Harvey D. Egan. New York: Crossroad, 1993.

■ Romania

The boundaries of the present state of Romania were essentially set after World War II, when Transylvania was taken from the defeated Hungary and made a part of Romania. As constituted, the newly reshaped country had some 91,700 square miles of territory. Today (2008) it has a population of 22,247,000.

The Romanian people can be traced to the ancient Dacians, who appear in history in the fourth century BCE, when several were sold as slaves in Athens. Their homeland was the Carpathian Mountains, which cut through what is now modern Romania. Rome conquered the region in 109 CE. The land north of the mountains, Transylvania, and south, Walachia, became Dacia Superior and Dacia Inferior, respectively. The Roman occupation, which lasted until 270, left a significant imprint on the region and gives the country its contemporary name. The withdrawal of Rome left the region open to successive waves of invading troops, though a somewhat stable period began in the seventh century with the incorporation of the area into the Bulgarian Empire.

Romania's history is marked by the invasion of the Mongols in 1241, when most of the records of its past were destroyed, and history essentially began anew in 1290 with the founding of the princedom of Walachia with headquarters at Curtea de Arges. At the same time, Hungary consolidated its control of Transylvania. Walachia struggled to remain independent from the more powerful Hungarians to the north and, increasingly in the 15th century, from the growing Ottoman Empire.

Roman Catholic Episcopal church and Holy Trinity monument in Timisoara, Romania. (iStockPhoto.com)

Wallachia became a Turkish province in 1417, but for the next century various attempts were made both to keep the Turks from occupying the land and to maintain the culture and religion of the people intact. Among the figures who came to the fore in the middle of the century was Prince Vlad (ca. 1431–ca. 1476), who became known for his efforts to unite the Wallachians and his battles against the Turkish armies. Considered a national hero by modern Romanians, he has become infamous in the West after his other name, Dracula (or son of Dracul, which in Romanian means "son of the dragon"), was given to the title character in Bram Stoker's vampire novel.

Although the Turkish advance was checked in 1529 at Vienna, Turkish dominance of Hungary and Wallachia remained through the rest of the century. There was a brief respite from Turkish rule beginning in the 1590s, but the Turks came into power again in the 17th century. Wallachia remained under Turkish control until Russia became involved. In 1812, Russia took control of the southeastern part of Moldavia and continued to put pressure on the Ottomans in the region. Step by step, greater levels of autonomy were introduced. In 1859, Alexandru Ion Ciza emerged as the ruler of a united Wallachia and Moldavia, which was recognized as the independent country of Romania in 1878 following the Russian Turkish War of 1877. Then in 1916, Romania aligned itself against Hungary and Austria in World War I, and it was awarded Transylvania when the Austro-Hungarian Empire was dismantled in 1918.

Romania was occupied by Germany during World War II. After the war, the country came under Russian influence, and in 1946 the Communists took control of

Romania

the government. In 1965, Nicolae Ceausescu (1918–1989) became head of the Communist Party and in 1967 president of the country. He began to pursue a policy somewhat independent of Russia, and emerged as a most brutal dictator. A combination of economic problems and government corruption led to massive discontent that culminated in the revolution of 1989 that drove Ceausescu from power and led to the establishment of a democratic government in the country.

Christianity was introduced into the Danube region, according to legend, by the Apostle Andrew in the first century. Documents are scarce, but a bishop resided at Tomis by the fourth century, and a bishop from Banat-Marisena attended the Ecumenical Council of 787. In subsequent centuries, Romania was on the battle line between the Byzantine Greek and the Roman Latin churches. The swing of Wallachia and Moldavia into the Greek camp was solidified during the two centuries of Bulgarian control. The work of Cyril and Methodius in introducing the Slavonic liturgy also influenced the developing church.

When Wallachia was founded as a separate state, Orthodoxy dominated. In 1359 an Orthodox bishop sent from Constantinople settled at Curtea de Arges. A second diocese was erected at Severin in 1370. Although Orthodoxy was the dominant force in Transylvania, the Roman Catholic Church was on the ascendancy. Benedictines had established themselves in Cluj and Saniob in the 11th century, and Franciscans and Dominicans arrived in the 13th century. From the 14th century, Orthodoxy became increasingly established in Wallachia and Catholicism in Transylvania. A bishopric was established in Moldavia in 1401.

As Hungary became the dominant force in Transylvania, the Orthodox Church was suppressed. In 1279 the Orthodox were stopped from building new churches and the Orthodox faith prohibited. The dominance of Roman Catholicism was bolstered by the arrival of many Germans into Transylvania. The Orthodox Church survived through the 17th century, but once Austria gained dominance of the region in 1687, systematic efforts to convert the Orthodox began. As part of its missionary thrust, Catholics founded the Romanian Catholic Church, an Eastern-rite church. Under threat of the loss of civil rights, the head of the Orthodox Church agreed to unite with Rome in 1698.

Early in the 16th century, an additional factor was introduced into Romanian religious life with the arrival of Protestants, both Lutherans and Reformed, from German-speaking areas to the west. Although they initially had their greatest success in the German-speaking communities, both a Hungarian- and a Romanian-speaking Protestant movement emerged. Transylvania also became home to an important (and the surviving) wing of Unitarianism (non-Trinitarian Christianity), which had also emerged in the 16th century and established itself briefly in Poland.

The progress of Christianity was checked somewhat by the conquest of the Ottomans, dedicated Muslims. Muslims from the area north of the Black Sea had entered what is now Romania as early as the 13th century, but others moved into the region following the spread of Ottoman control across Romania and into Hungary. Muslim strength was concentrated in the Danube River Valley, west of the Black Sea.

Independence in 1878 set the stage for a set of changes in Romanian religious life. Most important, in 1885, Orthodox believers established the Romanian Orthodox Church as an autocephalous body no longer under the administrative jurisdiction of the ecumenical patriarchate in Constantinople. Second, various Protestant/Free churches, most prominently the Baptists, saw an opportunity to plant their brand of Christianity in Romania. The original Baptist community was founded in 1856, but after 1877, Baptist churches began to appear across the country. Initial growth was in the German-speaking and Hungarian-speaking communities, but by the turn of the century a significant Romanian Baptist church had been formed. In 1917 there were 23,000 Baptists, of whom 11,000 were Hungarian, 10,000 Romanian, and only 1,000 German. Other new groups entering at this time were the Church of the Nazarene, the Christian Brethren, and the Seventh-day Adventist Church.

Pentecostalism began in Romania through a Romanian magazine published in the United States. The first prayer house opened in 1922, and in 1925 what became the Apostolic Church of God of Romania was organized. The Jehovah's Witnesses first appeared in 1912.

Religious life in Romania did not fare well through most of the 20th century, especially in the decades following World War II. The addition of Transylvania brought a score of new religions into Romania, where the Orthodox Church had a preferred role. Orthodoxy was hit with a schism in 1924, following its adoption of the Gregorian calendar, the Old Rite Romanian Orthodox Church being set up by those who continued to adhere to the Julian calendar. A law on religious organizations passed in 1928 that both favored some groups—those Christian churches that had a long history in the region—and prohibited the activity of the Jehovah's Witnesses, the Pentecostals, the Nazarenes, and a number of other smaller groups. Following the change in government after World War II, authorities moved to merge the Romanian Catholic Church into the Romanian Orthodox Church. This unhappy union led to the arrest of many who refused to discontinue Catholic rites.

The primary losers in Romania through the 20th century, however, were the Jews. Following their expulsion from Iberia (1492–1493), many Sephardic Jews moved to Romania. They were not allowed to organize until 1730. In the 19th century, especially in Transylvania, the Jewish community divided along Reformed and Orthodox lines. Jews were officially recognized in 1894 in Transylvania and in 1923 and 1928 in Romania. The federation of the Jewish Communities of Romania accommodated units for its two branches.

Romania

Religion	Followers in 1970	Followers in 2010	% of Population	Annual % growth 2000–2010	Followers in 2025	Followers in 2050
Christians	16,841,000	20,883,000	98.8	–0.40	19,326,000	15,807,000
Orthodox	16,194,000	19,340,000	91.5	0.01	18,000,000	14,780,000
Roman Catholics	2,834,000	1,880,000	8.9	–1.01	1,700,000	1,400,000
Protestants	1,586,000	1,910,000	9.0	2.59	1,800,000	1,500,000
Agnostics	1,703,000	150,000	0.7	–5.07	80,000	50,000
Muslims	250,000	75,000	0.4	–0.46	65,000	50,000
Atheists	1,356,000	25,000	0.1	–8.50	10,000	8,000
Jews	100,000	6,500	0.0	–0.47	6,000	5,500
New religionists	3,000	3,700	0.0	–0.47	3,000	2,500
Baha'is	0	1,900	0.0	–0.46	2,000	3,000
Chinese folk	0	1,200	0.0	–0.46	1,200	1,200
Buddhists	0	500	0.0	–0.46	800	800
Total population	**20,253,000**	**21,147,000**	**100.0**	**–0.47**	**19,494,000**	**15,928,000**

There were an estimated half-million Jews in Romania at the beginning of World War II. The majority were killed during the Holocaust, but more than 100,000 survived. During the Ceausescu era the government adopted a liberal immigration policy, and the majority of the community moved to Israel. As the new century begins, only some 10,000 Jews remain in Romania.

Islam survived in southeastern Romania, and in 1928 the community was divided into four muftiates. The mufti from Tulcea was recognized as the chief mufti, the leader of the Romanian Muslim community. There were some 185,000 Muslims at the time, although the community has decreased to around 55,000 today. There is a single muftiate headquartered in Constanta.

Surviving the Ceausescu era, Romania began a new period of religious freedom in 1989. Romania became a major target for evangelizing groups from both East and West, and it quickly jumped into a new level of religious pluralism. Among the groups that opened centers were the Baha'i Faith, The Family International/Children of God, the Church of Jesus Christ of Latter-day Saints, the Unification movement, the International Zen Association, the International Society for Krishna Consciousness, and the Movement of Spiritual Inner Awareness.

Since the revolution, 15 religious bodies have been recognized by the government. They are the Romanian Orthodox Church, the Romanian Catholic Church, the Roman Catholic Church (Latin-rite), the Reformed Church in Romania, the Evangelical Church of the Augsburg Confession in Romania (Lutheran), the Evangelical Synodal Presbyterial Church of the Augsburg Confession in Romania, the Unitarian Church, the Armenian Apostolic Church (Holy See of Echmiadzin), The Old Rite Romanian Orthodox Church, the Muslim community, the Jewish community, the Baptist Christian Church, the Seventh-day Adventist Church, the Pentecostal church, and the Romanian Evangelical Church. Numerous newer groups operate as religious associations, thereby receiving a form of government recognition but no public funds to assist their activities. As have many countries from the former Communist world, in the last two decades, Romania has tested numerous laws designed to limit various, especially minority, religions and privilege specific older groups, especially the Orthodox Church.

J. Gordon Melton

See also: Armenian Apostolic Church (Holy See of Echmiadzin); Baha'i Faith; Benedictines; Christian Brethren; Church of Jesus Christ of Latter-day Saints; Church of the Nazarene; Dominicans; Evangelical Church of the Augsburg Confession in Romania; Family International, The; Franciscans; International Society for Krishna Consciousness; International Zen

Association; Jehovah's Witnesses; Movement of Spiritual Inner Awareness; Old Rite Romanian Orthodox Church; Reformed Church in Romania; Roman Catholic Church; Romanian Greek Catholic Church; Romanian Orthodox Church; Seventh-day Adventist Church; Unification Movement.

References

Baron, Peter. *Romania Hermitages, Monasteries and Churches*. Royal Company, 1999.

Branzea, Nicolae I., and Stefan Ionita. *Religious Life in Romania.* Bucharest: Editura Paideia, 1999.

Butnaru, I. C. *The Silent Holocaust: Romania and Its Jews*. Westport, CT: Greenwood Press, 1992.

Clifton, Carmin. *Come Lord, Come: A History of the Church of Jesus Christ of Latter-day Saints in Romania*. N.p.: AuthorHouse, 2002.

Cuciuc, Constantin. *Atlasul Religiilor şi al Monumentelor Istorice Religioase din Romania.* Bucharest: Editura Gnosis, 1996.

Flora, Gravil, and Georgina Szilagyi. "Church and Society in Romania in the Period of Systemic Change." In *Religion and Social Change in Central and Eastern Europe,* edited by Irena Borowik and Miklos Tomka, 55–77. Krakow: Nomos, 2001.

Stan, Lavinia, and Lucian Turcescu. *Religion and Politics in Post-Communist Romania*. New York: Oxford University Press, 2007.

Talos, Vasile Alexandru. "Religious Pluralism in the Romanian Context." *Religion in Eastern Europe* 18, no. 4 (July 1998).

Romania, Islam in

The Romanian Muslim community has a variety of ethnic backgrounds, though most of Romanian Muslims are Turks and Tatars who came into what is now the easternmost part of Romania from the territory north of the Black Sea and later from the south as the Ottoman Empire expanded into Central Europe. Some of them came with the Petcheneg and the Cuman peoples, who settled in the area between the ninth and 12th centuries. A small number of Muslims are ethnic

King Carol I of Romania Mosque, built in 1910 in Constanta, Romania. Constanta is the center of Islam in Romania. (Gerald Kelsall/Dreamstime.com)

Albanians. Even Gypsies, known as *kaapti*, were converted to Islam. During several wars, Muslims from Crimea known as Circassians temporarily settled in the area and then moved to the south of the Danube.

Islam spread among the Petchenegs, Udis, Cumans, Tatars, and the Seljuk and the Osmanli Ottomans who originally resided in Central Asia. By the 10th century they were present north of the Black Sea and in Dobrogea. Islam gradually replaced the old religious practices, and the Uzbeks were the first to embrace the faith in Allah. During the reign of Khan Berke (1257–1267), the Turks from the north of the Black Sea and Dobrogea adhered to Islam. The subsequent waves of Turks coming from Central Asia and Anatolia formed large communities in what is now Romania, and Turkish geographical names have survived to this day (Babadag, Sarighiol, Medgidia, Techirghiol, Adamclisi, etc.). Gradually, the Muslim population increased in Dobrogea and in the towns along the Danube, which were exposed to the influence of the Muslim cultural centers from the south. Islam united the Tatar and Turkish populations and laid the foundations of several political and administrative institutions and an impressive culture. Islam brought about a spiritual revival for these populations and played an essential role in the preservation of the Turks' national identity.

As Islam pushed north into Hungary, the rulers of the Romanian countries, in an effort to preserve the independence of their principalities, attempted to limit the influence of Islam north of the Danube. For example, they were able to negotiate treaties with the sultans that allowed the Muslims who came to the area for trade to convert to Christianity. Thus, it was hoped that this would prevent the foundation of Muslim communities and the building of Islamic places of worship. In the 15th century, Dobrogea came under Ottoman administration and allowed the consolidation of Islam in the area. Mosques and *meshids* (smaller places of worship) were built during that time, and religious schools and courts were founded. The Sari Saltuk Mausoleum from Babadag, the Mischin Baba Mausoleum in Ada Kale (now moved to the Simian island), and several *cheshemels* (traditional wells) that have survived to this day date from the end of the 15th century.

Dobrogea was reintegrated into the Romanian state in 1878, and its particular cultural features as well as the political and administrative elements of the past were retained. The newspaper *Ikdam* reported in 1909 that the Turks from Dobrogea had 2 muftis paid by the government, 2 religious courts, more than 300 mosques, 107 mullahs, 100 imams, 81 muezzins, and 30 khaims. A law passed in 1880 to regulate Dobrogea's organization stated that the Muslim community was allowed to have two muftiates (Constanţa and Tulcea), as well as several Islamic religious courts; these would remain in operation until around 1930. The Muslim judge (the *cadi*) had a special competence in matters regarding the family, such as marriage, divorce, parental authority, guardianship, succession, and wills. The law of cults passed in 1928 recognized the organization of the Islamic community in four muftiates (Caliacra, Constanţa, Durostor, Tulcea). In Resolution 39818 issued by the Council of Ministers in 1937, the mufti from Tulcea was recognized as *basmufti* (chief mufti), the leader of all Muslims from Romania. In 1930 there were reported to be 185,486 Muslims in the country, many of them living in Durostor and Caliacra.

With funds from a donation by General Gazi Ali Pasa, a seminary for training Muslim clergy was founded in Babadag. In 1889 the Ministry of Cults and Public Instruction recognized and reorganized the Muslim seminary, which included also a Romanian language chair. Because of a drought and the consequent migration of people, the seminary was moved to Medgidia in 1901.

Through the early 20th century, many ethnic Turks residing in Romania returned to Turkey. Between the two World Wars, entire villages from Dobrogea were deserted. The number of places of Muslim worship also decreased. Of the 300 places of Islamic religious and cultural significance in existence by the turn of the 20th century, only about 80 have survived to this day. The Islamic community now has only one muftiate (in Constanţa), led by the chief mufti and an ecumenical council (the *surai islam*, made up of 23 members). The 1992 census recorded 55,988 Muslims in Romania, 0.2 percent of the country's population. The majority live in Dobrogea, but there are smaller communities in the port towns along the Danube. The Muslim community in Bucharest (about 300 to 500 believers) provides personnel for some embassies.

Muslim Community in Romania
Bd. Tomas nr. 41
Constanţa
Romania

Constantin Cuciuc

See also: Islam; Sufism.

References

Branzea, Nicolae I., and Stefan Ionita. *Religious Life in Romania*. Bucharest: Editura Paideia, 1999.

Cuciuc, Constantin. *Atlasul Religiilor si al Monumentelor Istorice Religicase din România*. Bucharest: Editura Gnosis, 1996.

Romanian Greek Catholic Church

An Eastern-rite church in communion with the Roman Catholic Church emerged in the late 17th century in

Romania following the retreat of the Turks from Transylvania in 1687. The new Hapsburg rulers of the Austro-Hungarian Empire encouraged the Orthodox faithful, the majority of Transylvanians, to change their allegiance to Rome and supported Jesuit missionaries to work toward that end. A combination of pressures, including the denial of full civil rights to Orthodox believers, led the head of the Orthodox church in Transylvania to agree to a union of his church with Rome in 1698. That agreement was approved at a synod two years later, and the Romanian Greek Catholic Church came into being.

The union held together until 1744, when a devout Orthodox monk began a revival of Orthodoxy and the government finally gave up its attempt to suppress it. In 1759 a new Orthodox bishop was consecrated for Transylvania. Two communities of about equal strength (the Romanian Orthodox and the Romanian Catholic) emerged, however, and some bitter feeling between the two groups remained. At the end of World War I, Transylvania was removed from Catholic Hungary and became a part of Orthodox Romania. By the end of the 1930s, there were 5 dioceses serving 1.5 million believers.

After World War II, the new Marxist government forced the Greek Catholics to break their ties to Rome and unite with the Romanian Orthodox Church. In 1948 the church was officially dissolved and its property turned over to the Orthodox officials. Shortly thereafter, all of the Catholic bishops were arrested. Five died in jail, and the sixth died in 1970 under house arrest.

The Romanian Greek Catholic Church was not able to revive until 1990, when the 1948 dissolution decree was rescinded after the fall of the Ceausescu government. Suddenly, three bishops who had been operating underground emerged. Pope John Paul II (1920–2005) immediately appointed bishops for all the vacant dioceses. The re-emergence of the church set off a continuing confrontation with the Romanian Orthodox Church. Greek Catholics demanded the immediate return of all the property seized in 1948. However, the Orthodox patriarch has been slow to turn over the property, as he insists that it is now serving members who have become Orthodox in faith. The church has been able to recover most of its former property, but a fight continues over disputed parishes. Some progress was noted following the visit of Pope John Paul II to Romania and his meeting with the Romanian Orthodox patriarch in 1999.

The Romanian Greek Catholic Church, United with Rome, is led by Metropolitan Lucian Muresan (b. 1931), who also serves as archbishop of Făgăraş and Alba Julia. On December 16, 2005, Pope Benedict XVI raised the Romanian Greek Catholic Church to the rank of Major Archepiscopal Church. With this act he also designated Metropolitan Muresan as Major Archbishop of Făgăraş and Alba Julia. In 2006, the church reported 764,000 adherents, with 1,225 worshipping communities served by 791 priests. There is one diocese located outside the country, St. George's Diocese based in Canton, Ohio.

Romanian Greek Catholic Church
Str. P. P. Aron 2
RO-3 175
Blaj AB
Romania

Constantin Cuciuc

See also: Roman Catholic Church; Romanian Orthodox Church.

References

Branzea, Nicolae I., and Stefan Ionita. *Religious Life in Romania.* Bucharest: Editura Paideia, 1999.

Cuciuc, Constantin. *Atlasul Religiilor şi al Monumentelor Istorice Religi case din România.* Bucharest: Editura Onosis, 1996.

Romanian Orthodox Church

Christianity reached the area west of Black Sea along the Danube River as early as the second century CE. Christian communities to the north of the Danube (present-day Romania) had close relations, including administrative relations, with the churches to the south (present-day Bulgaria), which were better organized and received pastoral guidance from the patriarch of Byzantium. In 535, Emperor Justinian (483–565) established the See of Tauresium in his native town (now the town of Taor, in the former Yugoslavia), and

View of Sf. Mihail si Gravril, a Romanian Orthodox church in Braila, Romania. (Nicu Mircea/Dreamstime.com)

the see had jurisdiction over some Romanian Christian communities. Although documents are rare, an episcopal office is mentioned as existing in Tomis (fourth–sixth centuries), and in 787, a bishop from Banat-Mariseena (today Cedad in Timis County) attended the seventh ecumenical council at Nicaea. The conversion to Christianity of people in Romania's neighboring countries had a great influence on the spread and consolidation of Christianity in Romania.

In 973 the new Hungarian state concluded an alliance with the powerful Catholic, Emperor Otto I (912–973), after which missionaries from the Roman Catholic Church were sent to the country to replace those from Byzantium. As a result of the influx of Roman Catholics into the region, the Balkans became one of the places where the line was drawn between Eastern Orthodoxy and Roman Catholicism in 1054, when the two churches formally separated.

In the meantime, the conquest of Bulgaria (1018) by the Byzantine King Basil II Bulgaroctonus (ca. 958–1025) allowed Byzantium to gain religious and political power over Romania. In succeeding years, the Orthodox Church was supported by the political authorities. The first centralized Romanian state, with its capital in Curtea de Argeş, was established in 1324 by Prince Basarab (d. 1352), the founder of Wallachia. His son adopted the Orthodox Church as a spiritual support for political life and asked that a bishop be sent from Constantinople. In 1359, Bishop Lachint from Vicina was accepted at Curtea de Argeş, and his jurisdiction also included Transylvania. A second episcopal see was established in Severn in 1370.

Romanian princes coming from Maramureş in 1350 organized the religious life of Moldavian locals, and during the reign of Prince Alexandru cel Bun (1400–1432), the patriarchate from Constantinople recognized Bishop Losif of Suceava (1401). In 1632 the capital of Moldavia (and the bishopric) was moved from Suceava to Lasi. While the Orthodox Church was spreading through Wallachia and Moldavia, its development in Transylvania was hindered when Hungary conquered the region and, with German backing, forced people to accept Catholicism. A Roman Catholic council in Hungary (1279) forbade Orthodox believers to build churches or to perform worship services according to Orthodox principles.

Pressure on both Roman Catholic and Orthodox believers followed the arrival of Calvinist Protestantism. Calvinist princes from Transylvania asked Orthodox believers to accept the Reformed faith, and some Orthodox bishops left as the Reformed Church in Romania grew in strength. Catholic authority was re-established after 1687, and again Catholic missionaries organized the conversion of Orthodox believers. The heightened pressure to convert was backed by the political authorities, leading to the acceptance of unity with Rome (1698–1701) and the foundation of the Romanian Greek Catholic Church. Orthodox converts were allowed to keep their Greek liturgy, but they acknowledged the authority of Rome. Forced conversions continued through the 18th century.

When Romania fell under Turkish rule in 1417, some semblance of local control remained and Christianity was left undisturbed. The Turkish hegemony was thrown off in the 1590s, but it returned in the next century. At about the same time, Russia began to meddle in the region as part of its drive for an ice-free port. The struggle to emerge as a nation free from the control of both Russia and the Ottoman Empire led to Romania's full independence in 1877.

After independence, the Romanian Orthodox Church proclaimed itself autocephalous, and in 1885 its independence was recognized by the Ecumenical Patriarchate. Following World War I, Transylvania was again united with Romania (1918), and the Orthodox Church was presented with a new opportunity. It considered Orthodox believers who had previously united with Rome to be still part of the Orthodox Church, and efforts were expended to reintegrate them back into Orthodoxy. The Romanian Constitution adopted in 1923 did not distinguish between the Romanian Greek Catholic Church and the Romanian Orthodox Church. The conflict between these two church bodies continues to the present.

Also following the war, steps were taken to unify the administration of the Romanian Orthodox Church. In 1920 a board was established to draw up the regulations of the church. The new "law and regulations of the organization of the Romanian Orthodox Church" appeared in 1925. The leading bishop was for the first time given the title of patriarch. The first Romanian patriarch, Miron Cristea (1868–1939), held the post from 1925 until his death in 1939. The church survived the upheavals of the 20th century, including the very repressive Marxist regime that exercised power from the end of World War II until 1989.

Today the Romanian Orthodox Church is organized according to its own regulations, drawn up by the synod and modified according to sociopolitical circumstances. Though independent administratively, it is one in faith and belief with the rest of the Orthodox world. The head of the Romanian Orthodox Church is the patriarch, and the Romanian Orthodox Patriarchate includes metropolitan bishoprics, archiepiscopates, and bishoprics.

In 1998 the church was divided into 10 archdioceses and 13 diocesan bishoprics. In 2006, it reported 18,806,000 members, 13,500 parishes, and 12,855 priests. The church also has canonical oversight of the Vicariate of the Serbian Orthodox Church in Romania, with 26,000 believers, and the Vicariate of the Ukrainian Orthodox Church, with 52,000 believers. Outside of Romania, there are bishops in Germany, France, and the United States who lead Romanian Orthodox believers who remain in communion with the Romanian Patriarchate residing in Western Europe and North America. The Orthodox Church oversees 14 theological institutes, most of them founded after 1989, with hundreds of students. It is a member of the World Council of Churches.

Romanian Orthodox Church
Aleea Patriahiei 2
70526 Bucharest, 4
Romania
http://www.patriarhia.ro/bor_eng/index_eng.htm

Constantin Cuciuc

See also: Ecumenical Patriarchate/Patriarchate of Constantinople; Reformed Church in Romania; Romanian Greek Catholic Church; Roman Catholic Church; World Council of Churches.

References

Branzea, Nicolae I., and Stefan Ionita. *Religious Life in Romania.* Bucharest: Editura Paideia, 1999.

Cuciuc, Constantin. *Atlasul Religiilor şi al Monumentelor Istorice Religicase din România.* Bucharest: Editura Gnosis, 1996.

Van Beek, Huibert. *A Handbook of the Churches and Councils: Profiles of Ecumenical Relationships.* Geneva: World Council of Churches, 2006.

Rome/Vatican City

Rome, Italy's largest city and capital, is located along the Tiber River some 30 miles from its mouth on the Tyrrhenian Sea. The city emerged to prominence as the center of the Roman Empire, and while serving that role became the setting for a number of foundational events in the establishment of the Christian church in the first century CE.

The Roman conquest of the Eastern Mediterranean provided the conditions in which Jesus was born and raised, and which then overshadowed his mature life and shaped his death. Following his arrest in Jerusalem, the Apostle Paul pleaded his case as a Roman citizen and was sent to Rome as a prisoner. He arrived

Saint Peter's Square in Vatican City. (Photka/Dreamstime.com)

around 60. Christianity likely had been established in the city earlier, as it caught the attention of the Emperor Nero, who in 64 targeted the church and attacked its members, who became scapegoats for the fire that swept through the city.

Both Rome and Christianity survived the first century, and the Christian movement continued to interact with events of the city. The second century would, for example, see the martyr's death of Bishop Ignatius, an act of suppression that like the others only seemed to spur Christianity's growth. The life of the church would be completely altered by the rise of the emperor Constantine (r. 305–337). Over the more than three decades of his rule, the persecutions ended and Christianity was first legalized and then privileged throughout the empire. Then, after Constantine shifted the center of the empire to Constantinople, the Western Latin-speaking church, slowly transforming into the Roman Catholic Church, would emerge as the major power structure permeating Western Europe. Simultaneously, the pope emerged as the temporal ruler of the Papal States, a country carved out of central Italy. The Papal States, with its capital in Rome, lasted until the unification of modern Italy in the 19th century. A remnant of the Papal States survives as the modern Vatican City, now consisting of a mere five acres of territory. It is the world's smallest country.

Prior to the Christian era, Rome was, of course, home to numerous Pagan temples. Rome's original ruler Servius Tullius (r. 578–534 BCE) integrated religion into the Roman civilization he helped establish. He is particularly credited with the rise of the cult of Diana on Aventine Hill. Her main temple has survived to the present. Most of the Pagan temples were either pulled down or transformed into Christian churches, but hundreds of the former temples survive, scattered about the city in various states of ruin. The most impressive of the surviving temples is the Pantheon, which was dedicated to the 12 Olympian gods, the main deities of the official Roman religion. The dome that spans some 142 feet in the central room was erected around the year 125 CE, then a major engineering accomplishment. It remained the largest dome in the world until the 15th century, when the Duomo in Florence, Italy, was constructed. The Pantheon has replaced previous temples on the same site, both of which had been destroyed by fire.

The earliest Christian sites in Rome were the catacombs, the places for the burial of the dead, which became home to the earthly remains of many Christians, including many later designated as saints. The catacombs contain more than 500,000 bodies in the more than 60 miles of their underground network.

As he began to privilege Christianity, Constantine also became the major force behind the transformation of Rome from a primarily Pagan to a primarily Christian city. He ordered the construction of the Church of Saint John Lateran, the first large basilica in the Christian world, which served as headquarters of the Roman Catholic Church and the center of papal authority for many centuries. In the Middle Ages, Saint John Lateran would be the site of some of the most important councils held by the Catholic Church. In spite of its being destroyed several times, it was on each occasion rebuilt, most recently in the 17th century.

Numerous Christian relics also survived through the centuries and are now located in Rome, some of the earliest dating to the initial gathering of artifacts by Constantine's mother, Helena (ca. 248–ca. 329). Among the more significant items, to be seen today at the Church of Saint John Lateran, is a staircase from Jerusalem that tradition suggests was walked upon by Jesus during the week between his grand entrance into Jerusalem (Palm Sunday) and crucifixion. In former years, the stairs functioned to connect the church with what was then the papal residence. Saint John Lateran's private papal chapel, the Sancta Sanctorum, also houses additional key relics, which, to believers, tie Rome to Christian origins in the Holy Land, for example, a portion of the True Cross, a lock of hair from the Virgin Mary, a fragment of bread from the Last Supper, and some bones from the two Johns (John the Baptist and John the Evangelist) for whom the church is named. Finally, the church also houses a set of Jewish artifacts originally brought to Rome by Vespasian following his sacking of Jerusalem in 70 CE.

The Church of Saint Mary Major is the first major church in Christendom dedicated to the Virgin Mary. According to legend, it originated from a vision of the Virgin in the fourth century during the reign of Pope Liberius (r. 352–366). In the middle of one of Rome's very hot summers, a wealthy Roman resident was told in the vision to build a church where he found snow falling the next morning. Simultaneously, the pope received a similar message in a dream. The next morning, to everyone's amazement, snow covered the Esquiline Hill, where a church was soon erected. That church would then be replaced in the fifth century with a large basilica dedicated in 435 in response to the proclamation of Mary as the Mother of God by the church council at Ephesus (431). The image of Mary in the church is referred to as Our Lady of the Snows.

The churches of Saint Mary Major and Saint John Lateran became the lead churches of the growing Christian community in Rome and the mothers of many congregations in the Archdiocese of Rome. They were also connected through the medieval era through a relic believed to be a full-length image of Jesus that dated to the Apostle Luke. It would periodically be carried in procession from the Lateran to Saint Mary's, where its arrival was seen symbolically as a reuniting of Jesus with his mother.

Christian life in Rome is also tied to the arrival of two of the most famous of Jesus' Apostles: Peter and Paul. Paul came to Rome around 60. Following his execution, he was reputedly buried outside the city walls in a cemetery belonging to a Roman lady named Lucina. During his reign, Constantine ordered the erection of a large basilica at this site. It came to be known as the Church of Saint Paul Outside the Walls. Peter is regarded by Roman Catholics as the first bishop of Rome. Also executed in the city, he was buried on the site of the present Vatican City. Constantine also built a large basilica over Peter's burial site. His basilica fell into disrepair during the period when the popes left Rome to live at Avignon, France (1309–1377). It was Pope Nicolas V (r. 1447–1455) who suggested rebuilding rather than repairing the old church. He was not aware that the effort would take a century and a half and be tied to demands from across Western Europe for church reform. Efforts to raise money to support the construction of Saint Peter's would occasion the emergence of Protestantism early in the 16th century and the eventual loss of most of northern and western European countries from the Catholic camp. The present St. Peter's Cathedral building was finally dedicated in 1626.

Saint Peter's dome is slightly larger than that of the Pantheon, but smaller than the Duomo in Florence, which had just been completed when the new Saint Peter's was originally conceived. The overall surface area of the interior is impressive at more than 160,000 square feet (compared to the 90,000 square feet covered by the cathedral in Milan, Italy, and the 84,000 square feet of Saint Paul's in London). The church houses a number of relics, many tracing their history to Saint Helena's search of the Holy Land in the fourth century, and has become the place where many of the church's most impressive services occur, including the canonization of saints and the coronation of successive popes.

Work on Saint Peter's was delayed occasionally by other projects. Pope Sixtus IV (r. 1471–1484), for example, directed his attention to the construction of a new chapel for the papal residence (the Vatican palace). Construction commenced in 1473 and over the next eight years the pope hired several famous Renaissance artists to decorate the walls, including Raphael, Bernini, and Sandro Botticelli. The work was, of course, capped by the paintings of Michelangelo, which cover some 12,000 square feet of the chapel. *The Creation* and *The Last Judgment* are generally judged the best work he ever completed.

With the establishment of Christianity's dominant religious role throughout Europe, Rome became a focus of pilgrimage. Three additional churches—Saint Lawrence Outside the Walls, the Holy Cross, and Saint Sebastian—would join Saint John Lateran, Saint Mary Major, Saint Paul Outside the Walls, and Saint Peter's Basilica as primary objects for visitation.

Today, on the streets around Vatican City, one finds the offices of the curia, the international administrative offices of the Catholic Church, numerous colleges and seminaries, the international headquarters of many ordered communities, and the offices of an uncounted number of official and unofficial Catholic organizations. Twelve buildings within Rome but not in the city, including, for example, the churches of Saint John Lateran, Saint Mary Major, and Saint Paul Outside the Walls, have been granted extraterritorial rights. They are exempted from either expropriation or taxation by the Italian government.

The importance of Rome as a world religious center was underscored in 2005, when following the death of Pope John Paul II (1920–2005), millions of television viewers watched the broadcast from Rome/Vatican City of the deceased pope's funeral services and the immediately following meetings at which his successor, Joseph Cardinal Ratzinger (b. 1927), who took the name Benedict XVI, was elected. That election occurred in the church in the Sistine Chapel, while the major public ceremonies were conducted in the single most important religious site in the city: Saint Peter's Cathedral.

Vatican City is considered to be a separate country, though, like a number of small countries, a variety of affairs generally conducted by a sovereign state are handled by Italy's government. Vatican City issues its own currency and stamps, has its own flag, and has its own police force. The complex political relationship between the governments of Vatican City and Italy, and the Roman Catholic Church, has led to an equally complex set of relationships between the Vatican and other governments and ecclesiastical entities worldwide.

In 1980, Vatican City and the church buildings granted extraterritorial status in Rome were included in the designation of the historic center of Rome as a World Heritage Site by the United Nations.

J. Gordon Melton

See also: Constantine the Great; Helena, Flavia Iulia; Martyrdom; Pilgrimage; Relics; Saints.

References

Barrett, David, ed. *The Encyclopedia of World Christianity*. 2nd ed. New York: Oxford University Press, 2001.

Hager, June. *Pilgrimage: A Chronicle of Christianity through the Churches of Rome*. London: Weidenfeld & Nicolson, 1999.

Hebblethwaite, P. *In the Vatican*. Oxford: Oxford University Press, 1987.

Introvigne, Massimo, Pier Luigi Zoccatelli, Nelly Ippolito Macrina, and Verónica Roldán. *Enciclopedia delle Religioni in Italia*. Leumann (Torino): Elledici, 2001.

Tylenda, Joseph N. *The Pilgrim's Guide to Rome's Principal Churches*. Collegeville, MN: Liturgical Press, 1993.

Romuva

Romuva (Lithuanian: sacred place, shrine) is a Lithuanian neo-Pagan movement that builds its faith and practice on Lithuanian folklore and other sources of pre-Christian belief. It is so far the only significant Lithuanian origin religious movement to arise at the turn of the 21st century, with 1,270 inhabitants of Lithuania identifying with it according to the census of 2001. In 2008, the Romuva movement had eight officially registered communities in Lithuania, most of those them united in the Old Baltic Faith Association. In 1997 Romuva initiated the World Congress of Ethnic Religions to facilitate ties with ethnic religions (surviving or reborn) of other countries around the world.

Early attempts to reconstruct the religion of pre-Christian Lithuania are to be found in Lithuania's national awakening movement of the 19th century. The most prominent promoters of the pre-Christian tradition were poet Andrius Vištelis (1837–1912) and Domas Šidlauskas (1878–1944); the latter also established a pagan shrine called Romuva and propagated a reconstruction of pre-Christian faith that he called Visuomybė (Lithuanian: universal faith). After the 1940 Soviet occupation, the movement was persecuted and disbanded. In 1967 Romuva was organized as a cultural society by Jonas Tinkūnas (b. 1939), who is also a prominent leader in the Romuva movement today. The new Romuva movement had no institutional ties with the pre-Soviet Visuomybė, and its main activities were the celebrations of folk holidays with the Christian elements removed, relying heavily on Lithuanian ethnic heritage and folklore in a belief that the pagan content is easily uncovered by removing the Roman Catholic veneer.

The neo-Pagan movement, persecuted in the Soviet period, was revived in 1988, and Romuva congregations were established in 1992 in Vilnius (the capital city of Lithuania) and Kaunas, with 10 communities registered in all by 2008 as well as among Lithuanians living in Chicago, Boston, and Toronto. Currently there are about 100 to 200 members and many more sympathizers, since Romuva's focus on the ethnic origins of Lithuania and on the propagation of ethnic culture makes the religion attractive and easily acceptable in the Lithuanian context. Romuva titles itself an "ethnic religion of Lithuania," is not conversionist, and has not spread beyond Lithuania except among the communities of ethnic Lithuanians in North America.

The beliefs of Romuva are not clearly and dogmatically defined and have peculiar interpretations within the different communities in the Romuva movement. Romuva claims to be a continuation of the pre-Christian (Pagan) religion of Lithuania and attempts to avoid inventions, which makes it difficult to define the doctrine or practice of the movement since no written scriptures or sources of the pre-Christian religion have survived. The movement largely depends on the ethnic culture, songs, ethnological myths, and anthropological reconstruction as the sources for its practices, and this leads to a plurality of perspectives within the movement. Generally, the concept of Darna (Harmony) is emphasized as the basis of morality and values, and ancient holidays are celebrated and ethnic particularities are observed in the belief that they facilitate the experience of the ancient religion. Different gods and goddesses of the pre-Christian pantheon (such as Dievas, Perkunas, and Laima) are invoked. They are often conceived as dependent realities, subordinate to the symbols they embody as well as the expressions of the sacredness that permeates all living and nonliving things. Celebrations of ancient holidays are the main activities within Romuva, usually held at ancient castle-hills or other sacred pre-Christian sites, like stones, hills, trees, groves, and rivers. None of the ancient shrines have survived and no shrines have been built by the movement, though building projects do exist.

Currently Romuva is trying to get state recognition as one of the traditional religions in Lithuania, along with the larger ones that have existed in the country for the last three centuries. The extent of Romuva's continuity with the pre-Christian faith of Lithuania is debated by scholars, who point to the existing differences from what is known of the pre-Christian religion as well as the impossibility of reviving a religion without any written sources or continuing priestly practice, which in Lithuania was discontinued a few centuries ago.

Despite the loose structure of the movement and undefined beliefs, the beginning of the 21st century saw some attempts at formalization: most independent communities were united into the Old Baltic Faith Association, which consequently consecrated a *krivis* (Lithuanian: high priest). There have also been attempts to express the beliefs of Romuva in a common creed.

Romuva (informal address)
A. Vivulskio St. 27–4
Vilnius LT-03114
Lithuania
http://www.romuva.lt/ (in Lithuanian)

Donatas Glodenis

References

Giedraitis, Liudvikas, ed. "Vaikštantys vandeniu." *Liaudies kultūra* 3 (2000): 1–7.

Trinkūnas, Jonas. *Baltų tikėjimas. Lietuvių pasaulėjauta, papraočiai, apeigos, ženklai.* Vilnius: Diemedžio Leidykla, 2000.

Trinkūnas, Jonas, ed. *Of Gods and Holidays: The Baltic Heritage.* Vilnius: Tvermė, 1999.

Rosh Hashanah

Rosh Hashanah is often referred to as the Jewish New Year though it is observed on the first day of the month of Tishri, which is the seventh month in the Hebrew calendar. It occurs at some point between September 5 and October 5 on the Common Era calendar. It starts the civil year in the Hebrew calendar, and is considered the new year for people, animals, and legal contracts. Rosh Hashanah may be adjusted a day, as it cannot fall on Sunday, Wednesday, or Friday.

Tradition acknowledges Rosh Hashanah as the point from which new calendar years as well as the sabbatical (*shmita*) and jubilee (*yovel*) years are designated. The dating of Rosh Hashanah was traditionally done by observing the Moon, which marked the move from one month to the next. Due to the difficulty in observing the Moon in some years, and to getting the word out to the areas farthest from Jerusalem, it became common to celebrate Rosh Hashanah for two days, a practice continued in today's Orthodox and Conservative Jewish communities. The two-day Rosh Hashanah is an official holiday in Israel.

The observance derives from the Torah (the Five Books of Moses, in which the Jewish law is laid down), and specifically from Leviticus 23:23–25, which reads, "And the LORD spoke unto Moses, saying: Speak unto the children of Israel, saying: In the seventh month, in the first day of the month, shall be a solemn rest unto you, a memorial proclaimed with the blast of horns, a holy convocation. Ye shall do no manner of servile work; and ye shall bring an offering made by fire unto the LORD." From this verse comes the practice of the blowing of the *shofar*, a trumpet made from a ram's horn. Its sounding is meant to awaken those within its reach from their soulful slumber. Rosh Hashanah are days of rest; hence many of the prohibitions on activity of the Sabbath are in effect.

The Talmud speculates that creation began on what would be the 25th day of the Hebrew month of Elul. Six days later, the first day of Tishri, humans were created. Thus Rosh Hashanah, among other things, commemorates the creation of the human race.

Ritually speaking, Rosh Hashanah serves the important function of initiating the High Holidays, the high point in the annual calendar of Jewish observance. The first 10 days of Tishri are a time for self-reflection, confession, and repentance, all leading to the last day, Yom Kippur, the Day of Atonement. The elements for the observance of Rosh Hashanah were spelled out in the Oral Law, which were subsequently written down in the Mishnah, a late-second-century attempt to commit the Oral Law to written form so it would not be lost in tumultuous times, and which became one of the two main parts of the great body of Jewish law, the Talmud.

On the day of the eve of Rosh Hashanah, the last day of the month of Elul, known as Erev Rosh Hashanah, Jews seek to end vows they have made that have not been fulfilled. If one has made a vow to do some-

Ultra-Orthodox Jews pray at the Western Wall in Jerusalem's Old City before the start of the holiday of Rosh Hashanah. (Andrea Basile/Dreamstime.com)

thing, the individual (a male) may gather a small group of cohorts and ask them to nullify the vow. The individual then joins in nullifying the vows of the others. This action is seen as part of starting the New Year with a blank slate.

On Rosh Hashanah, Jews worship together in the synagogue, using a special liturgy that includes scriptural readings, as on the Sabbath, and which emphasizes God's sovereignty. Worshippers greet each other with good wishes for the coming year. In their homes they eat festive meals that typically include apples and honey to symbolize hopes for a sweet year, and many homes display the New Year's cards that modern Jews have come to send to one another. Later in the day, some will walk to a nearby stream and throw in the contents of their pockets, symbolically casting off the sins of the old year. This ritual, called Tashlikh, points out one of the differences with the Sabbath. If Rosh Hashanah falls on a Monday, Tuesday, or Thursday, Tashlikh is observed on the afternoon of that day. If however, it falls on Saturday (the Sabbath), then Tashlikh is observed on the following Sunday afternoon, the second day of Rosh Hashanah, to avoid the prohibition against carrying on the Sabbath, which is considered work.

J. Gordon Melton

See also: Calendars, Religious; Conservative Judaism; Days of Awe; New Year's Day; Orthodox Judaism; Yom Kippur.

References

Cohen, Jeffrey M. *1,001 Questions and Answers on Rosh HaShanah and Yom Kippur*. New York: Jason Aronson, 1997.

Eckstein, Yecheil. *What You Should Know About Jews and Judaism*. Waco, TX: Word Books, 1984.

Greenberg, Irving. *The Jewish Way: Living the Holidays*. New York: Jason Aronson, 1998.

Posner, Raphael, Uri Kaploun, and Sherman Cohen, eds. *Jewish Liturgy: Prayer and Synagogue Service through the Ages*. New York: Leon Amiel Publisher/Jerusalem: Keter Publishing House, 1975.

Schauss, Hayyim. *The Jewish Festivals: A Guide to Their History and Observance*. New York: Schocken, 1996.

Ruhani Satsang

Ruhani Satsang (Science of Spirituality) was formally founded by Kirpal Singh (1894–1974) in 1950 in Delhi, India. According to Kirpal's own published accounts, he was chosen to be the spiritual successor of his guru, Sawan Singh (1858–1948) of Radha Soami Satsang, Beas. As Kirpal explains: "My Master, Hazur Baba Sawan Singh Ji Maharaj, a perfect Saint, had a great desire to form a common forum or platform, Ruhani Satsang [spiritual gathering], at which all persons, even though professing different faiths and religious beliefs, could be imparted the principles of Spirituality."

Kirpal's claims, however, were met by sharp resistance from the majority of Sawan Singh's following and blood relatives, who supported Jagat Singh (1884–1951) as the rightful successor at Radha Soami Satsang, Beas. This led to a distinct break between the two groups, and today they have no formal connection with each other beyond sharing a similar philosophy. This philosophy includes: (1) belief in a living human guru, (2) a strict vegetarian diet, (3) daily *shabd* yoga meditation, and (4) a high moral life, which includes abstaining from drugs and alcohol and sex before marriage.

Kirpal Singh initiated more than 80,000 people worldwide to the movement during his tenure and established Ruhani centers throughout India, Europe, and North and South America. He was also instrumental in establishing the World Fellowship of Religions in Delhi and in promoting other humanitarian projects. He authored a number of influential books on shabd yoga, including *The Crown of Life* and *Naam or Word*. His teachings were also highly influential among other new religious leaders, including Paul Twitchell (ca. 1909–1971), the founder of ECKANKAR, who was initiated by Kirpal Singh during his first tour of the United States in 1955.

Kirpal's death in August 1974 left his organization in disarray. Several disciples claimed to be his spiritual successor, and this led to the formation of a number of rival factions. Today several separate religious satsangs claim spiritual ties to the late Kirpal Singh. The Sawan-Kirpal Ruhani Mission was founded by Darshan Singh (1921–1989), Kirpal's eldest son, who was succeeded after his death by his eldest son, Rajinder Singh (b. 1946). Kirpal Light Satsang, formed by Thakar Singh (1929–2005), a disciple of Kirpal Singh and a close ally of Madam Hardevi, has been the subject of intense controversy in Germany and the United States due to widely reported allegations of sexual misconduct and child abuse on the part of the guru. Thakar Singh was succeeded by Baljit Singh in perhaps the clearest succession in the history of modern Sant Mat–related movements. Thakar Singh publicly announced Baljit as his successor before a large audience and videotaped the proceedings.

Sant Bani Ashram was established by Ajaib Singh (1926–1997), a disciple of Kirpal Singh and a former follower of Charan Singh (1916–1990) of Radha Soami Satsang, Beas, who recently died without formally appointing a successor. However, Sadhu Ram has emerged as one of Ajaib Singh's spiritual heirs and has gathered a core following. Of these groups, Sawan-Kirpal Ruhani Mission is by far the largest and most successful in terms of a global following, with well more than 200,000 followers.

Sawan-Kirpal Ruhani Mission
c/o Kirpal Ashram
2 Canal Rd.
Vijay, Magar, Delhi 110 001
India
http://www.sos.org/nc/main.htm or http://skrm.sos.org/

Kirpal Light Satsang
c/o KTS-NE P.O. Box 302
Kinderhook, NY 12106
http://www.santmat.net/

Sant Bani Ashram
Sanbornton, NH 03269
http://members.iex.net/~naam/

David Christopher Lane

See also: ECKANKAR; Radhasoami; Sikhism/Sant Mat.

References

Chadda, H. C., ed. *Seeing Is above All: Sant Darshan Singh's First Indian Tour*. Bowling Green, VA: Sawan Kirpal Publications, 1977.

Juergensmeyer, Mark. *Radhasoami Reality*. Princeton, NJ: Princeton University Press, 1991.

Lane, David C. Th*e Radhasoami Tradition: A Critical History of Guru Successorship*. New York: Garland Publishing, 1992.

Scotti, Juliet, and Ricki Linksman. *Kirpal Singh: The Story of a Saint*. Delhi: Sawan Kirpal, 1977.

Singh, Kirpal. *Surat Shabd Yoga: The Yoga of the Celestial Sound Current. Introduction for Western Readers*. Ed. by Robert Leverant. Berkeley, CA: Images Press, 1975.

Singh, Kirpal. *The Teachings of Kirpal Singh*. Ed. by Ruth Seader. Bowling Green, VA: Sawan Kirpal Publications, n.d.

Russell, Charles Taze

1852–1916

Charles Taze Russell was a Congregationalist church layman who became the founder of the Watch Tower Bible and Tract Society, the organization that would become publicly known as the Jehovah's Witnesses. He not only organized thousands of Bible students, but authored a number of books predicting the dawn of the biblically prophesied millennium of peace on Earth.

Russell was born February 15, 1852, in Allegheny, Pennsylvania. He was still a teenager when in 1869 he forsook the Congregational Church of his youth because his minister proved unable to answer the religious questions and doubts that had come to dominate his consciousness. During the 1870s, he began to read Adventist literature and in 1876 found himself drawn to the writings of Adventist writer/publisher Nelson Barbour (1822–1906), who convinced Russell that humanity was then living in a transition period that he termed the harvest time that heralded the imminent end of the age. Barbour suggested that the end of the Gentile times would be in 1914. Russell subsequently paid for the publication of Barbour's book *Three Worlds and the Plan of Redemption*, which appeared in 1877. Russell developed a chronology of the last days and released his own booklet, *The Object and Manner of the Lord's Return*.

In 1878, Russell discovered what he believed was a basic flaw in his thinking relative to the Greek word *parousia.* This word is most commonly translated "coming," as in the phrase "Jesus' second coming." Russell came to believe that parousia was better translated "presence." Having reworked the chronology essentially detailed by William Miller a generation earlier, Russell now asserted that Christ had become "present" in 1874. His new perspective led to his severing relations with Barbour and indeed with the larger Adventist community. Meanwhile, he had developed an Arian view of Christ, which affirmed Jesus as the Son of God and savior, but denied his full divinity. He also abandoned the idea of hell as a realm of eternal torment.

In 1879 he published the first issue of a new periodical, *Zion's Watch Tower and Herald of Christ's Presence,* through which he initiated a ministry to disseminate his new perspective. Two years later he founded Zion's Watch Tower Tract Society as a corporate home for his ministry, much of which consisted of publishing and distributing his books that presented a more systematic version of his revised theological position and informed the public of what was about to happen in human history. The first of a six-volume set of books that would announce the Dawn of the Millennium appeared in 1886. His followers would initially be called Dawnites.

Russell slowly built support from which he recruited agents (called colporteurs) to distribute both the periodical and his books. The colporteurs lived off the commissions from the literature they sold. In 1900 Russell opened an office in London from which the distribution of literature throughout Europe proceeded. His writings were soon being translated into all the major European languages. In 1908 he moved his American headquarters to Brooklyn, New York. He was becoming well known and his speeches would be reprinted in newspapers even as reporters sought him out to ask his opinions.

World War I broke out after Russell had been at work for more than 30 years. He had great expectations that his followers would live through the transition period. Many of his followers quickly concluded that the massive conflict heralded the end of the Gentile times just as Russell's book had suggested. Before the war ended, however, Russell died, on October 31, 1916, while traveling home from a speaking engagement in Los Angeles.

In the wake of his death, several different people vied for control of the Watch Tower Society. Joseph Franklin Rutherford (1869–1942), who spent time in prison during the war for his pacifist stance, emerged as the new president of the corporation. Reacting to the disappointment that the Gentile system was still in place after the war, Rutherford would begin the reorganization of the movement that included the imposition of a number of his own unique ideas, and in 1931 announced a new name for the movement, Jehovah's Witnesses. In the decade after the war, many of the Bible students who considered themselves orthodox students of Russell and his ideas broke with Rutherford and founded a set of different Bible student groups, some of which continue to exist. While the Witnesses continue to acknowledge Russell as their founder, the much smaller Bible student groups continue to publish and revere his writings.

Because of his theological divergences, more than his predictions of the end-times, Russell's contemporaries in the more mainstream Protestant churches denounced him. Conservative Protestants especially criticized him (and continue to criticize him) for his denial of the Trinity and with it the deity of Christ. His contemporaries were equally angered by Russell's role in popularizing the notion that those who did not accept Christ would after death be destroyed, rather than remain alive to experience eternal torment in hellfire. Many Protestants have, however, over the last century, also abandoned the idea of hell, and criticism of Russell for his opinion has diminished considerably in that regard. Russell has also been more positively evaluated on his support of Zionism. Not a popular opinion when he initially voiced support for a Jewish homeland, his opinions have been adopted by a number of evangelical Christians in the years since the establishment of the state of Israel.

Russell oversaw a relatively small, loosely organized group to which few saw any future at the time of his death. However, the long and dynamic leadership by Rutherford and the continued evangelical activity by his successors have turned the Jehovah's Witnesses into a global religion that has almost a million adherents in its homeland, is the second or third largest religious group in most European countries and has a measureable presence in more than 200 countries.

J. Gordon Melton

See also: Adventism; Arius; Congregationalism; Jehovah's Witnesses; Zionism.

References

Bergman, Jerry, *Jehovah's Witnesses and Kindred Groups: A Historical Compendium and Bibliography*. New York: Garland Publishing, 1984.

Horowitz, David, *Pastor Charles Taze Russell: An Early American Christian Zionist*. New York: Philosophical Library, 1986.

Penton, M. James, *Apocalypse Delayed: The Story of Jehovah's Witnesses*. 2nd ed. Toronto: University of Toronto Press, 1997.

Russell, Charles Taze. *The Divine Plan of the Ages*. Studies in the Scriptures. Vol. 1. 1886; rpt.: Rutherford, NJ: Dawn Bible Students Association, n.d. Reprint of original 1886 volume.

Russell, Charles Taze. *Pastor Russell's Sermons. A Choice Collection of His Most Important Discourses on All Phases of Christian Doctrine and Practice*. Brooklyn: International Bible Students Association, 1917.

Russell, Charles Taze. *What Pastor Russell Said: Charles Russell Answers Hundreds of Questions Regarding His Faith*. Rpt.: Scotts Valley, CA: CreateSpace, 2009

■ Russia

Russia is a name commonly applied to successive geo-political entities—Kievan Rus, which was the early

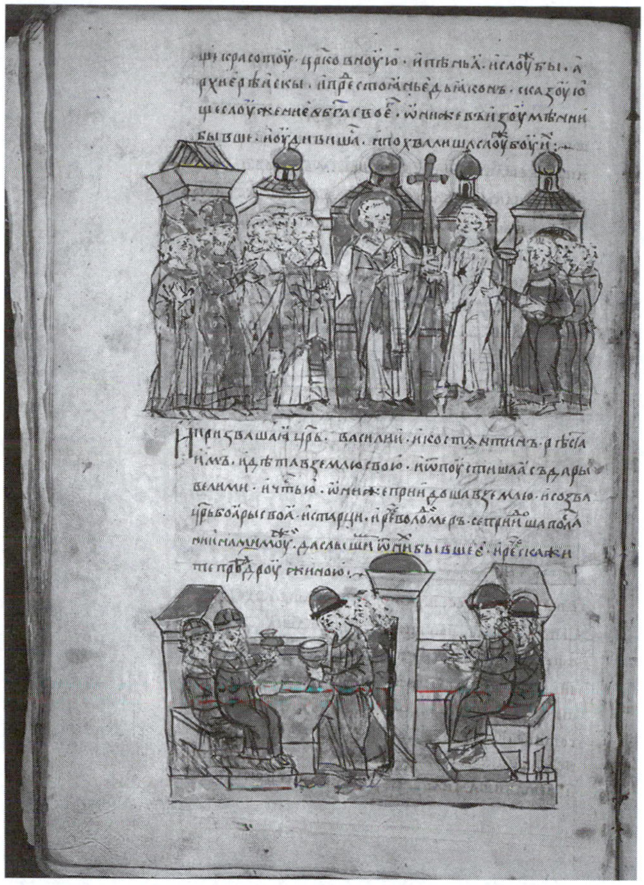

In a scene from the late-fifteenth-century *Radziwill Chronicle,* Russia officially becomes a Christian nation with the conversion of Vladimir I, prince of Kiev, about 988 CE. (Erich Lessing/Art Resource, NY)

state of the Eastern Slavs; the Duchy and later the Czardom of Muskovy; the Russian Empire; the Soviet Union; and currently the Russian Federation. Russia's current territory (10,610,162 square miles) extends over Eastern Europe and Northern Asia (or Eurasia). It borders 14 other countries with diverse cultural and religious traditions, including Eastern Orthodox, Roman Catholic, Protestant, Muslim, Confucian, and Buddhist. Its population (ca. 142 million, according to the 2002 census) comprises around 100 different ethnic groups. Ethnic Russians make up around 80 percent of the country's population and Russian is its official language. Eastern (Russian) Orthodoxy has long been Russia's dominant religious tradition, although all world religions have coexisted in the country—Christianity in all its major forms, Islam (both Sunni and Shia), Judaism, and Buddhism.

While having many features in common with other European countries, Russia's history has been marked by dramatic changes, in particular, the demise of the Russian Empire after the 1917 February and Bolshevik revolutions, the establishment of the Soviet Union in 1922, and seven decades of one-party rule and highly centralized state Socialism. The Soviet Union collapsed in December 1991, bringing about systemic political, economic, and social transformations. These changes had definitive effects on the religious history of the country, including its religious composition, on church-state relations, and on religious freedom. In addition, there are considerable differences between Russia's regions in terms of their religious composition, degree of diversity, history of church-state relations, and religious freedom.

Religion in Pre-Soviet Russia (before 1917) According to archaeological and anthropological research, a variety of pre-monotheistic beliefs and practices existed among Neolithic farming and hunting communities of Northern Eurasia. More specifically, although the prehistoric religion of Eastern Slavs remains under-researched, there is abundant evidence of developed nature and ancestor worship among them well before the emergence around the ninth century CE of their earliest state, which modern historians refer to as Kievan Rus.

With the adoption of Christianity by Grand Prince Vladimir (ca. 956–1015) in 988, Kievan Rus became part of Christendom, although vestiges of the earlier beliefs and practices long survived alongside the new faith in many parts of Russia.

From its beginning, the Russian Orthodox Church was linked to Byzantine (Eastern) Christianity. It thus inherited a rich and elaborate religious culture that emphasized aesthetic and ritualistic aspects of the faith and the preservation of tradition over reflective theology.

Byzantine Christianity developed the idea of symphony, that is, a symbiotic relationship between the secular and the ecclesiastical authorities. Unlike their Western counterparts, the Eastern churches did not have a central ecclesiastical authority; they were instead autonomous (autocephalous) and coterminous with each country.

Originally, from the 10th century, the Eastern Slavic lands came under jurisdiction of the metropolitans of Kiev, who were designated by the Ecumenical Patriarchate in Constantinople. Subsequently, in 1299, the seat of the Metropolitan moved to the northern principality of Vladimir and in 1325 to Moscow, following the ascendance of these cities as centers of political power. In 1589, the Russian Orthodox Church achieved formal independence from Constantinople. It founded the Moscow Patriarchate, which existed until 1721, when Peter the Great abolished it and replaced with the Holy Synod.

In the first half of the 13th century, Kievan Rus was successfully invaded by Mongolian tribes from the east, while Western Crusaders of the Teutonic Order alongside the Swedish army attempted to capture the northern city-states of Novgorod and Pskov. The next two centuries are often referred to as the "Tatar-Mongolian Yoke." During this time, Eastern Orthodoxy supplied the basis of a common identity among the otherwise disunited and politically subjugated Slavic population, distinguishing them from the Golden Horde (the Russian name for the Mongolian proto-state) that adopted Islam in the early 14th century, and from the Roman Catholic lands on the western frontiers.

Throughout the 14th and 16th centuries, the rulers of the Grand Duchy of Moscow appealed to the long-standing Orthodox tradition, utilizing the church's religious authority and symbolic power for the Russian Reconquista: the consolidation of eastern Slavic lands, their liberation from the Golden Horde, and the annexation of the khanates that emerged in the wake of its fragmentation. The historical coincidence of the fall of the Byzantine Empire (1453) with the ascendance of the Grand Duchy of Moscow gave rise to the concept of the Third Rome (first formulated by Abbot Filofey of Pskov in the early 16th century). This ideological construct encouraged the Moscow rulers to see themselves as legitimate heirs to the Roman and Byzantine empires. The expanding state regarded itself as having a mission to assert the true Orthodox faith among the colonized populations. The notions of Russia, Russian state, and Russian Orthodoxy were increasingly synonymous from the late 15th century on.

In the mid-1600s, however, the unity within the church as well as that between the ecclesiastical authority and the autocracy was interrupted by a major schism and conflict. Patriarch Nikon (1605–1681) introduced an ambitious reform that attempted to create uniformity in Russian liturgical books and rites by bringing them back in line with Greek (Byzantine) canons. The unintended consequence of the reform was a major split (*raskol*) within the church and the emergence of the Old Believers tradition in Eastern Orthodoxy. Soon after Nikon challenged monarchical authority, demanding that it defer to ecclesiastical authority. This led to Nikon's downfall, with the triumphant czar, Alexey Mikhailovich (1645–1672), making an important step toward establishing the church as politically subordinate to regal autocracy and reinforcing its crucial role of legitimizing that autocracy.

Russia's religious history reflects the distinctive features of the country's modernization, usually introduced "from above," and causing fears and anxieties about the potential erosion of the Orthodox ideological foundation of the autocracy. The modernizing and Westernizing reforms of Peter the Great (1682–1725) included changing ecclesiastical authority to approximate Protestant European models. In 1711 the Most Holy Synod, which was run by secular officials, replaced the Moscow Patriarchate in the administration of ecclesiastical affairs. The czar (who adopted the title of emperor in 1721) became "Head of the Church and Defender of the Faith," clergy were made state officials, and meticulous state control was imposed on congregational and parish life.

The Synodal period, which lasted until the 1917 February revolution, had mixed effects on the church and, more generally, on the relationship between religion and society. On the one hand, the Most Holy Synod was part of the state apparatus and as such was obliged to cooperate with the police in matters such as "subversive activities," censorship, adultery, and divorce. On the other hand, the church was fully protected by the state against competition with other faiths and had a monopoly on proselytizing. Furthermore, in the 19th century, when the ideological foundations of the autocracy seemed increasingly threatened by liberal ideologies, revolutionary movements, and the growing self-awareness of, and demands for, civil rights among ethnic minorities, the state proposed "the inseparable unity of Orthodoxy, the Autocracy, and the People."

This unity ideal was first formulated in 1832 by Minister of Education Count Uvarov.

The territorial expansion of the Russian Empire, as it was officially called between 1721 and February 1917, led to the inclusion of a variety of ethno-religious groups.

The 1897 census, the first and the only before 1917, indicated that 87 million out of 125 million, or 70 percent of the population, were Russian Orthodox, comprising predominantly ethnic Russians, the majority of Ukrainians and Belorussians, and many other smaller ethnic groups. Islam represented the most numerically significant religious minority, accounting for nearly 14 million (11 percent), according to the census. It must be noted, however, that this figure included Muslims of Central Asia and South Caucusus (Azerbaijan), which are not part of the post-Soviet Russian Federation, where the significant ethnic Muslims groups are mainly in the Middle Volga and Northern Caucasus areas. Additionally, Islam in Russia did not represent a single entity, but comprised a variety of different ethno-linguistic groups as well as internal divisions (both Sunni and Shia).

With the partitions of Poland in the late 18th and 19th centuries, Roman Catholicism became the third largest religion in the empire (around 11.5 million, or 9 percent of the population, according to the 1897 census), including most Poles, Lithuanians, and large proportions of Germans and Latvians. The inclusion of Poland also accounts for the fact that for more than a century the Russian Empire hosted the largest Jewish population in the world (6 million, or 5 percent in 1897), mainly concentrated in the western provinces (Poland, Ukraine, and Byelorussia). In addition, there were a considerable number of Protestants (around 4 million in 1897, mainly in the Duchy of Finland and the Baltic Provinces, also including German Mennonites but excluding Russian Protestant sectarians); Armenian Apostolics (more than a million); Buddhists (more than 430,000; mainly in Southern Siberia and Kalmyks in the Northern Caucasus); and shamanists in Siberia and in the Middle Volga region.

In the eyes of many, if not most, Russians, territorial expansion meant the extension of both Russian Orthodox territory and of the Orthodox state. Thus, Russia came to be seen as a vast contiguous Orthodox Empire with some enclaves of ethno-religious minorities. Russia's religious identity was of crucial political significance, meaning that religious dissent among ethnic Russians was a highly sensitive political issue.

Before the end of the 18th century, considerable efforts were made to convert colonized non-Christian populations to the Russian Orthodox faith, which at times involved coercion and violence. However, the state's overriding practical interest was in economic returns and social stability, which, by and large, made maintaining the religious status quo more desirable than missionary zeal. While continuing with aggressive efforts to convert Muslims in newly annexed territories, Peter the Great (1682–1725) guaranteed religious tolerance to foreigners willing to contribute to his reformist efforts. In the spirit of the "enlightened absolutism," Catherine the Great (1762–1796) favored more sophisticated methods of missionary work and government control over non-Orthodox minorities, introducing, among other things, semi-autonomous religious authorities for Muslims in the European part of the country. Little attempt at conversion was made with respect to Protestants. However, although they belonged to a variety of different groups, in 1832 all of them, except those who resided in the provinces of Poland and Finland, were placed under the jurisdiction of the Lutheran Church of St. Petersburg.

Two ethno-religious groups were subject to special policies. Separation was the preferred policy in relation to the Jewish population, although at times this was combined with attempts at assimilation and conversion to Orthodox Christianity. Catherine the Great, the "enlightened empress," still regarded the Jews as a potential threat to the Empire. She introduced the Pale of Settlement, a region along Russia's western borders outside which Jewish people were not allowed to settle. Generally, coercive attempts to convert non-Orthodox inhabitants never fully disappeared, and at times re-emerged with vengeance, in particular, toward those who were seen as "naturally Orthodox," such as the Uniates, the Slavic population of Western Ukraine and Byelorussia who retained Eastern Orthodox beliefs and practices, but accepted the papal authority of Rome.

In spite of the Orthodox hold on the land, a variety of alternative religions were introduced and coexisted

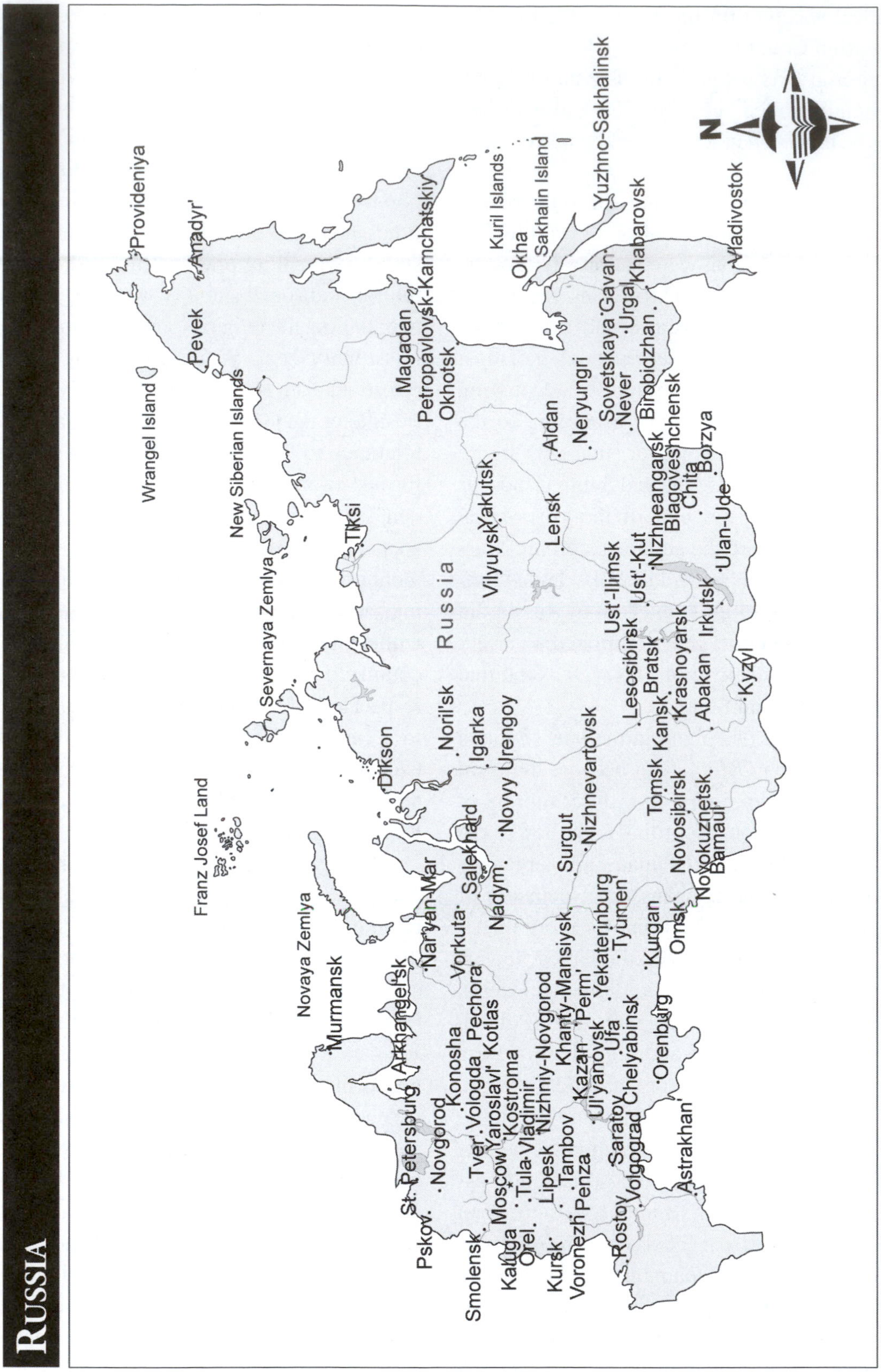
RUSSIA
Wrangel Island
Provideniya
Anadyr'
Pevek
New Siberian Islands
Magadan
Petropavlovsk-Kamchatskiy
Okhotsk
Kuril Islands
Sakhalin Island
Okha
Yuzhno-Sakhalinsk
Sovetskaya Gavan'
Urgal
Khabarovsk
Never
Birobidzhan
Vladivostok
Neryungri
Aldan
Blagoveshchensk
Borzya
Chita
Yakutsk
Lensk
Tiksi
Vilyuysk
Severnaya Zemlya
Russia
Ust'-Ilimsk
Ust'-Kut
Nizhneangarsk
Ulan-Ude
Irkutsk
Bratsk
Lesosibirsk
Krasnoyarsk
Abakan
Kyzyl
Kansk
Franz Josef Land
Dikson
Noril'sk
Igarka
Novyy Urengoy
Nizhnevartovsk
Tomsk
Novosibirsk
Novokuznetsk
Barnaul
Surgut
Nadym
Salekhard
Novaya Zemlya
Murmansk
Arkhangelsk
Nar'yan-Mar
Vorkuta
Pechora
Kotlas
Konosha
Vologda
Khanty-Mansiysk
Tyumen'
Yekaterinburg
Perm'
Kurgan
Omsk
Orenburg
Chelyabinsk
Ufa
Kazan'
Ul'yanovsk
Nizhniy-Novgorod
Kostroma
Yaroslavl'
Vladimir
Tver'
Novgorod
St. Petersburg
Pskov
Smolensk
Moscow
Tula
Kaluga
Orel
Kursk
Lipesk
Tambov
Penza
Voronezh
Saratov
Volgograd
Rostov
Astrakhan'
N

over the centuries. A prominent source of religious diversity in Russia was schismatic movements, the most significant of which were the Old Believers. The 17th and 18th centuries saw the growth of the Russian sectarian traditions of the Faith of Christ (or Believers in Christ; Russian: *khristovshchina*) and the Spiritual Christianity (Dukhvnoe Khristianstvo). These traditions gave rise to Russian Christian sects, such as the Flagellants (Khlysty), the Castrates (Skoptsy), the Doukhobors (Fighters for Spirit), the Molokan (Milk-Drinkers), and Subbotniks (Sabbath Observers). The teachings and practices of these sects suggest a degree of affinity with Western Protestantism and aspects of Judaism, or perhaps some more direct influence of these religions.

Freemasonry became popular among Russian nobles in the late 18th century and achieved particular prominence in the first two decades of the 20th century; almost all members of the Provisional Government (February–October 1917) were Free Masons. At different times, German Pietism and Spiritualism found a considerable following among Russian nobles and the intelligentsia. Helena P. Blavatsky (1831–1891), co-founder of the Theosophical Society, and Georges Gurdjieff (ca. 1872–1949), whose work continues through the Gurdjieff Foundation, came from Russia, although they mainly developed their teachings outside the country. The late 19th century was marked by active and often successful proselytizing by Western missionaries from groups such as the Baptists, Pentecostals, Jehovah's Witnesses, and Seventh-day Adventist Church.

It is important to note that much innovative philosophical thinking about religion took place outside the formal structures of the church. From the mid-19th century on in particular, writers such as Lev Tolstoy (1828–1910) and Fyodor Dostoevsky (1821–1881), and philosophers such as Vladimir Soloviev (1853–1900) and Nikolai Berdyaev (1874–1948), created intellectual and civic arenas for religious reflections and debates on politics, society, and moral issues.

Given the significance of Russian Orthodox identity to the empire, it is not surprising that, until the beginning of the 20th century, this enormous diversity was widely managed in a highly controlled manner. However, some important accommodations were made toward the major religious minorities and occasional privileges were given to some groups for pragmatic reasons. Thus, German Lutherans and Dutch Calvinists were offered guarantees of free practice of their faiths (on the condition of not proselytizing); the Mennonites were given religious freedom by Catherine the Great in exchange for their willingness to cultivate vast wastelands in the Southern European part of the empire. Religious affiliation defined the major legal categories and civil rights, with the primary division between those belonging to the Russian Orthodox Church (*pravoslavnye*) and people of "alien faiths" (*inovertsy*). Before 1905, proselytizing among ethnic Russians as well as their voluntary conversion to alien faiths were punishable as criminal offenses. There were also preventive measures, for instance, a ban on conducting Lutheran services in the Russian language.

Religious minorities were divided into three categories: (1) "recognized and tolerated," that is, ethnic religious groups who could practice their religions freely but not proselytize; (2) "tolerated and unrecognized," that is, major sects who were allowed to practice their religion with some restrictions on their civil rights; and (3) "tolerated and persecuted," that is, those who were seen as presenting particular dangers to the state and were subject to administrative exile and severe restrictions of civil rights. After the introduction of the Pale of Settlement for the Jewish population, czarist policy fluctuated between relative tolerance and severe repression. Consequently, the Pale of Settlement regulations were either inconsistently enforced or were reinforced by other highly restrictive laws, in particular, under Czar Alexander III (1881–1895). Laws such as the "May Laws" (1882) and the Edict of Expulsion (1886) enacted restrictions and bans on settlement, professions, economic activities, and education. In addition, the government at the very least condoned popular anti-Semitism ("Jews as Christ-killers"), the most violent expression of which were the pogroms, in particular, in the 1880s and 1900s.

The general situation with religious freedom began to change in the early 20th century with the introduction of the Edict of Toleration by Czar Nicolas II amid the popular uprising of 1905. This gave certain religious and civil rights to religious minorities and legitimized the freedom of individual religious choice. However, by that time, the state-church symbiosis had already produced its counter-image: Russian militant secularism and atheism.

Religion in the Soviet Union (1917–1991) During the Soviet period, the imposition of secularism and atheism by the Communist state over seven decades was a unique historical experience. This policy partly stemmed from the Marxist concept that religion was a "metaphysical vision" of class-divided and oppressive societies, and that Communist modernization would lead to religion withering away and being replaced by the materialist scientific outlook.

The actual Communist policy, however, was much more complicated and involved attempts both to eradicate religion and to manipulate it for political purposes. Immediately before and after the revolution, the general anti-religious stance was played down, with the Bolshevik government seeking allies among religious minorities, low-rank clergy, and ordinary believers (as they were oppressed in imperial Russia) against the hierarchy of the official church (as the main supporter of the oppressor). The 1918 Constitution of the Soviet Federal Socialist Republic stipulated the separation of the church from the state and the educational system from the church; it also guaranteed religious freedom, including the right of both religious and anti-religious meetings and propaganda. Ordinary Orthodox believers could continue worship and association, but the institutional structure of the church was considerably undermined by confiscations of property, although the clergy could still use church buildings. The church was formally allowed to engage in missionary work but it could no longer compete with virulent anti-religious campaigns conducted by the Communist Party and supported by the government.

By the end of the 1920s, however, the Bolsheviks had established a comprehensive machine for propagating atheism (for example, the Propaganda and Agitation Department in the Communist Party, the League of Young Communists, and the League of Militant Godless) and began an all-out war on religion, religious minorities included. This aimed at institutional destruction of the Orthodox Church and other religions and involved mass closures of churches, mosques, and other places of worship and repression of clergy, religious professionals, and activists. The 1929 Law on Religious Associations imposed severe restrictions and government control on religious activities and forcibly relegated religion to the private domain.

At the same time, the Communist government sought to socialize and re-socialize generations of Soviet people into atheism as part of a "political religion," that is, a set of prescribed Communist ideas, values, symbols, and rituals designed to unite people and provide a basis for their behavior. However, with the passage of time, the Soviet regime sought a degree of accommodation with religious institutions and believers; for instance, during the Great Patriotic War (1941–1945), the Moscow Patriarchate was restored together with some churches and monasteries. Nevertheless, up to the end of the Soviet regime, temporary thaws were followed by anti-religious campaigns, often launched by the same leaders. Even in the late 1980s, immediately before the collapse of the Soviet system, the Communist leadership still officially regarded atheist propaganda as one of its priorities.

During the seven decades of Communist modernization there remained some limited channels for transmitting religious culture. Although severely undermined and restricted, the Orthodox Church and other religious institutions continued to operate. In certain periods they were used for propagandist purposes both internally (in order to boost patriotic feelings), but mainly externally (to demonstrate Soviet achievements in guaranteeing human rights and freedoms). In search of historical continuity and moral examples, Soviet educationists increasingly turned to pre-revolutionary high culture, in particular, Russian classical literature with its wealth of religious themes, imagery, and symbols. Some elements of religious culture were preserved within émigré circles, and these were available to a very limited extent inside Russia. Finally, the generation of people brought up before the official assault on religion continued to have some influence in Soviet society.

The issues of incidence, dynamics, and forms of religious beliefs and practices during the different periods of the "construction of Communism" and among different sections of the population require further research. Nevertheless, there is much evidence to suggest that, while institutional forms of religion were significantly weakened, a considerable proportion of the population continued to regard themselves as religious even after the vicious anti-religious campaigns between 1918 and 1937. Thus, according to the 1937 census, the results of which remained unpublished until 1989, around 56.7 percent of those who provided answers claimed they were religious—at the time when Stalinist repressions were at their worst. In addition, some groups continued actively to practice their faith despite the government's attempts to suppress them and often at the risk of losing their freedom; the most conspicuous example of this was the group of the Initiativiniks (Initiators) that emerged among Russian evangelical Christians in the late 1950s.

The deepening crisis of the Soviet system from the 1970s on was accompanied by a growing interest in religion, including in the links between ethnicity and religion, and between religion and nationhood. Among other things, this interest showed itself in the activities of the All-Russian Society for Preservation of Historical and Cultural Monuments (VOOPIK), which in many cases was a code name for attempts to preserve and restore Russian Orthodox churches. It also expressed itself in the growing salience of religious themes in cinema, fine arts, and literature. At the same time, alternative religious thinking became increasingly popular in urban centers. From the 1970s on a range of grudgingly tolerated semi-underground and underground groups, activities and teachings emerged, such as the Agni-Yoga, practiced by the followers of Helena Roerich (1879–1955) and Nicholas Roerich (1874–1947); renewed interest in Nikolai Fyodorov's (1827–1903) ideas about immortality; and the first devotees of Hare Krishna.

The nationwide celebration of the millennium of Russian Orthodox Christianity in 1988 symbolized the beginning of the U-turn in the official policy toward religion. Immediately before the dissolution of the Soviet Union in December 1991, the 1990 Law on Freedom of Religions was passed by the Soviet Supreme Council (Parliament), which for the first time in Russia's history treated religious freedom as an "unalienable right of Russian citizens" and extended these rights to all those residing in Russia. The law contained strong clauses designed to prevent state agencies from interfering in religion and to guarantee the legal equality of all faiths.

Religion in Post-Soviet Russia The 1990s were characterized by the increased public prominence of religion that manifested itself in its high profile in the mass media, its engagement with politics, and the ubiquitous public display of religious symbols, in particular, those associated with the Russian Orthodox Church nationwide and with Islam in the regions with predominantly Muslim population (Tatarstan in the Volga area; Dagestan and Chechnya in the Northern Caucasus). How this increased visual prominence of religion is related to changes in religious affiliation and individual religiosity is much harder to assess, as polls yield different results, depending on their conceptualization of affiliation and religiosity and on the methodology employed. However, without doubt, there has been a considerable change in the number of religious communities, both registered and unregistered. The number of registered religious associations has risen from around 3,900 in 1991 to 21,000 in 2008. There have also been considerable changes in the composition of the Russian religious landscape. In 1991, out of officially registered associations, 78 percent were Russian Orthodox, 10 percent Muslim, and 3 percent Protestant. The figures for 2008 were 51 percent, 16.5 percent, and 21 percent, respectively.

Based on self-reporting, most polls indicate that since 1991 the number of those claiming to be religious has risen considerably, from around 40 percent to around 70 percent in 2000–2008. Up to 70 percent of respondents, or around 90 percent of all ethnic Russians, consider themselves Russian Orthodox, followed by those claiming affiliation with Islam—from 4 percent in 1991 to between 8 and 15 percent in different surveys, depending on the methodology employed. However, the incidences of active engagement with religious groups and of religious practice have remained low, with, for instance, between 2 and 7 percent of the nominally Russian Orthodox attending religious services on a weekly basis. With some regional exceptions, the figures for the other major religions are quite similar or even lower (in particular, for Judaism). In some statistical reports, however, figures for religious affiliation are based on ethnic criteria, according to which, for example, all Russians are considered Russian Orthodox and all Tatars are counted as Muslims, which results in very high figures for religious affiliation. This approach raises a range of methodological objections (for example, there is a considerable number of non-Orthodox ethnic Russians; at least 100,000 Tatars are Russian Orthodox, etc.). However, it also reflects ethno-religious politics in contemporary Russia, in particular, claims of its historic religions on representing core aspects of ethnicity and nationhood.

Since 1991, the ethno-religious religious structure of Russian society has been changing dramatically, largely following socio-demographic and cultural changes. Thus, immigration of ethnic Muslims from other parts of the former Soviet Union, combined with internal migration, led to an increased presence of Islam in Russia. On the other hand, between 1989 and 2008, the Jewish population has decreased by more than 50 percent (from an estimated 500,000 to 225,000), mainly following emigration and ethnic assimilation. Similar processes have occurred among ethnic Germans, resulting in the decreased numbers of Lutherans and Mennonites. There has been a growing interest in pre-Christian ethno-religious roots among some ethnic minorities, such as Mordvinians and Mari in the Middle Volga area, or Yakuts in Siberia and Adygs in the Northern Caucasus. Interest in shamanism has been growing among Buriats and Tuvinians. At the same time, the greater emphasis on individual religious choice and the immensely increased availability of spiritual alternatives have led to the growing numbers of those who opt out of their ethnic faiths.

We can discern three major trends that have simultaneously occurred and defined the distinctive scenario of religious life in post-communist Russia. First is the marked resurgence of the Russian Orthodox Church and its increasing prominence in Russian society and politics. Second, religions of ethnic minorities, such as Islam, Judaism, and Buddhism, have re-emerged as important aspects of identities of their constituent ethnic groups, with their professionals making considerable claims to represent these groups in Russian society and politics. Finally, increasing diversity has been caused by various new religious phenomena. These include more established groups from abroad, mainly Protestant and in particular, Pentecostal, and those that are usually defined as New Religious movements (NRMs). In addition, several Russian indigenous NRMs became prominent, such as the Mother of God Centre, and the Great White Brotherhood, and the Church of the Last Testament (the Vissarion movement). This increasing diversity touches on one of the most sensitive issues of the transitional period. On the one hand, in a post-Communist society such as Russia, religion is often seen as the most significant marker of national and ethnic identity, even as a reversal to the 1917 notion of the Russian Orthodox Land, and thus new and, by implication, "foreign," religions are given less legitimacy. On the other hand, the concept of a civic nation, with the accompanying recognition of the right to choose and practice religion freely, is embedded in the 1993 Constitution of the Russian Federation and shared by a considerable section of Russian society.

The resulting tensions were reflected in the introduction of the new 1997 Law on Freedom of Conscience and Religious Associations. While formally recognizing the basic religious freedoms and equality of all religions, the preamble to the law emphasized the historical role of Russian traditional religions as affiliated to major ethnic groups (Christianity, Islam, Judaism, and Buddhism) and in particular, the role of Russian Orthodoxy. At the same time, the Law differentiated between religious organizations that enjoy the full rights of a legal entity, and religious groups that can practice their faith freely but are institutionally severely restricted (they cannot own property, have educational establishments, publish literature, etc.). In order to obtain the status of a religious organization, an association has to provide evidence of its legal existence in the Russian Federation for 15 years prior to its application for registration. Given that most of the newer religious associations, in particular, those from abroad, would be very unlikely to have been able to legally exist in the Soviet Union, the law places serious restrictions on their activities and development.

So far, the 1997 law has had mixed effects. Although most religious associations, including NRMs, have been registered under the law, some were refused registration, and others, such as the Salvation Army

Russia

Religion	Followers in 1970	Followers in 2010	% of Population	Annual % growth 2000–2010	Followers in 2025	Followers in 2050
Christians	50,000,000	115,120,000	82.0	1.73	108,137,000	91,117,000
Orthodox	38,788,000	110,904,000	79.0	1.76	103,626,000	86,964,000
Independents	1,769,000	1,500,000	1.1	1.37	1,600,000	1,700,000
Protestants	928,000	1,300,000	0.9	0.02	1,400,000	1,250,000
Agnostics	36,629,000	6,500,000	4.6	–13.84	2,410,000	1,378,000
Muslims	10,100,000	15,400,000	11.0	0.41	15,500,000	13,500,000
Atheists	30,483,000	1,500,000	1.1	–10.24	400,000	200,000
Ethnoreligionists	535,000	980,000	0.7	–0.45	900,000	700,000
Buddhists	475,000	570,000	0.4	–0.48	600,000	650,000
Jews	2,168,000	180,000	0.1	–0.48	150,000	150,000
Hindus	0	46,000	0.0	1.16	60,000	80,000
Baha'is	2,000	17,000	0.0	–0.40	30,000	50,000
Sikhs	0	2,900	0.0	–0.47	3,000	3,000
New religionists	400	1,000	0.0	–0.49	1,200	1,400
Chinese folk	0	1,000	0.0	–0.47	2,000	3,000
Total population	**130,392,000**	**140,318,000**	**100.0**	**–0.48**	**128,193,000**	**107,832,000**

and the Moscow Branch of the Jehovah's Witnesses, were banned altogether following court decisions. In some cases the Russian Constitutional Court has interpreted the 1997 Law in favor of minority religions and overturned administrative decisions that had previously denied registration to them. Also, some groups (including the Salvation Army) have won cases against Russia in the European Court of Human Rights.

In the post-Soviet situation, many, including in state agencies, have turned to the Russian Orthodox Church as an important source of moral authority and social cohesion against what they perceive as the socially disruptive and morally corrosive forces of market economy, political instability, and geopolitical conflicts. In its turn, while remaining largely uninvolved in formal politics, the church draws on its considerably increased institutional strength and impact to reinforce its presence in major institutions such as the army and education. One expression of this has been a rapprochement between the church and the state agencies, which was achieved through official and semi-official agreements, and informal connections. On a more extreme side, political and ideological movements have appeared that promote their versions of Russian Orthodoxy as foci of their nationalist agendas (for example, the Eurasianists, the Orthodox Rus', the Great Russia). At the same time, certain new trends within minority religions have also found appeal among ethno-nationalist or trans-national political movements, such as new versions of Islam in the Northern Caucasus. Finally, the sharply enhanced political profile of religion, in particular, of the Russian Orthodox Church, has caused concern in some quarters about the secular nature of Russian society and government.

Marat S. Shterin

See also: Baptists; Ecumenical Patriarchate/Patriarchate of Constantinople; Great White Brotherhood; Gurdjieff Foundations; Jehovah's Witnesses; Molokans; Mother of God Centre; Old Believers (Russia); Russian Orthodox Church (Moscow Patriarchate); Salvation Army; Seventh-day Adventist Church; Theosophical Society (America).

References

Anderson, John. *Religion, State and Politics in the Soviet Union and Successor States, 1953–1993*. Cambridge: Cambridge University Press, 1994.

Billington, James H. *The Icon and the Axe: An Interpretative History of Russian Culture.* New York: Vintage Books, 1966.

Ellis, Jane. *The Russian Orthodox Church: Triumphalism and Defensiveness*. Basingstoke, NY: Macmillan, 1996.
Knox, Zoe. *Russian Society and the Orthodox Church: Religion in Russia after Communism*. London and New York: Routledge, 2005.
Lane, Christel. *The Rites and Rulers: Ritual in Industrial Society*. Cambridge: Cambridge University Press, 1981.
Steinberg, Mark, and Catherine Wanner. *Religion, Morality and Community in Post-Soviet Societies*. Bloomington and Indianapolis: Indiana University Press, 2008.
Witte John, Jr., and Michael Bordeaux, eds. *Proselytism and Orthodoxy in Russia: The New Wars for Souls*. Maryknoll, NY: Orbis, 1999.

Russia, Islam in

Contemporary Russia (or the Russian Federation) has the largest number of Muslims in Europe, with estimates ranging from 15 to 20 million people, or between 12 and 14.5 percent of the population. Muslim communities have been present in the country for more than 1,000 years and their histories are inextricably linked to that of the country as a whole. Most of Russia's Muslims live either in the Middle Volga region, mainly in the autonomous republics of Tatarstan and Baskhortostan, or in the Northern Caucasian republics of Dagestan, Chechnya, and Kabardino-Balkaria. Large groups of ethnic Muslims also reside in Russia's capital Moscow (between 1.5 and 2 million, according to different estimates), St. Petersburg, and many areas of Siberia. Islam in Russia comprises 38 ethnic groups with different languages, folk traditions, and historical legacies. The largest Muslim ethnic groups are Tatars (5,500,000), Bashkirs (1,600,000), Azeris (1,500,000), Chechens (1,300,000), Avars (800,000), Kazakhs (680,000), and Kabardinians (530,000). Most Russian Muslims are Sunni (90 percent) and 10 percent are Shia. Many Muslim ethnic groups have their politico-administrative homelands: Ingushetia, Dagestan, Chechnya, Kabardino-Balkaria, Karachaevo-Cherkesia, Tatarstan, and Bashkortostan.

The Kul Sharif Mosque and old kremlin, Kazan, Republic of Tatarstan, Russia. The original mosque was destroyed in 1552 when Russian forces, under Ivan IV ("The Terrible"), stormed Kazan. (Natalia Pavlova/Dreamstime.com)

Muslim communities first appeared in what is now the Russian Federation in the seventh century, when Arab Sassanids (from the area that is modern Iran) conquered the northeastern parts of the Caucasus Mountains (contemporary Dagestan), spreading the Shafii madhhab, one of four judicial schools within Sunni Islam. However, it was only in the early 19th century that Islam became the majority religion among the peoples of the Northern Caucasus. Its beliefs and practices coexisted for many centuries with pre-monotheistic religious cultures that included magic and worship of ancestors and deities of nature. Additionally, there was rivalry between Shafii and Hanafi madhhabs, with the former eventually prevailing among the Chechens and Ingushes in the 19th century.

The Middle Volga and the Western Urals constituted another area strongly influenced by Islam. From the eighth century on, they had trade connections with, and received missionaries from, Central Asian Muslims, and in 922, Islam became the official religion of the Kingdom of Volga Bulgars. Islam in this region survived the conquest of the Volga Bulgars by the Mongolian warriors in 1236, who initially tended to be tolerant toward religions of the subjugated populations.

Sufism began to proliferate in the Northern Caucasus as early as in the 12th century. By the early ninth century, brotherhoods of its Naqshbandiyya Order (*tariqa*) had assumed a significant role in the local social organization. From the 18th century, Naqshbandiyya Sufism became widespread also among the Volga Tatars, but its prominence never rivaled that of its Northern Caucasian counterpart; from the late 19th century, it began to wane in the face of the emerging Islamic renovation movements.

Interactions with its eastern Slavic Christian neighbors had a formative influence on the development of Muslim communities of northern Eurasia. Initially, they had only sporadic encounters with Kievan Rus, the early eastern Slavic state, which adopted Christianity in 988. However, following the Mongolian conquest in the 13th century, the situation changed dramatically, especially after 1313, when Khan Ozbek made Islam the official religion of the Golden Horde. Henceforth, the struggle against the "Mongolian Yoke" could be seen as synonymous with liberating Russian Orthodox lands from the Islamic Golden Horde. This association persisted in Russian culture for centuries and was reinforced by subsequent encounters with the Muslim world. Simultaneously, however, this perception was somewhat mitigated by collective memories of peaceful coexistence between ethnic Muslims and Russians in a single state over many centuries.

From the 14th century on, the geopolitical situation steadily reversed in favor of the expanding Russian state. In the 16th century, the Muscovite state conquered the descendants of the fragmented Golden Horde—the Khanates of Kazan in the Middle Volga (1552) and Astrakhan in the Volga delta (1556). Later, the rising Russian Empire (proclaimed in 1721 by Peter the Great) engaged in territorial expansion. It entered into a series of geopolitical conflicts with the Muslim powers on its southern borders, in particular, the Ottoman Empire and Iran. This resulted in annexation of the Crimean Khanate in 1783, the conquest of the Northern and Southern Caucuses (1780s–1850s), and the inclusion of the vast territories of Central Asia (1820s–1890s). By the end of the 19th century, at least 14 million (13 percent) subjects within the empire were Muslims, with some estimates putting their number as high as 20 million (following the argument that the 1897 census, the only one in Russian imperial history, tended to underestimate numbers of non-Russian ethnic minorities). Muslims belonged to a vast variety of cultures, languages, and versions of Islam, and had developed different historical memories of their relationships with the Russian Empire. The imperial policies toward Muslims, too, varied across different regions, groups and historical periods.

In the common spirit of the time, the conquest of the Khanates of Kazan and Astrakhan in the 1550s was followed by attempts to destroy Islamic institutions (for example demolition of mosques and confiscation of *waqf* [charitable property]), by brutality toward the local Muslim population and subsequent virulent efforts at Christianization. Occasionally, the government showed limited flexibility, in particular, toward local elites, preferring to co-opt them into the Russian nobility. In most cases, this advancement was conditional on conversion to the Russian Orthodox Church. However, and in general, the government pursued colonization of the majority Muslim regions by ethnic Russians. These policies of destruction and assimilation were largely driven by the fear that the inclusion of massed numbers of Muslims would corrode the Orthodox Christian identity of the expanding empire and the socio-political cohesion based on it. For their part, Muslims responded by occasional resistance and continuing migration from their ancestral territories, frequently to the Ottoman Empire.

However, Catherine the Great (1762–1796), influenced by the European Enlightenment and facing growing numbers of Muslim subjects, adopted a considerably more accommodating policy toward Islam. Christian proselytism among Muslims was banned, their landed nobility in the conquered Crimea retained their property, and permissions were liberally given to build new mosques and Koranic schools. In addition,

Catherine decreed the establishment of the Muhammadan Spiritual Assembly, a semi-autonomous administrative body to regulate Muslim activities in the European part of Russia. Rather than reflecting the empress's personal sympathies, this policy was designed to control Muslim population through more sophisticated means of co-opting the loyalty of Muslim nobility and clergy, encouraging them to follow what the Russian "enlightened" elite saw as the European way of life.

This approach was only partly institutionalized in the subsequent imperial policies in the 19th century, in particular, in the North Caucasian Mountains. Here the Russian conquest encountered strong resistance in which the organization, beliefs, and practices of Naqshbandiyya Sufi brotherhoods played a crucial role. Through the successive leaderships of Sheikh Mansur, a Sufi mystic and war leader (late 18th century); Ghazi Muhammad, a Dagestani Avar Koranic scholar (early 19th century); and, most important, Imam Shamil, also an Avar (1825–1859), a strong network of devoted Murids emerged. By the late 1850s, the Murids were defeated, but the tradition of Muridiyya had been established in the Northern Caucasus. A movement of committed Sufi warriors engaged in a battle for Islam and against the infidels emerged, for either the liberation of Muslim lands from non-Islamic invaders or the removal of "pagan" influences.

In late imperial Russia (late 19th through the early 20th centuries), the government's primary concern was the economic returns from Muslim territories, in particular, from Central Asia and the Caucasus, and consequently about maintaining a degree of stability in those areas. Traditional Islamic practices were more tolerated; educational establishments were allowed to function; and aggressive Orthodox Christian proselytism was often frowned upon by the Russian colonial authorities, more sophisticated missionary methods being preferred. Before 1917, there were around 26,000 functioning mosques in the Russian Empire. However, concerns about Muslim loyalty to the Orthodox Empire persisted. The government attempted to limit connections between local Muslims and their co-believers in the rest of the Islamic world. At times it outlawed certain versions and practices of Islam regarded as threatening. For example, in the 1850s–1860s, members of the (new) Qadiriyya Sufi Order gained a large following among Chechens and Ingushes. Also known as Zikrism (from *zikr,* its central practice of loudly exclaiming the name of Allah while dancing in a circle), the Order refused to obey the Russian authorities' demands for moderation. As the result, zikr and other key practices were banned. (It is interesting to note that Ramazan Kadyrov, the current president of Chechnya, comes from this Order. He is engaged in suppressing new and rival Islamic groups in the republic on the grounds of their extremism and threat to ethno-national cohesion.)

Even more significant were effects of wider socio-economic trends and policies. Russificiation continued, encouraging ethnic Russians to emigrate to the Muslim territories and imposing Russian as the official language. Consequently, traditional Islamic learning and education in local languages came to be associated with inferior social status and limited opportunities. In turn, this encouraged Muslim youth, particularly from more privileged backgrounds, to be educated in Russian, thus contributing to their increasing cultural separation from the Muslim world and diminishing their interest in Islamic thought.

However, the second half of the 19th century saw an emergence of new movements within Russian Muslims, in particular, among ethnic Tatars. Baha al-Din Vaisov, a Sufi mystic, led a radical revivalist movement that called Muslims to restore Islam to its pristine state as a community of devout equals, to purify it from Christian-style hierarchal authorities, and to terminate its subordination to the infidels' government. Popular mainly among rural Muslims, the movement was suppressed by the Russian authorities in the early 20th century. Also in the 1880s, a more significant movement—Jadidism (from Arabic *jaded,* "new")—emerged among Tatar intelligentsia. It rapidly spread among Central Asian and Crimean Muslims. The movement represented an innovative attempt to modernize Islam by introducing progressive educational methods and science into Islamic curriculum on the one hand, and liberating it from obscurantist accretions not rooted in the Koran on the other. The movement encountered hostility from Islamic conservatives of the Qadimiyya tradition (from Arabic *qadim*, "old") who saw it as a threat to the established Muslim authorities and ways of practicing the faith. At the same time it was treated with hostility by Russian officials who feared the prospect of the internal modernization and, by implication, increasing appeal of Islam at the expense of the Russification of Muslims. The beginning of the 20th century was also marked by growing political involvement of Muslims in the Russian Empire, which included formation of ethno-nationalist parties based on Islamic identity, Muslim factions in democratic and socialist movements, and pan-Islamic projects of creating supra-ethnic Islamic political entities.

The seven decades of the "construction of Communism" (1917–1991), and specifically, the antireligious policies and secularist and atheist ethos of the time, had major effects on Russia's Muslims. However, at certain periods the official policy also included pragmatic considerations, such as searching for political support from ethnic Muslims or the simple recognition of the role of Islam in local traditions. Initially, during the first decade after the 1917 Bolshevik revolution, the new government sent a signal that it regarded Muslims as a previously suppressed ethnic minority and therefore as potential allies. Some sections of Muslims responded positively, or pragmatically, by, for instance, forming regional Muslim Communist governments, Muslim Communist parties, and even a Muslim Red Army. However the Bolsheviks found more hostility in the mountainous regions of Chechnya and Dagestan.

The all-out assault on Islam began in the late 1920s. With the Stalinist policy of a "breakthrough" in the construction of Socialism, Islam was declared the major obstacle to the Socialist modernization of the traditionally Muslim regions and to the prosperity of individual Muslims. This accusation translated itself into mass closures and demolitions of mosques, repression of Islamic religious professionals, and banning of Islamic education and training. In 1929, Arabic script was abolished and replaced by Latin and later by Cyrillic, thus effectively separating Soviet Muslims from their religious heritage and increasing their political separation from the major centers of Islamic scholarship and culture. In the 1930s, a total ban was introduced on publication of Islamic literature, including the Koran, and on pilgrimages to Mecca (*hajj*), with only limited reversal of this policy after World War II. The Soviet assault on Islam was particularly harsh in the mountains of Chechnya and Dagestan, where Naqshbandiyya Sufi brotherhoods led irreconcilable guerrilla fighting against Bolshevism well into the 1930s. Following the eventual Soviet victory, Sufi brotherhoods were banned, their leaders executed or exiled, and properties confiscated. By 1948, even after the relative relaxation of anti-religious policies during World War II, only 416 mosques officially remained in the Russian Federation (1.5 percent of the 1917 figure), mainly in the Volga area. A single *madrasa*, Mir-Arab, in the entire Soviet Union was reopened in 1952 in the Uzbek city of Bukhara, later complemented by the Imam Al-Bukhari Institute in Tashkent. At the same time, the Communist government created four official administrations for Soviet Muslims, two of them in the current Russian Federation—the Spiritual Directorate of the Muslims of European Russia and Siberia and the Spiritual Directorate of the Northern Caucasus and Dagestan. These bodies were supposed to demonstrate to the outside world the freedom Islam enjoyed in the Soviet Union, and to secure loyalty of Muslims to the Soviet leadership. However, in reality they could only control a small section of Muslims, as Islamic practice does not require leadership by professional clergy to the same extent as in Orthodox Christianity.

The institutional destruction of Islam was compounded by the Soviet nationality policy. In the early years of the Bolshevik rule, some Islamic activists saw the apparent sympathy of the new government toward Muslims as an opportunity to realize their pan-Islamic ideas of creating large Muslim/Islamic political entities in Central Asia, Northern Caucasus, and the Middle Volga-Urals areas. Despite some initial success, these hopes proved to be short-lived. In the 1920s, Soviet "nationality policy" was informed by fears about political entities and loyalties developing based on Islam. Instead, it aimed to divide ethnic Muslim groups through drawing artificial administrative boundaries that split these groups and included mixed ethnicities. For instance, in the 1920s a considerable proportion of ethnic Tatars found themselves outside the Autonomous Republic of Tatarstan, becoming 30 percent of the population of Bashkortostan. The anti-Muslim stance of the Stalinist government showed itself most harshly in 1944, when between 600,000 and 800,000

Chechens, Ingushes, Crimean Tatars, and a number of smaller ethnic groups were accused of treason and collaboration with German armies and deported from their homelands to Siberia and Kazakhstan.

Although the most repressive aspects of Stalinism, such as the deportations, were rectified under the rule of Nikita Khrushchev (1954–1964), Islam as a faith remained a primary target of Khrushchev's anti-religious campaign, with particularly severe persecutions of Sufi brotherhoods, further closures of mosques, and enforced reduction in the number of clergy. However, in the late period of the Soviet Union (1970s–1980s), anti-religious campaigns subsided. The official stance was affected by the expediencies of foreign policy, oscillating between ideological recognition of the anti-imperialist potential of Islam (for example, in the 1979 Iranian Revolution) and reversal to the rhetoric about its backwardness (as a source of resistance to the 1979–1989 Soviet invasion of Afghanistan). At the same time, these events activated Islamic movements in the Soviet Union. Disillusioned by Socialism and influenced by the Afghan mujahedin, small underground fundamentalist groups emerged in Central Asia, and Sufi brotherhoods were increasingly influential in Chechnya and Dagestan.

Following the general liberalization under Mikhail Gorbachev (r. 1985–1991), restrictions on religious practice were considerably relaxed, and Soviet Muslims had better opportunities for reconnecting with their co-believers in other countries. In 1985 in the Russian Federation, in addition to around 190 officially registered mosques there were perhaps more than 300 unregistered ones; in the Chechen-Ingush Republic the proportion could be at least 10 times the official number. While Soviet secularization had considerable impact in some Muslim regions, in particular, in the Middle Volga-Urals and in Northwestern Caucasus, in other areas, such as Dagestan and Chechnya, the Sufi networks proved tenacious and contributed to Islam's continuing vitality. According to some estimates, by 1990, half of all Chechens belonged to Muridiyya brotherhoods. The fledgling Islamic revival was further reinforced by incipient financial and logistical support from the rest of the Muslim world, in particular, Saudi Arabia and Turkey.

The results of the Soviet anti-Islamic policy were somewhat paradoxical. The institutional devastation in the previous decades mainly undermined "high" Islam —the development of Islamic knowledge, thought, professional education, and culture. However, being less conditional on formal organization and professional clergy, Islam retained its vitality outside its institutional structures. Its role as a marker of ethnic identity was preserved—and in many aspects and places reinforced —through surviving folk practices (such as celebration of Uraza-bairam and Kurban-bairmam) and family socialization.

With the adoption of the 1990 Law on Freedom of Religions and following the end of the Soviet Union in December 1991, Islam in Russia entered what is often referred to as a period of resurgence. The number of registered Muslim communities grew dramatically: from around 100 in 1991 to around 3,800 in 2008. With inclusion of unregistered groups, the figure is likely to be much higher. Although the estimates vary widely, the number of mosques (both registered and unregistered) rose from a few hundred to at least 7,000. The acute need for religious professionals triggered a surge in Islamic educational establishments, although initially the demand was met more quantitatively than qualitatively. Recognized centers of high Islamic learning now include the Higher Islamic College in Moscow, the Russian Islamic Institute in Tatarstan, the Rizaetdin Fahreddin Institute in Bashkortostan, and Imam ash-Shafii Islamic University in Dagestan. In addition, an Islamic cultural milieu emerged, with organizations, services, and interest groups ranging from incipient Islamic banking and halal food outlets to Islamic fashion and film festivals, and from Muslim women's groups to Islamic political parties. Some developments resulted from the re-establishment of connections with the rest of the Islamic world: the flow of funds and missionaries from Islamic countries, such as Saudi Arabia, Pakistan, and Turkey on the one hand, and Russian Muslims visiting and studying abroad on the other. In 2006, 18,000 Russian Muslims performed hajj in Mecca. Nevertheless, the incidence of Islamic practice among ethnic Muslims remains relatively low, with only between 2 and 9 percent attending evening Friday prayer weekly, though it tends to be higher in some regions of the Northern Caucasus and among some immigrant Muslim groups in large cities. According to the 2008 Gallup Poll, around 15 percent of Russian Muslims never obey *salat* (the call to prayer), only 28 percent fast during the month of Ramadan, and around 50 percent drink alcohol.

In the 1990s, centralized administrative authorities of the Soviet period collapsed and were replaced by dozens of administrative structures claiming that they represent particular Muslim ethnic groups or visions of Islam. In reality, however, many of them are based on personal loyalties and commitments. The most influential administrative bodies are the Central Spiritual Directorate of Muslims, the Coordinating Committee of the Muslims of the Northern Caucasus, and the Council of Russia's Muftis.

The post-Soviet situation and profiles of Muslim communities were deeply affected by a number of interrelated processes, such as migration, ethnic revival and associated ethno-political conflicts, geopolitical issues, demographic and generational changes, and globalization of Islam.

After the collapse of the Soviet Union, large numbers of ethnic Muslims moved from their homelands in the Northern Caucasus and Central Asia to big cities, such as Moscow and St. Petersburg, in most cases trying to escape economic impoverishment or ethno-political conflicts. For instance, according to some estimates, at least 1,500,000 ethnic Muslims now live in Moscow and 200,000 in the largest Siberian city of Novosibirsk. One result of this was the formation of significant Muslim minority communities in major urban centers. Within some sections of ethnically Orthodox Christian majorities, this process caused anxieties about the changing ethno-demographic balance and fears of impending "Islamization."

In several regions, ethno-religious activists pressed for recognition of the central role of Islam in the cultural and social life of ethnic Tatars, Bashkirs, Chechens, and other communities. This open-ended trend manifested itself in demands for a greater role for Islam in social institutions and daily life, such as education, public morality (demands for Islamic censorship in Dagestan), the family (attempts at legalization of polygamy in some regions), and gender roles. In some cases, attempts were made to introduce elements of or the entire body of Sharia jurisprudence (in the village of Belozerye in Mordovia, and in parts of Dagestan and Chechnya). In some instances, ethno-religious identity became connected to claims for more political autonomy or even independence from the Russian Federation, for instance, the Ittifak movement in Tatarstan in the 1990s and the separatist groups in Chechnya. At the same time, some activists adopted Islamic agendas that transcended ethnic divisions. Some intended to unite and religiously educate all of Russia's Muslims (the Nur movement and the Union of Muslims of Russia in the 1990s). Others had pan-Islamic agendas that extended beyond the Russian Federation. Such activities considerably heightened the political profile of Islam and at times contributed to tensions and conflicts. A curious attempt at modernizing Islam has been made by Raphael Hakimov, an academic and presidential aide in the Republic of Tatarstan, who has been promoting "Euro-Islam," a liberal version of the religion suitable for modern European Muslims and reflecting a higher level of integration of the Tatar Muslims in European culture.

Geopolitical tensions and conflicts involving Islam had profound effects on Russia's Muslims and their communities, specifically after 9/11 and other terrorist acts. As elsewhere in Western countries, the extremist rhetoric and activities of some groups and networks outside Russia that declared a global jihad against the enemies of the faith anywhere in the world backlashed on ordinary Russian Muslims by provoking doubts and fears about their loyalty. What was earlier seen as a specific case of Chechen Islamic extremism, was now attributed to global trends in the relationships between "Islam" and "the West." The Chechen conflict itself began as predominantly ethno-political and only acquired the Islamic dimension as it unfolded, to some extent reflecting the later involvement of some international jihadists. Jihadist rhetoric found a receptive audience among a very small number of younger Russian Muslims, and those almost exclusively in regions already experiencing social tensions and political grievances, such as in Chechnya and elsewhere in the Northern Caucasus. Several terrorist acts in Russian cities, in particular, the 2004 tragic school siege in Beslan,

Northern Ossetia, contributed to creation of a negative image of Islam, amplified by the mass media.

Generational differences and demographic changes also contributed to the new profile of post-Soviet Islam. Younger Muslims make up a growing proportion of the population both in several traditionally Muslim regions and also among immigrants in large urban centers. They tend to be attracted to socially, and at times, politically, transformative forms of the religion, such as those offered by various groups within the Salafi strand of Sunni Islam, or what in Russia is often seen as an offshoot of Wahhabi Islam. Such groups commonly put emphasis on the transformation of the whole individual through a return to the "pure Islam" of the days of the Prophet. In practical terms, this means rejecting the traditional "ethnic" forms of Islam, living according to the prescriptions of sharia law and original Sunna, and studying the Koran in Arabic. These groups are particularly prominent in Dagestan and other parts of the Northern Caucasus but can also be found elsewhere in the Russian Federation, in particular, in large cities. Although most of them do not show politically extremist intentions, their existence has given rise to fears about terrorist networks covering the entire country. Many other Muslims often meet these groups with hostility, particularly those from more traditionally inclined Sufi brotherhoods, such as the Qadiriyya and Naqshbandiya Sufi orders. In the Northern Caucasus, some of the new groups became entangled with the Chechen rebels and engaged in armed conflicts involving Russian Federal forces (1999 in Dagestan and 2005 in Kabardino-Balkaria).

There have also emerged a variety of other new Islamic groups representing different currents and dimensions of contemporary Islam. These range from the highly politicized Hizb-Ut-Tahrir to the largely apolitical Tablighi Jamaat. Some are well known in both Muslim and Western countries and were introduced by missionaries. Examples are the Güllen movement of the followers of the Turkish Islamic thinker, Fethullah Gülen; Ahmadiyya Islam; and the new Sufi orders of Subud and Nimatullahi. There are also homegrown new groups, such as those led by Faisarhman Sattarov and Nurulla Moflukhanov in Tatarstan.

Many of these groups, in particular, those of foreign origins, have encountered considerable animosity from both more traditional Russian Muslims and the Russian authorities. Many of these reactions are affected by a shared discourse on Islamic extremism, often fueled by the mass media and the inflammatory politicized rhetoric that they spread. In this rhetoric, all foreign Islamic groups, particularly those connected to the Middle East and Turkey, tend to be seen as part or offshoots of a single extremist Islamist network. Almost invariably, these groups attract the attention of the Security Services, which use the 2002 law "On Fighting Extremist Activity," which contains loose definitions of religious extremism. The adoption of this law by the Duma (Lower House of Parliament) signified an important change in the official approach to Islamist extremism, which was now seen as a global phenomenon, with Russia as one of its main targets. In 2003, the Supreme Court banned 15 different international Islamic groups with records of violence or incitement of violence; however, the presence of most of them in the country is doubtful. Among these groups was Hizb-ut-Tahrir, the violent nature of which was never proven, its ideologically extreme aims notwithstanding. Since 2003, the police and security services have raided many new Islamic groups. In addition, in 2007, the Supreme Court began publishing "The Federal List of Extremist Materials." Among inflammatory and violence-inciting contemporary works, it also lists the books of Muhammad ibn Abd al-Wahhab (1703–1792), founder of Wahabiyya Islam, which are favored by contemporary jihadists, and of Said Nursi (1878–1960), a widely respected Turkish Islamic thinker.

At the same time, the Russian government consistently declared its support for Russian Muslims and its anti-Islamophobic credentials. In some situations, Russian Muslims found official support for expressions of their religious identity. Since 2003, the Russian government has repeatedly referred to its sizable Muslim minority as the basis for its intention to join Organization of Islamic Conference. However, inside the country, Islamophobia shows itself not so much in direct opposition to the religion but more in racist attitudes of some sections of society toward ethnic Muslims, which results in occasional racist attacks, in particular, by neo-Nazi style skinheads, and in harassment by the police.

Marat S. Shterin

See also: Ahmadiyya Movement in Islam; Bukhara; Globalization, Religion and; Hanafite School of Islam; Mecca; Moscow; Mosques; Muridîyya; Naqshbandiya Sufi Order; Pilgrimage; Qadiriyya Sufi Order; Ramadan; Russia; Russian Orthodox Church (Moscow Patriarchate); Shia Islam; Subud; Sufism; Wahhabi Islam.

References

Hunter, Shireen T. *Islam in Russia: The Politics of Identity and Security*. New York and London: M. E. Sharpe, 2004.

Malashenko, Alexei V. *Islamic Rebirth in Contemporary Russia*. Moscow: Carnegie Centre, 1998.

Pilkington, Hilary, and Galina M. Yemelianova, eds. *Private and Public Faces of Islam in Russia.* London and New York: Curzon, 2003.

Ro'i, Yaacov. *Islam in the Soviet Union: From the Second World War to Gorbachev*. New York: Columbia University Press, 2000.

Yemelianova, Galena. M. *Russia and Islam: A Historical Survey.* London: Palgrave, 2002

Russia, Protestantism in

Evangelical Lutheran church in St. Petersburg, Russia. (Maxim Toporskiy/Dreamstime.com)

Protestantism has been present in Russia in a variety of forms for nearly five centuries. It is currently the second largest and the fastest growing strain of Christianity in the country. Although Russia never had anything comparable to the Protestant Reformation in the West, some of its homegrown sectarian movements espoused ideas and practices that had a degree of affinity with those articulated in the antecedents and by the founders of Protestantism. Western Protestantism came to Russia in three different ways: through territorial expansion of the empire westward and northwestward; through voluntary settlement of Protestant groups, ethnic and otherwise; and through missionary activities among ethnic Russians.

Russian Sectarianism Long before the first Lutherans reached Russia in the 1520s, some Russian sectarian movements sought unmediated spiritual enlightenment and connection with God over and above the official dogma and church authority. These movements tended to emphasize direct mystical experience rather than rational thought, which can be partly explained by a lack of a developed theological tradition in pre-modern Russia. In the 1370s–1450s, the Strigol'niks ("Shearers," or "shorn-heads") attracted a large following in the northwestern cities of Novgorod and Pskov. They protested against the corruption and materialism of the official Russian Orthodox Church, called for a return to the pristine Christianity of the Apostles, and denounced priesthood. In the late 15th century, a diverse group of dissenters, named the Judizers by the Church, emerged in Novgorod and Moscow. Although some evidence suggests a Jewish influence, many of their diverse ideas, such as the rejection of the sacraments, monasticism, and professional clergy, were in tune with those of European pre-Reformation thinkers.

In the 17th and 18th centuries, when sectarianism flourished in Russia, followers of the Faith of Christ (Christovshchina) believed in personal experience of God through continuous recitation of the Lord's Prayer until their hearts received the Holy Spirit, which manifested itself in dancing, singing, glossolalia, and prophesying. They believed that their leaders spiritually embodied Christ and that, therefore, the kingdom of God was already spiritually present. While formally belonging to the official church, they held secret meetings and observed severe asceticism. Perhaps partly due to severe persecutions, some groups began to advocate and practice extreme forms of devotion to God through flagellation (the Flagellants; Russian: Khlysty) and later castration (the Castrates; Russian: Skoptsy).

The second half of the 18th and the 19th centuries saw the proliferation of Spiritual Christianity, in particular, the Dukhobors ("Spirit-wrestlers"), and the Molokans ("Milk-drinkers"). Both groups rejected Orthodox icons, sacraments, and hierarchy, and emphasized personal devotion and connection to God. In addition, a group of Molokans developed strong apocalyptic expectations, similar to those found in some Western Protestant sects.

Western Protestantism in Russia In the early 16th century, the rise of the Muscovite Czardom and its intensified trade connections coincided with the proliferation of Reformation movements in Western Europe. In the 1520s, the first German and Swedish Lutheran merchants came to Moscow and the northern city of Novgorod, followed by English and Dutch Calvinist traders, who were invited by Grand Prince Vasili III (1500–1533) and particularly his son Ivan IV ("The Terrible"; 1533–1582) to serve as specialists—builders, doctors, barbers, military advisors, and the like. Ivan IV's attitude to Western Protestants displayed a mixture of curiosity, tolerance, and suspicion, which was common in early Russian encounters with Protestantism. For example, he guaranteed English Protestants protection from coercive conversion to Russian Orthodoxy and allowed the building of a Lutheran church and a Reformed Calvinist church near the Kremlin. However, having grown suspicious of a possible heretical influence, he later had the churches demolished and segregated foreigners in a special German District in the outskirts of Moscow. However, settlement of foreign specialists and merchants continued: contemporary sources refer to at least 18,000 Protestants living in Russia in the mid-17th century.

Following Peter the Great's (1682–1725) extensive "Europeanizing" reforms, thousands of German and other European Protestants settled in the country and many became Russian subjects. This was further facilitated by Peter's legalization of mixed Orthodox-Protestant marriages and guarantees of free practice of Protestant faiths. In addition, by arranging numerous marriages with the German dynasties, Peter the Great paved the way for the German Lutheran nobility's settlement in Russia throughout the 18th century. Some of Peter's reforms themselves had an imprint of Protestantism, especially when he replaced the Patriarchate with the Most Holy Synod headed by a secular official, a form of ecclesiastical administration that was prompted by Peter's visit to England in 1698.

However, the numerical growth of Protestantism in Russia in the 18th century mainly resulted from territorial expansion to the northwest. Following its victory over Sweden in the Northern War (1700–1721), Russia annexed the Baltic lands and southern Finland with their predominantly Lutheran populations. In addition, thousands of Lutheran hostages were captured and settled throughout the Russian Empire. The Protestant population further increased after the inclusion of the rest of Finland (1809) and Poland (1815).

In the late 18th century, a new wave of Protestants came to Russia, invited by Catherine the Great to cultivate the wastelands in the Southern Ukraine, Volga, and Northern Caucasus regions. The majority of these new settlers were Lutherans, but a considerable proportion were Mennonites. Among the privileges granted to them by the empress was the freedom to practice their faith, declared by a special 1787 imperial decree. By the end of the 19th century, 1,800,000 Germans lived in Russia and around 75 percent of them were Lutherans. They created a distinctive ethnic group that shared many key elements of Russian culture, including the Russian language, but were distinguished by their faith. Many of the Lutherans and their families eventually became Russian Orthodox; some—or their descendants—made a considerable contribution to Russian culture and society (for example, Vitus Bering, the navigator; Sergey Witte, the statesman; and Alexander Blok, the poet).

Protestant Missionaries and New Russian Protestant Groups before 1917 In the 19th century Protestantism became increasingly prominent among ethnic Orthodox Russians. In the early 19th century, German Pietism became popular among the St. Petersburg nobility, with Czar Alexander I (1801–1825) being its major proponent. In addition, Alexander I favored the establishment in 1812 of the Russian Bible Society (RBS), an inter-denominational group devoted to the translation of the Bible into vernacular languages and its distribution among Russians and other ethnic groups. Between 1813 and 1826 (when the RBS was banned), many parts of the Bible were translated in Russian theological academies. The work was resumed in the 1860s under the editorship of Metropolitan Philaret of Moscow and was completed in 1876 when the Russian Synodal Bible was published. Subsequently, it became an important proselytizing tool of Western Protestant missionaries as well as a source of religious dissent among ethnic Orthodox Russians.

In the 1820s–1830s, German and English Pietists were proclaiming the Gospels in the German colonies in the South of Ukraine, in particular, introducing the practice of meeting for an hour of personal prayer and Bible study, or *Stunde* (German: "an hour"). From these colonies the practice spread to neighboring Ukrainian and Russian villages, giving rise to the movement of Russian Stundists in the 1850s–1860s. Initially Russian Stundists formally remained within the Russian Orthodox Church, but, faced with denunciation by the official church, some of them turned to Baptist missionaries; in the late 1860s, some Russians and Ukrainians accepted baptism by immersion. However, Russian Protestants share the view that the first Russian convert to baptism was Nikita Voronin from the Molokan background, who was baptized by a German missionary and later formed the first Russian Baptist community in Tiflis (modern Tbilisi, Georgia). In the 1860s and 1870s, together with the Ukraine, the Caucasus was the second Russian region where baptism enjoyed considerable success.

Another center of evangelical Christianity in the late 19th century was St. Petersburg, the imperial capital, where Lord Granville Radstock, an English aristocrat and evangelical missionary, introduced the Plymouth Brethren (the Christian Brethren) to members of the Russian nobility, such as Count M. Korf, Colonel V. Pashkov, and Count A. Bobrinksi (the then railways minister). The strenuous missionary activities of this group, known as the Russian Evangelical Christians, soon resulted in a considerable number of converts among the urban intelligentsia, students, urban artisans, and lower-rank military. In 1884, the Union of the Russian Evangelical Christians and Baptists was formed. By 1917, Baptists and evangelical Christians were among the fastest growing movements in Russia.

The last two decades of the 19th century saw missionary activities by a range of other Protestant groups. The Seventh-day Adventists, mainly from Germany and the United States, first attracted Russian converts in German colonies in the Caucasus and Ukraine, and later in the Baltic countries, Moscow and St. Petersburg. By 1917, there were around 7,000 Adventists in Russia. The first ethnic Russians converted to the Pentecostal Church in 1911 in Finland and then enjoyed rapid growth in the Caucasus, Ukraine, Estonia, Latvia, Moscow, and St. Petersburg; however, it became particularly successful in the first decade after the 1917 Bolshevik Revolution. There were also smaller groups of Presbyterians, Anglicans, Methodists, and Quakers.

In the late 1880s–1890s, newer Protestant groups, such as the Latter-day Saints (the Mormons) and the Salvation Army established their first missions in Russia. At the same time, Jehovah's Witnesses began to distribute Russian editions of their periodical *The Watchtower;* their founder Charles Taze Russell (1852–1916) visited Russia in 1891. In the same year one of the first Russian converts, Semyon Kozlitsky, was exiled to Siberia for his missionary activities.

Some wider historical developments contributed to the proliferation of Russian Protestant groups in the last five decades of the Russian Empire (1861–1917). The abolition of serfdom in 1861, followed by other reforms in the 1860s and 1870s, delivered millions of peasants who were losing their traditional ties with rural communities dominated by the Russian Orthodox Church and engaging in new economic activities. In addition, the Russian Orthodox Church was also losing its grip on the more educated classes who were becoming more open to spiritual alternatives. This created fertile soil for Protestant missionaries. On the other hand, the waves of Protestant spiritual revivals in the 19th-century United States and Western Europe produced a pool of missionaries eager to spread their faiths throughout the globe, in particular, taking advantage of the improved means of travel.

The official policy toward Russian Protestants in pre-1917 Russia was largely determined by the significance accorded to the Russian Orthodox identity of the empire on the one hand, and by the necessities and attractions of socio-economic and cultural exchange with the West on the other. On the most fundamental level, all Protestants were in the category of *inovertsy* ("people of alien faith"), which placed them below *pravoslavnye* (Russian Orthodox). However, some of them, such as German Lutherans, English Anglicans, and Dutch Calvinists, were associated with countries whose economic, military, and cultural achievements Russian Europeanizing elites sought to emulate and could offer skills and knowledge they were interested in using. In addition, Eastern Orthodox and Protestants shared an animosity to Roman Catholics. However, the freedom of worship by foreigners was strictly conditional on their non-proselytizing among ethnic Russians, even if the latter showed interest in the Protestant faith. One way of protecting them from the temptations of "alien faiths" was the spatial separation of Protestant foreigners from ethnic Russians, such as the German District in Moscow in the 16th and 17th centuries. This was relaxed under the "enlightened" monarchs of the 18th century, who even allowed Lutheran churches to be erected in central areas of Russian cities. However, the state never ceased to exercise political control of Protestant groups. In 1832, a decree by Nicolas I established a single state-controlled administration in St. Petersburg, which had jurisdiction over all Protestant groups in Russia (except Finland and Poland), irrespective of their differences. On the other hand, in different periods of Russian history, bans were introduced on anti-Lutheran propaganda and enforced conversion of Lutherans to other faiths (with the notion of Lutherans commonly applied to other established Protestant denominations, such as the Dutch Reformed Church).

In the last three decades of the 19th century, the proliferation of actively proselytizing Western Protestant groups presented a challenge to the imperial authorities, as it was seen as a threat to the unbreakable link between the Russian people and the Russian Orthodox Church. Torn between competing categorizations, the imperial authorities engaged in a flurry of legislative activities that oscillated between guaranteeing the freedom of worship to the traditionally respected Protestants and restricting the spread of undesirable sectarian groups. Konstantin Pobedonostsev, the highly influential ober-procurator (head) of the Most Holy Synod between 1880 and 1905, favored strict state control and persecution of "sectarian activities," first of all the Baptists and evangelical Christians, whom he officially declared the most dangerous anti-state and anti-church sect. Some Western missionaries, such as Lord Radstock, were banned from entering Russia, and their Russian co-believers, such as M. Korf and V. Pashkov, were forced to emigrate. However, the 1905 Edict of Toleration issued by Nicolas II legalized missionary activities and facilitated the organizational development of Protestant groups. The period of toleration was partially reversed immediately before and during World War I (1914–1918), as some influential czarist officials grew suspicious of the pro-German sympathies of Russian Protestants, which resulted in new restrictions and bans on their activities and exiles of their leaders.

Protestantism under the Soviet Regime (1917–1991)

The first years after the Bolshevik Revolution (1917–1920s) are often referred to as the "golden decade" of Russian Protestantism, in particular, of Baptist and evangelical groups. Despite their militant atheist stance and early anti-religious campaigns, initially the Bolsheviks treated the sectarians favorably as victims of persecution by the czarist state and church. The overall membership in these groups grew rapidly to at least 600,000 by 1929 (about 90 percent Baptists and evangelicals). Together with ethnic Protestants, the number of Russian Protestants was around a million (ca. one percent of the population). In an apparent show of affinity with the ethos of the new regime, Baptists and evangelicals set up their collective farms, cooperatives, and youth leagues (such as the Baptist Socialist Youth

League). Ivan Prokhanov (1869–1935), the prominent leader of Christian evangelicals, promoted the ideas of Christian Socialism and even attempted to establish Socialist Evangelical Christian communities. Within the first post-revolutionary decade, Seventh-day Adventist membership nearly doubled and reached 12,000. Pentecostalism, too, was growing rapidly, establishing a particularly strong presence in the Ukraine, where it had at least 25,000 members in about 400 communities. In 1929, Soviet Pentecostals formed the Union of Christians of the Evangelical Faith, which was affiliated with the international Assemblies of God.

However, these good fortunes were reversed from the mid-1920s on, particularly in the wake of the 1929 Law on Religious Associations. The official Soviet ideology began to present Baptists, evangelicals, and other groups as archenemies of the emerging "Communist society." Their categorization as "sectarian" was back in use in official propaganda and policy, this time in the service of state atheism. Their communities came under special surveillance by the security services, their members arrested and imprisoned and prayer houses shut down, their periodicals banned and educational activities terminated. After a short period of relative relaxation during and immediately after World War II, persecutions resumed in the mid-1950s, targeting Pentecostals, Adventists, and Baptists. Part of the Soviet-style control of the sectarians was destruction of their independent voluntary associations, such as the Union of Russian Baptists and Union of Evangelical Christians, and their replacement with state-controlled bodies, such as the Union of Evangelical Christians–Baptists of Russia (UECBR), founded in 1944. However, in the late 1950s–early 1960s a group that came to be known as the Initiativniks ("the Initiators") broke away from the UECBR, denouncing its politically subservient stance and forming an underground movement, the Council of Churches of Evangelical Christian Baptists. Jehovah's Witnesses suffered severe persecutions, in particular, during and after World War II. In 1949–1951 whole communities were sent to exile in Siberia, the Far East, and Kazakhstan, an inadvertent consequence of which became their particularly strong presence in these regions.

Protestant groups, ethnic and otherwise, enjoyed relatively more freedom and vibrancy in the Baltic Republic of Estonia. However, Lutheran Germans suffered a dramatic decline throughout the 20th century, as the two World Wars, famines, Stalinist repression, and economic disadvantages caused mass emigration, loss of life, and destruction of established communities. Overall, during the Soviet period, the profile of Russian Protestantism changed dramatically from being rooted in ethnic identity to becoming a matter of individual choice. This trend continued in the post-Soviet period.

Protestantism in post-Soviet Russia The introduction of the 1990 Law on Freedom of Religion and the collapse of the Soviet Union created favorable conditions for the proliferation of Protestant groups in post-Soviet Russia. The overall number of their communities grew from an estimated 510 in 1992 to around 4,000 registered communities in 2008, or ca. 20 percent of all registered religious organizations of the Russian Federation, with an estimated 2 million members. These figures are likely to be much higher if unregistered religious groups are accounted for. In some regions, particularly in Siberia and the Far East, the proportion of Protestant communities exceeds that of the Russian Orthodox Church. It has to be noted that Protestant communities normally use criteria of membership that are different from those of ethnic religions and tend to include only active and committed members.

Protestantism became highly visible in post-Soviet Russia, as Protestant communities tend to expect and encourage a high degree of religious commitment and social activism. In addition, newer Protestant groups tend to attract younger and more educated people, which imparts further vigor to their expression of faith and social activities. In some regions, these groups became actively involved in political life, mainly favoring politicians with democratic credentials.

In the post-Soviet era, Russian Protestantism became increasingly diverse. There was a revival of ethno-religious links, such as between remaining Russian Germans and Lutheranism, or between Finns and the Ingrian Lutheran Church. However, in some cases, ethnic Russians joined these groups too. Russian Baptists and evangelicals reconstituted their Union of the Evangelical Christians–Baptists of the Russian Federation and now have around 100,000 members in 1,400 local communities, slightly more than half of which are registered. Other communities, such as the Seventh-day Adventists, Methodists, the Quakers, the Presbyterians, the Anglicans, and the Mennonites also have between a few hundred and a few thousand members each. Most of these communities emerged as the result of missionary work of diverse groups of evangelizers and reflect their different versions of the Protestant tradition. For instance, there are quite different groups established by a range of Korean and American Methodists, Presbyterians, and others.

The proliferation of Charismatic and Pentecostal Christianity represents perhaps the most significant change in Russian Protestantism. Beginning from just dozens of unregistered communities in 1990, there were more than 1,500 registered Charismatic and Pentecostal communities in 2005, and perhaps an equal number of unregistered groups, with an estimated total membership ranging from 300,000 to 900,000, depending on the criteria of membership and statistics provided by their leadership. All Russian Pentecostal and Charismatic Christians share the beliefs in the "first blessing" of conversion; the "second blessing" of baptism by the Holy Spirit, evidenced in speaking in tongues; progressive sanctification; and individual holiness. However, three different strands can be identified among them, which in many ways reflect three generations of Russian Pentecostalism. The first, represented by the Christians of the Faith Union (or Fedotovtsy, after their leader Bishop Ivan Fedotov), is rooted within the generation of Pentecostals who resisted and survived Soviet persecutions and now tend to be more conservative, rejecting innovation, such as overt manifestations of miraculous healing, Western-style exuberant music and emotional worship, and personal prosperity theology. They are also distinguished by the practice of foot washing, symbolizing purity and humility. The second strand, represented by the Union of Evangelical Pentecostal Christians (led by Bishop Sergei Ryakhovski), remains relatively conservative but is more accommodating toward contemporary Western-style music and emotional forms of worship; however, they, too, dismiss the gospel of prosperity. Finally, the Russian adaptations of Charismatic Pentecostal Christianity are represented by the Word of Life Church founded by the Swedish Preacher Ulf Ekman, the New Generation Church movement, and the offshoots of the Embassy of God Church, originally established by the Nigerian evangelist Sunday Adelaja in the Ukraine.

The exponential growth and social activism of Protestant groups in post-Soviet Russia alarmed the Russian Orthodox Church and more nationalist factions of Russian society. The 1997 Law on Freedom of Conscience and Religious Associations was designed to restrict their growth by introducing a requirement for religious associations to provide a proof of lawful existence in Russia more than 15 years prior to application for registration as a full legal entity, unless they are part of a nationwide religious organization. Given that many Protestant groups were recent arrivals in Russia, they proved most vulnerable to this requirement. Some of them chose to join the Union of Evangelical Pentecostal Christians while others operate without registration, which places considerable restrictions on their activities. Another way of controlling the growth of Protestant groups was attempts to outlaw them through legal actions. In December 2001, a Moscow court banned the Moscow branch of the Salvation Army on the grounds that it was involved in unlawful activities as a "paramilitary organization." In October 2006, the European Court of Human Rights (ECHR) dismissed this decision. In 2004 another Moscow court banned the activities of the Jehovah's Witnesses in the city and ruled that they be "liquidated" as a legal entity. This was followed by several decisions against Jehovah's Witnesses in other Russian regions, one of which was successfully challenged in the ECHR in January 2007 (*Kuznetsov and Others v. Russia*). Although there is no evidence of a consistent anti-Protestant policy in Russia, there have been numerous decisions and actions by local authorities against them, such as restrictions on renting property, police raids and harassment, and visa restrictions for their pastors. These actions were often prompted by the renewed prominence of the anti-sectarian rhetoric, which portrays Protestant minority faiths as anti-social, anti-Russian, and morally corrosive. This rhetoric is echoed in some official and semi-official documents, such as the Doctrine of the National Security of the Russian Federation (2000), which sees missionary activities as part of the expansionist agendas by other states.

Russian Protestantism continues to play a considerable role in the country's religious life and society. It does this both directly (by introducing new forms of worship and social activism, emphasizing individual choice, and demanding more religious freedom) and indirectly (through challenging established assumptions about religious commitment and state management of religion).

Marat S. Shterin

See also: Assemblies of God; Atheism; Baptists; Calvinism; Christian Brethren; Church of Jesus Christ of Latter-Day Saints; Doukhobors; Jehovah's Witnesses; Lutheranism; Mennonites; Molokans; Pentecostalism; Russell, Charles Taze; Russian Orthodox Church (Moscow Patriarchate); Salvation Army; Seventh-day Adventist Church; Union of Evangelical Christians–Baptists of Russia.

References

Billington, James. *Icon and the Axe.* New York: Random House, 1966.

Coleman, Heather J. *Russian Baptists and Spiritual Revolution, 1905–1929*. Bloomington: Indiana University Press, 2005.

Heier, Edmund. *Religious Schism in the Russian Aristocracy, 1860–1900: Radstockism and Pashkovism*. The Hague, Netherlands: Nijhoff, 2005.

Nielsen, Niels C., Jr. *Christianity after Communism: Social, Political, and Cultural Struggle in Russia.* Boulder, CO: Westview Press, 1996.

Sawatsky, Walter. *Soviet Evangelicals since World War II.* Scottdale, PA: Herald Press, 1981.

Russian Orthodox Church (Moscow Patriarchate)

The Russian Orthodox Church (Moscow Patriarchate) is the primary representative of Eastern Orthodoxy in Russia. It is the largest Christian communion in Russia and additionally has a large following among the Russian diaspora internationally.

The newly installed Russian Orthodox Church patriarch Kirill, bottom center, conducts the enthronement service in Moscow's Christ the Saviour Cathedral, Russia, February 1, 2009. (AP Photo/Alexander Zemlianichenko)

Orthodox Christianity took root in what is now the Russian Federation long before Russia's emergence as a unified state. Originally, Orthodoxy had become the state religion of Kievan Rus in 988 CE, when Grand Prince Vladimir of Kiev (ca. 956–1015) decided to convert from traditional Pagan beliefs to the religion of Greeks, the Christianity of the Byzantine rite. From then Byzantine Christianity became the faith of the three peoples who trace their origins to the Rus of Kiev: Russians, Ukrainians, and Belarusians.

The princedom of Kiev entered a period of decline that culminated in 1240, when the city was destroyed during the Mongol invasion. By the 14th century, a new political center grew up around the principality of

Moscow, and the head of the church, the metropolitan of Kiev, took up residence there. Later, Moscow was declared the metropolitan see in its own right. Gradual centralization of political power in Moscow paved the way for the final formation of what would become the Russian Orthodox Church (ROC).

Initially, the ROC came under the titular jurisdiction of the Ecumenical Patriarchate in Constantinople, which appointed the Russian metropolitan and bishops. However, Russia gained more political power while Constantinople experienced gradual decline and finally fell to the Turks in 1453. In 1448, Grand Duke Vasily of Moscow (1415–1462) bade the Council of Russian Bishops to designate Bishop Jonas to the position of metropolitan. Not only was the Moscow metropolitan now independent, but henceforth the czar (and later the emperor) would be considered the champion and protector of the Orthodox faith in Russia. In 1589, the ROC achieved its full canonical independence (the so-called autocephaly), when Metropolitan Job (d. 1607) was enthroned by Ecumenical Patriarch Jeremiah II (r. 1585–1595) as the first Patriarch of Moscow and All Russia. It has become common to speak of Moscow as the "Third Rome," the first Rome being said to have fallen into heresy and the New Rome—Constantinople—having fallen under the Turks.

From the baptism of Kievan Rus and through most of the 17th century, relations between the Orthodox Church and the state in Russia were regulated by a concept developed in the Byzantine Empire. Its focal point was the idea of harmony between two collateral powers: the church (*sacerdotium*) and the monarchy (*imperium*). Each was considered supreme in its own sphere of life. The long-lasting administrative and, to a certain degree, political independence of the Orthodox Church from the Russian state also had a strong economic basis, given that about one-third of Russian lands were owned by monasteries.

In the early 16th century, the ROC became divided into two different camps: the monastic movements of "grabbers" (*stjazhateli*) led by Joseph Volockij and the "non-grabbers" (*nestjazhateli*) led by Nil Sorskij. The non-grabbers criticized the practice of extensive land ownership by monasteries. By contrast, the grabbers argued that lands (and other properties) owned by the church serve charitable purposes. The grabbers and non-grabbers also held different positions on the relationship between church and state. The non-grabbers believed in a clear-cut division between what "belongs to Caesar and to God." The grabbers instead backed strong union between church and state. While non-grabbers held the vision of the universal Orthodox Church, the grabbers promoted the national character of the ROC. The party of grabbers eventually won and the close union between the Orthodox Church and the Russian state was established.

In the mid-17th century a schism occurred in the ROC when Patriarch Nikon (1605–1681) initiated and resolutely enforced a number of church reforms. He introduced many elements and traditions of Greek Orthodoxy into ROC and changed prayer books so that they were in accordance with the original Greek texts. His actions resulted in the split of the ROC and emergence of the dissident Orthodox Old Believers movement, those who resisted reforms. Originally, Patriarch Nikon was supported by Czar Alexey, but by establishing "Greek Orders" in the ROC Nikon also pursued a political goal, namely, to achieve the supremacy of the church over the state. The confrontation between patriarch and monarch ended with the decisions of the Church Council of 1666–1667. The Council approved Nikon's reforms, but deposed him from the position of patriarch and sent him into exile.

The period of harmony and mutual independence in the relations between the church and the state came to an end under the reign of Emperor Peter the Great (1672–1725). In 1721, he abolished the position of patriarch as the head of the ROC and instituted instead the Holy Synod. All 12 members of the Holy Synod (3 bishops and 9 monastic or married clergy) were appointed or dismissed at the emperor's discretion. The Holy Synod was presided over by a secular official. The fundamental church reforms initiated by Peter the Great continued under the Empress Elizabeth (r. 1741–1762) and Catherine the Great (r. 1762–1796), who confiscated most of the church lands and enterprises (thus depriving the church of its economic independence) and closed more than half of the monasteries. From now on, the clergy of the ROC were regarded as the state's employees.

Through the Russian Empire, the ROC operated as the exclusive state church, and Orthodoxy came to be seen as emblematic of Russian statehood. Orthodox Christianity also played an important role in the geographic expansion of the Russian state. In fact, the state's cultural unity and integrity were based on three major premises: the influx of ethnically Russian colonists, the forced cultural-linguistic Russification, and the inclusion of new lands into the canonical territory of the ROC. The territorial growth of the Russian Empire resulted in the growing religious diversity of Russia's population. The ROC did little to convert the representatives of the other religions to the Orthodox faith. However, voluntary conversion to the Orthodox faith was socially rewarded by the state through much better career opportunities in any state institutions, including the army, education and administration. On the contrary, it was a crime for an Orthodox Christian to convert to any other religion. Marriages between Christians and non-Christians were forbidden. While followers of most of the non-Orthodox Christian churches were tolerated in terms of personal freedom to exercise their beliefs, only the ROC had the right for missionary activities and only ROC was present in the school system (the lessons on "God's order" were mandatory).

According to the 1897 census, of the Russian Empire's 125 million residents, 72 percent were Orthodox, 9.2 percent were Catholics, 3 percent were Protestants, 11.1 percent were Muslims, 4.2 percent were followers of Judaism, and 0.4 percent were Buddhists.

In August 1917, during the first stage of the Russian Revolution (after the abdication of the Emperor Nikolai II in February 1917), a synod of ROC bishops reestablished the patriarchal structure of the ROC and elected Metropolitan Tikhon (1865–1925) to the position of patriarch. The Communist revolution in October 1917, however, brought sweeping changes in the religious life of Russian society. Among the first laws adopted by the new Bolshevik authorities in January 1918 was a "Decree about separation of church from State and the school from the church." Originally, Patriarch Tikhon was an outspoken critic of the new Communist government, but he moderated his position after time spent in prison. His successor, Patriarch Sergius (1867–1944), created a model in church-state relations that would persist through almost 70 years of Communist rule in Russia: the ROC publicly supported government on all issues, while the state agreed to allow ROC a very restricted sphere of activity limited solely to liturgical worship.

In general, in the Soviet Union—the state that was declared atheistic—religion was effectively marginalized and ousted from public life in spite of the fact that the legislation of the Soviet Union formally always provided for freedom of conscience. The major target of the anti-religious policies of the Communist state was the ROC because it was directly associated with demolished Russian monarchy. By the mid-1930s, under Joseph Stalin's dictatorial rule, any forms of organized religious activities had become effectively illegal. Thousands of clergy had been arrested, put into concentration camps, expelled, or executed. The number of functioning parishes of the ROC dropped from 54,000 in 1914 to only 200 to 300 by the beginning of World War II. The majority of surviving parishes were located in Moldova, western Ukraine, and western Belarus—territories annexed to the Soviet Union only in 1939–1940. By 1939, only four of the Orthodox bishops that remained were free of arrest and continued to serve.

The policy of the outright persecution of the ROC changed significantly at the height of World War II. In September 1943, upon the personal initiative of Joseph Stalin, the Council of Bishops of the ROC was called and it elected a new patriarch. Several reasons contributed to the changes in the state policies toward ROC: usage of the social authority of the church in the political mobilization of the population in World War II; demonstrating to Western allies, most notably the United Kingdom and the United States, that religious freedom existed in the Soviet Union. It should also be noted that German military authorities allowed and even encouraged the restoration of the church's life in the occupied Russian territories, a policy that urged Stalin to take some steps toward winning the sympathies of believers.

The legalization and some restoration of the ROC in the late 1940s did not make the church free from the Communist rule. In fact, Stalin largely copied and rebuilt the system of state religious control that had existed in the Russian Empire. In 1943, the Council for the Affairs of the Russian Orthodox Church was founded, which was part of the Soviet government.

The Council for the Affairs of the Russian Orthodox Church and its successor (since 1965), the Council for Religious Affairs, not only controlled, but in many cases also administered the internal affairs of the ROC. Although Orthodox priests were appointed by the bishops to serve in the local parishes, they also needed to get permission from the Council for Religious Affairs. Similarly, the consecration of the new Orthodox bishops required the Council's approval. The ROC was allowed to engage in only one type of activity: the conducting of worship services. Neither church-based social work nor religious education of children was permitted. In exchange for their toleration on the part of the state, the leaders of the ROC were expected to publicly support and praise the Communist regime both domestically and abroad. Further, the ROC was expected to make regular financial "donations" to the state "Peace Foundation." Socially, both clergy and openly practicing lay members continued to suffer considerable civil discrimination. The Council for Religious Affairs ceased to exist only in 1991, the year of the breakup of the Soviet Union.

Beginning in the mid-1980s, Mikhail Gorbachev's (b. 1931) policy of political liberalization (commonly known as "perestroika") was accompanied by the gradual lifting of restrictions on religious activities. In 1988, the celebration of the Millennium of the Baptism of Russia was declared a national festival and was sponsored by the state. Gorbachev's reforms created the conditions for the dynamic development of the ROC. By 1988, the ROC had 6,893 active parishes divided into 67 dioceses and served by 6,700 priests. There were also 21 monasteries, 2 theological academies, and 3 theological seminaries. As of December 2008, the ROC counted 29,263 parishes divided into 157 dioceses and served by 27,216 priests. The church also has 804 monasteries and 87 educational institutions (including 5 theological academies, 38 theological seminaries, 39 theological schools, 3 Orthodox universities, and 2 theological institutes).

The early and mid-1990s witnessed the growth of the conservative wing and the rise of anti-ecumenical attitudes among church leaders. During two consecutive all-church Council of Bishops meetings in 1994 and 1997 the issue was raised to withdraw participation of the ROC from all ecumenical organizations including the World Council of Churches. These initiatives were turned down by the majority of the ROC bishops, but, at the same time, it was decided (at the 1997 Council of Bishops) to begin pan-Orthodox discussions and consultations on the advisability of continuing WCC membership. Both in 1994 and 1997, the Council of Bishops paid significant attention to the activity of the various foreign religious missionary groups working in Russia.

The perceived threat from foreign religious missionaries led the ROC to support a new national law "About freedom of conscience and about religious associations," which was adopted in September 1997. While this law acknowledges the equality of all religions in Russia, its introductory section emphasizes the special role of the Orthodox Church in Russian history, spirituality, and culture. Further, this law defined Orthodoxy, Islam, Judaism, Buddhism, and generally Christianity as "traditional religions," while restricting the activity of the new—for Russia—religious groups by imposing 15-year waiting period for their state registration. Effectively, it limits the activity of the unregistered groups to informal, private practice, and imposes many restrictions on the work of foreign missionaries.

The ROC enforces a strict ban on the participation of clergy in politics. Yet, in many ways, the ROC has significant influence on life in today's Russia. In August 2000, the all-church Council of Bishops approved the "Bases of the social concept of the Russian Orthodox Church," which articulated the church's relations with Russian society and state. This document emphasized the idea of collaboration between church and state in the various areas.

A number of agreements about cooperation have been signed during the past 15 years between the ROC and various Russian governmental agencies (including the Ministry of Internal Affairs in 1996, the Ministry of Defense in 1997, and the Ministry of Education in 1999). At the regional level, similar agreements on cooperation have been concluded between many individual dioceses of the ROC and the authorities of the Russian administrative provinces. In 1995, a special department of the ROC was established to maintain permanent contacts with the Russian military forces. By 2007, 2,072 military units had Orthodox chaplains.

The ROC is also acquiring more presence in the Russian public schools. In 1999, in a letter addressed to diocesan bishops, Patriarch Alexi II asked them to "pay special attention to the organization of the Orthodox education of children studying in state schools." By 2004, the subject of "The basics of the Orthodox culture" was included in the curricula of the state schools in more than 20 (out of 89) administrative regions of the Russian Federation. The "Coordinating Council for Cooperation" was created by the ROC and the Ministry of Education of Russia.

The 2000 all-church Council of Bishops also adopted the "Basic Principles of the Attitude of the Russian Orthodox Church toward the Other Christian Confessions." It asserted that Christian unity can only occur in the "bosom of the One, Holy, Catholic and Apostolic Church." Therefore, it could not recognize the equality of the different (especially Protestant) denominations. In spite of this stance, the ROC has remained a member of the World Council of Churches (WCC). In 2002, an agreement was reached between the ROC and the WCC to replace the WCC's parliamentary voting procedures with a consensus model of decision making, to more clearly distinguish between "confessional" and "inter-confessional" worship, and to create two models of WCC participation: "members" and "churches in association."

The last decade witnessed a sharp decline in relations between the ROC and the Roman Catholic Church. In 2002, the establishing of the four Catholic dioceses by the Holy See in Russia was perceived by the ROC as aggressive Catholic proselytism among the Russian Orthodox. The regular semiannual meetings between representatives of the ROC and Vatican officials have been broken. The ROC continues to object to a visit by the pope to Russia, insisting that any such visit must take place only after agreement between the ROC and the Catholic Church on issues related to Catholic proselytism in Russia and on relations between the Russian Orthodox and Greek Catholics ("Uniates") in western Ukraine.

The disintegration of the Soviet Union in 1991 had significant implications for the ROC. Indeed, in the Russian Empire and in the Soviet Union the ROC was a predominantly national church whose borders largely corresponded with the state borders. Quite differently, after the breakup of the Soviet Union, the ROC has become a transnational religious organization that extends far beyond the borders of the present Russian state. The headquarters of the ROC are still in Moscow, but 70 out of 157 dioceses and more than half of its parishes and clergy are not in Russia, but in the other former Soviet republics that now exist as independent countries. The branches of the ROC outside of the Russian Federation are given different measures of autonomy.

In some post-Soviet states, ROC dioceses and parishes remain under the direct supervision of the Moscow Patriarchate. There is one diocese in Lithuania and one in Azerbaijan. Kazakhstan is divided into three dioceses. The predominantly Islamic Central Asian post-Soviet states—including the republics of Uzbekistan, Kyrgyzstan, Turkmenistan, and Tadzhikistan—are united into one diocese headquartered at Tashkent, Uzbekistan. There are no parishes of the ROC in Georgia, where the Georgian Orthodox Church is autocephalous. The dioceses of the ROC in Byelorussia form the Byelarussian Exarchate—a regional grouping of dioceses united for purposes of day-to-day administration.

The Ukrainian, and Latvian Orthodox churches, the Estonian Apostolic Orthodox Church, and Orthodox Church of Moldavia have the status of the "autonomous and self-governing Churches." Yet, in many ways they remained linked to Moscow. In Ukraine, Byelorussia, Kazakhstan, and Moldova, the branches of the ROC are today the largest religious organizations of these independent states. In other former Soviet republics, especially in the Baltic and Central Asian states, the parishes and dioceses of the ROC serve as important ethno-cultural centers that consolidate the minority Slavic Russian-speaking population.

Outside the borders of the former Soviet Union, there are seven dioceses of the ROC in Western Europe (in Germany, Austria, Hungary, Netherlands, France, United Kingdom, Belgium). The South American diocese unites ROC parishes situated in Panama, Argentina, Colombia, Brazil, Chile, Peru, and Costa Rica. Although most North American parishes of the Russian tradition are part of the Orthodox Church in America, the smaller patriarchal parishes of the Russian Orthodox Church (31 in the United States and 25 in Canada) are in direct subordination to the Moscow Patriarchate, without local diocesan structures. There are also individual parishes of the ROC in Australia, the Czech Republic, Finland, Iran, Mexico, Mongolia, Morocco, Norway, Sweden, South Africa, and Tunisia. Two other national Orthodox Churches can be considered as "daughter churches" of ROC. The Orthodox Church of China was granted autonomy in 1957, and the Orthodox Church in Japan became autonomous in 1970.

The new situation of the ROC in today's Russia created conditions for reconciliation with the so-called Russian Orthodox Church outside of Russia (ROCOR) that had broken away from the ROC after the 1917 Bolshevik Revolution. At that time, more than a million Russians found themselves in exile in many countries, and a significant number of Russian Orthodox clergy came with them. In 1920, a meeting of more than 20 Russian Orthodox bishops in Istanbul created an autonomous church with the goal to serve the Russian emigrants. In 1928, the Bishops' Synod of the ROCOR refused to accept the call of Metropolitan Sergius, the temporary head of the ROC, for all Russian Orthodox bishops to refrain from political activity. Sergius also ordered that ROCOR be dissolved. By the mid-1930s, the ROC and ROCOR finally severed all relations. The headquarters of ROCOR originally located in Karlovci (Yugoslavia) moved in 1950 to New York City in the United States. The ROCOR, both lay members and clergy, was reinforced after World War II by a new wave of Russian emigrants—mostly displaced persons and those who had collaborated with Nazis in the occupied regions of the Soviet Union and who subsequently fled the country.

By the mid-1990s, several proposals and initiatives for a reconciliation between the ROCOR and the ROC led to an establishment of an official bilateral commission to examine the ways of reuniting the two churches. In May 2007, the full communion was re-established between the ROC and the ROCOR (which at that time had about 400 parishes and a number of monasteries spread worldwide). While the ROCOR remains independent in its internal affairs, it is also considered an indissoluble part of the ROC, and the election of the new ROCOR bishops and its head must be confirmed by the patriarch and Holy Synod of the ROC. The reunification of ROCOR and the ROC further expanded the global presence and influence of the ROC (especially in North America and Western Europe).

The complicated composition of the ROC makes it difficult to enumerate accurately its total membership. The estimates vary greatly between 90 and 120 million followers worldwide, thus making ROC the largest of all the Eastern Orthodox churches worldwide.

In Russia, according to the May 2008 national survey conducted by the All-Russia Public Opinion Research Center, 73 percent of respondents self-identify as followers of Orthodox Christianity as compared with only 49 percent in a similar survey administered in June 2001. The figure of 73 percent would mean that almost 110 million Russian citizens are Orthodox Christians. Yet, in the post-Communist Russian society there is a wide gap between regular religious participation and practice, on the one hand, and simply social-cultural identification with Orthodoxy, on the other hand. Indeed, the same May 2008 survey revealed that only 10 percent of Russians participate in the church's life regularly and follow religious requirements and practices. With the exception of the few traditionally Islamic and Buddhist administrative provinces of Russia, Orthodox Christianity is the predominant religion across the country.

Similarly, there is also no reliable information about Orthodox membership in the other Soviet republics. It is roughly estimated that the number of persons who identify themselves with the ROC is about 9 to 10 million in Ukraine, 8 million in Byelorussia, 7 to 7.5 million in Kazakhstan, 4 to 4.5 million in Moldavia, 2 million in Uzbekistan, and 1 million in Kyrgyzstan.

The Russian Orthodox Church has a hierarchical structure of governance. The supreme bodies of church authority are the Local Council (Pomestny Sobor), the Bishops' Council and the Holy Synod chaired by the Patriarch of Moscow and All Russia. The Local Council consists of the entire episcopate and representatives of the clergy, the monastic community, and the laity. It interprets the teaching of the Orthodox Church and deals with most important internal matters of church life, canonizes saints, elects the Patriarch of Moscow and All Russia, and establishes the procedure of such elections.

The Bishops' Council consists of all diocesan bishops and the bishops who direct Synodal departments and theological academies. The Bishops' Council must convene at least every four years. Its responsibilities include, among other things, preparation for a Local Council and monitoring the implementation of its decisions. It also adopts and amends the Statute of the Russian Orthodox Church; resolves basic theological, canonical, liturgical, and pastoral issues; defines the nature of relations with governmental bodies; maintains relations with other national Orthodox churches; and establishes, re-organizes, and dissolves dioceses and Synodal institutions.

The Holy Synod, chaired by the Patriarch of Moscow and All Russia, is the governing body of the ROC between Bishops' Councils. It is composed of the patriarch and six diocesan bishops: three of them permanent and three temporary members. His Holiness Patriarch of Moscow and All Russia is the first in honor among the bishops of the ROC. He governs the church together with the Holy Synod as its chairman. The patriarch is elected for life by the Local Council.

Today, ROC is headed by His Holiness Patriarch Kirill of Moscow and All Russia (b. 1946) who was elected patriarch of ROC in January 2009 after the death of Patriarch Alexy II, the head of ROC during 1990–2009. Prior to his current position, from 1989 to 2009, Metropolitan Kirill served as the head of the Department for External Church Relations of the Moscow Patriarchate.

Russian Orthodox Church (Moscow Patriarchate)
Department of External Relations,
Danilov Monastery, Danilovsky Val 22
115191 Moscow, Russian Federation
http://www.mospat.ru (in Russian)
http://www.mospat.ru/?lng=1 (in English)

Alexei D. Krindatch

See also: Eastern Orthodoxy; Ecumenical Patriarchate/Patriarchate of Constantinople; Estonian Apostolic Orthodox Church; Estonian Orthodox Church (Moscow Patriarchate); Istanbul; Old Believers (Russia); Orthodox Church in America; Orthodox Church in China; Roman Catholic Church; Russian Orthodox Church Outside of Russia; World Council of Churches.

References

Baltaden, S. K. *Seeking God: The Recovery of Religious Identity in Orthodox Russia, Ukraine, and Georgia*. De Kalb: Northern Illinois University Press, 1993.

Krindatch, Alexei. *Geography of Religions in Russia*. Decatur, GA: Glenmary Research Center, 1996.

Polonsky, A. 1998. "The Orthodox Church and Society in the Post-Communist Russia" (in Russian). In *Factor etnoconfessionalnoj samobytnosti v postsovetskom obshestve*. Moscow: Karnegi Center, 1998.

Pospielovsky, D. *The Russian Church under the Soviet Regime, 1917–1982*. Crestwood, NY: St. Vladimir's Seminary Press, 1984.

Roberson, R. *The Eastern Christian Churches: A Brief Survey*. 7th ed. Rome: Edizioni Orientalia Christiana, 2006.

Schmemann, Alexander. *The Historical Road of Eastern Orthodoxy*. Crestwood, NY: St. Vladimir's Seminary Press, 1977.

Ware, Timothy. *The Orthodox Church: New Edition.* London: Penguin Books, 1997.

Russian Orthodox Church Outside of Russia

In the years following the 1917 Russian Revolution and the defeat of the anticommunist White Armies, a first wave of emigration drove up to 2 million people into exile. A majority of them were members of the Russian Orthodox Church (Moscow Patriarchate), who now needed to organize their religious activities in new circumstances because communication with the Mother Church in Russia was difficult. Already cut from contact with the Moscow Patriarchate during the Civil War in Russia, hierarchs in the southern Russian zones under the control of the White Armies had created in May 1919 a Provisional Supreme Administration of the Church for South Russia. This move was approved by the church in November 1920, when a decree (*ukaz*) from Patriarch Tikhon (1865–1925) gave to bishops deprived of contact with the central administration of the church the right to organize themselves into a higher entity of ecclesiastical authority.

In November 1921 a council of Russian Orthodox emigrants gathered in Sremski Karlovci (Serbia). There were 13 bishops in exile among the 100 participants. Probably under pressure from the Soviet authorities, Patriarch Tikhon dissolved the Provisional Administration in 1922. The church in exile obeyed, but it immediately reorganized itself again in accordance with the patterns set in the 1920 decree: the Synod of Bishops would serve as the central church authority among the emigrants. This marked the beginning of what is known today as the Russian Orthodox Church Outside of Russia (ROCOR), also called the Russian Orthodox Church Abroad. Intermittent contacts with Moscow continued for a few years, insofar as the circumstances of those difficult times allowed, but a complete break came in 1927, when Metropolitan Sergius (1867–1944), administrator of the Moscow Patriarchate, requested a written expression of loyalty from the clergy in exile to the Soviet regime.

The Russian church in exile at first presented a united front, but soon divisions intervened, and large groups of Russian clergy and faithful in France (a stronghold of the emigration) and in the United States left the Russian Synod. In addition, during World War II and immediately following it, the ROCOR saw the loss of the numerous parishes in Eastern Europe and China, with emigrants resettling a second time in the West or in Australia. The headquarters of the synod had to leave Serbia, and finally relocated in 1949 in the United States. Due to the new geopolitical environment and the efforts of the Russian Orthodox Church under Soviet control to reinforce its links with the other Orthodox churches as well as other Christian denominations, active relations between the ROCOR and other religious bodies gradually decreased, although friendly contacts persisted with some, especially the Greek Orthodox Patriarchate of Jerusalem and the Serbian Orthodox Church. After the 1960s, the ROCOR itself also became increasingly critical of the involvement of Orthodox churches in the ecumenical movement. On the other hand, during the Soviet period, the ROCOR was held in high esteem by the believers of the so-called Catacomb Church, who led a clandestine religious life in Russia.

After the fall of the Soviet Union, some people or groups in Russia asked to be accepted into the jurisdiction of the ROCOR and formed a Free Russian Orthodox Church, but the movement did not grow very large and suffered divisions. In addition, some people in the ROCOR questioned those moves and pleaded for talks with the Moscow Patriarchate in order to find ways to restore the unity of the Russian Church. This created increasing tensions within the ROCOR between those open to a dialogue with the Patriarchate of Moscow and those who rejected entirely such overtures. This led to a first break within the ROCOR, when the aging Metropolitan Vitaly Ustinov (1910–2006), who had presided over the ROCOR since 1985, decided in 2001 to retire; very soon, however, he came to regret his decision and resumed his responsibilities, becoming the figure around whom people opposed to reunion with the Moscow Patriarchate rallied. The group following Metropolitan Vitaly took the name of the Russian Orthodox Church in Exile, but very soon became divided into competing factions.

In October 2000, the ROCOR Council of Bishops had decided to establish a committee to study the questions of unity of the Russian Church. Official visits to Russia and a formal dialogue soon started, with open encouragements from President Vladimir Putin—a fact that did not make opponents of reunification less suspicious. In May 2006, the IVth All-Diaspora Council of the ROCOR that took place in San Francisco agreed that a reunion was desirable, while a number of participants saw in the Russian Orthodox participation in the World Council of Churches a matter of concern, and would have expected an explicit renunciation of "Sergianism" (that is, the policy of allegiance to the state of Metropolitan Sergius); the Council of Bishops was entrusted with the task to assess how to proceed next. From that point, the pace toward reunion accelerated. The Act of Canonical Communion was solemnly signed in Moscow on May 17, 2007. According to the Act, the ROCOR is "an indissoluble, self-governing part of the Local Russian Orthodox Church," "independent in pastoral, educational, administrative, management, property, and civil matters, existing at the same time in canonical unity with the Fullness of the Russian Orthodox Church."

A majority of the ROCOR clergy and parish accepted the union. However, groups as well as entire parishes in various parts of the world (especially on the American continent) seceded from the ROCOR in repudiation of the move. Some of the dissenters have joined a group called the Russian Orthodox Church Abroad–Provisional Supreme Church Authority (ROCA-PSCA), under Metropolitan Agafangel Pashkovsky of Odessa, who was suspended from the ROCOR in 2007 "for disobeying lawful authority and inciting schism." Others joined Greek Old Calendarist or other Orthodox conservative groups. The ROCA-PSCA itself has entered into communion with one of the Greek Old Calendarist groups.

Although precise statistics are not available, it was estimated before the 2007 reunification that the ROCOR probably numbered less than 150,000 faithful, including converts of non-Russian origin.

Russian Orthodox Church Outside of Russia
75 E. 93rd St.
New York, NY 10128
http://www.russianorthodoxchurch.ws/ (in Russian and English)
http://rocorstudies.org/ (in Russian and English)
http://directory.stinnocentpress.com/ (ROCOR parish and clergy online directory)

Jean-François Mayer

See also: Greek Orthodox Patriarchate of Jerusalem; Russian Orthodox Church (Moscow Patriarchate); Serbian Orthodox Church.

References

Antić, Oxana. "The Russian Orthodox Church Abroad." In *Eastern Christianity and Politics in the Twentieth Century,* edited by Pedro Ramet, 135–145. Durham, NC, and London: Duke University Press, 1988.

Seide, Georg. *Verantwortung in der Diaspora: Die Russische Orthodoxe Kirche im Ausland.* Munich: Kyrill & Method Verlag, 1989.

Young, Alexey. *The Russian Orthodox Church Outside Russia: A History and Chronology.* San Bernardino, CA: Borgo Press, 1993.

Ruthenian Catholic Church

The Ruthenian Catholic Church is a Greek Byzantine church that has its base in the Carpathian Mountains of southwestern Ukraine, Slovakia, and southeastern Poland. Ruthenians speak a Ukrainian dialect but identify ethnically as Rusyns, not Ukrainians. Christianity began to be propagated late in the first millennium CE, and following the break between the Roman Catholic Church and Eastern Orthodoxy in 1054, the Ruthenian church adhered to Eastern Orthodoxy. At about the same time, the area came under Hungarian control.

In the centuries after Hungary, a Roman Catholic nation, established its rule in Slovakia and western Ukraine, priests began to agitate for the Orthodox Church to come into communion with Rome. In 1646, 63 Orthodox priests, primarily from what is today Slovakia, entered the Roman Catholic Church. The act of receiving them, called the Union of Uzhorod, occurred at a town on the Ukrainian-Slovakian border. Two additional acts of conversion to Roman Catholicism occurred in the Ukraine in 1664 and 1713. As a result of these events, Eastern Orthodoxy all but disappeared from the region.

Through the 18th century, a battle for control of the Ruthenians ensued between local bishops, who followed the Latin rite, and those priests who represented the Orthodox converts and continued to use a Slavic rite. Then in 1771, a Ruthenian bishop was elected and made the head of a Ruthenian eparchy (diocese). A Ruthenian seminary was established in 1778 at Uzhorod. Thus, the Ruthenian Catholic Church (also known as the Byzantine Catholic Church) emerged as a distinctive ethnic church that continued a variety of Eastern Orthodox traditions (including a married priesthood) and strongly identified with the Rusyn people of Transcarpathia.

Following World War I and the breakup of the Hungarian Empire, the region was incorporated into the new nation of Czechoslovakia, and in the 1920s one group left the church and returned to Orthodoxy. Then following World War II, the area east of Uzhorod became part of the Soviet Union. Pressure was exerted in the Ukraine to force the church back into Orthodoxy, and its parishes were placed under the Russian Orthodox

Church (Moscow Patriarchate) and its patriarch in Moscow. In like measure, an effort was made to destroy the Ruthenian church in Poland and Czechoslovakia. In the meantime, more than 500,000 Rusyns had migrated to the United States. However, they found that the American Roman Catholic hierarchy was opposed to the continuance of the traditional practices of the Ruthenian Church, especially the married priesthood. The majority of Rusyns in the United States reverted to Orthodoxy, and a few became Protestants.

The revival of the Ruthenian Catholic Church began after the disruption of the Soviet Union. In January 1991 the Vatican reestablished the Eparchy of Mukachevo (Ukraine) and appointed a new bishop. An estimated 500,000 Rusyn Catholics remained in the region. The seminary was reopened in Uzhorod in 1992. The status of the church in the Ukraine remains open, as both the Ukrainian Catholic Church and the Ukrainian Orthodox Church have been re-established in the now independent nation.

The first eparchy of the Ruthenian Catholic Church was established in the United States in 1924. There are now four American dioceses, with national leadership provided by the metropolitan, who resides in Pittsburgh, Pennsylvania. Some 200,000 Ruthenian Catholics reside in the United States. Ruthenian Catholics also reside in Australia and Western Europe, but the members are largely integrated into the Ukrainian Catholic Church.

Today, there are three distinct Ruthenian Catholic jurisdictions: (1) the eparchy of Mukačevo in Ukraine, which is immediately subject to the Holy See; the bishop of Mukačevo, currently Milan Šašík (b. 1952), is considered the head of the whole Ruthenian Catholic Church, but he exercises no authority over the other two jurisdictions; (2) the Ruthenian Byzantine Catholic Metropolitanate in the United States; and (3) the Apostolic Exarchate in the Czech Republic. The exact relationship between the three is still a matter of dispute.

In 2008, the membership of the three jurisdictions together was 598,000.

Ruthenian Catholic Church
Zakarpatska 18
294017 Uzhorod
Ukraine
http://www.byzcath.org (website of the Byzantine Catholic Churches in America)

J. Gordon Melton

See also: Eastern Orthodoxy; Roman Catholic Church; Russian Orthodox Church (Moscow Patriarchate); Ukraine, Eastern Orthodoxy in; Ukrainian Catholic Church.

References

Liesel, N. *The Eastern Catholic Liturgies: A Study in Words and Pictures.* Westminster, MD: Newman Press, 1960.

Roberson, Ronald G. *The Eastern Christian Churches: A Brief Survey.* 5th ed. Rome: Edizioni Orientalia Christiana, Pontificio Istituto Orientale, 1995.

■ Rwanda

Rwanda is a small country in the heart of the Great Lakes Region in Africa, just south of the equator. Rwanda became an independent nation in 1962, when Belgium handed over political authority to a democratically chosen government under Grégoire Kayibanda (1924–1976), Rwanda's first president. At the time, it counted 3.5 million inhabitants, of whom 95 percent were subsistence farmers who lived on the hills that are for the greater part covered with fertile soil.

By then, more than one-third of the population had been converted to Christianity, and particularly the Roman Catholic missionaries counted as the most successful in the world. The genocide of 1994, through which more than 800,000 people were slaughtered within less than 4 months, was a great disillusionment.

In 1885–1886, the Conference of Berlin allotted Rwanda to the German Empire, but only in 1896 did troops start to impose German authority. Before that date, the dreaded spears of the Rwandese kings had been able to keep slave traders from the coastal area and European explorers at a distance. The oral history of the kingdom was well recorded by the court aristocracy, and modern historians trace it back to the 14th or even the 10th century.

Rwanda

Religion	Followers in 1970	Followers in 2010	% of Population	Annual % growth 2000–2010	Followers in 2025	Followers in 2050
Christians	2,292,000	8,390,000	79.1	2.53	12,444,000	18,985,000
Roman Catholics	1,684,000	4,846,000	45.7	2.81	7,150,000	10,694,000
Protestants	332,000	2,060,000	19.4	1.95	3,200,000	5,100,000
Anglicans	162,000	1,150,000	10.8	4.56	1,680,000	2,500,000
Muslims	312,000	1,345,000	12.7	2.46	1,900,000	2,800,000
Ethnoreligionists	1,165,000	825,000	7.8	1.86	800,000	700,000
Agnostics	0	21,000	0.2	2.46	45,000	80,000
Baha'is	5,500	19,000	0.2	2.46	30,000	60,000
Hindus	1,000	500	0.0	2.47	1,000	2,000
Atheists	0	30	0.0	2.59	100	200
Total population	**3,776,000**	**10,601,000**	**100.0**	**2.46**	**15,220,000**	**22,627,000**

In the 18th century, anthropologists saw the Rwandese kingdom, in which the minority of Tutsi dominated the majority of Hutu and a small minority of Batwa, in the light of the Hamitic hypothesis, according to which the Batutsi belonged to the Nilo-Hamitic race. According to this hypothesis, the Batutsi had entered the country with their great herds of cattle in several stages in the 12th and 13th centuries. In the course of the last few centuries they had gradually subjected the Hutu agriculturalists of the Bantu race, who themselves had steadily deforested the hills since their arrival between the seventh and 10th centuries. These Bahutu had driven into the remaining forests the original pygmoid race of the Batwa, who were hunters.

Modern Rwandese historians and some Western scholars consider the Hamitic hypothesis as a way for European scholars to explain how highly developed cultures and organizations could be discovered in black Africa, where the "backward" Negro could not have created such civilizations. They claimed, therefore, that the Hamitic race was of Asian or even European origin (Sanders 1969). The fact is that the Rwandese oral history does not say anything about invading cattle farmers who gradually took the dominant position. The Banyarwanda (people of Rwanda)—the Tutsi, Hutu, and Twa—speak one language (Kinyarwanda, classified within the Bantu languages), share the same religious concepts and costumes, and have the same family traditions. The Hamitic hypothesis leaves unexplained why 15 out of the 18 Rwandese clans show a mixture of Batutsi, Bahutu, and Batwa.

Some lineages within the Batutsi group created their own identity, which in the 19th century strengthened the kingdom under the leadership of the Banyiginya clan, which is exclusively Batutsi. The kingdom developed an expansive power and gained hegemony over the greater part of Rwanda. This development created a growing tension between Bahutu and Batutsi, who were more and more seen as representing exclusive classes, although there always remained Batutsi without political influence and Bahutu who took leading positions in the Banyiginya kingdom. Until the beginning of the 20th century, a number of small more or less independent monarchies subsisted with a king (*mwami*) who belonged to the Bahutu group.

After World War I, the League of Nations conferred Rwanda to Belgium as a trustee area. The Belgian regime introduced an administrative reform in which leadership was exclusively given to Batutsi people. Thus, the distinction between Hutu and Tutsi was rigidified. The antagonism between classes turned into a struggle between what were considered different races, leading to a bloody social revolution in 1959 and continued turmoil within the Hutu-dominated government that assumed control from Belgium in 1962. At that point, some 10,000 Batutsi, many of them of the former ruling class, sought refuge in neighboring countries.

Denied the right to return, a second generation of these refugees, organized in the Rwandan Patriotic Front (FPR), attacked the country in 1990, heightening tensions between the two groups, now called Hutu and Tutsi, and culminating in the genocide of April–June 1994, in which more than 500,000 Tutsi and a considerable number of moderate Hutu were assassinated. Out of fear for the strong Tutsi-dominated invasion army, between 2 and 3 million Hutu then fled the country and stayed in refugee camps in Zaire/Congo and Tanzania until they were forced to return in 1996–1997. Upon their return they found a disrupted society of 8 million people, characterized by hatred, mistrust, grief, and mourning.

A government of national unity under the leadership of the FPR, carries out administrative reforms, and makes it illegal to speak of Hutu or Tutsi as different ethnic groups. Inspired by the autocratic leadership of Paul Kagamé, chosen as president in 2002, the nation experienced rapid economic development and radical social changes: an active policy of birth control, a transparent combat against HIV-AIDS, and national health insurance were introduced. Rwanda is characterized by a high participation of women in public affairs. In 2009 the shift from French to English was carried through as the basic language in administration and education.

From ancient times, the Rwandese people have been characterized by a religious consciousness that permeates all life—procreation, cattle breeding and agriculture, and the building of a homestead. They feel a strong relationship and even kinship with nature, which explains their respect for the environment. Humans are surrounded by an invisible world of spirits who influence human life. To this spiritual world belong the spirits of the ancestors (*abazimu*), who for some generations after their death participate in the life of the family. These ancestors need not be feared if people live in harmony and according to the rules of life that the forebears left as their testament. Illness, barrenness, and misfortune may be interpreted as punishment or revenge of the ancestors, reminding their offspring of the proper behavior. Ancestors are to be distinguished from bad spirits or malevolent forces (*amahembe* or *ibitega*), often of unknown origin. Bad forces may be used by personal enemies who act in a hidden way, only known and influenced by sorcerers (*abarozi*). In case of illness or misfortune, diviners (*abapfumu*) are consulted in order to detect the character and the meaning of the spiritual force behind it.

The idea of relations between human beings and God are fundamental notions in Rwandese religion. Humans are seen not as isolated persons but always in relationship to fellow humans and nature. The closest relationship is with the members of one's family, which includes several groups: the *inzu*, or minor lineage, one's father, mother, brothers and sisters; the *umuryango,* or major lineage, one's family in a larger sense; and the *ubwoko,* or clan, a broader entity of families, the membership of which is decisive for the rules of marriage. Individuals may enter into relationship with the spiritual world, enjoy the blessings from that world, and participate in its forces.

God, or Imana, is creator (Rurema) of the Earth and of the humans who reside there. Christian theologians have depicted Imana as transcendent, fitting the basic concept of God according to Christianity. Anthropologists have tended to describe Imana as the sacred dimension of life as it determines human destiny, gives fecundity, and yields wealth or poverty. According to some well-known myths, Imana once lived very close to people, and his most favorite activity was the cradling of babies. However, one day a young couple discovered Imana in their compound. They saw him as an intruding stranger, with their child in his arms. In defense the man aimed his arrow in the direction of Imana, who, since this unhappy misunderstanding, has never been seen again. According to an oft-cited proverb, Imana dwells all over the Earth during the day, but prefers to spend the night in the beloved Rwanda.

Traditional Rwandan religious consciousness involves no specific cultic manifestations of worship but is manifest in the celebration of the rites of passage, specifically the cults of Ryangombe, or *kubandwa*, and the cult of Nyabingi. Ryangombe is a mythical hero who died a tragic death. Before he died, he appealed in agony to the Batutsi, Bahutu, and Batwa peoples to be initiated into societies that honor him. The Ryangombe rite consists of cult sessions with dancing and singing, through which people are initiated into kubandwa societies. Initiates (*imandwa*) receive their own new secret name. Misfortunes, such as barrenness and illness, and natural disasters, such as drought, may intensify the Ryangombe cult sessions. Giving honor to Ryangombe provides protection against evil spirits. The Ryangombe cult has its parallels in other parts of

RWANDA

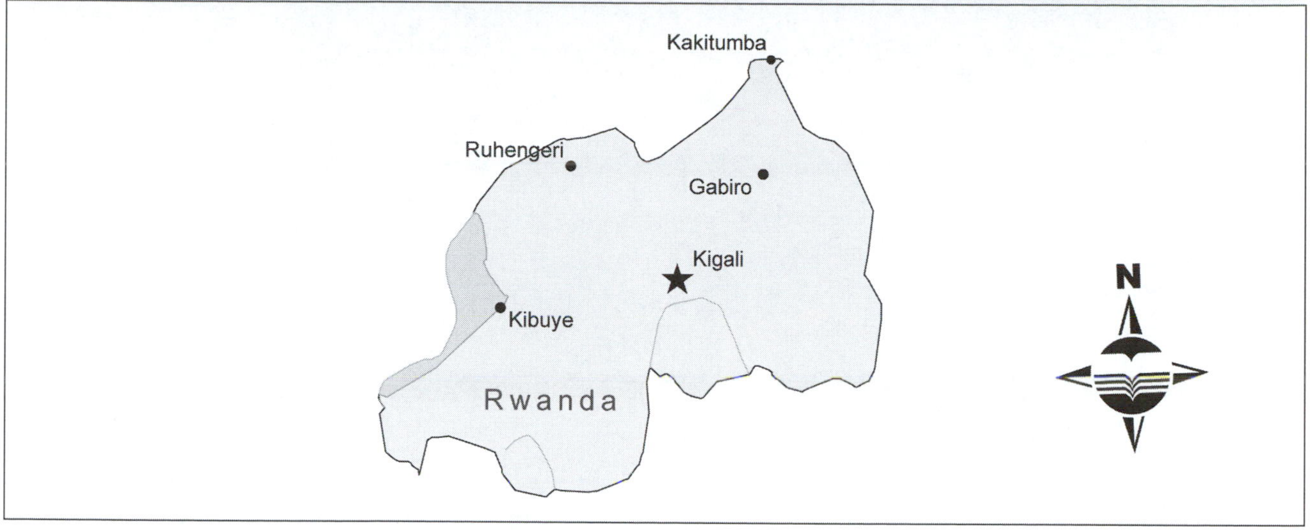

the Great Lakes region. Traditionally, as Hutu, Tutsi, and Twa participated together in it, the cult created social cohesion. Only the sacral king (*mwami*) could not participate in the initiation.

In the northern part of the country the cult of Nyabingi has a greater popularity. According to the myth, the woman named Nyabingi did not become a normal spirit (*umuzimu*) after her death, but instead she turned into a medium by whom one can be possessed through trance. Women may be cured from barrenness if they "have Nyabingi" (*bagirwa,* being possessed).

The first Christian missionaries to arrive in Rwanda were the White Fathers. This order of the Roman Catholic Church worked according to clear-cut missionary principles: gaining a deep knowledge of the people, establishing a four-year catechism according to the model of the ancient church, and trying to convert first the supreme political authority, who then will help with the conversion of the great masses. Rwanda, with its well-organized society headed by a king as absolute ruler, was an ideal place to apply these principles. Eager to precede Muslims and Protestants, the White Fathers quickly established parishes in all parts of the country, ten having been opened by the time the Germans were expelled in 1916.

In 1907 the first Protestant missionaries, German Lutherans, arrived as representatives of the Bethel Mission (the Evangelical Mission Society for German Eastern-Africa, or Evangelische Missionsgesellschaft für Deutsch-Ostafrika). One of their prominent missionaries, Ernst Johanssen (1864–1934), saw the African religion as a human answer to the divine revelation of the one God who communicates with all humankind. He studied Rwandese customs and religion in order "to trace the radiation of God's Glory hidden in the African religion." The German Lutherans founded eight missionary stations, along with two commercial missions to compete with the Muslim traders. When forced to leave in 1916, the Lutherans had already edited a translation of the four Gospels and a textbook in the Rwandese language.

The White Fathers continued their missionary work into the 1920s and provided the new patterns for structuring the Rwandan society. Missionaries became advisors to Belgian authorities, and Vicar Apostolic Léon Classe (1922–1943) especially promoted the influence of the Tutsi, being convinced that they were born to rule. By 1994 the Roman Catholic Church controlled more than half of all primary and secondary schools and sponsored a large number of hospitals.

In 1931, after King Yuhi V Musinga (1883–1944) refused to convert, Monseigneur Classe advised that he be dismissed and sent into exile. His successor, King Mutara III Rudahigwa (1913–1959), was baptized in 1943, and three years later he allocated his country to Christ. Prompted by the king's action, almost all the

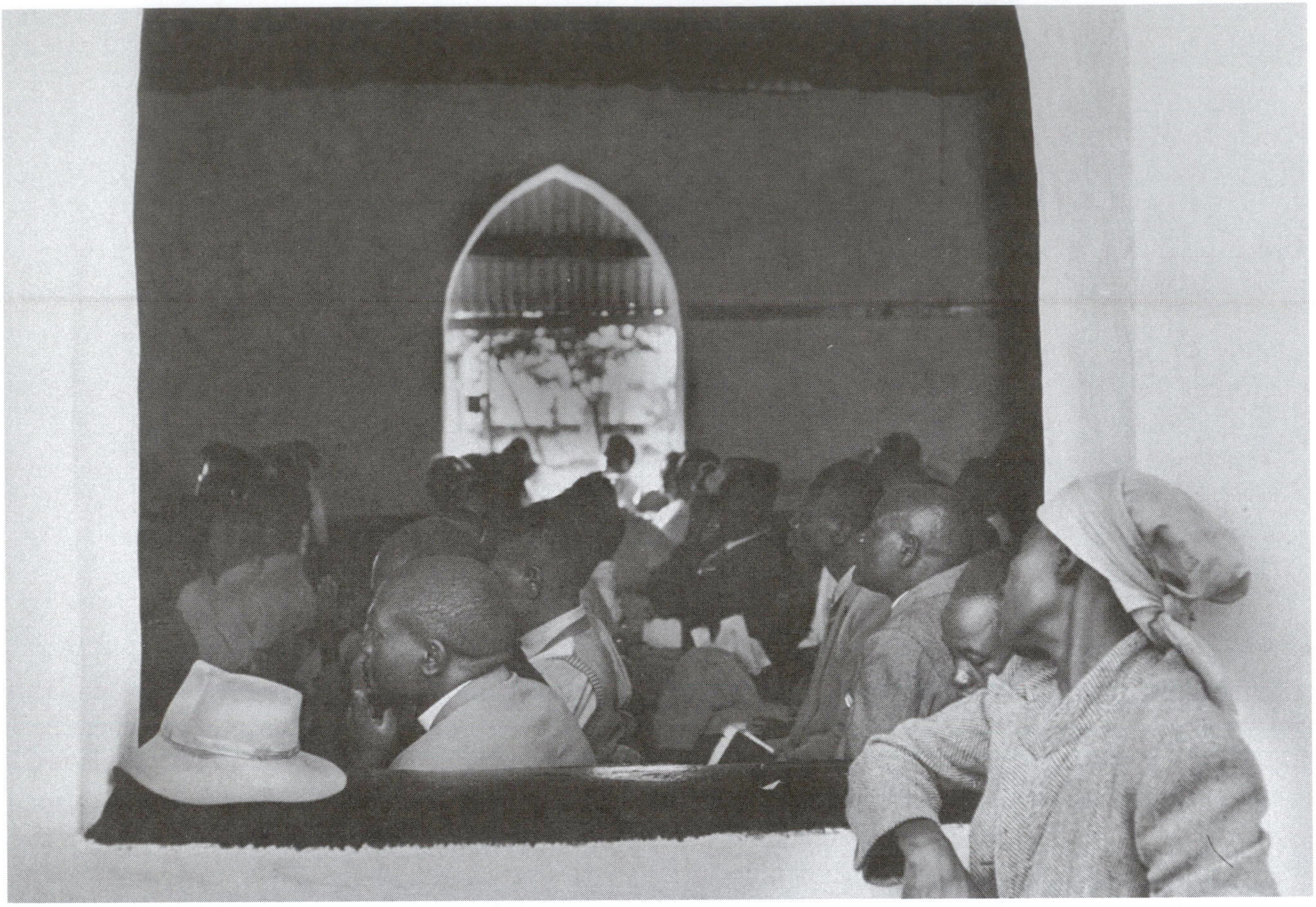

Crowd listens to American evangelist Billy Graham during his African crusade in Rwanda, 1960. (James Burke/Time Life Pictures/Getty Images)

aristocracy presented themselves for baptism, and the Hutu were encouraged to do the same. People spoke of the Tornado of Mission. From that time on, Christianity, and especially the Catholic Church, saw tremendous growth. In 1950, 25 percent of the population were counted as belonging to the Catholic Church, increasing to 34 percent in 1961 and 50 percent in 1988.

Only after World War II did leaders perceive the weakness of the missionary strategy. A new generation of priests, influenced by the ideas of Catholic Action and social democracy, saw the injustices of Rwandese class society. Previously, the rigid classification of the Rwandese as either Tutsi or Hutu resulted in their identification with the oppressors and the oppressed, respectively. Unfortunately, the new message of the equality of all people worked only to strengthen the identity of individuals as either Hutu or Tutsi, resulting in an even more rigid division of the population.

Catholic missionaries then began to promote the interests of the majority Hutu. On the eve of independence, the Hutu, supported by the church, started a social revolution. Under Rwanda's first president, Grégoire Kayibanda, the ruling party pursued a policy of ethnic equilibrium, through which jobs and positions were divided according to the percentage of Hutu (85 percent) and Tutsi (15 percent). This policy was continued by the successor government, led by General Juvénal Habyarimana (1937–1994), who took over power in a nearly bloodless military revolution in 1973.

After 1921 the Belgian Protestant Missionary Society (Société Belge des Missions Protestants au Congo) continued the work of the German Lutherans, thus accounting for the existence of a strong Presbyterian Church (rather than Lutheran) in the country. The Society represented a minority faction in Belgium, and its progress was initially hampered by lack of finances and personnel. In the course of time other Protestant missionary organizations followed: the Seventh-day Adventist Church from the United States (1916), Anglicans of the Church Missionary Society (1921), Danish Baptists (1938), Swedish Pentecostals (1940), and the Free Methodist Church (1942) from the United States. In 1994 the Union of Pentecostal churches outnumbered the mainline Protestant churches.

Within the Church Missionary Society, a revival movement developed that, in the 1930s and 1940s, exercised great influence among Protestants in neighboring Burundi, Uganda, Tanzania, and Kenya. This movement, called the East African Revival, typically sponsored "conventions," large meetings where people gathered for praying and singing, hearing sermons, and giving testimonies. The 1945 Kabale Convention attracted an international audience of 15,000. Devoted members of the movement, called *abake* (people on fire), or *abalokole* (those who are saved), experienced a heightened joy, visions and dreams, and an absence of any color bar between white and black. The abake struggled for equality between Hutu and Tutsi, promoted strong participation by women, and placed African leadership at the head of the movement. The movement led to independent churches in other countries, and in Rwanda it remains an influential movement within the Anglican community.

Around 1959–1962, the Protestant missions were transformed into independent church organizations, which then collaborated in founding the Conseil Protestant du Rwanda (CPR). From then on, an emancipation of the Protestants from foreign control became evident. The theological school in Butare, founded in 1971, developed into a Theological Faculty in which most mainline Protestants (including the Pentecostals) participate. In 1988 all Protestants together represented 20 percent of the population, less than half of that of Catholics. Today there are two ecumenical organizations serving the Protestant community, the Alliance Evangélique du Rwanda, which is affiliated with the World Evangelical Alliance, and the Protestant Council, which is affiliated with the All African Conference of Churches (AACC) and the World Council of Churches. The genocide of 1994 left all the churches in deep crisis. Almost one-third of the clergy had been Tutsi, of whom a majority were murdered. Those who had held leading positions, mostly Hutu, fled the country. Returning Tutsi refugees added to the controversy by attempting to seize leading positions. Past racial ideology and present internal problems prevented the churches from becoming healing communities. The Catholic Church was singled out for criticism by the new Tutsi-dominated government, which derided the church's assumed policy of divisionism, seen as the ultimate cause of the genocide.

After 1994 a number of new African Initiated Churches were created, most of them at the initiative of Tutsi returnees who did not want to reintegrate into the older churches that had been associated with the genocide. Thus, inadvertently and for the first time in Rwandese history, churches were founded on an ethnic basis. Most of these new communities participate in the Charismatic/Pentecostal movement, which is also influencing the older mainline churches. This new charismatic wave is characterized by strong eschatological preaching, baptism by immersion, and long sessions of ecstatic prayer. The Restoration Church, founded in 1994, is moreover characterized by a prosperity gospel. The Zion Temple Celebration Centres, founded by Apostel Paul Gitwaza in 1999, has created branches in Tanzania, Burundi, Congo, Denmark, Belgium, and the United States.

After 1994, Islam was no longer considered by the government and by the public news agencies to be an inferior religion. Muslims had been present in Rwanda since the beginning of the 20th century, the first being African soldiers serving in the German colonial army. The Germans also promoted the immigration of merchants and craftspeople, some of whom were Muslims, but at the same time they took measures to prevent any spread of Islam among the population.

The marginal position of Muslims in Rwanda was accentuated under Belgian rule, the Muslims being viewed as German partisans. Muslims were denied permission to create their own associations, and only in 1964 did Rwandese authorities recognize the Association of Muslims in Rwanda (AMUR). In 1970 about 8 percent of the population was Sunni Muslim. Then in 1994, Muslim Tutsis returning from their exile gave the community a new self-consciousness, claiming that Muslims had not participated in the genocide. Muslim missions began to attract great audiences. Schools were installed, and the end of Ramadan became an official national holiday. At his installation in January 2001, Sheikh Saleh Hategekimana claimed that Muslims, with about 120 mosques scattered throughout the country, represent 18 percent of the population.

Since 1996, the Centre for Theological Education and Documentation (CFD), related to the Presbyterian Church of Rwanda, has developed a dialogue program in which Protestants, Catholics, and Muslims participate. On a regular basis the Center organizes seminars where prominent leaders of these communities discuss together the social problems of the country.

Gerard van't Spijker

See also: African Initiated (Independent) Churches; African Traditional Religions; All Africa Conference of Churches; Church Missionary Society; Free Methodist Church; Roman Catholic Church; Seventh-day Adventist Church; World Council of Churches; World Evangelical Alliance.

References

Berger, Iris. *Religion and Resistance: East African Kingdoms in the Precolonial Period.* Tervuren, Belgium: Musée Royal de l'Afrique Centrale, Serie IN-80, no. 105, 1985.

Gatwa, Tharcisse. *The Churches and Ethnic Ideology in the Rwandan Crises 1900–1994.* Bletchley: Regnum, 2005.

Kasule, O. H. "Muslims in Rwanda: A Status Report." *Journal of the Institute of Muslim Minority Affairs* 3, nos. 1–2 (1982): 133–144.

Mamdani, Mahmood, *When Victims Become Killers. Colonialism, Nativism, and the Genocide in Rwanda.* Princeton, NJ: Princeton University Press, 2001.

Sanders, Edith. "The Hamitic Hypothesis: Its Origins and Function in Time Perspective." *Journal of African History* 10, no. 4 (1969): 521–532.

van't Spijker, Gerard. "Religion in Rwanda after the Genocide." *Studies in Interreligious Dialogue* 9, no. 2 (1999): 165–177.

Index